Duties and Liabilities of Public Accountants

Duties and Liabilities of Public Accountants

DENZIL Y. CAUSEY, JR., D.B.A., J.D., C.P.A.

Professor of Accounting
Mississippi State University

Revised Edition

DOW JONES-IRWIN   Homewood, Illinois   60430

ISBN 0-87094-325–1
Library of Congress Catalog Card No. 82-70156

Printed in the United States of America

1 2 3 4 5 6 7 8 9 0 K 9 8 7 6 5 4 3 2

Contents

Table of Cases

Foreword

One of the most striking developments in the public accounting profession in recent years has been the enormous increase in the legal liability of the auditor. The wave of litigation has affected the largest CPA firms and some of the smallest. Criminal charges against individuals as well as civil actions against CPA firms have created an awareness of this trend even among new staff members and among college students looking toward public accounting as a career.

The auditor can no longer achieve a comfortable sense of security by proclaiming that an annual audit is not designed or intended to detect fraud. Even the classical defense that the auditor performed his work in full compliance with generally accepted auditing standards may no longer afford protection. Perhaps most significant of all of these developments is the implicit challenge to the assumption that widespread collusion which makes a mockery of internal control systems is an unlikely phenomenon.

In the face of these startling changes in the environment of auditing, no clear answers are as yet apparent. As a first step, however, the independent public accountant must look long and hard at the specific cases that illuminate the path along which the public accounting profession is traveling. This book affords the practitioner and the student of accounting an opportunity to assess some of the significant events that have ushered in a new era in public accounting.

Robert F. Meigs*

---

* Coauthor, Walter B. Meigs, O. Ray. Whittington, and Robert F. Meigs, *Principles of Auditing*, 7th ed. (Homewood, Ill.: Richard D. Irwin, 1981).

Preface

Since the early 1960s there has been a great increase in litigation concerning the legal responsibility of professional persons, particularly public accountants. Changing concepts of duty and responsibility have begun to emerge.

The first objective of this book is to provide for the accountant, lawyer, and student a current and comprehensive statement as to emerging patterns of civil and criminal liability of public accountants along with a discussion of relevant auditing standards and procedures. Reprints of leading cases are provided to enable interested readers to pursue the subject further at their favorite beach, mountain retreat, desert inn, or even on an airliner en route without the inconvenience of going to a law library.

Because of the increasing importance of the subject for auditing courses and professional examinations, questions and problems have been added to facilitate use as a textbook. An instructor's manual is available from the publisher.

A second objective is to determine whether public accountants can improve their effectiveness in discharging their mission, while at the same time decreasing the risk of loss to themselves and users of their reports. Though Utopia may never be attained, this purpose will be achieved if general directions can be charted for the best course ahead.

I gratefully acknowledge suggestions and comments from William F. Crum during my initial research at the University of Southern California. The University of Texas at Austin funded my research during the summer of 1975.

Special appreciation is due my wife, Sandra, for her assistance throughout this work. She typed successive drafts of the manuscript and instructor's manual, assisted with preparation of footnotes, and helped with the copy editing.

Denzil Y. Causey, Jr.

PART ONE
TEXT

1

The Profession
Faces the Challenge

This chapter covers:

- OBJECTIVE OF THIS BOOK.
- PURPOSE OF THE ACCOUNTING AND AUDIT FUNCTION.
- THE AUDITING PROFESSION UNDER ATTACK.
- THE CONGRESS STARTS TO ACT.
- THE CONTINUING CONTROVERSY OVER PROFESSIONAL RESPONSIBILITY.
- REASONABLE APPLICATION OF PROFESSIONAL STANDARDS.
- A ROLE FOR UNIFORMITY AND CONSERVATISM.

OBJECTIVE OF THIS BOOK

The major objective of this book is to provide a comprehensive analysis of the legal relationships involved in public accounting practice. Practical pointers are interspersed throughout to help focus on guidelines that can help avoid particular legal entanglements.

PURPOSE OF THE ACCOUNTING AND AUDIT FUNCTION

In the broadest sense the function of accounting and of the audit by an independent public accountant is to

facilitate the operation of our economic system. Since economic systems differ, accounting and auditing need not be identical throughout the world. However, when one person is entrusted with the property of another, a need arises for accounting followed by an audit for verification of stewardship. Thus the audit of the stewardship function is as necessary in a communist or socialist society as in a capitalist one.

American accountants and auditors also play an important role in enabling our free market system to allocate private property rights to their highest valued uses as measured by dollar votes of demand. Perfect competition requires efficient markets supplied with complete information. The importance of information in the functioning of our securities market has been eloquently stated by Judge Timbers:

> The securities market performs the essential function of assessing the value that society places upon the efforts of a particular enterprise so that society can obtain the maximum amount of its preferred goods and services that our resources can produce. This function can be performed effectively only if the delicately calibrated balance of factors affecting demand and supply are allowed to have their impact upon the market place through an unrestricted flow of information. . . .[1]

Since accurate information is essential to the efficient use and exchange of property, it also forms the basis of our economic freedom.[2]

The auditor's responsibility in our system of competitive capitalism should be to ensure that material, relevant financial information, which is not misleading, is disseminated. More specifically, auditors can provide the means for investors to see that publicly

---

1. Chris-Craft Industries, Inc. v. Piper Aircraft Corp., 480 F.2d 341, 357 (2d Cir.), *rev'd on other grounds,* 430 U.S. 1 (1977).

2. Milton Friedman in *Capitalism and Freedom* (Chicago: University of Chicago Press, 1962), pp. 9–10, states that, although high levels of economic freedom have existed without political freedom, political freedom cannot exist without economic freedom.

For a discussion of these attributes of private property, see Harold Demsetz, "Toward a Theory of Property Rights," *American Economic Review: Papers and Proceedings of the Seventy-Ninth Annual Meeting of the American Economic Association,* May 1967, pp. 347–59. Also see Basil S. Yamey, "Accounting and the Rise of Capitalism: Further Notes on a Theme by Sombart," *Journal of Accounting Research,* Autumn 1964, pp. 117–36; on p. 117 Werner Sombart's view of the economic significance of accounting is summarized: "The main strands in this thesis may be set out as follows: by transforming assets into abstract values and by expressing quantitatively the results of business activities, double-entry bookkeeping clarified the aim of acquisitive business; moreover, it provided the rational basis on which the capitalist could choose the directions in which to employ his capital to best advantage; and finally, it made possible the separation of the business firm from its owners and hence the growth of large joint-stock businesses."

traded firms are managed in the public interest, not just for the private benefit of management. Unless this objective is achieved, the free market system will become a farce. Perhaps the most compelling responsibility of auditors is to enable investors to prevent the largest corporations of America from subverting democratic processes throughout the world by making bribes or illegal campaign contributions.[3] Failure here entails loss of political freedom.

The Securities and Exchange Commission (SEC) has repeatedly pointed out that the public accountant's duty to safeguard the public interest takes precedence over any duty to the client.[4] This responsibility is carried out through the independent verification of financial statements.

THE AUDITING PROFESSION UNDER ATTACK

Since the mid-1960s the auditing profession has faced increasingly heavy criticism from the financial press, the SEC, and others, along with an increasing flow of civil law suits. The profession has been even more alarmed that several auditors among the "Big Eight"[5] auditing firms have been subjected to criminal prosecutions, with some being convicted after jury trial.

Civil Litigation

In 1966 about 100 lawsuits filed by investors and creditors were pending against CPA firms.[6] In June 1968 *Fortune* reported that "there have been as many suits filed against auditors in the past 12 months as in the previous 12 years."[7] In the December 1970 issue of *Fortune,* it was reported that in an out-of-court settlement, "Lybrand, Ross Bros. & Montgomery [predecessor to Coopers & Lybrand], one of the 'Big Eight' accounting firms, agreed to pay $4,950,000 to the

shareholders and creditors of Mill Factors, an insolvent finance company."[8] Since that time many millions of dollars in settlements have been reported.[9]

According to the *Journal of Accountancy,* five accounting firms paid almost $44 million to settle Equity Funding claims: three accounting firms (Wolfson,

8. Arthur M. Louis, "A Fat Maverick Stirs Up the Accounting Profession," *Fortune,* December 1970, p. 97.

9. Some accounting firms have apparently made large settlement payments to their clients without finding any resulting independence problems. On March 20, 1980, *The Wall Street Journal* reported that Bankers Trust Co. obtained a settlement of almost $1 million from Price Waterhouse & Co. in a dispute over financial statements of one of the bank's borrowers and then requested shareholders to reappoint the firm as its own independent auditor. On March 12, 1979, *The Wall Street Journal* reported that C.I.T. Financial Corp received $3 million from its auditor, Touche Ross & Co., to settle a complaint against J. K. Lasser & Co. (acquired by Touche in 1977), and C.I.T. announced its belief that the independence of Touche was unaffected.

The June 1980 *Journal of Accountancy* reported that Seidman & Seidman paid $3.5 million to settle a lawsuit brought by stockholders of Cenco, Incorporated, a diversified medical supply company in Chicago. On January 30, 1980, *The Wall Street Journal* reported that Coopers & Lybrand agreed to pay $350,000 to a Methodist group that alleged that the accounting firm had failed "to warn the group's trustees soon enough that a former treasurer was funneling $5 million of the conference's pension funds into shaky loans to companies set up by the treasurer or his business friends."

On October 16, 1979, *The Wall Street Journal* reported that Omega-Alpha Inc. agreed to a $7.25 million settlement with two accounting firms in connection with its merger with Transcontinental Investing Corp. Touche Ross & Co., which had been the auditor for two Transcontinental subsidiaries, paid $6 million; and Hertz, Herson & Co., which had been the auditor for the parent, paid $1.25 million.

The November 1974 issue of *Dun's Review* reported a settlement of $400,000 by Haskins & Sells in connection with its audit of Orvis Brothers and another settlement of $875,000 by Arthur Andersen in connection with its audit of Whittaker Corp. *The Wall Street Journal,* September 4, 1973, reported that Arthur Young & Co. agreed to pay $950,000 to settle class-action claims by certain past and present stockholders of Commonwealth United. On June 5, 1974, *The Wall Street Journal* reported that Coopers & Lybrand and its insurers agreed to pay nearly $1.3 million to settle a lawsuit brought by the bankruptcy trustee of R. Hoe & Co., a printing press maker that went into bankruptcy. None of these settlements is an indication of wrongdoing or an admission of such. In fact, one story in *The Wall Street Journal* says: "That would make each share about $350,000, which in some circles is considered nuisance money"; see "Peat Marwick, Allen & Co. Inc., Others Quietly Settle Fraud Suit for $2.9 Million, *The Wall Street Journal,* December 9, 1974.

Discussion of some of the litigation can also be found in the following: T. A. Wise, "The Very Private World of Peat, Marwick, Mitchell," *Fortune,* July 1, 1966, p. 89 (discussion of litigation against the auditing firm of Peat, Marwick, Mitchell); "Trustee Issues Report on Westec; E & E Comments for Journal," *Journal of Accountancy,* February 1967, p. 7 (Richard T. Baker, managing partner of Ernst & Ernst, comments on litigation against the auditing firm of Ernst & Ernst concerning financial statements of Westec Corporation); Kenneth F. Byrd, "Accountancy and the Onslaught of Case Law in North America," *Accountant,* July 8, 1967, pp. 34–41 (discussion of major suits against auditing firms).

3. For an analysis of this problem as it relates to auditors, see the discussion at note 21.

4. *SEC Accounting Series Release No. 153,* "Touche Ross & Company" (1974).

5. The eight largest national CPA firms are listed alphabetically in the appendix to this chapter along with a list of the next four. Each of the Big Eight has from 50 to 125 offices in the United States and employs 4,000 to 9,000 U.S. staff members and support personnel in addition to 350 to 800 partners. For an interesting profile of each, see "An Audit of the Big Eight" in the July 17, 1978, issue of *Fortune,* p. 92.

6. "Auditors' Critics Seek Wider, Faster Action in Reform of Practices," *The Wall Street Journal,* November 15, 1966.

7. Arthur M. Louis, "The Accountants Are Changing the Rules," *Fortune,* June 15, 1968, p. 177.

Weiner & Co., Seidman and Seidman, and Haskins & Sells) paid $39 million, Joseph Froggett & Co. (acquired in 1972 by Coopers & Lybrand prior to the revelation of the scandal in 1973) paid $3.45 million, and Peat, Marwick, Mitchell & Co. paid $1.5 million.[10]

A $30 million verdict was entered against Touche Ross & Co. following an eight-month jury trial in connection with Touche audits of U.S. Financial Inc. The case was tried in state court in California where plaintiffs claimed only that Touche was negligent in failing to discover the management fraud.[11] According to later reports in *The Wall Street Journal,* an agreement was reached calling for at least $50 million to be paid to settle the U.S. Financial litigation by all defendants, including four former directors, auditors Touche Ross & Co., underwriters Goldman Sachs & Co., attorneys Brown, Wood, Fuller, Caldwell & Ivey, and lead bank Union Bancorp. The court awarded legal fees of $7.5 million and reimbursement of $873,000 in expenses to the plaintiffs' two law firms.[12]

On November 6, 1981, *The Wall Street Journal* reported a federal jury verdict in New York of $80 million in a fraud suit against Arthur Andersen & Co. by Fund of Funds (a major mutual fund during the 1960s). The controversy involved purchase of allegedly overvalued natural resource assets. Arthur Andersen reportedly will seek a new trial or appeal.

Criminal Prosecution

In 1968 a senior partner, a junior partner, and a senior associate in the CPA firm of Lybrand, Ross Bros. & Montgomery were convicted, after jury trial, of conspiracy to commit criminal fraud by knowingly certifying a false and misleading financial statement for Continental Vending Corporation for 1962.[13] Their sentences were limited to fines and probation. In 1972 they were given "full and complete pardons" by former President Richard M. Nixon.[14] This criminal case especially alarmed the accounting profession, because the court held that compliance with generally accepted accounting principles is not a complete defense against charges of certifying a false and misleading statement and that auditors have a duty to report major management misconduct.

Two partners and one employee of Arthur Andersen & Co. were indicted in 1972 in connection with the allegedly misleading financial reports of Four Seasons Nursing Centers. In 1974 a federal jury in Oklahoma acquitted the employee and one partner and deadlocked on the other partner.[15]

In 1975 a CPA was sentenced to a brief jail term after a jury convicted him of making false statements in the 1969 National Student Marketing (NSM) proxy statement. He had been partner in charge of auditing NSM in 1968 and 1969 for Peat, Marwick, Mitchell & Co.[16]

Also in 1975, three former auditors of Equity Funding Corp. of America were convicted, after jury trial, of multiple counts of securities fraud and filing false statements with the SEC. They were the partner in charge, an audit manager later hired by Equity Funding, and the replacement audit manager. The auditing firm involved was Wolfson, Weiner, Ratoff & Lapin. Although this firm was absorbed by Seidman and Seidman in 1972, Weiner and Block remained in charge of the Equity Funding audit. All three of the convicted auditors were sentenced to three months of actual jail time, four years of probation, and 2,000 hours of charity work.[17]

The Credibility Gap

By 1973 numerous situations where auditors failed to give clear warning of impending disaster or to discover massive fraud had caused auditors to lose credibility with the public.[18] The investment community had become convinced that auditors should reimburse stockholders for surprising losses from misrepresented financials. For example, one article in the financial press said:

10. "News Report," *Journal of Accountancy,* July 1978, p. 12.

11. "The USF Verdict against TR," *In Perspective* (published by Touche Ross & Co.) December 5, 1977.

12. *The Wall Street Journal,* November 29, 1978, and October 9, 1978.

13. *Aff'd in* United States v. Simon, 425 F.2d 796 (2d Cir. 1969), *cert. denied* 397 U.S. 1006 (1970).

14. *Journal of Accountancy,* February 1973, p. 3.

15. See *The Wall Street Journal:* "Eight Are Cited in Four Seasons Fraud Indictment," December 21, 1972; "Two Andersen CPAs Acquitted of Charges in Four Seasons Case," February 8, 1974.

16. United States v. Natelli, 527 F.2d 311 (2d Cir. 1975), *cert. denied,* 425 U.S. 934 (1976).

17. "Three Former Equity Funding Auditors Convicted of Fraud, Filing False Data," *The Wall Street Journal,* May 21, 1975. The convictions were sustained on appeal in United States v. Weiner, 578 F.2d 757 (9th Cir. 1978), *cert. denied,* 439 U.S. 981 (1978). The sentences were reported July 17, 1975, in *The Wall Street Journal.* In Weiner v. Mitchell, Silberberg & Knupp, 170 Cal. Rptr. 533 (Cal. App. 1981), Weiner's malpractice suit against his former attorneys for disclosure of confidential information to the SEC was dismissed because the criminal conviction indicated that the proximate cause of any damages was guilt and not disclosures by the attorneys.

18. "The Quality of Earnings Is under Attack," *Business Week,* December 23, 1972, pp. 74–76; "Accounting: New Numbers, Same Game," *Dun's Review,* August 1972, pp. 38–84; "Accounting: A Crisis over Fuller Disclosure," *Business Week,* April 22, 1972, pp. 54–60.

4

To many sophisticated business executives as well as ordinary stockholders, the idea that the auditors could not be responsible seems incredible. What else are auditors for, they ask, if not to verify the accuracy of a company's books?[19]

The Gap Widens

In the wake of Watergate investigations, numerous instances of illegal corporate campaign contributions for 1972 elections began to surface in 1973. Resulting SEC investigations then revealed that millions of dollars of corporate funds had been inaccurately recorded in the corporate books to facilitate making illegal or questionable payments both within the United States and abroad. Under SEC pressure, more than 60 of the nation's largest 1,000 corporations disclosed illegal or questionable payments.[20]

The implications of these practices were serious. Not only did the activities threaten our free democratic and economic processes, but they involved the following repercussions for the corporations and their investors:

1. The practices sometimes resulted in falsification of federal tax returns, and some of the corporate officials were reportedly indicted as a result of the tax filings.
2. Involvement by government contractors sometimes resulted in filing false cost data with the government.
3. The failure to accurately account for the expenditures may result in both civil and criminal liability under federal securities laws for participants as well as auditors who aid and abet the participants in their illegal activities.
4. Where members of management have knowledge of the matters, and in some cases, even instigated or personally participated in questionable or illegal payments, disclosure may be required under federal securities laws regardless of the size of the payment because such payments relate to the "integrity of management" and illegal activity usually carries with it substantial risks of significant repercussions.
5. The dependence of the enterprise on such activity for continued successful operation is usually unknown.

When these scandalous episodes of corporate illegality, unaccountability, and use of questionable business practices were reported, the public reaction was "Where was the auditor?" The public was even more dismayed to read accounts in the financial press that tended to indicate that some auditors had known about

19. "The War over Corporate Fraud," *Dun's Review,* November 1974, pp. 51–55.

20. Lockheed reportedly paid $7 million to a right-wing Japanese lobbyist named Yoshio Kodama, who was imprisoned after World War II as a war criminal (*The Wall Street Journal,* February 5, 1976); from 1970 through 1975 Lockheed bribes, extortion payments, and similar items were estimated as high as $38 million in a special report filed with the U.S. District Court in Washington and with the SEC pursuant to a consent decree; the payments were effected by use of off-the-books bank accounts, Swiss safe-deposit boxes, foreign consultants, and more than $10 million in cash and bearer checks paid in Japan (*The Wall Street Journal,* May 27, 1977).

A former Gulf Oil Corp. lobbyist admitted making $5 million in illegal corporate donations, mainly to oil-state politicians during 14 years ending in 1973. He indicated that he was not sure all the money he distributed went for campaign expenses. Gulf pleaded guilty to making illegal contributions to former President Richard M. Nixon, Senator Henry M. Jackson, D.-Wash., and former Representative Wilbur Mills, D.-Ark. (AP release of June 3, 1978). A November 26 *New York Times* dispatch indicated that Gulf acceded to a request from Charles Colson, an aide to Nixon, to finance a rebroadcast of the wedding of Tricia Nixon and Edward Cox and that a Gulf lobbyist had delivered $50,000 to Lyndon B. Johnson when he was vice president. A report filed with the SEC indicated a subsidiary in the Bahamas was used to "launder" approximately $10 million for both foreign and domestic use while apparently charging the funds to operating expenses. (*SEC Report on Questionable and Illegal Corporate Payments and Practices: CCH Federal Securities Law Reports Number 642,* May 19, 1976 (hereafter, *Report*), p. B-7.)

Minnesota Mining and Manufacturing Company had its director for civic affairs participate along with the president and vice president of finance in making political contributions, most of which were illegal. These activities also reportedly involved falsifying tax returns as well as the financial statements (*Report,* p. B-10).

At Northrop Corporation the chairman of the board and chief executive officer personally maintained an unrecorded cash fund and allegedly submitted false documents to federal investigators in connection with the Nixon contribution investigation (*Report,* p. B-18).

Ashland Oil Inc. made use of an officer's safe at corporate headquarters for illegal contributions. American Ship Building Company gave bonuses to employees who were directed to pay the taxes and contribute the remainder to various political figures (*Report,* p. B-1).

United Brands Co.'s $1.25 million bribe to Honduran government officials for a reduction on banana export taxes came to light in the SEC investigation into the suicide of United Chairman Eli Black, who broke a hole in a window with his briefcase and jumped off the 44th floor of New York's Pan Am Building ("A Record of Corporate Corruption," *Time,* February 23, 1976).

A report in *The Wall Street Journal,* November 26, 1975, indicated that Castle & Cooke payoffs in Latin America to expedite banana operations were charged to "first cost of fruit."

such matters and done nothing[21] or possibly, in some cases, acted as a conduit for the illegal payments.[22]

The SEC in Action

When the scandals of the 1960s broke, the SEC started aggressively issuing *Accounting Series Releases* dealing with accounting principles and began a more active enforcement program of administrative proceedings, injunctive proceedings, and reference of cases to the Department of Justice for criminal prosecution.

This SEC enforcement program has focused primarily on accountants, and more recently on lawyers, on the theory that these professionals are an essential element in accessing the securities market. Exercise of professional responsibility at critical points could prevent many questionable practices. The SEC enforcement program, along with investor lawsuits, was effective in making auditors tougher in standing up to clients and in prodding the profession toward expansion of its responsibility. However, the financial scandals continued.

THE CONGRESS STARTS TO ACT

Mindful of the information needs for our economic system[23] and increasingly aware of the failures of the accounting profession in meeting those needs, both houses of Congress started to investigate. These investigations tended to show that the SEC had been treating symptoms instead of the two real problems that surfaced during the course of the congressional investigations and hearings:

1. Auditors are not independent, either in appearance or mental attitude, from the management of firms that hire them and pay their fees.
2. Accounting rules consist of a collection of alternative practices, so there is no uniformity in reporting the same economic events.

The congressional findings were reported in three controversial but widely circulated reports:

1. *Federal Regulation and Regulatory Reform:* Report by the Subcommittee on Oversight and Investigations of the Committee on Interstate and Foreign Commerce, House of Representatives, 94th Congress, Second Session, October 1976 (hereafter, *Moss Report*).[24]
2. *The Accounting Establishment:* A Staff Study prepared by the Subcommittee on Reports, Accounting and Management of the Committee on Government Operations, United States Senate, December 1976 (hereafter, *Staff Study*).[25]
3. *Improving the Accountability of Publicly Owned Corporations and Their Auditors:* Report of the Subcommittee on Reports, Accounting and Management of the Committee on Governmental Affairs, United States Senate, November 1977 (hereafter, *Metcalf Report*).[26]

21. See "Data Laxity Laid to Merck Auditor: Andersen & Co. Is Said to Have Failed to Follow Up on Illegal Payments," *New York Times,* March 10, 1976; "Price Waterhouse Knew United Brands Paid Bribe but Didn't Require Disclosure," *The Wall Street Journal,* April 11, 1975. *The Wall Street Journal,* May 27, 1977, report of Lockheed payoffs has this account: "The report notes that Arthur Young & Co., the company's outside auditors, first uncovered questionable payments in 1971 and that internal auditors found some in 1973, at which time they were brought to the attention of the board's audit committee. In both instances, senior management was successful in keeping the information from other directors, the report states."

Auditors have never perceived themselves as whistle blowers, since the traditional view is to frown on "squealers" who do not have the team spirit. Although there is no legal protection for employees who speak out, they are coming forward as never before. Nader's Clearing House for Professional Responsibility received more than 6,000 letters from government and corporate tattlers during a two-year period. See "Disclosing Misdeeds of Corporations Can Backfire on Tattlers: Whistle Blowers Lose Jobs, Face Ostracism, Threats; Yet Many Take the Risk" in *The Wall Street Journal,* May 21, 1976.
22. See "Pullman Used Auditor to Make Payment Abroad: Arthur Young Apparently Served as Conduit for a 'Presumed' Tax Bribe" in *The Wall Street Journal,* October 25, 1976, which states: "Pullman didn't say so directly, but the auditor that served as the payment conduit apparently was Arthur Young & Co., which also helped conduct the investigation that turned up the questionable payments."
23. At page 30, the *Moss Report* states: "The securities markets rely on the continuing generation and updating of relevant, accurate, and timely information as the basis for informed capital-raising and capital-allocating decisions. The SEC's execution of the disclosure mission is essential both for the proper functioning of the capital markets and the economy as a whole. Disclosure starts from the basic operating unit of the economy, the corporation; provides the body of knowledge describing the operation of that and other units, hence the economy; and yields the factual basis for decisions by a number of economic actors: investors, financial analysts, economists, investment and commercial bankers, competitors, labor, consumers, government policy-makers, public administrators, and regulators. Ultimately, such information helps to form perceptions about the total economic environment. The circle is completed when a corporation's management or board responds to decisions made by outsiders who have acted on its own information. Management also is affected indirectly by individual and collective perceptions as to the state of the economy. It is difficult to overstate the need for relevant, accurate, and timely information about the basic unit of our free enterprise system."
24. See "Moss Report Says SEC Should Set Accounting/Auditing Rules; FASB's Armstrong Issues Rebuttal" in the December 1976 *Journal of Accountancy* at page 26.
25. The full text of the Summary was published in Official Releases, *Journal of Accountancy,* March 1977, pp. 104–20.
26. The full text was published in Official Releases, *Journal of Accountancy,* January 1978, pp. 88–96.

Lack of Independence

The *Staff Study* found that the Big Eight use their "dominance over the self-regulatory apparatus of the accounting profession, and the reliance of the SEC on the AICPA" to engage in a wide range of management advisory services that constitute a conflict of interest.

Lobbying Efforts. The *Staff Study* cited many examples of lobbying efforts by Big Eight auditors to show that accounting firms are not independent in appearance, but instead "readily identify with the self-interests" of their corporate clients.[27]

Executive Recruitment. The *Staff Study* questioned the potential conflict of interest whereby Big Eight auditors in effect run employment agencies as part of their management advisory services. This involves placement of marketing and management personnel as well as those in accounting. The *Staff Study* raised such questions as these:

Does the auditor have a stake in the operations where s/he placed the executive personnel?

Does the auditor retain an appearance of independence where the client's accounting executives have been placed by the auditor from the auditor's own staff?

Financial Management. The *Staff Study* found that the Big Eight extensively engage in installing financial management systems. The study raised questions as to whether auditors can independently audit their own work and whether it is a conflict of interest to use leverage as an auditor to sell management advisory services.

---

27. These items were among many examples cited:
    1. Haskins & Sells is auditor for several of the Nation's largest utilities and in Florida "represented the electric utilities to lobby against a bill in the state legislature which would have permitted utilities to charge customers only for the amount of taxes actually paid to the government."
    2. Peat, Marwick, Mitchell & Co. presented testimony before the House Ways and Means Committee on behalf of an oil and gas company.
    3. In testifying before state regulatory commissions Touche Ross & Co. "has supported controversial rate-making procedures which benefit utilities at the expense of consumers."
    4. Although Arthur Andersen & Co. states that the firm does not engage in lobbying activities, it engages in "public service" efforts and makes partisan statements that express the views of big-business lobbyists, such as its statement before the House Ways and Means Committee that "openly advocates retention of controversial foreign tax benefits for multinational corporations."

These examples raise questions as to whether auditors should be limited to representing consumer interests. Query whether business firms should be denied the benefit of CPA representation? Perhaps the answer is that independent auditing firms should not lobby for audit clients and should leave lobbying to CPAs who do not handle the audit work. Query whether auditing firms (as opposed to individuals) should take positions on public and political issues?

Lack of Uniform Accounting Rules

The Financial Accounting Standards Board (FASB) has spent years of effort and millions of dollars without being able to identify a uniform method for depreciation nor a uniform method of inventory costing. Corporate managements still remain free to choose from among alternative accounting principles in the following matters:

1. Depreciation.
2. Inventories.
3. Completed contract versus percentage of completion (there are two alternatives for *applying* percentage of completion).
4. Investment credit.
5. Uncertain revenue (recognized as cash is collected or after recovery of cost).

This dismal failure has hardly gone unnoticed in the financial press and the academic community, nor among practicing professionals and in the Congress. The *Moss Report* had this to say:

The FASB has accomplished virtually nothing toward resolving fundamental accounting problems plaguing the profession. These include the plethora of optional "generally accepted" accounting principles (GAAPs), the ambiguities inherent in many of those principles, and the manifestations of private accountants' lack of independence with respect to their corporate clients. Considering the FASB's record, the SEC's continued reliance on the private accounting profession is questionable.[28]

The *Staff Study* had this evaluation:

The complete inadequacy of the FASB's policies to prevent conflicts of interest is perhaps best illustrated by the recent departure of an FASB member from one of the "Big Eight" accounting firms who resigned prior to the end of his term in order to return to his firm. His resignation appears to violate an FASB rule prohibiting members from entering into formal or informal employment agreements while serving on the FASB. It seems doubtful that an FASB member would resign with an announcement of his intent to return to his previous business affiliation without some formal or informal agreement that he was wanted back and that there was an acceptable position for him. A "revolving door" arrangement between the FASB and the big accounting firms supporting it has apparently already begun.

A review of the FASB's activities confirms the finding of this study that there is no reason to expect the FASB to achieve serious reform by establishing a system of uniform and meaningful accounting standards.

---

28. *Moss Report*, pp. 32–33.

Such a system is needed to replace the present collection of flexible, alternative standards which have permitted the growth of "creative accounting" as an acceptable option to accurate financial reporting. A study sponsored by the AICPA has listed 31 separate kinds of business transactions with an aggregate of 80 different accounting alternatives for reporting the transactions.

During its three-year existence, the FASB has issued 12 "Statements of Accounting Standards." Those standards have addressed accounting problems of varying significance, but they have not resolved such problems in a manner which results in meaningful, as well as uniform, treatment of specific business transactions. Two of the standards have permitted alternative accounting methods, and none of them has seriously threatened the accounting prerogatives of various special interest groups in the established business community.[29]

The final *Metcalf Report,* unanimously approved by all members of the U.S. Senate Subcommittee on Reports, Accounting and Management, had this evaluation:

Uniformity in the development and application of accounting standards must be a major goal of the standard-setting system. Neither the SEC nor private sector bodies has clearly stated that uniformity must be achieved in a timely manner, notwithstanding some efforts which have been made to narrow differences and reduce alternatives. Yet, several witnesses testified that alternative standards for reporting the same type of business transaction not only are unnecessary, but have significantly hindered the development of clear, comparable financial statements. As an example, one witness described how annual revenues and earnings calculated by using the percentage-of-completion method for reporting long-term contracts can differ radically from reporting revenues and earnings of the same contracts as they are actually completed.

The subcommittee strongly believes that the clarity and comparability of corporate financial statements will be substantially improved if uniform accounting standards are used to report the same type of business transactions. Congress has previously indicated that uniform accounting standards are in the public interest by establishing the Cost Accounting Standards Board and directing the development of such standards for oil and gas producing companies.

Until uniformity is achieved, the public should be informed of the effect on financial statements from using a particular accounting standard to report a transaction, rather than using any of the acceptable alternatives. The independent auditor should give an opinion that the standards used are the most appropriate under the circumstances.

If the present standard-setting system is to become more responsive, the SEC must more vigorously oversee the system on behalf of the public. The standards and operation of the system should not be accepted automatically by the SEC, but should be evaluated and questioned to determine if they meet the public policies set forth in this report and by other actions of Congress. The SEC's annual report to Congress on accounting matters should comment on progress made in reaching these goals.[30]

The Report of the Public Review Board of Arthur Andersen & Co. contained in Andersen's 1977 annual report discussed efforts to restructure the FASB and offered this evaluation:

However, no amount of restructuring of organization and procedures, or conceptualizing about basic objectives, is going to substitute for the willingness to make tough decisions about which alternatives are preferable. Those decisions should be made by the FASB, not left to individual practitioners or accounting firms. We believe these decisions must be made now, by the profession and the FASB—rather than later, by the government.[31]

THE CONTINUING CONTROVERSY OVER PROFESSIONAL RESPONSIBILITY

The solution to problems facing the profession is made more difficult because of different perceptions of auditor responsibility held by the public (as represented by the SEC and the courts) and the American Institute of Certified Public Accountants (AICPA).

The AICPA View

The AICPA view of the auditor's duty to communicate differs importantly from that held by the SEC, the courts, and the public. These differences largely relate to the standard of communication required of public accountants and the conclusiveness of expert testimony in defining the standard.

AICPA positions on the standard of communication and conclusiveness of expert testimony are as follows:

1. The standard of communication required is measured by specific GAAP and GAAS and in absence of specific rules or customs by the views of experts (professional CPAs).
2. The jury (or court in case of trial without a jury) is never authorized to question the wisdom of the professional standard.

---

29. *Staff Study,* pp. 16–17.

30. *Metcalf Report,* p. 10.
31. Arthur Andersen & Co., *Annual Report,* August 31, 1977, at page 9 of the Report of the Public Review Board.

The auditor's duty as perceived from the AICPA position (1) does not require the auditor to blow the whistle on management misconduct[32] and (2) does not require an overall result of effective communication of material information to investors, but rather requires "fairness" only within the framework of GAAP.[33]

The AICPA view would place CPAs in the preferred position concerning standard of conduct and burden of proof that has been accorded to physicians and surgeons in medical malpractice cases. Courts traditionally have refused to question the usual medical practice as defined by expert witnesses.

The Courts' Views

The malpractice case generally requires proof of (1) the *usual* professional practice by testimony of experts,[34] (2) defendant's departure from the usual standard, (3) a loss or injury sustained by plaintiff, and (4) a causal relationship between plaintiff's loss and defendant's departure from the usual professional practice.

32. See, for example, *CCH AICPA Professional Standards* AU § 328.19, which provides: "Deciding whether there is a need to notify parties other than personnel within the client's organization of an illegal act is the responsibility of management. Generally, the auditor is under no obligation to notify those parties."

33. *CCH AICPA Professional Standards* AU § 411.03 provides: "The independent auditor's judgment concerning the 'fairness' of the overall presentation of financial statements should be applied within the framework of generally accepted accounting principles."

34. In Kemmerlin v. Wingate, 261 S.E.2d 50 (S.C. 1979), the malpractice suit against an accounting firm was dismissed because there was no evidence establishing the applicable standard of care. In Wright v. Williams, 47 Cal. App. 3d 810, 121 Cal. Rptr. 194 (Cal. App. 1975) the court held that in some attorney malpractice cases "the failure of attorney performance may be so clear that a trier of fact may find professional negligence unaided by the testimony of experts." However the court ruled that where the attorney is holding himself or herself out as a legal specialist and the claim is related to the claimed expertise, an expert witness must define the standard of care.

In Sorenson v. Fio Rito, 413 N.E.2d 47 (Ill. App. 1980), the court held the attorney's negligence in failing to timely file inheritance and estate tax forms was so explicit that expert testimony concerning the standard of care was unnecessary. Compare Sheetz v. Morgan, 424 N.E.2d 867 (Ill. App. 1981), where an attorney's failure to file a financing statement on an equipment lease caused a loss of a security interest and the court held that the failure did not constitute malpractice as a matter of law so that expert testimony was necessary.

In Coleco Industries, Inc. v. Berman, 423 F. Supp. 275 (E.D. Pa. 1976), *appealed on other issues,* 576 F.2d 569 (3d Cir. 1977), the court rejected the need for expert accounting testimony defining the professional standard in its note 59 because the errors were of a mechanical and computational nature.

In Escott v. BarChris Construction Corp., 283 F. Supp. 643, 703 (S.D.N.Y.), Judge McLean said, "Accountants should not be held to a standard higher than that recognized in the profession." However, the court did not find it necessary to discuss any expert opinion and instead determined that the auditor failed to carry out his own program properly, which presumably reflected those steps foreseeably required by professional standards: "He did not take some of the steps which Peat, Marwick's written program prescribed. . . ."

The usual standard for accounting practice is established by

1. Rules of state boards of public accountancy,[35]
2. SEC rules relating to publicly traded securities,[36]
3. Rules of the AICPA[37] and state societies of CPAs, and
4. IRS rules of practice.[38]

Standard of Communication. Where the profession has established specific standards, the professional duty will be limited to conformance if resulting financial statements fairly and meaningfully inform the investor.[39] Even if the auditor fails to follow professional standards, liability is imposed only when the resulting

35. In Lehmann v. State Board of Public Accountancy, 263 U.S. 394 (1923), the U.S. Supreme Court upheld the constitutionality of legislation empowering the Alabama State Board of Public Accountancy to revoke certificates for unprofessional conduct.

36. In Touche Ross & Co. v. SEC, 609 F.2d 570 (2d Cir. 1979), the court rejected an accounting firm's challenge to the SEC's authority to adopt its disciplinary rule 2(e) and to conduct a public disciplinary proceeding concerning the accounting firm's accounting practice.

37. The AICPA's right to make rules that affect members' clients was upheld in Appalachian Power Co. v. American Institute of CPAs, 177 F. Supp. 345 (S.D.N.Y. 1959), *aff'd per curiam,* 268 F.2d 844 (2d Cir. 1959), *cert. denied,* 361 U.S. 887 (1959).

AICPA rules bind all who practice regardless of AICPA membership. In Rhode Island Hospital Trust National Bank v. Swartz, Bresenoff, Yavner & Jacobs, 455 F.2d 847 (4th Cir. 1972), the court, in referring to AICPA pronouncements said: "While industry standards may not always be the maximum test of liability, certainly they should be deemed the minimum standard by which liability should be determined." In Stanley Bloch, Inc. v. Klein, 258 N.Y.S.2d 501 (N.Y. Sup. Ct. 1965), the court held that AICPA ethics rules fixed the standard of the profession.

For court decisions basing attorneys' malpractice on deviation from the attorneys' ethics code, *see* Woodruff v. Tomlin, 616 F.2d 924 (6th Cir. 1980) (duty of an attorney representing multiple clients in an auto accident to advise of a conflict of interest); Ishmael v. Millington, 50 Cal. Rptr. 592 (Cal. App. 1966) (failure of an attorney representing both parties in a divorce to disclose the conflict and advise of desirability of separate counsel); DeDaviess v. U-Haul Company of Southern Georgia, 267 S.E.2d 633 (Ga. App. 1980) (presentment of criminal charges to obtain an advantage in a civil matter as supporting a claim for malicious prosecution).

38. In Harary v. Blumenthal, 555 F.2d 1113 (2d Cir. 1977) the court upheld IRS' disbarment of a CPA from further practice before it. *See* Annot., Disciplinary Action Under 31 USCS § 1026 Authorizing Secretary of the Treasury to Suspend and Disbar any Person Representing Claimants from Further Practice Before the Treasury Department, 50 A.L.R. Fed. 817 (1980).

39. In Shahmoon v. General Development Corp., CCH Fed. Sec. L. Rep. ¶ 94,308 (S.D.N.Y. 1973), plaintiffs claimed damages under Section 10(b) of the Securities Exchange Act of 1934 and Section 17(a) of the Securities Act of 1933. Plaintiffs alleged damages of $150,000 from reliance on misleading statements in defendant's prospectus of accounts receivables, sales, and earnings for 1960 and 1961. Plaintiffs purchased stock and debentures and contended that the prospectus and financials should have disclosed that the installment purchasers of Florida land had no personal liability for GDC's accounts receivable. The court looked to GDC's methods, which it described as follows: "GDC recorded a homesite installment purchase as a sale at its full sale price at the time the purchaser made his first monthly payment. All costs, estimated and direct, relating to the sale were charged against

financials actually cause damage to plaintiffs.[40] Exemplary (punitive) damages are awarded only where defendant's conduct is willful, fraudulent, or wanton and reckless.[41]

---

income at that time as well, and anticipated future costs and expenses were recorded as estimated liabilities. During each accounting period, a charge against income was made for expected cancellations. The size of the charge which was arrived at was at best an estimated guess based upon past collection experience."

The report continues: "The published financial statements at issue were all audited and certified by Lybrand, Ross Bros. & Montgomery, a prominent accounting firm. They contained a full description of GDC's operations, including its accounting procedures, the way it dealt with delinquent accounts and installment purchases. They contained a fair presentation of GDC's financial position and the status of its home and homesite lot sales operations, on which this controversy is centered. These statements did not expressly indicate, however, that the purchaser was exempt from personal liability either in practice or by express contract provisions."

The court was impressed by the fact that GDC's accounting methods prevailed in the industry and that the SEC had never complained but had, in fact, required a GDC competitor to adopt GDC's methods. Under such circumstances the court could find nothing misleading and held: "Defendant's financial statements and accounting procedures cannot be considered fraudulent when they conform with generally accepted accounting procedures as that term is understood by at least a majority of accounting experts in the field and when the methods used are endorsed by the accounting profession as a whole."

In Colonial Realty Corporation v. Brunswick Corporation, 337 F. Supp. 546 (S.D.N.Y. 1971), plaintiff sued Brunswick Corporation, certain of its officers and directors, brokerage firms, and Brunswick's auditors (Arthur Andersen & Co.). Plaintiff claimed the prospectus and registration statement under the Securities Act of 1933 was misleading. More specifically, plaintiff claimed a financing arrangement with C.I.T. Corporation should have been shown as long-term debt, which would include and reveal the interest charge, instead of as a current liability, which did not involve revealing the interest charge. The financing arrangement related to installment obligations arising out of the sale of pinsetter equipment and interest was pegged at 6.5 percent over the prime lending rate. The court noted that the accounting judgments were made in good faith and based on generally accepted accounting principles. The court further called attention to the fact that the matter could not have been material in terms of causing loss because the interest rate was disclosed in Brunswick's 8-K report filed with the SEC and had been mentioned in *Fortune, Barron's,* and in a Loeb, Rhoades report on Brunswick that had been sent to plaintiff. Plaintiff could not under these circumstances claim it was misled or damaged.

In Crane Company v. Westinghouse Air Brake Company, 419 F.2d 787 (2d Cir. 1969), plaintiff sued under proxy rule 14a-9 (17 C.F.R. § 240, 14a-9), which the U.S. Supreme Court has held gives rise to a private right of action. Crane Company claimed Air Brake used misleading information in soliciting proxies in connection with Air Brake's proposed merger into American Standard, Inc. More specifically, Crane alleged that Standard's 1967 earnings were overstated by 25 percent because Standard failed to charge foreign currency losses of $3,333,000 against income; Rule 3-09 of Regulation S-X was cited. The court rejected the contention, however, noting that (1) the loss was as yet unrealized by conversion of foreign currencies into U.S. dollars, (2) the facts as to the unrealized loss were fully disclosed, (3) the loss was charged against a reserve that had been set up to absorb such losses and gains, and (4) expert testimony indicated the reserve was properly created in accordance with generally accepted accounting principles to cover the unrealized effects of foreign currency valuations. Apparently there were no defendant accountants involved.

40. In Bunge Corp. v. Eide, 372 F. Supp. 1058 (D.N.D. 1974), the defendant CPAs certified financial statements for 1963 through 1968, which valued inventories of sunflower seeds on the basis of

"local market," instead of cost quoted on the commodity exchange. There was no ready market quotation available for unprocessed sunflowers as there was for grain. In ruling for the defendant CPAs, the court noted that plaintiff was fully aware that the value of unprocessed sunflowers was stated in reports at the local market: "Defendants' method of stating unprocessed sunflower inventories at local market was not in accordance with generally accepted accounting principles. In all other respects, the financial statements and reports and auditing procedures were in accordance with generally accepted auditing procedures. There is no evidence that the sunflower inventories were sold for less than the stated valuations, and there is no evidence that the defendants' financial statements and audit reports on Gunkelman did not fairly reflect the financial condition of the company for the period covered by the reports."

Further, "the Court concludes the defendants did not materially misrepresent the financial condition of R.F. Gunkelman and Sons, and in extending credit, plaintiff's reliance was on Gunkelman principals and not on the reports of its accountants."

In Berkowitz v. Baron, 428 F. Supp. 1190 (S.D.N.Y. 1977), the accounting firm was found guilty of intentional misrepresentation. However, the damages were limited to $550, since the measure of damages was out-of-pocket losses, and the investors never paid the purchase price for the firm that went into bankruptcy.

In Vanderbilt Growth Fund, Inc. v. Superior Court, 164 Cal. Rptr. 621 (Cal. App. 1980), the motion by Arthur Young & Co. for summary judgment was granted because the securities in question were worthless both before and after the audit so that any negligence or breach of contract by the auditor could not have caused the loss.

For a complete analysis of recoverable damages, see the discussion in Chapter 5 at note 59.

41. Louisiana, Massachusetts, Nebraska, and Washington do not allow punitive damages. In Jones v. Miles, 656 F.2d 103 (5th Cir. 1981), the court set aside an award of punitive damages against a CPA and others because punitive damages cannot be recovered under section 10(b) of the Exchange Act, nor under section 12(2) of the Securities Act.

In Franklin Supply Co. v. Tolman, 454 F.2d 1059 (9th Cir. 1972), the appeals court set aside an award of $150,000 punitive damages against Peat, Marwick, Mitchell & Co. where Peat had been engaged by buyer (Franklin) and seller (Servicios) with each to split the fee to audit the subsidiary being sold (Peticon). The trial court held, based on testimony of plaintiff's expert witness, Eric Kohler (author of *Dictionary for Accountants*), that the audit report prepared by Peat, Marwick, Mitchell & Co. should have disclosed that the audit supervisor had been a member of the board of directors of the acquired firm (Peticon) during the 1959 contract negotiations and was an alternate director of the selling firm (Servicios) during the audit of Peticon.

In setting aside the award of punitive damages, the appeals court said: "Accepting the trial court's finding that Southerland should have made a written statement in the audit report of his association with Servicios as an alternative director and that he should have defined his understanding of the term 'current replacement value,' we do not agree that it must be concluded therefrom as a matter of law that Southerland and PMM were guilty of fraud. For actual fraud to exist, assuming Colorado law to apply, more than nondisclosure must exist. There must be actual concealment." The appeals court acknowledged that an auditor is liable for acting negligently or fraudulently but rejected the lower court's ruling that an auditor is a fiduciary. Since plaintiff had already recovered from the seller for damages due to overstatement of inventory, the recovery from the auditor was limited to the fee paid plus certain costs and expenses.

Compare Midwest Supply, Inc., d/b/a H & R Block Co. v. Waters, 510 P.2d 876 (Nev. 1973), where the court upheld $100,000 punitive damages for advertising accurate tax preparation while employing as tax return preparer a former construction worker who had received no formal training in tax return preparation.

When materially misleading financials cause losses, the courts can usually find violations of GAAP or GAAS. For example, in *Herzfeld v. Laventhol, Krekstein, Horwath & Horwath,* the court held the auditing firm liable for reporting profit on real estate transactions that were never consummated and rejected the accounting firm's argument that its responsibility was limited to the contents of its audit report.[42] The court buttressed its opinion by finding that the financials violated GAAP.

PRACTICAL POINTER

In order to avoid liability, accounting firms should refuse to associate themselves with materially misleading reports despite the fact that professional standards provide for qualified and adverse opinions or disclaimers of opinion. This is true even in the unaudited situation. Consider that paragraph 41 of *SSARS No. 1,* dealing with unaudited reports, provides: "If the accountant believes that modification of his standard report is not adequate to indicate the deficiencies in the financial statements taken as a whole, he should withdraw from the compilation or review engagement and provide no further services with respect to those financial statements." For a summary of cases involving both successful and unsuccessful use of disclaimers and qualified opinions see note 11 in Chapter 5. For cases dealing with the unaudited situation see note 33 in Chapter 5.

Conclusiveness of Expert Testimony. Where application of auditing standards requires expertise in (1) evaluating and testing internal controls, (2) statistical sampling of transactions, and (3) obtaining competent evidential matter, expert testimony will be conclusive. However, where communication of findings is involved, expert testimony as to compliance with GAAP will be persuasive but not conclusive.[43]

---

42. Herzfeld v. Laventhol, Krekstein, Horwath & Horwath, 540 F.2d 27 (2d Cir. 1976). The court said: "Laventhol . . . contends . . . that the only statement made by an auditor upon which an investor is entitled to rely is the auditor's opinion letter. We agree with none of these arguments."

43. For example, in the criminal case of United States v. Simon, 425 F.2d 796 (2d Cir. 1969), *cert. denied* 397 U.S. 1006 (1970), the trial court's charge to the jury is summarized by the U.S. Court of Appeals at pp. 805-806 of the opinion: "the 'critical test' was whether the financial statements as a whole 'fairly presented the financial position of Continental as of September 30, 1962, and whether it accurately reported the operations for fiscal 1962.' If they did not, the basic issue became whether defendants acted in good faith. Proof of compliance with generally accepted standards was 'evidence which may be very persuasive but not necessarily conclusive that he acted in good faith, and that the facts as certified were not materially false or misleading.' " In United States

Custom is relevant in establishing the standard for professional conduct because it suggests what is feasible, what is within the realm of knowledge, and what the far-reaching consequences of the court's decision might be.[44] If courts impose a standard higher than professional custom, liability may be imposed upon those doing everything that they have been taught and in all respects adhering to customary professional practice so that professionals will be unsure of the required standards of practice. Since laypersons are not conversant with the complexities of professional practice, expert testimony is necessary to establish the professional custom and its basis.[45]

Outside of the professions, the courts consistently hold that trades and businesses cannot concur in a careless or dangerous practice below the standard of reasonable prudence and thereby establish a negligent standard of care. In such cases, evidence of custom is not conclusive in determining the standard of conduct, but is admissible as one factor in determining the standard unless the custom is so hazardous that the negligence of those who follow it is patent.[46]

Although the courts have normally given preferred treatment to medical practitioners, inroads are now being made upon both the conclusiveness of medical custom and the necessity of expert medical testimony. Community standards, which reflected differences be-

---

v. Weiner, 578 F.2d 757 (9th Cir. 1978), the charge to the jury was that deviation from GAAP or GAAS was evidence, but not necessarily conclusive evidence, that the defendants did not act honestly and that the financials were materially misleading.

As to necessity of expert testimony, see note 34.

44. Darling v. Charleston Community Memorial Hosp., 33 Ill.2d 326, 331, 211 N.E.2d 253, 257 (1965); Annot., Propriety in Medical Malpractice Case, of Admitting Testimony Regarding Physician's Usual Custom or Habit in Order to Establish Nonliability, 10 A.L.R.4th 1243 (1981).

45. Annot., 81 A.L.R.2d 597 (1962); Annot., 68 A.L.R.2d 426 (1959).

46. Morris, "Custom and Negligence," 42 *Colum. L. Rev.* 1147 (1942). In Texas & Pac. Ry. v. Behymer, 189 U.S. 468, 470 (1903), the plaintiff (train brakeman) obeyed orders to get on top of train cars covered with ice and let brakes off. The engine then picked up the train cars and stopped suddenly, which upset plaintiff's balance so that he caught the bottom of his trousers on a projecting nail and was thrown between the cars. The United States Supreme Court rejected the argument that liability depended on "whether the freight train was handled in the usual way" and held that "this exception needs no discussion. The charge embodied one of the commonplaces of the law. What usually is done may be evidence of what ought to be done, but what ought to be done is fixed by a standard of reasonable prudence, whether it is complied with or not." *Also see* The T. J. Hooper, 60 F.2d 737 (2d Cir. 1932) (tugboat not equipped with radio set to receive storm warnings held unseaworthy); Marsh Wood Prod. Co. v. Babcock & Wilcox Co., 207 Wis. 209, 240 N.W. 392 (1932) (jury was authorized in finding failure to test steel used in boiler negligent despite contrary custom of manufacturers); Mayhew v. Sullivan Mining Co., 76 Me. 100, 112 (1884) (customary practice of leaving ladder-holes in the platforms of dark mines unguarded and unlit held inadmissible).

tween remote rural areas and large metropolitan centers, have been abandoned by many courts that now consider locality as only one factor in a decision. This eliminates the effect of the "conspiracy of silence" among local practitioners who will not testify, as well as the possibility of an unsatisfactory local standard.[47]

In cases of gross medical and surgical errors the doctrine of *res ipsa loquitur* (the thing speaks for itself) is invoked to establish a prima facie case without expert testimony. This doctrine is most commonly applied when foreign objects are left in the body,[48] when the injury occurs to a part of the body not under treatment,[49] or when burns are found on the body.[50] A few courts are now considering customary medical practice as only one of several factors in determining liability.[51] In *Helling v. Carey*[52] the plaintiff sued defendant ophthalmologists for alleged failure to detect the presence of open-angle glaucoma during a five-year period of treatment for eye irritation. When the plaintiff finally complained of loss of peripheral vision, the defendants tested her eye pressure and field of vision and discovered a permanent loss of most of her vision due to glaucoma. At the time of discovery, the plaintiff was 32 years of age. Defendants produced undisputed testimony of medical experts of customary practice, which did not require routine pressure tests for patients under 40 years of age because of the rarity of glaucoma in that age group. The court held, despite customary practice, the defendants were negligent as a matter of law and liable for the plaintiff's resulting blindness. Acknowledging that only 1 out of 25,000 persons under 40 years of age contracts glaucoma, the court said this individual was entitled to the same protection as those over 40 when this protection can be afforded by applying a simple test.

One way to interpret this decision is to view it as a balancing of the interest of two innocent parties; Justice Utter's concurring opinion states that when one of two innocent parties must bear the risk of loss, it should fall on the doctor since s/he could have prevented the disease. Another view might emphasize the remedial effect of requiring the medical profession to establish higher standards whenever customary practice fails to meet world demands by falling below the standard of reasonable prudence.

The SEC View

The SEC positions on the standard of communication and conclusiveness of expert testimony are as follows:

1. The auditor has an obligation that goes beyond specific GAAP and GAAS or professional custom to effectively communicate material information.[53]
2. If GAAP or GAAS are found lacking, the SEC will not hesitate to invoke its authority to establish meaningful standards of performance regardless of expert testimony as to professional standards.[54]

The auditor's duty as perceived from this position (1) requires accountants to blow the whistle on man-

---

47. 40 *Fordham L. Rev.* 435 (1971); 43 *Miss. L. J.* 587, 589 (1972); 44 *Wash. L. Rev.* 505 (1969); Annot., Malpractice Testimony; Competency of Physician or Surgeon from One Locality to Testify, in Malpractice Case, as to Standard of Care Required of Defendant Practicing in Another Locality, 37 A.L.R.3d 420 (1971).

48. Jefferson v. United States, 77 F. Supp. 706 D.Md. (1948) (towel); French v. Fischer, 50 Tenn. App. 587, 362 S.W.2d 926 (1962) (sponge); *Also see* Annot., Applicability of Res Ipsa Loquitur Where Plaintiff Must Prove Active or Gross Negligence, Willful Misconduct, Recklessness, or the Like, 23 A.L.R.3d 1083 (1969).

49. Evans v. Roberts, 172 Iowa 653, 154 N.W. 923 (1915) (tongue cut off when doctor was removing adenoids).

50. Montgomery v. Stary, 84 So. 2d 34 (Fla. 1955) (hot towels applied to newborn baby).

51. Note, "Medical Specialist May Be Found Negligent as a Matter of Law Despite Compliance with the Customary Practice of the Specialty," 28 *Vand. L. Rev.* 441 (1975).

52. Helling v. Carey 82 Wash. 2d 514, 519 P.2d 981 (1974).

53. *See In re* Associated Gas & Electric Co., 11 SEC 975, 1058–59 (1942), where the Commission said: "Too much attention to the question whether the financial statements formally complied with principles, practices and conventions accepted at the time should not be permitted to blind us to the basic question whether the financial statements performed the function of enlightenment, which is their only reason for existence."

54. Where intangible assets were valued on the basis of the par of the stock for various reasons and the respondent accounting firm attempted to justify the accounting based on uncontradicted testimony of members of other firms of certified public accountants, the Commission ruled: "While the opinions of qualified expert accountants may be helpful, this Commission must in the last analysis weigh the value of expert testimony against its own judgment of what is sound accounting practice." *SEC Accounting Series Release No. 73*, "In the Matter of Haskins & Sells and Andrew Stewart (1952)."

When the Commission rejected *Accounting Principles Board Opinion No. 2*, "Accounting for the Investment Credit," it was made clear that the Commission would decide for itself what constitutes generally accepted accounting principles. The Commission said its policy "is intended to support the development of accounting principles and methods of presentation by the profession but to leave the Commission free to obtain the information and disclosure contemplated by the securities laws and conformance with accounting principles which have gained general acceptance," *SEC Accounting Series Release No. 96*, "Accounting for the 'Investment Credit' " (1963).

In 1973 the Commission issued *Accounting Series Release No. 150,* which indicated that standards and practices promulgated by the FASB in its Statements and Interpretations would be considered as GAAP and those contrary as misleading. However, the SEC noted that it is necessary to depart from such pronouncements if failure to do so results in misleading statements. In *Accounting Series Release No. 153*, issued in 1974, the Commission established *new* GAAP and GAAS on its own, which should lay to rest any assumption that it is abdicating to the FASB or the AICPA. See the discussion in Chapter 3.

12

agement misconduct by reporting it to the SEC and the public and (2) requires *effective* communication of material information so as fairly and meaningfully to inform the lay investor.

The following comments contrast AICPA and Commission views with respect to the duty of effective communication:

> Fairness in presentation is a very important concept, and perhaps it is now blending into a legal concept even while it remains an accounting one with the same name. By "fairness in presentation" I mean that the financial statements reported on by the auditor must reflect the economic realities of the entire business operation—and I emphasize the word "realities"— and must not have been arrived at merely mechanically or by rote, even though all of the procedures and processes, when taken in segments, may each have comported with generally accepted accounting principles or generally accepted auditing standards.
>
> Hence, while GAAP and auditing standards are, of course, extremely useful tools in arriving at fair presentation, they are not necessarily insurers of that arrival. This statement may represent an inherent contradiction to accountants, who believe that proper adherence to generally accepted accounting principles and auditing standards must inevitably lead to fair presentation. But I think that that distinction is understandable to nonaccountants and even to laymen who are neither accountants nor lawyers.
>
> It will not do, in my opinion, to view accounting as a modular concept which has differences from reality, so that only initiates or experts can really understand it, and they must act as interpreters for everyone else. Rather, I think that intelligent and educated persons who are not accountants, but who are businessmen and who are investors and who are lawyers and others, must be able to look at it and be informed by—and certainly not misled by—accounting statements even though they are statements that are made in a complex discipline.[55]

REASONABLE APPLICATION OF PROFESSIONAL STANDARDS

In order to produce reasonable results, GAAP and GAAS must be reasonably applied. Under GAAP and GAAS, the auditor has little authority or responsibility to see that GAAP are reasonably applied. When there are no specific criteria for selecting alternative GAAP, the auditor is discouraged from challenging any of the available alternatives. This has given rise to various schemes calculated to produce misleading results, such as artful accounting, creative accounting, and salami accounting.

Artful accounting involves incomplete disclosure,

or disclosures buried in footnotes or in the auditor's report itself, or failure to give equal prominence to related matters. For example, where realization of income and the related receivables is doubtful, the auditor usually gives a "subject to realization" qualification in the report. Although disclaimers and qualifications have been effective in avoiding liability in some cases, they have not avoided liability where there has been a failure to communicate significant information that was known or should have been known to the CPA in the particular factual setting.[56]

Creative accounting involves the selective choice and/or corruption of accounting principles to present a misleading impression. Corruption is accomplished by applying accepted principles in inappropriate circumstances or in an unacceptable or misleading manner. Creative accounting sometimes goes even further and actually involves the structuring and implementing of transactions primarily for the sake of presenting an attractive financial picture with little or no regard for economic reality.[57]

Salami accounting is the practice of covering up past errors "whereby the amount of the error is sliced very thin and taken up gradually over future periods so as not to distort the main fare."[58] The incentive for salami accounting is that the auditor avoids having to blow the whistle on himself. Auditors seldom benefit from fraudulent schemes except for possibly retaining a client of dubious value; however, covering up past mistakes does provide a powerful incentive against full disclosure.

A ROLE FOR UNIFORMITY AND CONSERVATISM

If the accounting profession is to meet its challenge, uniformity and conservatism must be increasingly imposed on accounting practice. Alternative procedures give latitude in reporting that can ultimately result in investor losses.

Although both understatement and overstatement of income are undesirable, the major losses and finan-

---

55. Paul Gonson, "Disciplinary Proceedings and Other Remedies Available to the SEC," *Business Lawyer,* March 1975, p. 191. © 1975 by *Business Lawyer.*

56. One of the earliest court decisions involving auditor's liability warned that a "subject to realization" qualification is an unsatisfactory communication that assets are overstated. *See In re* London and General Bank, [1895] 2 Ch. 673. The case of Herzfeld v. Laventhol, Krekstein, Horwath & Horwath, 540 F.2d 27 (2d Cir. 1976), involved a similar problem. For a summary of court decisions relating to disclaimers and qualified opinions, see note 11 in Chapter 5. For cases dealing with the unaudited situation, see note 33 in Chapter 5.

57. See Staff of Securities and Exchange Commission, Report to Special Subcomm. on Investigations of the House Committee on Interstate and Foreign Commerce on the Financial Collapse of the Penn. Central Company, 92d Cong., 2d Sess. 33–83 (1972).

58. Henry P. Hill, "Responsibilities and Liabilities of Auditors and Accountants—An Accountant's View," *Business Lawyer,* March 1975, pp. 169–80 at 179–80.

cial scandals have resulted from overstatement of profits. Conservatism is supposedly a characteristic of financial reporting that involves selecting the lowest alternative for measuring income or assets, such as the lower-of-cost-or-market rule for valuing inventories. Events leading to the credibility gap have demonstrated that conservatism is not really an operational accounting concept. The credibility gap has resulted in large measure from unconservative accounting facilitated by permissive rules that permit alternative practices to produce unconservative results.

SUGGESTIONS FOR FURTHER READING

Litigation and Contemporary Disclosure

Gruenbaum, Samuel, H., and Marc I. Steinberg. "Accountants' Liability and Responsibility: Securities, Criminal and Common Law." *Loyola of Los Angeles Law Review,* March 1980, pp. 247–314.

Stern, Duke N. *An Accountant's Guide to Malpractice Liability.* Charlottesville, Va.: Michie Company, 1979.

"Symposium on Accounting and the Federal Securities Laws." *Vanderbilt Law Review,* January 1975, pp. 1–279.

The Credibility Gap

Briloff, Abraham J. *More Debits Than Credits: The Burnt Investor's Guide to Financial Statements.* New York: Harper & Row, 1976.

Dirks, Raymond L., and Leonard Gross. *The Great Wall Street Scandal.* New York: McGraw-Hill, 1974.

McClintick, David. *Stealing from the Rich: The Home-Stake Oil Swindle.* New York: M. Evans and Company, 1978.

QUESTIONS AND PROBLEMS

1. What are the two broad functions of audit services in America?
2. What is the relationship of accurate information to economic freedom and that of economic freedom to political freedom?
3. Is the auditor's primary responsibility to the public, or to the client who pays his or her fee, or to some other specific group?
4. What do you perceive as the underlying cause of the "credibility gap"?
5. Would the long-run interests of the auditing profession be served by limiting liability of auditors to $100,000 for any one engagement?
6. Should the auditor's responsibility for "fair" presentation include effective communication that adheres to a test of truth and candor so as to present material information without misleading? Should this standard make the auditor liable to investors for unintentional misrepresentation?
7. Define and distinguish (1) *artful accounting,* (2) *creative accounting,* and (3) *salami accounting.*
8. Discuss whether an auditing firm should serve as a consultant on rate making to a regulatory agency under each of the following circumstances:
    a. The auditing firm has numerous audit clients that will be directly affected by the rate making.
    b. The auditing firm has no clients affected by the specific regulatory agency, but the auditing firm has clients in the same industry regulated by other similar agencies.
    c. The auditing firm has no clients in the regulated industry.
9. Consider each of the following examples and discuss whether auditors should blow the whistle, and to whom, in order to fulfill their assigned social role:
    a. The president was recently convicted of petty larceny in a matter that did not involve the company.
    b. The president took an unauthorized pleasure trip to the Bahamas in the firm airplane, and all costs were charged to travel expenses.
    c. The firm padded cost figures submitted to the Department of Defense.
    d. The firm sold appreciated long-term investments at a gain to cover operating losses so that insiders could sell their stock.
    e. The firm falsified tax returns filed with the Internal Revenue Service.

APPENDIX

The Big Eight

The nation's eight largest accounting firms listed alphabetically:

Arthur Andersen & Co., 69 West Washington Street, Chicago, Illinois 60602.

Arthur Young & Co., 277 Park Avenue, New York, New York 10017.

Coopers & Lybrand, 1251 Avenue of the Americas, New York, New York 10020.

Deloitte Haskins & Sells, 1114 Avenue of the Americas, New York, New York 10036.

Ernst & Whinney, 1300 Union Commerce Building, Cleveland, Ohio 44115.

Peat, Marwick, Mitchell & Co., 345 Park Avenue, New York, New York 10154.

Price Waterhouse & Co., 1251 Avenue of the Americas, New York, New York 10020.

Touche Ross & Co., 1633 Broadway, New York, New York 10019.

The Next Four

The nation's four next largest accounting firms—after the Big Eight—listed alphabetically:

Alexander Grant & Co., 1 Huntington Quadrangle, New York, New York 10017.

Laventhol & Horwath, 919 Third Avenue, New York, New York 10022.

Main Hurdman, 55 East 52d Street, New York, New York 10055.

Seidman & Seidman, 15 Columbus Circle, New York, New York 10023.

2

Evolution of Responsibility and Independence

This chapter covers:

BEGINNINGS IN SCOTLAND AND ENGLAND

Independent checking and verification have existed as long as accounting, but a long evolution preceded the development of the responsibility of the modern auditing profession, which is constrained to give an independent, professional opinion on the financial statements that constitute management's report of stewardship. Evidence indicates that this evolution in responsibility is still taking place.

The Scottish and English auditors were the immediate antecedents of the American auditor. In England the Joint Stock Companies Act of 1844 enabled businessmen to establish a corporate entity with transferable shares by registration, although limited liability by registration was not available until 1855. The 1844 law required that a "full and fair" balance sheet be sent to each shareholder before ordinary shareholder meetings and that auditors be appointed to report on the balance sheet.[1] Littleton points out the distrust of directors evident in these early English laws, which required auditors to be stockholders but did not permit them to hold any office in the company.[2]

Although "full and fair" balance sheets were to be filed with the Registrar of Companies, there were no enforcement provisions concerning either the filing or the content of the balance sheets.[3] The early "audits" simply consisted of checking to see that disbursements were supported by vouchers, and some apparently considered them a farce.[4]

In 1856 Parliament dropped the compulsory accounting and audit requirement, leaving such matters for private contract. The 1856 act, as well as the later 1862 act, did contain a model set of articles providing for auditors, but a company could avoid these provisions by filing its own articles.[5] Although audit requirements were provided for banking companies (1879), and the publication of accounts was required for railways (1868), gas works (1871), and electric companies (1882), not until 1900 was an annual audit again made obligatory for all companies registered under the Companies Acts. When compulsory filing of

1. H. C. Edey and Prot Panitpakdi, "British Company Accounting and the Law 1844–1900," reprinted in *Studies in the History of Accounting,* ed. A. C. Littleton and B. S. Yamey (Homewood, Ill.: Richard D. Irwin, 1956), pp. 356–61.

2. A. C. Littleton, *Accounting Evolution to 1900* (New York: Russell & Russell, 1966), p. 289.

3. H. C. Edey, "Company Accounting in the Nineteenth and Twentieth Centuries," reprinted in *Contemporary Studies in the Evolution of Accounting Thought,* ed. Michael Chatfield (Belmont, Calif.: Dickenson Publishing, 1968), p. 136.

4. Littleton, *Accounting Evolution to 1900,* p. 290. Auditors historically "certified" the correctness of the financial statements. The word *certify* was abandoned as a result of concern over auditors' liability after the *Ultramares* case held auditors liable to third parties for fraud. See the editorial in the *Journal of Accountancy,* July 1931.

5. Edey and Panitpakdi, "British Company Accounting and the Law 1844–1900," pp. 361–62.

annual balance sheets was finally introduced in 1907, family businesses were exempted.[6]

The professional accountant developed major importance first in Scotland. In 1854 a Royal Charter was granted by Queen Victoria's Court to the Society of Accountants in Edinburgh. Two other Scottish societies followed. The three then agreed upon uniform examination and apprenticeship requirements for a single class of membership designated "C.A." for "chartered accountant." All three groups combined in 1951 under a new charter as the Institute of Chartered Accountants of Scotland.[7]

In England a formal charter was granted in 1880 to The Institute of Chartered Accountants in England and Wales. Except for original members, admission was established only after examination and apprenticeship of five years (three years for university graduates) under a member of the Institute. The apprenticeship was so important that they were paid no salary, but rather they paid from $250 to $2,500 for the privilege of working in the office. In contrast with the Scottish society, in which membership consists of only one class, members today are designated either fellows (FCA) or associates (ACA).[8]

Another organization, incorporated in England in 1885 as the Society of Incorporated Accountants and Auditors, permitted its members to use the designation "Incorporated Accountant." The members of the Institute of Chartered Accountants in England and Wales at first looked down on the Society, but its influence grew rapidly and its admission policies were similar to those of the Institute. Mr. Justice Warrington, when restricting the use of "Incorporated Accountant" to Society members in 1907, said the designation conferred a definite status indicating reliability and integrity. The Society was amalgamated with the Institute of Chartered Accountants in England and Wales in 1957.[9]

DEVELOPMENT OF AMERICAN AUDITING FROM SCOTTISH AND ENGLISH PRACTICE

During the late 1800s Scottish and British accountants began coming to the United States to check on British investments in American industries. As early as 1890 the London auditing firm of Price Waterhouse & Co. sent its first agent to the United States. In 1900 Arthur Lowes Dickenson, an English Chartered Accountant, came from England to take charge of American operations of the firm. Since 1902 the firm has been auditor for the United States Steel Company.[10]

George O. May, born in England in 1875, became an English Chartered Accountant in 1896 and entered the London office of Price Waterhouse & Co. in 1897. Shortly thereafter he was sent to the United States. He served as senior partner of the Price Waterhouse firm in America from 1911, when Dickenson retired, until his own retirement in 1940. During this period he greatly influenced American accounting and auditing practice. Carey says of May: "His speeches, articles, and writings probably have had more influence on American accounting than those of any other man."[11]

Colonel Robert Montgomery also had a profound influence on American audit practice. With little formal training, he became a lawyer, a CPA, an army colonel during the Spanish-American War, a professor at Columbia University, and president of predecessor groups to the American Institute of Certified Public Accountants (American Association of Public Accountants, 1912–14; American Institute of Accountants, 1935–36). Montgomery, although a native American, was influential in importing English auditing practice by editing for American use in 1905 the leading English textbook on auditing practice.[12] The first edition of this book was known as *Auditing,* written by Lawrence R. Dicksee and edited by Robert H. Montgomery. Successive editions were entitled *Auditing Theory and Practice* by Robert H. Montgomery. This book is kept up to date by members of the auditing firm of Coopers & Lybrand.[13]

In 1911 three Scots established the American antecedent of Peat, Marwick, Mitchell & Co., which is

6. Ibid., pp. 371–73.

7. James Don Edwards, "The Antecedents of American Public Accounting," reprinted in *Contemporary Studies in the Evolution of Accounting Thought,* ed. Michael Chatfield (Belmont, Calif.: Dickenson Publishing, 1968), p. 156; John L. Carey, *The Rise of the Accounting Profession,* vol. 1 (New York: American Institute of Certified Public Accountants, 1969), p. 19.

8. Edwards, "The Antecedents of American Public Accounting," pp. 157–65; Carey, *Rise of the Accounting Profession,* vol. 1, p. 20; Nicholas A. H. Stacey, *English Accountancy 1800–1954* (London: Gee and Company Publishers, 1954), pp. 24–31.

9. *Institute of Chartered Accountants in England and Wales* (London: William Heinemann, 1966).

10. Carey, *Rise of the Accounting Profession,* vol. 1, p. 28.

11. Ibid., p. 136. *Also see* George O. May, *Memoirs and Accounting Thought of George O. May,* ed. Paul Grady (New York: Ronald Press, 1962) and George O. May, *Twenty-Five Years of Accounting Responsibility: 1911–1936* (New York: American Institute Publishing, 1936).

12. Robert H. Montgomery, *Fifty Years of Accountancy* (New York: Ronald Press, 1939).

13. Lawrence R. Dicksee, *Auditing,* ed. Robert H. Montgomery (New York: Ronald Press, 1905), succeeded by Robert H. Montgomery, *Auditing Theory and Practice* (New York: Ronald Press, 1912), which was followed by later editions: 3d in 1921, 4th in 1927, 5th in 1934, 6th in 1940. The 7th edition, in 1949, was entitled *Auditing* by Robert H. Montgomery, Norman J. Lenhart, and Alvin R. Jennings, and the 8th, in 1957, was entitled *Montgomery's Auditing* by Norman J. Lenhart and Philip L. Defliese. The 9th edition appeared in 1975 is entitled *Montgomery's Auditing* by Philip L. Defliese, Kenneth P. Johnson, and Roderick K. MacLeod.

16

reportedly the world's largest auditing firm. General Electric Company was one of its early clients.[14]

The need for early American auditing was brought about primarily by pressure from bankers and investors. The industrial revolution, an arbitrarily selected period of 1760 to 1850, when the steam engine came into widespread use, brought forth need for increased capital, which could be provided by the business corporation. Most states passed laws between 1837 and 1900 permitting incorporation of any lawful business.[15]

In 1896 New York passed the first state law setting up the professional designation of Certified Public Accountant. The first uniform CPA exam prepared by the American Institute of Accountants was given in 1917 and was used by California, Colorado, Florida, Michigan, Missouri, Nebraska, New Hampshire, New Jersey, and Tennessee.[16]

The practice of British auditors had been to make bookkeeping-type audits that checked in detail the additions and postings in the books of account. The main purpose of the audit was supposed to be detection of fraud, but much of the fraud was accomplished by failure to account for cash receipts, which could not be detected by examining the books. Since no audits were required by law in the United States before the federal securities laws of 1933 and 1934, the client had to be convinced that the benefits were worth the cost. That need led to evaluation of the system of internal control to determine the scope of the examination, sampling methods, and reduction of time spent on details.[17]

FEDERAL SECURITIES LEGISLATION AS A RESULT OF DEMANDS OF INVESTORS

The number of investors in corporate stocks and bonds increased drastically between 1900 and 1930. This change brought with it increasing pressure for a shift in accounting objectives from information for management and bankers to information for stockholders and investors. Accounting came to serve a new audience, which was interested more in the income statement and less in the balance sheet. Yet some firms failed to provide any depreciation, and others omitted income statements altogether.[18]

Controversy and criticism over financial reporting

practices developed. Professor William Z. Ripley was an early critic of financial reporting, and his book *Main Street and Wall Street*,[19] published in 1927, got much attention. In 1932 Berle and Means pointed out methods of accounting manipulations and criticized the inadequacy of information given to investors in their book, *The Modern Corporation and Private Property*.[20]

The stock market crash of 1929, by reinforcing the controversy over financial reporting, helped bring about the Securities Act of 1933. This act required registration of new securities, including financial statements certified by an independent accountant, and gave the Federal Trade Commission authority to prescribe uniform accounting rules. Auditors' liability to any purchaser of the securities was established where the registration statement contained false financial statements certified by the auditor.

The Securities Exchange Act of 1934 created the Securities and Exchange Commission, which was charged with administering the 1933 Act. All listed companies were required to file annual reports, and pursuant to power granted in the act, the SEC requires the annual report to be certified by independent auditors.[21]

AUDITING STANDARDS AND PROCEDURES BEFORE THE McKESSON & ROBBINS CASE

As dissatisfaction with reported corporate financial information increased after 1900, William C. Redfield, the first secretary of commerce (Wilson administration), and officials of the Federal Reserve Board and the Federal Trade Commission became interested in bringing about reforms. Over 90 percent of the certifications by public accountants were the so-called balance sheet audits, which meant the certificate was based on examination of the books without personal observation of inventories or inspection of assets. The Federal Trade Commission was concerned about the lack of uniformity in such verifications. The Federal Reserve Board also took an interest in the matter, because bankers, of necessity, relied upon audited financial statements in making loans and, in turn, offered the commercial paper for discounting with Federal Reserve banks.

The Federal Trade Commission requested the American Institute of Accountants (since 1957 called the American Institute of Certified Public Accountants) to prepare a memorandum on "balance sheet au-

14. T. A. Wise, "The Very Private World of Peat, Marwick, Mitchell," *Fortune*, July 1, 1966, p. 91.

15. Eldon S. Hendriksen, *Accounting Theory*, rev. ed. (Homewood, Ill.: Richard D. Irwin, 1970), p. 50.

16. James Don Edwards, "Some Significant Developments of Public Accounting in the United States," reprinted in *Contemporary Studies in the Evolution of Accounting Thought*, ed. Michael Chatfield (Belmont, Calif.: Dickenson Publishing, 1968), pp. 199-206.

17. R. Gene Brown, "Changing Audit Objectives and Techniques," reprinted in *Contemporary Studies*, ed. Chatfield, pp. 181-82.

18. Hendriksen, *Accounting Theory*, p. 65.

19. William Z. Ripley, *Main Street and Wall Street* (Boston: Little, Brown, 1927).

20. Adolf A. Berle, Jr., and Gardiner C. Means, *The Modern Corporation and Private Property* (New York: Macmillan, 1933).

21. Carey, *Rise of the Accounting Profession*, vol. 1, pp. 170-94.

dits'' as a step toward standardization. An Institute committee including Robert Montgomery and George O. May was appointed in 1916 to confer with the secretary of commerce, the Federal Trade Commission, and the Federal Reserve Board in preparing such a memorandum. This committee adopted with little change the *Memorandum on Balance Sheet Audits*, which had been prepared in 1912 by John C. Scobie for internal use by Price Waterhouse & Co.[22] After approval by the Federal Trade Commission and acceptance by the Federal Reserve Board, the memorandum was published in the April 1917 issue of the *Federal Reserve Bulletin* and reissued in 1917 in pamphlet form under the misnomer *Uniform Accounting*.[23] It dealt with financial reporting and audit procedures and covered both the balance sheet and the income statement. In 1918 it was reissued as *Approved Methods for the Preparation of Balance-Sheet Statements*. In 1929 the Federal Reserve Board published a revised edition called *Verification of Financial Statements*.[24]

As accountants came to recognize the importance of the investor in financial reporting, the income statement increased in importance. In 1936 the Institute issued its revision of the memorandum under the title *Examination of Financial Statements by Independent Public Accountants*.[25] By the time the famous *McKesson & Robbins* case developed in 1938, the SEC was well established, but auditing standards still were basically as expressed in the 1936 revised statement, which did not require the auditor to observe or test the taking of a physical inventory or to confirm receivables. The New York State Society of CPAs in November 1938 adopted a resolution giving the auditor the right to rely on representations of management as to physical quantities and valuation of inventories.

IMPROVEMENT OF AUDITING STANDARDS AND PROCEDURES AFTER THE *McKESSON & ROBBINS* CASE

On Monday, December 5, 1938, a federal judge in Hartford, Connecticut, granted a petition for the appointment of a receiver for McKesson & Robbins, Inc.

The action was brought by stockholder Vincent W. Dennis, who alleged that waste and mismanagement had occurred and that the firm fraudulently included in its assets fictitious inventories and accounts receivable aggregating in excess of $10 million. The suit apparently was instigated by the firm's president, Frank Donald Coster, after he was confronted by Julian F. Thompson, treasurer and director, who had discovered the facts. On the following Thursday, trustees were appointed when the firm applied for reorganization under the Chandler Act, admitting that the last financial statements had overvalued assets by at least $10 million.[26]

The firm's 1937 financial statements had been audited by Price Waterhouse & Co. When George O. May, senior partner of Price Waterhouse, went to a meeting of stunned McKesson & Robbins executives on December 5, he assured them that as far as he knew the McKesson & Robbins books were in order. Subsequent investigation revealed, however, that of consolidated assets of over $87 million, approximately $10 million of inventory and $9 million of accounts receivable were fictitious.[27] The claim of McKesson's trustee against Price Waterhouse & Co. was subsequently settled without litigation upon the refund of $522,402.29, which had been paid by McKesson &

22. C. W. DeMond, *Price, Waterhouse & Co. in America* (New York: Comet Press, 1951), p. 125; May, *Memoirs*, p. 36; "Uniform Accounting," *Journal of Accountancy*, June 1917, pp. 401–33; T. A. Wise, "The Auditors Have Arrived" (Part I), *Fortune*, November 1960, p. 153; Hendriksen, *Accounting Theory*, pp. 60–61; Carey, *The Rise of the Accounting Profession*, vol. 1, pp. 129–32.

23. It was also published in the *Journal of Accountancy*, June 1919, pp. 401–33, and in *Canadian Chartered Accountant*, July 1917, pp. 5–33.

24. *Verification of Financial Statements*, rev. ed. (Washington, D.C.: U.S. Government Printing Office, 1929); *Journal of Accountancy*, May 1929, pp. 321–54.

25. *Examination of Financial Statements by Independent Public Accountants* (New York: American Institute of Accountants, January 1936).

26. *New York Times*, December 7, 1938, through December 9, 1938.

27. The incredible facts behind the case are completely unfolded in two articles that appeared in the *New Yorker*. The principal figure, Philip Musica, used the alias Frank Donald Coster. In 1909 Musica had pleaded guilty to fraud in connection with bribing customs examiners and importing far more cheese than disclosed by false invoices and bills of lading. After he had served less than six months, his sentence was commuted by President Taft.

Musica then organized the United States Hair Company and borrowed on human hair that he only pretended to buy. When he was caught, he entered a plea of guilty in 1913 as he had done before. But 22 banks had lost a total of about $600,000. When finally sentenced in 1916, after spending almost three years in prison, he received a suspended sentence and was placed on probation.

In 1920 Musica started in what appeared to be the pharmaceutical business, but he was actually involved in bootlegging alcohol during prohibition. In 1923 he ostensibly manufactured drugs under the name of Girard & Company, and by 1925 the firm's annual volume was nearly two million dollars. Although he was sole owner of Girard & Company, Musica had Price Waterhouse & Co. audit the books. He learned about current auditing practices, including the fact that auditors did not observe physical inventories unless specifically requested to do so. With financial support of bankers and a stock issue, Musica purchased in 1926 McKesson & Robbins, which was merged with his firm and moved to Fairfield.

On Friday, December 16, 1938, Musica shot himself after disclosure of his true identity and fictitious assets at McKesson & Robbins. Wardall, the trustee appointed by the United States District Court, kept the firm going. A reorganization plan was approved, the firm was returned to private ownership, and trading in McKesson & Robbins stock was resumed on the New York Stock Exchange on July 15, 1941. See Robert Shaplen, "Annals of Crime The Metamorphosis of Philip Musica," *New Yorker*, October 22, 1955, and October 29, 1955. The story is also covered in "America's Boldest Swindler," *Saturday Evening Post*, February 28, 1953, pp. 34–35.

Robbins to Price Waterhouse for all opinions subsequent to January 1, 1933.[28]

Trading of the McKesson stock was suspended so that all investors might have equal protection. When the SEC conducted its investigation, it found wide disagreement among auditors as to procedures to be employed in examination of inventories and receivables.[29]

The SEC findings[30] can be summarized as follows:

1. It found that the auditors, Price Waterhouse & Co., "failed to employ that degree of vigilance, inquisitiveness, and analysis of the evidence available that is necessary in a professional undertaking, and is recommended in all well-known and authoritative works on auditing." The SEC concluded that "meticulous verification of the inventory was not needed in this case to discover the fraud."

2. Though the profession had been emphasizing that auditors are not guarantors and should not be responsible for fraud detection, the SEC ruled: "We feel that the discovery of gross overstatements in the accounts is a major purpose of an audit even though it be conceded that it might not disclose every minor defalcation."

3. It commended the profession in adoption (subsequent to the scandal) of physical contact with clients' inventories and confirmation of accounts and notes receivable as normal procedures.

4. It pointed out that the activities of management must be included within the audit; therefore it was recommended that auditors be elected by stockholders and that nonofficer members of the board of directors make all nominations of auditors.

The SEC then suggested to the American Institute of Accountants that a distinction should be made between auditing "standards" and auditing "procedures." The SEC further amended Regulation S-X to require the auditor's certificate to state whether "the audit was made in accordance with generally accepted auditing standards applicable in the circumstances."[31]

Thus required to define such "standards," the Institute committee submitted a report in 1947, "Tentative Statement of Auditing Standards—Their Generally Accepted Significance and Scope." Auditing standards were said to deal with "quality of performance and objectives to be attained," while procedures "relate to acts to be performed." Confirmation of receivables and physical observation of inventories are thus procedures. The brochure was approved by the Institute membership in September 1948, and in 1954 it was replaced by the booklet *Generally Accepted Auditing Standards—Their Significance and Scope,* now superseded by *Statement on Auditing Standards No. 1.*[32]

Though interpretations change, the original auditing standards (as opposed to procedures) have remained unchanged:

General Standards

1. The examination is to be performed by a person or persons having adequate technical training and proficiency as an auditor.
2. In all matters relating to the assignment, an independence in mental attitude is to be maintained by the auditor or auditors.
3. Due professional care is to be exercised in the performance of the examination and the preparation of the report.

Standards of Field Work

1. The work is to be adequately planned and assistants, if any, are to be properly supervised.
2. There is to be a proper study and evaluation of the existing internal control as a basis for reliance thereon and for the determination of the resultant extent of the tests to which auditing procedures are to be restricted.
3. Sufficient competent evidential matter is to be obtained through inspection, observation, inquiries, and confirmations to afford a reasonable basis for an opinion regarding the financial statements under examination.

Standards of Reporting

1. The report shall state whether the financial statements are presented in accordance with generally accepted accounting principles.
2. The report shall state whether such principles have been consistently observed in the current period in relation to the preceding period.
3. Informative disclosures in the financial statements are to be regarded as reasonably adequate unless otherwise stated in the report.
4. The report shall either contain an expression of opinion regarding the financial statements, taken as a whole, or an assertion to the effect that an

28. DeMond, *Price, Waterhouse & Co. in America*, p. 273. At p. 4 the author notes that the style "Price, Waterhouse & Co." has remained the same since established in England in 1874, except for the later elimination of the comma.

29. Concerning inventories, Montgomery suggested in his fifth edition of *Auditing Theory and Practice*, published in 1934, at p. 182, that "physical tests should be made of a sufficient number of items to test the accuracy of the records." At p. 157 concerning accounts receivable, he said that "confirmation of accounts receivable is desirable but is not yet considered an essential part of every balance sheet examination."

30. *SEC Accounting Series Release No. 19,* "In the Matter of McKesson & Robbins, Inc." (1940).

31. Carey, *Rise of the Accounting Profession,* vol. 1, pp. 147-48.

32. *Statement on Auditing Standards No. 1,* p. 5.

opinion cannot be expressed. When an overall opinion cannot be expressed, the reasons therefor should be stated. In all cases where an auditor's name is associated with financial statements, the report should contain a clear-cut indication of the character of the auditor's examination, if any, and the degree of responsibility he is taking.[33]

Before the SEC had announced results of its investigation, the executive committee of the American Institute of Accountants in January 1939 authorized appointment of a committee on auditing procedure "to examine into auditing procedure and other related questions in the light of recent public discussion." The result was the beginning of a series of statements on auditing procedure. The first of these, issued in October 1939, was *Statement on Auditing Procedure No. 1:* "Extensions of Auditing Procedure," which thereafter required both observation and testing of a physical inventory and the confirmation of receivables.[34] The Committee on Auditing Procedure was succeeded by the Auditing Standards Executive Committee in 1973 and by the Auditing Standards Board in 1978.[35] AICPA ethics rule 202 requires adherence to auditing standards that are codified in a continuously updated loose-leaf service, *CCH AICPA Professional Standards.*

The *McKesson & Robbins* case was thus a major milestone in the development of American audit practice. Carey succinctly summarizes its effect:

> The *McKesson* case had been an abrasive experience for the profession as a whole—especially for those then in charge of the Institute's affairs—and most of all for the partners of the eminent accounting firm involved. Yet, if it cannot be said that the profession emerged with flying colors, it did come out of the affair without permanent injury. In fact, the results, in the long run, strengthened the profession's position. The importance of independent audits, and their unavoidable limitations, had been brought forcefully to the attention of many people who had given little

thought to the matter before. The constructive work resulting in *Statements on Auditing Procedure No. 1,* "Extensions of Auditing Procedure," led to a series of authoritative pronouncements on auditing standards and procedures, which . . . greatly strengthened the position of independent auditors.[36]

EVOLUTION OF THE AUDITOR'S REPORT

English Origins

The use of "auditor's certificate" to describe an audit report and "present fairly" as an attribute of financial statements has its origin in English practice. The English law, which abolished compulsory audits in 1856, included optional "model articles," which contained the following:

> The auditors . . . in every such Report . . . shall state whether, in their Opinion, the Balance Sheet is a *full and fair* Balance Sheet, . . . properly drawn up so as to exhibit a *true and correct* View of the State of the Company's Affairs. . . .[37] (Emphasis added.)

The auditor's reporting obligation during this permissive period was thus governed by the corporation's articles of incorporation. Illustrative of an audit report of the day is the following, made between 1874 and 1880:

> I certify that I have examined the above accounts and find them to be a true copy of those shewn in the books of the company.[38]

The English law of 1879, which provided for compulsory audits of banking companies, contained the following provision:

> The auditor or auditors shall make a report to the members on the accounts examined by him or them, and on every balance sheet laid before the company in general meeting during his or their tenure of office; and in every such report shall state whether, in his or their opinion, the balance-sheet referred to in the report is a *full and fair* balance-sheet properly drawn up, so as to exhibit a true and correct view of the state of the company's affairs, as shewn by the books of the company.[39] (Emphasis added.)

The following is an 1892 report under this act containing a "subject to realization" qualification:

33. Ibid.

34. In 1970 the Committee on Auditing Procedure of the AICPA issued *Statement on Auditing Procedure No. 43:* "Confirmation of Receivables and Observation of Inventories," which provides additional guidelines for the independent auditor in confirming receivables and observing inventories. It is codified at pp. 97–98 in *Statement on Auditing Standards No. 1,* issued in 1973 by the AICPA: "Restrictions imposed by the client on the scope of the examination most commonly concern the omission of the observation of inventory-taking or the confirmation of receivables by direct communication. In such cases when inventories or receivables are material, the independent auditor should indicate clearly in the scope paragraph (or in a middle paragraph) the limitations on his work and, generally, disclaim an opinion on the financial statements taken as a whole."

35. An excellent historical outline of the development of auditing procedures and standards is contained in *CCH AICPA Professional Standards,* AU Appendix A.

36. Carey, *Rise of the Accounting Profession,* vol. 2, p. 41.

37. 19 & 20 Vict., c. 47, Table B, art. 84.

38. This was the certificate of Locking discussed by the court in the first English case involving a suit against an auditor. See the opinion in Leeds Estate, Building and Investment Co. v. Shepherd, 36 Ch.D. 787 (1887).

39. This is quoted and discussed in the case of *In re* London and General Bank, 2 Ch. 673 (C.A. 1895).

We have examined the above balance-sheet and compared it with the books of the company; and we certify that it is a correct summary of the accounts therein recorded. The value of the assets as shewn on the balance-sheet is dependent upon realization.[40]

The English law of 1900, which made audits compulsory, specified that auditors must report to shareholders in general meeting their opinion as to whether the balance sheet "is properly drawn up so as to exhibit a true and correct view of the company's affairs. . . ." The auditors were also required to sign a *certificate* at the foot of the balance sheet stating whether "their requisitions as auditors had been complied with."[41] In 1907 the report and certificate were combined.[42]

In 1947 a law was enacted that represents the current English practice. It requires the auditor to state whether the financials give a "true and fair view," instead of a "true and correct" view, of the company's affairs.[43]

Early American Practice

American practice at first closely followed that of the English. The auditors' certificate in the *Ultramares* case for the year 1923 was as follows:

Touche, Niven & Co.
Public Accountants
Eighty Maiden Lane
New York
Certificate of Auditors

We have examined the accounts of Fred Stern & Co., Inc., for the year ending December 31, 1923, and hereby certify that the annexed balance sheet is in accordance therewith and with the information and explanations given us. We further certify that, subject to provision for federal taxes on income, the said statement, in our opinion, presents a true and correct view of the financial condition of Fred Stern & Co., Inc., as at December 31, 1923.

Touche, Niven & Co.
Public Accountants[44]

The decision of the Court of Appeals of New York in 1931 held that the auditor could be held liable to the third-party lender (Ultramares Corp.) for fraud, that is,

pretended audits, but not for ordinary negligence. This limited liability ruling was of such concern to accountants of that era that an editorial in the July 1931 *Journal of Accountancy* said that "the word 'certify' which has been used for many years is quite inappropriate and should be abandoned."

Origin of the Phrase *Generally Accepted Accounting Principles*

After the stock market crash of 1929, the already mounting dissatisfaction with financial reporting increased in intensity. Some reformers advocated uniform accounting rules for each industry. Federal legislation to deal with the problem appeared imminent. The New York Stock Exchange, which had rejected a proposal by the American Institute of Accountants in 1927 to cooperate in a consideration of financial reporting requirements, suddenly in 1930 reversed its position. George O. May was made chairman of a special American Institute of Accountants committee on cooperation with stock exchanges and in 1932 was also made chairman of another special Institute committee on development of accounting principles.[45]

In 1934 May's committees reported with a pamphlet entitled "Audits of Corporate Accounts," which contained correspondence with the Committee on Stock List of the New York Stock Exchange. A letter from George O. May dated September 22, 1932, deplored the selection of a "detailed set of rules which would become binding on all corporations of a given class." It advocated leaving "every corporation free to choose its own methods of accounting within the very broad limits to which reference has been made, but [it would] require disclosure of the methods employed and consistency in their application from year to year."[46]

The committees also proposed a new form of auditor's certificate that included "fairly present, in accordance with accepted principles of accounting consistently maintained by the Company." The purpose of this term was to identify "methods of accounting within the very broad limits." From 1940 the term was changed to "generally accepted accounting principles" in recommended forms of the short-form report.[47]

---

40. Ibid. The court found the auditor liable because the "subject to realization" qualification did not adequately communicate the state of affairs. For a more recent case with the same holding, see Herzfeld v. Laventhol, Krekstein, Horwath & Horwath, 540 F.2d 27 (2d Cir. 1976).

41. 63 & 64 Vict., c. 48, sec. 23.

42. Edw. VII, c. 50, sec. 19(2)(b).

43. 10 & 11 Geo. VI, c. 47, Second Schedule.

44. This certificate is quoted by the court in Ultramares Corp. v. Touche, 255 N.Y. 170, 174 N.E. 441 (1931).

45. Carey, *Rise of the Accounting Profession*, vol. 1, pp. 162–74.

46. The New York Stock Exchange announced that after July 1, 1933, all applicants for listing on the exchange must agree that future annual reports would be audited. No mention was made of disclosure of accounting methods. The requirements for audit were not extended to firms already listed. The committee report, "Audits of Corporate Accounts," is reprinted in George O. May, *Twenty-five Years of Accounting Responsibility 1911–1936* (New York: American Institute Publishing, 1936), pp. 112–44.

47. For a historical summary of the evolution of the audit report, see George Cochrane, "The Auditor's Report: Its Evolution in the U.S.A.," *Accountant*, November 4, 1950, pp. 448–60.

The new form of the report read as follows:

> We have examined the balance sheet of the ABC Company as of December 31, 1939, and the statements of income and surplus for the fiscal year then ended; have reviewed the system of internal control and the accounting procedures of the company, and, without making a detailed audit of the transactions, have examined or tested accounting records of the company and other supporting evidence by methods and to the extent we deemed appropriate.
>
> In our opinion, the accompanying balance sheet and related statement of income and surplus present fairly the position of the ABC Company at December 31, 1939, and the results of its operations for the fiscal year, in conformity with generally accepted accounting principles applied on a basis consistent with that of the preceding year.[48]

Generally Accepted Auditing Standards

When the SEC amended Regulation S-X in 1941 following the McKesson & Robbins scandal, the AICPA immediately added the following sentence to the end of the first paragraph of the above report:

> Our examination was made in accordance with generally accepted auditing standards in the circumstances and included all procedures we considered necessary.

Since auditing standards are *always* applicable, the wording of this sentence was changed to:

> Our examination was made in accordance with generally accepted auditing standards and included all procedures which we considered necessary in the circumstances.[49]

The Current Form

In 1949 the AICPA adopted the form used today except that the words *retained earnings* have been substituted for *surplus,* and a statement of changes in financial position is now covered by the report. The current form reads:

> (Scope paragraph)
> We have examined the balance sheet of X Company as of [at] December 31, 19XX, and the related statements of income, retained earnings and changes in financial position for the year then ended. Our examination was made in accordance with generally accepted auditing standards and, accordingly, included such tests of the accounting records and such other auditing procedures as we considered necessary in the circumstances.

> (Opinion paragraph)
> In our opinion, the financial statements referred to above present fairly the financial position of X Company as of [at] December 31, 19XX, and the results of its operations and the changes in its financial position for the year then ended, in conformity with generally accepted accounting principles applied on a basis consistent with that of the preceding year.[50]

Where financials for one or more prior periods are presented on a comparative basis, continuing auditors must modify the above report to include the prior financials in accordance with AU § 505.

EVOLUTION OF ACCOUNTING RULE MAKING

Accounting rule making in the United States has been primarily carried out in the private sector by the accounting profession. Discussion of the increasingly important role of the SEC in rule making for both generally accepted accounting principles (GAAP) and generally accepted auditing standards (GAAS) and its general supervision over the private accounting profession is reserved for Chapter 3. The profession has thus far primarily used three successive groups to establish GAAP: (1) the AICPA Committee on Accounting Procedure (1938-59), (2) the AICPA Accounting Principles Board (1959-73), and (3) the Financial Accounting Standards Board (1973 to the present).

The AICPA Committee on Accounting Procedure

In 1938 the Committee on Accounting Procedure of the American Institute of Accountants was made a standing committee and authorized to issue pronouncements on accounting principles and procedures. From 1939 to 1959 it issued 51 pronouncements called *Accounting Research Bulletins* (ARB). *Accounting Research Bulletin No. 43* represents a consolidation of the first 42 (except for 3 dealing with wartime problems and 8 dealing with terminology). *Accounting Research Bulletin No. 43, Accounting Terminology Bulletins,* and *Accounting Research Bulletin Nos.* 44 through 51 were printed together in *Accounting Research and Terminology Bulletins: Final Edition* after the Accounting Principles Board superseded the Committee in 1959.

The AICPA Accounting Principles Board

In 1959 the AICPA established the Accounting Principles Board to take over the work of the Commit-

48. Carey, *Rise of the Accounting Profession,* vol. 2, p. 154.
49. Ibid., pp. 154-55.

50. *CCH AICPA Professional Standards,* AU § 509.07.

tee on Accounting Procedure. The purpose of the change was a new approach "to narrow the areas of difference and inconsistency in practice."[51] It was thought that this could be accomplished by basing Board opinions on widely circulated research studies that would be carried out by an AICPA accounting research division.

In practice the APB differed very little from its predecessor, addressing itself to rather limited issues and leaving the door wide open for a large number of alternative practices with the choice being made by each firm's management. It issued 31 *Accounting Principles Board Opinions* dealing with details rather than basic principles.[52] The attempt to define postulates describing the environment underlying accounting principles and then the basic principles to serve as a guide to defining procedures met with failure when the APB rejected the research studies directed to these problems as "too radically different from present generally accepted accounting principles for acceptance at this time."[53]

In 1965 Paul Grady attempted a statement of existing concepts of "generally accepted accounting principles" with *Accounting Research Study No. 7: "Inventory of Generally Accepted Accounting Principles."* In 1970 the APB issued its *Statement No. 4: "Basic Concepts and Accounting Principles Underlying Financial Statements of Business Enterprises"* as an attempt to give a concise statement of existing generally accepted accounting principles. But these efforts at cataloging existing concepts did not "narrow the areas of difference and inconsistency in practice."

The Financial Accounting Standards Board

The controversy and dissatisfaction increased so that in 1971 the AICPA formed two study groups to consider these questions: (1) What should be the objectives underlying financial statements? (2) How should accounting principles be established?[54]

Former Securities and Exchange Commissioner Francis M. Wheat (at that time a Los Angeles attorney) was appointed chairman of the Study Group on Establishment of Accounting Principles. This group in 1972 recommended that the APB be replaced by a Financial Accounting Standards Board composed of seven full-time members who would cut all ties with CPA firms or business interests while serving a maximum of two five-year terms.[55] The AICPA Council (a 250-member policy-making group) immediately adopted the Wheat recommendations and established the Financial Accounting Standards Board (FASB).[56]

The organizational structure of the FASB is shown in Exhibit 2-1. Electors from six organizations appoint Financial Accounting Foundation (FAF) trustees, who approve the budget of the FASB, review the standard-setting function, and appoint the members of both the FASB and the Financial Accounting Standards Advisory Council. The current members of the FASB and their prior affiliations are shown in Exhibit 2-2. Interested persons can obtain copies of the Financial Accounting Foundation's Certificate of Incorporation (a Delaware corporation) and bylaws, FASB Rules of Procedure, and the FAF–FASB annual reports by writing to Publications Divison, FASB, High Ridge Park, Stamford, Connecticut 06905.

Failure of the FASB to Narrow Alternatives

Simple rules, comprehensible to users and accountants alike, could greatly improve the effectiveness of financial reports. However, the FASB has failed to deal with such relatively simple matters as specifying uniform standards for (1) depreciation, (2) inventory costing, and (3) profit recognition on long-term contracts. Not only is inconsistency permitted within each industry, there may be inconsistent methods within a single firm. The FASB has yet to deal with the accounting for management perquisites, bribes, and illegal contributions. Instead of addressing these problems, the FASB has issued a large and growing number of detailed pronouncements that it later finds necessary to explain with a large and growing number of interpretations.

So long as alternative principles exist, management retains power to influence the impression conveyed by financial reports. The effect of this influence can easily be misleading to investors who compare the reports with those of similar firms.

51. "Report to Council of the Special Committee on Research Program," *Journal of Accountancy,* December 1958, pp. 62–68.

52. The late Robert M. Trueblood in evaluating the first 10 years of the *APB Opinions* says, "In my view, most of them are too detailed and concern themselves unnecessarily with procedural matters." See "Ten Years of the APB: One Practitioner's Appraisal," *Journal of Accountancy,* January 1970, pp. 61–64. Mr. Trueblood was AICPA president 1965–66 and chairman of Touche Ross & Co. from 1963 until his death on February 7, 1974. He was chairman of the AICPA Study Group on the Objectives of Financial Statements.

53. *APB Statement No. 1* (New York: American Institute of Certified Public Accountants, 1962).

54. See "News Report," *Journal of Accountancy,* December 1971, pp. 10–12; May 1971, pp. 10–12.

55. "Accounting Board Should Be Supplanted by New Rules-Making Unit, Study Asserts," *The Wall Street Journal,* March 30, 1972, p. 6.

56. "AICPA Adopts Wheat Report on Accounting Standards Board," *Journal of Accountancy,* June 1972, pp. 10–12.

EXHIBIT 2–1
Organizational Structure of the Financial Accounting
Standards Board

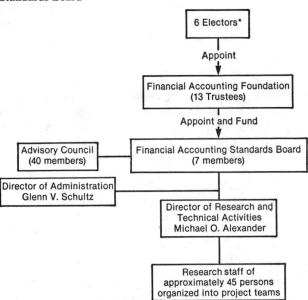

* Representatives from the American Accounting Association, American Institute of CPAs, Financial Analysts Federation, Financial Executives Institute, National Association of Accountants, and the Securities Industry Association.

EXHIBIT 2–2
The Financial Accounting Standards Board Membership

Member	Former Affiliation
Donald J. Kirk, Chairman	Partner, Price Waterhouse & Co.
Robert T. Sprouse, Vice Chairman	Professor of Accounting, Stanford University
Frank E. Block	Vice President, Bache Halsey Stuart Shields, Inc.
John W. March	Senior Partner, Arthur Andersen & Co.
Robert A. Morgan	Controller, Caterpillar Tractor Co.
David Mosso	Fiscal Assistant Secretary, U.S. Treasury Department
Ralph E. Walters	Director of Professional Standards, Touche Ross International

JUDICIAL ENFORCEMENT OF TECHNICAL STANDARDS

The AICPA ethics code[57] contains three major provisions that require public accountants to adhere to technical standards:

1. Ethics rule 202 requires auditors to comply with generally accepted auditing standards promulgated by the AICPA's Auditing Standards Board.[58]
2. Ethics rule 203 requires an exception in audit reports for material departures from official pronouncements of the FASB or unsuperseded *APB Opinions* and *Accounting Research Bulletins*.[59]
3. Ethics rule 204 requires public accountants to comply with technical standards promulgated by

the Management Advisory Services Executive Committee and the Accounting and Review Services Committee.[60]

Although it may not be possible for the AICPA to effectively police adherence to its ethics rules, the courts hold that AICPA rules provide minimum standards for all who practice public accounting. For example, in *Stanley L. Bloch, Inc. v. Klein*,[61] the court held that a balance sheet on a CPA's professional letterhead was audited, since AICPA ethics rules required a statement of any limitation of the CPA's responsibility. Similarly, in *Rhode Island Hospital Trust National Bank v. Swartz, Bresenoff, Yavner & Jacobs*,[62] the court referred to AICPA pronouncements and said:

> While industry standards may not always be the maximum test of liability, certainly they should be deemed the minimum standards by which liability should be determined.

MANAGEMENT CONTROL OF AUDITORS' TENURE

No law, ethics rule, or SEC regulation prevents corporate management from firing an auditor who refuses to agree to the propriety of management's finan-

57. The Code of Professional Ethics is located in volume 2 of *CCH AICPA Professional Standards*. The current version became effective in 1973 after approval by the AICPA membership.

58. *CCH AICPA Professional Standards*, ET § 202.01. The staff of the Auditing Standards Division has been authorized to issue interpretations to provide timely guidance; however, these are not as authoritative as pronouncements of the Auditing Standards Board. Auditing interpretations are located at AU § 9000 and following. Auditing standards at AU § 161.02 appear to require compliance with pronouncements of the AICPA Quality Control Standards Committee starting at QC § 10 located in volume 2 of *CCH AICPA Professional Standards*. Firms that are members of the AICPA Division for CPA Firms are bound by AICPA quality control standards.

59. *CCH AICPA Professional Standards*, ET § 203.01.

60. *CCH AICPA Professional Standards*, ET § 204.01.

61. Stanley L. Bloch, Inc. v. Klein, 258 N.Y.S.2d 501 (Sup. Ct. N.Y. 1965). For court decisions basing attorneys' malpractice on deviation from the attorneys' ethics code, *see* Woodruff v. Tomlin, 616 F.2d 924 (6th Cir. 1980) (duty of an attorney representing multiple clients in an auto accident to advise of a conflict of interest); Ishmael v. Millington, 50 Cal. Rptr. 592 (Cal. App. 1966) (failure of an attorney representing both parties in a divorce to disclose the conflict and advise of the desirability of separate counsel); De Daviess v. U-Haul Co. of Southern Georgia, 267 S.E.2d 633 (Ga. App. 1980) (presentment of criminal charges to obtain an advantage in a civil matter as supporting a claim for malicious prosecution).

62. Rhode Island Hospital Trust National Bank v. Swartz, Bresenoff, Yavner & Jacobs, 455 F.2d 847 (4th Cir. 1972).

cial statements.[63] Auditors are often summarily fired when any disagreement surfaces in the course of the audit. A notable example is provided in *SEC Accounting Series Release No. 153*.[64] In this case Touche Ross & Company (Touche) was fired in October 1971 at the time it was to commence the 1971 audit of U.S. Financial, Inc. (USF). USF then engaged Haskins & Sells (HS). On January 21, 1972, USF's chief executive officer terminated Haskins & Sells and on the following day USF again engaged Touche. In mid-February 1972 USF's audit committee submitted a report to the USF Board of Directors containing the following:

> 2. The January 1972 termination of HS was motivated in part by the inability of HS to complete the 1971 audit by the end of February, in part by an incompatibility which developed between management and HS and in part by potential disagreements as to matters of accounting principles.
>
> 3. The potential disagreements as to accounting principles between the management of USF and HS involved the question of when income should be recognized by USF in the following types of transactions: (a) Commissions, fees, and financing-type income received in cash by USF in 1971 from joint ventures or partnerships in which USF had an interest, where the cash received by USF came out of moneys loaned by USF. (b) Gains, profits and commissions income received by USF in 1971 where USF's profit or gain was represented at the end of 1971 by notes rather than cash, or where USF had a continuing cash investment in the transaction or had a contingent obligation to supply funds.[65]

At the time of these firings and rehirings USF's common stock was listed on the New York Stock Exchange. It had been listed on December 29, 1970, and was delisted on December 10, 1973.

The SEC determined that USF and certain officers, directors, and associates intentionally deceived Touche and that

> information furnished to the Commission indicated that Touche's conduct of the 1970 and 1971 audits in a number of respects did not meet the professional standards required of public accountants who practice before the Commission.
>
> Such information indicated that Touche failed to obtain sufficient independent evidentiary material to support its professional opinion in regard to a number of highly material transactions which were constructed by management in such a way as to make it appear that income had been earned when in fact it had not been. In connection with these transactions it also appeared that Touche failed to fully appraise the significance of information known to it and to extend sufficiently its auditing procedures under conditions which called for great professional skepticism. These transactions resulted in USF improperly recognizing millions of dollars of revenues and profits in 1970 and 1971.[66]

As a result of the above findings, Touche was censured by the Commission and subjected to remedial procedures.

This case dramatically illustrates the fact that the auditor operates in a legal environment which makes *effective* checking on management misconduct an improbability, if not an impossibility, since a firm is likely to be fired rather than allowed to investigate. This is only one example of many such situations.[67] The fact that the auditor is likely to be fired in any attempt to blow the whistle on management colors the whole relationship between client and auditor. It is not surprising that the SEC has difficulty in convincing the public accountant that the "first duty is to safeguard the public interest, not that of his client."[68]

Most state laws do not require corporations to appoint any auditors.[69] Corporations within the ambit of federal securities laws are required to issue financials audited by independent public accountants, but the auditor appointment process and his or her tenure are unregulated.

---

63. One possible exception is for corporations organized in Massachusetts, the only state that requires stockholder participation in selection of an auditor. This law provides (Mass. Ann. Laws ch. 156B, § 111): "The auditor to make the report for the then current fiscal year shall be selected by the stockholders at the annual meeting, or by the directors or a committee of the directors provided such election is ratified by stockholders. Any vacancy shall be filled by the directors or by such committee."

Another possible exception is for firms within the ambit of the Investment Company Act of 1940, which requires stockholder ratification or rejection of an auditor who is selected by disinterested directors. This act applies to firms trading in securities but excludes banks, insurance companies, savings and loan associations, and certain others. Audit reports under this act must be addressed both to the board of directors and to the security holders.

Whether such provisions as these prevent firing of auditors by management or management demands for auditor resignation is unclear.

64. *SEC Accounting Series Release No. 153,* "In the Matter of Touche Ross & Co." (1974).

65. Ibid.

66. Ibid.

67. For example, in Herzfeld v. Laventhol, Krekstein, Horwath & Horwath, 378 F. Supp. 112, 540 F.2d 27 (2d Cir. 1976), management pressure took other forms. A key transaction in the audit involved a contract for sale of real estate producing a $2,030,500 "profit." The client president warned the auditor that, in any discussions, the buyer must be handled with "kid gloves" to avoid losing him for future transactions. There was evidence that management insisted that all of the "profit" be included in current income and that the client's investment advisor threatened to sue the auditor if the planned private placement of securities fell through.

68. *SEC Accounting Series Release No. 153,* "In the Matter of Touche Ross & Co." (1974).

69. Douglas W. Hawes "Stockholder Appointment of Independent Auditors: A Proposal," 74 *Colum. L. Rev.* 1 at n. 70 (1974).

A few corporations have voluntarily provided in their bylaws or certificate of incorporation that auditors be appointed by stockholders. Vanderbilt professor Douglas W. Hawes found in a 1973 survey that 57 out of the top 100 corporations listed in the *Fortune 500* invited stockholder participation in the selection of the auditor. However, out of 7,000 firms that filed proxy statements with the SEC in 1973, only 3,121 gave stockholders any voice in the appointment of auditors.[70]

Where corporations do give stockholders a voice in auditor appointment, the most common procedure is for the board of directors to appoint the auditors and ask the stockholders to ratify or reject the appointment. Less common practices involve a request for stockholder "approval" of the appointment by the board of directors or a recommendation of an auditor by the board of directors.[71]

The legal effect of stockholder participation in the selection process is unclear. For example, where stockholder participation is solicited, does it bind the directors in making the appointment? Further, can the board of directors remove an auditor whose appointment is made with stockholder participation? The fact that there is no case authority on these issues shows that action taken with respect to auditor tenure goes unchallenged, with the auditor humbly bowing out.

New York Stock Exchange Requirements

Effective June 30, 1978, the NYSE started requiring listed firms to establish an audit committee comprised solely of outside directors. However, this provides no assurance that the NYSE can enforce the rule so as to provide tenure for the auditor.

SEC Disclosure Requirements

In 1974 the SEC amended Form 8-K to broaden the disclosure required when the auditor has resigned or is dismissed or replaced.[72] Firms making changes must state whether in the two most recent fiscal years and subsequent interim period there were any resolved or unresolved disagreements with the former auditor concerning accounting principles, auditing procedure, or financial disclosure. The filing must be accompanied by a letter from the former auditor giving his or her version of the termination.

Disagreements with auditors during the preceding 24 months must now be disclosed as notes to financial statements. Proxy materials must also disclose the current choice of auditor and any disagreements with auditors during the previous year and include a statement of the auditor's version.

Although disclosure requirements may discourage shopping for compliant auditors, they do not prevent the practice. Such requirements have shown, however, that the practice of pressuring auditors and firing those who do not succumb to pressure is a frequent occurrence.[73]

EVOLUTION OF INDEPENDENCE

According to Carey, the term *independent auditor* was first used in the sense of independent contractor. As the profession developed, accountants came to associate with it the characteristics of integrity, honesty, and objectivity.[74]

The Role of the SEC

The Securities Act of 1933 required audits by *independent* accountants, and the Federal Trade Commission's first regulations provided that accountants were not independent with respect to any client in whom they had *any* interest, directly or indirectly, or with whom they were connected as officer, director, or employee. After the Securities Exchange Act of 1934 created the SEC to take over administration of the Securities Act, the SEC was persuaded that the former rule was too harsh. SEC regulations issued in 1936 changed the rule to prohibit any *substantial* interest, direct or indirect. Disputes soon developed over the meaning of *substantial* and this caused the SEC to delete the word in 1950.

In 1972 the SEC issued *Accounting Series Release No. 126,* which has had an important effect in strengthening auditors' independence since it provides that within the scope of the federal securities laws:

1. Auditors may not engage in bookkeeping or write-up services for their clients.

---

70. Ibid. at p. 1.

71. Ibid. at pp. 21–22, n. 114–16.

72. See *SEC Accounting Series Release No. 165* (1974). Form 8-K is used to report specified events pursuant to sections 13 and 15(d) of the Securities Exchange Act of 1934.

73. For an excellent analysis of the problem, see Vanderbilt Professor Hawes's article, "Stockholder Appointment of Independent Auditors: A Proposal," 74 *Colum. L. Rev.* 1 (1974). Professor Hawes lists at p. 3 the following instances of firing: Peat, Marwick, Mitchell & Co. fired by Investors Funding Corporation ("Investors Funding Fires Peat Marwick in Dispute over Real-Estate Accounting," *The Wall Street Journal,* February 28, 1973); Alexander Grant & Co. fired by Allegheny Beverage Corporation over recognizing income from sale of vending machines, Form 8-K (April 7, 1972); Cerro Corporation fired Coopers & Lybrand over recognition of income of a newly acquired subsidiary and denied the auditor a meeting with the audit committee, Form 8-K (July 10, 1973).

74. Carey, *Rise of the Accounting Profession,* vol. 2, p. 175.

2. The auditor may not act as a conduit or agent between the client and a service bureau that performs record keeping by computer.
3. Normally an auditor cannot undertake an engagement when the client owes material amounts of unpaid fees for past services.
4. An auditor cannot be employed if family ties between the auditing firm and the client raise questions of independence.
5. Auditors cannot engage in business relations with their clients except as consumers in the normal course of business.
6. An auditor may not engage in occupations with conflicting interests such as attorney, broker-dealer, or competitor of a client.

The release specifically states that systems design and computer programming are appropriate activities for the auditor and do not interfere with independence. However, the release does not prohibit other consulting services.

The Role of the AICPA

The AICPA took no action on independence until 1941 when it adopted the rule that auditors could not have a substantial financial interest in publicly owned clients, and if they had such an interest, they had to disclose it. Since the SEC rule already prohibited auditor ownership of publicly held companies, the AICPA rule added nothing of substance.

In a 1960 AICPA meeting discussing independence, it was successfully argued that "integrity" sufficiently covered the matter and that a proposed rule prohibiting auditors from serving as director, officer, or employee was an attempt to legislate morality. Others said there was no valid reason why they should give up their directorships or minor offices in client enterprises that had been accepted as a "matter of convenience."[75] It was not until 1961 that the AICPA adopted a rule prohibiting auditors from serving as officers, directors, or employees of the client. The new rule dropped the "substantial interest" test and prohibited any direct or any material indirect financial interest during the period covered by the audit engagement. AICPA rules adopted in 1973 prohibit loans between the auditor and the client during the professional engagement.

The Dispute over Management Advisory Services (MAS)

Shortly after the 1961 adoption of the new AICPA rule prohibiting auditors from serving as directors, officers, or employees, the financial press, financial executives, several members of the academic community, and even the Congress began to question the propriety of auditor involvement in MAS. For example, here is a commentary from *Business Week:*

> And it has been the Big Eight, too, that have moved the most aggressively into such tangential fields as consulting, often through mergers with smaller, specialized regional and local accounting firms. Like drummers with wagon loads of new wares, most of the big CPA firms are stocking a full line of management advisory services these days. Peat, Marwick will help clients find a new president or top financial officer, or tell top executives they should switch part of their pay into tax shelters. Lybrand will help a company set up a new pension plan; Touche Ross and Ernst & Ernst will undertake detailed marketing plan strategy. Arthur Young will help a corporation defend itself against a takeover.
>
> But accountants are divided over where to draw the line on consulting to avoid conflicts—either in fact or in appearance—with their audit work.[76]

Some financial executives viewed auditor recommendations as sales pitches for the auditing firm's management services division. For example, one financial executive reported:

> Yes, there is a conflict of interest. The annual review of internal control usually goes beyond the financial audit and the resulting report then offers the assistance of the management services staff. It takes on the overtones of a sales promotion instead of an objective report on internal control matters.[77]

Some accounting professors have argued that advice leading to business decisions gives the auditor a financial interest in the company, an interest based on the "prestige as a successful advisor," so that the nature of that interest is not unlike that of an employee.[78] The late Manuel F. Cohen, former chairman of the SEC, indicated that consulting services that go beyond those related to information and control systems raise serious questions concerning the auditor's independence.[79] Senator William Proxmire questioned the propriety of serving, at the same time, as the auditor for the prime contractor on C-5A aircraft and as consultant to

75. Ibid., pp. 188–89.

76. "Accounting: A Crisis over Fuller Disclosure," *Business Week,* April 22, 1972, pp. 54–60.

77. George Hobgood and Joseph A. Sciarrino, "Management Looks at Audit Services," *Financial Executive,* April 1972, pp. 26–32 at 32.

78. R. K. Mautz and Hussein A. Sharaf, *The Philosophy of Auditing* (American Accounting Association, 1961), pp. 204–31; Arthur A. Schulte, Jr., "Compatibility of Management Consulting and Auditing," *Accounting Review,* July 1965, pp. 587–93; Abraham J. Briloff, "Old Myths and New Realities in Accountancy," *Accounting Review,* July 1966, pp. 484–95; William L. Raby, "Advocacy vs. Independence in Tax Liability Accrual," *Journal of Accountancy,* March 1972, pp. 40–47.

79. Carey, *Rise of the Accounting Profession,* vol. 2, pp. 198–99.

the government to reduce costs on government contracts. In the U.S. Senate hearings Senator Proxmire said:

> Mr. Fitzgerald, on the same day as your dismissal was announced it was revealed that your immediate superior . . . had hired as a consultant one of the partners in the Arthur Young and Co. accounting firm, the same firm that audits the books of the Lockheed Corp. Lockheed, of course, is the prime contractor of the C-5A. . . .
>
> Did anybody discuss with you . . . the conflict of interest . . . it was the auditing firm for Lockheed, it had a responsibility to Lockheed, was retained by Lockheed and paid by Lockheed. At the same time it was given responsibility for the Federal Government that could be, if zealously done, adverse to the Lockheed's interests.[80]

Senator Proxmire's question related to MAS for a third party that was not even an audit client.

In order to defend the status quo the AICPA issued its first statement relating to *independence in appearance* in 1963. While arguing that independence is a state of mind, it acknowledged that auditors should avoid relationships that have the appearance of a conflict of interest. In defense of the MAS practice the AICPA said:

> In the areas of management advisory services and tax practice, so long as the CPA's services consist of advice and technical assistance, the committee can discern no likelihood of a conflict of interest arising from such services. It is a rare instance for management to surrender the responsibility to make management decisions. However, should a member make such decisions on matters affecting the company's financial position or results of operations, it would appear that his objectivity might well be impaired. Consequently such situations should be avoided.
>
> In summary, it is the opinion of the committee that there is no ethical reason why a member or associate may not properly perform professional services, and at the same time serve the same client as independent auditor, so long as he does not make management decisions or take positions that might impair that objectivity.[81]

The matter of MAS practice for audit clients thus remains a controversial matter.

Current Standards of Independence

Independence is a qualitative standard that requires the CPA to act with integrity and objectivity in the performance of any and all services.[82] There are two distinctive aspects of independence:

1. Independence in fact.
2. Independence in appearance.[83]

Independence in fact is an objective, unbiased state of mind. Independence in appearance is the absence of affiliations or influencing factors that might lead to actual or presumptive conflicts of interest.

Scope of the Independence Requirement. CPAs engaged in performing audit services must have both independence in fact and independence in appearance. When performing management advisory services and tax practice, only independence in fact is required.[84] This means that judgments must be based on the true facts and applicable rules and that conclusions must be stated honestly and objectively. Although CPAs must not subordinate their judgment to others, they may resolve doubts in tax matters in favor of the client as long as all positions taken have reasonable support.[85] The CPA is encouraged to maintain independence in appearance regardless of the type of services being rendered. A tax client or MAS client may request an audit at any time, thus making independence in appearance necessary.

AICPA rules[86] limit the scope of independence requirements to (1) partners, (2) shareholders, and (3) professionals participating or located in an office participating in an engagement. Although associations as officer or employee are prohibited for the period covered by an audit, this does not relate to accounting firm *employees* who are not participating in the audit engagement.

---

80. Hearings on the Dismissal of A. Ernest Fitzgerald before the Subcomm. on Economy in Government of the Joint Economic Committee, 91st Cong., 1st Sess. (1969). Also see Berkeley Rice, *The C-5A Scandal* (Boston: Houghton Mifflin, 1971), pp. 100–101.

81. Carey, *Rise of the Accounting Profession*, vol. 2, pp. 193–94.

82. *CCH AICPA Professional Standards,* ET § 52.02 states: "Independence has traditionally been defined by the profession as the ability to act with integrity and objectivity."

83. *CCH AICPA Professional Standards,* ET § 52.10 provides: "When a CPA expresses an opinion on financial statements, not only the fact but also the appearance of integrity and objectivity is of particular importance."

84. *CCH AICPA Professional Standards,* ET § 52.11 provides: "Although the appearance of independence is not required in the case of management advisory services and tax practice, a CPA is encouraged to avoid the proscribed relationships with clients regardless of the type of services being rendered. In any event, the CPA, in all types of engagements, should *refuse to subordinate his professional judgment to others* and should express his conclusions honestly and objectively." (Emphasis added.)

85. Rule 102 of the *AICPA Code of Professional Ethics* provides: "A member shall not knowingly misrepresent facts, and when engaged in the practice of public accounting, including the rendering of tax and management advisory services, shall not subordinate his judgment to others. In tax practice, a member may resolve doubt in favor of his client as long as there is reasonable support for his position."

Revenue Ruling 78-344 provides that the fact that a tax preparer followed specific instructions of the client is no defense to the penalty under section 6694(a) of the Internal Revenue Code for negligent or intentional disregard of the regulations.

86. *CCH AICPA Professional Standards,* ET § 101.08.

The rules do not cover the matter, but nonprofessional support staff who have executive-team status, such as office managers and executive secretaries, should be independent. All office personnel should be cautioned as to improper use of confidential information.

Prohibited Financial Interests. Both AICPA and SEC rules prohibit *any* direct financial interest (material or immaterial) or *any material* indirect financial interest in the client.[87] A direct financial interest includes any interest of a spouse, dependent child, or relative who is either supported by the professional or living in a common household with the professional. It also includes any interest held by those who are subject to the CPA's supervision or control.

Indirect financial interests include nondependent children, brothers and sisters, grandparents, parents, parents-in-law, and the spouses of any of these. Financial interests of remote kin, such as uncles, aunts, cousins, nephews, nieces, are normally neither direct nor indirect financial interests of the CPA. Under AICPA rules, indirect interests are "material" if the kin's financial interest in the client is material to the kin's net worth. Under SEC rules the determination of materiality is primarily made with reference to the net worth of the CPA, his or her firm, and the net worth of the client. If the CPA does not and cannot reasonably know about such financial interests of kin, this fact eliminates any question as to the CPA's independence. The assessment of any relationships depends upon the circumstances, such as geographical proximity, strength of personal and other business relationships, and other factors which may pose a threat to objectivity.

Proscribed Period for Financial Interests. Both AICPA and SEC financial interest rules relate only to the period of the professional engagement and the date of the report. CPAs are permitted to have a financial interest during the period covered by the audit report provided (1) they take no part in auditor selection and, (2) they immediately dispose of their financial interests upon being appointed as auditor. Similarly, CPAs are permitted to acquire financial interests in former clients, and there is no loss of independence even where CPAs are required to reissue previous reports for purposes of SEC registration statements. In such circumstances the original date must be retained on the reis-

sued report. The SEC established these rules in *Accounting Series Release No. 79:*

> Situations arise in which it is not necessary to make a finding of lack of independence even though an accountant may have held a financial interest during the period of report but at a time when his independence was not a factor. For example, an accountant may be called upon to furnish a certificate in a registration statement for a former client in whom he now has a financial interest but with whom he maintained an independent relationship during the period covered by the audit and up to the date he issued his original certificate. Another example is where an accountant held stock in a company for which he had never had an engagement but sold it upon accepting an engagement. In these and other situations where it is clear from the facts that the independent status of the accountant is not prejudiced by a particular relationship, we will upon request advise the accountant that no action will be taken because of this relationship.

Loans and Unpaid Fees. Loans either to or from the client impair the accountant's independence. AICPA ethics rules specify that independence is impaired if the CPA

> had any loan to or from the enterprise or any officer, director or principal stockholder thereof. This latter proscription does not apply to the following loans from a financial institution when made under normal lending procedures, terms, and requirements:
> a. Loans obtained by a member or his firm which are not material in relation to the net worth of such borrower.
> b. Home mortgages.
> c. Other secured loans, except loans guaranteed by a member's firm which are otherwise unsecured.

Loans are distinguished from accounts that arise in the ordinary course of business. For example, where the CPA had a cash account with a brokerage firm client, independence was not impaired;[88] however, independence would be impaired if the CPA became either debtor or creditor.

If the client becomes delinquent in payment of the CPA's fee, the effect is similar to that of a loan with the CPA providing working capital to the client. According to SEC rules, the fees for the prior year's audit should be paid prior to commencing the current audit. AICPA rules (ET § 191.104) require payment for prior audits before issuance of the current audit report.

Pending or Threatened Litigation. AICPA Ethics Interpretation 101–6 understandably provides that independence is impaired if (1) litigation *by management* alleges deficient audit work and (2) litigation by the

87. SEC Regulation S-X, 17 C.F.R. § 210.2-01 provides: "For example, an accountant will be considered not independent with respect to any person or any of its parents or subsidiaries in whom he has, or had during the period of report, any direct financial interest; or with whom he is, or was during such period, connected as a promoter, underwriter, voting trustee, director, officer, or employee."

88. *CCH AICPA Professional Standards,* ET § 191.056.

auditor alleges fraud by the present management.[89] However, it is more difficult to understand the AICPA position that litigation by security holders against the auditor, along with the client company, management, officers, directors, and underwriters would not impair independence. The AICPA logic is that the relationship between management and the auditor is not altered. This seems to ignore the fact that the auditor's responsibility is to the public, and continuation permits a guilty auditor to participate with management in a cover-up of the past fraud. Of course, the mere filing of a lawsuit should not impair independence. However, once the case progresses through affidavits, depositions, and interrogatories to the point that there is a genuine issue for trial on the merits, the auditor should be required to withdraw. The public will not believe that an auditor is exercising independence during a lawsuit in which both the auditor and the management are charged with fraud.[90]

Civil or criminal litigation and administrative proceedings concerning the personnel to be involved in the audit raises questions as to disclosures in proxy materials for stockholder approval of the auditor. In *Lyman v. Standard Brands Inc.*[91] a stockholder brought a civil injunctive suit alleging that the defendant's proxy statement proposing stockholder ratification of the appointment of Arthur Andersen & Co. as auditors was false and misleading, and seeking injunctive relief to compel disclosure of Andersen's involvement in "the Four Seasons litigation." The central issue was whether this omission constituted material facts required to be disclosed under SEC proxy rule 14a-9, which provides:

> No solicitation . . . shall be made by means of any proxy statement . . . containing any statement which, at the time and in the light of the circumstances under which it is made, is false and misleading with respect to any material fact, or which omits to state any material fact necessary in order to make the statements therein not false or misleading or necessary to correct any statement in any earlier communication with respect to the solicitation of a proxy for the same

meeting or subject matter which has become false or misleading.[92]

The court, in distinguishing this case from those in which pending litigation directly affected the integrity or judgment of the directors soliciting proxies, ruled:

> The indictment of three employees in an Andersen office which has had no connection with the Standard Brands audit has only the most tenuous relationship to the shareholders' selection of the corporation's independent auditors. Had Andersen employees who had worked on or might in the future be assigned to the Standard Brands audit been indicted, the existence of that litigation might well be a material fact which must be disclosed to the Shareholders. However, the undisclosed fact here is so unrelated to the corporate integrity or fitness of Andersen that we conclude its omission would not have a "significant *propensity* to affect the voting process."[93]

Rejection of the plaintiff's injunctive suit intimates that indictment of those who had been associated with the audit would be material. Information that the firm's auditor was under disciplinary sanctions imposed by the SEC could well be material where the offending employees or partners were or would be personally involved in the firm's audit. Materiality depends on the decision being considered by the investor as well as the nature of the information. Thus in situations of annual reports, registration statements, or prospectuses, the question is whether the information would affect the investment decision, not the choice-of-auditor decision.

Reports Where Independence Is Lacking

Where independence is lacking, the reporting situation depends on whether the financial statements are those of a public or nonpublic entity. For a public entity the CPA must mark each page "Unaudited—see accompanying disclaimer of opinion." The disclaimer must read:

> We are not independent with respect to XYZ Company, and the accompanying balance sheet as of December 31, 19X1, and the related statements of income, retained earnings, and changes in financial position for the year then ended were not audited by us, and accordingly, we do not express an opinion on them.[94]

If the financial statements are those of a nonpublic

---

89. Interpretation 101-6 is reproduced in the January 1978 issue of the *Journal of Accountancy* at pages 86–87. For some examples of large settlements with clients that apparently did not impair independence, see note 9 in Chapter 1.

90. AICPA ethical standards are apparently identical with SEC rules as expressed in *Accounting Series Release No. 234:* "Independence of Accountants" (1977) with one exception: the AICPA contends that "immaterial" litigation over matters other than auditing (e.g., management consulting services) does not impair independence.

91. Lyman v. Standard Brands Inc., 364 F. Supp. 794 (1973). See note: "Disclosure of Litigation Involving Accountants Under SEC Proxy Rule 14a-9," 62 *Georgetown L.J.* 1229 (1974).

92. 17 C.F.R. 240.14a-9.

93. 364 F. Supp. 798.

94. *CCH AICPA Professional Standards,* AU § 504.08.

entity, the CPA must mark each page "See Accountant's Compilation Report" and use the following form:

> The accompanying balance sheet of XYZ Company as of December 31, 19XX, and the related statements of income, retained earnings, and changes in financial position for the year then ended have been compiled by me (us).
>
> A compilation is limited to presenting in the form of financial statements information that is the representation of management (owners). I (we) have not audited or reviewed the accompanying financial statements and, accordingly, do not express an opinion or any other form of assurance on them.
>
> I am (we are) not independent with respect to XYZ Company.[95]

CPAs are always prohibited from stating why they are not independent, since the public might make judgments as to the independence limitation and impart greater credibility as a result of the CPA's association.

Independence in the Future

The matter of independence will probably cause more problems for auditors than any other problem. The fact that a reputable auditing firm is willing to accept an audit client that has just fired a previous reputable auditor over matters of disclosure shows the profession has a long way to go in standing up to its responsibility of representing the public interest.

This condition has resulted in considerable loss of credibility and stature for the profession. A survey commissioned by Arthur Andersen & Co. revealed that "26 percent of corporate executives believe accounting firms do bend the rules in the client's favor." An even higher percentage, 50 percent or more, of professors, institutional investors, analysts, brokers, and government officials believe auditors bend the rules for clients. Nearly all the corporate social activists and members of the business press hold such views of auditors.[96]

An exemplary story involves a fictitious company that interviewed a dozen different auditors before finding a satisfactory one. The test was to ask each auditor, "What is two plus two?" The auditor who was selected replied, "What number did you have in mind?"[97] The story is too true to be funny.

---

95. *CCH AICPA Professional Standards*, AU § 100.22.

96. Arthur Andersen & Co., *Public Accounting in Transition* (1974), p. 68.

97. Abraham Briloff, *Unaccountable Accounting* (New York: Harper & Row, 1972), pp. 1–2. A cartoon in the *New Yorker* carried this legend: "In examining our books, Mr. Mathews promises to use generally accepted accounting principles, if you know what I mean."

Consider this account of an interview with the managing partner of Arthur Young & Co.'s New York office:

> "Realistically," he goes on, "management selects the auditors.". . .
>
> * * * * *
>
> "Real life" is also that outside auditors *report* to management—not to boards of directors as they are supposed to. . . .
>
> * * * * *
>
> "You can't be an adversary and do an audit of a company," he asserts.[98]

SUMMARY

In the late 1800s Scottish and British auditors started coming to the United States to check on British investments. They established offices in America and thus started the organized accounting profession in this country. Test checking and reliance upon internal controls developed as a practical approach to cost reduction.

From 1900 to 1930 drastic changes took place in the accounting audience as more and more persons acquired stocks and bonds and made demands for financial information. Accounting reports were no longer primarily for management and bankers, but came to serve stockholders and bondholders as well. The unsatisfactory financial reporting practices and the stock market crash of 1929 brought pressure for reforms that produced the Securities Act of 1933 and the Securities Exchange Act of 1934. Annual audits by independent auditors then became required by the SEC.

In 1938 the scandal at McKesson & Robbins, involving the discovery that the auditors had failed to detect fictitious inventories and assets, brought an extension of required auditing procedures to include confirming accounts receivable and observing and testing the taking of physical inventories, along with the development of *Statements on Auditing Standards*.

The FASB, like its predecessors, has failed to narrow alternative methods of accounting for depreciation, inventories, and profit recognition on long-term programs and construction projects. AICPA ethics rule 203 requires auditors to issue a qualified or adverse opinion whenever there are material departures from (1) *FASB Statements* and *Interpretations,* and (2) *APB Opinions* and *Accounting Research Bulletins* not superseded by FASB pronouncements.

Since there is no law, ethics rule, or SEC regulation

---

98. "But That Isn't Real Life," *Forbes,* May 15, 1976.

that prevents corporate management from firing an auditor who refuses to agree to the propriety of management's financial statements, auditors are sometimes fired when any disagreement surfaces during the course of an audit. The matter of auditor's tenure and independence is the most important problem for the profession for the foreseeable future.

SUGGESTIONS FOR FURTHER READING

Carey, John L. *The Rise of the Accounting Profession.* Vols. 1 and 2. New York: American Institute of Certified Public Accountants, 1969.

DeMond, C. W. *Price, Waterhouse & Co. in America.* New York: Comet Press, 1951.

Grady, Paul, ed. *Memoirs and Accounting Thought of George O. May.* New York: Ronald Press, 1962.

Hein, Leonard W. "The Auditor and the British Companies Acts." *Accounting Review,* July 1963, pp. 508–20.

Hendriksen, Eldon S. *Accounting Theory,* rev. ed. Homewood, Ill.: Richard D. Irwin, 1970.

May, George O. *Financial Accounting: A Distillation of Experience.* New York: Macmillan, 1943.

————. *Twenty-Five Years of Accounting Responsibility: 1911–1936.* New York: American Institute Publishing, 1936.

Miller, Norman C. *The Great Salad Oil Swindle.* Baltimore: Penguin Books, 1966.

Montgomery, Robert H. *Fifty Years of Accountancy.* New York: Ronald Press, 1939.

Our First Seventy-Five Years. New York: Haskins & Sells, 1970.

Ripley, W. Z. *Main Street and Wall Street.* Boston: Little, Brown, 1927.

Shaplen, Robert. "Annals of Crime—The Metamorphosis of Philip Musica." *New Yorker,* October 22, 1955, and October 29, 1955.

The First Fifty Years. Chicago: Arthur Andersen & Co., 1963.

The History of the Institute of Chartered Accountants in England and Wales 1880–1965. London: William Heinemann, 1966.

Thompson, Craig. "America's Boldest Swindler." *Saturday Evening Post,* February 28, 1953, pp. 34–35, 102, 105, 107.

QUESTIONS AND PROBLEMS

Discussion: Evolving Responsibility and Independence

1. Describe the antecedents of American accounting and auditing practice.
2. Who were pioneers in establishing the American accounting profession?
3. When did development of the organized accounting profession take place in America, and what were some of the principal events?
4. What brought about the Securities Act of 1933 and the Securities Exchange Act of 1934?
5. What effect did the *McKesson & Robbins* case have on American audit practice?
6. Discuss any identifiable long-term trends in auditing practice.
7. Explain the origins and contemporary use of the terms *auditor's certificate* and *present fairly.*

8. Who has the power, and who should have the power, to hire and fire auditors of firms having publicly traded securities?
9. Except in unusual circumstances, certain "official pronouncements" constitute the only generally accepted principles of accounting in areas covered therein. Detail each of the items that constitutes "official pronouncements."
10. Discuss two ways that management advisory services can conflict with an auditor's independence.
11. In the course of an audit, an auditor learns that firm X, an audit client, is failing. Firm Y, another audit client, has an important receivable due from X. Can the auditor make use of the information either in his capacity as *(a)* an auditor of Y, or *(b)* a management advisor to Y? (Reference to Chapter 8 and the discussion of the continuous flow of information required under the Securities Exchange Act may be helpful at this point.)
12. Describe the type of report issued when an auditor lacks independence.
13. *a.* Who should determine standards of full, fair, and accurate reporting in our society?
    b. If the responsibility should rest with the private sector, how should the public interest be represented?
14. What is an appropriate definition for accounting, and whom should accountants perceive as their audience?
15. What does the auditor say in his or her report and to whom should it be directed?

Auditing Standards

16. (From the May 1981 Uniform CPA Examination) Which of the following statements best describes the primary purpose of *Statements on Auditing Standards?*
    a. They are guides intended to set forth auditing procedures which are applicable to a variety of situations.
    b. They are procedural outlines intended to narrow the areas of inconsistency and divergence of auditor opinion.
    c. They are authoritative statements, enforced through the code of professional ethics, and are intended to limit the degree of auditor judgment.
    d. They are interpretations which are intended to clarify the meaning of "generally accepted auditing standards."
17. (From the May 1981 Uniform CPA Examination) The third general standard states that due care is to be exercised in the performance of the examination. This standard should be interpreted to mean that a CPA who undertakes an engagement assumes a duty to perform
    a. With reasonable diligence and without fault or error.
    b. As a professional who will assume responsibility for losses consequent upon error of judgment.
    c. To the satisfaction of the client and third parties who may rely upon it.
    d. As a professional possessing the degree of skill commonly possessed by others in the field.

18. (From the November 1980 Uniform CPA Examination)

    Auditing interpretations, which are issued by the staff of the AICPA Auditing Standards Division in order to provide timely guidance on the application of pronouncements of the Auditing Standards Board, are

    a. Less authoritative than a pronouncement of the Auditing Standards Board.

    b. Equally authoritative as a pronouncement of the Auditing Standards Board.

    c. More authoritative than a pronouncement of the Auditing Standards Board.

    d. Nonauthoritative opinions which are issued without consulting members of the Auditing Standards Board.

19. (From the November 1971 Uniform CPA Examination)

    The general group of the generally accepted auditing standards includes a requirement that

    a. The auditor maintain an independent mental attitude.

    b. The audit be conducted in conformity with generally accepted accounting principles.

    c. Assistants, if any, be properly supervised.

    d. There be a proper study and evaluation of internal control.

20. (From the November 1973 Uniform CPA Examination)

    The general group of the generally accepted auditing standards includes a requirement that

    a. The field work be adequately planned and supervised.

    b. The auditor's report state whether or not the financial statements conform to generally accepted accounting principles.

    c. Due professional care be exercised by the auditor.

    d. Informative disclosures in the financial statements be reasonably adequate.

21. (From the May 1975 Uniform CPA Examination)

    What is the general character of the three generally accepted auditing standards classified as standards of field work?

    a. The competence, independence, and professional care of persons performing the audit.

    b. Criteria for the content of the auditor's report on financial statements and related footnote disclosures.

    c. The criteria of audit planning and evidence gathering.

    d. The need to maintain an independence in mental attitude in all matters relating to the audit.

22. (From the November 1974 Uniform CPA Examination)

    What is the general character of the three generally accepted auditing standards classified as general standards?

    a. Criteria for competence, independence, and professional care of individuals performing the audit.

    b. Criteria for the content of the financial statements and related footnote disclosures.

    c. Criteria for the content of the auditor's report on financial statements and related footnote disclosures.

    d. The requirements for the planning of the audit and supervision of assistants, if any.

Auditors' Independence

23. (From the November 1969 Uniform CPA Examination)

    An auditor must not only appear to be independent; he must also be independent in fact.

    Required:

    a. Explain the concept of an "auditor's independence" as it applies to third-party reliance upon financial statements.

    b. (1) What determines whether or not an auditor is independent in fact?

       (2) What determines whether or not an auditor appears to be independent?

    c. Explain how an auditor may be independent in fact but not appear to be independent.

    d. Would a CPA be considered independent for an examination of the financial statements of a:

       (1) Church for which he is serving as treasurer without compensation? Explain.

       (2) Women's club for which his wife is serving as treasurer-bookkeeper if he is not to receive a fee for the examination? Explain.

    e. Write an opinion such as should accompany financial statements examined by a CPA who owns a direct financial interest in his nonpublic client.

24. Current ethical standards prohibit auditors from holding any

    a. Material direct financial interest in the client during the period covered by the financial statements.

    b. Substantial direct financial interest in the client during the period of the professional engagement and report.

    c. Direct financial interest in the client during the period of the professional engagement and report.

    d. Direct financial interest in the client during the period covered by the financial statements.

25. Under current ethical rules, a direct financial interest includes

    a. Only an interest held personally in the name of the auditor.

    b. The interest held by the auditor and the auditor's spouse and dependent children.

    c. The interest held by the auditor and the auditor's spouse, children, grandchildren, brothers, sisters, and parents.

    d. The auditor's household as well as all kin including uncles, aunts, cousins, nephews, and nieces.

26. In order to avoid impairing independence, current standards prohibit the auditor from serving as officer, director, or employee

    a. Only during the period covered by the financial statements.

    b. Only during the period of the professional engagement and report.

    c. Both during the period covered by the financial statements and the period of the professional engagement and report.

    d. Only during the period following the professional engagement.

27. When serving as auditor of a bank, independence would be impaired if

a. The auditor's home loan is obtained from the bank under normal lending procedures, terms, and requirements.

b. The auditor's auto loan is obtained from the bank under normal lending procedures, terms, and requirements.

c. A loan is obtained by the auditor's firm that is not material to the firm's net worth.

d. The bank has not paid the prior audit fee when issuing the current audit.

28. Under AICPA standards, independence is unimpaired by

a. Litigation by current management against the auditor alleging deficient audit work.

b. Litigation by the auditor alleging fraud by the current management.

c. Litigation by security holders alleging a fraudulent conspiracy by management and the auditor to loot the company.

d. Serving on the client's board of directors.

29. (From the May 1973 Uniform CPA Examination)

A CPA should reject a management advisory services engagement if

a. It would require him to make management decisions for an audit client.

b. His recommendations are to be subject to review by the client.

c. He audits the financial statements of a subsidiary of the prospective client.

d. The proposed engagement is not accounting-related.

30. (From the November 1973 Uniform CPA Examination)

Adams is the executive partner of Adams & Co., CPAs. One of its smaller clients is a large nonprofit charitable organization. The organization has asked Adams to be on its board of directors, which consists of a large number of the community's leaders. Membership on the board is honorary in nature. Adams & Co. would be considered to be independent

a. Under no circumstances.

b. As long as Adams' directorship was disclosed in the organization's financial statements.

c. As long as Adams was not directly in charge of the audit.

d. As long as Adams does not perform or give advice on management functions of the organization.

31. (From the November 1974 Uniform CPA Examination)

A client's management has asked you to consider a special study of a proposed modification of the system of internal control. It wishes to modify the existing system in approximately 18 months in conjunction with an upgrading of its computer system.

The scope of the study and evaluation to be reported on would be substantially more extensive than that required by a normal financial audit. The special report would be used solely for the internal information of management. Which of the following is the most appropriate response concerning the acceptance or rejection of the proposed engagement?

a. Explain that you are prohibited from accepting such an engagement because the client is not planning to allow distribution of the report to the general public upon request.

b. Explain that you can accept the engagement if it will not require decisions on your part which would impair your independence in connection with future audits of the client.

c. Explain that you are prohibited from accepting such an engagement because it would deal with a proposed rather than an existing system of controls.

d. Explain that you can accept the engagement but that there is a standard reporting format which you will be required to use when communicating your findings.

32. (From the November 1974 Uniform CPA Examination)

The certified public accounting firm of Lincoln, Johnson & Grant is the auditor for the Union Corporation. Mr. Lee, President of Union Corp., has asked the firm to perform management advisory services in the area of inventory management. Mr. Lee believes the procedures in this area are inefficient. Considering the dual engagement of the regular audit and the management services assignment, which of the following functions could impair the CPA firm's independence?

a. Identify the inventory-management problem as caused by the procedures presently operative in the purchasing, receiving, storage, and issuance operations.

b. Study and evaluate the inventory-management problem and suggest several alternative solutions.

c. Develop a time schedule for implementation of the solution adopted by Mr. Lee, to be carried out and supervised by Union Corp. personnel.

d. Supervise management of purchasing, receiving, storage, and issuance operations.

33. (From the November 1974 Uniform CPA Examination)

Fenn & Co., CPAs, has time available on a computer which it uses primarily for its own internal record keeping. Aware that the computer facilities of Delta Equipment Co., one of Fenn's audit clients, are inadequate for the company needs, Fenn offers to maintain on its computer certain routine accounting records for Delta. If Delta were to accept the offer and Fenn were to continue to function as independent auditor for Delta, then Fenn would be in violation of

a. SEC, but not AICPA, provisions pertaining to auditors' independence.

b. Both SEC and AICPA provisions pertaining to the auditors' independence.

c. AICPA, but not SEC, provisions pertaining to auditors' independence.

d. Neither AICPA nor SEC provisions pertaining to auditors' independence.

34. (From the May 1975 Uniform CPA Examination)

The AICPA Committee on Management Services has stated its belief that a CPA should not undertake a management advisory service engagement for implementation of the CPA's recommendations unless

a. The client does not understand the nature and implications of the recommended course of action.

b. The client has made a firm decision to proceed with

implementation based on his complete understanding and consideration of alternatives.

   c. The client does not have sufficient expertise within his organization to comprehend the significance of the changes being made.

   d. The CPA withdraws as independent auditor for the client.

35. (From the May 1975 Uniform CPA Examination)

   During the course of an audit, the client's controller asks your advice on how to revise the purchase journal so as to reduce the amount of time his staff takes in posting. How should you respond?

   a. Explain that under the AICPA Code of Professional Ethics you cannot give advice on management advisory service areas at the same time you are doing an audit.

   b. Explain that under the *AICPA Statement on Management Advisory Services* informal advice of this type is prohibited.

   c. Respond with definite recommendations based on your audit of these records but state that you will not assume any responsibility for any changes unless your specific recommendations are followed.

   d. Respond as practicable at the moment and express the basis for your response so it will be accepted for what it is.

36. (From the May 1975 Uniform CPA Examination)

   What is the meaning of the generally accepted auditing standard which requires that the auditor be independent?

   a. The auditor must be without bias with respect to the client under audit.

   b. The auditor must adopt a critical attitude during the audit.

   c. The auditor's sole obligation is to third parties.

   d. The auditor may have a direct ownership interest in his client's business if it is not material.

37. (From the May 1971 Uniform CPA Examination)

   With respect to examination of the financial statements of the Third National Bank, a CPA's appearance of independence ordinarily would not be impaired by his

   a. Obtaining a large loan for working capital purposes.

   b. Serving on the committee which approves the bank's loans.

   c. Utilizing the bank's time-sharing computer service.

   d. Owning a few inherited shares of Third National common stock.

38. (From the May 1971 Uniform CPA Examination)

   Mercury Company, an audit client of Eric Jones, CPA, is considering acquiring Hermes, Inc. Jones's independence as Mercury's auditor would be impaired if he were to

   a. Perform on behalf of Mercury a special examination of the financial affairs of Hermes.

   b. Render an opinion as to each party's compliance with financial convenants of the merger agreement.

   c. Arrange through mutual acquaintances the initial meeting between representatives of Mercury and Hermes.

   d. Negotiate the terms of the acquisition on behalf of Mercury.

3

Regulating and Policing the Profession

This chapter covers:

- STATE AND TERRITORIAL LICENSING BOARDS.
- THE AICPA AND STATE SOCIETIES OF CPAS.
- THE SECURITIES AND EXCHANGE COMMISSION.
- STATE AND FEDERAL COURTS.

Public regulation of professions must be limited to measures that are both *reasonable and necessary* for the protection of a compelling public interest. All too often, regulation is used to erect barriers and restrict competition, which results in less public service—not more. In some cases the regulations themselves are used to inflict injuries on the consuming public.[1]

Regulation of the accounting profession and enforcement of its standards of practice are dependent on the following organizations and authorities:

1. State and territorial licensing boards.
2. The AICPA and state societies of CPAs.

3. The Securities and Exchange Commission.
4. The U.S. Treasury Department (discussed in Chapter 12).
5. State and federal courts.

STATE AND TERRITORIAL LICENSING BOARDS

Courts hold that because of insufficient compelling public interest, states may not lawfully prohibit unlicensed persons from engaging in bookkeeping services. For example, in 1964 the Tennessee Court of Appeals said:

> The Courts have generally recognized that the practice of public accountancy is a highly skilled and technical . . . profession and, as such, may be regulated by the legislature within proper limits. . . . However, the Courts consistently have held that legislation which prohibits noncertified accountants from practicing the profession of accountancy is invalid as it infringes upon the rights of contract in matters of purely private concern bearing no perceptible relation to the general or public welfare. And, in so doing, the Courts have indicated that bookkeeping and similar technical services—as contrasted with auditing and expressing opinions on financial statements—do not involve a sufficient public interest to permit legislative interference with the normal right of an individual to deal with anyone he chooses. . . .[2]

The right to practice before the Internal Revenue Service is a federal right that cannot be impinged upon by the states.[3] While Oregon and California regulate tax return preparers, the rules exempt CPAs, enrolled agents, and attorneys, and the failure to provide this exemption might make the legislation unconstitutional. A Mississippi statute restricting the preparation of tax returns for compensation to CPAs and attorneys was held void as an unconstitutional exercise of the state's police power.[4]

Regulation of Professional Designations

Public accounting affects the public welfare; the states may thus exercise their police power to regulate

---

1. The Interstate Commerce Commission provides an interesting example. Carriers have competitive but differing rates. Where a carrier misrepresents rates to obtain business, a demand for the higher rate is not only permitted, but actually required. Regulation thus protects the carrier in inflicting injury on the public. *See* 9 Am. Jur. Carriers § 160 and 88 A.L.R.2d 1375.

   Government operations, as well as regulations frequently become oppressive. For example, some critics contend that Tennessee Valley Authority, designed to protect the environment, inflicts great injury on the environment.

2. State of Tennessee *ex rel.* State Board of Accountancy v. Bookkeepers Business Service Co., 382 S.W.2d 559 (Tenn. Ct. App. 1964). *Accord.*, Florida Accountants Ass'n v. Dandelake, 98 So. 2d 323 (Fla. 1957).

3. In Sperry v. Florida, 373 U.S. 379 (1963) the U.S. Supreme Court struck down a decision by the Florida Supreme Court holding that Sperry could not practice in Tampa as a Patent Attorney unless he was a member of the Florida bar. This implicitly overrules decisions holding that federal tax practice by CPAs constitutes unauthorized practice of law. For further discussion see Chapter 12.

4. Moore v. Grillis, 39 So. 2d 505 (Miss. 1949).

it.[5] All 54 U.S. jurisdictions (50 states plus Puerto Rico, the Virgin Islands, Guam, and the District of Columbia) now have laws regulating the use of the title *certified public accountant.* The majority of U.S. jurisdictions have "regulatory" statutes, most of which restrict to "certified public accountants" all *future* licenses to express opinions on financial representations. Most of these "regulatory" jurisdictions licensed, without examination, all noncertified accountants in practice at the time of adoption of the regulatory laws to continue to practice under the title *public accountant.* A minority of jurisdictions have "permissive" laws that permit anyone to use the designation *public accountant* and express opinions on financial statements. It is well settled that state laws that restrict use of the term *certified public accountant* and the initials CPA or PA to persons licensed by the state regulatory board are valid.[6]

The courts are divided as to whether or not the legislature may validly prohibit use of the word *accountant* by unlicensed persons. The better view is that the word *accountant* constitutes a professional designation, such as *lawyer* or *dentist,* and may thus be restricted to those having valid licenses to practice. In *Texas State Board of Public Accountancy v. W. L. Fulcher,*[7] the defendant presented himself to the public as an accountant. He was not a CPA or a licensed or registered public accountant under the state law. Although he did not issue audit opinions on financial statements, he did sign his name to financial reports and statements. *Fulcher & Fulcher, Accountants* appeared on both the building directory in the office building where he maintained an office and on the entrance doors to his office. The title *Fulcher & Company, Accountants* appeared in the return address on his business envelopes. In issuing its order enjoining the defendant from using the word *accountant* on his office signs and business envelopes, the Texas Court of Civil Appeals said:

As the affairs of the people change and progress, the police power progresses to meet the needs. . . . Today, the need to protect the public against fraud, deception and the consequences of ignorance or incompetence in the practice of most professions makes regulation necessary. The state may exact the requisite degree of skill and learning in professions which affect the public, or at least a substantial portion of the public, such as the practice of law, medicine, engineering, dentistry, and many others. . . .

The legislature, in effect, has determined that the public use of the term "accountant" is a holding out to the public that the person using that term holds a live permit to practice public accounting.

The Texas court did not prohibit unlicensed persons from doing accounting work but only restricted the use of the word *accountant* to those meeting licensing requirements. Since the status of the accountant has grown, laymen tend to place greater reliance upon those who use the title than is justified for unlicensed persons. This Texas decision is a forward-looking landmark in terms of eliminating the confusion of the layperson over differences in professional competence.

California followed the *Fulcher* reasoning in *People v. Hill*[8] and enjoined an unlicensed person from using the business name "A-ACCOUNTING—JACK M. HILL & CO." at his place of business, in the telephone directory, and on business correspondence. Unlike Texas, California has no statute prohibiting unlicensed persons from using the word *accountant.* However, the California court reached the same result by analysis of the definition of public accountancy as holding oneself "out to the public in any manner as one skilled in the knowledge, science and practice of accounting. . . ." In upholding the injunction the court said:

What does the public think when they see a company with the title "A-Accounting" advertising that name? Does not the very name connote that they are accountants ready and prepared to do accounting for the general public. . . .

By arguing that his conduct falls within the bookkeeping exemption contained in section 5052, appellant seeks to escape the provisions of the Accountancy Act. There is a great difference between bookkeeping and accounting. Had appellant advertised himself as

---

5. For an analysis of court decisions dealing with state regulation of public accounting practice, *see* Annot., Regulation of Accountants, 70 A.L.R.2d 433 (1960).

6. *See* Annot., Validity, Construction, and Application of Statute or Regulation Restricting Use of Terms Such As "Accountant," "Public Accountant," or "Certified Public Accountant," 4 A.L.R.4th 1201 (1981). States can also regulate the form of firm name. In McCaffrey v. Couper, 35 A.D.2d 129, 314 N.Y.S.2d 597 (App. Div. 1970), *aff'd without opinion,* 295 N.E.2d 651 (N.Y. App. 1973), the court held that public accountants had no constitutional right to continue to practice under the assumed trade name of Fiduciary Associates.

7. Texas State Board of Public Accountancy v. Fulcher, 515 S.W.2d 950 (Tex. Ct. App. 1974), writ of error denied in 1975. In the related case of Fulcher v. Texas State Board of Public Accountancy, 571 S.W.2d 366 (Tex. Ct. App. 1978), the court affirmed a permanent injunction preventing use of "public accounting offices, accounting practitioner, account, accounting, or any abbreviation or derivation thereof."

8. People v. Hill, 66 Cal. App. 3d 320, 136 Cal. Rptr. 30 (Ct. App. 1977). *Compare* Burton v. The Accountant's Society of Virginia, 194 S.E.2d 684 (Va. Sup. Ct. 1973) (statute that included an ambiguous prohibition against any holding out to the public as an "accountant" held applicable only to use of the title *public accountant* or *certified public accountant*); Tom Welch Accounting Service v. Walby, 138 N.W.2d 139 (Wis. 1965) (statute prohibiting unlicensed persons from using the title *certified public accountant* or *public accountant* did not prevent an unlicensed person from doing business under the name "Tom Welch Accounting Service" nor listing the name under the occupational heading *Accountants* in the yellow pages of the telephone directory).

"bookkeeper" or "bookkeeping" instead of "accounting," he would have been well within the law.

Other courts have struck down attempts to regulate the use of the word *accountant,* holding that such restrictions create ambiguity since unlicensed persons cannot be constitutionally prohibited from performing bookkeeping services. For example, in *Florida Accountants Association v. Dandelake*[9] the Florida Su-

---

9. Florida Accountants Association v. Dandelake, 98 So. 2d 323 (Fla. 1957). *Accord:* Washington Association of Accountants v. Washington State Board of Accountancy, CCH Accy. L. Rep. ¶64,097 (Superior Court of Washington for Thurston County 1973); Comprehensive Accounting Service Co. v. The Maryland State Board of Public Accountancy, 397 A.2d 1019 (Md. App. 1979).

In State Board of Accountancy of Florida v. Grady W. Hartley, CCH Accy. L. Rep. ¶64,084 (1972), a Florida trial court held that an unlicensed person can use the word *accountant* but cannot add to the term, either before or after, the words *enrolled* or *practicing.* The court ruled such persons can use the legend *enrolled to practice before the Internal Revenue Service* provided it is set forth apart from the designation *accountant.* This ruling was affirmed *per curiam* by the Florida District Court of Appeal for the First District on June 5, 1973, 279 So.2d 329 (Fla. App. 1973).

In another Florida case, the trial court ruled that an unlicensed accountant violated the accountancy law by (1) expressing an opinion on financial statements and (2) describing himself as an "accountant, a member of the Florida Accountants Association, and a member of the National Society of Public Accountants without using any language that he was not licensed" as required by the board. See the *Journal of Accountancy,* February 1975, p. 26.

preme Court struck down as unconstitutional the Florida statute prohibiting the practice of accounting by unlicensed accountants and held that so long as persons do not use the statutory title *certified public accountant* or *public accountant* or any other designation that might mislead or deceive the public, such persons have every right to work at their chosen profession and to call themselves accountants.

The solution for protecting the public, as well as the right of unlicensed persons to perform recordkeeping and elementary accounting services and such tax services as the taxing authorities permit, is to adopt words other than *accounting* and *accountant* to describe the work and persons not subject to regulation. A statutory provision regulating and narrowly defining *accounting* and *accountant,* while permitting unlicensed persons to engage in "bookkeeping and elementary services," should be a valid restriction on the use of the term *accountant.*

Requirements for Licensing of CPAs

Education and experience requirements for CPAs vary in the 54 jurisdictions (see Exhibit 3–1). All U.S. jurisdictions now require the passing of a two-and-a-half-day uniform exam prepared and graded by the AICPA as a prerequisite to obtaining a license to prac-

EXHIBIT 3–1
Combination of Education and Experience Required for CPAs

State or Territory	College Education Required		Years Experience Required	
	Years, Degree (D), or Graduate Study (G)	*Curriculum Specified*	*Public Accounting*	*Other*
Alabama	D	No[1]	2	
Alaska	D	Yes	2	2
	D	No	3	3
	2	No	4	4
Arizona	G	Yes	1	1
	D	Yes	2	2
Arkansas	G	Yes	1	1
	D	Yes	2	2
California	D	Yes	3	4
	2[2]	Yes	4	4
	0[3]	Yes	4	4
Colorado	G	Yes		
Connecticut	D	Yes	2	
Delaware	G	Yes	1	1
	D	Yes	2	2
	2	Yes	4	4
District of Columbia[4]	D	Yes	2	2

EXHIBIT 3-1 *(continued)*

State or Territory	College Education Required		Years Experience Required	
	Years, Degree (D), or Graduate Study (G)	Curriculum Specified	Public Accounting	Other
Florida	G	Yes		
Georgia	D	Yes	2	5
Guam	G	Yes	1	1
	D	Yes	2	2
Hawaii	G	Yes		
Idaho	4	Yes	1	2
Illinois[4]	4	Yes	1	1
	0[5]	Yes	3	3
Indiana	G	Yes	2	
	D	Yes	3	6
Iowa[4]	G	Yes	1	
	D	Yes	2	
	0	No	3	
Kansas	G	Yes[6]		
	D	Yes[6]	2	
Kentucky	G	Yes	1	4
	D	Yes	2	4
Louisiana	D	Yes	1	1[3]
Maine	G	No	1	
	D	No	2	
Maryland	D	Yes		
Massachusetts	G	Yes	2	4 to 6
	D	No	3	6 to 9
Michigan	D	Yes	2	2
Minnesota	G	Yes	1	1
	D	Yes	2	2
	D	No	3	3
	2	No	5	5
	0	No	6	6
Mississippi	D	Yes	1	1 to 3
Missouri[4]	D	Yes	2	
Montana	D	Yes		
	D	No	1	1
Nebraska	D	No	2	3
Nevada	D	Yes	2	2
New Hampshire	G	Yes	1	1
	4	No	2	2
New Jersey	D	Yes	2	4
New Mexico	4	Yes	1	
New York	G	Yes	1	1
	D	Yes	2	2
	0	No	15	

EXHIBIT 3–1 *(concluded)*

State or Territory	College Education Required — Years, Degree (D), or Graduate Study (G)	Curriculum Specified	Years Experience Required — Public Accounting	Other
North Carolina	G	Yes	1	1
	D	Yes	2	2
North Dakota	D	Yes		
	0	No	4	4
Ohio	G	Yes	1	1
	D	Yes	2	2
Oklahoma	D	Yes		
	0	No	3	3
Oregon	G	Yes	1	1
	D	Yes	2	2
	0	No	2	2
Puerto Rico	D	Yes		
	D	No	4	8
	0	No	6	12
Pennsylvania	G	Yes	1	
	D	Yes	2	
Rhode Island	G	Yes	1	
	D	Yes	2	
South Carolina	D	Yes	2	
South Dakota	D	Yes	1	
	0	No	1	
Tennessee	G	Yes	1	2
	D	Yes	2	3
Texas	G	Yes	1	1
	D	Yes	2	2
	2	Yes	6	6
Utah	G	Yes	1	
	D	Yes	2	
Vermont	1[7]	Yes	2	2
Virgin Islands	D	Yes	2	2
	D	No	3	3
	0	No	6	
Virginia	G	Yes	1	2
	D	Yes	2	3
Washington	D	Yes	1	2
	D	No	2	3
West Virginia	D	Yes		
Wisconsin	D	Yes	1½	
Wyoming	D	Yes	3	

[1] Only with a major in accounting can the exam be taken prior to the experience.
[2] Plus four years of study.
[3] Must demonstrate equivalency.
[4] Experience requirement is for permit to practice; none is required for the CPA certificate.
[5] Illinois accepts study in correspondence schools.
[6] No accounting courses are required for those having two years of experience.
[7] Thirty semester hours of accounting and related subjects including three hours of auditing.

tice as a CPA.[10] This exam is administered twice each year, in May and November, and is usually given in the following sequence:

Accounting Practice, Part I	(Wednesday, 1:30–6:00 P.M.)
Auditing	(Thursday, 8:30–12:00 M.)
Accounting Practice, Part II	(Thursday, 1:30–6:00 P.M.)
Business Law	((Friday, 8:30–12:00 M.)
Accounting Theory	(Friday, 1:30–5:00 P.M.)

Many jurisdictions require one or more years of experience either as a prerequisite for the CPA certificate or as a prerequisite for a permit to practice (required of those already having CPA certificates). The requirement of public accounting experience without specification as to the particular training required serves as a barrier to entry reminiscent of the medieval guild system and has little relation to professional competency. Meaningful experience requirements would focus on the activities composing the experience.

Many jurisdictions now require a CPA to have a college degree based on specified courses. The degree requirement serves only as a barrier to entry, as do some experience requirements, unless the curriculum is specified. An increasing number of states require continuing education as a condition to continued licensing of CPAs (see Exhibit 3–2).

Model Accountancy Bill. A model accountancy bill, available in booklet form from the AICPA,[11] contains a regulatory bill and provides for (1) required continuing education, (2) phasing in of a required fifth year of college study, and (3) omitting experience requirements for those having five years of college study that includes "an accounting concentration or its equivalent and such related subjects as the Board shall determine to be appropriate." An alternate proposed form of a model accountancy bill is available from the National Association of State Boards of Accountancy, 545 Fifth Avenue, New York, New York 10017. Both of these model bills are reproduced in *CCH Accountancy Law Reporter*.

Requirements for Due Process and Equal Protection. State boards of accounting must afford all applicants due process and equal protection under the law. Exercise of discretion by state boards must not be arbitrary and capricious. Due process of law requires state boards to conform to recognized rules of procedure. Applicants are thus entitled to be informed of everything considered by the board and must be given an opportunity to present relevant evidence prior to final rulings on their applications. Equal protection under the law requires that regulations must apply alike to all applicants similarly situated or be struck down as violations of the equal protection clause of the 14th Amendment of the U.S. Constitution.[12]

PRACTICAL POINTER

Attorney's fees may be recoverable against state boards that act in an arbitrary or capricious manner that indicates bad faith or violates civil rights protected by federal law. See court decisions dealing with the Attorney's Fees Act of 1976, 42 U.S.C. § 1988, and those dealing with inherent powers of federal courts under Rule 37(b) to award attorney's fees because of bad faith found either in actions that led to the lawsuit or in the conduct of the litigation.

EXHIBIT 3-2
States Requiring Continuing Education for CPAs

Required by Statute or Regulation

Alabama	Kansas	Ohio
Alaska	Louisiana	Oklahoma
Arizona	Maine	Oregon
Arkansas	Maryland	Pennsylvania
California	Massachusetts	Rhode Island
Colorado	Michigan	South Carolina
Connecticut	Minnesota	South Dakota
District of Columbia	Montana	Tennessee
Florida	Nebraska	Utah
Georgia	Nevada	Vermont
Hawaii	New Mexico	Washington
Indiana	North Carolina	Wyoming
Iowa	North Dakota	

*Required for Membership in
a State Society*

New Hampshire	Virginia	West Virginia

---

10. A guide to preparing for this examination entitled *Information for CPA Candidates* is furnished free in single copies to candidates by the AICPA, 1211 Avenue of the Americas, New York, N.Y. 10036.

11. *Model Accountancy Bill* (New York: American Institute of Certified Public Accountants, n.d.).

12. In Cenac v. Florida State Bd. of Accountancy, 399 So. 2d 1013 (Fla. App. 1981), Cenac, a Florida CPA, formed a corporation to consult on Medicare and Medicaid reimbursement. He informed the board, pursuant to statute, that he was permitting his CPA to be marked inoperative, thus exempting him from reestablishing his competency. When asked if he was a CPA, he would answer he was "nonpracticing." The court reversed the Florida Board's revocation of Cenac's certificate because the Board rejected the hearing officer's finding that Cenac was not practicing while failing to have adequate support for its decision.

In Ivancic v. Accountancy Bd. of Ohio, 221 N.E.2d 719 (Ohio App. 1966), the court held that it was an abuse of discretion to fail to declare the basis for rejecting an applicant. In Mercer v. Hemmings, 170 So. 2d 33 (Fla. 1965), *appeal dismissed*, 389 U.S. 46 (1067), the court held that a requirement for two years' residence in Florida prior to taking the CPA exam was void and unreasonable. In Lehmann v. State Bd. of Public Accountancy, 263 U.S. 394 (1922), the U.S. Supreme Court upheld an Alabama statute that provided for revocation of a CPA certificate for "unprofessional conduct" against the challenge that it was an unconstitutionally vague violation of due process. On state regulation generally, *see* Annot., Regulation of Accountants, 70 A.L.R.2d 433 (1960).

Invalidity of Citizenship Requirements

State laws requiring applicants for CPA certification to be U.S. citizens are held to be invalid and unconstitutional.[13] The 14th Amendment of the U.S. Constitution provides that no state shall "deprive any person of life, liberty, or property, without due process of law; nor deny to any person within its jurisdiction the equal protection of the laws." It has been held that the term *person* as used in the 14th Amendment includes lawfully admitted resident aliens, as well as citizens, and that equal protection of the law is afforded to citizens and aliens alike.[14] A legislative classification distinguishing between citizens and aliens can be sustained only if it reasonably protects a substantial public interest. Discrimination based on the fact of alienage must, in order to be valid, be shown to promote a compelling public interest.[15] Since citizenship does not bear any relation to the maintenance of minimum standards of competency in the practice of public accounting, such discrimination is unconstitutional.

In *In re Griffiths*[16] a resident alien was denied permission to take the Connecticut bar exam solely because he did not meet a citizenship requirement. The U.S. Supreme Court held such exclusion constituted a violation of the 14th Amendment because the state failed to show that the rule was related to its interest in the qualifications of those admitted to practice law.

Experience Requirements

Many states require "specified" experience before a person can be issued a CPA certificate or a permit to practice. The experience usually specified is "public accounting." Because these requirements do not provide for evaluation of equivalent training acquired through work with government or private industry, they may be subject to attack on constitutional grounds. Additionally, they place in the hands of licensed CPAs the power to exclude all others. Such apprenticeship requirements will be closely examined by the courts so that states will have to show that their conditions are reasonable and necessary means of effecting a compelling state interest.

Requirements Held Invalid. In *Welsh v. Arizona State Board of Accountancy,*[17] the Arizona Court of Appeals struck down a State Board of Accountancy ruling that experience with the Internal Revenue Service was not equivalent to employment by a CPA. The board made no effort to evaluate experience of applicants that consisted of (1) only write-up work in small CPA firms, (2) mainly write-up work and preparation of tax returns in large local CPA firms, and (3) comprehensive auditing training in national CPA firms. The board thus applied a more rigorous standard to the plaintiff than to those qualifying with CPA experience.

Following the *Welsh* case the Arizona statute was amended to require two years of experience

> in the office of a certified public accountant or public accountant, within private industry or a government agency, which employment shall have exposed the applicant to and provided him with experience in the practice of accounting, including examinations of financial statements and reporting thereon. . . .

The Arizona State Board chose to interpret this provision as requiring experience with the attest function of an independent auditor and denied a CPA certificate to an applicant having five years experience as an IRS agent.

In affirming the order requiring the Board to issue the certificate, the Arizona Court of appeals held:

> We have concluded that the history . . . demonstrates, as the trial court found, that the legislature did not intend to require attest function experience. Rather the inclusion of the environments of private industry and government as well as the failure to adopt the detailed attest function language of the House Bill or the language "in accordance with generally accepted auditing standards" are indicative of an intent to afford a broad interpretation to the experience requirement.[18]

In *Merrill v. McGinn,*[19] the Utah board refused to issue a CPA certificate to a plaintiff who had passed the CPA exam but lacked the required two years of "public accounting experience." The Utah Supreme Court sustained the lower court in requiring defendant to license plaintiff as a CPA because the denial of a license was "arbitrary, capricious, and without foundation in fact or law." The plaintiff had 15 years experience in large companies, including service as assistant controller in a firm with sales in 1973 of over

13. Michigan Attorney General's Opinion No. 4765, CCH Accy. L. Rep. ¶64,091 (1973); Virginia Attorney General's Opinion, CCH Accy. L. Rep. ¶64,094 (1973); Iowa Attorney General's Opinion, CCH Accy. L. Rep. ¶64,098 (1974).

14. It has been held that aliens cannot be discriminated against in the occupations of pawnbrokerage, Asakura v. Seattle, 265 U.S. 332 (1924); laundering, Yick Wo v. Hopkins, 118 U.S. 356 (1886); fishing, Takahashi v. Fish & Game Comm., 334 U.S. 410 (1948); Traux v. Raich, 239 U.S. 33 (1915); barbering, Templar v. Mich. State Brd. of Examiners of Barbers, 131 Mich. 254, 90 N.W. 1058 (1902); and soft drink sales, George v. Portland, 114 Ore. 418, 235 P. 681 (1925).

15. 3 Am. Jur. 2d Aliens & Citizens, §37 (1967).

16. *In re* Griffiths, 413 U.S. 717 (1973).

17. Welsh v. Arizona State Board of Accountancy, 484 P.2d 201 (1971). Compare Junco v. State Bd. of Accountancy, 390 So. 2d 329 (Fla. 1980), where the court refused to accept experience with the Internal Revenue Service as equivalent to experience with a CPA firm, the public service commission, or the state auditor general.

18. Arizona State Board of Accountancy v. Keebler, CCH Accy. Rep. ¶64,123 (Ct. of App. 1977).

19. Merrill v. McGinn, 30 Utah 2d 421, 518 P.2d 1392 (Utah 1974).

$175 million. The court found that the plaintiff's experience was equal to or superior to experience previously accepted as a substitute: auditor of Blue Cross and Blue Shield, agent for Internal Revenue Service, or accountant for Defense Auditing Agency.

A California attorney general's opinion[20] concluded that the California State Board of Accountancy could not require more experience of those employed in governmental accounting than required of those in public accounting if the governmental work is performed under a CPA and is equivalent to that experience otherwise accepted by the board.

Requirements Held Valid. In *Duggins v. North Carolina State Board of Certified Public Accountant Examiners*[21] the court held that plaintiff's experience as a tax lawyer under a lawyer who was also a CPA did not entitle him to his certificate even if it was exactly the same experience that an applicant working with a CPA in public practice would receive:

> The equal protection clauses of the state and federal constitutions are not violated by mere "incidental individual inequality" . . . whenever any classes are made the lines distinguishing them must be drawn. Of necessity some individuals will fall just short of the line while others will just barely cross it, and the differences between the two groups will often be slight. This result occurs regardless of where the line is drawn. To hold that the equal protection clauses prohibited this type of incidental individual inequality would be to effectively eliminate classification systems.

Discipline by State Boards

State licensing authorities set their own standards. *Fortune* reported that in some cases CPAs who have been expelled from the AICPA (one case even involving tax fraud) continue to practice undisturbed by state authorities.[22] Ingalls also indicates that enforcement procedures at the state level are not effective.[23]

In a study of disciplinary cases of the state board and state society in a large midwestern state, Loeb finds that not many cases are considered—under four per year for the state society and under three per year for the state board. Only about half of the cases result in sanctions, and most of those are for offenses against colleagues as opposed to client or public violations. The severity of sanctions imposed is not related to the number of past violations.[24]

Problems of State Regulation. Public accounting is necessarily national and international in scope, since it must be coextensive with the business firms subjected to audit. Although it is not practicable for a business firm to have a different auditor in each jurisdiction, state accountancy laws represent a diversity of standards with respect to ethics, interstate rights to practice, and qualifications for licenses to practice. This is clearly undesirable, since accounting and auditing rules are national in scope.

Although the AICPA has advocated uniform standards, little uniformity has been attained. AICPA ethics rules must be followed by AICPA members regardless of the member's licensing state. Although AICPA ethics rules should constitute minimum standards for the profession as a whole, each state follows its own policy as to ethics.

The AICPA advocates the following principles for state regulation of interstate practice:

1. Certificates should be issued to out-of-state CPAs on an equivalent standards basis, not by reciprocal agreements. The residence requirement for such a certificate should be satisfied by personal domicile, a place of business, or regular employment within the state.
2. An accounting firm should be permitted to use the CPA title if its local partners hold local certificates and every other partner holds a certificate from some state.
3. A CPA should have full freedom to enter any state to carry out engagements incident to his or her regular practice.
4. Reasonable provision should be made for the use of his or her title and the practice of the profession by a holder of a foreign certificate or license.

If the courts strike down as unreasonable burdens on interstate commerce any state laws that conflict with the AICPA position, then the public can get the auditing service that the public welfare requires.[25] Heimbucher, in an excellent article, "Fifty-Three Jurisdictions," points out that the diversity of state rules and

20. California Attorney General Opinion No. CV 73–219, CCH Accy. L. Rep. ¶64,106 (1975).
21. Duggins v. North Carolina State Board of Certified Public Accountant Examiners, 240 S.E.2d 401(N.C. 1978).
22. T. A. Wise, "The Auditors Have Arrived" (Part II), *Fortune*, December 1960, p. 148.
23. Ingalls, "Developing and Implementing Higher Professional Standards in Accounting," 30 *Law & Contemp. Prob.* 874, 878–79 (1965).
24. Stephen E. Loeb, "Enforcement of the Code of Ethics: A Survey," *Accounting Review*, January 1972, pp. 1–10.
25. The July 1980 *Journal of Accountancy* reported at page 16 that a federal court invalidated a Louisiana rule that required every member of a multistate accounting firm that practices in Louisiana to be licensed by the board. The court ruled that the board went beyond authority in the statute: "Rules and regulations of a board cannot enlarge, extend, or modify a governing statute or survive if in conflict."

prohibitions on interstate practice "reaches an absurdity."[26]

THE AICPA AND STATE SOCIETIES OF CPAS

The AICPA regulates its membership with the Code of Professional Ethics, which derives its authority from the AICPA bylaws. According to court decisions (see Chapter 1, note 37), AICPA rules are minimum standards required of all those practicing public accounting.

AICPA Right to Make Rules

The right of the AICPA to make and issue accounting rules was challenged in *Appalachian Power Co. v. American Institute of CPAs.*[27] The plaintiff sought an injunction to enjoin the AICPA from issuing an opinion (through its Committee on Accounting Procedure, which was superseded by the APB and later by the FASB) that charges made to income in recognition of the deferral of income taxes should not be credited to any account included in the stockholders' equity section of the balance sheet. The plaintiff had recorded more than $65 million in "earned surplus restricted for future federal income taxes." Plaintiff contended that as a result of this opinion, its auditors and the SEC would question its practice and that reclassification would limit the plaintiff's short-term borrowing capacity. The action was based on a New York doctrine of "prima facie tort" and brought in federal court on grounds of diversity of citizenship. The gist of prima facie tort is the infliction of *intentional* harm resulting in damage by an act that would otherwise be lawful. The court dismissed the action because there was no *intent* on the part of the AICPA to inflict injury on the plaintiff. The case still gives the AICPA authority to make auditing rules and the FASB (as successor to the Committee on Accounting Procedure) authority to make accounting rules.

Binding Technical Standards

Several AICPA ethics rules have the effect of creating binding technical standards for the entire public accounting industry. These are:

1. Rule 202 requires compliance by auditors with generally accepted auditing standards.
2. Rule 203 makes FASB financial reporting rules binding for auditors.
3. Rule 204 makes pronouncements of the Accounting and Review Services Committee binding for unaudited financial statements; it also makes pronouncements of the Management Advisory Services Executive Committee binding for management consulting engagements.

Membership in the AICPA Division of Firms,[28] which is composed of an SEC practice section and a private companies practice section, subjects the member to required continuing education, quality control standards, and peer review procedures.

Rule 203.   One of the most important AICPA rules is ethics rule 203, which states:

> A member shall not express an opinion that financial statements are presented in conformity with generally accepted accounting principles if such statements contain any departure from an accounting principle promulgated by the body designated by Council to establish such principles which has a *material effect on the statements as a whole,* unless the member can demonstrate that due to unusual circumstances the financial statements would otherwise have been misleading. In such cases the report must describe the departure, the approximate effects thereof, if practicable, and the reasons why compliance with the principle would result in a misleading statement. (Emphasis added.)

In the spring of 1973 the AICPA Council designated the FASB as the body to establish accounting principles pursuant to rule 203. It specified that the following principles are encompassed by rule 203:

1. *FASB Statements of Financial Accounting Standards and FASB Interpretations,* and
2. *Accounting Research Bulletins* (not to be confused with *Accounting Research Studies*) and *Accounting Principles Board Opinions* that are not superseded by action of the FASB.

Except in the "unusual circumstances" discussed in rule 203, an auditor must give either a qualified "except for" opinion or an adverse opinion wherever there is a deviation from official pronouncements. The

26. Clifford V. Heimbucher, "Fifty-Three Jurisdictions," *Journal of Accountancy,* November 1961, p. 45.

27. Appalachian Power Co. v. American Institute of CPAs, 177 F. Supp. 345 (S.D.N.Y. 1959), *aff'd per curiam,* 268 F.2d 844 (2d Cir. 1959), *cert. denied,* 361 U.S. 887 (1959). The voluminous pleadings, briefs, and rulings are reprinted in *Cases in Public Accounting Practice: The AICPA Injunction Case* (Chicago: Arthur Andersen & Co., 1960).

28. A group of 18 AICPA members sought to enjoin the AICPA's implementation of an SEC practice section and a private companies practice section until approved by the entire membership. On July 27, 1978, a New York trial court ruled for the AICPA and held that the Institute's board and council had the power to establish these "auxiliary bodies," which did not establish new classes of membership. See the September 1978 *Journal of Accountancy* at page 7.

qualified "except for" opinion states that "except for" the deviation from the pronouncement to which the qualification relates, the financial statements present fairly the financial position, results of operations, and changes in financial position in conformity with GAAP consistently applied. An adverse opinion states that financial statements do not present fairly the financial position, results of operations, or changes in financial position in conformity with GAAP. The choice between the qualified and adverse opinion is based upon materiality:

1. If the departure is immaterial, an unqualified opinion is issued.
2. If the departure is material but not so material as to impair the fairness of financial statements "taken as a whole," a qualified "except for" opinion is issued.
3. If the departure is so material that the financial statements taken as a whole are not presented fairly in conformity with generally accepted accounting principles, an adverse opinion is issued.

In evaluating materiality, one factor to be considered is the dollar magnitude of the effects. For example, if a departure regarding inventory valuation were material to current assets but immaterial to total assets, a qualified opinion might be issued. However, if the departure were material to total assets, an adverse opinion would be necessary. Materiality also depends on qualitative judgments, such as the significance of an item to a particular enterprise and the pervasiveness of the misstatement.[29]

Unusual Circumstances. The AICPA division of professional ethics in its interpretation 203–1 states:

> There is a strong presumption that adherence to officially established accounting principles would in nearly all instances result in financial statements that are not misleading.[30]

Under this interpretation "unusual circumstances" means that GAAP would, in the professional judgment of the auditor, produce misleading results. New legislation and the evolution of a new form of business transaction are given as examples of situations in which "unusual circumstances" might be involved. Examples of events that are *not* considered "unusual circumstances" are an unusual degree of materiality and the existence of conflicting industry practices.[31]

When the auditor determines that such unusual circumstances are present, the auditor expresses an *unqualified opinion,* despite the departure from official pronouncements, but explains in one or more separate paragraphs the information required by the rule, such as a description of the departure, its approximate effects, and the reasons the departure is necessary to avoid misleading results.[32]

Substantial Authoritative Support. Where matters are not governed by official pronouncements, GAAP are those principles that have "substantial authoritative support." AICPA rules provide:

> In the absence of pronouncements comprehended by Rule 203, the auditor should consider other possible sources of established accounting principles, such as AICPA accounting interpretations, AICPA industry audit guides and accounting guides, and industry accounting practices. Depending on their relevance in the circumstances, the auditor may also wish to refer to APB statements of position, pronouncements of other professional associations and regulatory agencies, such as the Securities and Exchange Commission, and accounting textbooks and articles. . . . [Independent auditors] should also be alert to changes that become acceptable as a result of common usage in business, rather than as a result of pronouncements.[33]

Competitive Bidding

The AICPA formerly had a rule prohibiting competitive bidding, which read: "A member or associate shall not make a competitive bid for a professional engagement. Competitive bidding for public accounting services is not in the public interest, is a form of solicitation, and is unprofessional." In *United States v. American Institute of Certified Public Accountants,*[34] the Antitrust Division of the Department of Justice brought suit under the Sherman Act to enjoin the prohibition of competitive bidding. The AICPA then agreed to the entry of a final judgment, enjoining it from prohibiting or limiting price quotations and requiring it to delete the competitive bidding rule from its ethics code.

State society rules that prohibit competitive bidding are now invalid as violations of federal antitrust laws. For example, in *United States v. Texas State Board of Public Accountancy,*[35] the court held that the state board rule prohibiting competitive bidding was void as

29. *CCH AICPA Professional Standards,* AU § 509.16.
30. *CCH AICPA Professional Standards,* ET § 203.02.
31. Ibid.
32. Ibid.
33. *CCH AICPA Professional Standards,* AU § 411.06.
34. United States v. American Institute of Certified Public Accountants, CCH Accy. L. Rep. §64,082 (1972).
35. United States v. Texas State Board of Public Accountancy, 592 F.2d 919 (5th Cir.), *cert. denied,* 100 S. Ct. 262 (1979). In National Society of Professional Engineers v. United States, 435 U.S. 679 (1978), the U.S. Supreme Court held that an agreement not to engage in competitive bidding violated the Sherman Act. Similarly, in Goldfarb v. Virginia State Bar, 421 U.S. 773 (1975), the U.S. Supreme Court struck down a bar association's minimum fee schedule as a violation of the Sherman Act.

a violation of the Sherman Act. The court rejected the board's claim of immunity from the Sherman Act because the prohibitions on competitive bidding were established by the board and not by the legislature.

Although state laws prohibiting competitive bidding get around the Sherman Act, they may violate the right to freedom of speech guaranteed under the First Amendment. In *Bates v. State Bar of Arizona,*[36] the U.S. Supreme Court upheld the right of attorneys to advertise fixed fees for standardized services. IRS amendments to its rules of practice indicate that advertising fixed fees for standardized services is permissible. Presumably the IRS rules would preempt and supersede any contrary state laws as well as ethics rules of private associations.

Advertising and Personal Solicitation

Following the U.S. Supreme Court ruling in *Bates v. State Bar of Arizona*[37] that prohibitions on advertising violated the free speech rights of attorneys, the AICPA adopted a new ethics rule 502:

> A member shall not seek to obtain clients by advertising or other forms of solicitation in a manner that is false, misleading or deceptive.

Interpretation 502-1 provides that the ad may quote both fixed fees and hourly rates. The AICPA membership voted in 1979 to delete its rule against personal solicitation as well as its rule on encroachment.

In *Ohralik v. Ohio State Bar Association,*[38] the U.S. Supreme Court upheld the discipline of an attorney for in-person solicitation. The evil that the court addressed was urging of services on young accident victims at a time when they were especially incapable of making informed judgments, using a tape recorder to ensure evidence of assent, and refusing to withdraw only a day later. These considerations have no relationship whatever to an invitation to lunch for members of an audit committee of a prospective corporate client. Although a rule prohibits the open direct contact, it presumably permits use of a marketing consultant to catalog the identity, clubs, etc., of prospective clients for indirect personal solicitation. Many persons see nothing immoral in direct contacts. For example, the conclusion of the *Metcalf Report,* unanimously approved by all members of the subcommittee, had this to say:

Restraints on Market Entry

One element which is essential to improving the professional environment for independent auditors is the removal of artificial restrictions on the auditor's ability to communicate with potential clients. The subcommittee believes these restrictions have been detrimental to the public because they have prevented the free flow of information needed by users of accounting services to evaluate properly the types, amounts, and prices of services offered by the accounting profession. In the absence of such information, the public—including even sophisticated users in banking, the investment community, and business—have tended to associate quality accounting services solely with the Nation's eight largest accounting firms whose names are well known.

Smaller accounting firms have not been able to compete effectively for publicly owned clients and larger businesses due to the lack of information on their ability to perform quality auditing and accounting services. Subcommittee members have been impressed with the accounting expertise shown by representatives of smaller firms, and believe that the trend toward concentration in the supply of accounting services to publicly owned corporations could be reversed if such firms were permitted to inform existing and potential clients of their abilities. The key to avoiding development of a "first class" and "second class" accounting profession is public knowledge that smaller firms can perform as well as large firms.

The public will receive the best accounting services in an environment which provides competition in pricing and innovation, but is balanced by a strong program to assure that professionalism and independence are not compromised. Accounting firms practicing in such an environment can inform the public of their abilities if the appropriate means become available. Thus, the subcommittee believes there must be an immediate end to artificial professional restrictions against advertising, talking with another firm's clients, and talking with another firm's employees about possible employment without first informing that firm. Prohibitions by accounting organizations in some States against competitive bidding should also be removed.[39]

Discipline by the AICPA and State Societies

The majority of the more than 200,000 CPAs in the United States are members of the AICPA and thus subject to its discipline. Authority relationships at the AICPA are diagrammed in Exhibit 3-3. Since 1975 the AICPA has jointly operated ethics enforcement with the state societies of CPAs. Complaints are received

36. Bates v. State Bar of Arizona, 433 U.S. 350 (1977). *Also see* In the Matter of R.M.J., 50 U.S.L.W. 4185 (1981), where the U.S. Supreme Court reversed discipline of a St. Louis attorney for using direct-mail advertising.

37. Ibid.

38. Ohralik v. Ohio State Bar Ass'n., 436 U.S. 350 (1978).

39. U.S. Senate Subcommittee on Reports, Accounting and Management, *Improving the Accountability of Publicly Owned Corporations and Their Auditors,* reprinted in the January 1978 issue of the *Journal of Accountancy* at pages 88–96.

EXHIBIT 3-3A
Flow of Responsibility of the AICPA

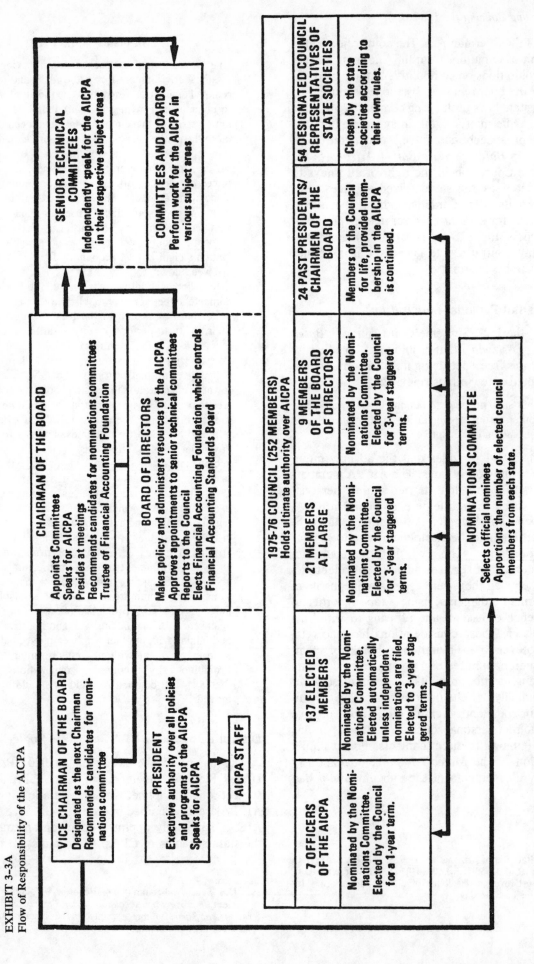

EXHIBIT 3-3B
Organization of the AICPA Staff

| | | | PRESIDENT | | | |
| | | | P.B. Chenok | | | |

```
VICE PRESIDENT          VICE PRESIDENT      VICE PRESIDENT      VICE PRESIDENT      VICE PRESIDENT          GENERAL COUNSEL
COMMUNICATIONS          GOVERNMENT          AUDITING            TECHNICAL           REVIEW AND              AND SECRETARY
AND EDUCATION           RELATIONS           D. Carmichael       T. Kelley           REGULATION              D. Schneeman
D. Roberts              T. Barreaux                                                 W. Bruschi
```

MANAGING DIRECTOR CPE — R. Cruse

VICE PRESIDENT ADMINISTRATIVE SERVICES — D. Adams

- INDUSTRY AND PRACTICE MANAGEMENT — N. Myers
- PUBLIC RELATIONS — B. Smith
- PUBLICATIONS
- RELATIONS WITH EDUCATORS — J. MacNeill
- STATE SOCIETY RELATIONS — D. Roberts
- International Relations
- Meetings and Travel

- FEDERAL GOVERNMENT RELATIONS — J. Moraglio
- FEDERAL LEGISLATIVE AFFAIRS — N. Nichols
- FEDERAL TAXATION — K. Thomas

- AUDITING STANDARDS

- ACCOUNTING STANDARDS — P. Rosenfield
- DIVISION FOR CPA FIRMS
  - PRIVATE COMPANIES PRACTICE SECTION — J. Mitchell
  - SEC PRACTICE SECTION — T. Kelley
  - QUALITY CONTROL REVIEW — T. Felix
- MANAGEMENT ADVISORY SERVICES — M. Kuttner
- TECHNICAL INFORMATION — G. Dick
- International Standards

- EXAMINATIONS — M. Rothkopf
- PROFESSIONAL ETHICS — H. Finkston
  - Information Retrieval
  - Practice Review
  - State Legislation

- COMPUTER SERVICES — D. Adams
- CONTROLLER — F. Di Pascali
- INFORMATION SERVICES — M. O'Driscoll
- OFFICE MANAGEMENT — R. Ade
- PERSONNEL — N. Nestler
- Library
- Purchasing

- Trial Board (under GENERAL COUNSEL AND SECRETARY)

Source: AICPA Committee Handbook: 1980–1981. (Used with permission.)

by either the AICPA Ethics Division or the State Society Ethics Committee. If the complaint involves issues of broad national concern, multistate jurisdiction, or litigation, the AICPA Ethics Division retains direct control. Otherwise the state society conducts the investigation. If further action is warranted, the case is presented to one of 12 regional trial boards. The National Review Board (elected by the AICPA council) consists of 36 practicing members of the AICPA. It has review jurisdiction as well as original jurisdiction where requested by the respondent.

The maximum penalty that the Joint Trial Board can impose is expulsion from membership, which does not affect the right to practice as a CPA. Penalties can be imposed only for violating enumerated provisions, which unfortunately do not include "substandard auditing."

The *Metcalf Staff Study* stated "The standard of ethics followed by the AICPA for partners of large national accounting firms appears to be that disciplinary action for ethics violations must be predicated upon a final verdict of guilty in a court of law." The *Study* gives as an example the fact that the AICPA took no action against partners of Peat, Marwick, Mitchell & Co. after the SEC cited the firm in ASR 173 for improper auditing in five separate cases. Another example cited was the AICPA finding that the former Secretary of Commerce, Maurice H. Stans, did not bring discredit to the profession when he pled guilty to certain offenses relating to the Watergate scandal.[40] The *Study* concludes:

> The results of the AICPA's activities regarding professional ethics and acceptable practice standards are detrimental to the vast majority of CPAs who perform their services with competence, care and pride. By seeking lower standards for all accountants in order to defend the few who are negligent or incompetent, the AICPA contributes to the erosion of public confidence in the usefulness of accounting services.[41]

Other observers have also been critical of AICPA discipline. Professor Abraham Briloff characterizes action of the AICPA Trial Board as "moving in the manner of those false guides referred to in the Scriptures—who swallow camels yet strain at gnats."[42] He gives the following account of confronting Wallace Olsen, the first paid AICPA president and formerly the chairman of the AICPA Ethics Committee:

> In mid-1971 . . . I confronted Mr. Olsen with the challenge: Why has the AICPA not taken disciplinary action in BarChris, Mill Factors, Yale Express, and the other matters which have already run the legal labyrinth? His response was phrased in rhetorical questions: Did I know how voluminous the record was in BarChris alone? How could the Ethics Committee, comprised of unpaid members with only limited personnel support, find the time to make the necessary probe, especially when the members serve as volunteers while pursuing their regular practices? Clearly, I had no answer . . . except to conclude that . . . the more egregious the violation the less likely it will be that its perpetrator will be subjected to judgment by his peers.[43]

Marshall S. Armstrong, a former AICPA president and later an FASB chairman, after hearing many comments by practitioners concerning the apparent lack of effective enforcement of the ethics code, concluded:

> In my view, there is an absence of spirited enforcement of the Code of Professional Ethics throughout the profession as a whole. If such a condition were allowed to continue, the result could be gradual loss of the privilege of self-discipline without our realizing it.[44]

The AICPA has no subpoena power, and according to the January 22, 1973, issue of *The Wall Street Journal*, accounting firms refuse to provide information while litigation is pending because they fear it will be subpoenaed and hurt their position in court. In fairness to the AICPA it should be observed that neither lawyers nor physicians have been able to cope effectively with the problem of policing their profession.[45]

THE SECURITIES AND EXCHANGE COMMISSION

The Securities and Exchange Commission presumably has the power to make and enforce both account-

---

40. The November 2, 1973, *Washington Post* reported that Maurice Stans solicited illegal campaign contributions from Peat, Marwick, Mitchell & Co. and told the firm's senior partner: "Don't worry about the statute. The fact that you're a government contractor is all the more reason for you to give." Upon advice of counsel, Peat rejected the request.

41. *Staff Study,* p. 126. See Chapter 1 at note 25.

42. Abraham J. Briloff, "The Accounting Profession at the Hump of the Decades," *Financial Analysts Journal,* May–June 1970, p. 64.

43. Abraham J. Briloff, "We Often Paint Fakes," 28 *Vand. L. Rev.* 165, 198 (January 1975).

44. Marshall S. Armstrong, "Organizing the Disciplinary Effort of the Accounting Profession," *CPA,* February 1971, p. 2.

45. Watergate revealed one possible reason for this: the biggest crooks are sometimes the most respected and powerful members of the establishment. In 1887 Lord Acton wrote: "Power tends to corrupt and absolute power corrupts absolutely."

ing and auditing rules.[46] There is growing sentiment that nonpublic companies should not be required to provide all the detailed disclosures required for public companies. However, SEC antifraud rules and resulting civil liabilities apply to both public and nonpublic firms and their auditors.

Rule Making

Despite its broad powers, the Commission has historically followed the practice of letting the private accounting profession take the lead in rule making.[47] This has been especially true with respect to reports to stockholders, which have been relatively unregulated, as opposed to the detailed regulations relating to financial statements that must be "filed" with the SEC.

In *Accounting Series Release No. 1*,[48] issued in 1937, the SEC announced a program of publication "of opinions on accounting principles for the purpose of contributing to the development of uniform standards and practice in major accounting questions." In 1938 the Commission announced that supplemental disclo-

sures could not substitute for failure to follow specific Commission rules:

> In cases where financial statements filed with this Commission pursuant to its rules and regulations under the Securities Act of 1933 or the Securities Exchange Act of 1934 are prepared in accordance with accounting principles for which there is no substantial authoritative support, such financial statements will be presumed to be misleading or inaccurate despite disclosures contained in the certificate of the accountant or in footnotes to the statements provided the matters involved are material. In cases where there is a difference of opinion between the Commission and the registrant as to the proper principles of accounting to be followed, disclosure will be accepted in lieu of correction of the financial statements themselves only if the points involved are such that there is substantial authoritative support for the practices followed by the registrant and the position of the Commission has not previously been expressed in rules, regulations, or other official releases of the Commission, including the published opinions of its chief accountant.[49]

The Commission still follows this statement of policy. It requires correction of financials that do not comply with GAAP and will accept neither a qualified "except for" nor an adverse auditor's opinion in lieu of correction. The Commission will sometimes accept an auditor's opinion containing "subject to" qualifications relating to uncertainties inherent in balance sheet accounts.

The Commission has consistently indicated its intention to give great weight to principles established by the accounting profession, but to retain for itself the right to make the final decision to protect the public interest. For example, where intangible assets were valued on the basis of the par of the stock for various reasons and the respondent accounting firm attempted to justify the accounting based on uncontradicted testimony of members of other firms of certified public accountants, the Commission ruled: "While the opinions of qualified expert accountants may be helpful, this Commission must in the last analysis weigh the value of expert testimony against its own judgment of what is sound accounting practice."[50]

The Commission also made clear it would decide for itself what constitutes generally accepted accounting principles when it rejected *Accounting Principles Board Opinion No. 2:* "Accounting for the Investment Credit." The Commission said its policy

---

46. Section 19(a) of the Securities Act of 1933 and Section 13(b) of the Securities Exchange Act of 1934, respectively, empower the SEC to (1) determine "such rules and regulations as may be necessary to carry out the provisions of this title, including . . . defining accounting . . . terms" and "among other things . . . the methods to be followed in the preparation of accounts," and (2) prescribe "the form or forms in which the required information shall be set forth, the items or details to be shown in the balance sheet and the earnings statement, and the methods to be followed in the preparation of reports. . . ."

Items 25 and 26 of Schedule A of the Securities Act of 1933 provide for financial statements "certified by an independent public or certified accountant." Sections 7 and 10 of this act, respectively, require inclusion of items 25 and 26 in registration statements and prospectuses. Section 13(a) of the Securities Exchange Act of 1934 requires issuers of registered securities to "file with the Commission, in accordance with such rules and regulations as the Commission may prescribe as necessary or appropriate for the proper protection of investors and to insure fair dealing in the security . . . such annual reports . . . certified if required by the rules and regulations of the Commission by independent public accountants, and such quarterly reports . . . as the Commission may prescribe." The SEC prescribed forms, which also constitute part of the rules and regulations, require annual reports to be certified.

47. Before the crisis over disclosure that occurred in the 1960s, the accounting profession resisted an aggressive SEC role. A redraft of SEC Regulation S-X, which was to address more extensively accounting principles, brought strong objections from the AICPA in 1950 and from the American Accounting Association in 1951. See "Accountants Dissent on Many of SEC's Proposed Changes in Regulation S-X," *Journal of Accountancy*, October 1950, pp. 312–20; Samuel J. Broad, "The Need for Continuing Change in Accounting Principles and Practices," *Journal of Accountancy*, November 1950, pp. 405–13; and the report of the American Accounting Association resolution in the *Accounting Review*, November 1951, p. 19.

48. *SEC Accounting Series Release No. 1*, "Treatment of Losses Resulting from Revaluation of Assets" (1937).

---

49. *SEC Accounting Series Release No. 4*, "Administrative Policy on Financial Statements" (1938).

50. *SEC Accounting Series Release No. 73*, "In the Matter of Haskins & Sells and Andrew Stewart" (1952).

is intended to support the development of accounting principles and methods of presentation by the profession but to leave the Commission free to obtain the information and disclosure contemplated by the securities laws and conformance with accounting principles which have gained general acceptance.[51]

In 1973 the Commission announced strong support of the FASB in *Accounting Series Release No. 150,* indicating that

> principles, standards and practices promulgated by the FASB in its Statements and Interpretations [and those *Accounting Research Bulletins* and *APB Opinions* not superseded by statements of the FASB] will be considered as having substantial authoritative support, and those contrary to such FASB promulgations will be considered to have no such support.[52]

The Commission noted that AICPA ethics rule 203 provides that departures from such official pronouncements are necessary if, due to unusual circumstances, failure to do so would make the statements misleading. The Commission said that in such cases, "the use of other principles may be accepted or required by the Commission."

Some observers thought that this release meant the Commission was abdicating its rule-making function despite the fact that the release stated that "the Commission will continue to identify areas where investor information needs exist and will determine the appropriate methods of disclosure to meet these needs." *Accounting Series Release No. 153,* issued in 1974, has now laid to rest any such conjecture.[53] There the Commission established both new GAAP and new GAAS. In the principles area, the Commission ruled that an absolute guarantee against loss from ownership of properties makes recognition of profit on the sale improper. In the auditing area, the Commission ruled that all audit engagements should include "a specific review to determine any private involvement of the management and other related persons in corporate transactions reflected in financial statements under examination." Also in the auditing area, the Commission ruled:

When one auditor succeeds another, be it on the same engagement or on a different one, it is important that the successor obtain access to and carefully review the results of the predecessor's work. In most instances, this will entail some review of the predecessor's work papers. In other instances, it may require discussions with those responsible for the predecessor's work. If a client refuses to permit such discussions, such a refusal should constitute a reason for rejecting the engagement. It is essential that both the successor and the predecessor be fully advised of the reasons surrounding the termination and the new engagement, of any questions raised or problems encountered in the audit by the terminated firm, and of any other relevant circumstances, so that the public interest that the accounting profession is supposed to protect will be properly served.[54]

Enforcement

SEC rules provide that where "it appears that there may be violation of the acts administered by the Commission or the rules and regulations thereunder, a preliminary examination is generally made."[55] If it appears that a violation has been or is about to be committed, the Commission may order a formal investigation.[56] If the investigation reveals that a violation has taken place, the Commission can institute administrative proceedings looking to the imposition of remedial sanctions, institute civil injunctive actions, or refer cases to the Department of Justice for criminal prosecution.[57]

The choice of remedy or combination of remedies by the Commission depends upon the degree of egregiousness of the violation; the extent of knowledge, intent, or awareness by the perpetrator; and involvement or lack of involvement of violations of ethics, or federal securities laws, or both. Generally, violations of law result in injunctive actions, while violations of ethics are handled by administrative proceedings.[58] The first two of these possible enforcement alternatives are discussed below; the third, criminal prosecution, is discussed in Chapter 9.

Administrative Proceedings. SEC rule 2(e),[59] provides for discipline of accountants[60] and other persons

---

51. *SEC Accounting Series Release No. 96,* Accounting for the 'Investment Credit' " (1963).

52. *SEC Accounting Series Release No. 150,* "Statement of Policy on the Establishment and Improvement of Accounting Principles and Standards" (1973). Arthur Andersen & Company brought suit against the SEC, urging the court to declare *Accounting Series Release No. 150* void as an unlawful delegation of rule-making power. The case was dismissed because Andersen was unable to prove any economic loss and thus had no standing to sue. See Arthur Andersen v. SEC, CCH Fed. Sec. L. Rep ¶ 96,374 (N.D. Ill. 1978).

53. *SEC Accounting Series Release No. 153,* Touche Ross & Co. (1974).

54. Ibid.

55. 17 C.F.R. § 202.5.

56. Ibid.

57. Ibid.

58. Paul Gonson, "Disciplinary Proceedings and Other Remedies Available to the SEC," 30 *Business Lawyer* 191, 200 (March 1975). © 1975 by *Business Lawyer.*

59. 17 C.F.R. § 201.2(e).

60. In Touche Ross & Co. v. SEC, 609 F.2d (2d Cir. 1979), the court rejected an accounting firm's challenge to the SEC's authority to adopt rule 2(e) and to conduct a public proceeding concerning its audit practices.

who "practice" before the Commission. "Practice before the Commission" includes transacting any business with it and preparing any statement, opinion, or other paper by any attorney, accountant, engineer, or other expert, filed with the Commission with the preparer's consent.[61]

Rule 2(e) provides for imposing sanctions in three different situations:

1. After notice and opportunity for hearing, persons who are unqualified, unethical, or who have violated federal securities laws may be temporarily or permanently denied the privilege of practice.
2. Any person is automatically suspended from practice (without a hearing) upon *(a)* revocation or suspension of his or her professional license by a state or territory, or *(b)* conviction of a felony or of a misdemeanor involving moral turpitude.
3. The Commission may, without a hearing, temporarily suspend any professional who *(a)* has been enjoined from violation of federal securities laws in any action brought by the Commission, or *(b)* has been found by the Commission in any administrative proceeding, or by a court in an action brought by the Commission, to have violated or aided and abetted the violation of federal securities laws. If the person temporarily suspended does not, within 30 days, petition the Commission to lift the suspension, such suspension becomes permanent.

In all three situations, an application for reinstatement may be made at any time. Only in situation 1 is the applicant *entitled* to a hearing on the application; however, in situations 2 and 3, hearings may be granted at the discretion of the Commission.

Hearings under rule 2(e) are usually private, pursuant to rule 2(e)(7), which provides that hearings "shall be nonpublic unless the Commission on its own motion or at the request of a party otherwise directs." The SEC applies a preponderance-of-the-evidence standard of proof and is not required to use the stricter clear-and-convincing standard.[62]

Where the Commission finds inadequacies in professional conduct, it either communicates its displeasure privately or announces its remedial sanctions, usually with the name of the offender, in its *Accounting Series Releases;* the specific remedy is determined by the seriousness of the offense.

SEC Civil Injunctive Actions. The SEC has statutory authority under each of the six statutes that it administers to bring civil injunctive suits against any person engaged, about to engage, or who has engaged in violations of the laws or related rules and regulations.[63] Unlike the typically private administrative proceedings under rule 2(e), these cases are tried in public before a federal district judge without a jury and with SEC staff attorneys representing the government.

The objective of an injunctive action is to obtain a permanent injunction, which is a court order requiring a defendant either to comply with a law or refrain from violating a law.[64] In itself, an injunction does nothing more than require any enjoined individuals to obey the law. The effects that flow from an injunction can, however, be very severe. Violation of an injunction can result in either civil or criminal contempt proceedings. Civil contempt involves compelling future action so that any imprisonment imposed will usually run until the defendant complies with the court order. Criminal contempt involves punishment for past violations of court orders and any imprisonment imposed is limited to a fixed term. Injunctions may thus convert civil violations into criminal acts.

Accountants and other professionals enjoined from violating federal securities laws can be temporarily suspended from practice under rule 2(e). At any hearing held on a suspension under these circumstances, the professional is assumed to have committed the alleged misconduct even if the injunction was a result of a consent decree entered without admission or denial of the allegations. The only matters that may be considered here are mitigating circumstances that should prevent censure or temporary or permanent disqualification of the professional from practice before the Commission. It is thus imperative for an accountant, who is a defendant in a Commission injunctive action, to negotiate the 2(e) consequences along with any negotiations for settlement of the injunctive action.

In years past the test for granting an injunction was whether previous violations provided a reasonable likelihood of future violations that would cause public injury.[65] However, more recent decisions have indi-

61. 17 C.F.R. § 201.2(g).
62. Steadman v. SEC, 101 S. Ct. 999 (1981).

63. Statutory authorities: (1) Securities Act of 1933: Section 20(b); (2) Securities Exchange Act of 1934: Section 21(e); (3) Public Utility Holding Company Act of 1935: Section 18(f); (4) Trust Indenture Act of 1939: Section 321(a); (5) Investment Company Act of 1940: Sections 36 and 42(e); (6) Investment Advisers Act of 1940: Section 209(e).

64. Three types of injunctions are recognized under rule 65 of the Federal Rules of Civil Procedure: (1) a temporary restraining order, (2) a preliminary injunction (temporary injunction or injunction *pendente lite*), and (3) a permanent injunction. Under rule 65, a temporary restraining order may be granted without notice to the restrained party if irreparable injury will result and if a showing is made of any efforts to give notice and reasons why notice should not be required. Temporary restraining orders are limited to a duration of 10 days.

65. In SEC v. Capital Gains Research Bureau, 375 U.S. 180, 193 (1963) the U.S. Supreme Court held that it is not necessary in a civil injunctive suit to establish all the elements required in a suit for money damages.

cated a more literal interpretation and more restrictive application of federal securities laws.[66] An injunction is now viewed as a "drastic remedy" that must be justified by something more than past violations. This involves showing a realistic likelihood of recurrence.[67]

Inconsistent and Ineffective Policies. There are problems with the SEC's current enforcement program. Practitioners in small CPA firms are identified by name and routinely barred or suspended from practice, but offending individuals in national firms are not identified or individually sanctioned. The SEC has concluded that national firms involve "institutional problems," and the firm or office of the firm is given a short suspension from accepting new clients. Available evidence shows that this sanction has no effect whatever on growth of the national firm or retention of the firm's share of the market.[68] Even if it did, such an adverse effect would be unfair to the many honest professionals associated with the firm.

The *Staff Study* contains this analysis of the problem:

> After receiving complaints that individual CPAs and small accounting firms are treated unfairly by the SEC, the subcommittee staff reviewed the SEC's procedures designed to ensure that independent auditors perform their responsibilities properly. The staff's review of SEC disciplinary proceedings against independent auditors since 1969 showed that individual CPAs and small accounting firms apparently were treated more harshly than large national accounting firms by the SEC. The subcommittee asked the SEC to explain its uneven application of enforcement sanctions. The SEC response raises questions about its disciplinary program.
>
> The SEC response emphasizes that its primary enforcement procedure, a Rule 2(e) proceeding to determine the fitness of an independent auditor to practice

before the SEC, is remedial rather than punitive in nature. Nevertheless, disciplinary sanctions against individual CPAs and small accounting firms have included public identification of the offending individuals, as well as permanent disqualification from practice before the SEC.

> Offending individuals in large national accounting firms have not been identified to the public. Disciplinary sanctions usually have required only that external quality reviews be conducted and, occasionally, a short temporary suspension from accepting new clients.
>
> The discrepancies in the SEC's disciplinary procedures are most apparent in regard to the three "Big Eight" firms which have been disciplined by the SEC —Arthur Andersen & Co., Peat, Marwick, Mitchell & Co., and Touche Ross & Co. None of the individual offenders was named, and the SEC agreed to the participation of CPAs from other large accounting firms in quality reviews, the results of which were kept confidential. The mild sanctions imposed by the SEC are especially significant because the SEC found that partners from Arthur Andersen & Co. and Peat, Marwick, Mitchell & Co. intentionally misled the SEC's staff in its investigations.[69]

Better tailoring of SEC enforcement could be achieved by action that encourages or requires the accounting firm to dissociate itself from those few individuals who engage in unacceptable conduct. The importance of purging such individuals from accounting firms increases in direct proportion to the person's level in the firm. Certainly there are many cases in which the evidence will not support a criminal indictment of the individuals, yet the misconduct does relate primarily to individuals as opposed to the firm. Imposing sanctions on the entire firm in such circumstances may be counterproductive, but severing such individuals from the accounting firm may benefit the firm and at the same time protect the public interest.

Another current problem of SEC enforcement is that the consent judgments are entered with the defendant neither admitting nor denying the allegations. Shortly afterward, the defendant may make a public statement denying all of the allegations. This situation is confusing both to the public and the profession. If the enforcement is to be remedial, then those subjected to discipline should be forced to acknowledge the impropriety or remain silent.[70] A consent settle-

66. In Aaron v. SEC, 100 S. Ct. 1945 (1980), the U.S. Supreme Court held that the SEC is required to establish scienter to enjoin violations of § 10(b) of the Exchange Act and § 17(a)(1) of the Securities Act but need not establish scienter to enjoin violation of sections 17(a)(2) and 17(a)(3) of the Securities Act.

The granting of an injunction is largely discretionary with the trial court. *See* SEC v. Koracorp Industries, Inc., 575 F.2d 692 (9th Cir.), *cert. denied*, 439 U.S. 953 (1978) (denial of injunction against Arthur Andersen & Co. affirmed); SEC v. National Student Marketing, CCH Fed. SEC. L. Rep. ¶ 96,540 (D.D.C. 1978) (denial of injunction despite finding that attorneys acted with scienter); SEC v. Arthur Young & Co., 590 F.2d 785 (9th Cir. 1979) (SEC failed to establish on appeal that there was no reasonable basis for denial of the injunction).

67. SEC v. Commonwealth Chemical Securities, 574 F.2d 90, 99 (2d Cir. 1978).

68. Consider this from the July 17, 1978, issue of *Fortune:* "Oddly enough, the fierce struggle for business has not brought much relative movement among the Big Eight. . . . Since only three of the firms publish financial statements . . . , precise comparisons are not possible, but the available figures indicate that the Big Eight have all been growing at about the same pace in recent years."

69. *Staff Study*, pp. 180–181.

70. Since such admissions would be admissible in private damage suits, defendants would be willing to admit only those things that they will be forced to admit in those actions. This does not close the door on obtaining such admissions but only limits the possibilities. Some commentators argue that the consent settlement itself should now constitute a collateral estoppel with respect to liability in a private damage suit. *See* Comment, "The Effect of SEC Injunctions in Subsequent Private Damage Actions—Rachal v. Hill," 71 *Col. L. Rev.* 1329 (1972).

ment with the wrongdoer claiming innocence is not the proper approach toward professional conduct.

STATE AND FEDERAL COURTS

State courts enforce contractual obligations of CPAs to their clients (see Chapter 5) and obligations imposed on CPAs by state law to avoid negligent or willful injury to the general public (see Chapter 6). Federal courts enforce CPA obligations imposed by federal civil laws (Chapter 8) and federal criminal laws (Chapter 9). Federal courts will also enforce state civil laws where there is diversity of citizenship and a claim exceeding $10,000.

In the case of *Stanley L. Bloch, Inc. v. Klein*,[71] decided in 1965, the court seems to suggest the machinery for establishing uniformity in the enforcement of accounting and auditing standards. The court held that ethical and technical standards promulgated by the AICPA apply in determining liability of public accountants regardless of whether they are members. The case dealt with public accountants who violated an AICPA rule by issuing a balance sheet on their letterhead without stating the responsibility assumed. The court quoted the AICPA rule and said:

> Defendants' failure to place any qualification notice on the subject balance sheet, therefore, clearly constituted a violation of the emphasized portion of the cited rule which, without any doubt, *fixes the existing and accepted standards of their profession.* (Emphasis added.)

Similarly the United States Court of Appeals for the Fourth Circuit held in its 1972 decision of *Rhode Island Hospital Trust National Bank v. Swartz, Bresenoff, Yavner & Jacobs*[72] that AICPA rules constitute minimum standards for the profession.

Considering that the majority of CPAs are members of the AICPA and that the influence of the AICPA in the accounting and auditing sphere is important, it seems quite reasonable to hold all public accountants to AICPA standards. The law requires any professional to adhere to the standard of conduct and skill usually possessed by members of the profession in the community (see Chapter 5).

Thus the groundwork is set for the uniform application of AICPA standards, with the SEC acting as a watchdog for the public by checking on the adequacy of those standards. This procedure has some similarity to a judicial process suggested by some writers who have proposed an accounting court.[73]

SUMMARY

In a democracy, regulations must be limited to those reasonably necessary to protect compelling public interests. State and territorial licensing boards may lawfully regulate public accounting, but cannot prohibit unlicensed persons from engaging in bookkeeping services. Texas courts, in a landmark decision, established the right of state boards to regulate the word *accountant* as a professional designation similar to *lawyer* or *dentist.* California followed the Texas lead in limiting use of the term *accountant.*

Education, experience, and continuing education requirements for CPAs vary throughout the 54 U.S. jurisdictions. However, all jurisdictions require the passing of a uniform CPA exam prepared and graded by the AICPA.

CPA applicants are entitled to due process and equal protection under the law. State laws requiring CPA applicants to be U.S. citizens are unconstitutional.

The right of the AICPA to issue pronouncements has been sustained, and presumably the FASB is successor to this right with respect to accounting (as opposed to auditing) rules. Whenever there is a departure from "official pronouncements" that has a material effect on financial statements, AICPA rules require that, except in "unusual circumstances," auditors must give either a qualified opinion or adverse opinion, depending on the materiality.

As a result of the U.S. Supreme Court decision in *Bates,* all professionals can now advertise.

The SEC generally will not accept "except for" qualified opinions in lieu of correction of the financial statements. Although the SEC fully supports the FASB and has declared that *FASB Statements of Financial Accounting Standards* constitute principles having "substantial authoritative support" and contrary ones as having no support, it retains for itself the final authority in disclosure required to protect the public interest.

71. Stanley L. Bloch, Inc. v. Klein, 258 N.Y.S.2d 501 (Sup. Ct. N.Y. Cty. 1965). The case was not appealed, and the judgment was satisfied; see "News Report," *Journal of Accountancy,* July 1965.

For court decisions basing attorneys' malpractice on deviation from the attorneys' ethics code, see Woodruff v. Tomlin, 616 F.2d 924 (6th Cir. 1980) (duty of an attorney representing multiple clients in an auto accident to advise of a conflict of interest); Ishmael v. Millington, 50 Cal. Rptr. 592 (Cal. App. 1966) (failure of an attorney representing both parties in a divorce to disclose the conflict and advise of the desirability of separate counsel). *Also see* Chapter 1, note 37.

72. Rhode Island Hospital Trust National Bank v. Swartz, Bresenoff, Yavner & Jacobs, 455 F.2d 847 (4th Cir. 1972).

73. A. A. Berle, Jr., in "Accounting and the Law," *Accounting Review,* March 1938, pp. 9-15, at p. 14 suggested establishing a Board of Accounting Appeals for deciding accounting questions raised in connection with practice before federal agencies. Also see Leonard Spacek, "The Need for an Accounting Court," *Accounting Review,* July 1958, pp. 368-79; Arthur Andersen & Co., *Establishing Accounting Principles—A Crisis in Decision Making* (1965), pp. 23-42; Carey, *The Rise of the Accounting Profession,* vol. 2, pp. 124-27.

The SEC enforces its regulations through administrative proceedings, civil injunctive actions, and referral of cases to the Department of Justice for criminal prosecution.

State courts enforce contractual obligations to CPA clients and additional obligations imposed by state laws. Federal courts enforce obligations imposed under federal securities laws. Federal courts also enforce obligations imposed under state laws if there is diversity of citizenship and the claim exceeds $10,000.

SUGGESTIONS FOR FURTHER READING

Annot. "Disciplinary Action against Attorney or Accountant for Misconduct Related to Preparation of Tax Returns for Others." 81 *American Law Reports* 3d 1140, 1977.

Annot. "Federal Income Tax Conviction as Constituting Nonprofessional Misconduct Warranting Disciplinary Action against Attorney." 63 *American Law Reports* 3d 512, 1976.

Annot. "Federal Income Tax Conviction as Involving Moral Turpitude Warranting Disciplinary Action against Attorney." 63 *American Law Reports* 3d 476, 1976.

Annot. "Regulation of Accountants." 70 *American Law Reports* 2d 433, 1960.

Bernstein, Peter W. "Competition Comes to Accounting." *Fortune,* July 17, 1978, pp. 88–94.

Cases in Public Accounting Practice: The AICPA Injunction Case. Chicago: Arthur Andersen & Co., 1960.

Gonson, Paul. "Disciplinary Proceedings and Other Remedies Available to the SEC." *Business Lawyer,* March 1975, pp. 191–205.

NOTE. "Disclosure of Litigation Involving Accountants Under SEC Proxy Rule 14a-9." *Georgetown Law Review* 62 (1974) pp. 1229–42.

QUESTIONS AND PROBLEMS

Discussion: Regulating and Policing

1. Contrast and compare jurisdictions that have regulatory accountancy laws with permissive jurisdictions.
2. Should use of the word *accountant* be regulated? Explain the pros and cons.
3. What combination of requirements for education, experience, and continuing education do you recommend to state boards of accountancy?
4. Identify some problems that occur as a result of 54 different jurisdictions regulating the licensing of the accounting profession.
5. Describe three types of audit reports that a CPA might legitimately issue when a client fails to follow "official pronouncements." State the circumstances that distinguish the use of these three reports.
6. Discuss the legal and ethical considerations for each of the following approaches to setting audit fees:
   a. Quoting hourly rates with an estimated total fee for the engagement.
   b. Quoting hourly rates with a guaranteed ceiling for the engagement.
   c. Quoting a fixed fee with assurance that the prospective client desires to use the firm's services subject to acceptable fee negotiations.
   d. Quoting a competitive bid: a fixed fee with knowledge that the prospective client is obtaining fixed quotations from other firms.
7. Discuss the legal and ethical considerations for each of the following approaches to obtaining clients:
   a. Running an ad in a newspaper or magazine.
   b. Advertising on radio or television.
   c. Sending personalized direct mail pieces to prospective clients.
   d. Inviting audit committees to lunch and making a sales presentation.
   e. Establishing hit lists of prospective clients and structuring activities and memberships to make contacts with those having influence as to the choice of auditor.
8. What, if any, recognition has the SEC given to FASB rule making?
9. Does the SEC make accounting and auditing rules? If so, give an example of each.
10. What three major courses of action are open to the SEC in enforcing federal securities laws? Have all three been used against accountants?
11. Since an injunction only tells a person to obey the law, which everyone is supposed to do anyway, why is a civil injunctive action against an accountant a serious matter?
12. Who must adhere to AICPA ethics rules and auditing standards?

Auditor Enforcement of Generally Accepted Accounting Principles

13. "Official pronouncements" that, except for unusual circumstances, constitute the only generally accepted accounting principles for areas covered are
   a. *Accounting Research Bulletins* and *APB Opinions.*
   b. *FASB Statements of Financial Accounting Standards and Interpretations* issued by the FASB.
   c. AICPA accounting guides.
   d. All items included in *a* and *b* above.
   e. All items included in *a, b,* and *c* above.
14. Where departures from "official pronouncements" have a material effect on financial statements, the auditor should (except in unusual circumstances)
   a. Give a disclaimer of opinion or qualified opinion.
   b. Give a disclaimer of opinion or adverse opinion.
   c. Give a qualified opinion or adverse opinion.
   d. Give a disclaimer of opinion on financial statements as a whole while giving a piecemeal opinion on accounts with which the auditor is satisfied.
   e. None of the above.
15. "Unusual circumstances" where literal application of official pronouncements would have the effect of rendering financial statements misleading would most likely exist
   a. When applying *APB Opinion No. 16* to business combinations.

b. In the event of new legislation or evolution of a new form of business transaction.

c. In the event of an unusual degree of materiality.

d. Where there are conflicting industry practices.

e. All of the above.

16. In areas not covered by "official pronouncements," generally accepted accounting principles are those that

a. Would be followed by a reasonable person.

b. A prudent person would adopt in the circumstances.

c. Have substantial authoritative support.

d. Are usually found in textbooks.

e. Are discussed in articles appearing in accounting journals.

17. (From the November 1973 Uniform CPA Examination)

Clark, CPA, wishes to express an opinion that the financial statements of Smith Co. are presented in conformity with generally accepted accounting principles; however, the financial statements contain a material departure from *APB No. 5*.

a. Under any circumstances, Clark would be in violation of the Code of Professional Ethics if he were to issue such an opinion.

b. Clark should disclaim an opinion.

c. Clark may issue the opinion he desires if he can demonstrate that due to unusual circumstances the financial statements of Smith Co. would otherwise have been misleading.

d. This specific situation is not covered by the rules established by the Code of Professional Ethics.

18. (From the May 1974 Uniform CPA Examination)

The AICPA Code of Professional Ethics derives its authority from the

a. Bylaws of the American Institute of CPAs.

b. Financial Accounting Standards Board.

c. Federal government.

d. Securities and Exchange Commission.

19. (From the May 1975 Uniform CPA Examination)

According to court decisions, the generally accepted auditing standards established by the AICPA apply

a. Only to the AICPA membership.

b. To all CPAs.

c. Only to those who choose to follow them.

d. Only when conducting audits subject to AICPA jurisdiction.

APPENDIX

Addresses of Boards of Accountancy for Fifty-four U.S. Jurisdictions

Alabama State Board of Public Accountancy
1103 South Perry Street
Montgomery, Alabama 36104

Alaska State Board of Public Accountancy
Department of Commerce
Pouch D
Juneau, Alaska 99811

Arizona State Board of Accountancy
1645 West Jefferson Street
Phoenix, Arizona 85007

Arkansas State Board of Accountancy
1515 West 7th
Suite 320
Little Rock, Arkansas 72202

California State Board of Accountancy
2135 Butano Drive
Sacramento, California 95825

Colorado State Board of Accountancy
1525 Sherman Street
Denver, Colorado 80203

Connecticut State Board of Accountancy
20 Grand Street
Hartford, Connecticut 06106

Delaware State Board of Accountancy
P.O. Box 121
Newark, Delaware 19711

District of Columbia Board of Accountancy
Bureau of Occupations and Professions
614 "H" Street, N.W. #109
Washington, D.C. 20001

Florida State Board of Accountancy
P.O. Box 13475, University Station
Gainesville, Florida 32604

State Examining Boards
166 Pryor Street, S.W.
Atlanta, Georgia 30303

Territorial Board of Public Accountancy
P.O. Box P
Agana, Guam 96910

Hawaii State Board of Accountancy
Department of Regulatory Agencies
P.O. Box 3469
Honolulu, Hawaii 96801

Idaho State Board of Certified
  Public Accountancy
P.O. Box 2896
Boise, Idaho 83701

Committee on Accountancy
Administration Building
University of Illinois at Urbana-Champaign
Urbana, Illinois 61801

Indiana State Board of Public Accountancy
910 State Office Building
Indianapolis, Indiana 46204

Iowa Board of Accountancy
Jewett Bldg.
904 Grand Avenue
Des Moines, Iowa 50309

Kansas Board of Accountancy
503 Kansas, Room 236
Topeka, Kansas 66603

Kentucky State Board of Accountancy
310 West Liberty
Louisville, Kentucky 40202

State Board of Certified Public Accountants
Masonic Temple Building
333 St. Charles Avenue
New Orleans, Louisiana 70130

Maine Board of Accountancy
84 Harlow Street
Bangor, Maine 04401

Maryland State Board of Public Accountancy
One South Calvert Bldg., Room 802
Baltimore, Maryland 21202

Massachusetts Board of Public Accountancy
100 Cambridge Street, Room 1524
Boston, Massachusetts 02202

Michigan State Board of Accountancy
P.O. Box 30018
920 South Washington
Lansing, Michigan 48909

Minnesota State Board of Accountancy
Metro Square Building
St. Paul, Minnesota 55101

Mississippi State Board of Public Accountancy
4795 McWillie Drive
Jackson, Mississippi 39206

Missouri State Board of Accountancy
3523 North Ten Mile Drive
P.O. Box 613
Jefferson City, Missouri 65102

Montana State Board of Public Accountancy
LaLonde Bldg.
Helena, Montana 59601

Nebraska State Board of Public Accountancy
State Capitol Bldg., Room 2301
Lincoln, Nebraska 68509

Nevada State Board of Accountancy
Security Bank Bldg.
1 East Liberty Street
Reno, Nevada 89501

New Hampshire Board of Accountancy
1 Tremont Street
Concord, New Hampshire 03301

New Jersey State Board of CPAs
1100 Raymond Blvd.
Newark, New Jersey 07102

New Mexico State Board of Public Accountancy
6101 Marble, N.E.
Albuquerque, New Mexico 87110

NYS Board for Public Accountancy
State Education Dept., Room 1839
Twin Tower Bldg.
99 Washington Avenue
Albany, New York 12201

North Carolina State Board of Certified
   Public Accountant Examiners
209 Lennox Building, P.O. Box 2248
Chapel Hill, North Carolina 27514

North Dakota State Board of Accountancy
Box 8104, University Station
Grand Forks, North Dakota 58202

Accountancy Board of Ohio
65 South Front St.
Columbus, Ohio 43215

Oklahoma State Board of Public Accountancy
265 West Court, Lincoln Office Plaza
4545 Lincoln Blvd.
Oklahoma City, Oklahoma 73105

Oregon State Board of Accountancy
Fourth Floor, Labor & Industries Bldg.
Salem, Oregon 97310

Pennsylvania State Board of Examiners
   of Public Accountants
279 Boas Street, Room 301
P.O. Box 2649
Harrisburg, Pennsylvania 17120

Puerto Rico Board of Accountancy
P.O. Box 3271, 261 Tanca Street
San Juan, Puerto Rico 00904

Rhode Island Board of Accountancy
100 North Main Street
Providence, Rhode Island 02903

South Carolina Board of Accountancy
P.O. Box 11376
Columbia, South Carolina 29211

South Dakota State Board of Accountancy
1501 South Prairie Ave.
Sioux Falls, South Dakota 57101

Tennessee State Board of Accountancy
706 Church Street
Nashville, Tennessee 37203

Texas State Board of Public Accountancy
3301 Northland Drive
Austin, Texas 78731

Utah Committee for Public Accountancy
Department of Registration
330 East Fourth South, Room 207
Salt Lake City, Utah 84111

Vermont State Board of Accountancy
10 Baldwin Street
Montpelier, Vermont 05602

Virgin Islands Board of Public Accountancy
P.O. Box 511, 4AB Royal Strand Bldg.
Charlotte Amalie, St. Thomas Christiansted, St. Croix
Virgin Islands 00820

Dept. of Professional and Occupational
 Registration
P.O. Box 1-X
Richmond, Virginia 23202

Washington State Board of Accountancy
210 East Union, Suite H
Olympia, Washington 98504

West Virginia Board of Accountancy
Charleston National Plaza
Charleston, West Virginia 25301

Accounting Examining Board
1400 E. Washington Avenue
Madison, Wisconsin 53702

Wyoming Board of Certified Public Accountants
200 W. 25th Street
Cheyenne, Wyoming 82002

4

Working Papers and Confidential Communications

This chapter covers:

- LEGAL RIGHTS TO WORKING PAPERS.
- LIMITATIONS ON DISPOSITION OF ACCOUNTANTS' WORKING PAPERS.
- REFUSING CLIENT ACCESS TO WORKING PAPERS TO ENFORCE A FEE.
- THE ACCOUNTANT-CLIENT PRIVILEGE.
- ACCESS TO ACCOUNTANTS' WORKING PAPERS.
- CPA FIRM MANUALS AND PERSONNEL RECORDS.
- TESTIMONY GIVEN TO THE SEC.
- MUNICIPAL AND STATE RECORDS AND STATE AUDITOR'S WORKING PAPERS.
- THE AICPA CONFIDENTIALITY RULE.

LEGAL RIGHTS TO WORKING PAPERS

CCH AICPA Professional Standards, AU § 338.03 defines working papers as follows:

Working papers are the records kept by the independent auditor of the procedures he followed, the tests he performed, the information he obtained, and the conclusions he reached pertinent to his examination. Working papers, accordingly, may include work programs, analyses, memoranda, letters of confirma-

tion and representation, abstracts of company documents, and schedules or commentaries prepared or obtained by the auditor.[1]

Where public accountants are employed as independent contractors, it is well settled that the working papers they prepare remain their property.[2] It is essential for the accountants to retain possession of their working papers in case their competence in performance is questioned. In several jurisdictions, accountancy laws specifically provide that working papers remain the property of the accountant.[3]

Damages for Wrongful Taking of Accountants' Working Papers

Although the previous year's working papers are important for planning the current year's work, working papers for earlier years have little value to the accountant. They are retained primarily to demonstrate the adequacy of work performed in the event the quality of the work is questioned. In *Ablah v. Eyman,*[4] the issue of damages arose when the public accountant was wrongfully deprived of his working papers in a replevin action by the client. The court held that the accountant could waive the tort suit for the amount of his loss and sue on the quasi-contract obligation of the former client to pay for the value of the use of the working papers in the then current audit by the IRS:

> The rule is known as the resulting benefit rule . . . , and it is based . . . upon the principle that no one should be allowed to enrich himself unjustly at the expense of another; also, upon the premise that where property has been wrongfully detained from another, the law imposes a duty to return it and to pay the value of the use, which may be treated as the result of an implied contract.

---

1. *CCH AICPA Professional Standards*, AU § 338.05 provides that working papers generally would include: (1) data reconciling reports with client records, (2) work programs, (3) a review of the system of internal control, (4) evidence of testing of accounts, (5) explanation of resolution of exceptions and unusual matters, and (6) commentaries indicating conclusions concerning matters of significance.

2. Annot., Ownership of, and Literary Property in, Working Papers and Data of Accountant, 90 A.L.R.2d 784 (1963).

3. Alaska, Arizona, California, Colorado, Florida, Hawaii, Kentucky, Maryland, Massachusetts, Missouri, Nebraska, Nevada, New Hampshire, Ohio, Oregon, Pennsylvania, Rhode Island, Tennessee, Utah, Virginia, Washington, West Virginia, Wisconsin, Puerto Rico, and the Virgin Islands.

4. Ablah v. Eyman, 365 P.2d 181 (Kan. 1961).

LIMITATIONS ON DISPOSITION OF ACCOUNTANTS' WORKING PAPERS

Although public accountants own their working papers, this is a limited and custodial ownership. They cannot sell or transfer the working papers to another without the client's consent.

The AICPA Committee on Professional Ethics has ruled that the seller of an accounting practice has a duty to obtain permission of the client before making working papers and other documents available to a purchaser. Although a partner in an accounting firm may appropriately will his or her interest in partnership papers to the surviving partners, working papers of a deceased sole practitioner must be destroyed after (1) returning to clients any papers that they furnished, and (2) assuring there are no claims against the estate that would require preservation of the papers for protection of the estate.

In an early New York case (not reported in the official reports), a sole CPA practitioner bequeathed to his secretary all of his office files and records. The court held:

> Deceased was an accountant by profession. In his office files no doubt are papers which represent work done by him for clients and such papers contain no doubt information given to deceased in confidence. In respect of such working papers and data of a confidential nature, it is the duty and obligation of the executrix to return to the clients of deceased such copies of papers or other data as they furnish to deceased, or if that cannot be done to destroy such papers. The executrix should likewise destroy the work sheets of deceased relating to such confidential work. Before taking the irrevocable step of destruction of any record, the executrix must assure herself that there is no basis for claims against the estate which would require the preservation of the papers for the protection of the estate. Insofar as the office files and records are non-confidential, they will pass under this provision of the will. Though the accounting has shown that such items have no value they are nevertheless tangible things which are capable of manual delivery and so the executrix should make them available to the legatee so that the latter may take them at her own cost. If possession of them is not sought by the legatee within a reasonable time after notice that they are available, such articles may be destroyed by the executrix.[5]

REFUSING CLIENT ACCESS TO WORKING PAPERS TO ENFORCE A FEE

At common law the only persons having a lien for their services on articles coming into their possession are attorneys, warehousers, and bailees employed to change, alter, repair, or otherwise by their services add value to property. Where accountants only examine books and records, as when performing an audit, they do not have benefit of the common-law lien. However, some courts have recognized an accountant's lien on books and records that the accountant altered or improved.[6]

Regardless of the legal right to retain working papers or the client's books and records to enforce payment of the fee, AICPA ethics interpretation 501-1 requires the CPA to surrender books, records, and working papers that constitute books and records upon request by the client, regardless of whether or not the fee is paid. The California State Board of Accountancy vigorously enforces its rule 68, which is the equivalent of the AICPA rule. Under these rules the CPA must furnish the following items upon request, regardless of payment of the fee:

Worksheets in lieu of journals or ledgers.

Worksheets containing adjusting and closing entries and supporting details, such as depreciation schedules.

Supporting detail used in arriving at final figures incorporated in a tax return or financial statement.

Although CPAs can charge for supplying such copies, they may not insist upon payment as a condition precedent. However, where CPAs have returned all client books and records and furnished copies of required

---

5. This excerpt is from report of *Estate of William H. Dennis* in Saul Levy, *Accountants' Legal Responsibility* (New York: American Institute of Accountants, 1954), p. 267. The author notes at pp. 56–57 that the case, decided by the New York Surrogate's Court, February 15, 1936, does not appear in the official reports but appeared at 95 N.Y.L.J. 827. Also see the discussion in the *Journal of Accountancy*, April 1936, pp. 246–50.

6. Annot., Right of Accountant to Lien Upon Client's Books and Records in Former's Possession, 76 A.L.R.2d 1315 (1961). In Goethel v. First Properties Int'l, Ltd., 363 So. 2d 1117 (Fla. App. 1978), both an attorney and a CPA claimed a lien for fees on a corporate client's books and records; however, the court required the books and records returned, upon substitution of a cash bond by the corporation, because the corporation needed the books and records to defend against the claims.

Compare Whitlock v. PKW Supply Co., 269 S.E.2d 36 (Ga. App. 1980) (tax return preparer refused to deliver or file tax returns until fee was paid and client recovered $5,000 which was the reasonable cost of completing the abandoned obligation); Ambort v. Tarica, 258 S.E.2d 755 (Ga. App. 1979) (in absence of actual damages, client could recover nominal damages for CPA's wrongful withholding of business records); Linebaugh v. Helvig, 615 P.2d 366 (Or. App. 1980) (tax return preparer had a legal duty to return records to a client within a reasonable time after receiving either a verbal or written request); Thomas v. Adams, 271 So. 2d 684 (La. App. 1972) (CPA held not liable to client where evidence indicated that CPA had furnished one copy of adjusting entries to client but refused to furnish another copy until fee was paid).

supporting data, they have discharged their obligation and need not comply with subsequent requests to again furnish such records.

PRACTICAL POINTERS

1. Always anticipate the duty to supply books and records at the start of the engagement, and require advance retainers or progress payments to cover this cost. In some cases it may be prudent to have the client sign a receipt acknowledging delivery of books and records and a copy of any working papers constituting books and records.
2. Consider whether preparing tax returns on a cash-on-delivery basis can cause you to run afoul of the rules. Cash in advance of preparation may be a more prudent practice.

THE ACCOUNTANT-CLIENT PRIVILEGE

The common law recognized a need for protecting certain interests and relationships so that communications between attorney and client and husband and wife were privileged. When such privileged information is offered in court, the holder of the privilege (for example, the client, husband, or wife) can object and prevent its introduction. Another familiar rule of privilege is the privilege of a witness against self-incrimination provided by the Fifth Amendment of the Federal Constitution. These rules are in no way devised to aid in the search for truth. Rather, they are designed to shut out the truth where the sacrifice is warranted to protect full and honest disclosure between the parties to certain relationships.

At common law there is no privilege that an accountant or the client may invoke to prevent disclosure of client communications to the accountant. According to Carey and Doherty:

> There is a difference of opinion within the profession as to whether or not statutory provisions creating privileged communications between clients and CPAs are desirable. It is universally agreed that a CPA should not voluntarily disclose any information in his possession about a client's affairs, but there is some doubt whether it is in the public interest to impede the courts in the administration of justice by preventing them by law from calling CPAs as witnesses.[7]

Desirable or not, 19 U.S. jurisdictions have adopted

statutes creating an accountant-client privilege.[8] The statutes vary in that (1) some apply only to CPAs and others extend to all public accountants; (2) some provide that the privilege is not applicable with respect to criminal[9] or bankruptcy laws; (3) some exclude certain services, such as audits and reports on financial statements; and (4) some statutes do not state clearly whether the client or the accountant has the benefit of the privilege. Illinois[10] and New Mexico[11] statutes have been construed as creating an accountant's privilege, which can be invoked only by the accountant. Florida,[12] Colorado,[13] and Indiana[14] courts have held that the privilege can be invoked only by the client. In *People v. Zimbelman*[15] the Supreme Court of Colorado denied defendant's motion to suppress evidence obtained from a CPA who audited the corporate books. The corporation was the client and the victim. The defendant, as half owner of the corporate stock, was not permitted to invoke Colorado's accountant-client privilege statute, since the corporate victim was the client and holder of the privilege.

The accountant-client privilege has been held inapplicable to communications by one joint venturer to the joint venture's accountant in a suit by the other joint venturer.[16] Similarly, it is inapplicable to communications to the accountant engaged by a corporation in a suit by stockholders of the firm.[17]

Rule 501 of the *Rules of Evidence for United States Courts and Magistrates* provides that whenever state law supplies the rule of decision, rules of privilege shall be determined in accordance with state law. However, where the suit is based on federal law, only the common law privileges of husband-wife and attorney-client are recognized.

Neither the attorney-client nor the accountant-client privilege can be claimed as to information fur-

---

7.   John L. Carey and William O. Doherty, *Ethical Standards of the Accounting Profession* (New York: American Institute of Certified Public Accountants, 1966), p. 134.

8.   Jurisdictions that have adopted the accountant-client privilege are Arizona, Colorado, Florida, Georgia, Illinois, Indiana, Iowa, Kentucky, Louisiana, Maryland, Michigan, Missouri, Montana, Nevada, New Mexico, Pennsylvania, Puerto Rico, Tennessee, and Texas. The Texas privilege is virtually nullified by its many exceptions.

9.   For interpretation of Louisiana's privilege statute excluding criminal proceedings, *see* State v. McKinnon, 317 So. 2d 184 (La. 1975). Accord: State v. Obrien, 601 P.2d 341 (Ariz. 1979).

10.   Dorfman v. Rombs, 218 F. Supp. 905 (N.D. Ill. 1963); Palmer v. Fisher, 228 F.2d 603 (7th Cir. 1955).

11.   Ash v. Retier Co., 429 P.2d 653 (N.M. 1967).

12.   Savino v. Luciano, 92 So. 2d 817 (Fla. 1957).

13.   Weck v. District Court, 158 Colo. 521, 408 P.2d 987 (1965).

14.   Ernst & Ernst v. Underwriters Nat'l Assurance Co., 381 N.E.2d 897 (Ind. App. 1978) (accountant could not claim the privilege in a negligence suit by the client).

15.   People v. Zimbelman, 572 P.2d 830 (S. Ct. Colo. 1977).

16.   Gearhart v. Etheridge, 208 S.E.2d 460 (Ga. 1974).

17.   Pattie Lea, Inc. v. District Court, 423 P.2d 27 (Colo. 1967).

nished to a tax return preparer, regardless of whether the preparer is an accountant or attorney.[18] If the accountant is employed by an attorney to assist with the defense of a tax fraud case, communications to the accountant are protected by the attorney-client privilege as well as the attorney-work-product rule.[19] However, if tax returns are prepared, the privilege is waived as to all data supporting the filed returns.[20]

Presumably the accountant-client privilege could never be applicable to material information relevant to financial statements with which the accountant is associated. Professional standards require adequate disclosure of relevant information, and the accountant must withdraw if the client refuses to consent to a full disclosure.[21]

ACCESS TO ACCOUNTANTS' WORKING PAPERS

In a suit by the client or third parties, accountants are usually required to produce their working papers for inspection or copying despite a state accountant-client privilege statute. The reasons are that courts usually hold that the accountant-client privilege belongs to the client (not to the accountant), and the privilege is of doubtful applicability in audit engagements.[22] It has been held inapplicable in federal tax cases so that working papers must be produced in response to an IRS summons, regardless of whether they are in the possession of the accountant, client, or attorney.[23]

Grand juries have broad investigatory powers, and they may require production of working papers without demonstrating probable cause that a crime has been or is being committed.[24] Although IRS special agents and other persons investigating criminal conduct may obtain search warrants to seize business records, they must show probable cause that a crime has been or is being committed, and the search warrant must identify the things to be searched and seized.[25] Since accountants' working papers are not "private," there can be no claim of Fifth Amendment protection from self-incrimination whenever their production is sought.[26]

Where accountants serve as expert witnesses, opposing parties have a right to discover their opinions and to examine their supporting working papers before trial. In *Inspiration Consolidated Copper Co. v. Lumbermens Mutual Casualty Co.*,[27] Price Waterhouse & Co. had acted as regular auditor for many years and had prepared two sets of working papers as an expert witness: one set would support testimony at the trial, and the other set would not be used. The claim, based on New York law, was in federal court based on diversity of citizenship. Since New York had no accountant-client privilege, the court required production of Price's working papers prepared as regular auditor. Since rule 26 of the *Federal Rules of Civil Procedure* permits discovery of opinions of experts who are expected to testify and the basis for the testimony, the court required production of working papers to the extent they related to Price's expected expert testimony. The court did not require production of working papers prepared as an expert that would not be the basis of testimony.

The SEC has especially broad investigative powers, and its subpoena power is coextensive with its investigatory power. In *SEC v. Arthur Young & Co.*[28] the SEC launched a broad investigation into suspected self-dealing and looting by the management of SCA Services, Inc., a publicly held corporation engaged in waste disposal services. Arthur Young resisted the SEC subpoena that required production of the entire working papers. In rejecting Young's challenge the U.S. Court of Appeals for the District of Columbia Circuit held:

> Carefully analyzed, appellant's stance on relevance is largely another outcropping of its distaste for the size of the production summoned. The essence of its claim is that the Commission has embarked upon an illegal fishing expedition into its files. That would have

---

18. *See* Annot., What Constitutes Privileged Communications with Preparer of Federal Tax Returns so as to Render Communication Inadmissible in Federal Tax Prosecution, 36 A.L.R. Fed. 686 (1978).

19. *In re* Grand Jury Proceedings, 601 F.2d 162 (5th Cir. 1979).

20. United States v. Cote, 465 F.2d 142 (8th Cir. 1972).

21. The third standard of reporting at AU § 430.01 states, "Informative disclosures in the financial statements are to be regarded as reasonably adequate unless otherwise stated in the report." *SSARS No. 1*, dealing with unaudited financials of nonpublic entities, provides in paragraph 12 that whenever the accountant is aware that the information is incorrect, incomplete, or otherwise unsatisfactory, the accountant should withdraw if the entity refuses to provide additional or revised information.

22. See the discussion at note 14. In State of Ohio v. Arthur Andersen & Co., 570 F.2d 1370 (10th Cir. 1978), the court upheld preclusionary sanctions and an award of $59,949 costs and expenses because of Andersen's alleged unreasonable resistance to discovery. In Fein v. Numex Corp., CCH Fed. Sec. L. Rep. ¶ 98,355 (S.D.N.Y. 1981), the court required the accounting firm to produce its working papers and held it had no standing to challenge the complaint despite the fact that it could yet be named as a defendant to the suit.

23. See the discussion and citations in Chapter 12 at note 41.

24. Ibid., note 46.

25. Ibid., note 44.

26. Ibid., note 43.

27. Inspiration Consolidated Copper Co. v. Lumbermens Mutual Casualty Co., 60 F.R.D. 205 (S.D.N.Y. 1973).

28. SEC v. Arthur Young & Co., 584 F.2d 1018 (D.C. Cir. 1978), *cert denied*, 439 U.S. 1071 (1979).

been a potent argument in the early era of administrative law, but it retains scarcely any of its clout today. As Professor Davis observes, "[t]he older cases strongly condemn roving inquiries into private books and records, but the recent cases permit such roving inquiries to whatever extent seems to be necessary to make the power of investigation effective."

The court noted that there is a continuing general duty to respond to governmental process and that subpoenaed parties can legitimately be required to absorb reasonable expenses of compliance. However, it modified the order of the district court to afford Arthur Young the opportunity to seek reimbursement for cost of compliance after identification by the SEC of documents desired.

Shareholders of closely held corporations have a right to inspect books and records of the corporation, and in some instances this involves the accountants' working papers.[29] Directors have sweeping access to all information about a corporation. Their right to information is more extensive than shareholder rights.

CPA FIRM MANUALS AND PERSONNEL RECORDS

Many CPA firms expend considerable effort producing internal manuals on accounting and auditing. Such accounting and auditing manuals are treated as confidential and constitute trade secrets; plaintiffs may require their production only upon showing actual need or necessity for the plaintiff's case. In *Rosen v. Dick*[30] the plaintiff sought to examine internal literature of Arthur Andersen & Co., including the second edition of Andersen's *Audit Objectives and Procedures* and Andersen's "Industry Research Binder" pertaining to cattle ranching or cattle farming. In limiting production to essentials, the court said:

Andersen further contends that the accounting and auditing manuals and procedures in question are in the nature of trade secrets, and as such are only discoverable upon the higher showing of actual need or necessity. 4 Moore, Federal Practice ¶ 26.60[4] (2d ed. 1970); *Hartley Pen Co. v. United States District Court for the Southern District of California*, 287 F.2d, 324 (9th Cir. 1961); *Eastman Kodak Co. v. International Harvester Co.*, 14 Fed. Rules Serv. 2d 1272 (S.D.N.Y. 1970).

The internal accounting and auditing manuals of Andersen are properly termed "trade secrets." Clearly, they are carefully protected internally and are the product of much effort on the part of Andersen.

However, in this case I think a showing of necessity has been made. In order to show fraud or negligence, even measured against generally accepted accounting practices, plaintiff must establish by a preponderance of the evidence that Andersen's actions did not meet that standard. It will be necessary for plaintiff to be aware of these procedures to conduct a meaningful deposition of the accountants who worked on the audits in question. Evidence that is acquired from those depositions will have a direct bearing on the outcome of the case. I find sufficient need, therefore, to overcome the trade secret barrier, protected, of course, by the proper restrictive order.

In *New York Stock Exchange v. Sloan*[31] the court held that there were strong policy reasons for nondisclosure of a CPA firm's personnel files containing confidential evaluation of employees. When balanced against the stricter standard for relevancy, the court denied access because it would (1) invade employees' privacy and (2) hamper the ability of firms to maintain standards and improve performance. As to relevancy the court noted the material dealt with what the firm's management thought of the employees it assigned to the audit as opposed to performance on the particular audit.

TESTIMONY GIVEN TO THE SEC

In *Goldberg v. Touche Ross & Co.*[32] the court held that plaintiff in an antifraud suit is entitled to the CPAs' copy of the transcript of testimony before the SEC. This included a 61-page statement by the firm as well as testimony by employees and partners. The CPA firm was also required to produce working papers for the audit subsequent to the period of the alleged fraud, since it was when working on this audit that the CPA withdrew its certification for the period of the alleged fraud.

MUNICIPAL AND STATE RECORDS AND STATE AUDITOR'S WORKING PAPERS

Any citizen has an interest in the execution of the laws and has a right to inspect municipal and state records.[33] Thus in *Nowack v. Fuller*[34] the court held

---

29. *See* Annot., What Corporate Documents are Subject to Shareholder's Right to Inspection, 88 A.L.R.3d 663 (1978).

30. Rosen v. Dick, CCH Fed. L. Rep. ¶ 94,989 (1975).

31. New York Stock Exchange v. Sloan, CCH Fed. Sec. L. Rep. ¶ 95,774 (S.D.N.Y. 1976).

32. Goldberg v. Touche Ross & Co., CCH Fed. Sec. L. Rep. ¶ 95,759 (S.D.N.Y. 1976).

33. *See* Am. Jur. 2d, Records and Recording Laws §§ 22, 23 (1973).

34. Nowack v. Fuller, 219 N.W. 749 (Mich. 1928); Annot., Enforceability by Mandamus of Right to Inspect Public Records, 60 A.L.R. 1357, 1373 (1929); 169 A.L.R. 653 (1947).

that a newspaper publisher had a common-law right to inspect records in the state auditor's office.

THE AICPA CONFIDENTIALITY RULE

AICPA ethics rules prohibit disclosure of *confidential* information obtained from clients except (1) when necessary to avoid violation of auditing standards and accounting principles, (2) when necessary to comply with an enforceable subpoena or summons, (3) in connection with a voluntary quality review authorized by the AICPA, or (4) when it is necessary to respond to an inquiry made by the AICPA ethics division, AICPA Trial Board, state CPA society, or state regulatory authority.[35] The rules have the effect of preventing the CPA from being a volunteer and impose a duty to draw the court's attention to a state accountant-client privilege statute whenever it may apply. However, the rule does not prevent access to information by virtue of legal proceedings described earlier in this chapter.

SUMMARY

Where public accountants are employed as independent contractors, working papers that they prepare remain their property. However, this is a custodial type of ownership, and accountants cannot sell or transfer their working papers to another without the client's consent.

At common law the only privileged communications were husband-wife and attorney-client. Nineteen states have created an accountant-client privilege that is of dubious value to the accountant. No such state accountant-client privilege is recognized in a federal tax matter nor in litigation based on federal laws. The privilege is usually unavailable when the accountant is sued by the client or a third party.

AICPA ethics rule 301 prohibits disclosure of confidential information obtained from clients except (1) when necessary to avoid violation of auditing standards and accounting principles, (2) when necessary to comply with an enforceable subpoena or summons, (3) in connection with a voluntary quality review authorized by the AICPA, or (4) when it is necessary to respond to an inquiry made by the AICPA ethics division, AICPA Trial Board, state CPA society, or state regulatory authority.

SUGGESTIONS FOR FURTHER READING

Annot. "What Corporate Documents Are Subject to Shareholder's Right to Inspection." 88 *American Law Reports* 3d 663, 1978.

---

35. *CCH AICPA Professional Standards*, ET § 301.01.

O'Neal, F. Hodge, and Stephen R. Thompson. "Vulnerability of Professional-Client Privilege in Shareholder Litigation." *Business Lawyer*, July 1976, pp. 1775–97.

QUESTIONS AND PROBLEMS

Working Papers

1. (From the November 1980 Uniform CPA Examination)
   A CPA's retention of client records as a means of enforcing payment of an overdue audit fee is an action that is
   a. Not addressed by the AICPA Code of Professional Ethics.
   b. Acceptable if sanctioned by the state laws.
   c. Prohibited under the AICPA rules of conduct.
   d. A violation of generally accepted auditing standards.

2. (From the November 1973 Uniform CPA Examination)
   Poust, CPA, has sold his public-accounting practice to Lyons, CPA.
   a. Poust must obtain permission from his clients before making available working papers and other documents to Lyons.
   b. Poust must obtain permission from his clients for only audit-related working papers and other documents before making them available to Lyons.
   c. Poust must return the working papers and other documents to his clients, and Lyons must solicit the clients for his use of the materials.
   d. Poust must obtain permission from his clients for only tax-related working papers and other documents before making them available to Lyons.

3. (From the November 1963 Uniform CPA Examination)
   The X Corporation engaged Y, a CPA, to examine its financial statements. Nothing was expressly agreed between the parties as to the ownership of Y's working papers.
   In a subsequent year the client engaged another firm to examine its statements. The client demanded the return of the working papers from Y.

   Required:
   a. To whom do the working papers belong? Explain the reasons why this is the rule.
   b. What restrictions, if any, are placed upon the ownership of the working papers? Explain.

4. (From the May 1981 Uniform CPA Examination)
   The CPA firm of Knox & Knox has been subpoenaed to testify and produce its correspondence and workpapers in connection with a lawsuit brought by a third party against one of their clients. Knox considers the subpoenaed documents to be privileged communication and therefore seeks to avoid admission of such evidence in the lawsuit. Which of the following is correct?
   a. Federal law recognizes such a privilege if the accountant is a certified public accountant.
   b. The privilege is available regarding the working papers, since the CPA is deemed to own them.
   c. The privileged communication rule as it applies to

the CPA-client relationship is the same as that of attorney-client.

    d. In the absence of a specific statutory provision, the law does not recognize the existence of the privileged communication rule between a CPA and his client.

5. (From the May 1981 Uniform CPA Examination)

    The AICPA Code of Professional Ethics states that a CPA shall not disclose any confidential information obtained in the course of a professional engagement except with the consent of the client. This rule should be understood to preclude a CPA from responding to an inquiry made by

    a. The trial board of the AICPA.
    b. An investigative body of a state CPA society.
    c. A CPA-shareholder of the client corporation.
    d. An AICPA voluntary quality review body.

Client Communications

6. (From the May 1975 Uniform CPA Examination)

    The AICPA Code of Professional Ethics states that a CPA shall not disclose any confidential information obtained in the course of a professional engagement except with the consent of his client. In which one of the situations given below would disclosure by a CPA be in violation of the code?

    a. Disclosing confidential information in order to properly discharge the CPA's responsibilities in accordance with his profession's standards.
    b. Disclosing confidential information in compliance with a subpoena issued by a court.
    c. Disclosing confidential information to another accountant interested in purchasing the CPA's practice.
    d. Disclosing confidential information in a review of the CPA's professional practice by the AICPA Quality Review Committee.

7. (From the May 1975 Uniform CPA Examination)

    In connection with a lawsuit, a third party attempts to gain access to the auditor's working papers. The client's defense of privileged communication will be successful only to the extent it is protected by the

    a. Auditor's acquiescence in use of this defense.

    b. Common law.
    c. AICPA Code of Professional Ethics.
    d. State law.

8. (From the May 1964 Uniform CPA Examination)

    Peter is a certified public accountant, and Frank is one of his clients. Frank was sued, and Peter was called as a witness by the opposing party. After being sworn in, Peter was asked certain questions which related to confidential business matters of Frank which came to Peter's attention in his professional accounting capacity. Frank's attorney immediately objected to the questions, claiming that the admission of such evidence would be violative of the "privileged communication" rule.

Required:

    a. Explain the meaning of the term *privileged communication.*
    b. What is the policy factor which has led to the recognition of privileged communication as a valid reason for the exclusion of evidence?
    c. Indicate the most common types of relationships that give rise to privileged communication.
    d. Based upon the attorney's objection, what will the result be in the above fact situation according to the common-law rule? Explain.

9. (From the November 1973 Uniform CPA Examination)

    Parker Products, Inc., is suing Flagstone Specialties, Inc., your client in the state court system, alleging a breach of contract. The contract provided for Flagstone to construct a piece of highly technical equipment at Flagstone's cost plus a fixed fee. Specifically, Parker alleges that Flagstone has calculated costs incorrectly, loading the contract billings with inappropriate costs. Parker seeks to recover the excess costs.

    Charles Lake, your CPA firm's partner in charge of the Flagstone account, has been subpoenaed by Parker to testify. Neither Lake nor the firm wishes to become involved in the litigation. Furthermore, if Lake testifies, some of the facts he would reveal might be prejudicial to the client.

Required:

    a. Must Lake testify? Explain.
    b. If the cause of action had been such that the suit would have been brought in a federal court, must Lake testify? Explain.

5

Accountant-Client Relationships

This chapter covers:

- CONTRACTUAL RIGHTS OF PUBLIC ACCOUNTANTS.
- CIVIL LIABILITY TO CLIENTS.
- SUBROGATION RIGHTS OF A SURETY COMPANY.

CONTRACTUAL RIGHTS OF PUBLIC ACCOUNTANTS

Rights to Fees: Generally

Where the amount of the fee is not specified in advance, courts permit recovery for the reasonable value of the services rendered. For example, in *Noble v. Hunt*,[1] the CPA sued for fees for handling the client's tax case before the IRS and the United States Tax Court. Since the parties had not agreed as to the amount of the fee in advance, the CPA sued on a *quantum meruit* basis and not on a liquidated amount. The appellate court upheld the following charge to the jury by the lower court:

The court charges you that the reasonable value of the services rendered, if not fixed by contract, would be of or the amount that is generally charged by certified public accountants for the same or like services in the same community and under the same or similar circumstances as exist in the case now on trial.

This was held to be a correct statement of the Georgia rule that permits recovery in the absence of an express contractual amount for "the ordinary and reasonable charge made for such services by members of similar standing in the same profession."

PRACTICAL POINTERS

1. It is generally advisable to have an engagement letter specifying the fee or billing rate. Otherwise it may be necessary to present expert testimony as to the value of services in the event of suit for the fee. One adverse effect of a written contract is that it may extend the time period during which the CPA can be sued for deficient work.
2. Some CPAs provide in the engagement letter that the client will sign a promissory note for past due fees. Others present a note for signature when the fee becomes past due. This has several advantages:
   a. The standard note provides for interest and payment of attorney's fees and cost of collection;
   b. It limits the area of dispute in case of suit; and
   c. Some malpractice insurers do not consider the suit on a note to be a suit for a fee when answering the application question: Have you ever sued for a fee?
3. One of the most important aspects of the engagement letter is to specify the method of progress billing and payment and/or advance retainers. Although CPAs often advise others on setting credit limits, they sometimes ignore this aspect of their own practice.

In Mitchell and Pickering v. Louis Isaacson, Inc., 229 S.E. 535 (Ga. App. 1976), the CPA testified as to reasonable value, and testimony by independent experts was not required. Because the issue of reasonable value is for the jury, the court reversed a directed verdict for the CPA in Austin v. R. W. Raines Enterprises, Inc., 264 S.E.2d 121 (N.C. App. 1980).

In Schiffman v. H. L. Raburn & Co., 255 So. 2d 332 (Ala. App.) *cert. denied*, 255 So. 2d 338 (1971), the agreement by the corporation's president to be jointly liable for the CPA's services to the corporation was enforced since it was not a suretyship agreement that was void under the statute of frauds. *Compare* Harry L. Beacham and Co., Ltd. v. Belanger, 388 So. 2d 101 (La. App. 1980), where the CPA's invoice covered services to a bankrupt corporation as well as services for its officer. There was no evidence that the officer agreed to be responsible for the corporation's debt and without a breakdown of the invoice for services to the officer, there was no basis for an award based on quantum meruit.

---

1. Noble v. Hunt, 99 S.E.2d 345 (Ga. App. 1957). There are four alternative bases for a suit for the fee: (1) amount or rate specified in the contract, (2) a reasonable fee on a contract with fee unspecified, (3) quantum meruit (implied contract) for value of services, or (4) account stated (after the client has agreed that the account is correct and due).

In a suit on account stated it is not necessary to prove the reasonableness of the fees; *see* Rhode, Titchenal, Bauman & Scripter v. Shattuck, 619 P.2d 507 (Colo. App. 1980) (client did not protest accounting firm's bills and admitted owing sums charged); Intercompany Services Corp. v. Kleeb, 231 S.E.2d 505 (Ga. App. 1976) (where client accepted bills as correct when presented, CPA was not required to prove value).

66

Minor errors or inaccuracies do not affect the right to be paid provided the work performed is of substantial value.[2] Where work is performed on the basis of an estimate, substantially higher fees may be justified, especially where the client permits work to continue after learning of additional work required.

Although oral engagements are generally enforceable, the provision in the Statute of Frauds voiding oral contracts that cannot be performed within one year applies to contracts for services. The rule that part performance takes an oral contract out of the statute of frauds is inapplicable to contracts for services. The Uniform Commercial Code is applicable only to the sale of goods and does not apply to engagements for professional services.

Rights to Fees upon Discharge

Because of the confidential nature of accounting practice, courts permit the client to terminate the relationship with the professional with or without cause. The courts of all jurisdictions agree that a practitioner who is wrongfully discharged under a contract fixing a stipulated fee, whether contingent or noncontingent, can recover the reasonable value of services rendered to the date of discharge on a *quantum meruit* basis.[3] Wrongful discharge for this purpose includes cases where the client's conduct or lack of cooperation has prevented performance.[4] Some jurisdictions take the view that the wrongfully discharged practitioner is limited to *quantum meruit*, but the majority permit recovery in full of a noncontingent fee on the theory of constructive performance. However, a deduction from the full fee may be allowed for savings of such out-of-pocket items as travel expenses, but no abatement is allowed for overhead or cost of accounting services. Where there has been substantial or full performance on a contingent fee contract prior to wrongful discharge, recovery may be allowed for the full fee.

In *Adams v. Fisher*[5] attorney McGraw was employed under a contingent fee agreement. The client then discharged McGraw and employed attorney Myrick under a contingent fee agreement. McGraw filed a motion to establish an equitable charging lien on any recovery by the client. The trial judge ordered McGraw's fee, based on *quantum meruit*, paid out of the new attorney's fee. However, the appeals court reversed and held that the client must pay McGraw for the *quantum meruit* value of his services and must also pay Myrick his full contingent fee. This rule ensures the client's right to discharge with or without cause, but also makes the client responsible for such actions.

Delegation and Impossibility

Executory contracts for personal services or those involving confidential relationships are not assignable by either party unless otherwise provided or the other party consents.[6] Where full performance is prevented by an act of God, the majority view is that the value of beneficial services previously rendered may be recovered. However, there can be no recovery for part performance of an indivisible contract (e.g., to perform an audit or to prepare a Form 1040) if the failure of performance is a substantial failure of consideration.[7] Thus where public accountants die or become seriously disabled so that they cannot carry out the engagement, the contractual obligations of both parties are generally discharged, since the contract is for services of a personal nature that are then impossible to perform.

Suits for Fees

Before filing suit for an unpaid fee, it is advisable to carefully evaluate the risk of a counterclaim for deficient work. If the work was carefully performed and documented with supporting working papers so that the risk of malpractice seems small, a suit may be advisable. However, always consider the time and expense factor while assuming that a counterclaim for deficient work is a likely defensive measure. Although the counterclaim may turn out to be frivolous, it usually should be reported to the malpractice insurance carrier to avoid any loss of coverage due to a breach of the notice requirement in the policy.

Consider the Iowa case of *Ryan v. Kanne*,[8] where the CPA undertook to prepare an unaudited balance sheet to facilitate the attraction of investors for incorporation of a financially weak proprietorship. Although the CPA had estimated his fee at $500 to $750, he was allowed to continue work after it was evident that his estimate was too low. When the CPA's bill for more than $3,400 remained unpaid, he sued the newly

---

2. In Ryan v. Kanne, 170 N.W.2d 395 (Iowa 1969), the court allowed recovery of the fee despite substantial errors in the report. For cases resulting in refund of the fee, see note 41.

3. *See* Annot., Measure or Basis of Attorney's Recovery on Express Contract Fixing Noncontingent Fees, Where He Is Discharged Without Cause or Fault on His Part, 54 A.L.R.2d 604 (1957), and Annot., Limitation to Quantum Meruit Recovery, Where Attorney Employed Under Contingent Fee Contract Is Discharged Without Cause, 92 A.L.R.3d (1979). *Compare* Griswold v. Heat Inc., 229 A.2d 183 (N.H. 1967), where the CPA was entitled to recover on his contract for $200 per month for five years despite termination by client.

4. As to what constitutes justifiable cause for voluntary withdrawal so as to permit recovery of compensation, *see* Annot., Circumstances under Which Attorney Retains Right to Compensation Notwithstanding Voluntary Withdrawal from Case, 88 A.L.R.3d 246 (1978).

5. Adams v. Fisher, 390 So. 2d 1248 (Fla. App. 1980).

6. *See* 6 Am. Jur. 2d, *Assignments* § 11.

7. *See* 17 Am. Jur. 2d, *Contracts* §§ 383, 413, 506.

8. Ryan v. Kanne, 170 N.W.2d 395 (Iowa 1969).

formed corporation on the theory that there was an obligation to pay for benefits bestowed. Although the court entered judgment for the full fee, it held the CPA liable on the counterclaim for more than $23,000 because the CPA had understated the payables after orally representing to investors that his figure was reliable.

PRACTICAL POINTERS

1. Avoid the situation in which buyer and seller make the sale price dependent upon the accountant's determination of earnings or book value. Any negligence here will be the cause of a loss to either buyer or seller.

2. For examples of disputes over methods followed, see *Franklin Supply Co. v. Tolman*, 454 F.2d 1059 (9th Cir. 1972) (dispute over whether *current replacement value* meant prices on the salvage market or prices from usual sources of supply), and *Kohler v. Kohler Co.*, 319 F.2d 634 (7th Cir. 1963) (CPA did not consider differences in pension cost accounting when estimating the value of closely held corporate stock).

3. In *Aluma Kraft Mfg. Co. v. Elmer Fox & Co.*, 493 S.W.2d 378 (Mo. App. 1973), the court upheld a complaint that charged that *negligent* auditors knew their report would be used by third parties to determine book value to be paid for Aluma Kraft stock.

4. In *Gammel v. Ernst & Ernst*, 245 Minn. 249, 72 N.W.2d 364 (1955), the court held that the CPA is not relieved of negligence or clothed with judicial immunity as a quasi-arbitrator when sale price of corporate stock is made dependent upon the CPA's determination of earnings; the CPA in such situation must select the alternate accounting practice *fairly applicable* to the situation.

Failure to Secure Local License

Where practitioners fail to obtain licenses required for regulatory purposes (as opposed to revenue purposes), the courts may not enforce contracts to pay for the services rendered. For example, in *Bauman and Vogel, C.P.A. v. Del Vecchio*,[9] the court rejected the

---

9. Bauman and Vogel, C.P.A. v. Del Vecchio, 423 F. Supp. 1041 (E.D. Pa. 1976). *Similarly*, in Ronaldson v. Moss Watkins, Inc. 127 So. 467 (La. App. 1930), a CPA from Beaumont, Texas, sued for an audit performed at Lake Charles, Louisiana. The Louisiana court held that the CPA's failure to obtain a Louisiana CPA certificate, as required by Louisiana law, made the contract to pay for his services void and unenforceable. However, *compare* Respess v. Rex Spinning Co., 133 S.E. 391 (N.C. 1926), where Georgia CPAs contacted in Atlanta were permitted to recover for an audit "in the rough with pencil" performed in North Carolina, since they returned to Atlanta and "made up their report."

New Jersey CPA firm's suit for a fee for systems work because the CPA was not licensed in Pennsylvania, where the services were performed.

Disclaimers and Qualifications

Courts reject contractual provisions that exempt professionals from all liability for their own negligence on the grounds of public policy.[10] Disclaimers and qualifications have been effective in avoiding liability in some cases, but they have not avoided liability where there has been a failure to communicate significant information that was known or should have been known to the CPA in the particular factual setting.[11]

---

10. *See* 57 Am. Jur. 2d *Negligence* § 20, and Annot., Validity of Contractual Provision by One Other Than Carrier or Employer for Exemption from Liability, or Indemnification, for Consequences of Own Negligence, 175 A.L.R. 8 (1948). In some cases, contracts that provide for assumption of risk, indemnification, or reasonably limit liability are enforced, but such provisions are strictly construed against the party seeking their protection. For related decisions in the medical area, *see* Annot., Validity and Construction of Contract Exempting Hospital or Doctor from Liability for Negligence to Patient, 6 A.L.R.3d 704 (1966).

11. For cases involving effective use of disclaimers and qualifications, *see the following:*

California: In Lindner v. Barlow, Davis & Wood, 27 Cal. Rptr. 101 (Cal. App. 1962), the CPAs who prepared plaintiff's tax returns appended a written statement to the effect that such returns were based upon information not independently verified. The court found that the CPAs were justified in relying upon W-2 forms as to taxability, since this was the customary practice of CPAs in San Francisco.

Colorado: In Stephens Industries, Inc. v. Haskins & Sells, 438 F.2d 357 (10th Cir. 1971), the court applied Colorado law and held the auditor not liable where (1) the audit engagement specifically relieved the auditors of responsibility for accounts receivable, (2) the auditor's opinion contained a notation that the auditors did not confirm accounts receivable or review their collectibility, and (3) the balance sheet indicated that the accounts receivable balance had not been adjusted for uncollectible accounts.

England: In Hedley Byrne & Co. Ltd. v. Heller & Partners, Ltd., [1964] A.C. 465 (1963), the English House of Lords held that bankers are liable for negligence when gratuitously giving credit information to those who foreseeably will rely upon it; however, insertion of the words "For your private use and without responsibility on the part of this bank or its officials" was held to have prevented reliance resulting in legal responsibility.

New York: In C.I.T. Financial Corp. v. Glover, 224 F.2d 44 (2d Cir. 1955), the auditors escaped liability for an audit report that included a disclaimer as to valuation of loan collateral that proved to be overvalued.

Ohio: In Beardsley v. Ernst, 191 N.E. 808 (Ohio App. 1934), the defendant auditors were held not liable where the report showed that the consolidated statements were based on statements from abroad as to foreign subsidiaries.

For cases involving ineffective use of disclaimers and qualifications, *see*:

England: In the case of *In re* London and General Bank, [1895] 2 Ch. 673, the court held the auditor liable to the receiver for negligence because a "subject to realization" qualification was an unsatisfactory communication that loans and securities were overvalued.

Federal: In Herzfeld v. Laventhol, Krekstein, Horwath & Horwath, 540 F.2d 27 (2d Cir. 1976), the CPAs were held liable under

Contingent Fee Engagements

Although AICPA ethics rule 302 prohibits contingent fees, an exception is provided for tax matters "if determined based on the results of judicial proceedings or the findings of governmental agencies." Therefore it is appropriate to set the fee for representing the taxpayer in an administrative appeal before the IRS Appellate Division as a percentage of the amount saved on a tax assessment. For example, in *Gladding v. Langrall, Muir & Noppinger*[12] the court enforced an agreement to pay a substantial contingent fee despite only a few hours of time expended by the CPA firm.

Since a properly prepared tax return results in a proper tax liability, it is unethical to base a fee on the amount of tax liability. However, the fee can be based on the amount saved upon processing a claim for refund since there will be an IRS determination. For example, in *Jorge v. Rosen*[13] the court upheld an agreement to pay 20 percent of any amount refunded and 20 percent of any amount received as a credit on future federal income taxes.

CIVIL LIABILITY TO CLIENTS

When public accountants fail in their duty to carry out their contracts for services, liability to clients may be based either on breach of contract or on a tort action for negligence. Breach of contract liability is based on failure to carry out a duty created by mutual assent of the parties, whereas tort liability is based upon failure to carry out a duty created by either social policy or social policy and contract.[14] For example, negligence may result from breach of a duty to the public at large, such as in driving an automobile (social policy but no contract), or from failure of a professional to use due care in discharging a contract (social policy and contract).

Although modern statutes have largely abolished the requirement that a complaint be stated in a technical form of contract or tort, the distinction still retains considerable importance for such matters as jurisdiction, venue, statutes of limitation, proof, and measure of damages. Under a breach of contract theory, the plaintiff may have the advantages of attachment or summary judgment or may use the claim as a set-off or counterclaim. The defense of contributory negligence cannot be raised as a defense to a charge of breach of contract, but it may bar a tort claim. Contract claims, as opposed to tort claims, may be assignable. The measure of damages in contract may be different from tort, since in breach of contract actions the damages give plaintiffs benefit of their bargain, whereas in tort plaintiffs are compensated for their loss.[15] Punitive damages ordinarily cannot be recovered in contract actions but may be recovered in tort. The malpractice case (tort) usually requires expert testimony to show a failure to exercise the ability and skill commonly possessed by public accountants in the locality, whereas

---

section 10(b) of the Exchange Act to an investor in a private placement because the subject to realization qualification did not effectively erase the misrepresentation created by the financial statements, which included profit on real estate transactions that were never consummated.

New York: In State Street Trust Co. v. Ernst, 278 N.Y. 104, 15 N.E.2d 416 (1938), a single copy of a qualifying letter concerning the audit was sent some thirty days after delivery of an original and 10 copies of the certified financials. In holding the auditor liable to a third party for recklessness in overvaluation of accounts receivable, the court characterized withholding the explanatory letter as equivalent of active misrepresentation.

In Stanley L. Bloch, Inc. v. Klein, 258 N.Y.S.2d 501 (N.Y. Sup. Ct. 1965), the court found the CPA liable to the client for defective audit work where the CPA failed to append an appropriate disclaimer to the balance sheet to indicate that it was not audited.

In 1136 Tenants' Corp. v. Max Rothenberg & Co., 27 App. Div. 2d 830, 277 N.Y.S.2d 996 (1967), aff'd, 21 N.Y.2d 995, 290 N.Y.S.2d 919, 238 N.E.2d 322 (N.Y. Ct. App. 1968), the CPA was held liable for failure to inquire or communicate concerning suspicious circumstances despite a legend on the financials stating "No independent verifications were undertaken thereon."

Rhode Island: In Rhode Island Hospital Trust Nat'l Bank v. Swartz, Bresenoff, Yavner & Jacobs, 455 F.2d 847 (4th Cir. 1972), the court held that the CPA was negligent in failing to give a clear explanation of the reason for the disclaimer of opinion.

12. Gladding v. Langrall, Muir & Noppinger, 401 A.2d 662 (Md. App. 1979).

13. Jorge v. Rosen, 208 So. 2d 644 (Fla. App. 1968).

14. According to Prosser, the earliest cases involving overlapping of tort and contract involved persons in public callings where the remedy took the form of pure tort (trespass on the case, i.e., where wrongful force was indirect). The defendant's "assumpsit" or undertaking then became the basis for the action, and with development of the doctrine of consideration, contract became a basis of liability, but the tort remedy survived. See W. Prosser, *Law of Torts*, 613–618, 4th ed. (St. Paul, Minn.: West Publishing Co., 1971). The theory for extension of contract liability is well stated in Flint & Walling Mfg. Co. v. Becket, 167 Ind. 491, 498; 79 N.E. 503, 505 (1906): "If a defendant may be held liable for the neglect of a duty imposed on him, independent of any contract, by operation of law, *a fortiori* ought he to be held liable when he has come under an obligation to use care as a result of an undertaking founded on consideration. Where the duty has its roots in contract, the undertaking to observe due care may be implied from the relationship, and should it be the fact that a breach of the agreement also constitutes such a failure to exercise care as amounts to a tort, the plaintiff may elect, as the common-law authorities have it, to sue in case or in assumpsit."

15. Damages for breach of contract are limited, under the rule of Hadley v. Baxendale, 9 Ex. 341, 156 Eng. Rep. 145 (1854), to those foreseeable at the time of contract. In a tort action damages are limited to those resulting from "proximate cause" of the negligence. Although there is great confusion in the law as to the meaning of proximate cause, one test is foreseeability from the point of the negligence. In Palsgraf v. Long Island R. R. Co., 248 N.Y. 339, 162 N.E. 99 (1928), "proximate cause" was held not to include "unforeseeable plaintiffs." For a discussion of unforeseeable consequences in the law of tort, see W. Prosser, *Law of Torts* 250–70, 4th ed. (1971).

For a complete analysis of recoverable damages, see the discussion starting at note 59.

under contract theory such testimony may not be required.

The statute of limitation commences running in a contract action at the time of the breach. Since the cause of action in tort often occurs only at the time of the injury,[16] the statute may begin running only at that time. But some courts, without regard to the form of action, hold that fraud or concealment tolls the statute, or that the statute starts running from the time the negligence was, or should have been, discovered. Plaintiff's attorney will usually plead as many alternative theories of the action as possible, for example, negligence, express warranty, implied warranty, fraud and deceit, to avoid being barred by the statute of limitations; defense attorneys will usually scrutinize each of plaintiff's theories and move to dismiss claims that are barred.[17]

There still exists some confusion as to whether the plaintiff may elect either remedy, but the election privilege would give maximum protection to the injured party. Some courts characterize a complete nonperformance as a breach of contract only and distinguish it from a defective performance, which is said to be both breach of contract and negligence.[18]

The most difficult problem arises in attempting to characterize a defective performance as either tort or contract. Some torts based on negligence occur solely as a breach of a duty to the public at large, such as negligent operation of an automobile, and no confusion with contract is possible. But when a contractual relation creates the duty, negligence in performance may create an action in either tort or contract. Sometimes it is said that negligent performance of duties owing from physician to patient, employer to employee, or landlord to tenant is regarded as tort, since negligence is considered the "gravamen of the action."[19] Such cases are similar to that of an auditor who assumes the obligation to exercise due care. But when an accountant agrees to do a specific thing, such as prepare and file the plaintiff's income tax return, or a physician is specifically employed to remove a wart from the patient's foot, the gist of the action seems to be contract. Claims based both on contract theory and tort theory have been sustained against accountants.[20]

Perhaps under modern pleading, which allows tort and contract to be joined as alternative claims in the same suit, the plaintiff will be permitted to plead and prove both theories and take advantage of the theory that gives the more advantageous remedy. Corbin argues that when the wrong involves both a breach of contract and a tort, the plaintiff should be given the advantage of the more liberal rule of damages.[21]

Conditions for Determining Negligence

Negligence is deviation from a standard of behavior that in most cases is that of a reasonable person. But professionals or others who undertake work calling for special skill must employ the knowledge, skill, and judgment usually possessed by members of their profession in the particular locality. The responsibility of those offering special skills is set forth in an often-quoted passage:

> In all those employments where peculiar skill is requisite, if one offers his services, he is understood as holding himself out to the public as possessing the degree of skill commonly possessed by others in the same employment, and if his pretensions are unfounded, he commits a species of fraud upon every man who employs him in reliance on his public profes-

---

16. If the act (which later produces injury) is itself a legal injury, the cause of action may accrue immediately on commission of the tort. For discussion, *see* Atkins v. Crosland, 417 S.W.2d 150 (Texas 1967), where it was held that the statute of limitations did not begin to run on taxpayer's claim against an accountant until assessment of tax deficiency by the Internal Revenue Service.

17. *See* Annot., Application of Statute of Limitations to Damage Actions Against Public Accountants for Negligence in Performance of Professional Services, 26 A.L.R.3d 1438 (1969).

18. W. Prosser, *Law of Torts* 614, 618–19, 4th ed. (1971).

19. For a discussion of the early authorities, *see* Dantzler Lumber & Export Co. v. Columbia Casualty, 115 Fla. 541, 156 So. 116 (1934), where the court quotes the following: "Whenever there is carelessness, recklessness, want of reasonable skill, or the violation or disregard of a duty which the law implies from the conditions or attendant circumstances, and individual injury results therefrom, an action on the case lies in favor of the party injured; and if the transaction had its origin in a contract, which places the parties in such relation, as that, in performing or attempting to perform the service promised, the tort or wrong is committed, then the breach of the contract is not the gravamen of the suit. There may be no technical breach of the letter of the contract. The contract, in such case, is mere inducement, and should be so

stated in pleading. It induces, causes, creates the conditions or state of things, which furnishes the occasion of the tort. The wrongful act, outside of the letter of the contract, is the gravamen of the complaint; and in all such cases, the remedy is an action on the case." For a contrary view, *see* City of East Grand Forks v. Steele, 121 Minn. 296, 141 N.W. 181 (1913), where it was alleged that an auditor negligently failed to discover fraud, and it was held that the gist or gravamen of the action was breach of contract, and that losses for embezzlement were not within contemplation of the parties. Thus plaintiff was limited to a claim for refund of the audit fee.

Also see the discussion of overlapping remedies in L. B. Laboratories, Inc. v. Mitchell, 39 Cal. 2d 56, 244 P.2d 385 (1952).

20. For a case holding that a breach of an agreement to perform an audit can be based only in tort, *see* Carr v. Lipshie, 9 N.Y. 2d 983, 218 N.Y.S.2d 62, 176 N.E.2d 512 (1961). However, the New York rule announced in *Carr* seems to be in a state of flux. *See* Taylor v. G I Export Corp., 78 F.R.D. (494 E.D.N.Y. 1978). In L. B. Laboratories, Inc. v. Mitchell, 39 Cal. 2d 56, 244 P.2d 385 (1952), it was held that an action for breach of an agreement to prepare and file plaintiff's tax return was in contract.

21. A. Corbin, *Contracts* § 1019 n. 59 (1951). *Also see* Loss, *Securities Regulation* at 1624 (2d ed., 1961), stating that "it is a generally accepted rule that where two theories of damages lie, claimant is entitled to the greater of the two." Damages are discussed generally at note 59.

sion. But no man, whether skilled or unskilled, undertakes that the task he assumes shall be performed successfully, and without fault or error; he undertakes for good faith and integrity, but not for infallibility, and he is liable to his employer for negligence, bad faith, or dishonesty, but not for losses consequent upon mere errors of judgment.[22]

The requisites for liability for negligence are (1) a duty with respect to a standard of conduct, (2) a failure to act in accordance with the duty, (3) causal connection between negligence and injury, and (4) actual loss or damage to the plaintiff. An unavoidable accident that is unintentional and could not have been foreseen or prevented by reasonable precautions does not result in liability. Examples of such a situation are runaway horses, a driver of a car who is struck with a heart attack, or a child who runs in front of a car.[23]

English Precedents

American law, like American auditing, was derived from the English practice. Most of our states passed early laws adopting all English statutes and decisions in force not repugnant to our way of life or otherwise superseded by specific American statutes or rulings. Thus if a matter had not been specifically considered by our legislature or courts, the English law would govern. Since both American law and auditing have their roots in England, the early English cases are important in tracing the development of auditing standards and liability of the American public accountant.

English statutes provided for recovery by the liquidator of a company against the promoters, directors, or other officers for misfeasance or breach of trust.[24] The word *officer* in the statute was held to include recovery against accountants.[25] Since the statutes provided for recovery for breach of a duty to independently report financial condition, the cases constitute legal authority for interpretation of an auditor's contractual duties without regard to the statute.

Apparently the first English case that involved a suit against an auditor was *Leeds Estate, Building and Investment Co. v. Shepherd*,[26] decided in 1887. The

company was formed in 1869 under the Companies Act of 1862 for lending money on security. Its articles tied compensation of directors to dividends paid, restricted dividends to payments out of profits, and required an income statement and balance sheet to be presented at least once a year at a general meeting. The articles further provided that the accounts of the company should be examined at least once a year and the correctness of the balance sheet ascertained by one or more auditors who should state "whether in their opinion the balance-sheet is a full and fair balance-sheet containing the particulars required by these regulations, and properly drawn up so as to exhibit a true and correct view as to the state of the company's affairs." Such a report had to be read, along with the report of the directors, at the general meeting.

The manager of the company prepared balance sheets that overstated assets, and as a result, dividends were paid out of capital. When the company went into voluntary liquidation in 1882, the liquidator brought an action for damages for the benefit of creditors against the directors, manager, and auditor.

Locking, the auditor, was a clerk in a bank at the time of his first appointment. His certificate from 1874 to 1880 was in this form: "I certify that I have examined the above accounts and find them to be a true copy of those shewn in the books of the company." In 1870 Locking included in his certificate the statement:

> The vouchers and receipts correspond in all cases with the payments debited. I have gone carefully into the items shewn in the stock account, and consider the dividend which it is proposed to declare a just and fair division.

In 1871 he wrote the directors a letter discussing the stock account:

> I do not consider the estimate overdrawn or likely to give any shareholder cause to object. Of course, it would have been better if the parties had agreed to divide nothing for a few years till a good accumulation had taken place, but a dividend is no doubt a necessity.[27]

At the trial Locking contended his duty was confined to seeing that the balance sheet was as represented by the books of the company. The court, however, found that the duty was as set forth in the articles of the company and that the auditor's statement that he had not seen the articles of association afforded him no excuse because he knew of their existence. Justice Stirling found that the auditor, along with the manager and directors, breached his duty to the company:

> It was in my opinion the duty of the auditor not to

22. T. Cooley, *Torts* 335, 4th ed. (1932). The passage is quoted, for example, in Smith v. London Assurance Corp., 109 App. Div. 882, 96 N.Y.S. 820 (1905).

23. Prosser, *Law of Torts* 140–143, 4th ed. (1971).

24. Section 10 of the Companies Act of 1890 replaced section 165 of the Companies Act of 1862. Both laws were passed to facilitate recovery by the liquidator of a company for breaches of trust and misfeasance.

25. *See In re* London and General Bank, 2 Ch. 673 (C.A. 1895).

26. Leeds Estate, Building and Investment Co. v. Shepherd, 36 Ch.D. 787 (1887). In this case the attorney for the auditor pointed out to the court: " . . . this is the first time that an auditor has ever been made a Defendant to an action of this character."

27. Ibid. at 792.

confine himself merely to the task of verifying the arithmetical accuracy of the balance-sheet, but to inquire into its substantial accuracy, and to ascertain that it contained the particulars specified in the articles of association (and consequently a proper income and expenditure account), and was properly drawn up, so as to contain a true and correct representation of the company's affairs.[28]

In re London and General Bank[29] was decided eight years later, in 1895. Banking companies registered after 1879 were required to have accounts audited by an auditor elected annually by stockholders. The auditor was required to state whether the balance sheet of the firm was "full and fair." Theobald, the auditor, made a detailed report to the directors showing the unsatisfactory state of loans and securities, which was the most important balance-sheet item, being stated at £346,975. But the only qualification in his report to stockholders was that "the value of the assets as shewn on the balance-sheet is dependent upon realization." Although this statement was unusual in an auditor's report, the court held the auditor's duty was to convey information, not just to arouse inquiry. In holding the auditor liable, along with the directors, to the receiver for dividends paid out of capital, the court applied the doctrine of *res ipsa loquitur* (the thing speaks for itself) to find that the improper audit was the proximate cause of the improper dividend.

If the unsatisfactory nature of the loans and securities had been disclosed to stockholders, as well as to directors, the auditor's duty would have been discharged, since the auditor "is not an insurer" or guarantor.[30] Although the auditor's investigation was adequate, the court found that he failed in his *duty to communicate information*.

---

28. Ibid. at 802.

29. *In re* London and General Bank, [1895] 2 Ch. 673.

30. The court in this 1895 case says of the auditor's duty: "An auditor, however, is not bound to do more than exercise reasonable care and skill in making inquiries and investigations. He is not an insurer; he does not guarantee that the books do correctly show the true position of the company's affairs; he does not guarantee that his balance sheet is accurate according to the books of the company. If he did he would be responsible for an error on his part, even if he were himself deceived, without any want of reasonable care on his part—say, by the fraudulent concealment of a book from him. His obligation is not so onerous as this.

"Such I take to be the duty of the auditor; he must be honest—that is, he must not certify what he does not believe to be true, and he must take reasonable care and skill before he believes that what he certifies is true. What is reasonable care in any particular case must depend upon the circumstances of that case. Where there is nothing to excite suspicion, very little inquiry will be reasonable and sufficient; and in practice, I believe, business men select a few cases haphazard, see that they are right, and assume that others like them are correct also. Where suspicion is aroused more care is obviously necessary, but still an auditor is not bound to exercise more than reasonable care and skill even in a case of suspicion; and he is perfectly justified in acting on the opinion of an expert where special knowledge is required."

In re Kingston Cotton Mill Company,[31] decided in 1896, involved a suit by the liquidator against the company auditors to recover dividends paid out of capital because of the auditors' failure to discover that the inventory was overstated. The auditors had accepted the manager's certificates that the inventory sheets showed the correct values and quantities and had placed on the balance sheet the words "As per manager's certificate" immediately preceding the figures. Although the auditors could easily have tested the accuracy of the inventory sheets, they failed to do so.

The court held the auditors justified in relying on the manager's certificate since (1) auditors do not guarantee correctness, (2) it is not the auditor's duty to take stock, and (3) the entry in the balance sheet showed that the auditors took the item from the manager. Justice Lopes said:

> An auditor is not bound to be a detective, or as was said, to approach his work with suspicion or with a foregone conclusion that there is something wrong. He is a watch-dog, but not a bloodhound.[32]

Negligence Applied to American Public Accounting Practice

The public accountant's duties depend upon the nature of the engagement[33] and relationship of the par-

---

31. *In re* Kingston Cotton Mill Co., 2 Ch. 279 (C.A. 1896).

32. Ibid.

33. The accountant assumes less responsibility where the financials are unaudited and a number of cases have been successfully defended on this basis. *See* MacNerland v. Barnes, 199 S.E.2d 567 (Ga. Ct. App. 1973) (accountant held not liable to investor for negligence where accountant disclaimed because of lack of independence; however, it was held that accountant could be liable for negligence in performing agreement with plaintiff to verify certain major accounts); Rich v. Touche Ross & Co., 415 F. Supp. 95 (S.D.N.Y. 1976) (federal securities law fraud suit by customers of stock brokerage firm against CPA firm dismissed since there could have been no reliance upon financials marked "unaudited"); Katz v. Realty Equities Corp. of New York, 406 F. Supp. 802 (S.D.N.Y. 1976) (summary judgment for CPA firm granted in federal securities law fraud suit by investors because the CPA firm refused to certify the financials and refusal was communicated to the shareholders); O'Neal v. Atlas Auto. Finance Corp. 11 A.2d 782 (Pa. Super. 1940) (jury found for CPA on claim for unpaid fee and against defendant's counterclaim for negligent failure to discover fraud by the bookkeeper because, contrary to the client's contention, the engagement contemplated only a limited examination and financial review); Ronaldson v. Moss Watkins, Inc., 127 So. 467 (La. App. 1930) (the CPA was held not liable for errors since a detailed audit was not contemplated in the engagement).

In Seedkem, Inc. v. Safranek, 466 F. Supp. 340 (D. Neb. 1979), applying Nebraska and Indiana law, the court refused to dismiss a negligence suit against a CPA who maintained books and records and issued an unaudited disclaimer where plaintiff alleged that the CPA foresaw or should have foreseen plaintiff's use of the financials in extending credit. In Coleco Indus., Inc. v. Berman, 423 F. Supp. 275 (E.D. Pa. 1976), *appealed on other issues*, 567 F.2d 569 (3d Cir. 1977) (applying New Jersey and Pennsylvania law) the accountant was held liable for "obvious and mechanical" errors in unaudited financials; Heating and Air Conditioning Associates,

72

ties.[34] A finding of lack of due care (negligence) can be based upon failure to adhere to a specific undertaking[35] or an implied duty[36] that would have disclosed a fraudulent practice or a misrepresentation of financial condition. An engagement to perform an audit implies duties to verify the cash,[37] confirm accounts receivable,[38] observe physical inventories, and generally adhere to accepted professional standards.[39] However, an auditor is not a guarantor, and an audit cannot be relied upon to discover fraud, especially where it does not materially affect financial position. But if the auditor's negligence prevents discovery of fraud and results in losses that could, by the discovery, have been prevented, the auditor may be liable.[40] Even if such further losses cannot be shown, it has been held that the client can recover the fee paid for the negligent audit.[41]

Under the doctrine of *respondeat superior*[42] and the law of agency,[43] the accounting firm is liable for acts of its employees. Liability attaches only as a result of transactions arising in the course of the employment and does not apply if the employee clearly departs from the legitimate scope of the employment. Similarly, an accounting firm is liable for acts of its partners.[44]

Failure to Discover Embezzlement. A number of early American decisions established liability for failure to discover embezzlement.[45] The accountant is liable only for losses that take place after the fraud

Inc. v. Myerly, 222 S.E.2d 545, *cert. denied*, 225 S.E.2d 323 (N.C. 1976) (verdict for CPAs on claim for embezzlement losses because an engagement to prepare an unaudited financial statement does not require checking for accuracy or investigation of honesty of employees).

Also see Ryan v. Kanne at note 8 and *1136 Tenants' Corp. v. Max Rothenberg & Co.* at notes 47, 48, and 49.

34. Except to the extent that liability extends to third parties, the plaintiff must be a party to the contract. Thus in Blank v. Kaitz, 216 N.E.2d 110 (Mass. 1966), where the accountant contracted with the corporation, the court held that the directors had no standing to sue. For discussion of liability to third parties see Chapter 6.

35. In Smith v. London Assurance Corp., 109 App. Div. 882, 96 N.Y.S. 820 (1905), it was held that a cause of action is stated by allegation that embezzlement losses resulted from breach of a specific agreement to frequently check the cash account. The matter was raised on counterclaim to a suit by the auditors for their fee.

In Maryland Casualty Co. v. Cook, 35 F. Supp. 160 (E.D. Mich. 1940), the written audit contract contained specifications creating both specific and implied duties, the fulfillment of which would have led the auditor to discover the embezzlement.

36. In Dantzler Lumber & Export Co. v. Columbia Casualty Co., 115 Fla. 541, 156 So. 116 (1934), the complaint stated a cause of action in tort for negligence where it alleged that pursuant to employment of defendants as auditors, the duty arose to examine every cash transaction and investigate supporting data; that the auditors failed to discover fraud because of lack of due care in discharging the duty; and that further loss from embezzlement occurred. On both specific and implied duties of auditors, *see* Board of County Commissioners v. Baker, 152 Kan. 164, 102 P.2d 1006 (1940).

37. National Surety Corp. v. Lybrand, 256 App. Div. 226, 9 N.Y.S.2d 554 (1939).

38. Cereal Byproducts Company v. Hall, 8 Ill. App. 2d 331, 132 N.E.2d 27, *aff'd*, 15 Ill.2d 313, 155 N.E.2d 14 (1958).

39. Stanley L. Bloch, Inc. v. Klein, 258 N.Y.S.2d 501 (1965).

40. See note 45.

41. Board of County Comm'rs v. Baker, 102 P.2d 1006 (Kan. 1940) (auditor's failure to discover discrepancies apparently involving defalcations was fundamental breach that justified refund of fee); Stanley L. Bloch, Inc. v. Klein, 258 N.Y.S.2d 501 (Sup. Ct. N.Y. Cty. 1965) (failure to discover inventory discrepancy required return of fee, however, damages from remaining in business were too remote); Craig v. Anyon, 208 N.Y.S.2d 259, *aff'd* 152 N.E.

431 (N.Y. App. Div. 1925) (return of fee required by failure to discover embezzlement, but defalcation losses too remote where client represented that employee could be trusted); City of East Grand Forks v. Steel, 141 N.W. 181 (Minn. 1913) (cause of action for breach of contract stated by allegation that embezzlement losses resulted from auditor's negligence, but defalcation losses were too remote to be recovered from auditor without showing special circumstances).

42. The maxim *respondeat superior* means "let the master answer" and is applied where the relation of master and servant exists between a defendant and wrongdoer with respect to the transaction causing injury. In Sharp v. Coopers & Lybrand, 649 F.2d 175 (3d Cir. 1981), the court imposed liability on an accounting firm for acts of its employee basing application of *respondeat superior* on an accounting firm's strict duty to supervise its employees.

43. In the case of Matter of F. W. Koenecke & Sons, Inc., 605 F.2d 310 (7th Cir. 1979), the court applied Illinois law in holding an accounting firm liable to the client for fraud of the firm's senior accountant who participated in a diversion of funds. Without considering the adequacy of supervision, the court quoted from the Restatement of the Law of Agency: "A principal who puts a servant or other agent in a position which enables the agent, while acting within his authority, to commit fraud upon third persons is subject to liability to such third persons for the fraud."

In the landmark Ultramares Corp. v. Touche, 174 N.E. 441 (N.Y. 1931), the court said: "Whatever wrong was committed by the defendants was not their personal act or omission, but that of their subordinates. This does not relieve them, however, of liability to answer in damages for the consequences of the wrong. . . . The question is merely this, whether the defendants, having delegated the performance of this work to agents of their own selection, are responsible for the manner in which the business of the agency was done. As to that the answer is not doubtful."

44. See §§ 13 and 14 of the Uniform Partnership Act.

45. Smith v. London Assurance Corp., 96 N.Y.S.2d 820 (N.Y. App. Div. 1905) (cause of action stated by allegation that embezzlement losses resulted from breach of a specific agreement to frequently check the cash account); Dantzler Lumber & Export Co. v. Columbia Casualty Co., 156 So. 116 (Fla. 1934) (cause of action in tort stated by allegation that auditor's negligence resulted in failure to discover embezzlement); National Surety Corp. v. Lybrand, 9 N.Y.S.2d 554 (N.Y. App. Div. 1939) (the question of the auditors' liability for negligence in failing to discover embezzlement should have been submitted to the jury); Maryland Casualty Co. v. Cook, 35 F. Supp. 160 (E.D. Mich. 1940) (apparently applying Michigan law, accounting firm held liable for breach of contract for failing to discover embezzlement where following audit procedures specified in the contract would have uncovered the fraud); Cereal Byproducts Co. v. Hall, 132 N.E.2d 27, *aff'd*, 155 N.E.2d 14 (Ill. 1956) (auditor held liable for failure to discover embezzlement by virtue of accepting the bookkeeper's list of accounts receivable not to be confirmed).

should have been discovered by application of the procedures usually applied for the particular engagement.

The auditor's responsibility for detection of fraud was expanded by the 1977 adoption of *Statement on Auditing Standards No. 16,* now at AU § 327.05. It provides:

> Under generally accepted auditing standards the independent auditor has the responsibility within the inherent limitations of the auditing process to plan his examination to search for errors or irregularities that would have a material effect on the financial statements, and to exercise due skill and care in the conduct of that examination.

The more typical embezzlement claim arises as a result of the failure to discover embezzlement by lapping or kiting of checks when performing an audit. For example, in *National Surety Corp. v. Lybrand,*[46] the surety on a fidelity bond paid the loss and sued the auditors as assignee of the client. The embezzlement was perpetrated by lapping and kiting of checks. The various auditors never noticed that the makers of checks recorded on various deposit slips differed from the accounts credited on the books. In one instance the auditor compiled a list of transfers between banks that revealed the kiting. However the auditor either disregarded the schedule or failed to understand its significance. In reversing the lower court's dismissal and remanding for trial, the court reviewed the various authorities on auditing that refer to testing composition of deposits, scheduling interbank transfers, accounting for unissued checks, and obtaining confirmation from the bank and said:

> It is undisputed that cash in bank can be verified absolutely.

> * * * * *

> It was for the jury to say whether the practice of "lapping" and "kiting" of checks should have put the defendants upon inquiry which would have led to discovery of the defalcations, and whether, if defendants had exercised ordinary care and used proper methods of accounting as established by the expert testimony, they would have observed checks drawn out of numerical order. If they had checked "outstandings," they would have noted that the check or checks used by Wallach at the audit dates were returned with the cancelled vouchers accompanying the next bank statement. Again, if there had been any substantial compliance with the requirements for verifying cash in banks, the cash shortages would have been detected, as the jury might have found. Their representations that there had been a verification of cash was a pretense of knowledge when they did not know the condition of the bank accounts and had no reasonable basis

to assume that they did. This, the jury could have found, amounted to at least a constructive fraud.

PRACTICAL POINTER

As experts on internal control, CPAs are expected to advise on unusual control weaknesses relative to the size and type of the client, regardless of the nature of the engagement. For example, a CPA received a call from the client's bookkeeper, who said: "We know you are busy during tax season, but we would like to get our bank account reconciled and wonder if I can take over that function." The CPA assented and, as a result, the bookkeeper was able to embezzle the funds without detection. When the claim was presented to a defense attorney, he said "Pay it." The CPA had agreed to a change in procedure that facilitated the fraud without discussing the change with the client.

In *1136 Tenants' Corp. v. Max Rothenberg & Co.,*[47] a CPA firm was held liable to the client (owners of a co-op apartment house) for embezzlement by the managing agent. The managing agent who had hired the CPA firm pled guilty to embezzlement and then testified in the civil suit against the CPAs that the CPAs were engaged to perform an audit despite the fact that an audit might have revealed his embezzlement.

This was a controversial case for several reasons. The CPAs first moved to dismiss the suit because the legend, "No independent verifications were undertaken thereon," showed that the financials were unaudited. However the New York Appellate Division refused to dismiss and held that even if the CPA "acted as but a robot, merely doing copy work," there was an issue as to whether there were suspicious circumstances that imposed a duty on the CPA firm to warn the client.[48] When the case went to trial, judgment was entered for the plaintiff for more than $237,000, despite the fact that the CPAs were employed for $600 annually to "write-up" the books from statements and facts submitted by plaintiff's managing agent. In affirming, the New York Appellate Division found an engagement to audit, noting that the CPAs admitted performing services that went beyond the scope of a write-up.

---

46. See note 45.

47. See notes 48 and 49.

48. 1136 Tenants' Corp. v. Max Rothenberg & Co., 27 App. Div. 2d 830, 277 N.Y.S.2d 996 (1967), *aff'd,* 21 N.Y.2d 995, 290 N.Y.S.2d 919, 238 N.E.2d 322 (N.Y. Ct. App. 1968). According to the opinion of the two judges who dissented from the three-judge majority, the affidavits and examination before trial showed that defendant was employed for $600 annually to "write-up" the books from statements and facts submitted by plaintiff's managing agent.

Work sheets indicated that the CPAs examined the bank statement and bills, and one work sheet entitled "Missing Invoices 1/1/63—12/31/63" showed more than $44,000 of invoices missing from the records.[49]

PRACTICAL POINTERS

1. An audit is the highest level of service performed in connection with financial statements. Any time an accounting firm is engaged to perform a lesser service relative to financial statements, it is imperative to obtain a written contract with the client setting forth the limitations of the engagement.

2. Financial statements should always be accompanied by a statement indicating the responsibility the CPA has assumed. In *Stanley L. Bloch, Inc. v. Klein,* 258 N.Y.S.2d 501 (Sup. Ct. N.Y. County 1965), the court held that the failure to place a qualification on financial statements issued on the CPA's professional letterhead meant that the plaintiff could assume that the figures were audited.

In *Bonhiver v. Graff*[50] a local CPA firm was engaged to write-up the books and records for an insurance company. In performing the write-up work, the CPAs failed to investigate and discover the true nature of a number of transactions whereby the fraud was taking place. The court held the CPA liable to the receiver for the company for the amount of unpaid claims. The court treated the suit by the receiver as a claim by the client. The receiver's claim was limited to rights of creditors, since the owners had perpetrated the fraud. The unique aspect of this case is that the CPAs were held liable despite the fact that they had never prepared a financial statement for the company.

---

49. 1136 Tenants' Corp. v. Max Rothenberg & Co., 36 App. Div. 2d 804, 319 N.Y.S.2d 1007 (1971); 30 N.Y.2d 585, 330 N.Y.S.2d 800 (1972).

The AICPA-NYSSCPA brief submitted to the Court of Appeals of the State of New York is reprinted in the *Journal of Accountancy,* November 1971, pp. 68–73, following the full text of the decision of the Appellate Division. Previously the AICPA-NYSSCPA submitted to the Appellate Division a brief that is reprinted in the *Journal of Accountancy,* March 1971, pp. 57–62. This brief quotes from the opinion of the trial court, which stated that a "certain amount of auditing procedure is required even in a 'write-up.'"

50. Bonhiver v. Graff, 248 N.W.2d 291 (S. Ct. Minn. 1976). This case resulted in liability for write-up work to a nonclient insurance agent as well as to the receiver. Liability to third parties is discussed in Chapter 6.

PRACTICAL POINTERS

1. Preparation of unaudited financial statements for nonpublic entities is governed by pronouncements of the AICPA Accounting and Review Services Committee—*Statements on Standards for Accounting and Review Services (SSARS). SSARS No. 1* indicates in paragraph 11 that based on knowledge of the industry and stated qualifications of client personnel, the CPA may become aware of the need to assist with bookkeeping or adjusting the books. Thus whenever client personnel do not know LIFO from FIFO, the CPA should check on calculation of significant inventories. Similarly, when the client personnel are not sophisticated in estimating bad debt losses, the CPA should supervise preparation of an aging schedule for significant receivables.

2. Paragraph 12 of *SSARS No. 1* states that where CPAs become aware, by virtue of inquiry or procedures, that information supplied by an entity is incorrect, incomplete, or otherwise unsatisfactory for compiling financial statements, they should obtain additional or revised information and withdraw from the engagement if the entity refuses to supply the information. Consider whether issuing financial statements or trial balances to be used as financial statements violates this provision where they contain a suspense account or unclassified items. The fact that the item remains unclassified tends to indicate that its materiality has not been investigated, especially if its investigation leads to discovery of fraud.

Loss of Client Books and Records. In *Cook & Nichols, Inc. v. Peat, Marwick, Mitchell & Co.,*[51] the client alleged that the accounting firm lost its books and records. The court held that the damages for loss of property that has no market value is measured by the value to the owner giving due regard to the owner's prospective uses of the property.

Negligence in Tax Practice. Where a tax return preparer's negligence results in assessment of additional taxes, penalties, and interest, the preparer is usually liable only for the penalties. There is usually no liability for the interest, since the client had the use of the money. There is usually no liability for the taxes, since the client owed the taxes without regard to any negligence by the preparer. Court decisions relating to tax practice are discussed in Chapter 12.

---

51. Cook & Nichols, Inc. v. Peat, Marwick, Mitchell & Co., 480 S.W.2d 542 (Tenn. App. 1971).

Breach of Fiduciary Duty. An accounting firm is not a fiduciary when it performs an audit.[52] However, where accountants serve on the board of directors,[53] undertake to do the bookkeeping,[54] advise concerning financial affairs,[55] or prosecute a claim for tax refund,[56] they are held to be fiduciaries. A fiduciary is not privileged to deal at arm's length, but must adhere to the highest standard of candor and fairness. The fiduciary relationship shifts the burden of proof so that a CPA entrusted with the client's money has the duty to provide a full and complete accounting to the client.

In *Reid v. Silver*,[57] plaintiff had been engaged in design and manufacture of "Rose Marie Reid" swim suits. She entrusted more than $1.4 million to a CPA for investment purposes. The court, applying Illinois law, held that Silver was a fiduciary and required him to furnish a full and complete accounting of all of his actions in handling plaintiff's moneys, property, and business affairs from the beginning of their relationship.

Other Errors. In *Professional Rodeo Cowboys Ass'n, Inc. v. Wilch, Smith & Brock*,[58] an accounting firm was held liable for an error that caused the wrong cowboy to be declared champion. The court held the accounting firm liable for costs of settlement of the resulting dispute with contestants, including the fee of the attorney engaged to effect the settlement.

Measure of Damages

According to Prosser,[59] American courts are divided as to two measures of damages for misrepresentation, and few courts follow either rule with complete consistency. One rule, said to represent the majority view, is to give plaintiffs the benefit of their bargain. This rule allows plaintiffs to recover the difference between the actual value of what was received and the value as measured by the false representation. This rule is consistent with a breach-of-contract theory of suit. The other measure, called the out-of-pocket rule,

---

52. In Franklin Supply Co. v. Tolman, 454 F.2d 1059 (9th Cir. 1972) (applying Colorado and Venezuela law) the court said: "The duty of PMM was not to act as a fiduciary for Franklin; it was, rather, to act independently, objectively and impartially, and with the skills which it represented to its clients that it possessed, to make accurate determinations of fact. It would be liable for acting negligently or fradulently.

"We do not say that a certified public accountant may never be a fiduciary. We do say it was not here."

In Shofstall v. Allied Van Lines, Inc., 455 F. Supp. 351 (N.D. Ill. 1978), the court held there was no fiduciary relation between a purchaser of corporate stock and the corporation's auditor.

53. In Security-First Nat'l Bank of Los Angeles v. Lutz, 297 F.2d 159 (9th Cir. 1961), *modified on other issues*, 322 F.2d 348 (9th Cir. 1963), where the accountant served as part of management and was a member of the board of directors, the court based his liability on his fiduciary relationship. It brought him within California Civil Code § 1573, which defines *constructive fraud* as a breach of duty without fraudulent intent imposed where a fiduciary relationship exists between the parties. *Compare* Blakely v. Lisac, 357 F. Supp. 255 (D. Or. 1972), where the court held that the accountant, who also served as a director, was liable to investors under section 10(b) of the Exchange Act for unaudited financials that disclosed the liability for financing equipment without revealing that the equipment was unusable and that a judgment against the seller was uncollectible.

54. In Cafritz v. Corporation Audit Co., 60 F. Supp. 627 (D.C. 1945), plaintiff employed the Corporation Audit Company to maintain books and records and to prepare tax returns for himself and for several of his corporations. It was alleged that defendant caused certain monies to be paid out of plaintiff's bank account for benefit of defendant and that defendant refused to surrender plaintiff's checkbooks and cancelled checks. In holding that the fiduciary relation shifted the burden to defendant to prove proper disposition of the money, the court said:

It is plaintiff's contention that there existed a fiduciary relation, while this is vigorously denied by the defendants. Whether a fiduciary relation exists or not is always a question of fact. As stated by Pomeroy, *Equity Jurisprudence,* § 956, "Courts of equity have carefully refrained from defining the particular instances of fiduciary relations in such a manner that other and perhaps new instances might be excluded. It is settled by an overwhelming weight of authority that the principle extends to every possible case in which a fiduciary relation exists as a fact, in which there is confidence reposed on one side and the resulting superiority and influence on the other. The relation and the duties involved in it may be moral, social, domestic or merely personal." . . .

It is well established that where the defendant . . . stands as one occupying a fiduciary relation toward the plaintiff, because of money or property intrusted to him, the burden is upon him to show that he has performed his trust and the manner of its performance.

55. In Squyres v. Christian, 242 S.W.2d 786 (Tex. App. 1951), the CPA was engaged by an uneducated man to handle income tax matters and to advise and counsel concerning financial affairs. The CPA borrowed $7,000 from the client and misrepresented that the statute of limitations would never run against the note. When the client's widow brought suit on the note, the CPA pleaded the statute of limitations. The court found a fiduciary relationship and held that where a party occupies a position of influence and trust,

it is necessary to show the fairness of the transactions when it is attacked for fraud by the other party.

In Shwayder Chemical Metallurgy Corp. v. Baum, 206 N.W.2d 484 (Mich. App. 1973), an employee of a CPA who prepared a financial study and analysis of operations was a fiduciary and could be enjoined from using confidential client information in establishing a competing business.

Compare Midland Nat'l Bank of Minneapolis v. Perranoski, 299 N.W.2d 404 (Minn. 1980), where the court held that a CPA who acted as a seller of partnership interests and who held himself out as an investment advisor was not a fiduciary with respect to investors who were advised by their own legal counsel prior to investing.

56. In Jorge v. Rosen, 208 So. 2d 644 (Fla. App. 3d Dist. 1968), an accountant prosecuting a claim for refund of federal taxes was held to be a fiduciary; however, the contingent fee agreement was binding, since it was reasonable and executed after the client obtained independent counsel and advice.

57. Reid v. Silver, 354 F.2d 600 (7th Cir. 1965).

58. Professional Rodeo Cowboys Ass'n, Inc. v. Wilch, Smith & Brock, 589 P.2d 510 (Colo. App. 1978).

59. Prosser, *Law of Torts* 733–5, 4th ed. (1971).

76

gives plaintiffs the difference between the amount paid and the value received. This rule is consistent with a negligence or fraud theory. It should be the maximum recovery permitted for a third party who has no contract with the accountant, especially where liability is based on negligence instead of fraud.

Courts have applied a variety of measures of damages in imposing liability on accountants. These have included:

1. Return of accounting fees paid by the client.[60]
2. Embezzlement losses that take place after the fraud should have been discovered.[61]
3. Funds diverted by the accounting firm's employee.[62]
4. Funds embezzled by the CPA's partner.[63]
5. Funds diverted by the client and not disclosed by the CPA (in a suit by a third party).[64]
6. Amount of credit or loans lost in reliance on erroneous financials (in a suit by a third party).[65]

7. Accounting or legal fees incurred to correct deficient work.[66]
8. Excessive amount paid to purchase a business at book value.[67]
9. Dividends paid as a result of overstated profits and financial position.[68]
10. Excess cost of replacing stocks that were sold due to erroneous tax advice.[69]
11. Penalties assessed by the IRS as a result of late or erroneous filing of tax returns.[70]
12. Income taxes paid in error and no longer recoverable because of the three-year limitation period.[71]
13. Income taxes paid on a transaction that the CPA advised would be nontaxable.[72]
14. Corporate income taxes assessed as a result of late filing of a subchapter S election.[73]

60. City of East Grand Forks v. Steele, 141 N.W. 181 (Minn. 1913) (damages for losses resulting from defalcations and insolvency too remote without a showing of proximate cause from improper audit; however, return of audit fee was recoverable upon proper proof); Craig v. Anyon, 152 N.E. 431 (N.Y. 1925) (judgment against auditor for return of fee but, because of contributory negligence of client, auditor was not liable for embezzlement losses); Board of County Comm'rs. v. Baker, 102 P.2d 1006 (Kan. 1940) (judgment for return of entire fee based on fundamental breach of contract to audit in accordance with specified standards).

61. Smith v. London Assur. Corp. 96 N.Y.S. 820 (N.Y. App. Div. 1905) (denial of motion to dismiss claim against auditor for embezzlement losses); Dantzler Lumber & Export Co. v. Columbia Casualty Co., 156 So. 116 (Fla. 1934) (denial of motion to dismiss suit for embezzlement losses); National Surety Corp. v. Lybrand, 9 N.Y.S.2d 554 (App. Div. 1939) (claim against three successive auditors for embezzlement losses had to be submitted to the jury); Cereal Byproducts Co. v. Hall, 155 N.E.2d 14 (Ill. 1956) (judgment for accountants reversed and liability imposed for embezzlement losses); 1136 Tenants' Corp. v. Max Rothenberg & Co., 319 N.Y.S.2d 1007 (1971), aff'd, 281 N.E.2d 846 (1972) (judgment for embezzlement losses where accountants were aware of missing invoices); Bonhiver v. Graff, 248 N.W.2d 291 (Minn. 1976) (judgment for embezzlement losses where accountant performing bookkeeping failed to investigate and discover the true nature of a number of transactions by which the fraud was taking place).

62. Matter of F. W. Koenecke & Sons, Inc. 605 F.2d 310 (7th Cir. 1979) (applying Illinois law, CPA firm held liable to trustee in bankruptcy where accounting senior's false entries concealed diversion by senior and management in collusion).

63. Duke v. Hoch, 468 F.2d 973 (5th Cir. 1972) (applying Florida law, innocent partners were held liable for a partner's diversion of funds, which was not insured by the particular malpractice insurance policy).

64. United States Nat'l Bank of Or. v. Fought, 612 P.2d 754 (Or. App. 1980). (CPAs held liable for continuing to supply financial information without disclosing client's breach of agreement with bank to deposit all receipts in bank-controlled cash collateral account).

65. Shatterproof Glass Corp. v. James, 466 S.W.2d 873 (Tex. App. 1971) (auditors owed a duty of due care to third party that they knew would use the financials in advancing funds).

66. Professional Rodeo Cowboys Ass'n v. Wilch, Smith & Brock, 589 P.2d 510 (Colo. App. 1978) (CPAs liable for attorney's fees to settle dispute that resulted from error); Stanley L. Bloch, Inc. v. Klein, 258 N.Y.S.2d 501 (Sup. Ct. N.Y. County 1965) (CPA liable for return of fee plus accounting fee for corrected report); Ryan v. Kanne, 170 N.W.2d 395 (Iowa 1969) (CPA liable for return of fee plus accounting fee for a corrected report); Slaughter v. Eugene C. Roddie d/b/a/ Roddie Tax Service, 249 So. 2d 584 (La. App. 1971) (tax preparer held liable for CPA's fee for correcting erroneous tax work); Sorenson v. Fio Rito, 413 N.E.2d 47 (Ill. App. 1980) (attorney liable for legal fees incurred by former client in attempting to obtain refund of penalties and interest resulting from attorney's failure to timely file estate tax returns); also see, Annot., Attorneys' Fees Incurred in Litigation with Third Person as Damages in Action for Breach of Contract, 4 A.L.R.3d 270 (1965).

67. Aluma Kraft Mfg. Co. v. Elmer Fox & Co., 493 S.W.2d 378 (Mo. App. 1973) (refusal to dismiss complaint that alleged auditors knew their report would be used to determine book value to be paid for client's stock).

68. In re London and General Bank, [1895] 2 Ch. 673 (auditor held liable to receiver for dividends paid out of capital).

69. Rassieur v. Charles, 188 S.W.2d 817 (Mo. 1945) (accountants liable for loss on reacquisition of shares where they erroneously advised that the sale of the shares would produce a tax loss that could be used to offset a taxable gain).

70. L.B. Laboratories, Inc. v. Mitchell, 244 P.2d 385 (Cal. 1952) (CPA held liable for IRS penalties that resulted from his failure to timely prepare client's tax return).

71. Lindner v. Barlow, Davis & Wood, 27 Cal. Rptr. 101 (Cal. App. 1963) (client was unable to recover taxes paid on closed years against CPAs because CPAs proved that they applied usual standard of care).

72. Bancroft v. Indemnity Ins. Co. of North America, 203 F. Supp. 49 (W.D. La. 1962), aff'd mem. 309 F.2d 959 (5th Cir. 1963) (CPA held liable for a tax assessment of over $35,000 on two transactions executed by the taxpayer in reliance upon the CPA's erroneous advice that no taxes would result).

73. Feldman v. Granger, 257 A.2d 421 (Md. App. 1969) (CPA was sued for taxes, penalties, and interest that resulted from failure to timely file client's subchapter S election; however, the claim against the CPA was barred by the three-year statute of limitations, which started to run upon the taxpayer's receipt of a notice of deficiency from the IRS).

15. The difference between the actual value of an investment and the value based on the CPA's erroneous financial statements (sometimes in a suit by a third party).[74]
16. Total funds invested (in an action to rescind against a CPA firm that aided and assisted the sale of limited partnerships that should have been registered under state blue-sky law).[75]
17. The value to the owner of books and records lost by the CPA.[76]
18. The cost of settling a dispute where the CPA's error caused the wrong cowboy to be declared champion.[77]
19. Loss of reputation to a general agent who represented that the insurance firm was sound in reliance upon the insurance commissioner, who in turn relied upon the CPA.[78]

Punitive damages are damages awarded plaintiff for the purpose of punishing the defendant for wrongful conduct. Punitive damages are not allowed in Louisiana, Massachusetts, Nebraska, and Washington. Punitive damages are unlikely in a professional malpractice case because plaintiff must generally prove malicious or willful and wanton conduct by defendant. For example, in *Stern v. Abramson*[79] the court held that allegations of gross negligence by auditors that caused losses to plaintiff's tobacco store by virtue of the manager's embezzlement did not constitute malice nor willful and wanton conduct so as to permit recovery of punitive damages. However, in one case, an award of $100,000 in punitive damages was sustained on appeal where the tax return was prepared by a former construction worker who had received no formal training in tax-return preparation.[80]

In a case involving alleged malpractice by an attorney, the state supreme court reversed a judgment for plaintiff based on mental anguish because there was no proof of extreme and outrageous conduct.[81]

For other aspects of damages, see the following:

1. Single recovery limitation at Chapter 7 note 17.
2. Plaintiffs duty to minimize damages at Chapter 7 note 36.
3. Proximate cause requirements at Chapter 7 note 7.

SUBROGATION RIGHTS OF A SURETY COMPANY

It is well settled that an insurer, upon payment of a loss, becomes entitled to (subrogated to) any right of action that the insured had against any third person who caused the loss. Where the insurer pays embezzlement losses, should the insurer be able to sue on the client's claim against a negligent auditor, as well as on the client's claim against the embezzler? It has been held that the insurer does have the right to proceed against the auditor,[82] except where (1) recovery can be obtained from the party bearing primary responsibility for the loss,[83] or (2) the client (or the client's assignor)

74. Teich v. Arthur Andersen & Co., 40 Misc. 2d 519, 243 N.Y.S.2d 368 (Sup. Ct. 1963), *rev'd per curiam,* 24 App. Div. 2d 749, 263 N.Y.S.2d 932 (1965) (despite fact that plaintiff's stock investment had risen, he could recover any excess that he paid over what the price would have been without the alleged misrepresentation); Ryan v. Kanne, 170 N.W.2d 395 (Iowa 1965) (recovery against CPA by corporation that assumed assets and liabilities of a proprietorship for understatement of accounts payable).

75. Hild v. Woodcrest Ass'n, 391 N.E.2d 1047 (Ohio Common Pleas 1977) (CPA firm held liable for restoring investor to former position where suit for rescission of sale of limited partnerships was based on failure to register securities under state blue-sky laws and CPA's aiding and assisting the seller).

76. Cook & Nichols, Inc. v. Peat, Marwick, Mitchell & Co., 480 S.W.2d 542 (Tenn. App. 1971) (measure of damages for books and records allegedly lost by accounting firm is the value to the owner, considering their purpose and prospective use).

77. Professional Rodeo Cowboys Ass'n v. Wilch, Smith & Brock, 589 P.2d 510 (Colo. App. 1978) (where the accounting firm's error caused the wrong cowboy to be declared champion, the accounting firm was liable for costs of settling the dispute, including the cost of awarding equal prize money to both cowboys who were declared co-champions plus the attorney's fees incurred by the sponsor as well as those incurred by both cowboys).

78. Bonhiver v. Graff, 248 N.W.2d 291 (Minn. 1976) (CPA held liable for $10,000 representing general damages for loss of business reputation).

79. Stern v. Abramson, 376 A.2d 221 (N.J. Super. 1977).

80. Midwest Supply, Inc. v. Waters, 510 P.2d 876 (Nev. 1973).

81. Selsnick v. Horton, 620 P.2d 1256 (Nev. 1980).

82. In Dantzler Lumber & Export Co. v. Columbia Casualty Co., 115 Fla. 441, 156 So. 116 (1934), the Supreme Court of Florida held that upon payment to an insured party, the insurer was subrogated in a corresponding amount to the assured's right of action against any other person responsible for the loss. The court considered the gist of the action alleging auditors' negligent failure to discover embezzlement as being in tort. *Accord:* Maryland Casualty Co. v. Cook, 35 F. Supp. 160 (D. Mich.) (apparently applying Michigan law); Western Surety Co. v. Loy, 594 P.2d 257 (Kan. App. 1979).

In National Surety Corp. v. Lybrand, 256 App. Div. 226, 9 N.Y.S.2d 554 (1939), the bonding company paid the embezzlement loss and sued the auditor as assignee of the client.

In American Indemnity Co. v. Ernst & Ernst, 106 S.W.2d 763 (Tex. Civ. App.-Waco 1937), the court ruled the action by a bonding company alleging auditors' negligent failure to discover embezzlement could only be in tort, and the claim was held to be barred by the statute of limitations governing tort actions.

83. Where the county treasurer was primarily responsible for defalcations of his deputy and had given part payment and a collectible note for the balance, the surety company was estopped from collecting the loss from the auditors, Fidelity & Deposit Co. of Maryland v. Atherton, 47 N.M. 443, 144 P.2d 157 (1943).

78

was guilty of fraud or contributory negligence in connection with the loss.[84]

Malpractice insurance usually covers an auditor's negligent failure to discover fraud, while a fidelity bond covers the loss from fraud. After paying on the fidelity bond, the bonding company sues to get reimbursement from the auditor's malpractice insurance. To avoid such suits the AICPA persuaded many surety companies issuing fidelity bonds to agree not to sue auditors unless an impartial committee found dishonest or criminal acts or gross negligence.[85] The problems that such an accommodation presents for public policy are (1) whether the public at large should bear the cost of "ordinary" negligence of accountants and (2) how to distinguish between ordinary and gross negligence. Considering the time and expense of litigation and the fact that the insurance industry would be bearing costs on both sides, however, the accommodation seems to be a practical solution. The problem for the CPA is that not all surety companies joined in this agreement, and there is some doubt as to whether it is binding or irrevocable.

SUMMARY

Where the amount of the fee is not specified in advance, accountants are entitled to recover the ordinary and reasonable charge made for such services in the particular community by members of similar standing in the profession. Minor errors or inaccuracies do not affect the right to be paid, provided the work performed is of substantial value.

Executory contracts for personal services or those involving confidential relationships are not assignable by either party unless otherwise provided or the other party consents. Where full performance is prevented by an act of God, the majority view is that the value of beneficial services previously rendered may be recovered. However, there can be no recovery for part performance of an indivisible contract (e.g., to perform an audit or to prepare a tax return) if the failure of performance is a substantial failure of consideration.

Negligence is the failure to apply the usual standard of care. The requisites for liability for negligence are (1) a duty with respect to a standard of conduct, (2) a

failure to act in accordance with the duty, (3) causal connection between negligence and injury, and (4) actual loss or damage to the plaintiff. An unavoidable accident that is unintentional and could not have been foreseen or prevented by reasonable precautions does not result in liability.

Accountants are liable for defalcation losses that would have been prevented by the exercise of the usual standard of care for the particular engagement. Audit engagements usually involve verification of cash in bank, including tests of composition of deposits, accounting for unissued checks, obtaining confirmation from the bank, and preparing a schedule of interbank transfers. Generally accepted auditing standards require the auditor to plan the engagement to search for material fraud.

Under the law of agency, accounting firms are responsible for fraud of their employees perpetrated within the scope of the employment. Where CPAs act as financial, business, or investment advisors, they are held to be fiduciaries, which requires the highest standard of candor and good faith.

Where surety companies pay defalcation losses, they become entitled to sue on their insured's claim against a negligent accountant. Although some surety companies agreed not to sue CPAs unless a committee first found gross negligence, not all such firms signed, and there is some doubt as to whether the agreement is enforceable or irrevocable.

SUGGESTIONS FOR FURTHER READING

American Jurisprudence Legal Forms 2d. Vol. 1, chap. 5, "Accountants." New York: Lawyers Co-operative Publishing, 1971.

American Jurisprudence Pleading and Practice Forms Annotated. Rev. ed., vol. 1, "Accountants." New York: Lawyers Co-operative Publishing, 1967.

Annot. "Accountant's Malpractice Liability to Client." 92 *American Law Reports* 3d 396, 1979.

Prosser, William L. *Law of Torts.* 4th ed. St. Paul, Minn.: West Publishing, 1971.

Stern, Duke Nordlinger. *An Accountant's Guide to Malpractice Liability.* Charlottesville, Va.: Michie Co., 1979.

QUESTIONS AND PROBLEMS

Rights and Liabilities

1. Define the following terms:
   a. *Tort*
   b. *Negligence*
   c. *Respondeat superior*
   d. *Fiduciary*
2. Contrast and compare breach of contract with tort by giving examples of conduct that can be *(a)* only the tort of negligence but not breach of contract, *(b)* only breach of contract but not tort, and *(c)* both breach of

---

84. Rock River Savings & Loan Ass'n v. American States Ins. Co., 594 F.2d 633 (7th Cir. 1979) (applying Illinois law, subrogation claim against accounting firm barred where stockholders' transferors participated in fraud that caused the loss). For subrogation suits dismissed because of contributory negligence of the insured (not involving accounting firms), *see:* Allstate Ins. Co. v. Town of Ville Platte, 269 So. 2d 298 (La. App. 1972); and Holt v. Myers, 494 S.W.2d 430 (Mo. App. 1973).

85. John L. Carey, "Defalcation in Relation to Audit, Internal Control and Fidelity Bonds," *Journal of Accountancy,* April 1947, p. 353.

contract and the tort of negligence, depending upon how one views the conduct.

3. What are the four requisites for liability for negligence?

4. What is the legal responsibility of an auditor to the client?

5. When does a failure of an auditor cause him or her to forfeit the fee?

6. Under current professional standards, what is the auditor's responsibility for detection of fraud?

7. What is the meaning of *subrogation,* and how does it relate to auditors' liability?

8. (From the May 1981 Uniform CPA Examination)
DMO Enterprise, Inc., engaged the accounting firm of Martin, Seals & Anderson to perform its annual audit. The firm performed the audit in a competent, nonnegligent manner and billed DMO for $16,000, the agreed fee. Shortly after delivery of the audited financial statements, Hightower, the assistant controller, disappeared, taking with him $28,000 of DMO's funds. It was then discovered that Hightower had been engaged in a highly sophisticated, novel defalcation scheme during the past year. He had previously embezzled $35,000 of DMO funds. DMO has refused to pay the accounting firm's fee and is seeking to recover the $63,000 that was stolen by Hightower. Which of the following is correct?

a. The accountants cannot recover their fee and are liable for $63,000.

b. The accountants are entitled to collect their fee and are not liable for $63,000.

c. DMO is entitled to rescind the audit contract and thus is not liable for the $16,000 fee, but it cannot recover damages.

d. DMO is entitled to recover the $28,000 defalcation, and is not liable for the $16,000 fee.

9. (From the November 1970 Uniform CPA Examination)
Each of the following five sentences states a legal conclusion relating to the lettered material. You are to determine whether the legal conclusion is true or false according to the *Uniform Commercial Code and the general principles of contract law.*

Davis, a CPA, has a one-year retainer agreement with Franklin Corporation. Davis is to examine the financial statements, prepare tax returns, and be available for consultation on financial matters. The retainer provides for an annual fee of $12,000. Davis has a claim for $3,000 for services rendered to the Corporation prior to the execution of the retainer agreement. Davis performs the required services for the first four months and is paid therefor. Davis then is required to retire completely from practice because of a severe heart attack and assigns to Leeds, another CPA, his $3,000 claim against the Franklin Corporation and his rights and duties under the retainer agreement.

a. Davis's assignment of his $3,000 claim against the Franklin Corporation is valid, even without Franklin's consent to such assignment.

b. Franklin Corporation is not legally obligated under the retainer agreement to accept Leeds as its CPA for the remaining period.

c. Franklin Corporation may recover a judgment against Davis for breach of contract.

d. If Leeds sues Franklin Corporation, the latter may assert against Leeds all defenses it had against Davis before Davis assigned the claim to Leeds.

e. The assignment to be valid must be in writing.

10. (From the May 1965 Uniform CPA Examination)
Keen, a certified public accountant and sole practitioner, was retained by Arthur and Son, a partnership, to audit the company books and prepare a report on the financial statements for submission to several prospective partners as part of a planned expansion of the firm. Keen's fee was fixed on a per diem basis. After a period of intensive work, Keen had completed about half of the necessary field work when he suffered a paralyzing stroke. He was forced to abandon all his work, and in fact retired from the profession. The planned expansion of the firm failed to materialize because the prospective partners would act only upon the basis of the report which Keen was to have submitted and lost interest when the report was not available.

Required:

a. Arthur & Son sues Keen for breach of his contract. Will it recover? *Explain.*

b. Keen sues Arthur & Sons for his fee for the work he was able to complete or, in the alternative, for the reasonable value of the services performed. Will he recover? *Explain.*

c. Arthur & Son demand from Keen all of the working papers relative to the engagement, including several cancelled checks, the articles of copartnership, and some other records of the firm. Will the firm succeed in its demand? *Explain.*

11. (From the November 1977 Uniform CPA Examination)
A CPA was engaged by Jackson & Wilcox, a small retail partnership, to examine its financial statements. The CPA discovered that due to other commitments, the engagement could not be completed on time. The CPA, therefore, unilaterally delegated the duty to Vincent, an equally competent CPA. Under these circumstances, which of the following is true?

a. The duty to perform the audit engagement is delegable in that it is determined by an objective standard.

b. If Jackson & Wilcox refuses to accept Vincent because of a personal dislike of Vincent by one of the partners, Jackson & Wilcox will be liable for breach of contract.

c. Jackson & Wilcox must accept the delegation in that Vincent is equally competent.

d. The duty to perform the audit engagement is nondelegable and Jackson & Wilcox need not accept Vincent as a substitute if they do not wish to do so.

12. (From the November 1977 Uniform CPA Examination)
Gaspard & Devlin, a medium-sized CPA firm, employed Marshall as a staff accountant. Marshall was negligent in auditing several of the firm's clients. Under these circumstances which of the following statements is true?

a. Gaspard & Devlin is not liable for Marshall's negligence because CPAs are generally considered to be independent contractors.

b. Gaspard & Devlin would *not* be liable for Marshall's negligence if Marshall disobeyed specific instructions in the performance of the audits.

c. Gaspard & Devlin can recover against its insurer on its malpractice policy, even if one of the partners was also negligent in reviewing Marshall's work.

d. Marshall would have no personal liability for negligence.

Verification of Cash

13. (From the May 1971 Uniform CPA Examination)

The cashier of Baker Company covered a shortage in his cash working fund with cash obtained on December 31 from a local bank by cashing an unrecorded check drawn on the Company's New York bank. The auditor would discover this manipulation by

a. Preparing independent bank reconciliations as of December 31.

b. Counting the cash working fund at the close of business on December 31.

c. Investigating items returned with the bank cutoff statements.

d. Confirming the December 31 bank balances.

14. (From the November 1971 Uniform CPA Examination)
Kiting most likely would be detected by:

a. Tracing the amounts of daily deposits from the cash receipts journal to bank statements.

b. Confirming accounts receivable by direct communication with debtors.

c. Preparing a four-column proof of cash.

d. Preparing a schedule of interbank transfers.

15. (From the May 1973 Uniform CPA Examination)
Lapping would most likely be detected by:

a. Examination of canceled checks clearing in the bank cutoff period.

b. Confirming year-end bank balances.

c. Preparing a schedule of interbank transfers.

d. Investigating responses to account receivable confirmations.

6

Liability to Third Parties at Common Law

This chapter covers:

- THE THIRD-PARTY PROBLEM.
- HISTORICAL PERSPECTIVE OF CONDITIONS FOR IMPOSING LIABILITY.
- FRAUD AS THE TEST FOR THIRD-PARTY LIABILITY.
- NEGLIGENCE AS THE TEST FOR THIRD-PARTY LIABILITY.
- CIVIL ACTIONS UNDER STATE AND FEDERAL STATUTES.
- THIRD-PARTY LIABILITY FOR NEGLIGENCE OF GOVERNMENTAL AUDITORS.

THE THIRD-PARTY PROBLEM

Public accountants generally assume that their reports are used and relied upon by persons other than their clients. Financial statements "are designed to serve the needs of a variety of users, *particularly owners and creditors*."[1] Although the most important function of the auditor is to provide an independent check for owners and creditors, these primary users are not usually parties to the contract for audit services; that is, they are not in "privity" with the auditor. Under what, if any, circumstances should these parties be allowed to recover from the auditor for losses that they incur as a result of the auditor's malpractice?

The large number of parties having a direct or indirect economic interest in financial statements makes finding a solution difficult. Thus in the *Ultramares* case Judge Cardozo balked at the prospect of holding the negligent auditor liable "in an indeterminate amount for an indeterminate time to an indeterminate class."[2] If responsibility is to be imposed where specific users are identified, then to what extent will it be imposed, and what criteria will be used to determine the specific users to whom the auditor should be responsible?

Liability imposed should have some relation to the responsibility reasonably assumed and the compensation paid. Although the auditing procedures and standards should be of the same quality regardless of the group expected to rely upon the audit report, auditors must know the identity of the particular group of persons to whom they will be responsible if they are to include in their fee a charge for the risk and responsibility assumed. Even where auditors can foresee the uses and users of their reports, indefinite rules as to measurement of damages make evaluation of risk of loss difficult.[3]

HISTORICAL PERSPECTIVE OF CONDITIONS FOR IMPOSING LIABILITY

Various tests have been applied by the courts in defining accountants' third-party liability at common law. In Exhibit 6–1, stop 1 on the scale represents early development in the law—third parties had to show fraud to recover from an auditor. Although there is some conflict, *Ultramares* also embraced stop 2, which holds the auditor liable to third parties where there is recklessness or gross negligence. At stop 3 liability is imposed for ordinary negligence where the particular third-party user and transaction are identified at the time of the engagement. *Ultramares* may embrace this test under the formulation of "primary beneficiary" where the "end and aim" of the audit report is to shape the conduct of an identified third party. Stops 4 and 5 represent the current trend of the law as discussed later in this chapter.

English Precedents

The rule in England is that only parties to a contract may enforce it. In 1833 it was held in *Price v. Easton*[4]

---

1. *Statement of the Accounting Principles Board No. 4:* "Basic Concepts and Accounting Principles Underlying Financial Statements of Business Enterprises" (New York: American Institute of Certified Public Accountants, 1970), pp. 6, 18–19.

2. Ultramares Corp. v. Touche, 255 N.Y. 170, 174 N.E. 441 (1931).

3. See the discussion of damages in Chapter 5 at note 59.

4. Price v. Easton, 4 Barn. & Adol. 433 (1833). This case was followed by Tweddle v. Atkinson, 1 Best & S. 393 (1861), and Dunlop Pneumatic Tyre Co. v. Selfridge & Co., [1915] A.C. 847.

EXHIBIT 6-1
Tests for Third-Party Liability and Related Court Decisions

Tests		Court Decisions
Fraud (knowing misrepresentation)	①→	*Ultramares Corp.* (New York)
Recklessness (gross negligence)	←②→	*State Street Trust* (New York) *Duro Sportswear* (New York)
Ordinary negligence (particular plaintiff and transaction foreseen)	←③→	*C.I.T. Financial Corp.* (New York) *Ryan v. Kanne* (Iowa) *White v. Guarente* (New York) *Hedley Byrne* (England)
Ordinary negligence (class of user and type of transaction foreseen)	←④	*Rusch Factors* (Rhode Island) *Rhode Island Hospital* (Rhode Island) *Shatterproof Glass* (Texas) *Aluma Kraft* (Missouri) *Bonhiver v. Graff* (Minnesota) *Merit Insurance* (Illinois) *Haig v. Bamford* (Canada)
Ordinary negligence (balancing of policy factors, including foreseeability)	←⑤→	*Biakanja v. Irving* (California)* *Guy v. Liederbach* (Pennsylvania)†

*Defining liability of a notary public.
†Defining liability of an attorney.

that although the plaintiff was entitled to a sum of money from the defendant, the plaintiff could not sue because he was not a party to the contract. In 1842 the English Court of Exchequer in *Winterbottom v. Wright*[5] held that an injured passenger, who was not a party to a contract to maintain a stagecoach, could not sue on the contract. Because of the strong words of Lord Abinger, who foresaw "the most absurd and outrageous consequences"[6] unless the operation of contracts was confined to the parties, the case was misinterpreted to mean there could be no suit in tort by such an injured party.[7]

In 1883, however, in *Heaven v. Pender*,[8] Brett, who later became Lord Esher, found the supplier of a scaffold for the painting of a ship liable to the painter even in the absence of privity of contract. In his famous

dictum he attempted to state a formula of duty for the law of torts:

> Whenever one person is by circumstances placed in such a position with regard to another that every one of ordinary sense who did think would at once recognize that if he did not use ordinary care and skill in his own conduct with regard to those circumstances he would cause danger of injury to the person or property of the other, a duty arises to use ordinary care and skill to avoid such danger.

The formula is very broad and could justify accountants' liability to virtually anyone expected to use the accountants' work. Lord Esher later rejected his own formula in *Le Lievre v. Gould*.[9]

In 1889 *Derry v. Peek*[10] became the basis for a dividing line for third-party liability for negligent language. It was held that there was no liability to third parties for negligent language that resulted only in pecuniary loss, although liability to third parties could be established if the negligent misrepresentation resulted in loss of life, limb, or health. The case involved directors who, in a prospectus designed to induce stock subscriptions, misrepresented that the company had the right to use steam or mechanical power instead of horses. Although there was no reasonable ground for such a belief, the House of Lords concluded that the defendants honestly believed the statement and that the plaintiff could not recover, because the misrepresentation was only negligent, as opposed to intentional.

It was held that a false statement made through carelessness and without reasonable ground for believing it to be true could be evidence of fraud. However, if it was made in the honest belief that it was true, it was not fraudulent and could not render the person liable in deceit. Lord Herschell summarized the authorities as follows:

> First, in order to sustain an action of deceit, there must be proof of fraud, and nothing short of that will suffice. Secondly, fraud is proved when it is shown that a false representation has been made (1) knowingly, or (2) without belief in its truth, or (3) recklessly, careless whether it be true or false. Although I have treated the second and third as distinct cases, I think the third is but an instance of the second, for one who makes a

5. Winterbottom v. Wright, 10 M. & W. 109, 152 Eng. Rep. 402 (Ex. 1842).

6. Ibid. at 114, 152 Eng. Rep. at 405. In Lord Abinger's speech he said: "there is no privity of contract between these parties; and if the plaintiff can sue, every passenger, or even any person passing along the road who was injured by the upsetting of the coach, might bring a similar action. Unless we confine the operation of such contracts as this to the parties who entered into them, the most absurd and outrageous consequences, to which I can see no limit, would ensue."

7. W. Prosser, *Law of Torts* 622, 4th ed. (St. Paul, Minn.: West Publishing, 1971).

8. Heaven v. Pender, 11 Q.B.D. 503 (1883).

9. Le Lievre v. Gould, [1893] 1 Q.B. 491 (C.A.). Another formula for duty, which was proposed by Lord Atkin in Donoghue v. Stevenson, [1932] A.C. 579, indicates the objective but provides no criteria: "You must take reasonable care to avoid acts or omissions which you can reasonably foresee would be likely to injure your neighbor. Who, then, in law is my neighbor? The answer seems to be persons who are so closely and directly affected by my act that I ought reasonably to have them in contemplation as being so affected when I am directing my mind to the acts or omissions which are called in question."

10. Derry v. Peek, 14 A.C. 337 (1889).

statement under such circumstances can have no real belief in the truth of what he states. To prevent a false statement being fraudulent, there must, I think, always be an honest belief in its truth. And this probably covers the whole ground, for one who knowingly alleges that which is false, has obviously no such honest belief. Thirdly, if fraud be proved, the motive of the person guilty of it is immaterial. It matters not that there was no intention to cheat or injure the person to whom the statement was made.

According to Prosser, *Derry v. Peek* has been the subject of great controversy and is not necessarily supported by American courts, which "render lip service to it, and yet allow recovery in deceit for misrepresentation which falls short of actual intent to deceive."[11] American courts may find a remedy in deceit, negligence, or warranty, but Prosser believed the result should be based on responsibility of the defendant as opposed to the form of action.

English courts continued to follow *Derry v. Peek* until 1963. During this period there was no liability to third parties for *negligent* misrepresentation except when a special duty to be careful was imposed by contract, a fiduciary relationship, or likelihood of physical damage to person or property. Thus in 1893 in *Le Lievre v. Gould*[12] it was held that an architect who negligently gave certificates of progress for the construction of a building was not liable to a lender for losses incurred in relying on the certificates. Lord Bowen said:

> But the law of England does not go to that extent: it does not consider that what a man writes on paper is like a gun or other dangerous instrument, and unless he intended to deceive, the law does not, in the absence of contract, hold him responsible for drawing his certificate carelessly.

In 1951 in *Candler v. Crane, Christmas & Co.*[13] the English Court of Appeal specifically held that a firm of accountants was not liable to third parties for negligence even though the accountants presented the statement directly to the third party who intended to rely upon it. A company had been formed by Ogilvie, who was chairman and managing director for life. The defendant accountants were employed "to prepare the accounts of the company and to write up the books." The accountants entrusted the work to a clerk, who accepted Ogilvie's statements without verification. This same clerk met with plaintiff Candler, a prospective investor, and presented a draft of the accounts. It was represented that the accounts would be certified, and they were in fact later certified by defendants in

the same form as exhibited at the meeting. After the meeting Candler invested £2,000, which was lost.

The accounts that Candler saw gave "an altogether inaccurate picture of the position of the company" and admittedly the clerk "had entirely failed to use proper care and skill in the preparation and presentation of the accounts." But the court held that Candler could not recover from the accountants, since there was no fraud and the accountants' only duty to a third party was to produce accounts that they honestly believed to be the accounts of the company.

But the reasoning in the now famous dissent of Lord Denning eventually was to form the basis for the law of England:

> I think that the law would fail to serve the best interests of the community if it should hold that accountants and auditors owe a duty to no one but their client. Its influence would be most marked in cases where their client is a company or firm controlled by one man. It would encourage accountants to accept the information which the one man gives them, without verifying it; and to prepare and present the accounts rather as a lawyer prepares and presents a case, putting the best appearance on the accounts they can without expressing their personal opinion of them. This is, to my way of thinking, an entirely wrong approach. There is a great difference between the lawyer and the accountant. The lawyer is never called upon to express his personal belief in the truth of his client's case, whereas the accountant, who certifies the accounts of his client, is always called upon to express his personal opinion whether the accounts exhibit a true and correct view of his client's affairs; and he is required to do this not so much for the satisfaction of his own client but more for the guidance of shareholders, investors, revenue authorities, and others who may have to rely on the accounts in serious matters of business. If we should decide this case in favour of the accountants there will be no reason why accountants should ever verify the word of the one man in a one-man company, because there will be no one to complain about it. The one man who gives them wrong information will not complain if they do not verify it. He wants their backing for the misleading information he gives them, and he can only get it if they accept his word without verification. It is just what he wants so as to gain his own ends. And the persons who are misled cannot complain because the accountants owe no duty to them. If such be the law, I think it is to be regretted, for it means that the accountant's certificate, which should be a safeguard, becomes a snare for those who rely on it. I do not myself think that it is the law. In my opinion accountants owe a duty of care not only to their own clients, but also to all those whom they know will rely on their accounts in the transactions for which those accounts are prepared.

In 1963 the House of Lords overruled *Candler v. Crane, Christmas & Co.* by holding in *Hedley Byrne &*

11. Prosser, *Law of Torts* 700, 4th ed. (1971).
12. Le Lievre v. Gould, [1893] 1 Q.B. 491 (C.A.).
13. Candler v. Crane, Christmas & Co., [1951] 2 K.B. 164.

Co. Ltd. v. Heller & Partners, Ltd.[14] that one who undertakes to give advice is liable for negligence to third parties, who foreseeably may rely upon it. The plaintiffs were advertising agents who sued defendant bankers for losses incurred through reliance on the bankers' negligent credit report. Although the defendants made their report gratuitously, they would have been held liable for negligence except that they prefaced their report with the words, "For your private use and without responsibility on the part of this bank or its officials." The case of *Le Lievre v. Gould* was distinguished because there the defendant architect did not know that his certificate would be relied upon by the plaintiff.

The extent to which *Derry v. Peek* has been limited is not yet clear. Apparently in a case where reliance by third parties cannot be sufficiently foreseen it remains good law in England. In *Le Lievre v. Gould* Lord Bowen pointed out that *Derry v. Peek* decided "there is no duty enforceable in law to be careful." Duty is limited to those who can establish a relationship of proximity. But proximity may be found where information, in itself gratuitous, is given in the course of defendant's business or professional relations as opposed to social relations, such as curbstone information by an attorney or physician to one who is not a client or patient.[15]

The Institute of Chartered Accountants in England and Wales obtained counsel's advice as to the effect of *Hedley Byrne* on accountants' liability to third parties. Counsel's opinion was that third parties may recover from negligent accountants

> in circumstances where the accountants knew or ought to have known that the reports, accounts or financial statements in question were being prepared for the specific purpose or transaction which gave rise to the loss and that they would be shown to and relied on by third parties in that particular connection.[16]

Early American Decisions

The 1889 decision of the English House of Lords in *Derry v. Peek* limiting liability for deceit to intentional misrepresentation greatly influenced American courts. The case was the origin of the early American rule denying liability to third parties for merely *negligent* misrepresentations. Prosser indicates that although the majority of American courts "purport to accept it as sound law," many have devised "more or less ingenious fictions and formulae" that permit them to get around it.

As early as 1859 there were indications that American courts might come to treat the third-party problem differently from the English. The New York court in *Lawrence v. Fox*[17] broke with the English rule that only one who is "privity" to a contract may sue to enforce it. This case started a movement throughout America permitting third-party donee and creditor beneficiaries to enforce contracts made for their benefit.[18]

But these early rights were given to American third parties only where the promisor's contractual duties were limited to the third party. If the promisor also had duties of performance to the promisee, then third parties were said to be incidental beneficiaries and could not bring suit. For example, if A promised to audit B's accounts and render reports to B and to B's bank, the bank was considered only an incidental beneficiary and could not bring suit for breach of the contract. If the auditor's only duty was to the bank, however, then the bank could bring suit. Under such rules it was not necessary that the third party be identified at the time the contract was made—but the party had to be identified by the time of performance.[19]

In the tort area the English rule established in *Winterbottom v. Wright* fell in 1916 when Judge Cardozo's famous opinion in *MacPherson v. Buick Motor Co.*[20] extended third-party liability to manufacturers of articles that would be dangerous if negligently made:

> If the nature of a thing is such that it is reasonably certain to place life and limb in peril when negligently made, it is then a thing of danger. Its nature gives warning of the consequences to be expected. If to the element of danger there is added knowledge that the thing will be used by persons other than the purchaser and used without new tests, then irrespective of contract, the manufacturer of this thing of danger is under a duty to make it carefully. That is as far as we are required to go for the decision of this case.

The result of *MacPherson v. Buick Motor Co.* was finally reached in England in *Donoghue v. Stevenson*[21] in 1932.

14. Hedley Byrne & Co. v. Heller & Partners, Ltd., [1964] A.C. 465 (1963).

15. Prosser, *Law of Torts* 706, n. 31 4th ed. (1971).

16. Accountants' Liability to Third Parties. The Hedley Byrne Decision," reprinted from the August 7, 1965, issue of the *Accountant* in the *Journal of Accountancy*, October 1965, pp. 66–67.

17. Lawrence v. Fox, 20 N.Y. 268 (1859).

18. L. Simpson, *Contracts*, 241–46, 2d ed. (St. Paul, Minn.: West Publishing, 1965). For an analysis of court decisions, see 4 A. Corbin, *Contracts* §788 (1951).

19. Ibid. For an analysis of court decisions, see 4 A. Corbin, *Contracts* §781 (1951).

20. MacPherson v. Buick Motor Co., 217 N.Y. 382, 111 N.E. 1050 (1916).

21. Donoghue v. Stevenson, [1932] A.C. 562. This case involved ginger beer in a bottle with no opportunity to the distributor or consumer for inspection and discovery of any defect. Lord Atkin announced his neighbor theory of duty (*supra* at note 9), and Lord

Landell v. Lybrand,[22] decided in 1919, was the earliest American case dealing with the CPA's liability to a third party (i.e., a party having no contract with the CPA). The plaintiff claimed to have purchased stock in reliance on a false report that the auditors negligently prepared. The Pennsylvania Supreme Court noted there was no averment of intent to deceive and held that, in absence of contract, defendants could not be liable to the plaintiff for negligence.

Judge Cardozo extended more liability to third parties with his 1922 opinion in *Glanzer v. Shepard*.[23] The plaintiff was buyer of 905 bags of beans; payment was to be based on weight sheets certified by public weighers. The seller informed the defendant weighers that the beans had been sold to the plaintiff and requested defendant weighers to make a return of the weight and furnish the plaintiff with a copy. Although the seller paid for the services, the court held that the buyer could recover from defendant weighers for damages due to incorrect weight. The court stressed that the defendant knew the weighing was performed "with the very end and aim of shaping the conduct of another." Citing *MacPherson v. Buick Motor Co.*, the court said:

> In such circumstances, assumption of the task of weighing was the assumption of a duty to weigh carefully for the benefit of all whose conduct was to be governed. We do not need to state the duty in terms of contract or of privity. Growing out of a contract, it has none the less an origin not exclusively contractual. Given the contract and the relation, the duty is imposed by law.

The court went on to add that a similar result could be reached by an extension of the third-party beneficiary theory of *Lawrence v. Fox*:

> We state the defendants' obligation, therefore, in terms not of contract merely, but of duty. Other forms of statement are possible. They involve, at most, a change of emphasis. We may see here, if we please, a phase or an extension of the rule in *Lawrence v. Fox* (20 N.Y. 268) as amplified recently in *Seaver v. Ransom* (224 N.Y. 233). If we fix our gaze upon that as-

pect, we shall stress the element of contract, and treat the defendants' promise as embracing the rendition of a service, which though ordered and paid for by one, was either wholly or in part for the benefit of another.

FRAUD AS THE TEST FOR THIRD-PARTY LIABILITY

Liability for Fraud Established

Ultramares Corp. v. Touche[24] established the rule that public accountants are liable to third parties for deceit but held they cannot be liable to *unidentified* third parties for negligence.

Ultramares Corporation, the plaintiff, was engaged in business as a lender on receivables. The defendant public accountants were engaged to prepare and certify a December 31, 1923, balance sheet for Fred Stern & Co., Inc. Defendant auditors knew that in the usual course of business the certified balance sheet would be exhibited by Stern to banks, creditors, stockholders, purchasers, or sellers, according to the needs of the occasion, as the basis for financial dealings. Accordingly they supplied 32 copies certified with serial numbers as counterpart originals for this purpose.

At the time of the audit, the plaintiff had never advanced funds to the company and was not otherwise identified to the auditors. Loans later made by the plaintiff could be foreseen in only a general way; that is, such loans were within the wide "range of transactions in which a certificate of audit might be expected to play a part."

The *Ultramares* case was the first American decision to establish the auditor's liability to third parties for deceit. According to Prosser the action of deceit dates back to 1201 but owes its modern origin to the 1789 case of *Pasley v. Freeman*, which established tort liability for deceit where the parties had no contract. The elements of the cause of action are (1) false representation, (2) scienter: either knowledge of falsity or insufficient basis of information, (3) intent to induce action in reliance, (4) justifiable reliance, and (5) resulting damage.[25]

After *Derry v. Peek* in 1889, deceit could not be sustained if the defendant believed the false representation, even though the belief had no reasonable basis. But Judge Cardozo, speaking in *Ultramares* for the unanimous Court of Appeals of New York, said:

> No such charity of construction exonerates accountants, who by the very nature of their calling profess to speak with knowledge when certifying to an agreement between the audit and the entries.

MacMillan explained the evolution of the common law in the following terms: "The criterion of judgment must adjust and adapt itself to the changing circumstances of life. The categories of negligence are never closed. . . . Where there is room for diversity of view, it is in determining what circumstances will establish such a relationship between the parties as to give rise, on the one side, to a duty to take care, and on the other side to a right to have care taken."

22. *Landell v. Lybrand*, 264 Pa. 406, 107 Atl. 783 (1919). This case is apparently no longer law in Pennsylvania. *See Guy v. Leiderbach*, 421 A.2d 333 (Pa. Super. 1980), where the court ruled that a beneficiary under a will can sue the attorney who drafted it on both negligence and contract theories despite the absence of a contractual relationship.

23. *Glanzer v. Shepard*, 233 N.Y. 236, 135 N.E. 275 (1922).

24. *Ultramares Corp. v. Touche*, 255 N.Y. 179, 174 N.E. 441 (1931).

25. W. Prosser, *Law of Torts* 685–86, 4th ed. (1971).

It was therefore held that certification of a balance sheet without information leading to a sincere or genuine belief could constitute deceit. Defendants had certified the balance sheet for Fred Stern & Co., Inc., on December 31, 1923, showing capital and surplus intact, but in reality the corporation was insolvent. Since the defendants could not show verification of $706,000 of fictitious receivables, Judge Cardozo ruled that a jury could find the defendants had certified a statement as true to their own knowledge when they had no knowledge on the subject.

Liability for Negligence Rejected

In holding that the plaintiff in *Ultramares* could not sue the auditor for negligence, the proximity of the parties was distinguished from *Glanzer v. Shepard,* where public weighers knew of both the transaction and the identity of the plaintiff buyer. Judge Cardozo noted that in *Glanzer* "the bond was so close as to approach that of privity." In fact the nexus was so close that the duty of the weighers could be viewed as an extension of *Lawrence v. Fox,* because the weighing was primarily for the benefit of the plaintiff and only incidentally for the promisee. Only the lack of proximity and foreseeability in *Ultramares* caused Judge Cardozo to say:

> If liability for negligence exists, a thoughtless slip or blunder, the failure to detect a theft or forgery beneath the cover of deceptive entries, may expose accountants to a liability in an indeterminate amount for an indeterminate time to an indeterminate class.

If, in analogy to *Glanzer,* the auditor had been told to supply an audit report for the use of the plaintiff lender in evaluating a loan, Cardozo might well have held the auditor liable to the lender for negligence. But such facts were not placed before the court.

Ultramares Becomes a Landmark

The prestige of the New York court and more especially of its chief judge, Benjamin Nathan Cardozo, was such that the *Ultramares* case immediately was established as a landmark. Cardozo's decisions adapting common-law principles to modern needs influenced courts throughout the English-speaking world. His opinions in *MacPherson v. Buick Motor Co.* (1916), *Glanzer v. Shepard* (1922), and *Palsgraf v. Long Island R.R.* (1928) constitute an important part of the law of torts. His thinking in *MacPherson v. Buick Motor Co.* was adopted by the English House of Lords in the celebrated case of *Donoghue v. Stevenson* in 1932. When Cardozo took his seat on the Supreme Court of the United States in 1932, the New York court had become the most forward-looking state

court—the second most distinguished court in the nation.[26]

Ultramares Interpreted and Then Rejected

The *Ultramares* decision soon proved to be subject to widely differing interpretations. In the 1937 decision of *O'Connor v. Ludlam,*[27] involving a purchaser of preferred stock foreseen to the auditor, the court instructed the jury that the auditors could not be held liable if they had honestly believed their reports unless they rendered them with "no knowledge on the subject." Based on this instruction, the jury ruled in favor of the auditors, and the verdict was sustained upon appeal.

In the 1938 decision of *State Street Trust Co. v. Ernst,*[28] the court held the auditor liable to a bank on the basis of reckless conduct for which it coined the term *gross negligence.* This was followed in 1954 by *Duro Sportswear, Inc. v. Cogen,*[29] which held the CPA firm liable on the basis of "gross negligence" to a purchaser of the corporation's stock who relied upon the audited financial statements.

In the 1955 decision of *C.I.T. Financial Corp. v. Glover,*[30] the court held that auditors are liable to third parties for ordinary negligence if the reports they prepare are for the identified third party's "primary benefit" in connection with the transaction that results in loss. The jury found, however, that the defendant CPAs were not liable to the plaintiff lender because (1) the defendants' representations were not negligently false and misleading and (2) the reports were not for the primary benefit of the plaintiff, so there was no duty to use due care for the plaintiff's benefit.

In the years that have since followed, the great majority of courts that have considered the matter have now rejected the *Ultramares* rule.[31] Accountants are generally held liable for ordinary negligence to third parties whose reliance is foreseen to the account-

26. Biography by Felix Frankfurter in *Supplement Two* of *Dictionary of American Biography* (New York: Charles Scribner's Sons, 1958), pp. 93–96; *Encyclopaedia Britannica* (Chicago: Encyclopaedia Britannica, 1968); Seavey, "Mr. Justice Cardozo and the Law of Torts," *52 Harv. L. Rev.* 372–404 (1938–39).

27. O'Connor v. Ludlam, 92 F.2d 50 (2d Cir. 1937), *cert denied,* 302 U.S. 758 (applying New York law).

28. State Street Trust Co. v. Ernst, 278 N.Y. 104, 15 N.E.2d 416 (1938).

29. Duro Sportswear, Inc. v. Cogen, 131 N.Y.S.2d 20 (Sup. Ct. 1954), *aff'd mem.,* 285 App. Div. 864, 137 N.Y.S.2d 829 (1955).

30. C.I.T. Financial Corp. v. Glover, 224 F.2d 44 (2d Cir. 1955) (apparently applying New York Law). See Saul Levy, "The C.I.T. Case," *Journal of Accountancy,* October 1955, pp. 31–42, which contains a reprint of the case along with excerpts from the charge to the jury.

31. California: Biakanja v. Irving, 320 P.2d 16 (Cal. 1958) (notary public who prepares a will may be liable for negligence to a beneficiary under the will); Lucas v. Hamm, 364 P.2d 685 (Cal. 1961),

ants at the time of the engagement. Even the New York Court of Appeals has sharply limited *Ultra-*

cert. denied, 368 U.S. 987 (1962) (attorney who prepares a will may be liable for negligence to a beneficiary under the will).

Canada: Haig v. Bamford, Wicken and Gibson, [1976] 3 W.W.R. 331 (Supreme Court of Canada) (Chartered accountants held liable for negligence to an investor of equity capital where they knew the audited financials would be used to raise equity capital but did not know the identity of the particular investor. The court found the class of persons sufficiently small and limited as to justify a duty of due care because it was unlawful for the private company to offer securities to the general public.)

England: Hedley Byrne & Co. Ltd. v. Heller & Partners, Ltd., [1964] A.C. 465 (1963) (One who undertakes to give gratuitous advice is liable to third parties who foreseeably may rely upon it. No liability was imposed on the bank that furnished credit information because of the disclaimer "For your private use and without responsibility on the part of this bank or its officials.")

Illinois: Merit Ins. v. Colao, 603 F.2d 654 (7th Cir. 1979) (Auditors may be held liable for negligence to one of a relatively small group of third parties who foreseeably will rely upon the audit report).

Indiana: Seedkem, Inc. v. Safranek, 466 F. Supp. 340 (D. Neb. 1979) (applying law of Nebraska, where defendant resided, and law of Indiana, the place of reliance) (Court refused to dismiss complaint by third party alleging negligence by CPA who maintained books and records and issued unaudited financial statements).

Iowa: Ryan v. Kanne, 170 N.W.2d 395 (Iowa 1969) (CPA held liable for negligence to corporation that was formed by using the CPA's unaudited balance sheet of a proprietorship).

Minnesota: Bonhiver v. Graff, 248 N.W.2d 291 (Minn. 1976) (CPA held liable for negligent bookkeeping entries to third-party insurance agent).

Missouri: Aluma Kraft Mfg. Co. v. Elmer Fox & Co., 493 S.W.2d 378 (Mo. App. 1973) (complaint held good where it alleged that negligent auditors knew that their report would be used to determine book value to be paid by the plaintiff for Aluma Kraft stock).

Nebraska: See Indiana.

New Jersey: Coleco Indus., Inc. v. Berman, 423 F. Supp. 275 (E.D. Pa. 1976), appealed on other issues, 567 F.2d 569 (3d Cir. 1977) (applying New Jersey and Pennsylvania law) (accountant who was aware of the purpose and use of the report held liable for negligence to sellers of corporate stock who warranted the financials).

New York: White v. Guarente, 43 N.Y.2d 356, 372 N.E.2d 315 (N.Y. App. 1977) (auditor/tax preparer may be held liable to limited partners for negligence); Resnick v. Touche Ross & Co., 470 F. Supp. 1020 (S.D.N.Y. 1979) (allegation of recklessness against accounting firm by third-party investor held sufficient).

Pennsylvania: Guy v. Liederbach, 421 A.2d 333 (Pa. Super. 1980) (attorney who draws a will may be liable to a beneficiary under the will for negligence). Also see New Jersey.

Rhode Island: Rusch Factors v. Levin, 284 F. Supp. 85 (D.R.I. 1968) (CPA who knows financial statements are being prepared for submission to a lender may be held liable to the lender for negligence); Rhode Island Hospital Trust Nat'l Bank v. Swartz, Bresenoff, Yavner & Jacobs, 455 F.2d 847 (4th Cir. 1972) (auditors may be liable for negligence to foreseen and limited classes).

Texas: Shatterproof Glass Corp. v. James, 466 S.W.2d 873 (Tex. App. 1971) (Where an auditor was advised that the purpose of the audit was for use of an identified creditor, the auditor was required to use ordinary care for the creditor's benefit).

Utah: Milliner v. Elmer Fox & Co., 529 P.2d 806 (Utah 1974) (The court embraced the foreseeability rule but dismissed the suit against the accounting firm, holding that unidentified future purchasers of corporate shares are an unlimited class whose reliance cannot be reasonably foreseen).

mares[32] by holding that accountants are liable for ordinary negligence to third party users who are identified, limited, and foreseen at the time of the negligent conduct. Only a few jurisdictions still cling to the notion that accountants are liable to third parties only upon proof of intentional misrepresentation or gross negligence.[33]

PRACTICAL POINTERS

1. Consider the fact that continuing to serve as the client's accountant without disclosing that the client is engaging in a material breach of contract may constitute fraud. In *United States Nat'l Bank of Or. v. Fought,* 612 P.2d 754 (Or. App. 1980), the CPAs knew that the bank would rely upon them for information in connection with a bank-controlled cash collateral account that required deposit of all receipts and prior bank approval of all checks. The court held the CPAs were guilty of fraud and liable for $105,000 because they continued to supply information and lists of checks with-

---

32. See note 31, New York.

33. Florida courts have apparently adopted the foreseeability rule with respect to attorneys and other professionals, but apply the strict *Ultramares* rule to accountant cases. For Florida cases rejecting accountants' third-party liability for negligence, *see:* Investment Corp. of Fla. v. Buchman, 208 So. 2d 291 (Fla. App. 1968) (negligence liability rejected despite the fact that the auditor knew the audit would be relied upon by the investor/plaintiff); Canaveral Capital Corp. v. Bruce, 214 So. 2d 505 (Fla. App. 1968); Dubbin v. Touche Ross & Co., 324 So. 2d 128 (Fla. App. 1976); Mulligan v. Wallace, 349 So. 2d 745 (Fla. App. 1977); Investors Tax Sheltered Real Estate, Ltd. v. Laventhol, Krekstein, Horwath & Horwath, 370 So. 2d 815 (Fla. App. 1979); Nortek, Inc. v. Alexander Grant & Co., 532 F.2d 1013 (5th Cir. 1967).

For Florida cases adopting the foreseeability rule, *see* McAbee v. Edwards, 340 So. 2d 1167 (Fla. App. 1976) (attorney who draws will may be liable for negligence to a beneficiary under the will); Kovaleski v. Tallahassee Title, 363 So. 2d 1156 (Fla. App. 1978) (title abstractor may be liable to a third party for negligence).

In Stephens Indus., Inc. v. Haskins & Sells, 438 F.2d 357 (10th Cir. 1971), the United States Court of Appeals for the 10th Circuit, applying its view of Colorado law, rejected the contention that auditors were liable for negligence to a third-party purchaser of corporate stock of car-rental firms. Allegedly, the auditor knew that the plaintiff would rely on the audit report and that the report misrepresented accounts receivable. The audit engagement specifically relieved the auditors of responsibility for accounts receivable, and the auditors' opinion contained a notation that the auditors did not confirm accounts receivable or review their collectibility. The notes to the balance sheet also indicated that the accounts receivable balance was not adjusted for uncollectible accounts.

The court did not discuss whether it is appropriate to give an auditor's opinion on financial statements as a whole when the engagement does not include confirmation of accounts receivable. This issue seems certain to arise in future cases, since the AICPA guidelines now provide that where confirmation of material receivables or observation of material inventories is omitted, the auditor should generally "disclaim an opinion on the financial statements taken as a whole."

out disclosing that they knew the client had diverted receipts in this amount.

2. Failure to withdraw a previously issued report when you learn it is no longer reliable may constitute fraud. In *Fischer v. Kletz,* 266 F. Supp. 180 (S.D.N.Y. 1967), investors alleged that the auditors failed to disclose subsequently acquired information that made their previously issued audit report misleading. Applying New York law to a common-law count for deceit, the court quoted Prosser (*Law of Torts,* p. 696, 4th ed.) on an exception to the general rule that there is no liability in deceit for nondisclosure:

> Again, one who has made a statement, and subsequently acquires new information which makes it untrue or misleading, must disclose such information to any one whom he knows to be still acting on the basis of the original statement—as, for example, where there is a serious decline in the profits of a business pending its sale.
>
> The court noted that the liability question involved policy issues requiring a balancing of interests and refused to decide the matter on a motion to dismiss prior to full development of the facts.

NEGLIGENCE AS THE TEST FOR THIRD-PARTY LIABILITY

Courts have applied three different tests in holding public accountants and other professionals liable to third parties for ordinary negligence:

1. Whether the particular plaintiff and the loss transaction were foreseen at the time of the engagement,
2. Whether the class of plaintiff and type of transaction were foreseen at the time of the engagement, or
3. Whether a balancing of public policy factors, including foreseeability of the injury at the time of the engagement, justify imposing liability.

Particular Plaintiff and Transaction Foreseen

In *Ryan v. Kanne,*[34] decided in 1969, the Iowa Supreme Court dropped the "primary benefit" test and extended to third parties the right to recover against auditors for ordinary negligence if (1) the auditor knows the engagement is for the benefit and guidance of the third party and (2) the third party is identified before the statement or report is submitted by the auditor.

Plaintiffs in the case were certified public accountants who filed suit for their fee against James A. Kanne, Mid-States Enterprises, Inc., and Kanne Lumber and Supply, Inc. Kanne Lumber and Supply, Inc. filed a counterclaim for negligence against the accountants. The accountants' defense was that the corporation was not a client and could not sue them for negligence. Thus the CPAs found themselves in the incongruous position of suing a corporation for a fee while at the same time claiming they did not owe a duty of care to the corporation. Although the court awarded the plaintiff CPAs their fee of $3,434.67 plus interest and costs, the newly formed corporation recovered a judgment based on ordinary negligence of the accountants for $23,042.94. The judgment against the accountants was based on understatement of accounts payable plus the cost of a corrected report.

In *White v. Guarente,*[35] decided by the New York Court of Appeals in 1977, the court held that an accountant retained by a limited partnership to perform auditing and tax-return services may be held liable for negligence to an identifiable group of limited partners. Since the decision was on a motion by defendant Arthur Andersen & Co. to dismiss, the court did not pass on the validity of the allegations. It was alleged that Andersen knew or should have known that the general partners were withdrawing funds in violation of the partnership agreement and that the financials misrepresented the value of restricted securities held by the enterprise. The court said:

> Here, the services of the accountant were not extended to a faceless or unresolved class of persons, but rather to a known group possessed of vested rights, marked by a definable limit and made up of certain components. . . . The instant situation did not involve prospective limited partners, unknown at the time and who might be induced to join, but rather actual limited partners, fixed and determined. Here, accountant Andersen was retained to perform an audit and prepare the tax returns of Associates, known to be a limited partnership, and the accountant must have been aware that a limited partner would necessarily rely on or make use of the audit and tax returns of the partnership, or at least constituents of them, in order to properly prepare his or her own tax returns. This was within the contemplation of the accounting retainer. In such circumstances, assumption of the task of auditing and preparing the returns was the assumption of a duty to audit and prepare carefully for the benefit of those in the fixed, definable and contemplated group whose conduct was to be governed, since, given the contract and the relation, the duty is imposed by law and it is not necessary to state the duty in terms of contract or privity. . . .

---

34. Ryan v. Kanne, 170 N.W.2d 395 (Iowa 1969).

35. White v. Guarente, 43 N.Y.2d 356, 372 N.E.2d 315 (N.Y. 1977).

Class of User and Type of Transaction Foreseen

Business ethics of the past as expressed in *caveat emptor* are rapidly giving way to concepts of public responsibility. Prosser observed that "the law appears to be working toward the ultimate conclusion that full disclosure of all material facts must be made whenever elementary fair conduct demands it."[36]

This movement is reflected in § 522, Tentative Draft No. 12 of *Restatement of the Law Second: Torts,* which is a statement of what some scholars think the law should be:

> 1. One who, in the course of his business, profession or employment, or in a transaction in which he has a pecuniary interest, supplies false information for the guidance of others in their business transactions, is subject to liability for pecuniary loss caused to them by their justifiable reliance upon the information, if he fails to exercise reasonable care or competence in obtaining or communicating the information.
>
> 2. Except as stated in subsection (3), the liability stated in subsection (1) is limited to loss suffered
>
> a. By the person or one of the persons for whose benefit and guidance he intends to supply the information, or knows that the recipient intends to supply it.
>
> b. Through reliance upon it in a transaction which he intends the information to influence, or knows that the recipient so intends, or in a substantially similar transaction.[37]

Illustrations that follow § 522 show that when a CPA is not informed of the use of the reports but knows of their customary use in a wide variety of transactions the CPA would not be liable for ordinary negligence to a lender who suffered loss. If the client informs the CPA of loan negotiations with X Bank in mind, then the CPA would be liable to either X Bank or Y Bank in connection with a loan. The CPA is also liable if the loan is mentioned without reference to a specific bank. But if the CPA is told that the reports are to be used for bank credit, there would be no negligence liability in connection with trade credit. Similarly if the CPA is informed that a trade creditor will use the statements as a basis for extending trade credit, the CPA is not liable if the trade creditor buys the controlling interest in the corporation's stock and suffers loss.

The Federal District Court in *Rusch Factors, Inc. v. Levin*[38] construed the above *Restatement* illustrations as applications of the *Glanzer* principle to accountants. The case was in federal court only because of diversity of citizenship and subject matter in excess of $10,000. The court's application of the restatement principles was therefore viewed as application of state law.

The plaintiff, Rusch Factors, had requested certified financial statements as prerequisite to a loan. The defendant accountant prepared statements that allegedly showed the corporate borrower as solvent when it was insolvent. The borrower then submitted the statements to the plaintiff, who relied upon them in lending $337,000. The borrower went into receivership, and the lender brought suit against the accountant for loss of $121,000 as a result of reliance upon the allegedly negligent misrepresentations in the certified financial statements. In denying the defendant's motion to dismiss based on absence of privity of contract, the court, following the *Restatement,* said:

> With respect, then, to the plaintiff's negligence theory, the Court holds that an accountant should be liable in negligence for careless financial misrepresentations relied upon by actually foreseen and limited classes of persons. According to the plaintiff's complaint in the instant case, the defendant knew that his certification was to be used for, and had as its very aim and purpose, the reliance of potential financiers of the Rhode Island corporation. The defendant's motion is, therefore, denied.

The Court of Civil Appeals of Texas also followed the *Restatement* in its 1971 decision in *Shatterproof Glass Corp. v. James.*[39] The defendant certified public accountants were advised that the plaintiff was considering making "Paschal Enterprises" a distributor and that the plaintiff acted as "bankers" for its distributors. Allegedly the defendants prepared in 1963 a certified audit report that represented a net worth for Paschal Enterprises of approximately $173,000, whereas in reality the liabilities exceeded assets by approximately $150,000. The plaintiff claimed damages of $425,000 for an uncollectible loan to Paschal Enterprises made in reliance on the audit report. The court held that the defendants owed the plaintiffs a duty to exercise due care:

> We find and hold that within the scope defined in Restatement, Second, Torts, § 552 (Tent. Draft No. 12, 1966), an accountant may be held liable to third parties who rely upon financial statements, audits, etc., prepared by the accountant in cases where the latter fails to exercise ordinary care in the preparation of such statements, audits, etc., and the third party because of such reliance suffers financial loss or damage.

Similarly, in the 1973 decision of *Aluma Kraft Man-*

36. W. Prosser, *Law of Torts* 698, 4th ed. (1971).

37. *Restatement of the Law Second: Torts: Tentative Draft No. 12,* 14 (1966).

38. Rusch Factors, Inc. v. Levin, 284 F. Supp. 85 (D.R.I. 1968).

39. Shatterproof Glass Corp. v. James, 466 S.W.2d 873 (Tex. 1971).

ufacturing Co. v. Elmer Fox & Co.,[40] the court held that the complaint, which alleged that *negligent* auditors knew that their report would be used to determine book value to be paid by the plaintiff for Aluma Kraft stock, stated a good claim for relief.

In the 1972 decision of *Rhode Island Hospital Trust National Bank v. Swartz*[41] the United States Court of Appeals for the Fourth Circuit, applying Rhode Island law, cited both the *Restatement* and *Rusch Factors, Inc. v. Levin* and concluded that Rhode Island law would hold auditors liable for negligence in careless financial misrepresentations relied upon by actually foreseen and limited classes of persons.

This case is unusual in that it holds that an auditor may be liable for negligence to a third party despite the auditor's disclaimer of an opinion on the fairness of the financial statements. The reason given by the auditor for the disclaimer was:

> *Additions* to fixed assets in 1963 *were found* to include principally warehouse improvements and installation of machinery and equipment in Providence, Rhode Island, Brunswick, Georgia, and Palm Beach, Florida. Practically *all of this work was done by company employees and materials and overhead was borne by the International Trading Corporation and its affiliates.* Unfortunately, fully complete detailed cost records were not kept of these capital improvements and no exact determination could be made as to the actual cost of said improvements. (Emphasis added by the court.)

The court found that *no* cost records were kept, and capital improvements were fictitious; yet the disclaimer referred only to the problem of valuation and did not question the existence of the improvements. Accordingly, the court held that the auditor was negligent in failing to give a clear explanation of the reasons for the qualification and of the effect on financial position and results of operations as required by *CCH AICPA Professional Standards* § 509.32–33. The court's ruling, similar to the earlier holding in *Stanley L. Bloch, Inc. v. Klein* (see Chapter 5), was that AICPA rules constitute minimum standards for the profession.

The Minnesota case of *Bonhiver v. Graff*[42] decided in 1976 involved the third-party claim of a general insurance agent against a CPA who had undertaken to get the insurance firm's books up to date. The CPA never prepared financial statements, but displayed incomplete working papers to a team of examiners sent by the Minnesota Commissioner of Insurance. The CPA failed to investigate and discover the true nature of a number of transactions by which a massive fraud by management was being carried out. In sustaining the agent's suit against the CPA for negligence, the court rejected the idea that liability for negligence requires foreseeability as to the particular plaintiffs and embraced the *Restatement* concept of imposing liability for foreseeable classes. The court seemed to have some difficulty in identifying the particular classes falling within the foreseeability rule; however, it identified the plaintiff as within a protected class:

> Wherever the line will eventually be drawn between those who can recover from the negligent accountant and those who cannot, we feel that on the facts of this case Delmont falls on the side of those who can recover. Delmont was one of two general agents of American Allied. When rumors of American Allied collapse began to spread, Delmont suspended American Allied sales and Frank Delmont personally went to the commissioner in order to determine the status of the company. When the commissioner reassured Delmont that American Allied was financially sound, he resumed sales. This personal reliance, indirect though it may be through the commissioner, was reasonable on the part of Delmont and sufficient to accord him protection against defendants' negligence.

Negligence Liability Justified by Public Policy Factors

Some courts weigh various policy factors relating to each factual situation in deciding whether to impose liability for negligence to a nonclient third party. These include:

1. The extent to which the transaction was intended to affect the plaintiff.
2. The foreseeability of plaintiff's loss or injury.
3. The degree of certainty of plaintiff's loss or injury.
4. The closeness of the connection between the defendant's conduct and plaintiff's loss or injury.
5. The moral blame associated with defendant's conduct.
6. The policy of preventing future harm.

The California Supreme Court looked to these policy factors in deciding that a notary public who undertook to prepare a will could be held liable for negligence to a beneficiary under a will.[43] In a later case the California Supreme Court held that an attorney could also be held liable for negligence to the beneficiary of a will.[44]

40. Aluma Kraft Mfg. Co. v. Elmer Fox & Co., 493 S.W.2d 378 (Mo. Ct. App. 1973).
41. Rhode Island Hospital Trust National Bank v. Swartz, Bresenoff, Yavner & Jacobs, 455 F.2d 847 (4th Cir. 1972).
42. Bonhiver v. Graff, 248 N.W.2d 291 (S. Ct. Minn. 1976).
43. Biakanja v. Irving, 49 Cal. 2d 647, 320 P.2d 16 (1958).
44. Lucas v. Hamm, 364 P.2d 685 (1961), *cert. denied* 368 U.S. 987 (1962).

In a case of first impression in Pennsylvania, an appellate court adopted this balancing test in ruling that an attorney could be held liable to a beneficiary under a will on both negligence and contract (third-party beneficiary) theories.[45]

PRACTICAL POINTERS

1. Consider limiting compilations to internal use to avoid liability to third parties. (See the sample engagement letter in Chapter 13).

2. Whenever you have a limited partnership client, never prepare financials restricted to internal use; you know the limited partners must have access to the information and they are not internal management.

3. Always assume you may be liable to third parties. Some ingenious third parties have been able to sue as the client: they sue the client for misrepresentation, and in the same action the client files a third-party complaint against the accountant for *negligence*. For an illustration including counts for both negligence and breach of contract, see *Taylor v. G I Export Corp.*, 78 F.R.D. 494 (E.D.N.Y. 1978).

CIVIL ACTIONS UNDER STATE AND FEDERAL STATUTES

Accountants have been held liable to third parties in connection with tax advice and sale of tax-sheltered investments based on both state blue-sky laws and federal securities laws. These situations are discussed in Chapter 12. Liability under federal securities laws is broadly covered in Chapter 8. Although every state has laws imposing penalties for violation of its securities laws,[46] some provide for recovery of more damages than are available under either common law or federal securities laws. For example, Florida law provides for recovery of "the full amount paid by the purchaser together with interest, damages, court costs, and reasonable attorneys fees, including appeals, upon tender of the securities sold or of the contract made."[47]

New York courts now hold that the New York penal statute implies a civil cause of action.[48] New York General Business Law § 352-C makes it a misdemeanor to engage in fraud or misrepresentation "where engaged in to induce or promote the issuance, distribution, exchange, sale, negotiation or purchase . . . of any securities. . . . "

THIRD-PARTY LIABILITY FOR NEGLIGENCE OF GOVERNMENTAL AUDITORS

There is some question as to whether the U.S., state, and local governmental units and the employees performing audit functions may be held liable to third parties for negligence. In *Social Security Administration Federal Credit Union v. United States*[49] the credit union brought suit under the Federal Tort Claims Act to recover embezzlement losses on the ground that federal examiners were negligent in failing to discover it. In finding that the examiners had no duty to the credit union, the court considered the limited (1) scope of federal supervision, (2) number of federal examiners, and (3) qualifications and low pay (most were not CPAs).

In other factual situations, it is quite possible that liability may be imposed. For example, in *United States v. Neustadt*,[50] purchasers of a home recovered damages from the United States because of negligence of an agent of the federal housing commissioner in making an appraisal of the property. In affirming the verdict, the court noted that the Tort Claims Act excludes any claim for misrepresentation or deceit but found that the wrongful conduct was the negligent appraisal itself and not merely or chiefly the communication to the plaintiff. The court also cited a precedent involving a ship collision where the Coast Guard negligently failed to find a submerged channel light and the bulletin contained a misrepresentation of facts.

SUMMARY

Public accountants recognize that a primary function of audits is to supply information to persons who are not their clients. If their liability is to be related to responsibility reasonably assumed and compensation paid, then public accountants must know the identity of the particular group of persons and possible transactions for which they will be responsible so as to make their fee commensurate with the risk and responsibility assumed.

Public accountants are liable to third parties for gross negligence (for example, certifying without

---

45. *Guy v. Liederbach*, 421 A.2d (Pa. Super. 1980).

46. For citation of all the statutes and discussion of their interstate application, see Note, "Interstate Scope of the Uniform Securities Act," 1974 *Wash. U.L.Q.* 421 (1974).

47. F.S.A. § 517.211.

48. *Barnes v. Peat, Marwick, Mitchell & Co.*, 69 Misc. 2d 1068 (Spec. Term 1972), *aff'd*, 42 App. Div. 2d 15 (1st Dept. 1973).

49. Social Security Administration Fed. Credit Union v. United States, 138 F. Supp. 639 (D. Md. 1956).

50. United States v. Neustadt, 281 F.2d 596 (4th Cir. 1960).

knowledge) in a common-law action of deceit. Where the public accountant's work is primarily for the benefit of an identified third-party plaintiff, the auditor is liable for ordinary negligence.

The trend is toward increasing responsibility and holding public accountants liable for ordinary negligence to third persons where the accountant can reasonably foresee the parties and the transactions giving rise to loss.

SUGGESTIONS FOR FURTHER READING

Annot. "Liability of Public Accountant to Third Parties." 46 *American Law Reports* 3d 979, 1972.

Causey, Denzil Y., Jr. "Foreseeability as a Determinant of Audit Responsibility." *Accounting Review*, April 1973, pp. 258-67.

Prosser, William L. *Law of Torts.* 4th ed. St. Paul, Minn.: West Publishing, 1971.

————. "Misrepresentation and Third Persons." *Vanderbilt Law Review,* March 1966, pp. 231-55.

Stern, Duke Nordlinger. *An Accountant's Guide to Malpractice Liability.* Charlottesville, Va.: Michie Company, 1979.

QUESTIONS AND PROBLEMS

1. Who are the users for whom audit reports are designed? Do they usually have a contract with the auditor?
2. If the accountant focuses on the needs of investors and creditors, will the reports serve other interested parties? If you think not, explain why and give specific illustrations.
3. Enumerate two shades of foreseeability that the courts use as conditions for imposing auditors' liability to third parties.
4. In what circumstances may a third-party beneficiary recover on a contract?
5. What trend do you perceive with respect to rights of third parties to recover for the auditor's failure to carry out duties created by contract?
6. Distinguish the *Ultramares* case from *Glanzer.* In what ways are the cases similar? If the auditor in *Ultramares* had been requested to send a report directly to the third-party lender, do you think the court would have reached the result in *Glanzer*?
7. Does *State Street Trust Co. v. Ernst* extend the auditor's liability beyond *Ultramares?* If so, how?
8. (From the November 1979 Uniform CPA Exam)
   Part a. Marcall is a limited partner of Guarcross, a limited partnership, and is suing a CPA firm which was retained by the limited partnership to perform auditing and tax-return preparation services. Guarcross was formed for the purpose of investing in a diversified portfolio of risk capital securities. The partnership agreement included the following provisions:

   The initial capital contribution of each limited partner shall not be less than $250,000; no partner may withdraw any part of his interest in the partnership, except at the end of any fiscal year upon giving written notice of such intention not less than 30 days prior to the end of such year; the books and records of the partnership shall be audited as of the end of the fiscal year by a certified public accountant designated by the general partners; and proper and complete books of account shall be kept and shall be open to inspection by any of the partners or his or her accredited representative.

   Marcall's claim of malpractice against the CPA firm centers on the firm's alleged failure to comment, in its audit report, on the withdrawal by the general partners of $2 million of their $2.6 million capital investment based on back-dated notices, and the lumping together of the $2 million withdrawals with $49,000 in withdrawals by limited partners so that a reader of the financial statement would not be likely to realize that the two general partners had withdrawn a major portion of their investments.

   The CPA firm's contention is that its contract was made with the limited partnership, not its partners. It further contends that since the CPA firm had no privity of contract with the third-party limited partners, the limited partners have no right of action for negligence.

   Required:
   Answer the following, setting forth reasons for any conclusions stated: Discuss the various theories Marcall would rely upon in order to prevail in a lawsuit against the CPA firm.

   Part b. Farr & Madison, CPAs, audited Glamour, Inc. Their audit was deficient in several respects:
   (1) Farr and Madison failed to verify properly certain receivables which later proved to be fictitious.
   (2) With respect to other receivables, although they made a cursory check, they did not detect many accounts which were long overdue and obviously uncollectible.
   (3) No physical inventory was taken of the securities claimed to be in Glamour's possession, which in fact had been sold. Both the securities and cash received from the sales were listed on the balance sheet as assets.

   There is no indication that Farr & Madison actually believed that the financial statements were false. Subsequent creditors, not known to Farr & Madison, are now suing based upon the deficiencies in the audit described above. Farr and Madison moved to dismiss the lawsuit against it on the basis that the firm did not have actual knowledge of falsity and therefore did not commit fraud.

   Required:
   Answer the following, setting forth reasons for any conclusions stated: May the creditors recover without demonstrating Farr & Madison had actual knowledge of falsity?

7

Common-Law Defenses

This chapter covers:

- COMPLIANCE WITH THE USUAL PROFESSIONAL STANDARD.
- LACK OF RELIANCE OR CAUSATION.
- RELEASE OR SATISFACTION OF RECOVERABLE LOSSES.
- FAILURE OF AN UNFORESEEABLE THIRD PARTY TO PROVE RECKLESS CONDUCT.
- STATUTES OF LIMITATION.
- RIGHTS TO INDEMNITY, CONTRIBUTION, OR DAMAGES FOR WRONGFUL SUIT.
- PLAINTIFF'S FAILURE TO MINIMIZE DAMAGES.
- PLAINTIFF'S CONTRIBUTORY NEGLIGENCE.
- PRIVILEGE IN A DEFAMATION CASE.

COMPLIANCE WITH THE USUAL PROFESSIONAL STANDARD

In order to prove a malpractice claim, plaintiffs must prove that the defendant deviated from the usual professional standard in the community. Plaintiffs are not entitled to perfection, nor to the performance provided by the best CPAs—only average care and competence. Unless the deviation from average standards is patent, such as failure to prepare a tax return in time for filing, it is necessary for plaintiffs to present expert

testimony[1] to show the usual professional practice in the particular community and then prove defendant's deviation from it. The fact that advice or financials prove wrong does not necessarily indicate malpractice. This is true in all functional areas, such as auditing, tax-return preparation, tax advice, investment advice, and accounting services.

Auditing

CPAs do not guarantee audited financials, but rather represent that they have applied usual professional standards with respect to them. While application of usual professional standards would likely uncover kiting or lapping, it would not necessarily reveal forged checks. An auditor is generally expected to observe the inventory count and either control the inventory count tags or observe the client's control, however, the fact that the inventory and profits are materially wrong does not necessarily establish that the auditor is guilty of malpractice. For example, in *Delmar Vineyard v. Timmons*[2] there was evidence that the CPA omitted some payables and used the wrong percentage in converting retail inventory to cost. In rejecting the claim for malpractice the court said:

> Generally, it is established law throughout this country that an accountant does not guarantee correct judgment, or even the best professional judgment, but merely reasonable care and competence. . . .
>
> The standard of care applicable to the conduct of audits by public accountants is the same as that applied to doctors, lawyers, architects, engineers and others furnishing skilled services for compensation and that standard requires reasonable care and competence therein.

Tax Return Preparation

Tax return preparation involves evaluating many gray-zone items that ultimately may be resolved either way. The tax preparer is not responsible for an adverse determination of such items. If the preparer makes an error that results in penalties, interest, and additional taxes, there is usually no liability for the additional taxes, since the client owed the taxes anyway. However, the preparer could be liable for taxes erroneously paid that are now barred by the three-year limitation period for filing amended returns. There should be no

---

1. See notes 34 and 37 in Chapter 1. In Lucas v. Hamm, 364 P.2d 685 (Cal. 1961), *cert. denied*, 368 U.S. 987 (1962), the court ruled as a matter of law that alleged violation of the rule against perpetuities by an attorney drawing a will did not constitute negligence.

2. Delmar Vineyard v. Timmons, 486 S.W.2d 914 (Tenn. App. 1972).

94

liability for the interest, since the client had the use of the money. There is no liability for the penalties if the preparer applied the usual standard of care with respect to the situation.

Consider *Lindner v. Barlow, Davis & Wood*[3] where the CPAs prepared five years of federal income tax returns. They relied on W–2 forms in assuming that corporate payments to a widow were taxable. After an attorney obtained a refund of taxes for the three open years, the widow sued the CPAs for taxes paid in the two closed years. The CPAs proved that they followed the "usual practice" in San Francisco, which was to accept W–2 forms as evidence of taxability. In rejecting the malpractice claim, the court quoted the following:

> Accountants have been recognized as a skilled professional class . . . subject generally to the same rules of liability for negligence in the practice of their profession as are members of other skilled professions. . . .
>
> They have a duty to exercise the *ordinary* skill and competence of members of their profession, and a failure to discharge that duty will subject them to liability for negligence. Those who hire such persons *are not justified in expecting infallibility*, but can expect only reasonable care and competence. *They purchase service, not insurance*.

Tax Advice

Sometimes CPAs give tax advice based on a Circuit Court of Appeals decision only to have the matter decided adversely in the circuit where the advice is applied. At other times it may be necessary to give advice in situations where there is a lack of judicial authority at the time the advice is given, and later decisions may prove the advice wrong. These situations do not constitute malpractice provided the CPA applied the usual standard of care.

Consider *Smith v. St. Paul Fire & Marine Ins. Co.*[4] where the lawyer gave tax advice and prepared a return where there was a lack of authority on the particular matter. A later court decision proved the advice and resulting tax return wrong. In rejecting the claim for malpractice, the court noted that other competent practitioners were giving similar advice at the time and said:

> An attorney who acts in good faith and in an honest belief that his advice and acts are well founded and in the best interest of his client is not answerable for a mere error of judgment or for a mistake on a point of

law which has not been settled by the court of last resort in his State and on which reasonable doubt may be entertained by well-informed lawyers.

Investment Advice

Public accountants who act as investment advisors are bound to exercise care in recommending a particular investment but, in absence of a specific agreement, do not guarantee the soundness of investments they recommend. Thus, in *Midland Nat'l Bank of Minneapolis v. Perranoski*[5] the CPA was held not liable to investors, despite the fact that the investors lost their investment and had to pay an additional sum to cover creditors because the investments involved a partnership instead of a limited partnership or corporation. In finding the CPA not liable, the court said it would have been unreasonable to expect the CPA to foresee the fall in cattle prices that caused the losses.

Accounting Services

The CPA performing accounting services is responsible only for the usual standard of care involved in the particular engagement. CPAs have been held not liable for errors or embezzlement because of the limited nature of the particular engagement.[6]

LACK OF RELIANCE OR CAUSATION

Even if the conduct of public accountants falls below the usual standard of care, they are not liable unless the particular failure caused someone a loss. Regardless of whether plaintiffs are clients or third parties, they must prove that they relied on the accountant's work so as to relate their loss to the malpractice.[7] Some claims against accountants have been

3. Lindner v. Barlow, Davis & Wood, 27 Cal. Rptr. 101 (Cal. App. 1963).

4. Smith v. St. Paul Fire & Marine Ins. Co., 366 F. Supp. 1283 (M.D. La. 1973), *aff'd per curiam*, 500 F.2d 1131 (5th Cir. 1974).

5. Midland Nat'l Bank of Minneapolis v. Perranoski, 299 N.W.2d 404 (Minn. 1980).

6. For cases holding the CPA not liable because the financials were not audited, see note 33 in Chapter 5. For cases holding the CPA not liable because of a disclaimer, see note 11 in Chapter 5.

7. Kemmerlin v. Wingate, 261 S.E.2d 50 (S.C. 1979) (malpractice suit by client dismissed because there was no evidence of damages proximately caused by accounting firm's negligence); Vernon J. Rockler & Co. v. Glickman, Isenberg, Lurie & Co., 273 N.W.2d 647 (Minn. 1978) (client's closing of short sales out of investment account and loss of capital gains treatment was based on necessity and not upon tax advice given by CPA); Delmar Vineyard v. Timmons, 486 S.W.2d 914 (Tenn. App. 1972) (owners of a retail store could not recover losses incurred from continuing in business where they did not rely upon the audit and agreed with the CPA as to the cost ratio used in deriving the inventory); Stanley L. Bloch, Inc. v. Klein, 258 N.Y.S.2d 501 (Sup. Ct. N.Y. Cty. 1965) (client could not recover losses from remaining in business because other available information concerning the situation indicated a lack of reliance upon the CPA's work); Flagg v. Seng, 60 P.2d 1004 (Cal. 1936) (the trustee in bankruptcy could not recover from auditors for unlawful dividends where the auditors booked

dismissed because the plaintiffs never saw the allegedly erroneous reports or saw them after the transaction that resulted in loss.[8]

The case of *Vanderbilt Growth Fund, Inc. v. Superior Court*[9] provides a good illustration of the reliance/causation defense. Client firms sued Arthur Young & Co. alleging that it failed to determine that certain restricted securities had been overvalued. Arthur Young's motion for summary judgment was properly granted because AY demonstrated that the securities were worthless both before and after the audit so that any negligence or breach of contract by AY could not have caused plaintiffs' losses where they merely continued their investment.

The case of *Bunge Corp. v. Eide*[10] is another good example of the reliance/causation defense. The plaintiff was engaged in financing of grain for the CPA's audit client. In audit reports for 1963 through 1968, the CPAs permitted sunflower seeds to be valued at local market (there was no quoted market). The defendants disclaimed an opinion in their report for the period ending June 30, 1969, because of errors in quantities and prices. The errors were all "one way" and overstated quantities and values:

> Because of the inadequate inventory procedures we were unable to substantiate the correctness of inventory quantity, quality and price. Because inventories enter materially into the determination of financial position and results of operations, we express no opinion on the accompanying financial statements.

In a note to the accompanying financial statements the defendants stated:

It has been the practice in prior years to value unprocessed sunflower inventories at cost plus a "market escalation." Inasmuch as there is not a ready market quotation available for unprocessed sunflowers as there is in the case of grain, the company has changed their method of valuation of unprocessed sunflowers from an approximate market value to cost. Had this method of valuation been used in the preceding year, the net loss for the current year would have been $149,536.00.

The court noted that *AICPA Accounting Research Bulletin No. 43* provides:

> Only in exceptional cases may inventories properly be stated above cost. For example, precious metals having a fixed inventory value with no substantial cost of marketing may be stated at such inventory value; any other exceptions must be justifiable by inability to determine appropriate approximate costs, immediate marketability at quoted market price, and the characteristic of unit interchangeability. Where goods are stated above cost, this fact should be fully disclosed.

The court refused to impose liability on the CPAs, despite a finding that "defendants' method of stating unprocessed sunflower inventories at local market was not in accordance with generally accepted accounting principles."

The case was tried in a federal court only because of diversity of citizenship, and the court was thus obliged to apply state law. Although there were no North Dakota decisions on the point, the court speculated that North Dakota would impose liability for negligence only to a "primary beneficiary" of the audit report. The court found it unnecessary to resolve the issue, however. Reasoning that there was insufficient reliance by the plaintiff on the audit reports and that the defendants did not *materially* misrepresent the financial condition, the court held there was insufficient causation to impose liability, even under a negligence standard. The court found that the plaintiffs knew the value of the unprocessed sunflowers was stated at local market and that the plaintiffs relied on their discussions with Gunkelman principals, not on the audit reports.

Effects of Disclaimers on Justifiable Reliance

A number of courts have held that the CPA's disclaimer was such that reliance was not warranted so that the CPA was not liable.[11] Several courts have held that reliance is not warranted where the CPA indicates the financials are not audited.[12]

---

gains on the exchanges of real estate and land acquired for corporate stock on orders of the directors, who were in no way deceived by the auditors); Donovan Constr. Co. of Minn. v. Woosley, 358 F. Supp. 375 (W.D. Ark. 1973) (applying Arkansas law) (suit dismissed since plaintiff did not rely upon certified financial statements in entering into loss contracts); Eikelburger v. Rogers, 549 P.2d 748 (Nev. 1976) (judgment was entered for CPA sued for errors in statements prepared for opposing party in litigation with plaintiffs because plaintiffs did not rely on them and to the contrary challenged them in the litigation) (query whether the statements were subject to the absolute privilege conferred on witnesses and others involved in judicial proceedings?)

For the effect on justifiable reliance of a disclaimer or an indication that the financials were not audited, see notes 11 and 33 in Chapter 5.

8. Landy v. FDIC, 486 F.2d 139, 168 (3d Cir. 1973), *cert. denied,* 416 U.S. 960 (1974) (claims dismissed for those plaintiffs who had not seen CPA's report distributed only to bank directors); Wessel v. Buhler, 437 F.2d 279 (9th Cir. 1971) (unaudited financials were prepared by CPA on two dates and audited financials on another; assuming they were misleading, there could be no liability since none were disseminated and plaintiff stockholders never saw them until after the litigation began).

9. Vanderbilt Growth Fund, Inc. v. Superior Court, 164 Cal. Rptr. 621 (Cal. App. 1980).

10. Bunge Corp. v. Eide, 372 F. Supp. 1058 (D.N.D. 1974) (applying North Dakota law).

11. See note 11 in Chapter 5.
12. See note 33 in Chapter 5.

In *Stephens Indus., Inc. v. Haskins & Sells,*[13] the auditor was held not liable to a third party investor where the audit engagement specifically relieved the auditor of responsibility for accounts receivable, the auditor's opinion contained a notation that disclaimed confirmation and review of their collectibility, and notes to the balance sheet indicated that the accounts receivable balance had not been adjusted for uncollectible accounts. The court did not discuss whether it is appropriate to give an auditor's opinion on financial statements as a whole when the engagement does not include confirmation of accounts receivable. This issue seems certain to arise in such cases in the future, since GAAS now provide that the auditor should generally disclaim an opinion where confirmation of receivables or observation of inventories is omitted.

PRACTICAL POINTER

If the auditor is to benefit from a disclaimer or qualification, it is important that it be clearly and fully communicated simultaneously with related financial information. In *State Street Trust Co. v. Ernst*, 15 N.E.2d 416 (1938), *rehearing denied*, 16 N.E.2d 851, the auditor was held liable to a third-party creditor on the basis of fraud where only one copy of an explanatory letter followed the 10 copies of the financial statements by one month. The letter explained limitations on scope of the audit and reservations as to the financial statements.

In *Rhode Island Hospital Trust Nat'l Bank v. Swartz, Bresenoff, Yavner & Jacobs*, 455 F.2d 847 (4th Cir. 1972), the auditors discussed additions to fixed assets, stating "fully complete detailed cost records were not kept of these capital improvements," when in fact there were no capital improvements. The court held this was negligence, which made the auditors liable to the lender if, upon remand, the lower court made a finding of reliance in making the loan.

Shifting Reliance to Other Auditors

Apparently an auditor can divide responsibility with other auditors so long as the audit report clearly explains the divided responsibility. AICPA auditing rules require an auditor using the work of another auditor to make "inquiries concerning the professional reputation and independence of the other auditor" and "adopt appropriate measures to assure the coordination of his activities with those of the other auditor in order to achieve a proper review of matters affecting the consolidating or combining of accounts."

The auditor must elect whether to accept full responsibility (other auditors are not mentioned in the report) or to divide responsibility with other auditors (the report must indicate clearly the division of responsibility). Where responsibility is divided by the mention of other auditors, it is not necessary to name the other auditors. The other auditors may be named, but only under circumstances where their express permission is obtained and their report is presented together with the report of the principal auditor. When other auditors are mentioned, the report should disclose the magnitude of the portion of the financials examined by other auditors by stating the dollar amounts or percentages of one or more of the following: total assets, total revenues, and other appropriate criteria.[14]

In *Beardsley v. Ernst,*[15] decided in 1934, the defendant auditors were held not liable to third parties for false financial statements when their certificate showed that consolidated statements were based on statements from abroad with respect to foreign constituent companies. The certificate read:

> We hereby certify that we have examined the books of account and records of International Match Corporation and its American Subsidiary company at December 31, 1929, and have received statements from abroad with respect to the foreign constituent companies as of the same date. Based upon our examination and information submitted to us it is our opinion that the annexed Consolidated Balance Sheet sets forth the financial condition of the combined companies at the date stated, and that the related Consolidated Income and Surplus Account is correct.

The plaintiff had purchased bonds and preferred stock in reliance upon the auditors' certification of the consolidated financial statements for 1929 and 1930. The Ohio court noted that *Ultramares* had held that an action for fraudulent misrepresentation by auditors could be sustained if "the defendant accountants made a statement as true to their own knowledge when they had no knowledge on the subject." But in holding for the auditors the court noted that the language used in the certificates showed that the auditors had not examined the books and records of the foreign constituent companies.

---

13. Stephens Indus., Inc. v. Haskins & Sells, 438 F.2d 357 (10th Cir. 1971 (applying Colorado law).

14. *CCH AICPA Professional Standards,* AU § 543.

15. Beardsley v. Ernst, 191 N.E. 808 (Ohio 1934). A financial disaster in Canada resulted from auditors of a parent company relying on opinions of other auditors for subsidiary companies whose receivables caused trouble. Professor A. Beedle of the University of British Columbia had this to say: "If there is any lesson to be learned from the Atlantic disaster, it is that the auditor of a parent company, in expressing an unqualified opinion on consolidated financial statements, must take full responsibility for the opinions of auditors of subsidiary companies and that he should be liable, within the framework of the law of agency, for the consequences of their shortcomings." See "Atlantic Acceptance Corporation—A Sorry Affair," *Journal of Accountancy,* August 1971, pp. 63-67.

Although an auditor may rely on the work of other auditors and divide responsibility by appropriate wording in the certificates, reliance may not be placed on unaudited data. Failure to disclaim in such a case could be construed as making statements without knowledge and thus could result in liability to third parties.

AICPA standards are still lacking in that they fail to require the certifying auditor to accept responsibility for substantially all of the assets on any certified balance sheet.

Effect of Silent Withdrawal upon Reliance

Where public accountants voluntarily or involuntarily withdraw, there is apparently no liability for remaining silent if there has been no association with the client's financial representations. For example, in *Gold v. DCL, Inc.*[16] a suit against Price Waterhouse & Co. was dismissed, since Price was fired prior to issuing what would have been a qualified opinion. The court held that Price had no duty to publicly announce its *intended* qualification upon DCL's announcement of *unaudited* earnings, although the company ignored Price's warning to say the earnings were subject to remarketing certain inventory items.

PRACTICAL POINTER

Where the CPA learns that the client is misleading or attempting to mislead others, the CPA should consult legal counsel as to whether the factual setting permits withdrawal in silence. The CPA's own counsel may want to consider the propriety of a meeting with the client and the client's counsel to discuss disclosure responsibilities. For related cases, see *Spectrum Financial Companies v. Marconsult, Inc.*, 608 F.2d 377 (9th Cir. 1979), *cert. denied*, 446 S.Ct. 936 (1980) (although the certified financials had never been seen by plaintiffs, the court found there was a triable issue as to the accounting firm's duty to disclose that a buyer had been found for what was essentially worthless stock); *Mallis v. Bankers Trust Co.*, 615 F.2d 68 (2d Cir. 1980) (there was a triable issue as to whether the bank was liable for negligence under New York law for failure to disclose to the buyer that the stock certificate that the bank held as loan collateral had been recalled by the issuer).

Exceptions to Reliance Requirement under Federal Securities Laws

The requirement for proof of reliance/causation has been modified in some instances where the claims are based on federal securities laws as opposed to the common law. Since there is no way to prove reliance upon an omission, reliance is presumed upon proof of a material omission. Where the securities are publicly traded, it is presumed that misrepresentations are reflected in the market price and affect all who trade until there is a full disclosure of the true facts. For discussion of these situations under federal securities laws, see Chapter 8.

RELEASE OR SATISFACTION OF RECOVERABLE LOSSES

Single-Recovery Limitation

The general rule of law is that where the plaintiff's claim is paid in full, the plaintiff is barred from any further recovery. Partial recoveries reduce *pro tanto* any amount recoverable for the injuries. The rule applies both where wrongdoers acted in concert and where wrongdoers acted independently to produce a single, indivisible result.[17] Thus where the seller of a business and a CPA, either acting in concert or independently, misrepresent the financial position, the plaintiff buyer cannot recover his full loss twice.

The only exception to the single-recovery limitation is made under the "collateral source doctrine," which provides that compensation or indemnity received by an injured party from a collateral source, wholly independent of the wrongdoer and to which he has not contributed, will not diminish the damages otherwise recoverable from the wrongdoer.

In *Franklin Supply Co. v. Tolman*,[18] Franklin Supply Co. (Franklin) agreed to purchase the stock of a Venezuela corporation, Petroleum Industry Consul-

---

17. W. Prosser, *Law of Torts* 300, 4th ed. (1971).

18. Franklin Supply Co. v. Tolman, 454 F.2d 1059 (9th Cir. 1972). This case involved an interesting interpretation of the lower-of-cost-or-market rule for valuation of inventory. The court found that Peat, Marwick, Mitchell's interpretation of replacement value as "current costs from usual and regular sources of supply" had substantial support. PMM presented testimony from the late Robert Trueblood and Carman Blough to support this view. An audit prepared by Arthur Andersen & Co., which was introduced in evidence, had reexamined inventory valuations and, by using the price of *surplus* materials on the local market for replacement value, reduced the PMM figure by approximately $465,000.

Apparently basing the rulings on testimony by Eric Kohler, the author of *Kohler's Dictionary for Accountants,* the court found that the audit report should have disclosed (1) that PMM's audit supervisor was an alternate director of Servicios and (2) the basis of prices used in determining "current replacement value." The appellate court ruled, however, that such "nondisclosure," as opposed to active concealment, would not support the trial court's award of punitive damages.

---

16. Gold v. DCL, Inc., CCH Fed. Sec. L. Rep. ¶ 94,036 (S.D.N.Y. 1973). *Also see* Grimm v. Whitney-Fidalgo Seafoods, Inc., CCH Fed. Sec. L. Rep. ¶ 96,029 (S.D.N.Y. 1973) (action dismissed since Price Waterhouse & Co. had not audited nor compiled interim financials).

tants C.A. (Peticon), from Servicios Hydrocarb C.A. (Servicios) at the book value of the stock with inventory to be valued at the lower of cost or current replacement value. The parties employed Peat, Marwick, Mitchell & Co. (PMM), auditors for Servicios, to perform an audit of Peticon, with the parties to share the accounting fee equally.

A lawsuit between Franklin and Servicios concerning alleged overvaluation of the inventory was settled by a price reduction of $200,000 with a stipulation providing for a reservation of rights by Franklin against PMM. Franklin then sued PMM. The U.S. Court of Appeals for the 9th Circuit affirmed the trial court's finding of damages of $200,000, based on overpricing of inventory, but held that the plaintiff had already been compensated by that amount in the settlement with Servicios and was not entitled to a double recovery from PMM. The Court of Appeals held that the "collateral source doctrine" did not apply, since both Servicios and PMM were charged with causing the same injury.

Release of Joint Tortfeasors

The common-law rule is that the release of one joint tortfeasor releases all of them, even if there is a specific reservation of rights against those not parties to the settlement. The basis for the rule is that each joint tortfeasor is liable for the entire injury and that the injured party is entitled to only one satisfaction. This rule has been abrogated by statute in some jurisdictions and is avoided in others by recognizing the device of a convenant not to sue, whereby the liability continues but the injured party agrees not to enforce any rights against the settling party. Apparently only Washington and Virginia adhere to the strict common-law rule. Regardless of any reservation of rights or agreement to the contrary, any amount received must be credited to reduce the damages recoverable from anyone liable for the loss.[19]

PRACTICAL POINTER

Accounting defendants should carefully scrutinize the language used in any settlements and releases executed with other parties responsible for the same loss. The wording of the documents may have released all parties. Consider *MacKethan v. Burrus, Cootes and Burrus*, 545 F.2d 1388 (4th Cir. 1976), where the receiver of a savings and loan corporation obtained a jury verdict of $1.1 million against an accounting partnership and its three partners based on allegations of aiding and abetting violations of section 10(b) of the Exchange Act. However, the receiver had previously settled with other defendants for $6 million. Despite the fact that total losses claimed were between $10 and $11 million, the court held that the judgment against the accounting firm of $1.1 million was satisfied by the $6 million settlement. To obtain an unsatisfied judgment, plaintiff's verdict must have exceeded the $6 million settlement.

Limits on Recoverable Losses

In a fraud case, the damages are limited to plaintiff's out-of-pocket losses. Thus in *Berkowitz v. Baron*[20] the CPA was held liable on a fraud theory after a long trial in federal court. However, damages against the accounting firm were limited to investor expenditures of $550, since the investors never paid the purchase price for the acquired firm, which went into bankruptcy. For a comprehensive analysis of recoverable damages, see Chapter 5 at note 59.

FAILURE OF AN UNFORESEEABLE THIRD PARTY TO PROVE RECKLESS CONDUCT

While public accountants are liable to clients and foreseeable third parties for negligence, others must prove fraud or recklessness that constitutes an extreme departure from professional standards. In order to provide a reasonable limit for professional responsibility, liability should be imposed to unforeseeable plaintiffs only where the danger that caused the loss was foreseeable at the time of the deficient work. In this way recklessness is measured by the perceived risk and the egregiousness of the conduct in the particular factual setting.

The case of *McLean v. Alexander*[21] provides an example of the reckless test under section 10(b) of the Exchange Act, which is also helpful for evaluating third-party, common-law liability. The court refused to hold the CPA liable for a scheme to defraud an investor of more than $1 million in a private placement where the only audit deficiencies involved accounts receivable that proved to be consignments. In confirming accounts receivable of less than $75,000, the CPA had no reason to anticipate a danger of such magnitude or that the only product of the technologically oriented client was unmarketable. However, had the CPA been sued on a common-law negligence theory, the plaintiff might have prevailed if the *investor had been sufficiently foreseen* at the time of defective performance.

The distinctions applied above afford a reasonable standard for professional conduct. Due care must be

---

19. W. Prosser, *Law of Torts* 301-5, 4th ed. (1971).

20. Berkowitz v. Baron, 428 F. Supp. 1190 (S.D.N.Y. 1977).
21. McLean v. Alexander, 599 F.2d 1190 (3d Cir. 1979).

applied for the benefit of foreseeable third parties. CPAs are also required to avoid extreme departures from professional standards that constitute foreseeable dangers to unforeseen third parties.

STATUTES OF LIMITATION

Each state has limitation periods during which suit can be brought on claims of various types so that the statutes of the particular state must be consulted. The period often differs, depending upon whether the theory of the suit is contract, tort, or fraud. Since the time period is sometimes longer for suits on written contracts than for oral contracts, an engagement letter can have the effect of providing a longer period during which the accountant can be sued for malpractice.

The general rule is that the statute of limitations starts running on a breach-of-contract claim from the date of the breach, while it starts running on a negligence or fraud suit when the negligence or fraud was or could have been discovered with reasonable diligence.[22]

It is good defensive strategy to argue that a claim involving a tax error is premature until the matter is determined by the Tax Court and then to invoke the statute. For example, in *Bronstein v. Kalchiem & Kalchiem, Ltd.,*[23] the client sued an attorney for negligent tax advice following an adverse ruling and notice of

deficiency by the IRS Appeals Division. The court dismissed the suit, holding it was premature, since it was filed prior to a determination by the Tax Court. However, in *Feldman v. Granger,*[24] the taxpayer waited until resolution by the Tax Court to sue the accounting firm for failure to timely file a subchapter S election, and the court ruled that the suit was time barred, since the statute started to run upon receiving the notice of tax deficiency from the IRS.

A number of courts reject the discovery rule and hold that the statute runs on malpractice claims from the time of the defective performance. Thus, in *Owyhee County v. Rife,*[25] the court held that the statute of limitations started running on a CPA's alleged failure to detect embezzlement from the time of delivery of the audit reports. New York applies a continuous representation rule under which the statute of limitation starts running only when the client consults another professional, on the theory that only then would a layperson be able to discover the professional malpractice.[26] Delaware denies the statute of limitations defense altogether where it is alleged that the accounting firm is engaged in a conspiracy with directors to defraud.[27]

RIGHTS TO INDEMNITY, CONTRIBUTION, OR DAMAGES FOR WRONGFUL SUIT

Indemnity and Contribution

Indemnity is the shifting of the total loss from one required to pay it to another who should bear it. Contribution distributes the loss so that each party pays a proportionate share.

A negligent auditor ought to be able to claim indemnity from those who are guilty of willful and conscious wrongdoing. According to Prosser, indemnity is not limited to those who are personally free from fault. He states:

> There is in addition considerable language in the cases to the effect that one whose negligence has consisted

22. For cases that follow this general rule, *see:* L.B. Laboratories, Inc. v. Mitchell, 244 P.2d 385 (Cal. 1952), in a suit against a CPA for breach of a written contract to timely prepare a tax return the court assumed the statute started running from the date of the breach but was tolled until plaintiff discovered that the tax return had not been filed; Glick v. Sabin, 368 N.E.2d 625 (Ill. App. 1977), discovery rule applied to allegations that CPAs were aiding and abetting and knew or should have known of defalcations; Sato v. Van Denburgh, 599 P.2d 181 (Ariz. 1979), discovery rule applied to a claim by a partner that the CPA was negligent in maintaining partnership books; Nellas v. Loucas, 191 S.E.2d 160 (W. Va. 1972), heirs were permitted to show special circumstances why the statute of limitations should not bar a suit against an attorney for late filing of an estate tax return; Moonie v. Lynch, 64 Cal. Rptr. 55 (Cal. App. 1967), limitation period on a negligence claim against CPA for IRS penalties started running when the negligent act was or with reasonable diligence could have been discovered; Atkins v. Crosland, 417 S.W.2d 150 (Tex. 1967), limitation period started running on claim against accountant when tax deficiency was assessed by the IRS; Chisholm v. Scott, 526 P.2d 1300 (N.M. App. 1974), limitation period started running when the IRS gave written notice of the assessment to the taxpayer; Isaacson, Stopler & Co. v. Artisan's Savings Bank, 330 A.2d 130 (Del. 1974), limitation period started running when, following an audit, the taxpayer received the first communication from the IRS concerning the deficiency); Briskin v. Ernst & Ernst, 589 F.2d 1363 (9th Cir. 1978), the California statute of limitations started running on a fraud claim when the plaintiff knew or in the exercise of reasonable diligence should have known of the alleged fraud.

23. Bronstein v. Kalchiem & Kalchiem, Ltd., 414 N.E.2d 96 (Ill. App. 1980). In Philip v. Giles, 620 S.W.2d 750 (Tex. App. 1981), the court dismissed a malpractice suit against an attorney for erroneous tax advice because the IRS had never assessed taxes and the cause of action accrues when tax liability is "determined" and not from the duty to report income accurately.

24. Feldman v. Granger, 257 A.2d 421 (Md. 1969).

25. Owyhee County v. Rife, 593 P.2d 995 (Idaho 1979). In Carr v. Lipshie, 176 N.E.2d 512 (N.Y. 1961) the court held that a malpractice claim for a deficient audit was barred, since the three-year tort limitation period ran from the defective performance. In Bonhiver v. Graff, 248 N.W.2d 291 (Minn. 1976) the court held the statute of limitations on the receiver's claim ran from the time the cause of action accrued, which occurred when the last negligent act was committed by the CPA. However, the claim of the general agent did not accrue until the collapse of the insurance company, which started the limitation period on the general agent's claim.

26. Wilkin v. Dana R. Pickup & Co., 357 N.Y.S.2d 125 (Sup. Ct. Allegany Cty. 1973) (statute did not start running on a claim against an accounting firm for an alleged error on a tax return until the taxpayer consulted other tax specialists).

27. Laventhol, Krekstein, Horwath & Horwath v. Tuckman, 372 A.2d 168 (Del. 1976).

100

of mere passive neglect may have indemnity from an active wrongdoer. Where this has validity, it appears to be in situations where only one tortfeasor, by his active conduct, has created a danger to the plaintiff, and the other has merely failed to discover or to remedy it.

* * * * *

Carrying this to a possible logical conclusion, it has been suggested that one who is liable merely for ordinary negligence should have indemnity from another who has been guilty of intentionally wrongful or reckless conduct. There is, however, no visible support for such a proposition . . . and it has been firmly rejected when the question has arisen.[28]

In the majority of jurisdictions, a negligent accountant has at least a right of contribution against others whose wrongful actions combined with the auditor's negligence to cause the loss. Six American jurisdictions have allowed a right of contribution from a joint tortfeasor without legislation,[29] and 25 states have enacted legislation to permit contribution.[30] The apportionment of loss is made by requiring each defendant, or each solvent defendant, to bear an equal share or by distributing the liability on the basis of comparative fault of the defendants.[31] The right of auditors to contribution under federal securities laws has been clearly established (see the discussion in Chapter 8).

Damages for Wrongful Suit

Courts have inherent power to assess attorneys fees when the losing party has acted in bad faith, vexatiously, wantonly, or for oppressive reasons.[32] Bad faith may be found in the actions that led to the lawsuit as well as in the conduct of the litigation.

In *Stratton Group, Ltd. v. Sprayregen*[33] the court dismissed a negligence claim against an accounting firm because there was no contractual relation and dismissed the claim under section 10(b) of the Exchange Act because there was no purchase or sale after the date of the auditor's report. The court said:

Again, in light of the frivolous nature of the suits filed against Laventhol, I find this an appropriate situation in which to assess costs and attorneys fees against the Sprayregens on a pro rata basis.

In *Coopers & Lybrand v. Levitt*[34] the accounting firm's suit for malicious prosecution and malicious abuse of process was dismissed. There was no allegation of a final determination in its favor to support the claim for malicious prosecution and no showing of a perversion of process for an illegal or improper purpose to support the claim of abuse of process.

Indemnity Pursuant to Charter of the Client Company

Laws of Kansas, the Bahamas, possibly laws of other states, and the federal securities laws may entitle defendant auditors who are found nonnegligent to indemnification for their costs and expenses. In *Koch Industries Inc. v. Vosko*[35] the defendant-auditors, Arthur Young & Co., were awarded indemnity for costs and expenses of litigation of $466,260.65.

The *Koch* case involved a suit by Koch Industries, Inc. (Koch), a Kansas corporation, against Vosko, the seller of stock of Atlas Petroleum, Ltd. (Atlas Pete), and Arthur Young, auditor of Atlas Pete. Koch claimed damages for fraud, negligence, violation of the Securities Act, and punitive damages. Vosko filed a counterclaim against Koch, and both Vosko and Arthur Young filed third-party claims against Atlas Pete. The trial court found the plaintiff guilty of fraud but found no fraud chargeable to either Vosko or Arthur Young. The trial court also made *no* finding that Arthur Young was negligent. The U.S. Court of Appeals held:

This leaves the challenge by Koch to an award by the trial court to Arthur Young, a "servant" of Atlas Pete, as indemnity for the costs and expenses of litigation. This award was in the amount of $466,260.65, and was entered directly against Koch Industries. The appellant argues that such an award is against public policy in Kansas, also under the Securities Act, and that Arthur Young was not the "auditor" or a servant of

28. W. Prosser, *Law of Torts* 312, 4th ed. (1971).

29. Iowa, Maine, Minnesota, New York, Wisconsin, and the Virgin Islands. *See* Annot.: Contribution Between Negligent Tortfeasors at Common Law, 60 A.L.R.2d 1366.

30. Alaska, Arkansas, Delaware, Georgia, Hawaii, Kansas, Kentucky, Louisiana, Maryland, Massachusetts, Michigan, Mississippi, Missouri, Nevada, New Jersey, New Mexico, North Carolina, North Dakota, Pennsylvania, Rhode Island, South Dakota, Tennessee, Texas, Virginia, and West Virginia.

Where the United States is a joint tortfeasor, its right to and liability for contribution is, pursuant to the Federal Tort Claims Act, determined under local law. In England, contribution between negligent joint tortfeasors has been established by statute.

31. Only eight American jurisdictions allocate contribution on a relative fault basis: Arkansas, Delaware, Hawaii, Maine, New York, South Dakota, Wisconsin, and the Virgin Islands. *See* Annot.: Contribution or Indemnity between Joint Tortfeasors on Basis of Relative Fault, 53 A.L.R.3d 184. For a court decision applying Delaware's relative fault approach (90 percent of the fault allocated to management and 10 percent to the auditor), *see* McLean v. Alexander, 449 F. Supp. 1251 (D. Del. 1978), *rev'd on other grounds,* 599 F.2d 1190 (3d Cir. 1979).

32. Roadway Express, Inc. v. Piper, 100 U.S. 2455 (1980).

33. Stratton Group, Ltd. v. Sprayregen, 466 F. Supp. 1180 (S.D.N.Y. 1979).

34. Coopers & Lybrand v. Levitt, 384 N.Y.S.2d 804 (App. Div. 1976).

35. Koch Indus., Inc. v. Vosko, 494 F.2d 713 (10th Cir. 1974).

Atlas Pete, and thus not entitled to indemnity under Article 84 of the Charter of Atlas Pete.

The award of indemnity to Arthur Young is in accord with Kansas law. Talley v. Skelly Oil Co., 199 Kan. 767, 433 P.2d 425; Hunter v. American Rentals, Inc., 189 Kan. 615, 371 P.2d 131; K.S.A. § 17-6305 (1972 Cum. Supp.)

As to federal law relating to the Securities Act claims, we find no policy contrary to an award to a party for legal expenses in successfully defending. Globus v. Law Research Service, Inc., 418 F.2d 1276 (2d Cir.), is not contrary. The court there said: "Thus it is important to emphasize at the outset that at this time we consider only the case where the underwriter has committed a sin graver than ordinary negligence." This issue was tried as an indemnification matter only, and the Bahamian law permits such recovery against a company there organized under these circumstances. Arthur Young & Company conducted the audit for the preparation of this report for Occidental, and they were formally engaged to do so. They were thus within the scope of the indemnity provision in the charter. Again there was no finding or conclusion that Arthur Young & Company was negligent. Since the award was not against public policy in the forum, was in accordance with Bahamian law, and no challenge was made to the fact that the costs were incurred, it must be upheld on this appeal. Proof was introduced to support the claimed amount. The award was against Koch Industries, and this is also proper in view of the manipulation by Koch of Atlas Pete assets and statements made during trial as to the judgment.

The Court of Appeals held that Vosko was not entitled to indemnity for his expenses of suit because he was not a corporate officer acting in the execution of the officer's duties under the corporate charter provision providing for indemnity. Apparently Arthur Young was deemed such an officer and was allowed recovery against Koch, not Atlas Pete, only because Koch had reduced Atlas Pete's assets to zero.

PLAINTIFF'S FAILURE TO MINIMIZE DAMAGES

In *Cook & Nichols, Inc. v. Peat, Marwick, Mitchell & Co.*[36] a joint venturer sued an accounting firm alleging that it negligently lost the books and records of the joint venture. The jury awarded a verdict of $30,000, which the lower court reduced to $250. In remanding for a new trial the appellate court ruled that the measure of damages for loss of personal property which has no market value, such as books and records, is the value of the property to the owner. The appeals court also ruled that the jury should be instructed on the

duty to mitigate damages because the accounting firm made its working papers available, but plaintiff refused to use them. The court said:

> Generally, one who is injured by the wrongful or negligent act of another, whether by tort or breach of contract, is bound to exercise reasonable care and diligence to avoid loss or to minimize or lessen the resulting damage, and to the extent that his damages are the result of his active and unreasonable enhancement thereof, or due to his failure to exercise such care and negligence, he cannot recover.

PLAINTIFF'S CONTRIBUTORY NEGLIGENCE

The case of *Craig v. Anyon*,[37] decided in 1926, is said to represent the rule that the client's contributory negligence may be a defense to an auditor sued by the client.[38] In that case the plaintiffs were partners in a brokerage business. The defendant auditing firm failed to discover that an employee had embezzled more than $1.25 million over a period of nearly five years. The court ruled that, on the basis of the facts as proved, defendants could be liable only for the $2,000 paid as compensation for their services and not for the embezzlement loss. Plaintiffs had restricted certain activities of the auditors. For example: "Plaintiffs refused to allow statements to be sent to customers." The case seems to hold that although the defendants were negligent and obligated to return their fee, either the negligence was not the *proximate cause* of the embezzlement loss or the losses were not *direct consequences* of the contract breach, such as were contemplated by the parties when entering into the contract.

In *National Surety Corp. v. Lybrand*[39] the court rejected a defense of contributory negligence:

> Accountants, as we know, are commonly employed for the very purpose of detecting defalcations which the employer's negligence has made possible. Accordingly, we see no reason to hold that the accountant is not liable to his employer in such cases.

The courts have not sufficiently dealt with the matter so as to establish a clear standard of conduct to be expected from the client-plaintiff in suits against the auditor. In a 1933 Canadian case[40] the client failed to set up a recommended and improved internal control

---

36. Cook & Nichols, Inc. v. Peat, Marwick, Mitchell & Co., 480 S.W.2d 542 (Tenn. App. 1971).

37. Craig v. Anyon, 212 App. Div. 55, 208 N.Y.S. 259, *aff'd mem.*, 242 N.Y. 569, 152 N.E. 431 (1926).

38. See discussion in C. Hawkins, "Professional Negligence Liability of Public Accountants," 12 *Vand. L. Rev.* 797–824 (1959).

39. National Surety Corp. v. Lybrand, 256 App. Div. 226, 9 N.Y.S.2d 554 (1939).

40. International Laboratories, Ltd. v. Dewar, 3 D.L.R. 665, 41 Manitoba R. 329 (1933).

system, complained about the amount of the fee, and instructed the auditor to limit the scope of future examinations. Later the client sued the auditor for negligence in failing to detect fraud. The court held that contributory negligence was a good and complete defense. In another case it was held that leaving the entire management of a federal credit union to the manager without routine checks was contributory negligence.[41]

In a 1958 Illinois case,[42] however, the court found that contributory negligence was not demonstrated where the plaintiff's president had requested the auditors not to confirm certain accounts receivable. The court noted that when the president gave the auditors a list of accounts receivable not to be confirmed, his action implied no authority for the bookkeeper to do likewise. The case implies that the president has such authority. AICPA standards since 1970, however, have required disclaimer of an opinion when client-imposed restrictions limit confirmation of material amounts of receivables or observation of material amounts of inventories.[43]

The court in *Shapiro v. Glekel*[44] does the best job of cutting out the underbrush in the contributory negligence thicket. The case involved a suit by the trustee in bankruptcy of a corporation against Ernst & Ernst. Plaintiff alleged that Ernst & Ernst's negligence caused Beck Industries, Inc., to overstate its earnings and financial condition, thereby causing Beck directors to engage in an ill-advised program of acquisitions. Ernst & Ernst moved to dismiss on the ground that, according to the pleadings, the president and the chairman of the executive board of Beck knew or should have known that Beck's earnings were materially less, and its financial condition materially worse than as represented in the financials. Ernst & Ernst argued that this knowledge must be attributed to the corporation and hence to the trustee so as to bar the claim. In refusing to dismiss the claim the court held:

> The Court is convinced that the correct rule of contributory negligence applicable in accountant's liability cases, such as at bar, is that expressed in *Lybrand,* namely, that the "negligence of the employer is a defense only when it has contributed to the accountant's failure to perform his contract and to report the truth."

Where the contributory negligence defense is rejected, the accounting firm may be able to invoke the comparative negligence doctrine which requires apportionment of losses between plaintiff and defendant according to their relative fault. The comparative negligence doctrine has been adopted by statute in 31 states: Colorado, Connecticut, Georgia, Hawaii, Idaho, Kansas, Louisiana, Maine, Massachusetts, Minnesota, Mississippi, Montana, Nebraska, Nevada, New Hampshire, New Jersey, New York, North Dakota, Ohio, Oklahoma, Oregon, Pennsylvania, Rhode Island, South Dakota, Tennessee, Texas, Utah, Vermont, Washington, Wisconsin, and Wyoming. Seven other states have adopted the doctrine by judicial decision: Alaska, California, Florida, Illinois, Michigan, New Mexico, and West Virginia.

PRIVILEGE IN A DEFAMATION CASE

Defamation involves oral communications (slander) or written communications (libel) to third parties that injure plaintiff's reputation. Living persons, corporations, and partnerships can defame and be defamed. Because of the historical development of the law, negligence is not an essential element to either libel or slander. There is no liability for an unintentional publication, as where a third party unexpectedly opens and reads a letter addressed to plaintiff.

While truth is always a good defense to defamation, the burden of proving truth is on the defendant, since defamatory statements are presumed false. An immediate retraction may eliminate damages, and a later retraction may mitigate damages.

Plaintiffs may recover for libel without proof of actual damages, but slander requires proof of specific damages, except for oral statements that plaintiff is (1) guilty of crime, (2) afflicted by veneral disease or leprosy, (3) unfit in performing in a trade, business, or profession, or (4) an unchaste woman or a homosexual.

Absolute Privilege

Absolute privilege confers absolute immunity from liability for defamation. It is based on public policy considerations that favor complete freedom of expression in these limited situations:

1. Judicial proceedings, including judges, jurors, witnesses, parties, and attorneys.
2. Quasi-judicial proceedings, including administrative officers, boards, and commissions involved in applying the law to facts.
3. Legislators in the course of their functions, such as debate, voting, reporting, or committee work.
4. Executive officers in discharging governmental duties.

41. Social Security Administration Baltimore F.C.U. v. United States, 138 F. Supp. 639 (D. Md. 1956). Although the federal examiners examined the books periodically, the court did not find that the government had violated any duty owed to the credit union.

42. Cereal Byproducts Co. v. Hall, 8 Ill. App. 2d 331, 132 N.E.2d 27 (1956), aff'd, 15 Ill. 2d 313, 155 N.E.2d 14 (1958).

43. *CCH AICPA Professional Standards,* AU § 509.12 provides: "When restrictions that significantly limit the scope of the audit are imposed by the client, the auditor generally should disclaim an opinion on the financial statements."

44. Shapiro v. Glekel, 380 F. Supp. 1053 (S.D.N.Y. 1974).

In *Angel v. Ward,*[45] a CPA telephoned the IRS to complain about the competence and behavior of a revenue agent. The IRS requested the CPA to put the comments in writing for an evidentiary file that would be used to terminate the agent's employment. Upon termination, the revenue agent sued the CPA firm for libel. In dismissing the suit the court held that the CPA had the benefit of the absolute privilege:

> A defamatory statement made in the due course of a judicial proceeding is absolutely privileged. . . . The privilege attending communications made in the course of judicial proceedings has been extended to protect communications in an administrative proceeding only where the administrative officer or agency in the proceeding in question is exercising a judicial or quasi-judicial function. . . .
>
> Mr. Allen in his solicitation of defendants' letter was acting for and on behalf of the Internal Revenue Service in a governmental matter. He was in the process of evaluating plaintiff in connection with her employment. The agency decided to terminate plaintiff's employment, and Mr. Allen was preparing an evidentiary file to support the termination decision. The proceeding was quasi-judicial in nature, and defendants' communications were absolutely privileged. . . .
>
> We hold that the trial court properly entered summary judgment on plaintiff's libel claim.

Qualified Privilege

The common law recognizes a qualified privilege which provides immunity from liability for defamation so long as the statement is made in good faith without knowledge of its falsity. The qualified privilege applies to all communications reasonably related to one's personal or business affairs. Persons likely to deal with, employ, or extend credit may be informed about credit, character, or misconduct. Citizens are privileged to give information to authorities for prevention or punishment of crime and to complain about the conduct of public officials, including school teachers and IRS agents. The common-law qualified privilege extends to fair comment on matters of public proceedings.

In *Ross v. Gallant, Farrow & Co., P.C.,*[46] the business manager of a local union sued a CPA firm because the CPAs' audit report indicated that expenditures for Christmas party gifts, printing expenses, and two automobiles were unauthorized. At the trial, witnesses testified both ways as to their interpretations of the union constitution and bylaws. However, the court held that CPAs performing an audit have a qualified

privilege and dismissed the suit because the plaintiff failed to prove that the CPAs were motivated by malice. Malice, the court held, involves making a defamatory statement with knowledge of its falsity or in reckless disregard of whether it was true or false.

Constitutional Privilege

In *New York Times Co. v. Sullivan,*[47] the United States Supreme Court held that the First Amendment right to free speech confers a qualified privilege that protects false statements of fact provided they are made without malice. Malice for this purpose means with knowledge of falsity or in reckless disregard for the truth. The privilege cannot be defeated by subjective ill will and desire to do harm, nor by negligence in publishing without verification. While the scope of this privilege is broad—embracing (1) matters of public concern, (2) public figures and news, and (3) reports of public proceedings—it clearly does not justify intrusion into the private life of someone who is otherwise obscure and unknown.

SUMMARY

Professional persons do not guarantee their work. They undertake only to comply with the usual professional standard for the particular community. Where plaintiffs do not rely upon the accountant's work, it is not the cause of their injury and they cannot recover, despite flagrant conduct by the accountant. Plaintiffs are entitled to only one recovery and may not recover from the accountant if the losses have been recovered from another wrongdoer jointly responsible for the injury.

While public accountants are liable to clients and foreseeable third parties for negligence, unforeseeable plaintiffs must prove knowledge of falsity or recklessness that constitutes an extreme departure from professional standards. In order to provide a reasonable limit for professional responsibility, liability should be imposed to unforeseeable plaintiffs only where the danger that caused the loss was foreseeable at the time of the deficient work.

Each state has established limitation periods for bringing suits of various types. Generally the designated period starts running on a contract claim at the time of the breach and on a negligence or fraud claim when the negligence was or should have been discovered.

A negligent accountant generally has the right of contribution against others who are jointly liable for the loss. Courts have inherent power to assess attorneys' fees when the losing party has acted in bad faith,

---

45. Angel v. Ward, 258 S.E.2d 788 (N.C. App. 1979).

46. Ross v. Gallant, Farrow & Co., P.C., 551 P.2d 79 (Ariz. App. 1976).

47. New York Times Co. v. Sullivan, 376 U.S. 254 (1964).

vexatiously, wantonly, or for oppressive reasons. Contributory negligence is a defense to a malpractice claim only when it has contributed to the accountant's failure to perform.

Defamation involves oral communications (slander) or written communications (libel) to third parties that injure plaintiff's reputation. Absolute privilege provides absolute immunity from liability for (1) judicial proceedings, (2) quasi-judicial proceedings, (3) legislators, and (4) executive officers. The qualified privilege provides immunity for statements made in good faith without knowledge of falsity. It extends to fair comment on matters of public concern, public figures, news, and public proceedings. The First Amendment provides a constitutional privilege that protects false statements of fact made without malice.

SUGGESTIONS FOR FURTHER READING

Annot. "Release of One Joint Tortfeasor as Discharging Liability of Others." 73 *American Law Reports* 2d 403, 1960.

Annot. "Testimony before or Communications to Private Professional Society's Judicial Commission, Ethics Committee, or the Like as Privileged." 9 *American Law Reports* 4th 807, 1981.

Annot. "Tortfeasor's General Release of Cotortfeasor as Affecting Former's Right to Contribution against Cotortfeasor." 34 *American Law Reports* 3d 1374, 1970.

Annot. "Validity and Effect of Agreement with One Cotortfeasor Setting His Maximum Liability and Providing for Reduction or Extinguishment Thereof Relative to Recovery against Nonagreeing Cotortfeasor." 65 *American Law Reports* 3d 602, 1975.

Annot. "What Law Governs Right to Contribution or Indemnity between Tortfeasors?" 95 *American Law Reports* 3d 927, 1974.

Annot. "When Statute of Limitations Commences to Run against Claim for Contribution or Indemnity Based on Tort." 57 *American Law Reports* 3d 867, 1974.

Dean, Reagan W. "Summary Judgment Motions in Medical Malpractice Actions." *Georgia State Bar Journal,* August 1981, pp. 44–46.

QUESTIONS AND PROBLEMS

1. (From the May 1981 Uniform CPA Examination)

    If a CPA firm is being sued for common-law fraud by a third party, based upon materially false financial statements, which of the following is the best defense which the accountants could assert?
    a. Lack of privity.
    b. Lack of reliance.
    c. A disclaimer contained in the engagement letter.
    d. Contributory negligence on the part of the client.

2. (From the November 1978 Uniform CPA Examination)

    Magnus Enterprises engaged a CPA firm to perform the annual examination of its financial statements. Which of the following is a correct statement with respect to the CPA firm's liability to Magnus for negligence?
    a. Such liability can *not* be varied by agreement of the parties.
    b. The CPA firm will be liable for any fraudulent scheme it does *not* detect.
    c. The CPA firm will *not* be liable if it can show that it

exercised the ordinary care and skill of a reasonable man in the conduct of his own affairs.
    d. The CPA firm must *not* only exercise reasonable care in what it does, but also must possess at least that degree of accounting knowledge and skill expected of a CPA.

3. (From the November 1978 Uniform CPA Examination)

    The Apex Surety Company wrote a general fidelity bond covering defalcations by the employees of Watson, Inc. Thereafter, Grand, an employee of Watson, embezzled $18,900 of company funds. When his activities were discovered, Apex paid Watson the full amount in accordance with the terms of the fidelity bond, and then sought recovery against Watson's auditors, Kane & Dobbs, CPAs. Which of the following would be Kane & Dobbs' best defense?
    a. Apex is *not* in privity of contract.
    b. The shortages were the result of clever forgeries and collusive fraud which would *not* be detected by an examination made in accordance with generally accepted auditing standards.
    c. Kane & Dobbs were *not* guilty either of gross negligence or fraud.
    d. Kane & Dobbs were *not* aware of the Apex-Watson surety relationship.

4. Grover, CPA, has released the audit report on Local 10 of the fruit packers' union, wherein he disclosed that certain expenditures were unauthorized. The *minimum* proof required to establish a prima facie defamation claim by the manager of the local is that the
    a. Statement concerning unauthorized expenditures was negligent.
    b. Statement concerning unauthorized expenditures was defamatory.
    c. CPA refused, upon request, to retract the statement concerning unauthorized expenditures.
    d. Statement concerning unauthorized expenditures was made with full knowledge of its falsity.

5. James Jones, CPA, failed to discover embezzlement in connection with his first audit of Equipment Corporation. Losses prior to the audit amounted to $100,000, and $50,000 was embezzled after the audit work was completed but prior to discovery by management. Which statement below best describes the CPA's liability to the client?
    a. Regardless of the methods used by the embezzler, the CPA is liable for $150,000.
    b. Regardless of the methods used by the embezzler, the CPA is liable for $50,000.
    c. If the application of the usual auditing practices would have resulted in discovery of the embezzlement, the CPA is liable for $100,000.
    d. If the application of the usual auditing practices would have resulted in discovery of the embezzlement, the CPA is liable for $50,000.

Reliance on Work of Other Auditors

6. a. To what extent can an auditor rely on the work of other auditors?
    b. If reliance is placed on the work of other auditors, what duties are imposed on the reliant auditor?

7. (From the May 1971 Uniform CPA Examination)

If another auditor's examination of a subsidiary company's financial statement results in an unqualified opinion, the auditor of the parent company may express an unqualified opinion on the fairness of the consolidated statements provided that, as a minimum, he

   a. Assumes responsibility for the proper performance of the work done by the subsidiary's auditor.
   b. Reviews the working papers of the subsidiary's auditor.
   c. Is satisfied as to the independence and professional reputation of the subsidiary's auditor.
   d. Performs his own examination of the subsidiary's financial statements.

8. (From the November 1971 Uniform CPA Examination)

A CPA was engaged to examine the consolidated financial statements of the Kauffman Tool Company and its Canadian subsidiary. He arranged for a reputable firm of Canadian chartered accountants to conduct the examination of the Canadian subsidiary's financial statements. The CPA reviewed both the audit program and the working papers prepared by the Canadian firm and is willing to accept full responsibility for the performance of the examination of the subsidiary's financial statements. The Canadian chartered accountants expressed an unqualified opinion on the subsidiary's financial statements, and the CPA has no exceptions on the parent's statements or the procedures used to prepare the consolidated statements. Under these circumstances, the CPA's report on the consolidated statements

   a. Should include a piecemeal opinion covering the parent's statements and a qualified opinion as to the Canadian subsidiary.
   b. Need make no reference to the chartered accountants' examination.
   c. Must include a reference to the chartered accountants' examination in the scope paragraph or a middle paragraph together with an unqualified opinion paragraph.
   d. Must include a qualification of the opinion paragraph stating that the CPA's unqualified opinion is based in part upon the chartered accountants' examination.

9. (From the November 1973 Uniform CPA Examination)

Grauer, Inc., carries its investment in Salvemini Corporation at equity. Grauer's investment in Salvemini accounts for 45 percent of the total assets of Grauer. Grauer and Salvemini are not audited by the same CPA. In order for Grauer's auditor to issue an unqualified opinion in regard to the value of Grauer's investment in Salvemini and the income derived therefrom, Grauer's auditor

   a. Needs to obtain only Salvemini's unaudited financial statements.
   b. Needs to obtain only Salvemini's audited financial statements.
   c. Must obtain Salvemini's audited financial statements and make inquiries concerning the professional reputation and independence of Salvemini's auditor.

   d. Must review the working paper of Salvemini's auditor.

10. (From the November 1974 Uniform CPA Examination)

Jackson, CPA, is the principal auditor for the Jones Corp. He requests another CPA to perform the examination of a subsidiary corporation which is located in a distant state. Jackson has satisfied himself as to the independence, professional reputation, and conduct of the examination of the other auditor. What reference, if any, must Jackson make to the work of the other CPA, assuming that he is willing to accept responsibility for his work?

   a. He should indicate the extent of the other auditor's work in the scope paragraph of his own report and state in the opinion paragraph he accepts full responsibility for the work.
   b. He need not make any reference to the examination or report of the other CPA.
   c. He should make certain that the report of the other CPA accompanies his own.
   d. He should indicate the extent of the other auditor's work in the scope paragraph of his own report, but he need not make any reference to it in the opinion paragraph.

11. (From the May 1975 Uniform CPA Examination)

Abbot, CPA, as principal auditor for consolidated financial statements is using a qualified report of another auditor. Abbot does not consider the qualification material relative to the consolidated financial statements. What recognition, if any, must Abbot make in his report to the report of the other audit?

   a. He need make no reference.
   b. He must refer to the qualification of the other auditor and qualify his report likewise.
   c. He must include the other auditor's report with his report but need not qualify his own report.
   d. He must include the other auditor's report with his report and give an explanation of its significance.

12. (From the May 1975 Uniform CPA Examination)

Russo, CPA, succeeded Brown, CPA, as auditor of Sunshine Corp. for the calender year 1974. Brown had issued an unqualified report for the calendar year 1973. What must Russo do to establish the basis for expressing his opinion on the financial statements with regard to opening balances?

   a. Russo must apply appropriate auditing procedures to all account balances at the beginning of the period so as to satisfy himself that they are properly stated and may not rely on any work done by Brown.
   b. Russo may review Brown's work papers and thereby reduce the scope of audit tests he would otherwise have to do.
   c. Russo may rely on the prior year's financial statements, since an unqualified opinion was issued, but should not make reference in his report to Brown's report.
   d. Russo may rely on the prior year's financial statements, since an unqualified opinion was issued, but must refer in a middle paragraph of his report to Brown's report of the prior year.

8

Civil Liability under
Federal Securities
Laws

This chapter covers:

- ADVENT OF THE SEC.
- THE SECURITIES ACT.
- THE EXCHANGE ACT.
- THE INVESTMENT ADVISERS ACT OF 1940.
- CLASS ACTIONS AND DERIVATIVE SUITS.
- VENUE AND JURISDICTION.
- RIGHT TO JURY TRIAL.

ADVENT OF THE SEC

Federal securities laws are the result of an evolution in adapting to perceived needs for regulation of the sale of investments. In 1719 the failure of the Mississippi Company organized by John Law created a financial scandal in France, and a similar occurrence in England in 1720 involved the failure of the South Sea Company, which enjoyed a monopoly from the British government for trading with South America and the Pacific Islands.[1]

The English Bubble Act of 1720, which prohibited taking subscriptions for false or irregular charters and apparently served to protect those who had legal charters, was finally repealed in 1825. In 1844 the English Companies Act required registration of prospectuses

offering corporate shares, but it was also found lacking in its disclosure requirements. In 1890 Parliament passed the Directors Liability Act, reversing the result that had been reached by the House of Lords in *Derry v. Peek* and subjecting corporate directors and promoters to civil liability for false statements in a prospectus without proof of scienter.[2]

The first effective disclosure requirements in England came with the Companies Act of 1900, which contained an elaborate prescription of the contents of the prospectus. Lord Davey's committee report of 1895, which preceded the legislation, expressed the new philosophy that later was to characterize American legislation. Lord Davey noted that a person invited to subscribe to a new undertaking has practically no opportunity to make an independent inquiry and that the maxim of "Caveat Emptor has . . . but a limited application in such cases."[3]

By 1933 most of the American states had enacted blue-sky laws regulating the sale of securities. But state laws were not adequate to deal with the problem of protecting the investing public in an interstate economy. After severe losses from dishonest practices, arguments for reform were made by such critics as Louis D. Brandeis in his book *Other People's Money and How the Bankers Use It*.[4] When the stock market crash of 1929 reinforced such arguments, many persons became convinced that federal legislation was necessary. Three different approaches to federal control were advocated: (1) strict enforcement of criminal laws without power to enjoin fraud, (2) a disclosure law following the English approach, and (3) administrative evaluation of the soundness of the investment.[5] President Roosevelt chose the English disclosure approach and in recommending federal securities legislation in 1933 said:

> Of course, the Federal Government cannot and should not take any action which might be construed as approving or guaranteeing that newly issued securities are sound in the sense that their value will be maintained or that the properties which they represent will earn a profit.
>
> There is, however, an obligation upon us to insist that every issue of new securities to be sold in interstate commerce shall be accompanied by full publicity and information, and that no essentially important element attending the issue shall be concealed from the buying public.
>
> This proposal adds to the ancient rule of caveat emptor, the further doctrine *"Let the seller also be-*

1. 1 L. Loss, *Securities Regulation* 4, 2d ed. (Boston: Little, Brown, 1961).

2. Ibid. at 4–7.

3. Ibid. at 6–7.

4. Louis D. Brandeis, *Other People's Money and How the Bankers Use It* (New York: Frederick A. Stokes, 1914).

5. 1 L. Loss, *Securities Regulation* 121–22, 2nd ed. (1961).

ware." It puts the burden of telling the whole truth on the seller. It should give impetus to honest dealing in securities and thereby bring back public confidence.[6] (Emphasis added.)

The Securities and Exchange Commission (hereafter, Commission) was established by the Securities Exchange Act of 1934 (hereafter, Exchange Act) to administer the Exchange Act and to take over administration of the Securities Act of 1933 (hereafter, Securities Act). The President appoints the five members of the Commission to five-year terms and designates one as chairperson. The organizational structure of the Commission staff, including the locations of regional and branch offices, is shown in Exhibit 8-1.

The Commission currently administers and enforces the following six laws:

1. The Securities Act (15 U.S.C. §§ 77a and following).
2. The Exchange Act (15 U.S.C. §§ 78 and following).
3. The Public Utility Holding Company Act of 1935 (15 U.S.C. §§ 79 and following).
4. The Trust Indenture Act of 1939 (15 U.S.C. §§ 77aaa and following).
5. The Investment Company Act of 1940 (15 U.S.C. §§ 80a–1 and following).
6. The Investment Advisers Act of 1940 (15 U.S.C. §§ 80b–1 and following).

The Commission also serves as adviser to federal courts in corporate reorganization proceedings under chapter 11 of the Bankruptcy Reform Act of 1978 (11 U.S.C. § 1109). The Commission further has rulemaking and enforcement responsibility under the Securities Investor Protection Act of 1970 (15 U.S.C. §§ 78aaa and following).

Each of the six main laws administered by the Commission either specifically or by implication imposes civil liabilities.[7]

THE SECURITIES ACT

The Securities Act is known as the truth in securities law. Section 5 of the act makes it unlawful to use "any means or instruments of transportation or communication in interstate commerce or of the mails" in connection with the sale or delivery of securities *unless a registration statement is in effect.*[8]

This law generally relates only to the *initial* distribution of an issue of securities as opposed to the subsequent trading in the securities.

The jurisdictional reach of the act is extensive, so that unless an exemption is applicable, the law applies. Use of the telephone (an instrument of communication in interstate commerce)—even for an intrastate call to discuss a possible investment—satisfies the jurisdictional requirements.[9] Similarly, an intrastate mailing of an advertisement invokes the act.[10]

The definition of *security* under section 2(1) of the act is very broad.[11] In holding that units of a citrus grove development, coupled with a contract for cultivating, marketing, and remitting of net proceeds, were investment contracts covered by the law, the U.S. Supreme Court indicated that form must be disregarded for substance and economic reality and stated that a security is "a contract, transaction or scheme whereby a person invests his money in a common enterprise and is led to expect profits solely from the efforts of a third party, it being immaterial whether the shares in the enterprise are evidenced by formal certificates or by nominal interests in the physical assets employed in the enterprise."[12]

In *Exchange National Bank of Chicago v. Touche Ross & Co.,*[13] plaintiff sued Touche under both the Securities Act and the Exchange Act along with a pendent negligence claim under state law. Plaintiff claimed

---

6. Message of March 29, 1933, 77 *Cong. Rec.* 937 (1933).

7. Express provisions imposing civil liability are found in sections 11 and 12 of the Securities Act (15 U.S.C. §§ 77k, 77l); sections 9(e), 16(b), and 18 of the Exchange Act [15 U.S.C. §§ 78i(e), 78p(b), 78r]; sections 16(a) and 17(b) of the Public Utility Holding Company Act of 1935 [15 U.S.C. §§ 79p(a), 79q(b)]; and Section 30(f) of the Investment Company Act of 1940 [15 U.S.C. § 80a–29(f)]. Provisions implying civil liability are sections 10(b) and 14 of the Exchange Act and a strictly limited remedy under section 206 of the Advisers Act.

8. Securities Act of 1933 § 5, 15 U.S.C. § 77e. Offers, but not sales, may be made by means of a prospectus after the registration statement is filed but prior to its effective date.

9. Myzel v. Fields, 386 F.2d 718 (8th Cir. 1967), *cert. denied,* 390 U.S. 951 (1968).

10. SEC v. Truckee Showboat, Inc., 157 F. Supp. 824 (S.D. Cal. 1957).

11. Section 2(1) defines *security* as "any note, stock, treasury stock, bond, debenture, evidence of indebtedness, certificate of interest or participation in any profit-sharing agreement, collateral-trust certificate, preorganization certificate or subscription, transferable share, investment contract, voting-trust certificate, certificate of deposit for a security, fractional undivided interest in oil, gas, or other mineral rights, or in general, any interest or instrument commonly known as a 'security,' or any certificate of interest or participation in, temporary or interim certificate for, receipt for, guarantee of, or warrant or right to subscribe to or purchase, any of the foregoing."

In Canfield v. Rapp & Son, Inc., 654 F.2d 459 (7th Cir. 1981) the court held that purchase of all of the stock of a corporation and assumption of management was not within the scope of federal securities laws.

12. SEC v. W. J. Howey Co., 328 U.S. 293 at 298–99 (1946). Limited partnership interests have been held to be securities. *See* Pawgan v. Silverstein, 265 F. Supp. 898 (S.D.N.Y. 1967). Real estate condominiums and franchises can also be securities if the seller is to operate them and remit the profits.

13. Exchange National Bank of Chicago v. Touche Ross & Co., 544 F.2d 1126 (2d Cir. 1976).

EXHIBIT 8-1
Organizational Structure of the Securities and Exchange Commission

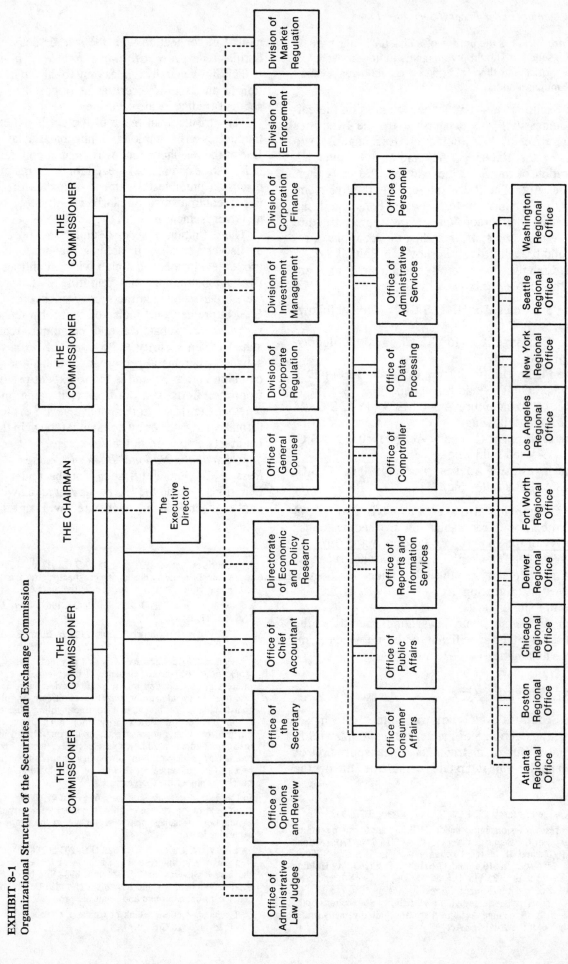

Source: *The Work of the Securities and Exchange Commission,* March 1978, p. v.

to have relied upon Touche's audit in acquiring three notes aggregating $1 million in connection with the financing of a New York brokerage firm. Touche moved to dismiss on the grounds that such notes were not securities within either the Securities Act or the Exchange Act. In denying the Touche motion the court noted that, in the context of the federal securities laws, home mortgages, consumer loans, and notes formalizing open accounts are not securities. In other situations the court concluded it would look to the language of the laws themselves. The Exchange Act defines security as including any note except one having a maturity not exceeding nine months. The Securities Act provides that any note is a security but exempts from registration provisions (not from antifraud provisions) any note "which arises out of a current transaction or the proceeds of which have been or are to be used for current transactions, and which has a maturity at the time of issuance of not exceeding nine months. . . ."

Exemptions

Sections 3[14] and 4[15] of the act contain exemptions from the registration requirements for certain specified securities and transactions. It should be noted, however, that the exemption applies only to the registration requirement, so that antifraud, civil liability, and any Exchange Act reporting provisions remain applicable. Some of the main exemptions from registration are:

1. Securities of governmental units (federal, state, and local) and securities issued or guaranteed by banks [§ 3(a)(2)].
2. Short-term obligations not exceeding nine months [§ 3(a)(3)].
3. Securities issued by religious, educational, or charitable organizations [§ 3(a)(4)].
4. Securities issued by carriers subject to the Interstate Commerce Act [§ 3(a)(6)].
5. Intrastate offerings [§ 3(a)(11)]. (Regulated by SEC rule 147.)
6. Small offerings not to exceed $5 million as implemented by SEC regulations [§ 3(b)]. (Regulated by several SEC rules: Regulation A for offerings up to $1.5 million in 12 months, rule 240 for offerings of up to $100,000 in 12 months, rule 242 for offerings up to $2 million in 6 months to an unlimited number of "accredited investors" and no more than 35 other persons.)
7. Securities issued under the Small Business Investment Act [§ 3(c)], as per SEC Regulation E.
8. Private offerings to a limited number of sophisticated investors who do not need protection afforded by the act (the act refers to "transactions by an issuer not involving any public offering") [§ 4(2)]. (Regulated by SEC rule 146.)
9. Offers and sales to "accredited investors" if there is no public solicitation and the aggregate amount of the offering is $5 million or less [§ 4(6)].

The Intrastate Exemption. Section 3(a)(11) of the Securities Act [U.S.C. § 77c(a)(11)] provides an exemption from registration for

> any security which is a part of an issue offered and sold only to persons resident within a single State or Territory, where the issuer of such security is a person resident and doing business within, or, if a corporation, incorporated by and doing business within, such State or Territory.

Since the act exempts intrastate issues, *not* individual transactions, an offer or sale of a single share to a nonresident will retroactively destroy the exemption for the entire issue.[16] The word *intrastate* refers only to the domicile of the issuer, offerees, and purchasers, not to the instrumentalities used in the sale. A Texas corporation would not lose the exemption by virtue of selling securities through the mail to a Texas resident temporarily in Arizona. However, the exemption is lost if a Texas corporation makes sales in Texas to a resident of Arizona temporarily in Texas. It is unwise to rely on the intrastate exemption where securities are sold on the installment plan, since the purchaser may move prior to consummation of the sale and delivery of the securities.

Rule 147 (17 C.F.R. § 230.147) provides a "safe harbor" rule for meeting the requirements; that is, the requirements may be otherwise satisfied, but compliance with the rule gives assurance of compliance. The factors considered by the rule, and hence by the Commission, for meeting the "doing business" test include the percentage of revenues received from within the state, the percentage of assets located within the state, the percentage of proceeds of the issue to be expended within the state, and whether the principal office is located within the state.

Rule 147 also requires that issuers take precautions to ensure that until nine months from the last sale, resales are made only to residents. This involves placing a restrictive legend on the securities, restricting the transfer agent accordingly, disclosing the restriction to offerees, and obtaining a written representation from each purchaser concerning the purchaser's residence.

The intrastate exemption is only an exemption from registration requirements. There is no exemption from

---

14. Securities Act of 1933 § 3, 15 U.S.C. § 77c.

15. Securities Act of 1933 § 4, 15 U.S.C. § 77d.

16. SEC v. Hillsborough Inv. Corp., 173 F. Supp. 86 (D.N.H. 1958).

civil liability under section 12(2) of the Act nor section 10(b) of the Exchange Act. Securities acquired under the intrastate exemption may be resold to nonresidents after they have come to rest in the hands of residents acquiring for investment and not for purposes of resale.

The Small Offering Exemption. Section 3(b) of the act provides that

> the Commission may from time to time by its rules and regulations, and subject to such terms and conditions as may be prescribed therein, add any class of securities to the securities exempted as provided in this section, if it finds that the enforcement of this title with respect to such securities is not necessary in the public interest and for the protection of investors by reason of the small amount involved or the limited character of the public offering; but no issue of securities shall be exempted under this subsection where the aggregate amount at which such issue is offered to the public exceeds $5 million.

Pursuant to this statute the Commission has adopted rules providing three different options for avoiding registration of small issues: (1) Regulation A, (2) rule 240, and (3) rule 242. None of these options provides an exemption from civil liability provisions under sections 12(2) of the act or section 10(b) of the Exchange Act. Under rules 240 and 242, no general solicitation nor general advertising is permitted. Securities acquired under rules 240 and 242 are "unregistered" (restricted) securities that can be resold only in exempt transactions or disposed of gradually after a two-year waiting period under rule 144.

Regulation A (17 C.F.R. §§ 230.251 to 230.262) provides a simplified registration form for public offerings of securities that do not exceed $1.5 million in one year. Before offering securities under Regulation A, an offering circular must be filed with the Commission's regional office nearest the issuer's principal place of business for 10 days (excluding Saturdays, Sundays, and holidays). The practice, however, is to wait until the Commission staff has communicated its comments before offering the securities. Except for firms required to file certified financials under the Exchange Act, certified financials are not required for Regulation A filings. The circular must include a balance sheet as of a date within 90 days prior to filing and income statements for the two preceding fiscal years.

Rule 240 provides an exemption from registration for closely held issuers who sell a maximum of $100,000 of securities within 12 months with a limitation of all security holders to 100 or fewer persons.

Rule 242 provides an exemption from registration for sale of $2 million of securities within any six-month period to an unlimited number of "accredited investors" and no more than 35 other persons.

The Private Offering Exemption. Section 4(2) provides an exemption from the registration requirements

of section 5 for "transactions by an issuer not involving any public offering." In 1974 the Commission adopted rule 146 (17 C.F.R. § 230.146), which provides a "safe harbor" of assurance of exempt status for situations meeting requirements of the rule. Failure to meet requirements of the rule does not disqualify the transaction from exemption. The rule requires that (1) no general advertising be used in the offer and sale of the securities; (2) all offerees or their representatives be persons with knowledge and experience in financial and business matters; (3) offerees who must depend on representatives for "knowledge and experience" must be able to bear the economic risk of the investment; (4) all offerees, or their representatives, have access to the type of information that registration would disclose, or it must be furnished if reasonably available; (5) there can be no more than 35 purchasers of the issuer's securities in any 12-month period (sales for cash to any person aggregating $150,000 or more are excluded in the count); and (6) certain steps must be taken to prevent the resale of the securities in violation of Commission rule 144, which governs resale of restricted securities that have not been covered by a filed registration statement.

Securities sold under this exemption should contain a typed or stamped legend limiting resale except upon opinion by counsel satisfactory to the issuer; the opinion must state that registration is not required. Further, the issuer usually notifies the transfer agent to refuse transfer of the stock.

In evaluating the disclosure requirement of the rule, one commentator observed:

> Although in some cases the rule may permit a nonreporting issuer to make an offering in the absence of audited financial statements required by the relevant registration form, dependence on unaudited statements may increase the potential liability of those associated with the offering (by eliminating the right reasonably to rely upon auditing experts) if the unaudited statements turn out to be materially in error. In addition, the issuer's financials must presumably be stated in conformity with regulation S-X. . . .[17]

In *Doran v. Petroleum Management Co.*[18] the U.S. Court of Appeals for the Fifth Circuit used a four-factor test for evaluating the private placement exemption:

---

17. Robert H. Kinderman, Jr., "The Private Offering Exemption: An Examination of Its Availability under and outside Rule 146," 30 *Business Lawyer* 921, 1935–36 (April 1975).

18. Doran v. Petroleum Management Co., 545 F.2d 893 (5th Cir. 1977). In SEC v. Ralston Purina, 346 U.S. 119 (1953), the U.S. Supreme Court held that, in a private placement, offers must be restricted to those who, by virtue of their knowledge and sophistication, do not need the protection of the Securities Act; the Court rejected the SEC's former 25-person test and indicated that no particular numbers are prescribed.

The relevant factors include the numbers of offerees and their relationship to each other and the issuer, the number of units offered, the size of the offering, and the manner of the offering. . . . These factors serve as guideposts to the court in attempting to determine whether subjecting the offering to registration requirements would further the purposes of the 1933 Act.

The court considered the first factor as critical, since it requires that all offerees (as opposed to purchasers) be adequately informed. Although the court accepted the disjunctive test that offerees have either information or access to information that would be disclosed in a registration statement, the court took a practical view of "access." To prove access, the issuer must show that the offeree has a realistic opportunity to learn essential facts by virtue of possessing sufficient investment sophistication to seek the relevant information by asking the right questions.

Restricted Securities

Securities acquired under rules 146 (private placement), 240, and 242, as well as those acquired under section 4(6), are "restricted securities" and cannot be resold except under strictly limited and defined conditions. This is true despite the fact that there may be other securities of this same class that are publicly traded. Securities owned by controlling persons may not be resold because a controlling interest is tantamount to a new public offering so that a registration statement is required.

SEC rule 144[19] gives partial relief to facilitate the sale of restricted securities, as well as a controlling interest, by permitting these investors to dribble out their shares in small lots over a period of time. The quantity of securities sold in any three-month period is limited to the greater of (1) 1 percent of the outstanding securities of the class or (2) the average weekly trading volume during the four calendar weeks preceding the sale. Securities must be held two years following the payment of the full purchase price before taking advantage of rule 144. However, the two-year requirement does not apply to controlling persons who acquired their securities in a public market instead of through rules 146, 240, 242, or section 4(6).

PRACTICAL POINTERS

1. Auditors should be aware of restrictions on resale, since under *FASB No. 12* restricted stock does not meet the definition of *marketable*.

2. Always examine certificates for marketable securities to assure there is no restrictive legend. (*FASB Interpretation No. 16* provides that the marketable category includes shares that can be dribbled out within one year under rule 144.)

3. Restricted securities should be classified as nonmarketable and valued at the lower-of-cost or the discounted-appraisal value that reflects the restriction.

The Registration and Selling Process

The Securities Act is designed to require disclosure of information relative to a new public offering of securities through the registration statement and prospectus. The prospectus is an information booklet containing certified financial statements. It constitutes part of the registration statement which must be filed with the Commission.

The act provides that the effective date of a registration statement (the day securities may be sold) will be the 20th day after filing or such earlier date as the Commission may determine. Each amendment creates a new filing date unless the amendment is filed with the consent of the Commission. In order to provide the SEC staff with an opportunity to comment on any inadequacies in disclosure, the practice is to file a "delaying amendment" to indefinitely postpone the effective date. The Commission's comment letter may take one of several forms:

1. It may indicate that the disclosures are so inadequate that the registrant should start over and refile.
2. It may suggest specific amendments or additions.
3. It may offer no objections leaving full responsibility on the registrant for the adequacy of disclosures.

After all indicated deficiencies are corrected, the registrant files a completing amendment, which indicates the public offering price, the underwriter's commission and the expected proceeds, and a request for acceleration of the effective date to the date desired by the registrant, given the then current fluctuations in the securities market.

Selling Activities. During the *prefiling period* (before filing the proposed registration statement with the Commission), there can be neither news releases calculated to soften the market nor other sales activity. During the *waiting period* (after filing the proposed registration statement but before the effective date), the underwriter may (1) make oral offers but no sales, (2) announce the planned public offering in a "tombstone ad," and (3) distribute copies of the preliminary prospectus. The preliminary prospectus is called a "red herring," since it bears a red-ink caption, "Pre-

---

19. 17 C.F.R. § 230.144.

liminary Prospectus," and a warning that the information is subject to amendment. It generally does not contain the price information because this will be decided just before the effective date and will depend upon then current market conditions. After the effective date, the underwriter can make sales and distribute sales literature; however, the first written communication delivered to a prospective investor must be the final prospectus containing the price information supplied by amendment. Where sales are made orally, the prospectus must accompany the confirmation of sale.

The Registration Team. The issuer's attorney is in charge of the preparation of the registration statement and coordinates the work of the issuer, auditor, underwriter, and other experts, such as engineers. The underwriter usually undertakes the selling effort on a nonbinding letter of intent and becomes bound just before the effective date of the registration statement. Depending upon the financial standing of the issuer, the underwriter may agree (1) to purchase all the securities net of underwriting fees on the effective date, or (2) to make a best-efforts attempt to sell the securities on behalf of the issuer. Before filing the registration statement it must be reviewed for accuracy by the accountant and other experts, underwriter, and board of directors of the issuer.

Disclosure Requirements and Enforcement

Regulation S-X[20] prescribes the form and content of financial statements filed with the Commission under the 1933 and 1934 acts, the Public Utilities Holding Company Act of 1935, and the Investment Company Act of 1940. Rule 2–01 of Regulation S-X prescribes qualifications for public accountants.[21] Rule 2–02 sets forth the requirements for certificates of public accountants to financial statements filed with the Commission.[22]

The Commission enforces its Securities Act disclosure requirements by (1) issuing a stop order suspending the effectiveness of a registration statement (after 15 days' notice and opportunity for hearing),[23] (2) issuing an order refusing to permit a registration statement from becoming effective (after 10-days' notice and opportunity for hearing),[24] and (3) referring matters to the Attorney General for possible criminal proceedings. In making its decision to issue a stop order, the Commission can (1) demand production of books and papers, (2) examine the issuer, underwriter, or others under oath, and (3) require the production of a balance sheet and an income statement certified by a public or certified accountant approved by the Commission. The failure of an issuer or underwriter to cooperate with such examination constitutes proper ground for issuance of a stop order.[25]

Any person aggrieved by an order of the Commission may obtain review in the U.S. Court of Appeals for the circuit where the person resides or has the principal place of business or in the U.S. Court of Appeals for the District of Columbia.[26]

Liability under Section 11

Due Diligence. Section 11 of the act establishes liability of public accountants to third-party investors when the accountant makes an untrue statement of a material fact (or omits a material fact) in a registration statement.[27] The public accountant can avoid liability by the "due diligence" defense of showing that after reasonable investigation, s/he had reasonable ground to believe and did believe at the time the registration statement became effective that the statements therein were true.[28] The law provides that in determining "what constitutes reasonable investigation and reasonable ground for belief, the standard of reasonableness shall be that required of a prudent man in the management of his own property."[29]

Since the certifying accountants' liability under section 11 is conditioned on false statements as of the effective date, it is important for the accountants to

20. SEC Reg. S-X, 17 C.F.R. § 210.
21. SEC Reg. S-X, 17 C.F.R. § 210.2–01.
22. SEC Reg. S-X, 17 C.F.R. § 210.2–02.
23. Securities Act of 1933 § 8(d), 15 U.S.C. § 77(h)(d).
24. Securities Act of 1933 § 8(b), 15 U.S.C. § 77(h)(b).
25. Securities Act of 1933 § 8(e), 15 U.S.C. § 77(h)(e).
26. Securities Act of 1933 § 9, 15 U.S.C. § 77(i).
27. Section 11 of the Securities Act of 1933, 15 U.S.C. § 77k (1970). Essential allegations in a complaint filed under the 1933 act are set forth in 7 *Am. Jr. Pl. and Pr. Forms* 609–10, rev. ed. (1969). Suit can be maintained against any person who (a) signed the registration statement, (b) was director or partner at time of filing, (c) was named in the registration statement as about to become director or partner, (d) was an accountant, engineer, or appraiser named as having prepared or certified any part of the registration statement, and (e) was an underwriter of the security. Section 12 also imposes liability on one offering or selling securities (a) by means of false written or oral statements or (b) without registration.
28. Section 11(b) of the Securities Act of 1933, 15 U.S.C. § 77k(b), which is the "due diligence" defense, provides: "Notwithstanding the provisions of subsection (a) of this section no person, other than the issuer, shall be liable as provided therein who shall sustain the burden of proof—(3) that . . . (B) as regards any part of the registration statement purporting to be made upon his authority as an expert . . . (i) he had, after reasonable investigation, reasonable ground to believe and did believe, at the time such part of the registration statement became effective, that the statements therein were true and that there was no omission to state a material fact required to be stated therein or necessary to make the statements therein not misleading. . . ."
29. Securities Act of 1933 § 11(c), 15 U.S.C. § 77k(c) (1970).

exercise due diligence to see that statements they certify are correct at that time. For this purpose they customarily carry out a due-diligence review called an S-1 review, after Form S-1, which is one of the most commonly applicable forms for financial statements filed in a registration statement.

The law imposes the same requirement of due diligence on directors, underwriters, and accountants. While directors, underwriters, and other experts have benefit of the due-diligence defense, the issuer is liable for misstatements and has no due-diligence defense. The position of underwriter is in a sense adverse to directors, since they cannot rely on information furnished by directors without verification, but must make a reasonable investigation of their own. According to Loss,[30] professor of law at Harvard, the underwriters usually arrange a due diligence meeting while waiting for the registration statement to become effective. Loss advises that in view of the potential liability such a meeting should be a serious matter for representatives of the issuer, the issuer's attorney, underwriters, the underwriters' attorney, the public accountant, and any other experts.[31] The underwriter has a possible, but not yet clearly defined, defense under section 11(b)(3)(c), which permits reliance upon expert accountants except where there is reason for doubt. In order to show reliance upon auditors, underwriters ask auditors for "comfort letters" assuring that there is no reason to doubt any of the statements, especially those subsequent to the certification date. In an apparent effort to limit the expanding scope of the auditor's responsibility, AICPA standards limit the assurances which the accountant should provide for the underwriter.[32]

Limited Scope of Section 11 Liability. Section 11 of the 1933 act extends liability only to misleading statements in the registration statement. Although this does include the prospectus, it does not extend liability to periodic reports filed with the SEC, nor to annual reports distributed to stockholders. Since a registration statement is filed only when a corporation is making a new public offering, the extension of auditor's liability to third parties under the 1933 act is quite limited. In *Grimm v. Whitney-Fidalgo Seafoods, Inc.,* the court held that the liability of accountants under section 11 is limited to those financials included within the auditor's opinion:

> Price asserts, correctly, that its liability under section 11 is limited to those materials it prepared or which others prepared on its authority, and that "[j]ust

what has been certified can be determined within the four corners of the prospectus."[33]

The right of suit given to "any person acquiring such security" relates only to one acquiring the specific securities offered through the registration statement.[34] Where the registration statement covers additional securities of an already outstanding class, plaintiffs who purchased in the open market must be able to trace their particular securities to those issued under the registration statement.[35] And where the registration statement covers a new issue of preferred stock, there is no liability to a purchaser of common stock even though the purchaser can prove reliance.[36] Where plaintiffs cannot trace their *specific* shares to the registration statement, they can possibly still recover under the 1934 act, but such recovery is conditioned on proof of more than ordinary negligence.

Standard of Conduct. Section 11 puts the burden of proving due diligence on the defendant public accountants because in such complex situations the information and evidence would be known to them and largely unavailable to investors. Since negligence is the failure to exercise due care, some observers have concluded that the statute provides essentially a negligence standard.[37] Section 11 provides liability for material misstatements or omissions; however, liability is incurred at common law only where the auditor fails to exercise the professional skill usually possessed by members of the profession. Since few cases involving liability of accountants have been decided under section 11, the required standard of conduct is not yet well defined.

Reliance. Section 11 requires reliance as an element of the plaintiff's case *only where* the plaintiff

30. 3 L. Loss, *Securities Regulation* 1730–31, 2nd ed. (1961).

31. Ibid. at 1731.

32. The rules concerning letters for underwriters are now codified in *CCH AICPA Professional Standards,* AU § 630.

33. Grimm v. Whitney-Fidalgo Seafoods, Inc., CCH Fed. Sec. L. Rep. ¶ 96,029 (S.D.N.Y. 1973). *Accord,* McFarland v. Memorex Corp., CCH Fed. Sec. L. Rep. ¶ 97,368 (N.D. Cal. 1980). These cases must be carefully placed in context by considering the criminal conviction under the Exchange Act in United States v. Natelli, 527 F.2d 311 (1975), *cert. denied,* 425 U.S. 934 (1976), for unaudited data in a proxy statement: "We do not think this means, in terms of professional standards, that the accountant may shut his eyes in reckless disregard of his knowledge that highly suspicious figures, known to him to be suspicious, were being included in the unaudited earnings figures with which he was 'associated' in the proxy statement." Furthermore, professional standards now give the auditor limited responsibility with respect to "other information" in annual reports to shareholders and Exchange Act filings (see *CCH AICPA Professional Standards,* AU § 550).

34. 3 L. Loss, *Securities Regulation* 1731, 2nd ed. (1961).

35. Barnes v. Osofsky, 373 F.2d 269 (2d Cir. 1967); Colonial Realty Corp. v. Brunswick Corp., 257 F. Supp. 875 (S.D.N.Y. 1966).

36. Fischman v. Raytheon Mfg. Co. 9 F.R.D. 707 (S.D.N.Y. 1949); 188 F.2d 783 (2d Cir. 1951).

37. 3 L. Loss, *Securities Regulation* 1730, 2nd ed. (1961). The U.S. Supreme Court expressed this in dictum in the *Hochfelder* case.

purchases the security after the issuance of an earnings statement covering a period of at least 12 months following the effective date of the registration statement. When reliance is required, it is not necessary to prove that the plaintiff read the registration statement.

Materiality. Section 11 liability is conditioned on the omission or misstatement of a material fact. This is an *objective* test of whether there is a substantial likelihood that a reasonable investor would consider it important in making investment decisions.[38] This element should not be confused with *reliance* (discussed above), which relates to the subjective effect of the misstatement on conduct of the *particular* plaintiff.

Measure of Damages. Section 11(e) of the 1933 act establishes the measure of damages. The accountant is made liable for the difference between the amount paid and the market value of the security at the time of suit; if the security has been sold, the amount recoverable is the difference in amount paid and sale price. Recovery is limited, however, to the price at which the security was offered to the public. If the securities are sold after suit, but before judgment, the plaintiff cannot recover any decrease in value after suit, but the defendant is given benefit of any increase in value after suit. It is, therefore, to the plaintiff's advantage to sell the security before filing suit.

Statute of Limitations. The time limitation provides that action must be brought within one year after the untruth or omission was or should have been discovered, but no more than three years after the security was offered to the public.[39]

Defenses under Section 11

Defenses available to the accountant are:

1. Statements are true and are not misleading.
2. Misstatement was immaterial.
3. Plaintiffs purchased after the issuance of an earnings statement covering 12 months following the effective date of the registration statement and did not rely on it.
4. Accountant exercised due diligence.

5. Damage does not relate to the misstatement by the accountant.[40]
6. Plaintiff had prior knowledge of the falsity of the misrepresentations.[41]
7. Statute of limitations has run.

The only elements that the plaintiff must prove are related to the first three items. Once the plaintiffs prove a material misstatement, the burden shifts to the defendant to prove items 4 through 7 in order to avoid liability.

Section 11(e) contains a provision that enables courts to require the plaintiffs to provide security, so that if the suit is found to be without merit, the defendant can be reimbursed for costs and reasonable attorneys' fees. In *Aid Auto Stores, Inc. v. Cannon*[42] the court awarded defendant costs and attorney's fees of $8,480 based on a finding that plaintiff's claims under both section 11 of the Securities Act and section 10(b) of the Exchange Act met the test of bordering on frivolity or brought in bad faith.

Rights of Contribution. Section 11(f) of the act specifically enables the defendants to claim contribution from other parties:

> All or any one or more of the persons specified in subsection (a) shall be jointly and severally liable, and every person who becomes liable to make any payment under this section may recover contribution as in cases of contract from any person who, if sued separately, would have been liable to make the same payment, unless the person who has become liable was, and the other was not, guilty of fraudulent misrepresentation.

Cases under Section 11

Shonts v. Hirliman. In the first case involving accountants, *Shonts v. Hirliman,*[43] the court held there was no liability for failure to disclose an obligation to pay $35,000 minimum annual rental under a lease. The accountants' certificate was dated January 19, 1937. A telegram (which did not refer to a minimum annual rental) dated January 31, 1937, committed the company to a rental arrangement and was followed by for-

---

38. In TSC Industries, Inc. v. Northway, Inc., 426 U.S. 438, 449 (1976), the U.S. Supreme Court said: "An omitted fact is material if there is a substantial likelihood that a reasonable shareholder would consider it important in deciding how to vote." Thus it is not necessary to prove that disclosure of an omission would cause a change in the investment decision. See Chapter 13 for a complete analysis of materiality.

39. Securities Act of 1933 § 13, 15 U.S.C. § 77m (1970). In Morse v. Peat, Marwick, Mitchell & Co., CCH Fed. Sec. L. Rep. ¶ 96,444 (S.D.N.Y. 1977), the court held that the statute of limitations starts to run on the effective date of the registration statement. In Summer v. Land & Leisure, Inc., 664 F.2d 965 (5th Cir. 1981), the court held that claims against an accounting firm were barred because normal tolling rules do not apply to sections 11 and 12(2) of the Securities Act.

40. Section 11(e) states that "if the defendant proves that any portion or all of such damages represents other than the depreciation in value of such security resulting from such part of the registration statement, with respect to which his liability is asserted, not being true or omitting to state a material fact required to be stated therein or necessary to make the statements therein not misleading, such portion of or all such damages shall not be recoverable."

41. Section 11(a), which imposes liability, contains the exception: "unless it is proved that at the time of such acquisition he knew of such untruth or omission."

42. Aid Auto Stores Inc. v. Cannon, CCH Fed. Sec. L. Rep. ¶ 94,971 (S.D.N.Y. 1975).

43. Shonts v. Hirliman, 28 F. Supp. 478 (D.C.S.D. Cal. 1939).

mal leasing on March 9, 1937. The plaintiffs stressed the failure to disclose the minimum annual rental in amendments to the registration statement dated January 23, 1937, and February 1, 1937. In finding that the accountants could not be charged with misrepresentation of events occurring after their certification the court held:

> The rental arranagement was not called to their attention. There was no entry on the books at their disposal, from which, by further inquiry, they might have discovered that there was such an undertaking. Absent these, they cannot be charged with a misrepresentation which was made later—long after their certification.

This ruling has been criticized as ignoring the statute that requires "reasonable grounds for belief at the time the registration statement becomes effective."[44] The accounting profession has recognized the duty to go beyond the requirements of *Shonts v. Hirliman. Statement on Auditing Procedure No. 47:* "Subsequent Events," issued in September 1971, provides:

> To sustain the burden of proof that he has made a "reasonable investigation" as required under the Securities Act of 1933, the auditor should extend his procedures with respect to subsequent events from the date of his report up to the effective date or as close thereto as is reasonable and practicable in the circumstances.[45]

The required extension of procedures includes (1) comparison of unaudited data with the audited statements, (2) inquiries to the client's officers, executives, and legal counsel, and (3) other procedures necessary to dispose of questions that arise.

The BarChris Case. Another case involving accountants under section 11 is *Escott v. BarChris Construction Corp.*[46] BarChris was engaged in construction of bowling centers that in most cases included bar and restaurant facilities. The business was an outgrowth of a partnership formed by Vitolo and Pugliese in 1946. Pugliese supervised construction work, and Vitolo was concerned with obtaining new business. According to the prospectus, net sales had increased (in round figures) from $800,000 in 1956 to over $9,165,000 in 1960.

BarChris was in constant need of cash to finance its growing operations. BarChris filed a registration statement for debentures in preliminary form on March 30, 1961, and filed amendments on May 11 and May 16. The closing of financing took place on May 24

when BarChris received the net proceeds of financing. On October 29, 1962, a petition was filed under chapter XI of the Bankruptcy Act.

Purchasers of debentures brought suit against (1) persons who signed the registration statement, (2) the underwriters (eight investment banking firms), and (3) BarChris's auditors, Peat, Marwick, Mitchell & Co. (PMM), under section 11 of the Securities Act of 1933, alleging that the registration statement contained material false statements and material omissions. PMM pleaded the due-diligence defense for an expert.

PMM audited BarChris's financial statements for 1958, 1959, and 1960. The 1960 figures were set forth in the registration statement. PMM also undertook an S-1 review in connection with the registration. Most of the actual audit was performed by a senior accountant, Berardi, who was not yet a CPA. He had no previous experience with the bowling industry, and this was his first job as senior accountant. He was assisted by junior accountants. In the words of the court, "He could hardly have been given a more difficult assignment." Among other things, the court found that Berardi failed to discover that Capitol Lanes had not been sold, which affected both sales and the liability side of the balance sheet.

The purpose of the S-1 review was to ascertain whether, subsequent to the certified balance sheet, any material changes had occurred that should be disclosed to prevent the balance sheet figures from being misleading. The court held:

> There had been a material change for the worse in BarChris's financial position. That change was sufficiently serious so that the failure to disclose it made the 1960 figures misleading. Berardi did not discover it. As far as results were concerned, his S-1 review was useless.
>
> Accountants should not be held to a standard higher than that recognized in their profession. I do not do so here. Berardi's review did not come up to that standard. He did not take some of the steps which Peat, Marwick's written program prescribed. He did not spend an adequate amount of time on a task of this magnitude. Most important of all, he was too easily satisfied with glib answers to his inquiries.
>
> This is not to say that he should have made a complete audit. But there were enough danger signals in the materials which he did examine to require some further investigation on his part. Generally accepted accounting standards required such further investigation under these circumstances. It is not always sufficient merely to ask questions.
>
> Here again, the burden of proof is on Peat, Marwick. I find that that burden has not been satisfied. I conclude that Peat, Marwick has not established its due diligence defense.

The *BarChris* case was reportedly settled without a judicial determination of the sufficiency of

---

44. 3 L. Loss, *Securities Regulation* 1732–33, 2nd ed. (1961).

45. This rule is now codified in *CCH AICPA Professional Standards,* AU § 710.08.

46. Escott v. BarChris Construction Corp., 283 F. Supp. 643 (S.D.N.Y. 1968).

the underwriters' statement of claim against Peat, Marwick on the basis of Peat Marwick's comfort letter.[47]

BarChris and Accounting Principles. In *BarChris* the judge found that Capitol Lanes had not been sold when it was apparently the subject of a sale and leaseback by a subsidiary. In 1960, when the sale and leaseback took place, the only specific rule was that there should be disclosure of material obligations under long-term leases and that "in addition, in the year in which the transaction originates, there should be disclosure of the principal details of any important sale-and-lease transaction."[48]

In 1964 the Accounting Principles Board established an accounting principle for recognition of gain on a sale and leaseback:

> The Board is of the opinion that the sale and the leaseback usually cannot be accounted for as independent transactions. Neither the sale price nor the annual rental can be objectively evaluated independently of the other. Consequently, material gains or losses resulting from the sale of properties which are the subject of sale-and-leaseback transactions, together with the related tax effect, should be amortized over the life of the lease as an adjustment of the rental cost (or, if the leased property is capitalized, as an adjustment of depreciation).[49]

BarChris demonstrates that the courts may impose liability on accountants where a failure to portray economic realities produces materially misleading results regardless of the absence of specific accounting rules.

Section 12(2) Liability

Section 12(2) imposes liability on any person who:

> offers or sells a security . . . by means of a prospectus or oral communication, which includes an untrue statement of a material fact or omits to state a material fact necessary in order to make the statements, in light of the circumstances under which they were made, not misleading . . .

Liability is imposed in favor of the purchaser of the security from the person who offers or sells the security for:

the consideration paid for such security with interest thereon, less the amount of income received thereon, upon the tender of such security or for damages if he no longer owns the security.

Since accountants are not usually offerors or sellers, some courts have held they cannot be held liable under section 12(2).[50] However, other courts have held that active participation in the selling effort or related activities can result in accountants' liability for aiding and abetting a section 12(2) violation.[51] Section 12(2) applies regardless of an exemption from registration requirements, and *prospectus* is broadly construed to include "commercial paper reports," confirmations of sales, and implied representations.

In a case not involving accounting defendants, the court held that section 12(2) imposes liability without regard to reliance by plaintiffs on the misrepresentation or omission. Liability is based on sales "*by means of* a prospectus or oral communication, which includes an untrue statement of a material fact or omits to state a material fact." The court held:

> Although the "by means of" language in the statute requires some causal connection between the misleading representation or omission and plaintiff's purchase, defendants' interpretation is much too stringent. It is well settled that § 12(2) imposes liability without regard to whether the buyer relied on the misrepresentation or omission.[52]

47. Henry B. Reiling and Russell A. Taussig, "Recent Liability Cases—Implications for Accountants," *Journal of Accountancy,* September 1970, pp. 47–48.

48. *Accounting Research and Terminology Bulletins: Final Edition* (New York: American Institute of Certified Public Accountants, 1961), Bulletin 43, p. 126.

49. *APB Opinion No. 5:* "Reporting of Leases in Financial Statements of Lessee" (New York: American Institute of Certified Public Accountants, 1964), ¶ 21.

50. Dorfman v. First Boston Corp., 336 F. Supp. 1089 (E.D.Pa. 1972) (complaint by purchaser of bonds of a Penn Central subsidiary dismissed because it failed to allege that Peat, Marwick, Mitchell & Co. sold securities in violation of section 12(2); however, the court noted that liability could be imposed on an agent "who takes an active part in negotiating a sale for the direct seller"); Kramer v. Scientific Control Corp., 452 F. Supp. 812 (E.D.Pa. 1978) (complaint by purchaser of stock dismissed against Arthur Andersen & Co. because a prerequisite to imposition of liability based on § 12(2) is strict privity between buyer and the immediate seller); Lorber v. Beebe, 407 F. Supp. 279 (S.D.N.Y. 1976) (complaint against Price Waterhouse & Co. dismissed because under section 12(2) plaintiff must show that defendant was seller or someone aiding and abetting the seller and that the sale was effected by means of written or oral communications from seller to plaintiff).

51. *In re* Caesar's Palace Securities Litigation, 360 F. Supp. 366, 378–383 (S.D.N.Y. 1973) (accountants may be held liable under section 12(2) upon proof of conspiracy with the seller); Sandusky Land, Ltd. v. Uniplan Groups, Inc., 400 F. Supp. 440 (N.D. Ohio 1975) (motion to dismiss of Haskins & Sells denied where investors in a limited partnership tax shelter alleged reliance upon the accounting firm's written opinion as to the flow through of tax benefits which were disallowed by the IRS); Vogel v. Trahan, CCH Fed. Sec. L. Rep. ¶ 97,303 (E.D. Pa. 1980) (motions to dismiss by accounting firms that prepared the financials for the limited partnership offering circular and the accounting firm that advised as to availability of tax deductions denied because section 12(2) liability may be imposed on accounting defendants who aid and abet section 12(2) violations).

52. Sanders v. John Nuveen & Co., Inc., 619 F.2d 1222 (7th Cir. 1980).

PRACTICAL POINTER

Active participation in the sale of securities may result in (1) liability under § 12(1) of the Securities Act if securities, such as limited partnerships, are not registered and are not exempt from registration, (2) liability for negligent misrepresentation under § 12(2) of the Securities Act, and (3) being required to register as an investment adviser under the Investment Advisers Act of 1940.

THE EXCHANGE ACT

Disclosure Requirements and Enforcement

The Exchange Act deals primarily with trading in securities. All securities (1) sold on a national security exchange[53] or (2) issued by firms having assets in excess of $1 million and 500 or more holders of a class of equity securities[54] come under the continuous disclosure provisions of the act.

Under section 13 the Commission is empowered to require issuers of registered securities to file annual reports, quarterly reports, and information required to keep the registration statement current. The initial registration for trading is similar to registration under the 1933 act. The annual reports must be certified by independent public accountants if required by the rules and regulations of the Commission.[55] The Commission's power to make accounting and auditing rules is discussed in Chapter 3.

When management solicits proxies relating to an annual meeting at which directors are to be elected, *proxy statements and annual reports* must be furnished. Proxy statements must disclose management's direct and indirect security holdings, compensation for the five highest paid individuals receiving more than $50,000 per year, and occupation and business relationships of nominees.[56]

Each annual report must contain

> audited balance sheets as of the end of each of the two most recent fiscal years and audited statements of income and changes in financial position for each of the

three most recent fiscal years prepared in accordance with Regulation S-X. . . .[57]

It must also include data for the last five years on sales; income (loss) from continuing operations; income (loss) from continuing operations per common share; total assets; long-term obligations and redeemable preferred stock and certain specified ratios. Management's discussion and analysis of financial condition and results of operations must also be provided. The proxy statement or annual report must offer to provide, without charge, a copy of the issuer's annual report (Form 10-K or 12-K) filed with the Commission.

Even where proxies are not solicited by management, the issuer must, before the annual meeting of stockholders, file with the Commission and transmit to all holders of record substantially equivalent information as required for proxy solicitations.[58] Seven copies of each such annual report must be furnished to the Commission for information only, but the law provides these are not "filed" and thus avoids possible liability under section 18 for false and misleading statements.[59]

The Commission enforces the Exchange Act disclosure requirements by subjecting violators to (1) summary suspension of trading for 10 days or less,[60] (2) administrative hearings, followed by an order suspending trading for 12 months or less,[61] (3) civil injunctive proceedings in federal district courts,[62] or (4) reference of matters to the Attorney General who, in his discretion, may institute criminal proceedings.[63] Section 21 of the act gives the Commission power to (1) conduct investigations of violations, (2) subpoena witnesses and compel production of records, and (3) enforce subpoenas through federal district courts.

Any persons aggrieved by an order of the Commission may obtain review of the order in the U.S. Court of Appeals for the circuit where they reside or have their principal place of business or in the U.S. Court of Appeals for the District of Columbia.[64]

---

53. Securities Exchange Act of 1934 § 12(a), 15 U.S.C. § 78l(a).

54. Securities Exchange Act of 1934 § 12(g), 15 U.S.C. § 78l(g).

55. Securities Exchange Act of 1934 § 13(a), 15 U.S.C. § 78m(a). The SEC–prescribed forms, which also constitute part of the rules and regulations, require certified financial statements.

56. Securities Exchange Act of 1934 § 14, 15 U.S.C. § 78n; rule 14a-3, 17 C.F.R. § 240.14a-3; Schedule 14A, § 240.14a-101.

57. Rule 14a-3, 17 C.F.R. § 240.14a-3, adopted pursuant to Securities Exchange Act of 1934 § 14(a), 15 U.S.C. § 78n(c).

58. Securities Exchange Act of 1934 § 14(c), 15 U.S.C. § 78(c).

59. Rule 14a-3, 17 C.F.R. § 240.14a-3, adopted pursuant to Securities Exchange Act of 1934 § 14(a), 15 U.S.C. § 78n(a).

60. Securities Exchange Act of 1934 § 12(k), 15 U.S.C. § 782(k). In SEC v. Sloan, 436 U.S. 103 (1978), the U.S. Supreme Court held that the SEC is not empowered to tack successive 10-day summary suspension orders based on a single set of circumstances.

61. Ibid.

62. Securities Exchange Act of 1934 § 21, 15 U.S.C. § 78u.

63. Ibid.

64. Securities Exchange Act of 1934 § 25, 15 U.S.C. § 78y.

Liability under Section 10(b)

Section 10(b) and rule 10b-5 contain no express provisions for any civil liability, but federal courts have construed the provisions as establishing civil remedies for any violation. Section 10(b) is wide in scope, since liability can be based on any false statements without regard to whether they are "filed" with the SEC.

Section 10(b) of the 1934 act provides:

> It shall be unlawful for any person, directly or indirectly, by the use of any means or instrumentality of interstate commerce or of the mails, or of any facility of any national securities exchange—
>
> (b) to use or employ, in connection with the purchase or sale of any security registered on a national securities exchange or any security not so registered, any manipulative or deceptive device or contrivance in contravention of such rules and regulations as the Commission may prescribe as necessary or appropriate in the public interest or for the protection of investors.[65]

The law was further amplified by rule 10b-5 promulgated by the SEC:

> It shall be unlawful for any person, directly or indirectly, by the use of any means or instrumentality of interstate commerce, or of the mails, or of any facility of any national securities exchange,
>
> *a.* To employ any device, scheme, or artifice to defraud,
>
> *b.* To make any untrue statement of a material fact or to omit to state a material fact necessary in order to make the statement made, in the light of the circumstances under which they were made, not misleading, or
>
> *c.* To engage in any act, practice, or course of business which operates or would operate as a fraud or deceit upon any person, in connection with the purchase or sale of any security.[66]

Standard of Conduct. The standard of conduct for imposing civil liability under section 10(b) was decided in a 1976 landmark decision by the U.S. Supreme Court in *Ernst & Ernst v. Hochfelder.*[67] The case arose as a result of an audit of First Securities Company of Chicago, a small brokerage firm registered with the SEC as a broker-dealer and member of the Midwest Stock Exchange and National Association of Securities Dealers, Inc.

Leston B. Nay, president and 92 percent stockholder of First Securities, left a suicide note in 1968 in which he described First Securities as bankrupt due to his embezzlement of certain escrow accounts. Nay

had induced customers to invest in an "escrow" account that would yield a high rate of return. Customers made such investments from 1962 through 1966. Ernst & Ernst had been retained from 1946 through their last audit in November 1967.

The plaintiffs, who were investors in the escrow account, sued Ernst & Ernst, claiming that negligence of Ernst & Ernst, aided and abetted Nay's 10b-5 violations. It was alleged that Ernst & Ernst should have discovered the mail rule that required all mail addressed to Nay to be held unopened during his absence and that further investigation would have revealed or prevented the fraud.

The United States Supreme Court dismissed the claim against Ernst & Ernst and held that auditors are liable under section 10(b) only upon proof of intent to deceive, manipulate, or defraud. The Court reserved judgment as to whether reckless behavior would be sufficient to impose liability.

While lower courts have held that recklessness is a sufficient basis for imposing liability,[68] complaints against accountants are dismissed where the plaintiffs fail to identify specific items that were knowingly or recklessly misrepresented prior to plaintiffs' purchase of the investment.[69]

Cases Imposing Liability on Accountants. In *Herzfeld v. Laventhol, Krekstein, Horwath & Horwath,*[70] decided by the U.S. Court of Appeals for the Second Circuit shortly after the Supreme Court decision in *Hochfelder,* the court held the accounting firm liable to an investor in a private placement of securities. The

65. Securities Exchange Act of 1934 § 10(b), 15 U.S.C. § 78j.

66. 17 C.F.R. § 240.10b-5.

67. Ernst & Ernst v. Hochfelder, 425 U.S. 185 (1976).

68. Rolf v. Blyth, Eastman, Dillon & Co., 570 F.2d 38 (2d Cir.), *cert. denied,* 439 U.S. 1039 (1978); McLean v. Alexander, 599 F.2d 1190 (3d Cir. 1979); First Va. Bankshares v. Benson, 559 F.2d 1307 (5th Cir. 1977), *cert. denied,* 435 U.S. 952 (1978); Mansbach v. Prescott, Ball & Turben, 598 F.2d 1017 (6th Cir. 1979); Sundstrand Corp. v. Sun Chem. Corp., 553 F.2d 1033 (7th Cir.), *cert. denied,* 434 U.S. 875; Nelson v. Serwold, 576 F.2d 1332 (9th Cir.), *cert. denied,* 439 U.S. 970 (1978). For an analysis of recklessness as "scienter," see Louis Haimoff, "Holmes Looks at Hochfelder and 10b-5," *Business Lawyer,* November 1976, pp. 147–75.

Can a pattern of negligent conduct constitute scienter? Consider this from Hubshman v. Alexander Grant & Co., CCH Fed. Sec. L. Rep. ¶ 95,923 (S.D.N.Y. 1977): "While, taken separately, these claims might only be indicative of negligence or professional malpractice; when taken together they may read to support plaintiffs' allegations of a pattern of behavior from which plaintiffs may draw an inference of scienter, on information and belief."

69. Denny v. Barber, 576 F.2d 465 (2d Cir. 1978) (F.R. Cir. P. 9(b) requires fraud to be alleged with particularity). The problem of pleading fraud with particularity can be avoided by suing under sections 11 or 12(2) of the Securities Act where liability is imposed for negligence. *See* McFarland v. Memorex Corp., CCH Fed. Sec. L. Rep. ¶ 97,368 (N.D. Cal. 1980).

70. Herzfeld v. Laventhol, Krekstein, Horwath & Horwath, 540 F.2d 27 (2d Cir. 1976). For an extensive analysis, *see* Denzil Y. Causey, Jr., *"Herzfeld* Revisited after *Hochfelder:* The 'Scienter' Standard Applied to the Reporting of Uncertainties," *American Business Law Journal,* Fall 1976, pp. 252–67.

critical part of the audit involved a real estate purchase and resale transaction that converted a net loss to a net profit. Each agreement was on an identical printed form titled "Agreement for Sale of Real Estate." The first was a purchase of nursing home properties on November 22, and the second was for the resale on November 26. There was reference to an attached Exhibit A schedule of the property, which was apparently never attached. The purchase involved $5,000 down on a price of over $13 million, and the sale involved $25,000 down on a sale price of over $15 million. Although this transaction was never closed, Laventhol included $235,000 in current profit by adding a down payment of $25,000 to another payment of $25,000 that had *not* been made and then adding $185,000 liquidated damages provided for nonperformance by the buyer.

Under pressure by the client, Laventhol changed the $1,795,500 "unrealized gross profit" referred to in the income statement to "deferred gross profit." This second report contained a qualified "subject to collectibility of the balance receivable" clause. Neither the purchase nor sale was consummated, and over a year later the company filed a petition under chapter XI of the Bankruptcy Act. The court rejected Laventhol's argument that the only statement made by an auditor upon which an investor is entitled to rely is the auditor's opinion letter. In imposing liability for scienter under section 10(b) the court noted that the investor checked the Laventhol income statement and said:

> In reliance upon this corroborative Laventhol financial statement, Herzfeld completed his investment in FGL securities. . . .

* * * * *

> The issue here is not one of negligence, but of the "materially misleading" treatment of facts known to Laventhol in its submitted audit.
>
> The function of an accountant is not merely to verify the correctness of the addition and subtraction of the company's bookkeepers. Nor does it take a fiscal wizard to appreciate the elemental and universal accounting principle that revenue should not be recognized until the "earning process is complete or virtually complete," and "an exchange has taken place." Insofar as FGL's [the client's] interest in Monterey transactions is concerned, the earning process had hardly commenced, let alone neared completion."

* * * * *

The vice of the report was its representation that the Monterey transactions were consummated and the concomitant statement that current and deferred profit had been realized. This would have been remedied by simply not recognizing the sales as completed transactions for the period ending November 30, 1969.

* * * * *

The accountants here are not being cast in damages for negligent nonfeasance or misfeasance, but because of their active participation in the preparation and issuance of false and materially misleading accounting reports upon which Herzfeld relied to his damage.

In the case of *Sharp v. Coopers & Lybrand*,[71] the U.S. Court of Appeals for the Third Circuit held an accounting firm liable to investors under section 10(b) for recklessness in writing a tax opinion letter. This case involved "scienter" of the accounting firm's employee for which the firm was held responsible under the doctrine of *respondeat superior* (let the master answer) based on an accounting firm's strict duty to supervise its employees.

Cases Rejecting Accountants' Liability. In several cases, courts have held that the accounting firm's conduct did not amount to recklessness.[72] In a split decision the Sixth Circuit reversed a lower court which held Peat, Marwick, Mitchell & Co. liable under section 10(b) for failure to disclose pervasive internal control weaknesses in its audit report.[73]

In another split decision the Third Circuit reversed the lower court that held a local CPA firm liable under section 10(b) to a sophisticated investor who acquired stock in a private placement.[74] The controversy focused on less than $75,000 of receivables which represented 40 percent of total assets but less than 5 percent of the purchase price. Some of the receivables were in dispute, but most involved consignments instead of amounts owed on account. The court held the CPAs were not liable because they knew nothing of the fraud whereby the sellers made the buyer believe that the company's only product was selling well, when in fact they knew it was defective and unmarketable. The court quoted this test for recklessness:

> Reckless conduct may be defined as highly unreasonable conduct involving not merely simple, or even inexcusable negligence, but an extreme departure from

71. Sharp v. Coopers & Lybrand, 649 F.2d 175 (3d Cir. 1981), *cert. filed*, Sept. 2, 1981. Compare Hickman v. Groesbeck, 389 F. Supp. 769 (D. Utah 1974), where the court dismissed the action against a CPA firm that prepared its tax-opinion letter on the basis of facts related over the telephone with no independent verification because the CPAs could not have been expected to know about the fraud.

72. In Pegasus Fund v. Laraneta, 617 F.2d 1335 (9th Cir. 1980), the court dismissed the claim against Arthur Young & Co. because the allegation, that AY failed to discover that restricted securities carried at cost were practically worthless, was at most ordinary negligence.

In Oleck v. Fischer, 623 F.2d 791 (2d Cir. 1980), the appeals court affirmed the lower court's finding that Arthur Andersen & Co. did not act recklessly because it relied on cash projections in issuing its unqualified opinion. However, in clarifying the lower court's finding as to a footnote, it said; "An objective reader of the controversial footnote might well wonder whether the auditors had been overly accomodating to their client's desire to have the transaction look like a wash."

73. Adams v. Standard Knitting Mills, 623 F.2d 422 (6th Cir. 1980).

74. McLean v. Alexander, 599 F.2d 1190 (3d Cir. 1979).

the standards of ordinary care, and which presents a danger of misleading buyers or sellers that is either known to the defendant or is so obvious that the actor must have been aware of it.

Jurisdictional Requirements. Jurisdiction of section 10(b) is invoked by direct or indirect use of (1) any means or instrument of interstate commerce, (2) the mails, or (3) any facility of any national securities exchange. Civil liability can be imposed whenever the jurisdictional means are used directly or indirectly in connection with the wrongful conduct. Evidence that defendants go from one state to another in connection with the sale establishes jurisdiction regardless of the method of transportation.[75] It is not necessary that the misrepresentation or omission be conveyed by the jurisdictional means.[76] The transportation or communication need not be illegal so long as it is related to the illegal conduct or scheme.[77] Clearing a check for remitting of proceeds[78] or later efforts at a cover-up by use of the jurisdictional means is sufficient to invoke jurisdiction.[79]

Since the rule refers to "use of any means or instrumentality of interstate commerce" as opposed to "in interstate commerce," an intrastate telephone call is sufficient to invoke jurisdiction, since a telephone connected to interstate wires is a "means or instrumentality of commerce."[80] Similarly, since the rule refers to use of the mails, the mailing of intrastate letters invokes the rule.[81] The jurisdictional reach is so extensive that the matter is now infrequently disputed in litigation.[82] There is no requirement that the securities be traded on an exchange or over-the-counter market nor that they be subject to any filing require-ments of either the Securities Act or the Exchange Act. In *Wachovia Bank and Trust Co. v. National Student Marketing Corp.*[83] the U.S. Court of Appeals for the District of Columbia Circuit rejected the arguments by Peat, Marwick, Mitchell & Co. (Marketing's auditor) and White & Case (Marketing's counsel) that section 10(b) did not afford a civil remedy to purchasers of newly issued securities in a private placement exempt from SEC filing requirements.

"In Connection With." Section 10(b) of the Exchange Act and rule 10b-5 make it unlawful to use deceptive devices or to make misleading statements "in connection with the purchase or sale of any security." Both the statute and the rule contain the quoted language. In the case of *Blue Chip Stamps v. Manor Drug Stores*[84] the U.S. Supreme Court held that "in connection with" requires that plaintiffs in private damage actions under the rule be actual purchasers or sellers of the securities,[85] however, this requirement does not extend to defendants.

Auditors at first attempted to defend against suits under section 10(b) on the ground that as auditors they are neither purchasers nor sellers and cannot be liable in the absence of privity with plaintiffs. Courts had

---

75. Hill York Corp. v. American Int'l Franchises, Inc., 448 F.2d 680 (5th Cir. 1971).

76. MacClain v. Bules, 275 F.2d 431 (8th Cir. 1960); Blackwell v. Bentsen, 203 F.2d 690 (5th Cir. 1953); Schillner v. H. Vaughan Clarke & Co., 134 F.2d 875 (2d Cir. 1943).

77. Kopald-Quinn & Co. v. United States, 101 F.2d 628 (5th Cir.), *cert. denied sub. nom.* Ricebaum v. United States, 307 U.S. 628 (1939) (delivery of confirmation).

78. Little v. United States, 331 F.2d 287 (8th Cir. 1964); Kann v. United States, 323 U.S. 88, 93 (1944).

79. United States v. Riedel, 126 F.2d 81, 83 (7th Cir. 1942).

80. Spilker v. Shane Laboratories, Inc., 520 F.2d 523 (9th Cir. 1975); Nemitz v. Cunny, 221 F. Supp. 571 (N.D. Ill. 1963); Myzel v. Fields, 386 F.2d 718 (8th Cir. 1967), *cert. denied,* 390 U.S. 951 (1968). *Contra:* Rosen v. Albern Color Research, Inc., 218 F. Supp. 473 (E.D. Pa. 1963).

81. Northern Trust Co. v. Essaness Theatres Corp., 103 F. Supp. 954, 962 (N.D. Ill. 1952).

82. In Gordon v. Lipoff, 320 F. Supp. 905 (W.D. Mo. 1970), the court dismissed a section 10(b) suit against an accounting firm that alleged "The means of interstate commerce and the mails were used at every step of the course of conduct described in the narrative" without any specific facts. The court held the use of the mails and the fraudulent act must bear a distinct relationship to the purchase or sale of securities.

83. Wachovia Bank and Trust Co. v. National Student Marketing Corp. 650 F.2d 342 (D.C. Cir. 1980), *cert. denied,* _____ U.S. _____ (1981).

84. Blue Chip Stamps v. Manor Drug Stores, 421 U.S. 723 (1975).

85. For suits against accounting firms dismissed because of failure of plaintiffs to meet the purchase or sale requirement, *see* Rothstein v. Seidman and Seidman, 410 F. Supp. 244 (S.D.N.Y. 1976), action dismissed because plaintiff invested prior to auditor's report containing alleged misrepresentations; Wittenberg v. Continental Real Estate Partners, 478 F. Supp. 504 (D. Mass. 1979), action against Price Waterhouse & Co. dismissed where alleged misrepresentation occurred after plaintiffs invested; Mendelsohn v. Capital Underwriters, Inc., CCH Fed. Sec. L. Rep. ¶ 97,169 (N.D. Cal. 1979), action against Harris, Kerr, Forster & Co. by limited partners dismissed because any alleged misrepresentations occurred after plaintiffs' investment.

In Rich v. Touche Ross & Co., 415 F. Supp. 95 (S.D.N.Y. 1976), investors claimed their stockbroker's auditor was responsible for their losses, which resulted from leaving their securities in the broker's possession. The court rejected their claims, which were "in connection with a bailment" and not in connection with the purchase or sale of securities.

The securities purchased or sold may be those of a different company from the one having misrepresented financials if there is a close relationship. For example, in Braun v. Northern Ohio Bank, CCH Fed. Sec. L. Rep. ¶ 95,906 (N.D. Ohio 1977), the court, in denying the motion to dismiss of Peat, Marwick, Mitchell & Co., said: "This risk [oral testimony] is controlled if there must not only be a purchase of a security, as the *Birnbaum* rule requires, but the Rule 10b-5 action involving that security must be based upon misrepresentations with regard to the financial condition of the same or closely related company. Without attempting to list all types of relationships that might meet this requirement, standing should at least be granted where the company has a direct management interest in, or proposes to merge with or acquire the company whose securities are purchased." Similarly in Competitive Assocs., Inc. v. Laventhol, Krekstein, Horwath & Horwath, 516 F.2d 811 (2d Cir. 1975), the court held the "in connection with" requirement as to plaintiffs was satisfied by alleging a fraudulent scheme "directly related to the trading process."

little difficulty in rejecting such arguments in the face of allegations of "conspiracy with the issuer" or "aiding and abetting the issuer."[86] It is now well settled that auditors need be neither buyers nor sellers nor in privity with plaintiffs to be liable under section 10(b).[87] However, in order to impose secondary liability on an accounting firm for aiding and abetting, plaintiffs must allege and prove three prerequisites:

1. The existence of a securities law violation by the primary party.
2. "Knowledge" of the violation on the part of the accountant.
3. "Substantial assistance" by the accountant in the achievement of the primary violation.[88]

---

86. In H. L. Green Co. v. Childree, 185 F. Supp. 95 (S.D.N.Y. 1960), plaintiff was a corporation that issued its stock in exchange for stock of another corporation, and defendants were certified public accountants. It was alleged that defendants knowingly prepared false financial statements pursuant to a conspiracy to defraud. The complaint was held to state a claim under section 10(b), and the court rejected the contentions that (1) a merger was not a "purchase or sale" and (2) preparation of a false financial statement does not make the accountant a participant in the sale.

In Miller v. Bargain City, U.S.A., Inc., 229 F. Supp. 33 (E.D. Pa. 1964), plaintiffs purchased stock in Bargain City, U.S.A., Inc., over the counter after consulting Standard & Poor's most recent report and alleged that defendants engaged in a conspiracy in filing false financial statements with the SEC in violation of section 10(b). On defendants' motion to dismiss, the court rejected the argument that because the alleged fraud was covered in section 18, the claim could not be brought under section 10(b). The court also rejected defendants' contention that plaintiffs must show privity of contract with defendants to recover under section 10(b).

87. In Feldberg v. O'Connell, 338 F. Supp. 744 (D. Mass. 1972), limited partner plaintiffs sued the auditors who certified the limited partnership's financials. Plaintiffs alleged they were misled as to the true financial condition and as a result refrained, to their loss, from taking any steps to dissolve the partnership. The court held that allegations that the partnership was to be liquidated was sufficient to constitute a sale of securities and to state a valid claim against the auditor under section 10(b).

In Heit v. Weitzen, 402 F.2d 909 (2d Cir. 1968), cert. denied, 395 U.S. 903 (1969), the complaints essentially involved failure to disclose that a substantial amount of income for fiscal year 1964 was derived from various overcharges on government contracts and that defendants had knowledge or notice of the falsity. The Heit court followed the rule established in *Texas Gulf Sulphur:* The "in connection with" requirement of rule 10b-5 is satisfied if a false representation would cause reasonable investors to purchase and sell in reliance thereon.

In Blakely v. Lisac, 357 F. Supp. 255 (D. Ore. 1972), the court held the accountant liable for unaudited data in a prospectus. The data correctly indicated liability for the financing of an equipment purchase but failed to reveal that the equipment was unusable and that a judgment against the seller was uncollectible.

88. In IIT v. Cornfeld, 619 F.2d 909 (2d Cir. 1980), the court enumerated these prerequisites and dismissed the complaint against Arthur Andersen & Co. for aiding and abetting a section 10(b) violation because there were no allegations of knowledge or recklessness and no showing of substantial assistance. *Compare* Clark v. Cameron-Brown Co., CCH Fed. Sec. L. Rep. ¶ 97,539 (M.D.N.C. 1980), where the court refused to dismiss a complaint by investors in a real estate investment trust alleging that Peat, Marwick, Mitchell & Co. aided and abetted a section 10(b) violation. The court held that allegations of knowingly certifying false financial statements fulfilled the "substantial assistance" element.

Materiality. Liability under section 10(b), as well as any other disclosure liability under the federal securities laws, is conditioned upon misstatement or omission of "material" information. Materiality is viewed as an objective, rather than as a subjective, standard. The issue is whether a reasonable investor, not the particular investor, would attach importance to the alleged misrepresentation or omission.[89]

Reliance and Causation. Since a damage action is compensatory, courts traditionally have required proof that reliance caused the resulting injury in any action for misrepresentation. There are at least three distinctive factual situations that may affect the method of proving the element of reliance and causation. First, if the securities are publicly traded so as to establish a market price, misrepresentation will affect the trading and the price. Certainly analysts, brokers, and others read financial statements and incorporate the information into their evaluation and hence into the market price so that material misrepresentation will inevitably injure all who trade. In this situation, proof of materiality constitutes causation in fact. This is called the "fraud on the market" theory.[90]

In a second situation, the misconduct primarily involves a failure to disclose, as opposed to active misrepresentation, so it is impossible to prove *reliance* on

---

89. See note 38.

90. Blackie v. Barrack, 524 F.2d 891, 906–07 (9th Cir. 1975), cert. denied, 429 U.S. 816 (1976); Schlick v. Penn-Dixie Cement Corp., 507 F.2d 374, 381 (2d Cir. 1974), cert. denied, 421 U.S. 976 (1975); Heit v. Weitzen, 402 F.2d 909, 913 (2d Cir. 1968), cert. denied, 395 U.S. 903 (1969).

In Shores v. Sklar, 647 F.2d 462 (5th Cir. 1981), the court embraced the "fraud on the market" theory in a case apparently including a CPA defendant. In reversing the dismissal of the section 10(b) claim because the plaintiff never saw the offering circular, the court held: "The requisite element of causation in fact would be established if Bishop proved the scheme was intended to and did bring the Bonds onto the market fraudulently and proved he relied on the integrity of the offerings of the securities market. His lack of reliance on the Offering Circular, only one component of the overall scheme, is not determinative. . . . Bishop's burden of proof will be to show that (1) the defendants knowingly conspired to bring securities onto the market which were not entitled to be marketed, intending to defraud purchasers, (2) Bishop reasonably relied on the Bonds' availability on the market as an indication of their apparent genuineness, and (3) as a result of the scheme to defraud, he suffered a loss."

In Spectrum Financial Cos. v. Marconsult, Inc., 608 F.2d 377 (9th Cir. 1979), cert. denied, 446 U.S. 936, the plaintiffs who acquired Marconsult stock never saw the financial statements audited by Harris, Kerr, Forster & Co. (HKF). In refusing to dismiss the suit against HKF the court got around the reliance requirement by noting that HKF knew the California Commissioner of Corporations would rely on its audit report.

Compare Mills v. Electric Auto-Lite Co., 396 U.S. 375 (1970), where proxy solicitation material failed to disclose a conflict of interest. At page 385, Mr. Justice Harlan stated the causation principle as follows: "Where there has been a finding of materiality, a shareholder has made a sufficient showing of causal relationship between the violation and the injury for which he seeks redress if, as here, he proves that the proxy solicitation itself, rather than the particular defect in the solicitation materials, was an essential link in the accomplishment of the transaction."

the omission. Persons who trade in the security are injured by not having the benefit of reliance on the omitted disclosures. In this situation it is necessary to prove only that the facts withheld are material in the sense that a reasonable investor would have considered them important in making an investment decision.[91]

In a third possible situation there is not an active market to establish a market price and the misconduct consists of active misrepresentations. In this case the plaintiffs will fail unless they can prove that they relied upon the misrepresentations and that such reliance proximately caused their loss.[92]

In order for the plaintiff to avoid proving reliance, it may be necessary to carefully frame the theory of the case, including allegations and proof, to either avoid alleging misrepresentations or to carefully relate misrepresentations to their effect on the market as opposed to the effect on the plaintiff. Where plaintiff failed to do this, the Eighth Circuit dismissed a complaint against Arthur Young & Co. and said:

> Though other theories of this case might have been devised, we find that the thrust of what Vervaecke actually pleaded was the use of fraudulent misstatement and omission within the four corners of an offering prospectus which mislead *him* and other bond purchasers. . . .
>
> Since this is not a case in which Vervaecke may presume reliance, he was obligated to state facts sufficient to raise a genuine factual dispute with regard to his actual reliance on the misleading documents.[93]

Measure of Damages. Injured plaintiffs are allowed to recover their "out-of-pocket" losses, which is the difference between the contract price and the real or actual value on the transaction date. Actual value is established by looking to the market price when the misrepresentation or omission is cured. Where there are other intervening factors, the actual value is hard to determine. Accordingly, some courts have used other methods, such as the difference between purchase price and amount received on resale.[94]

---

91. In Affiliated Ute Citizens v. United States, 406 U.S. 128 (1972), a bank and its employees made purchases of stock from unsophisticated Indian shareholders without disclosing the higher price prevailing in a secondary market fostered by the bank. At common law the claim of the Indian plaintiffs would have failed for lack of proof of reliance. However, the U.S. Supreme Court held that under 10b-5 damage actions involving nondisclosure, reliance is proved by showing the materiality of the omission: "Under the circumstances of this case involving primarily a failure to disclose, positive proof of reliance is not a prerequisite to recovery. All that is necessary is that the facts withheld be material in the sense that a reasonable investor might have considered them important in the making of this decision. . . . This obligation to disclose and this withholding of a material fact establish the requisite element of causation in fact."

In Sharp v. Coopers & Lybrand, 649 F.2d 175 (3d Cir. 1981), *cert. filed*, Sept. 2, 1981, the court held that plaintiffs were entitled to a rebuttable presumption of reliance because the accounting firm's tax opinion letter allegedly contained both omissions and misrepresentations in violation of section 10(b).

In Tucker v. Arthur Andersen & Co., CCH Fed. Sec. L. Rep. ¶ 95,107 (1975), the court noted that plaintiffs alleged both omissions (concealment of an embezzlement scheme after its discovery and failure to disclose a lack of adequate financial controls) and misrepresentations (misstatement of assets and net income) and indicated that it would allow a presumption of reliance if the plaintiffs could prove that there were either material misrepresentations that affected the market or material omissions.

The defendant can always rebut causation or presumption of reliance by showing that the misrepresentation or omission had no effect on plaintiff's conduct. Thus in Competitive Assocs., Inc. v. Laventhol, Krekstein, Horwath & Horwath, 516 F.2d 811 (2d Cir. 1975), the court held that a showing of reliance is not required where a comprehensive scheme to defraud includes omissions and misrepresentations and substantial collateral conduct. However, upon remand the case was dismissed because evidence showed that the accounting firm's reports were not relevant in plaintiff's decision to hire a portfolio manager. *See* CCH Fed. Sec. L. Rep. ¶ 97,150 (S.D.N.Y. 1979).

92. In Lorber v. Beebe, 407 F. Supp. 279 (S.D.N.Y. 1976), the court demonstrates at page 296 that where plaintiff claims damages for misstatement of earnings, the evidence must show plaintiff's reliance upon the price-earnings ratio in making the investment decision.

In Capital Investments, Inc. v. Bank of Sturgeon Bay, 430 F. Supp. 534 (E.D. Wis. 1977), plaintiffs were estopped from suing an accounting firm in federal court under section 10(b), where a state court had decided in a negligence action that plaintiffs had not relied upon the alleged misrepresentations in selling their stock.

93. Vervaecke v. Chiles, Heider & Co., 578 F.2d 713 (8th Cir. 1978). *Compare* Rifkin v. Crowe, 574 F.2d 256 (5th Cir. 1978), where plaintiffs sued Price Waterhouse & Co. in connection with Price's audit of Recognition Equipment, Inc., claiming the 1969 profit was a result of improperly capitalizing millions of dollars of research and development expenses plus the failure to eliminate profit on sales to a 49-percent-owned subsidiary. In reversing dismissal by the district court the Fifth Circuit noted that plaintiffs' testimony would support recovery under even the most restricted reliance requirement. Rifkin stated in his deposition: "I read every document I received from the Company and to the extent I read it, I relied on it." He also took into account information in *Moody's, The Wall Street Journal,* and the *New York Times.* In making purchases he also relied on the fact that the market price of a stock reflects the information in the financial statements: "I think the buyer of a security has a right to rely on the fact that the stock value bears some reasonable relationship to the financial statements circulated in the investment market. . . . Investors are entitled to rely on the fairness of a price set by the general investment community. . . ."

In Societe Generale DeBanque v. Touche Ross & Co., 69 F.R.D. 24 (S.D. Cal. 1975), the court considered, among others, the dominoes theory used to establish a common core of reliance in a class action suit. Like standing dominoes, one misrepresentation can cause subsequent statements to fall into inaccuracy and distortion when considered by themselves or compared with previous misstatements. There is a commonality of reliance because each investor is, in essence, relying on the same misrepresentations, regardless of the document consulted.

94. Only actual damages are recoverable because of section 28 of the Exchange Act which states: "No person permitted to maintain a suit for damages under the provisions of this title shall recover . . . a total amount in excess of his actual damages on account of the act complained of."

Measuring damages as the difference between the purchase price and (1) the amount received on resale or (2) the value when the

Defenses under Section 10(b)

Some of the more important defenses under section 10(b) are:

1. There is no proof of scienter—intent to deceive, manipulate, or defraud.
2. The defendants' conduct did not cause the plaintiffs any loss (that is, there is a lack of reliance or materiality).
3. The plaintiff failed to exercise due diligence.
4. The statute of limitations has run.
5. Other parties should indemnify or, at least, contribute to the loss.
6. Satisfaction of judgment.

Plaintiffs' Due Diligence. While plaintiffs are not required to prove that they exercised due diligence, they may be required to negate their own recklessness if the defendant puts it in issue. Thus the Second Circuit held (in a case not involving accountants):

> While we have no quarrel whatever with the result in *Hirsch* and *Edwards & Hanly* on the facts there presented, we hold that in the light of *Ernst & Ernst* a plaintiff's burden is simply to negate recklessness when the defendant puts that in issue, not to establish due care.[95]

The Third Circuit requires that plaintiffs act reasonably, permits plaintiffs to presume that other parties are honest, and shifts to defendants the burden of proving that plaintiffs acted unreasonably.[96] The

Seventh and Tenth Circuits agree with the Third and hold that where plaintiffs can show justifiable reliance, there is no duty to investigate except where representations are patently false.[97] The Fifth and Ninth Circuits consider the matter a factual question as to whether plaintiffs acted recklessly.[98]

Most of the decisions can be reconciled by analysis of the relationship between defendants' conduct and plaintiffs' losses: Would the elimination of grossly improper conduct by the defendants have resulted in avoidance of plaintiffs' losses? This eliminates placing the burden on either plaintiff or defendant in order to focus on the effect of the particular conduct by defendants.

Statute of Limitations. Since section 10(b) and rule 10b-5 make no express provision for civil liability, they contain no statute of limitations. Federal courts, therefore, look to laws of the forum state and select the statute of limitations applicable to the state action that is most similar to a civil suit under section 10(b) and rule 10b-5. The courts generally select the limitation period for the forum state's blue-sky law. The result is considerable lack of uniformity for 10b-5 limitations throughout the country.

While state laws determine the length of the limitation period, federal law determines when the period commences. In *Homberg v. Armbrecht*,[99] the U.S. Supreme Court established the equitable tolling doctrine, which tolls the statute of limitations for fraud until the plaintiff knows or by exercise of due diligence should know of the fraud. In its decision of *American Pipe & Construction Co. v. Utah*,[100] the Court also held that filing a class action tolls the statute for all class members whether present or absent.

---

fraud is discovered, can be justified as a rescission alternative under section 29(b) of the Exchange Act which states: "Every contract made in violation of any provision of this title or of any rule or regulation thereunder . . . shall be void." However, the rescission measure should generally be applied only where there is a contract relation between plaintiff and defendant.

For the "value line" method of computing the actual value, *see* Green v. Occidental Petroleum Corp., 541 F.2d 1335, 334–6 (9th Cir. 1976). *Compare* Elkind v. Liggett & Myers, Inc., 635 F.2d 156 (2d Cir. 1980), where the court held that damages under section 10(b) should be limited to disgorgement of any profit earned by the wrongdoer.

95. Mallis v. Bankers Trust Co., 615 F.2d 68 (2d Cir. 1980). In Hirsch v. duPont, 553 F.2d 750 (2d Cir. 1977), the Second Circuit held that Haskins & Sells was not liable in connection with its audit of a stock brokerage firm because Haskins & Sells had no duty to disclose (under GAAP applicable in 1969) a violation of the New York Stock Exchange's net capital rule and that the information was either immaterial or should have been discovered by due diligence.

96. Straub v. Vaisman & Co., Inc., 540 F.2d 591 (3d Cir. 1976). *Straub* involved a broker/dealer who sold in excess of market price while having a controlling interest and inside information about the imminence of bankruptcy. In rejecting the broker/dealer's argument that plaintiff failed to exercise due diligence, the court said: "A sophisticated investor is not barred by reliance upon the honesty of those with whom he deals in the absence of knowledge that the trust is misplaced. Integrity is still the mainstay of commerce and makes it possible for an almost limitless number of transactions to take place without resort to the courts."

97. Sundstrand Corp. v. Sun Chemical Corp., 553 F.2d 1033 (7th Cir. 1977). In Holdsworth v. Strong, 545 F.2d 687 (10th Cir. 1976), husband and wife plaintiffs claimed their sale of a minority interest in a closely held corporation called Sans-Copy was induced by fraud. The court rejected the defense of plaintiffs' lack of due diligence despite the fact that the plaintiff husband was both a CPA and an attorney.

98. Dupuy v. Dupuy, 551 F.2d 1005 (5th Cir.), *cert. denied*, 434 U.S. 911 (1977), involved sale of stock to a brother who knew, but failed to disclose, that it was worth a small fortune. The court held the evidence supported the jury's finding that plaintiff was not reckless in the circumstances. In Rosenbloom v. Adams, Scott & Conway, Inc., 552 F.2d 1336 (9th Cir. 1977), the court held that plaintiff's insider status as a majority shareholder and director did not foreclose a suit under section 10(b) alleging fraudulent inducement to sell since plaintiff's access to information was a factual matter.

99. Homberg v. Armbrecht, 327 U.S. 392 (1946). *Also see* Robertson v. Seidman & Seidman, 609 F.2d 583 (2d Cir. 1979), which reversed a lower court ruling that the statute of limitations on a 10(b) claim started to run prior to an SEC Opinion and Order that named the accounting firm as a participant in the fraud.

100. American Pipe & Constr. Co. v. Utah, 414 U.S. 538 (1974). *Also see* Briskin v. Ernst & Ernst, 589 F.2d 1363 (9th Cir. 1978), where the court held that plaintiffs who joined after the action was commenced were entitled to the relationback principle.

Auditors' Right of Contribution. It is now well settled that a defendant auditor sued under section 10(b) can file a third-party complaint for contribution against management or others who caused the problem.[101] For example in *Laventhol, Krekstein, Horwath & Horwath v. Horwitch,*[102] the court held that the accounting firm could claim contribution against management on federal claims regardless of management's settlement with plaintiffs. The court also permitted the accounting firm to claim indemnity from management on common-law claims to whatever extent permitted by the applicable state law. However, full indemnity is not usually allowed especially where there is evidence that the auditor had knowledge of the misrepresentations.

Satisfaction of Judgment. In *MacKethan v. Burrus, Cootes and Burrus,*[103] the receiver of a savings and loan corporation obtained a jury verdict of $1.1 million against an accounting partnership and its three partners based on allegations of aiding and abetting section 10(b) violations. However, the receiver had previously settled with other defendants for $6 million. Upon appeal the court held the judgment against the accounting firm was satisfied. The accounting firm could be liable only for the amount of a verdict that exceeded $6 million, since payments by one of several parties liable for a loss reduces the total liability for all.

Continuous Disclosure Requirements of Section 10(b)

The much celebrated case of *SEC v. Texas Gulf Sulphur Co.*[104] involved a misleading company press release that tended to dispel rumors of an ore strike near Timmins, Ontario. The SEC brought an action under section 10(b) to recover insider profits on stock purchases prior to April 17, 1964, when the ore strike was made known to the public. It was held that the framers of the press release did not exercise due diligence and that a press release should include basic facts that were known or reasonably should be known to the authors of the press release. The court decided that the insider profits would be held in escrow for five years subject to disposition upon application of the SEC and other interested persons, including payment of judgments against insiders arising out of the events.

Although public accountants were not involved, the case is of great importance to accountants because it imposes a duty on managements of publicly held firms to make prompt public disclosures of news or information that reasonably can be expected to have a material effect on the market for the firms' securities. Information can be withheld *only* when there is a legitimate business purpose. During this period, insiders can neither trade nor divulge the information to others who trade and must take steps to keep the information secret.

Broker-dealers who come into possession of material nonpublic information in their underwriting activities cannot use that information for the benefit of themselves or their customers. Violation of this rule results in liability to all those who trade without benefit of the information.[105]

Auditors' Liability under Section 14

Section 14 of the Exchange Act, and related SEC rules, makes it unlawful to make false or misleading statements in soliciting proxies. In *J. I. Case Co. v. Borak*[106] the U.S. Supreme Court held that this provision provides an implied civil remedy for either the corporation or the shareholders. In *Ernst & Ernst v. Hochfelder* the Supreme Court noted, with neither approval nor disapproval, that the Second Circuit had

---

101. See James M. Fischer, "Contribution in 10b-5 Actions," *Business Lawyer,* April 1978, pp. 1821–44. Liability for contribution is eliminated by settlement for one's full share. *See* Herzfeld v. Laventhol, Krekstein, Horwath & Horwath, 540 F.2d 27 (2d Cir. 1976). The auditor's third-party complaint may be grounds for denial of a separate trial for the various defendants since culpability is a matter of degree that should be determined by the same jury. *See* State Mut. Assurance Co. v. Arthur Andersen & Co., 63 F.R.D. 389 (1974).

102. Laventhol, Krekstein, Horwath & Horwath v. Horwitch, 637 F.2d 672 (9th Cir. 1980). Compare *In re* Investors Funding Corp. of New York, CCH Fed. Sec. L. Rep. ¶ 97,667 (S.D.N.Y. 1980), where the court held that accounting defendants could not file claims for indemnification and contribution in the debtor-company's reorganization proceeding because (1) indemnification is contrary to federal securities laws, and (2) the Bankruptcy Act authorizes disallowance of unliquidated claims for contribution that would otherwise delay and interfere with the reorganization plan.

For a case dealing with collateral estoppel as a defense to an accounting firm's claim for contribution, *see* Tucker v. Arthur Andersen, 646 F.2d 721 (2d Cir. 1981).

103. MacKethan v. Burrus, Cootes and Burrus, 545 F.2d 1388 (4th Cir. 1976).

104. SEC v. Texas Gulf Sulphur Co., 258 F. Supp. 262 (S.D.N.Y. 1966), *rev'd and remanded,* 401 F.2d 833 (2d Cir. 1968), *on remand,* 312 F. Supp. 77 (S.D.N.Y. 1970), *aff'd,* 446 F.2d 1301 (2d Cir. 1971), *cert. denied* 92 S. Ct. 651 (1971).

105. Shapiro v. Merrill Lynch, Pierce, Fenner & Smith, Inc., 495 F.2d 228 (2d Cir. 1974); Slade v. Shearson Hammill & Co., 517 F.2d 398 (2d Cir. 1974). Query whether a CPA who gains inside information is liable for making use of it in another engagement that involves either (1) auditing or (2) management advisory services, or must he insist on immediate public disclosure to protect his own position? In Chiarella v. United States, 445 U.S. 222 (1980), the U.S. Supreme Court reversed the criminal conviction under § 10(b) of a printer who was able to identify target firms in corporate takeover bids and used the information for trading purposes. The court held that Chiarella was not a corporate insider, that he received no confidential information from the target companies whose stock he purchased, and that he had no disclosure duties. SEC rule 14e-3 (17 C.F.R. § 240.14e-3), adopted since *Chiarella,* prohibits trading on inside information about a tender offer.

106. J. I. Case Co. v. Borak, 377 U.S. 426 (1964).

adopted a negligence standard of culpability for section 14.

Thus in the *Clinton Oil*[107] case the court applied a negligence standard for direct liability. In rejecting the contention that auditors cannot be liable under section 14, the court said:

> The Court does not believe that direct liability can be imposed upon Elmer Fox because Elmer Fox, as an accounting firm, was not involved in the *solicitation* of the proxy.
>
> * * * * *
>
> The Court, nevertheless, believes that Elmer Fox may be subjected to liability for aiding or abetting in the alleged violation of § 14(a).
>
> * * * * *
>
> To subject Elmer Fox to liability under § 14(a) for aiding and abetting, the plaintiff must prove Elmer Fox knowingly and substantially assisted in the wrongdoing which resulted in injury to plaintiffs.

Thus the court applied a negligence standard of culpability for direct violations and a scienter standard for the conduct of auditors.

Auditors' Liability under Section 17

Section 17 gives the SEC power to regulate the accounting for broker/dealers, and SEC rules require independent accountants to certify their financials. However, in *Touche Ross & Co. v. Redington,*[108] the U.S. Supreme Court held that section 17 does not create an implied civil right of action that permits a broker-dealers' customers to sue the broker-dealers' auditors.

Auditors' Liability under Section 18

Under section 18 of the 1934 act any person who makes any "false and misleading" statement in documents "filed" under the act is liable to any person "who, in reliance upon such statement, shall have purchased or sold a security at a price which was affected by the statement." Since the defendants can avoid liability if they proved that they acted in good faith and had no knowledge that the statement was false or misleading, the apparent effect is to make gross negligence the test for liability, so that public accountants are in the same position as at common law, where they can be sued by third parties for gross negligence.

Scope of liability under section 18 is very narrow, since it relates only to documents "filed." Rules 14(a)

and (c) specifically state that annual reports to shareholders are not deemed filed with the Commission or subject to the liabilities of section 18.

Fischer v. Kletz[109] involved certified financial statements for Yale Express System, Inc., for 1963, and the auditor, while doing "special studies" of past and current income and expenses, allegedly discovered that the statements were false. The plaintiffs contended the falsity was known to the auditors prior to June 29, 1964, when Yale filed with the SEC a 10-K report that contained the certified statements. The auditors denied such discovery prior to or at the time of filing. On the basis of such factual dispute the court refused to dismiss the claim under section 18, apparently adopting the plaintiffs' contention that if the allegations were true, then liability under section 18 would be established.

THE INVESTMENT ADVISERS ACT OF 1940

The Investment Advisers Act of 1940 was enacted to protect investors, who pay for investment services, from dishonest and self-dealing practices. Sections 206(1) and (2) of the Advisers Act provide:

> It shall be unlawful for any investment adviser, by use of the mails or any means or instrumentality of interstate commerce, directly or indirectly—
> 1. To employ any device, scheme, or artifice to defraud any client or prospective client.
> 2. To engage in any transaction, practice or course of business which operates as a fraud or deceit upon any client or prospective client. . . .

In a five-to-four decision the U.S. Supreme Court held in *Transamerica Mortgage Advisors, Inc. v. Lewis*[110] that the only private remedy under the Investment Advisers Act of 1940 is for rescission of a contract with an investment adviser.

CLASS ACTIONS AND DERIVATIVE SUITS

Class Actions

Rule 23 of the Federal Rules of Civil Procedure was amended in 1966 to liberalize the conditions under which purchasers, sellers, or holders of securities can institute collective lawsuits on behalf of themselves and as representatives of the class of persons similarly situated. The rule requires that common questions of law or fact must predominate over questions affecting the individual members. The attorney for the class can arrange with the court for a contingent fee on the total recovery.

---

107. *In re* Clinton Oil Company Securities Litigation, CCH Fed. Sec. L. Rep. ¶ 96,015 (D. Kan. 1977).

108. Touche Ross & Co. v. Redington, 442 U.S. 560 (1979).

109. Fischer v. Kletz, 266 F. Supp. 180 (S.D.N.Y. 1967).

110. Transamerica Mortgage Advisors, Inc. v. Lewis, 444 U.S. 11 (1979).

The ruling in *Eisen v. Carlisle & Jacquelin*[111] made the maintenance of class actions potentially more expensive for plaintiffs. The U.S. Supreme Court held that individual notice must be sent to all class members whose names and addresses may be ascertained through reasonable effort and that the plaintiff must pay for the cost of notice as part of the ordinary burden of financing the suit. Rule 23(c)(2) specifies the content of the notice as follows:

> The notice shall advise each member that (a) the court will exclude him from the class if he so requests by a specified date; (b) the judgment, whether favorable or not, will include all members who do not request exclusion; and (c) any member who does not request exclusion may, if he desires, enter an appearance through his counsel.

This case has not greatly reduced utility of class actions since (1) the Court's opinion permits plaintiffs to redefine the class into smaller subclasses, (2) individual notice is not required where names and addresses cannot be obtained by reasonable effort, and (3) the cost of providing notice is a recoverable cost if the action is successful.

Another case limiting the use of class actions is *Zahn v. International Paper Co.*[112] The plaintiffs sought to represent themselves and a class of 200 lakefront property owners allegedly damaged by the defendant's discharges into a lake. The case was brought in federal court, not because of a federal claim, but because of claims under state law, which may be brought in federal court where there is diversity of citizenship and the amount in controversy exceeds $10,000. The U.S. Supreme Court held that *each* plaintiff must have a claim of the requisite amount and that the amounts claimed by various plaintiffs cannot be added together to satisfy jurisdictional requirements. Auditors can take little comfort from the *Zahn*

decision, however, since claims under section 10(b) of the Exchange Act or section 11 of the Securities Act are federal claims not requiring any jurisdictional amount.

Class actions are particularly applicable to suits under section 11 of the Securities Act, since any misrepresentation in the registration statement and prospectus will be common to all members of the class. There is no reliance requirement under section 11 for plaintiffs who purchase prior to issuance of a report on earnings for the 12 months following registration. The *BarChris* case was, for example, a class action.

In actions under section 10(b) of the Exchange Act, the necessity for a common core of reliance may make a class action inappropriate except for the situations where reliance can be presumed (see the discussion of reliance under the Exchange Act above).

In *Coopers & Lybrand v. Livesay*[113] the U.S. Supreme Court held that decisions of trial judges certifying or decertifying a class are not appealable as a matter of right; however, district judges may be requested to certify their orders for interlocutory review. If so certified, the matter is then discretionary with the particular U.S. Court of Appeals.

Derivative Suits

Derivative suits are judicially fashioned remedies to enable minority shareholders to bring an action to recover on behalf of the corporation not only against faithless officers and directors, but also against third parties whom the corporate management refused to pursue.[114] Such actions can be brought either in state court on common-law principles as modified by state statutes, or in federal courts. The federal court action can be based on diversity of citizenship (and thus based on state substantive law) or on federal securities laws. If the action is in federal court on the basis of federal claims, claims under state law can be included under the pendent jurisdiction of the court.

---

111. Eisen v. Carlisle & Jacquelin, 417 U.S. 156 (1974). This case was amplified in Oppenheimer Fund, Inc. v. Sanders, 437 U.S. 340 (1978) where the U.S. Supreme Court held that a district court has the discretion to order a defendant to perform one of the tasks necessary to send notice where the defendant can perform it with less difficulty and expense, but that ordering a defendant to pay $16,000 to enable plaintiffs to identify their own class was an abuse of discretion. *Also see* Gold v. Ernst & Ernst, 574 F.2d 662 (2d Cir. 1978), where the court held that plaintiff must bear all necessary costs to determine names and addresses of class members whose securities are held in "street names," but suggested making maximum use of letters of inquiry and subpoenas duces tecum so as to minimize costs.

In *In re* Viatron Computer Systems Corp. Litigation, 614 F.2d 11 (1st Cir. 1980), the court held that Arthur Andersen & Co. had no standing to challenge the method of giving notice to the class of a settlement by the underwriter.

112. Zahn v. International Paper Co., 414 U.S. 291 (1973).

113. Coopers & Lybrand v. Livesay, 437 U.S. 463 (1978).

114. The U.S. Supreme Court traced the history of derivative suits in Ross v. Bernhard, 396 U.S. 531, 534 (1969). The remedy was made available in equity because the common law did not permit stockholders to call corporate managers to account in actions at law. Preconditions for the suit are (1) a valid claim on which the corporation could have sued, and (2) the corporation's refusal to proceed after demand upon it to do so. In Greenspun v. Del E. Webb Corp., 634 F.2d 1204 (9th Cir. 1980), the court dismissed a derivative suit because the demand for "corrective action" was presented only to the president/director of the corporation and its general counsel and not to the entire board of directors. In Burks v. Lasker, 441 U.S. 471 (1979), the U.S. Supreme Court held that federal courts should apply state law in deciding whether independent directors have the power to discontinue derivative suits.

Not all violations of federal law result in a federal claim that can be asserted in a derivative suit. In *Cort v. Ash*[115] a stockholder brought suit derivatively on behalf of Bethlehem Steel Corp. against Cort, who was chairman of the Bethlehem board. Bethlehem had used general corporate funds in the election campaign of 1972 to run ads countering statements made by presidential candidate George McGovern, who had called for big business to pay its fair share of the tax burden. Reprints of the ad were included with quarterly dividend checks prior to the election. The suit claimed an implied right of action under the federal statute that provided criminal penalties for corporate contributions in federal election campaigns.

In rejecting the argument that this particular criminal statute provided a private remedy, the U.S. Supreme Court identified four factors that determine whether a private remedy is implicit in a statute not expressly providing one:

1. Is plaintiff one of the class for whose special benefit the statute was enacted?
2. Is there any explicit or implicit indication of legislative intent to create or deny a federal right of action?
3. Is it consistent with the purpose of the legislative scheme to imply a remedy?
4. Is the cause of action one traditionally relegated to state law so that a federal remedy would be inappropriate?

The main factor in the Court's decision was that the purpose of this law was to assure that federal elections are free from the power of money and to eliminate the hold of business interests on political parties. The feeling that corporate officials had no moral right to use corporate funds for contribution to political parties without consent of shareholders was, at best, a secondary consideration.

Class Actions versus Derivative Suits

In *Schlick v. Castle*[116] the plaintiff brought a derivative action growing out of the merger on May 14, 1973, of Continental Steel Corporation into Penn-Dixie Cement Corporation. The factual allegations of the parties claimed violations of federal law [including section 10(b)], and most of the requested relief was similar to a class action then pending. The defendants argued for dismissal on two grounds: (1) the merged corporation no longer has existence and cannot sue derivatively, and (2) a class action, not a derivative suit, is the only manner in which the claims may be asserted. The court rejected the first argument, saying:

> It seems incongruous and inequitable that former directors and the surviving corporation should be immune from suit for fraud in a merger because the merged corporation in technical terms no longer exists, when the fraud under attack was the very means by which the merged corporation's existence was ended.

As to the second defense the court held that defendants were correct that the plaintiff could not recover twice. However, in upholding the derivative suit and transferring it to be heard with the class action suit, the court said:

> In the context of some cases, and potentially in this case, a derivative suit may be a proper and even preferable procedure. Certainly at this early stage the defendants' arguments are not sufficient to require that the derivative suit should be dismissed.
>
> In some cases where the corporation in whose name a derivative suit is brought no longer exists, courts have been able to provide relief by passing the recovery through directly to the shareholders, often limiting the class of shareholders to exclude shareholders who were wrongdoers.
>
> See e.g., *deHaas v. Empire Petroleum Co.*, 300 F. Supp. 834, 838 (D. Colo. 1969), modified, 435 F.2d 1223 (10th Cir. 1970); *Johnson v. American Gen. Ins. Co.*, 296 F. Supp. 802, 809 (D.D.C. 1969); *Miller v. Steinbach*, 268 F. Supp. 255, 269 (S.D.N.Y. 1967); Note, *Individual Pro Rata Recovery in Shareholder Derivative Suits*, 69 Harv. L. Rev. 1314 (1956); cf. *Perlman v. Feldman*, 219 F.2d 173, 178 (2d Cir. 1955), *cert. denied*, 349 U.S. 952 (1955). These cases may reflect in the end the fashioning of class action remedies in derivative suits. The success of such efforts indicates, however, that the important question in a suit such as this one is not the procedural theory but the substantive right asserted by the plaintiff and whether a remedy can be fashioned that can afford relief. So long as the substantive allegations state a claim for relief, no reason appears why in the first instance the plaintiff should not have the option of selecting the procedural mode for his suit.

A derivative suit against auditors apparently enables plaintiffs to recover for negligence upon the common-law count, since the corporation is the nominal plaintiff. However, such suits are not likely since it is difficult to prove that the corporation, as opposed to its security holders, were damaged by any action of the auditors.

115.   Cort v. Ash, 422 U.S. 66 (1975). In Rochelle v. Marine Grace Trust Co. of N.Y., 535 F.2d 523 (9th Cir. 1976), the court held that a reorganization trustee could maintain in federal court a stockholders' common law derivative suit against an accounting firm because of the independent source of federal jurisdiction conferred by the Bankruptcy Act.

116.   Schlick v. Castle, CCH Fed. Sec. L. Rep. ¶ 94,909 (1974).

VENUE AND JURISDICTION

Venue is the place where an action is brought for trial. Jurisdiction is authority over the parties and the subject matter. Once venue is established, the court can obtain personal jurisdiction over the defendants by virtue of the nationwide service of process provisions of section 22(a) of the Securities Act and section 27 of the Exchange Act.

Section 22(a) of the Securities Act, 15 U.S.C. § 77v(a), establishes venue for any suit arising under the act "in the district wherein the defendant is found or is an inhabitant or transacts business, or in the district where the offer or sale took place, if the defendant participated therein. . . ." Section 27 of the Securities Exchange Act of 1934, 15 U.S.C. § 78aa, establishes venue for any suit under the act in any district "wherein any act or transaction constituting the violation occurred . . . or in the district wherein the defendant is found or is an inhabitant or transacts business. . . ." Both of these sections provide that "process in such cases may be served in any other district of which the defendant is an inhabitant or wherever the defendant may be found."

Where suits involve claims under more than one federal securities act, venue properly laid for claims under one act satisfactorily establishes venue for the other. Venue for an Exchange Act claim is proper if there is any one act within the forum district that represents more than an immaterial part of the alleged illegal events. In a multiple defendant suit, where a common scheme of acts or transactions to violate the securities laws is alleged, venue for any defendant establishes venue for all other defendants, even in the absence of contact by any one defendant with the district. This is called the coconspirator theory of venue.

In *Arpet, Ltd. v. Homans*[117] it was alleged that all defendants were liable under the 1933 and 1934 acts for engaging in a common fraudulent scheme involving the sale of notes and stock to the plaintiff. Financing statements had been filed in the forum district, and one defendant had transacted business in the forum district. Therefore, the court ruled that venue was properly laid in the district and that a defendant certified public accountant and a defendant lawyer, who were served in New York City, had to defend suit in the Western District of Pennsylvania although they had no contact with the forum district. Similarly, it was held in *Rosen v. Dick*[118] that a director could be properly served by registered mail in Switzerland in an action brought in the Southern District of New York for violation of section 10(b) of the Exchange Act.

A divided U.S. Supreme Court held in *Radzanower v. Touche Ross & Co.*[119] that the more restrictive venue provision of the National Bank Act governed venue in a suit against a national banking association and that the suit could be brought only in the district where the association was established.

RIGHT TO JURY TRIAL

There is no "complexity" exception to the Seventh Amendment right to a jury trial in civil cases. Thus the Ninth Circuit reversed a lower court that struck demands for a jury trial because of the complexity involved in a suit by investors against the issuer and its attorneys and auditors that combined claims under federal and state securities laws with common-law negligence and fraud claims.[120]

SUMMARY

A long history of misrepresentation, increasing importance of securities markets in the interstate economy, and the Great Depression of 1929 brought about the realization that the doctrine of caveat emptor was inappropriate in the offering and trading of securities. The Securities Act of 1933 was concerned primarily with the quantity and quality of disclosure of information on new public offerings of securities. The Securities Exchange Act of 1934 created the Securities and Exchange Commission to administer both the 1933 and 1934 acts and established disclosure requirements, primarily in connection with the trading of securities as opposed to new offerings.

Section 11 of the 1933 act makes public accountants and others liable to investors for untrue statements in materials "filed" with the SEC pursuant to a new offering. To avoid liability public accountants must assume the burden of showing they exercised "due diligence." This is the equivalent of a negligence standard for imposing liability.

Although section 10(b) of the Exchange Act contains no express provision establishing civil liability, the courts have held that a private right of action is implied to effectuate its purpose of eliminating fraud in the trading of securities. The U.S. Supreme Court, in the case of *Ernst & Ernst v. Hochfelder,* rejected a suit based on negligence and held that liability can be imposed under section 10(b) only upon proof of scienter, which is defined as intent to deceive, manipulate, or defraud.

Class actions are collective lawsuits where the plaintiff represents a class of persons similarly situated. Derivative suits are judicially fashioned remedies

117. Arpet, Ltd. v. Homans, CCH Fed. Sec. L. Rep. ¶ 95,052 (W.D. Pa. 1975).

118. Rosen v. Dick, CCH Fed. Sec. L. Rep. ¶ 94,590 (1974).

119. Radzanower v. Touche Ross & Co., 426 U.S. 148 (1976).

120. *In re* U.S. Financial Securities Litigation, 609 F.2d 411 (9th Cir. 1970).

to enable minority shareholders to recover on behalf of a corporation for mismanagement by those having a fiduciary responsibility. A plaintiff can choose the most appropriate remedy.

SUGGESTIONS FOR FURTHER READING

Annot. "In Pari Delicto as Defense in Private Action for Violation of Securities Act or Securities Exchange Act." 26 *American Law Reports* Fed. 682, 1976.

Bloomenthal, Harold S. *Securities and Federal Corporate Law.* Vols. 3 and 3A. New York: Clark Boardman Company, 1974.

Gruenbaum, Samuel H., and Marc I. Steinberg. "Accountants' Liability and Responsibility: Securities, Criminal and Common Law." *Loyola of Los Angeles Law Review,* March 1980, pp. 247–314.

Jacobs, Arnold S. *The Impact of Rule 10b-5.* Vols. 5 and 5A. New York: Clark Boardman Company, 1974.

Loss, Louis. *Securities Regulation.* Vols. 1, 2, and 3. 2nd ed. Boston: Little, Brown, 1961. _____. *Securities Regulation: Supplement to Second Edition.* Vols. 4, 5, and 6. Boston: Little, Brown, 1969.

QUESTIONS AND PROBLEMS

Federal Securities Laws

1. What is the philosophy behind the federal securities laws?
2. How many commissioners compose the Securities and Exchange Commission, and how are they and their chairperson selected?
3. (From the May 1977 Uniform CPA Examination)
   The Securities and Exchange Commission is not empowered to
   a. Obtain an injunction which will suspend trading in a given security.
   b. Sue for treble damages.
   c. Institute criminal proceedings against accountants.
   d. Suspend a broker-dealer.
4. (From the May 1977 Uniform CPA Examination)
   One of the major purposes of federal security regulation is to
   a. Establish the qualifications for accountants who are members of the profession.
   b. Eliminate incompetent attorneys and accountants who participate in the registration of securities to be offered to the public.
   c. Provide a set of uniform standards and tests for accountants, attorneys, and others who practice before the Securities and Exchange Commission.
   d. Provide sufficient information to the investing public who purchases securities in the marketplace.

The Securities Act

5. What is the principal concern of the Securities Act of 1933?
6. What is the jurisdictional reach of the Securities Act?
7. Explain the conditions necessary to qualify for each of the following exemptions from the Securities Act:
   a. The intrastate exemption.
   b. The private-offering exemption.
8. Explain and contrast three different categories of the small-offering exemption.
9. How can the Commission enforce its Securities Act disclosure requirements?
10. Describe the extent of an auditor's exposure to civil liability under the 1933 act.
11. When is proof of reliance necessary under section 11 of the Securities Act?
12. What is an S-1 review?
13. What are some crucial steps that the auditor in *Bar-Chris* might have taken to help avoid liability?
14. (From the November 1973 Uniform CPA Examination)
    The Securities Act of 1933 applies to the
    a. Sale in interstate commerce of insurance and regular annuity contracts.
    b. Sale by a dealer of securities issued by a bank.
    c. Sale through a broker of a controlling person's investment in a public corporation.
    d. Sale in interstate commerce of bonds issued by a charitable foundation.
15. (From the May 1981 Uniform CPA Examination)
    Major, Major & Sharpe, CPAs, are the auditors of MacLain Industries. In connection with the public offering of $10 million of MacLain securities, Major expressed an unqualified opinion as to the financial statements. Subsequent to the offering, certain misstatements and omissions were revealed. Major has been sued by the purchasers of the stock offered pursuant to the registration statement which included the financial statements audited by Major. In the ensuing lawsuit by the MacLain investors, Major will be able to avoid liability if
    a. The errors and omissions were caused primarily by MacLain.
    b. It can be shown that at least some of the investors did *not* actually read the audited financial statements.
    c. It can prove due diligence in the audit of the financial statements of MacLain.
    d. MacLain had expressly assumed any liability in connection with the public offering.
16. (From the November 1980 Uniform CPA Examination)
    Theobold Construction Company, Inc., is considering a public stock offering for the first time. It wishes to raise $1.2 million by a common stock offering and do this in the least expensive manner. In this connection, it is considering making an offering pursuant to Regulation A. Which of the following statements is correct regarding such an offering?
    a. Such an offering can *not* be made to more than 250 people.
    b. The maximum amount of securities permitted to be offered under Regulation A is $1 million.
    c. Only those corporations which have had an initial registration under the Securities Act of 1933 are eligible.
    d. Even if Regulation A applies, Theobold is required to distribute an offering circular.
17. (From the November 1980 Uniform CPA Examination)
    Which of the following statements is correct regard-

130

ing qualification for the private placement exemption from registration under the Securities Act of 1933?

a. The instrumentalities of interstate commerce must *not* be used.

b. The securities must be offered to *not* more than 35 persons.

c. The minimum amount of securities purchased by each offeree must *not* be less than $100,000.

d. The offerees *must* have access to or be furnished with the kind of information that would be available in a registration statement.

18. (From the November 1977 Uniform CPA Examination)

Josephs & Paul is a growing, medium-sized partnership of CPAs. One of the firm's major clients is considering offering its stock to the public. This will be the firm's first client to go public. Which of the following is true with respect to this engagement?

a. If the client is a service corporation, the Securities Act of 1933 will *not* apply.

b. If the client is *not* going to be listed on an organized exchange, the Securities Exchange Act of 1934 will *not* apply.

c. The Securities Act of 1933 imposes important additional potential liability on Josephs & Paul.

d. As long as Josephs & Paul engages exclusively in intrastate business, the federal securities laws will *not* apply.

19. (From the May 1980 Uniform CPA Examination)

The directors of Clarion Corporation, their accountants, and their attorneys met to discuss the desirability of this highly successful corporation going public. In this connection, the discussion turned to the potential liability of the corporation and the parties involved in the preparation and signing of the registration statement under the Securities Act of 1933. Craft, Watkins, and Glenn are the largest shareholders. Craft is the Chairman of the Board; Watkins is the Vice Chairman; and Glenn is the Chief Executive Officer. It has been decided that they will sign the registration statement. There are two other directors who are also executives and shareholders of the corporation. All of the board members are going to have a percentage of their shares included in the offering. The firm of Witherspoon & Friendly, CPAs, will issue an opinion as to the financial statements of the corporation which will accompany the filing of the registration statement, and Blackstone & Abernathy, Attorneys-at-Law, will render legal services and provide any necessary opinion letters.

Required:

Answer the following, setting forth reasons for any conclusions stated: Discuss the types of potential liability and defenses pursuant to the Securities Act of 1933 that each of the above parties or classes of parties may be subject to as a result of going public.

The Exchange Act

20. What are the criteria that subject firms to continuous disclosure under the 1934 act?

21. How does the Commission enforce the Exchange Act disclosure requirements?

22. Explain the meaning and applicability of the "in con-

nection with the purchase or sale of any security" phrase that is found in section 10(b) of the Exchange Act.

23. Discuss the test of materiality under section 10(b) and whether it is an objective or subjective standard.

24. Explain three different factual situations and the effect that each has on proof of reliance under section 10(b) of the Exchange Act.

25. Describe the extent of an auditor's exposure to civil liability under the Exchange Act.

26. Contrast the auditor's liability under section 18 of the Exchange Act and liability at common law.

27. What is a class action lawsuit, and how does it differ from a stockholders' derivative suit?

28. (From the November 1980 Uniform CPA Examination)

Which of the following statements concerning the scope of Section 10(b) of the Securities Exchange Act of 1934 is correct?

a. In order to come within its scope, a transaction must have taken place on a national stock exchange.

b. It applies exclusively to securities of corporations registered under the Securities Exchange Act of 1934.

c. There is an exemption from its application for securities registered under the Securities Act of 1933.

d. It applies to purchases as well as sales of securities in interstate commerce.

29. (From the November 1980 Uniform CPA Examination)

The Securities Exchange Act of 1934 requires that certain persons register and that the securities of certain issuers be registered. In respect to such registration under the 1934 Act, which of the following statements is *incorrect*?

a. All securities offered under the Securities Act of 1933 also must be registered under the 1934 Act.

b. National securities exchanges must register.

c. The equity securities of issuers, which are traded on a national securities exchange, must be registered.

d. The equity securities of issuers having in excess of $1 million in assets and 500 or more stockholders which are traded in interstate commerce must be registered.

30. (From the May 1981 Uniform CPA Examination)

Donalds & Company, CPAs, audited the financial statements included in the annual report submitted by Markum Securities, Inc., to the Securities and Exchange Commission. The audit was improper in several respects. Markum is now insolvent and unable to satisfy the claims of its customers. The customers have instituted legal action against Donalds based upon section 10(b) and rule 10b-5 of the Securities Exchange Act of 1934. Which of the following is likely to be Donalds' best defense?

a. They did *not* intentionally certify false financial statements.

b. Section 10(b) does *not* apply to them.

c. They were *not* in privity of contract with the creditors.

d. Their engagement letter specifically disclaimed any liability to any party which resulted from Markum's fraudulent conduct.

9

Criminal Liability

This chapter covers:

- ENGLISH PRECEDENTS.
- AMERICAN STATE LAWS.
- FEDERAL DISCLOSURE ACTS.

ENGLISH PRECEDENTS

Although misrepresentation may result in much greater loss than burglary or armed robbery, the common law has been extremely slow to apply criminal sanctions that require a clear and consistent standard of disclosure in commercial transactions. Common law is the unwritten law as distinguished from statutory law. Only when custom and usage have been established from time immemorial are they considered to constitute common law. Thus our ancestors naturally brought with them the common law of England. Most American states passed early statutes adopting the English common law as modified by acts of Parliament except where it was repugnant to our conditions and way of life. Some states adopted acts of parliament in force as of the Declaration of Independence in 1776, while other states adopted English statutes in force as of 1607, the date of the first English settlement at Jamestown, Virginia.[1] Since our law, as well as our audit practice, was derived from the English, Americans have a special interest in English precedents for auditor's liability.

Under early English common law, directly defraud-

ing the government or public at large was punishable, but defrauding a private person was punishable only if false tokens or symbols were used, such as false weights and measures. The theory was that criminal liability would be imposed only where common prudence could not protect the public. Thus selling an unsound horse for a sound one (called "jockeyship"), asking to look at a promissory note and carrying it away, obtaining credit by falsehood, or putting a stone in a single pound of butter were not punishable at early common law.[2] The limited concept of criminal responsibility was expressed by the statement, "We are not to indict a man for making a fool of another."[3]

To remedy this deficiency in the punishing of fraud, the English Parliament in 1757 passed the statute that was the forerunner of American statutes on the subject:

> Be it enacted . . . that all persons who knowingly and designedly, by false pretense or pretenses, shall obtain from any person or persons, money, goods, wares, or merchandises, with intent to cheat or defraud any person or persons of the same . . . shall be deemed offenders against law and public peace, and shall be fined or imprisoned, or put in the pillory, or publickly whipped, or be transported, as soon as conveniently may be.[4]

The English courts were slow to give effect to the new statute. In the case of *Rex v. Wheatley*[5] in 1761 (only four years after the new statute) the new law was apparently ignored. A brewer was indicted for pretending to deliver 18 gallons of beer when he knowingly delivered only 16. Lord Mansfield said:

> I think this case not indictable; it only amounting to unfair dealing with, and an infraction on, a private man, whose own carelessness it was not to measure the cask. All indictable cheats are where the public in general may be injured, as by using false weights, measures, or tokens; or where there is a conspiracy.

Similarly, full effect was not given to the statute in *Rex v. Pear,*[6] decided 18 years later in 1779, where Pear hired a horse and immediately sold it. The crime of embezzlement was not yet established, and by a majority of 7 out of 11 judges, Pear was found guilty of larceny, which was a felony. Although larceny required a taking from possession, it was reasoned that because the owner did not know of the plan to sell the

---

1. 1 W. Burdick, *The Law of Crime* (New York: Matthew Bender & Co., 1946), pp. 15–47.

2. 2 W. Burdick, *The Law of Crime* (New York: Matthew Bender & Co., 1946), pp. 461–65; 2 R. Anderson, *Wharton's Criminal Law and Procedure* (New York: Lawyers Co-operative Publishing, 1957), pp. 303–04.

3. Regina v. Jones, 1 Salk, 379 (1703).

4. 30 Geo. II, c. 24 (1757).

5. Rex v. Wheatley, 97 Eng. Rep. 746 (1761).

6. Rex v. Pear, 168 Eng. Rep. 208 (1779).

horse, he never gave possession. The majority of the judges thought a charge of false pretenses, a misdemeanor, was inapplicable.

In 1789 in *Rex v. Young*[7] the defendant falsely represented that a bet had been made on a race that was a sure thing, inducing Thomas to give money to cover his share of the bet. A conviction under the new statute was finally affirmed. But the law was soon held to apply only to misrepresentation of a past or existing fact. In *Rex v. Goodhall*[8] in 1821 a vendor would not extend credit. Goodhall agreed to return his payment with the delivery boy but never paid for the delivery. Goodhall's conviction was overturned, because (1) Goodhall's representation related to future conduct, and (2) common prudence could have avoided the loss.[9]

The false pretenses statute would be applicable only to directors, officers, or accountants who received money or property as a result of false statements or who conspired with one receiving money or property. Therefore, Parliament passed the Larceny Act of 1861, which provides that any corporate officer or director who

> shall make, circulate or publish, or concur in making, circulating or publishing, any written statement or account which he shall know to be false in any material particular, with intent to deceive or defraud any member, shareholder, or creditor of such body corporate or public company, or with intent to induce any person to become a shareholder or partner therein, or to entrust or advance any property to such body corporate or public company, or enter into any security for the benefit thereof, shall be guilty of a misdemeanour.[10]

This act was first construed in 1931 in *Rex v. Kylsant and Morland,*[11] which involved the affairs of the Royal Mail Steam Packet Company. The case is commonly referred to as the *Royal Mail* case. Lord

Kylsant was found guilty and sentenced to 12 months imprisonment for making, publishing, and circulating a false prospectus, but was acquitted on the charge of making, circulating, or publishing false annual reports for 1926 and 1927. Harold John Morland, the firm's auditor and a partner in the accounting firm of Price, Waterhouse & Co., was acquitted on the charge of aiding and abetting Lord Kylsant in connection with the annual reports.

Lord Kylsant, a most distinguished figure, no doubt would have preferred trial by judge rather than by jury. His family had held a baronetcy since Edward I, and his ancestors included the Emperor Maximum and Vortigen, King of the Bretons. His titles included Lord Lieutenant of Hereford, Vice-Admiral of North Wales, and Vice-Chairman of the Representative Body of the Church of Wales. He had been a member of Parliament, president of the London Chamber of Commerce, and president of the Federation of Chambers of Commerce of the British Empire. He was chairman and director of the Royal Mail Steam Packet Company, which had been developed largely through his personal efforts and which in 1931 was one of the largest shipping companies in the world.[12]

The Royal Mail Steam Packet Company was also one of the oldest English shipping companies, having been formed in 1839 by Royal Charter.[13] Before the Companies Acts a corporation could be created only by the special act of the Crown or Parliament. Only a few of these chartered companies existed, and in 1931 they were not within the reporting requirements of the Companies Act of 1900, which had been amended in 1929. Rather each was governed by its own charter, which in the case of the Royal Mail Company provided:

> Previously to every yearly general meeting an account shall be prepared by the Court of Directors of the debts and assets of the said corporation with an account of the profits made in the year ending 31st December preceding such general meeting for the time being, as near as the same can be ascertained, and with all such information as may to the directors seem necessary to be given or as may be required by any bye-laws of the corporation, which accounts shall be signed by at least one of the directors of the corporation and shall be laid before such meeting to be audited and settled as aforesaid.[14]

During the years 1921 to 1927 the firm did not earn sufficient profits to pay its dividends, but paid profits out of past earnings. Liability for taxes had been over-

7. Rex v. Young, 3 Durn. & E. 98 (1789).

8. Rex v. Goodhall, 168 Eng. Rep. 898 (1821).

9. For a discussion of the spread of the doctrine of *Rex* v. *Goodhall* and the resulting unsatisfactory state of the law, *see* Pearce, "Theft by False Promises," 101 *U. Pa. L. Rev.* 967 (1953).

10. The Larceny Act of 1861, 24 & 25 Vict. c. 96.

11. The lower court's conviction of Lord Kylsant was affirmed by the Court of Criminal Appeal in Rex v. Kylsant, [1932] 1 K.B. 442 (1931). Although there is no official report of the original criminal trial, a copy of an official Transcript of Trial is reportedly in the Yale Law Library. *See* MacIntyre, "Criminal Provisions of the Securities Act and Analogies to Similar Criminal Statutes," 43 *Yale L. J.* 254, 256 n. 17 (1933). The case is extensively reported in the *Times* (London), July 21–25 and 28–31, 1931. Part of the transcript of the lower court proceedings is reprinted in R.W.V. Dickerson, *Accountants and the Law of Negligence* (Toronto, Canada: Canadian Institute of Chartered Accountants, 1966), pp. 456–94. *Also see* "Rex v. Kylsant-A New Golden Rule for Prospectuses," 45 *Harv. L. Rev.* 1078 (1932).

12. MacIntyre, "Criminal Provisions," *supra* note 11 at 257.

13. Dickerson, *Accountants and the Law,* p. 460.

14. Ibid. (Reprinted with permission from The Canadian Institute of Chartered Accountants, Toronto, Canada.)

stated from the profitable war years and carried on the books under "Sundry balances, accounts not closed and debts owing by the Co." Refunds due from tax payments made to the government were not set out, and as the tax matter was adjusted, transfers were made to profit and loss.[15] The stockholders were never informed, however, that current profits were insufficient to pay the dividends.[16] Expert accountants who testified agreed that some point could be reached where disclosure must be made of increases in profit and loss from taxation reserves, but they concurred that the words "adjustment of taxation reserves," which Morland had placed in the profit and loss account for the first time in 1925 and which reappeared in 1926 and 1927, constituted adequate disclosure.[17] The result of operations was referred to as "Balance for the year including dividends on shares in allied and other companies, adjustment of taxation reserves, less depreciation of fleet, etc."[18]

The Crown argued that the reports were misleading because disclosure was not in layman's language. However, expert testimony apparently convinced the jury that, on the basis of the state of accounting at the time, there was no criminal conduct.

The prospectus, however, was another matter. The stated object of the debenture offering was to provide additional capital for a new freehold building and for the general purposes of the company. One of the actual purposes was to pay off a bank overdraft. Another part of the prospectus relevant to the trial was the following statement:

> The interest on the present issue of debenture stock will amount to 100,000l. per annum. Although this company, in common with other shipping companies, has suffered from the depression in the shipping industry, the audited accounts of the company show that during the past ten years the average annual balance available (including profits of the insurance fund), after providing for depreciation and interest on existing debenture stocks, has been sufficient to pay, the interest on the present issue more than five times over. After providing for all taxation, depreciation of the fleet, & c., adding to the reserves and payment of dividends on the preference stocks, the dividends on the ordinary stock during the last seventeen years have been. . . .[19]

The quoted statement misled because it implied that the firm continued to have profits adequate to pay dividends. The truth was that large profits were earned during World War I, but following the war profits were nil and had not covered dividends.

In affirming Lord Kylsant's conviction, the Court of Criminal Appeal quoted from an 1896 opinion of Lord Halsbury:

> If by a number of statements you intentionally give a false impression and induce a person to act upon it, it is not the less false although if one takes each statement by itself there may be a difficulty in showing that any specific statement is untrue.[20]

The court noted that the figures apparently disclosed the financial position, but actually concealed it by implying that the company was in a sound financial position, and that a prudent investor could safely invest in its debentures.

The *Royal Mail* case presents the critical issue to be raised in criminal disclosure litigation for the next several decades. Did the defendants try to mislead the average prudent investor by conveying erroneous impressions while taking care to cover themselves under generally accepted accounting principles?[21] If the defendants know that their carefully prepared statements will mislead the ordinary prudent investor, then criminal liability will be imposed.

AMERICAN STATE LAWS

Most American states enacted statutes making the obtaining of money by false pretenses a criminal offense.[22] Unless the auditor received money or property, or aided or abetted, or conspired with one receiving money or property, he would not incur liability under such statutes. Public accountancy statutes in some states provide criminal penalties for public accountants who willfully falsify reports or statements.[23] State accountancy laws also generally provide for revocation or suspension of the right to practice for those engaging in unethical conduct.[24] Some states have

15. Ibid., pp. 471–72; MacIntyre, "Criminal Provisions," *supra* note 11 at 258.

16. MacIntyre, "Criminal Provisions," *supra* note 11 at 258 n. 30.

17. Dickerson, *Accountants and the Law*, pp. 488–89.

18. MacIntyre, "Criminal Provisions," *supra* note 11 at 259.

19. Rex v. Kylsant, [1932] 1 K.B. 442 (1931).

20. Ibid.

21. Peter E. Fleming, who was prosecutor in the *Continental Vending* case *infra*, said: "The consideration you must ask yourself when you certify to a financial statement, or where you have something to do with other information which you know is going to the public, is whether your statements communicate the true financial condition which you supposedly are reporting upon; not whether you can get away with it under accepted accounting principles but whether in fact it is misleading, because that in my estimation is truly the single accepted accounting principle." See J. McCord, ed., *Accountants' Liability* (New York: Practising Law Institute, 1969), p. 232.

22. 2 R. Anderson, *Wharton's Criminal Law,* 1957, p. 305.

23. Wiley Daniel Rich, *Legal Responsibilities and Rights of Public Accountants* (New York: American Institute Publishing, 1935), p. 109.

24. Annot., "Regulation of Accountants," 70 A.L.R. 2d 433, 459 (1960).

enacted statutes that provide criminal penalties for false statements in a prospectus.[25] Twenty states have adopted section 101 of the Uniform Securities Act,[26] which is similar to SEC rule 10b-5 (see Chapter 8) and provides:

> It is unlawful for any person, in connection with the offer, sale, or purchase of any security, directly or indirectly—
>
> 1. To employ any device, scheme or artifice to defraud.
>
> 2. To make any untrue statement of a material fact or to omit to state a material fact necessary in order to make the statements made, in light of the circumstances under which they were made, not misleading.
>
> 3. To engage in any act, practice, or course of business which operates or would operate as a fraud or deceit upon any person.[27]

State criminal laws dealing with disclosure, like state civil provisions, are not really adequate to regulate interstate problems. Perhaps this inadequacy accounts for what seems to be public indifference toward enforcement of state blue-sky and disclosure laws.

FEDERAL DISCLOSURE STATUTES

Public accountants can run afoul of several federal laws which provide criminal penalties in connection with disclosure. Section 24 of the Securities Act of 1933[28] provides criminal penalties for willfully making an untrue statement or omitting any material fact in a registration statement. Violations of the antifraud provisions of section 17 are also punishable under section 24. The 1933 act has been effective in discouraging inadequate disclosure in connection with new offerings because of its tough liability provisions. Few civil (see Chapter 8) and criminal cases *infra* have been decided involving accountants.

Section 32(a) of the Securities Exchange Act of 1934[29] provides criminal penalties for willfully making

false or misleading statements in reports required to be filed under the act. This provision extends criminal liability to 10-K financial reports filed with the SEC. Violations of the antifraud provisions of section 10(b) are also punishable under section 32(a). Although the SEC conducts all of its own civil litigation, it, like other government departments and agencies, refers criminal matters to the Department of Justice.[30] A more aggressive policy in the SEC could therefore result in prosecution of more public accountants under this law.

Public accountants can incur criminal liability under the Federal False Statements Statute[31] for any false statement in any matter within the jurisdiction of any federal department or agency. Knowingly filing any false statement with the SEC is clearly within the statute. Since SEC rules require proxy materials and annual reports to be furnished to stockholders, such statements are "within the jurisdiction" so as to impose criminal liability.

Criminal liability of auditors can also be based on the Federal Mail Fraud Statute in connection with a mailing of or a conspiracy to mail false financial statements.[32]

---

25. MacIntyre, "Criminal Provisions," *supra* note 11 at 263-64.

26. For a brief comparative survey of state disclosure laws, see Comment, "Opening a Pandora's Box—Disclosure under the Florida Securities Act," 23 *U. Miami L. Rev.* 593, 595 (1969).

27. Uniform Securities Act, § 101, 9C U.L.A.

28. The Securities Act of 1933 § 24, 15 U.S.C. § 77x, provides: "Any person who willfully violates any of the provisions of this title, or the rules and regulations promulgated by the Commission under authority thereof, of any person who willfully, in a registration statement filed under this title, makes any untrue statement of a material fact or omits to state any material fact required to be stated therein or necessary to make the statements therein not misleading, shall upon conviction be fined not more than $10,000 or imprisoned not more than five years, or both."

29. The Securities Exchange Act of 1934 § 32(a), 15 U.S.C. § 78ff(a), provides: "Any person who willfully violates any provisions of this title, or any rule or regulation thereunder the violation of which is made unlawful or the observance of which is required

under the terms of this title, or any person who willfully and knowingly makes, or causes to be made, any statement in any application, report, or document required to be filed under this title or any rule or regulation thereunder or any undertaking contained in a registration statement as provided in subsection (d) of section 15 of this title or by any self-regulatory organization in connection with an application for membership or participation therein or to become associated with a member thereof, which statement was false or misleading with respect to any material fact, shall upon conviction be fined not more than $10,000, or imprisoned not more than five years, or both, except that when such person is an exchange, a fine not exceeding $500,000 may be imposed; but no person shall be subject to imprisonment under this section for the violation of any rule or regulation if he proves that he had no knowledge of such rule or regulation."

30. McCord, ed., *Accountants' Liability,* 1969, p. 122.

31. The Federal False Statements Statute provides at 18 U.S.C. § 1001: "Whoever, in any matter within the jurisdiction of any department or agency of the United States knowingly and willfully falsifies, conceals or covers up by any trick, scheme, or device a material fact, or makes any false, fictitious or fraudulent statements or representations, or makes or uses any false writing or document knowing the same to contain any false, fictitious or fraudulent statement or entry, shall be fined not more than $10,000 or imprisoned not more than five years, or both."

32. The Federal Mail Fraud Statute provides at 18 U.S.C. § 1341: "Whoever, having devised or intending to devise any scheme or artifice to defraud, for obtaining money or property by means of false or fraudulent pretenses, representations, or promises, or to sell, dispose of, loan, exchange, alter, give away, distribute, supply, or furnish or procure for unlawful use any counterfeit or spurious article, for the purpose of executing such scheme or artifice or attempting so to do, places in any post office or authorized depository for mail matter, any matter or thing whatever to be sent or delivered by the Postal Service, or takes or receives therefrom, any such matter or thing, or knowingly causes to be delivered by mail according to the direction thereon, or at the place at which it is directed to be delivered by the person to whom it is addressed, any such matter or thing, shall be fined not more than $1,000 or imprisoned not more than five years, or both."

Conspiracy by two or more persons to commit any offense against the United States is punishable if one or more persons acts to effect the object of the conspiracy.[33] Whoever aids, abets, counsels, commands, induces, or procures commission of an offense against the United States is also punishable as a principal.[34]

When public accountants engage in tax practice, they may be subjected to prosecution for criminal violations of the U.S. criminal code as well as violations of criminal provisions of the Internal Revenue Code. A discussion of these provisions and convictions of accountants is contained in Chapter 12.

Elements of Proof: Falsity and Intent

Under section 32 of the Exchange Act, the government must prove that a "willful" violation of a substantive provision occurred or that a false statement was "willfully and knowingly" made in a required filing.[35] Under section 24 of the Securities Act, it is necessary to prove only willfulness.[36] Under antifraud provisions contained in section 17 of the Securities Act and section 10(b) of the Exchange Act the government must prove either specific intent to defraud or scienter (guilty knowledge).[37] Specific intent can be proved by showing actual knowledge or reckless disregard of the truth of the statements.

The trial court in *United States v. Natelli*[38] instructed the jury that they could infer the defendant acted willfully and knowingly if he "deliberately closed his eyes to the obvious or to the facts that certainly would be observed or ascertained in the course of his accounting work" or if he "recklessly stated as facts matters of which he knew he was ignorant." Similarly, in *United States v. Benjamin*[39] the conviction of a CPA for a willful criminal violation of the Securities Act was upheld. The court, in using a test for intent similar to that used by Cardozo in establishing civil liability to third parties, said the government's burden was met by proving "that a defendant deliberately closed his eyes to facts he had a duty to see." The court noted that other circuits had even held "the willfulness requirement of the Securities Act to be satisfied in fraud cases by proof of representations which due diligence would have shown to be untrue."

In the Equity Funding Corp. of America case, the jury convicted three auditors despite defense testimony that Equity Funding officers kept secrets from the auditors. The jury apparently believed that the auditors issued their reports in willful or reckless disregard for the truth.[40] On May 21, 1975, *The Wall Street Journal* had this account:

> One of the jurors, Armando Carrillo, told reporters after the verdict was handed down that the jury agreed "there wasn't any direct evidence that they were involved" in Equity Funding's fraud. Rather, Mr. Carrillo said, "It was the signing of these statements when they (the defendants) didn't know they were true" that impressed the jury.

Evidence of motive for misdeeds of accountants usually relates to covering up past mistakes or building a practice through bending the rules. However, in *United States v. Zane*,[41] the government introduced evidence tending to show that the auditors received an additional $5,000 fee to certify to a nonexistent certificate of deposit. In order to cover diversion of corporate funds, a certificate of deposit was purchased in the corporation's name with funds from the simultaneous sale of the certificate. The accountants certified to existence of the nonexistent $500,000 certificate based on a letter from the seller. The accountants claimed that their acquittal on a conspiracy charge required a dismissal on the charge of filing a false Form 10-K with the SEC. However, their arguments were rejected, with each receiving a sentence of two years with four months to be served and the balance suspended.

Circumstantial evidence is sufficient to prove intent. For example, in *United States v. Bruce*[42] a Florida CPA was convicted on two counts of fraud in connection with financial statements prepared for a prospectus for a firm incorporated in Atlanta, Georgia, in 1966. The organizers first approached an accountant with a national accounting firm, but the firm rejected the engagement because the policy of the firm on the use of appraisal values in financial statements for newly formed companies would not allow what the promoters wanted.

The CPA was tried before the court without a jury; upon appeal he contended that he should have been acquitted since his work was purely a professional service, involving matters of judgment, and was not per

---

33. 18 U.S.C. § 371.

34. 18 U.S.C. § 2.

35. See note 29.

36. See note 28.

37. Troutman v. United States, 100 F.2d 628 (10th Cir. 1938).

38. United States v. Natelli, 527 F.2d 311 (1975), *cert. denied*, 425 U.S. 934 (1976).

39. United States v. Benjamin, 328 F.2d 854, 863 (2d Cir. 1964).

40. On July 17, 1975, *The Wall Street Journal* reported that the convicted auditors were sentenced to a suspended two-year prison term, three months of actual jail time, four years of probation, and 2,000 hours of charity work. The conviction was affirmed in United States v. Weiner, 578 F.2d 757 (9th Cir. 1978). The charge to the jury was that deviation from GAAP or GAAS was evidence, but not necessarily conclusive evidence, that the defendants did not act honestly and that the financials were materially misleading. Reprinted by permission of *The Wall Street Journal,* © Dow Jones & Company, Inc., 1975. All rights reserved.

41. United States v. Zane, 495 F.2d 683 (2d Cir. 1974).

42. United States v. Bruce, 488 F.2d 1224 (5th Cir. 1973).

se false. The CPA had compiled and formulated financial data in two different prospectuses, the first offered to the public on January 31, 1967, and the second showing 1968 income and expenses.

The U.S. Fifth Circuit Court of Appeals said:

> As to the second prospectus, Judge Edenfield found that "all of the defendants *knew and could not have failed to know* (emphasis added) that the business they were conducting was a fraud"; that while the Company had collected "over $200,000 from the sale of stock and investment certificates, it had not devoted a single dollar of the Company's assets to the purposes for which the corporation was purportedly created, but instead had squandered and spent vast sums of the Company's assets . . . all without having earned one dime for stockholders or investors."
>
> Essentially, a scheme to defraud is measured by a nontechnical standard. "It is a reflection of moral uprightness, of fundamental honesty, fair play and right dealing in the general and business life of members of society," *Gregory v. United States,* 5 Cir., 1958, 253 F.2d 104, 109.
>
> The scheme need not be fraudulent upon its face or misrepresent any material fact. All that is necessary is that it be a scheme reasonably calculated to *deceive* persons of ordinary prudence and comprehension. The intent of the crime is shown by the scheme itself— here, the active promotion of a company known to be inescapably insolvent by making impossible representations of possible wealth to potential investors. . . .

United States v. White,[43] decided in 1941, is another example of circumstantial evidence used to prove the requisite intent. A public accountant was convicted of using the mails to defraud, violating section 17 of the Securities Act of 1933, and conspiring with others to commit the crimes. The charges related to financial statements in registration statements and prospectuses under the Securities Act of 1933. The auditor's defense was that he had taken facts either from the books or from what management told him. The prosecution based its case on the inference that anyone with the auditor's experience and intelligence would have been aware of the irregularity. The court, after reviewing numerous items of questionable accounting that taken individually did not demonstrate knowledge of falsity, noted that a "cumulation of instances" may have much greater probative force than any one alone. Such instances included purchasing accounts receivable at substantial discounts, then writing them up and recognizing profit before realization on the basis of estimates by management.

In affirming conviction of the auditor the court said:

> We do not say that his guilt was demonstrated, but enough was proved to subject him to the hazard of a verdict; faced with the choice of finding him a knave or a fool, we cannot say that the jury was bound to acquit him; fair men might have had no compunction in refusing to believe that he was so credulous or so ill-acquainted with his calling as a finding of innocence demanded.

Duty to Disclose Management Misconduct

In 1970 the United States Supreme Court denied *certiorari* in *United States v. Simon,*[44] known as the *Continental Vending* case. In this case, as in many other civil and criminal cases involving public accountants, the auditors had no apparent motive for wrongdoing and reaped no personal benefit from any of the transactions. This case was particularly unfortunate; it involved some disclosure problems not settled by auditing standards and accounting principles, and new disclosure responsibility was in effect enunciated in a criminal proceeding. However, the general theory of the public prosecutor had been enunciated in the *Royal Mail* case over 30 years earlier: Knowingly and intentionally misleading the ordinary prudent investor constitutes criminal conduct.

A senior partner, a junior partner, and a senior associate in the accounting firm of Lybrand, Ross Bros. & Montgomery were convicted of a conspiracy to violate the Federal Mail Fraud Statute and the Securities Exchange Act of 1934 by knowingly drawing up and certifying a false and misleading financial statement of Continental Vending Machine Corporation for the year ending September 30, 1962, and the use of the mails to distribute the statement in violation of the Federal Mail Fraud Statute.

The controversy over disclosure related to a loan which Continental, the audited company, made to Valley Commercial Corporation, an affiliate. Valley in turn loaned the money to Roth, who was president of Continental, supervised operations of Valley, and owned about 25 percent of the stock of both companies. Roth was unable to repay the money to Valley, and Valley in turn could not pay Continental. Roth put up security for the loan, but about 80 percent of the security was stock and debentures of Continental itself.

The disclosure required by the auditors clearly showed a deteriorating financial position, and when the annual reports were mailed, Continental's stock prices fell. The auditors then withdrew their opinion on the statements because of the fall in value of the collateral. When a Continental check to the Internal Revenue Service bounced, an investigation was started, the plant was padlocked, and bankruptcy followed.

43. United States v. White, 124 F.2d 181 (2d Cir. 1941).

44. United States v. Simon, 425 F.2d 796 (2d Cir. 1969), *cert. denied,* 397 U.S. 1006 (1970).

The thrust of the government's case was built on the points that (1) the defendants concealed, but should have disclosed, that Roth got the money and (2) because the collateral was inappropriate, its nature should have been disclosed. The financial statements certified by the defendants contained the following note:

> The amount receivable from Valley Commercial Corp. (an affiliated company of which Mr. Harold Roth is an officer, director and stockholder) bears interest at 12 percent a year. Such amount, less the balance of the notes payable to that company, is secured by the assignment to the Company of Valley's equity in certain marketable securities. As of February 15, 1963, the amount of such equity at current market quotations exceeded the net amount receivable.

The issues in the case are clearly revealed when comparison is made with the following note that the government contends was required:

> The amount receivable from Valley Commercial Corp. (an affiliated company of which Mr. Harold Roth is an officer, director and stockholder), which bears interest at 12 percent a year, was uncollectible at September 30, 1962, since Valley had loaned approximately the same amount to Mr. Roth who was unable to pay. Since that date Mr. Roth and others have pledged as security for the repayment of his obligation to Valley and its obligation to Continental (now $3,900,000 against which Continental's liability to Valley cannot be offset) securities which, as of February 15, 1963, had a market value of $2,978,000. Approximately 80 percent of such securities are stock and convertible debentures of the Company.

The government contended disclosure was misleading because:

1. Continental's footnote should have disclosed that Roth got the money.
2. Since 80 percent of the collateral was securities issued by Continental and hence unsuitable security, the nature of the collateral should have been disclosed.
3. Continental's footnote improperly showed that the net amount of receivables from Valley was secured, but the liability to Valley was composed of negotiable notes that were discounted with outsiders. Defendants admitted that they made an error in netting the two accounts.
4. Continental's footnote referred to the secured position at February 15, 1963, without disclosing that the Valley receivable had increased.

The defendants contended that compliance with generally accepted accounting principles was a conclusive defense to criminal charges of misrepresentation. The court rejected the defendants' argument, however, and held that the critical test is whether the financial statements, as a whole, fairly present the financial position and accurately report operations (see Chapter 1 at note 43).

An important rule established by *Continental Vending* is that an auditor must disclose improper activities of the client or the client's officers when such activities are known to the auditor and may reasonably affect the audited financial statements.[45] This duty of disclosure, though now imposed by this criminal case, is yet to be defined by the profession itself. The court opinion does not define exactly what conduct is improper but leaves it for the auditor to decide when a corporation is operated, not in the interest of all stockholders, but for the private benefit of an insider. The court's only guidelines are:

> We join defendants' counsel in assuming that the mere fact that a company has made advances to an affiliate does not ordinarily impose a duty on an accountant to investigate what the affiliate has done with them or even to disclose that the affiliate has made a loan to a common officer if this has come to his attention. But it simply cannot be true that an accountant is under no duty to disclose what he knows when he has reason to believe that, to a material extent, a corporation is being operated not to carry out its business in the interest of all the stockholders but for the private benefit of its president. For a court to say that all this is immaterial as a matter of law if only such loans are thought to be collectible would be to say that independent accountants have no responsibility to reveal known dishonesty by a high corporate officer. If certification does not at least imply that the corporation has not been looted by insiders so far as the accountants know, or, if it has been, that the diversion has been made good beyond peradventure (or adequately reserved against) and effective steps taken to prevent a recurrence, it would mean nothing, and the reliance placed on it by the public would be a snare and a delusion. Generally accepted accounting principles instruct an accountant what to do in the usual case where he has no reason to doubt that the affairs of the corporation are being honestly conducted. Once he has reason to believe that this basic assumption is false, an entirely different situation confronts him. Then, as the Lybrand firm stated in its letter accepting the Continental engagement, he must "extend his procedures to determine whether or not such suspicions are justified." If as a result of such an extension or, as here, without it, he finds his suspicions to be confirmed, full disclosure must be the rule, unless he has

---

45. David Isbell, an attorney, argues that "the criminal prosecution certainly served as leverage to force the settlement of the companion civil suit, in the amount of $2.1 million." He contends that the loss resulting from Continental's collapse was not caused by any failure of disclosure and the charges "would not have supported a civil damage action even though they did support a criminal action." See David B. Isbell, "The Continental Vending Case: Lessons for the Profession," *Journal of Accountancy,* August 1970, pp. 33–40.

made sure the wrong has been righted and procedures to avoid a repetition have been established. At least this must be true when the dishonesty he had discovered is not some minor peccadillo but a diversion so large as to imperil if not destroy the very solvency of the enterprise.

The court also ruled that the jury could consider the failure to disclose composition of collateral, because the nature of the collateral made it unsuitable.

> As men experienced in financial matters . . . they must have known that the one kind of property ideally unsuitable to collateralize a receivable . . . would be securities of the very corporation whose solvency was at issue, particularly when the 1962 report revealed a serious operating loss.

Courts may well give more weight to accounting principles when they are clear and specific. But in *Continental* the expert witnesses were divided as to whether the disclosure was in accordance with generally accepted accounting principles. The accounting profession should therefore take a hard look at establishing guidelines for reporting of collateral and should specifically adopt the court's rule that securities issued by the client cannot be considered collateral. The question of disclosure of insider misconduct also needs careful attention.

Duty to Disclose Errors in Prior Audits

Where an auditor makes an honest mistake, s/he has a duty to disclose the error as soon as s/he learns of it. The failure to do so results in civil liability, whether in connection with tax returns (see Chapter 12) or audits (see Chapter 13). Such failure also results in criminal liability because the requisite intent to mislead is present. An auditor's attempt to cover up the prior error in connection with subsequent work provides evidence of the criminal intent.

In *United States v. Natelli*[46] the U.S. Court of Appeals for the Second Circuit upheld the conviction of Anthony M. Natelli, an audit partner of Peat, Marwick, Mitchell & Co., in the *National Student Marketing Corp.* (NSM) case. The conviction was based on two specifications of Natelli's having knowingly filed a false 1969 proxy statement: (1) knowingly failing to disclose in the 1969 NSM proxy statement that about

$1 million in sales originally reported by NSM in 1968 had been written off as nonexistent by understating the 1968 figures given for companies acquired by NSM the following year and thus substantially overstating NSM's 1968 sales and profits, and (2) exaggerating NSM's unaudited results for the nine months ended May 31, 1969, by reporting earnings of $702,270, while knowing that NSM had no earnings.

Concerning the *first specification,* Judge Gurfein found that the auditors clearly had a duty to disclose the error in the 1968 financials:

> A simple desire to right the wrong that had been perpetrated on the stockholders and others (in the original statements) should have dictated that course. The failure to make open disclosure could hardly have been inadvertent, or a jury at least could so find.

Duty to Disclose Known Falsity of Unaudited Financials

In the *Natelli* case the second specification of filing a false proxy statement concerns unaudited financials. The AICPA filed an *amicus curiae* brief, which addressed itself only to this matter. It contended that the trial court failed to distinguish the auditor's responsibility for unaudited financials from his responsibility for audited financials. Commenting on unaudited financials, it said:

> If [the auditor] is "associated" with such statements, his duty is limited to insisting upon disclosure of material departures from generally accepted accounting principles which are in fact known to him; he has no affirmative duty to satisfy himself that the statements are not misleading.[47]

The Appeals Court rejected the AICPA contention that the trial judge's instructions should have made a distinction between audited and unaudited financials and said:

> The issue is not what an auditor is generally under a duty to do with respect to an unaudited statement, but what these defendants had a duty to do in these unusual and highly suspicious circumstances.

Pro Forma Financials

Pro forma financials are financial statements that reflect transactions not yet consummated. The SEC has recognized the usefulness of pro forma statements and sometimes requires them in registration statements or proxy statements. For example, where two firms are about to be merged, pro forma statements

46. United States v. Natelli, 527 F.2d 311 (1975), *cert. denied,* 425 U.S. 934 (1976). In further proceedings in United States v. Natelli at 553 F.2d 5 (2d Cir. 1977), *cert. denied,* 434 U.S. 819 (1978), the United States Court of Appeals for the Second Circuit denied Natelli's bid for a new trial, stating: "Upon analysis, Natelli's argument is reduced to the claim that he is entitled to a new trial to produce the testimony of Randell which in our view is at best questionable, was previously available and in any event would not be of any significant assistance to Natelli. The order below is therefore affirmed."

47. "AICPA Brief in Natelli-Scansaroli," *Journal of Accountancy,* May 1975, p. 69.

may be needed to portray the merged balance sheet and past income on a merged basis.[48]

Rule 201E of the AICPA *Code of Professional Ethics* provides:

> A member shall not permit his name to be used in conjunction with any forecast of future transactions in a manner which may lead to the belief that the member vouches for the achievability of the forecast.

This rule does not prohibit a member from preparing either pro forma or forecasted statements or associating his or her name with them. It does require the CPA to state that s/he does not vouch for the accuracy of any forecast, and full disclosure must be made of (1) sources of information, (2) assumptions, (3) character of the work performed, and (4) responsibility the CPA is assuming.[49] In *United States v. Benjamin*[50] the defendant certified public accountant had prepared reports containing "pro forma" balance sheets and contended that he had sheltered himself with the words *pro forma* and that he did not know the reports were to be used in stock sales. But the court found that he knew his reports were being used with brokers selling the stock. The court also found that knowledge of falsity was clearly shown by (1) inclusion as an asset of over $700,000 of "unrecovered development costs" of a dormant mining company known to have been through insolvency proceedings, and (2) assertion, in a profit and loss statement, that six companies were "acquired within the last few months" when the accountant knew that at least some had never been acquired. The court noted that the second report, extolling the prospects of the $8.7 million company, was delivered in a setting where the defendant accountant had not been able to obtain a $200 advance, in a hotel which had turned off food and telephone service for nonpayment of bills.

The court concluded that the words *pro forma* do not justify showing ownership of property that was neither owned nor the subject of firm arrangements for acquisition. When a public accountant prepares such a report, he has a duty to make sure that the transactions are bona fide by investigating arrangements for acquisition and provision for payment. His opinion on such statements should be given only when the nature of the transactions to be effected is clearly described.

The court affirmed the CPA's conviction, along with that of a lawyer and a promoter, for willfully conspiring by use of interstate commerce to sell unregistered securities and to defraud in the sale of securities, in violation of the Securities Act of 1933 as implemented criminally by section 24.[51]

The case of *Getchell v. United States,*[52] decided in 1960, also involved a certified public accountant in connection with promotion of a new corporation. The accountant was to have become treasurer, comptroller, and a director of a new corporation, Florida Alpha Pulp Corporation, which was to make alpha-cellulose (paper pulp) from cabbage palms by a "secret" process. The court held the evidence insufficient to convict the accountant for violation of section 17(a)(1) of the Securities Act of 1933,[53] which makes it unlawful to defraud in the sale of securities by use of the mails or other instruments of interstate commerce. In reversing the conviction the court said his "chief fault was that he authored too rosy a 'pro forma' statement or estimate of anticipated profits."[54]

SUMMARY

At early common law, private frauds were not punishable unless some false tokens or symbols, such as false weights or measures, were used. Gradually criminal responsibility was extended to cover all types of private fraud. The conviction of Lord Kylsant in *Rex v. Kylsant and Morland* in 1931 established a precedent for extension of criminal penalties to those who knowingly mislead the ordinary prudent investor, even though the statements are true when taken individually.

In our American economy the needs of investors can be met only if uniform standards of responsibility are imposed throughout the nation. Accordingly the federal government has taken the lead in establishing criminal responsibility for those involved in frauds affecting the interstate securities markets. Federal criminal penalties are imposed on those willfully making false financial disclosures by the securities laws, the Federal False Statements Statute, the Federal Mail Fraud Statute, and federal statutes providing penalties for those who conspire, aid, or abet in commission of federal crimes.

An auditor may incur both civil and criminal penalties if s/he fails to disclose (1) management misconduct threatening the solvency of the enterprise, or (2) previous honest audit errors of great materiality. Preparation of pro forma statements constitutes one of the

48. Louis H. Rappaport, *SEC Accounting Practice and Procedure,* 3d ed. (New York: Ronald Press, 1972), pp. 19.1–19.2

49. See "Interpretation under Rule 201—Forecasts," *CCH AICPA Professional Standards,* ET § 201.03 and discussion under "Forecasts and Projections" in Chapter 13.

50. United States v. Benjamin, 328 F.2d 854 (2d Cir. 1964).

51. The CPA, promoter, and lawyer were convicted for violation of the Securities Act of 1933, §§ 5, (a) and (c), and 17(a), 15 U.S.C. §§ 77e, (a) and (c), and 77q(a), implemented criminally by § 24 of the act, 15 U.S.C. § 77x.

52. Getchell v. United States, 282 F.2d 681 (5th Cir. 1960).

53. 15 U.S.C. § 77q(a)(1).

54. Getchell v. United States, *supra* note 52 at 689.

highest risk engagements for an auditor. In such engagements, special care must be taken to ascertain the integrity of the client.

The *Continental Vending* case extended criminal liability to public accountants who knowingly fail to disclose insider misconduct that may materially affect financial position. It established the rule that compliance with GAAP is not a conclusive defense to charges of criminal fraud.

The trend is toward stricter enforcement of criminal, as well as civil, provisions against accountants with increased public awareness as expressed by Judge Friendly: "In our complex society the accountant's certificate and the lawyer's opinion can be instruments for inflicting pecuniary loss more potent than the chisel or the crowbar."[55]

SUGGESTIONS FOR FURTHER READING

Anderson, Ronald A. *Wharton's Criminal Law and Procedure*. Vol. 2. New York: Lawyers Co-operative Publishing 1957, pp. 301–94.

Burdick, William L. *The Law of Crime*. Vol. 2. New York: Matthew Bender & Co., 1946, pp. 456–513.

Dickerson, R. W. V. *Accountants and the Law of Negligence*. Toronto, Canada: Canadian Institute of Chartered Accountants, 1966.

Dunfee, Thomas W., and Irvin N. Gleim. "Criminal Liability of Accountants: Sources and Policies." *American Business Law Journal*, Spring 1971, pp. 1–20.

"Federal Criminal and Administrative Controls for Auditors: The Need for a Consistent Standard." *Washington University Law Quarterly*, Spring 1969, pp. 187–229.

Isbell, David B. "The Continental Vending Case: Lessons for the Profession." *Journal of Accountancy*, August 1970, pp. 33–40.

Robertson, Wyndham. "Those Daring Young Con Men of Equity Funding." *Fortune*, August 1973, pp. 81–132.

"The Criminal Liability of Public Accountants: A Study of United States v. Simon." *Notre Dame Lawyer*, Spring 1971, pp. 564–603.

QUESTIONS AND PROBLEMS

1. What long-term trends in criminal responsibility do you perceive?
2. What federal statutes provide penalties for false disclosures?
3. What are the implications of the *Continental Vending* case?
4. When must an auditor disclose "insider" misconduct?
5. What are the duties and responsibilities of a public accountant with respect to pro forma statements?

---

55. United States v. Benjamin, 328 F.2d 854 (2d Cir. 1964).

6. (From the November 1961 Uniform CPA Examination)
   In addition to the civil liability imposed upon the accountant, certain federal statutes impose criminal liability on those preparing financial statements. List three well-known statutes which have so imposed liability and with which accountants are frequently concerned.

7. (From the May 1962 Uniform CPA Examination)
   As a certified public accountant you have been asked to examine and give your opinion on pro forma financial statements of a client.

   Required:
   a. Define *pro forma financial statements*.
   b. List and briefly discuss the conditions necessary for giving an opinion on pro forma financial statements.

8. (From the May 1973 Uniform CPA Examination)
   The CPA who regularly examines Viola Corporation's financial statements has been asked to prepare pro forma income statements for the next five years. If the statements are to be based upon the Corporation's operating assumptions and are for internal use only, the CPA should
   a. Reject the engagement because the statements are to be based upon assumptions.
   b. Reject the engagement because the statements are for internal use.
   c. Accept the engagement, provided full disclosure is made of the assumptions used and the extent of the CPA's responsibility.
   d. Accept the engagement, provided Viola certifies in writing that the statements are for internal use only.

9. (From the November 1977 Uniform CPA Examination)
   A CPA is subject to *criminal* liability if the CPA
   a. Refuses to turn over the working papers to the client.
   b. Performs an audit in a negligent manner.
   c. Willfully omits a material fact required to be stated in a registration statement.
   d. Willfully breaches the contract with the client.

10. (From the November 1977 Uniform CPA Examination)
    Under which of the following circumstances could an auditor consider rendering an opinion on pro forma statements that give effect to proposed transactions?
    a. When the pro forma statements include amounts based on financial projections.
    b. When the time interval between the date of the financial statements and consummation of the transactions is relatively long.
    c. When certain subsequent events have some chance of interfering with the consummation of the transactions.
    d. When the proposed transactions are subject to a definitive agreement among the parties.

10

Malpractice Insurance

This chapter covers:

- TYPES OF COVERAGE.
- POLICY LIMITS AND PREMIUMS.
- EXCLUSIONS.
- DUTIES OF THE CARRIER.
- DUTIES OF THE INSURED.
- CLAIMS MANAGEMENT.
- LOSS PREVENTION/RISK MANAGEMENT.

TYPES OF COVERAGE

Malpractice insurance coverage is classified as "claims made" or "occurrence" coverage. Claims-made policies generally cover claims discovered and reported to the carrier during the policy period, regardless of when the malpractice occurred. Occurrence policies generally cover all malpractice that occurs within the policy period, regardless of when the claim is discovered. Claims-made coverage has become prevalent because it avoids the "tail" associated with occurrence coverage. At the end of the policy year the insurance carrier can establish reserves and evaluate loss experience which is not possible with occurrence coverage.

There are three problems to be avoided in maintaining coverage. These are:

1. The sole practitioner who retires and discontinues a claims-made policy.
2. The obtaining of coverage for prior acts for practitioners who have practiced without coverage.

3. Uninsured gaps that can result from shifting back and forth between carriers who offer different types of coverage.

The Retiring Sole Practitioner

The sole practitioner who retires and discontinues claims-made coverage will be uninsured for claims that are discovered during retirement. This problem can be solved by continuing to carry a "nonpracticing policy" that is available at modest cost.

Prior Acts Coverage

Some claims-made policies insure only claims that occur after a retroactive date and are reported to the carrier by the end of the policy period. Those who have never had malpractice coverage will remain without coverage for occurrences prior to the retroactive date. Therefore it is important to obtain coverage for acts occurring by the end of the policy period that are reported by the end of the policy period. Some companies sell a "tail" policy to cover the prior acts problem.

Uninsured Gaps

The uninsured gaps problem is illustrated by the case of *Gereboff v. Home Indemnity Co.*[1] The CPAs prepared financials in 1968 allegedly taking the bookkeeper's word for receivables in the form of an adding machine tape on which the indicated total exceeded the true total. The problem was not discovered until 1971 at which time the client indicated it would be handled as a family matter since the bookkeeper was a member of the family. However, in 1973 the CPAs were sued by the executor of the estate of one of the owners. The CPAs then brought suit against the three malpractice insurance carriers that insured them at the relevant times:

1. In 1968 Home Indemnity Co. provided claims-made coverage for all claims reported during the policy period or within one year thereafter. This policy did not apply since the claim was not reported during the period of coverage.
2. In 1971 St. Paul Fire and Marine provided occurrence coverage plus claims-made coverage for claims reported within the policy period. However, this policy did not apply since the matter did not occur in 1971 and the CPAs did not report the matter to the carrier in 1971.
3. In 1973 American Home Assurance Company provided coverage for claims "arising out of pro-

---

1. Gereboff v. Home Indemnity Co., 383 A.2d 1024 (R.I. 1978).

fessional services performed during the policy period" which were reported during the policy period. This policy did not afford coverage because of the occurrence limitation that insured only services performed during the policy period.

Thus an occurrence-type limitation following claims-made coverage must be avoided in order to eliminate gaps in coverage.

POLICY LIMITS AND PREMIUMS

In order to provide catastrophic coverage for the smaller CPA firm, it is necessary to carry $1 million of coverage for each professional up to a maximum of $10 million. In contrast, many Big Eight firms are insured with Lloyds of London and may have a deductible of $5 or $6 million. The better policies for small firms should not charge cost of defense against the policy limits but may charge the deductible.

The premiums are usually based on the number of professionals associated with the firm. Rates vary depending upon the geographic location of the firm. Firms located in New York, Los Angeles, and Miami are apt to pay higher premiums because of the amount of litigation in those areas.

EXCLUSIONS

Affirmative Dishonesty

Virtually all policies exclude affirmative dishonesty of the firm or its partners from coverage. Better policies insure the innocent partner from liability for a dishonest partner. This problem is illustrated by *Berylson v. American Surety Co. of New York*[2] where the CPA sued his malpractice carrier to recover $42,500 in legal expenses for defending a criminal indictment charging him with willfully filing a false income tax return. The suit was dismissed because the policy covered neglect, error, or omission but excluded dishonesty, misrepresentation, or fraud committed with intent to deceive or defraud.

Coverage for innocent partners is an important consideration. Under section 14 of the Uniform Partnership Act, the partnership is responsible for the money misapplied by a partner. Under section 15, all partners are personally liable for the full amount of such losses. In *Duke v. Hoch*,[3] two innocent CPA partners found themselves uninsured for their partner's alleged misappropriation of $40,000 of client funds.

Liability under Federal Securities Laws

Some policies exclude all liability under federal securities laws. These policies should be considered unacceptable since civil liability and antifraud provisions of federal securities laws apply whenever securities (including limited partnerships) are sold by use of the mails or telephone regardless of an exemption from SEC filing requirements. For further discussion of this problem, see Chapter 8.

Punitive Damages

Some policies simply fail to cover punitive damages by undertaking to pay "compensatory" damages. Other policies exclude punitive damages. Prior to these practices there was some doubt as to whether public policy considerations permitted insurance for punitive damages which are generally recoverable only for flagrant conduct.

DUTIES OF THE CARRIER

The courts hold that there is an implied duty of good faith on the part of the insurance carrier which requires the carrier to exercise due care to protect the insured. Some courts reach this result by speaking in terms of the carrier's negligence instead of its duty of good faith.

Investigation and Settlement

Courts generally hold that the carrier must promptly investigate all claims and make an effort to protect the insured by attempting to settle claims of clear liability within the policy limits. Where the carrier fails to do so, the courts may hold the carrier liable for the resulting verdict that exceeds the policy limits. This is especially true if the carrier has rejected the legal counsel's recommendation to accept a settlement offer at or near the policy limits.

Defense

Policies generally undertake to provide a legal defense for the insured. Since the policy insures "damages," there is no duty to defend a revocation of license or other disciplinary proceeding nor an SEC enforcement action. However, the duty to defend is broader than the duty to pay damages. In *St. Paul Fire & Marine Insurance Co. v. Clarence-Rainess & Co.*,[4] the insurance carrier disclaimed the duty to defend

---

2. Berylson v. American Surety Co. of New York, 220 N.Y.S.2d 532 (Sup. Ct. N.Y. Cty. 1961).

3. Duke v. Hoch, 468 F.2d 973 (5th Cir. 1972) (applying Florida law).

4. St. Paul Fire & Marine Ins. Co. v. Clarence-Rainess & Co., 355 N.Y.S.2d 169 (Sup. Ct. 1972), *aff'd without opinion*, 340 N.Y.S.2d 587 (App. Div. 1973).

because some theories of the suit involved affirmative dishonesty excluded from the coverage. However, the court held that the duty to defend arises whenever some of the claim falls within the coverage, and the carrier was required to reimburse the accounting firm for the reasonable costs that it had incurred.

In *St. Paul Fire & Marine Ins. Co. v. Weiner,*[5] the carrier contended that criminal conviction of the insured CPAs relieved it of the duty to defend the related civil suits because of the affirmative dishonesty exclusion. However, the court rejected this argument because the liability issues and time periods were not identical in the civil and criminal actions.

Where the carrier undertakes to defend without reserving the right to contest coverage of any resulting damage verdict, it is bound to pay up to the limit of the policy. In order to avoid this result, carriers sometimes undertake to defend on a reservation of rights basis. In *Rimar v. Continental Casualty Co.,*[6] the court held that reservation of rights to contest coverage creates a conflict of interest between the insured and the carrier which gives the insured CPA the right to select legal counsel to be paid by the insurance carrier.

DUTIES OF THE INSURED

Under the terms of virtually all policies, the insured is required to give immediate written notice to the carrier of any claim or of any occurrence that may lead to a claim within the coverage of the policy. A claim is any formal allegation of having performed professional services in a deficient manner. Examples include a demand to make good a loss by the client, being served with a lawsuit, or being served with a counterclaim for deficient work when you sue for a fee. An occurrence is your awareness of deficient performance or when the client believes your work is deficient. Examples include mention of dissatisfaction by the client or your knowledge of an error that remains unknown to the client.

Policies give the carrier the right to control the defense and negotiate settlements. An admission of liability by the insured is a breach of the insured's duties under the policy and can result in loss of coverage for the claim. Never offer to pay the loss, admit responsibility, or say your insurance company will take care of it without obtaining prior approval of your insurance carrier.

The doctrine of "trivial occurrence" sometimes may be invoked to excuse the failure to give notice, especially where the failure has not resulted in any

damage to the case. Some CPAs elect to pay such small items as the $100 IRS negligence penalty with no notice to the carrier. However, the failure to give notice may result in loss of coverage on any other losses resulting from the same event.

CLAIMS MANAGEMENT

Where an obvious tax error by the CPA causes IRS penalties, the best course of conduct is to assure the client that you will take care of the matter and make good any loss. Doing this avoids the cost the client might incur in retaining other professionals to straighten out the matter. It also minimizes the cost of defense and loss of time on a matter of clear liability while retaining the client and the client's goodwill and possibly increasing the client's confidence. *However, remember that if you want malpractice insurance coverage on the claim, do not accept responsibility without getting prior consent of the carrier.*

LOSS PREVENTION/RISK MANAGEMENT

An accounting firm that is a well-managed, highly competent, and profitable operation serving honest, successful clients is the best approach to loss control. This necessarily involves some degree of specialization to permit a high level of expertise in each activity. Regardless of firm size, activities should be limited to those where there is a realistic potential for excellence with one person responsible for each activity on a firm-wide basis. Special controls should be placed on high-risk activities, such as writing tax-opinion letters or preparing financials to raise capital for a new venture.

A good, internal, client-accounting system which affords *prompt* client billing is a sometimes neglected element in loss control. This is especially effective when coupled with a policy of advance retainers, interest on past-due balances, and credit limits. This can avoid collection-related problems that often cause a deterioration in client relationships. Another loss-control technique worth considering is to place one partner in charge of developing a records-retention policy and file control on a firm-wide basis. Regardless of loss control techniques, we all make mistakes so that malpractice insurance is an essential ingredient in a risk-management program.

SUMMARY

Malpractice coverage is written on either a claims-made or occurrence basis with the claims-made basis becoming prevalent. Important considerations in obtaining malpractice insurance are to

5. St. Paul Fire & Marine Ins. Co. v. Weiner, 606 F.2d 684 (9th Cir. 1979) (applying California law).

6. Rimar v. Continental Cas. Co., 376 N.Y.S.2d 309 (App. Div. 1975).

144

1. Obtain coverage for innocent partners for affirmative dishonesty of others.
2. Obtain coverage for liability under federal securities laws, regardless of the fact that the firm does not do SEC filings.

Claims and occurrences must be reported in writing to the carrier. Never accept liability without obtaining prior approval of the carrier.

SUGGESTIONS FOR FURTHER READING

Annot. "Liability Insurance: Clause with Respect to Notice of Accident or Claim, etc., or with Respect to Forwarding Suit Papers." 18 *American Law Reports* 2d 443, 1951.

Annot. "Liability Insurance: Failure or Refusal of Insured to Attend Trial or to Testify as Breach of Cooperation Clause." 9 *American Law Reports* 4th 218, 1981.

QUESTIONS AND PROBLEMS

1. Define these terms:
   a. Claims-made coverage.
   b. Occurrence coverage.
2. What are the principal variables that affect the cost of malpractice insurance?
3. Identify (a) usual exclusions and (b) exclusions to be avoided when selecting malpractice insurance.
4. In what circumstances is an insurance carrier liable for a judgment in excess of the policy limits?
5. What is the effect of a carrier defending the insured on a "reservation-of-rights" basis?
6. What is the likely result where a CPA negotiates a favorable settlement of a malpractice claim before informing the insurance carrier?
7. Identify some loss-control techniques for a CPA firm.

11

Business and Competitive Practices

This chapter covers:

- UNFAIR TRADE PRACTICES.
- NONCOMPETITION AGREEMENTS.
- THE PROFESSIONAL CORPORATION.

UNFAIR TRADE PRACTICES

Solicitation of the Employer's Clients

Solicitation of firm clients while still associated with the firm may constitute an unfair trade practice. In *Biever, Drees & Nordell v. Coutts*[1] the employee of a CPA firm conducted periodic audits of certain Minnesota school districts. While still employed, he contacted these clients and indicated that he, as an individual, was interested in performing the audit work and recounted his past experience with such audits. At the time of this solicitation, he had not informed the employer CPA firm that he was contemplating leaving nor that he was contacting firm clients on his own behalf. There was no written or oral agreement concerning the employment relation. After the employee's voluntary termination in June 1979, the firm obtained a court order enjoining the former employee from performing audit or other services for such clients through

December 31, 1981. In upholding the injunction the North Dakota Supreme Court held that if an employee solicits the employer's customers in anticipation of starting a competing business, the employer is entitled to an injunction for a sufficient length of time to permit it to compete on even terms.

Misleading Advertising

Regulation by state boards and societies concerning advertising and solicitation is covered in Chapter 3, and regulation of tax practice is discussed in Chapter 12. In addition to those rules, the Federal Trade Commission Act empowers the FTC to order a cessation of advertising which constitutes an unfair or deceptive practice. In *Beneficial Corp. v. FTC,*[2] the FTC entered an order directing Beneficial to cease and desist from advertising and solicitation practices and ordered a total ban on use of Beneficial's copyrighted terms *Instant Tax Refund Plan* and *Instant Tax Refund Loan.* Upon Beneficial's petition for review, the court found that evidence supported the conclusion that Beneficial's advertising was deceptive, since customers failed to understand that Beneficial was offering only its normal loan service with normal finance charges. However, the court ruled that in placing a total ban on the use of the copyrighted terms, the Commission framed an overbroad remedial order which went further than reasonably necessary to accomplish its remedial objective. Therefore the court affirmed the order except for the total ban on use of the copyrighted terms.

NONCOMPETITION AGREEMENTS

At common law, restrictions on competition are not favored. Noncompetition convenants in employment and partnership agreements are enforced only if the restraints are reasonably limited in time and territory and are otherwise reasonable considering the interest of the employer and the effect on the employee. Restrictive covenants on the sellers of businesses are subject to more latitude and are not necessarily invalid because of the absence of a time limitation. The stronger bargaining position of a seller of a business makes the restrictive covenant more reasonable than those restricting employees in earning a livelihood.

Several states have enacted statutes dealing with this matter, while in others the courts' interpretation of the common-law rules are subject to wide variation. Therefore it is necessary to consult the statutes and court decisions for the particular jurisdiction. If noncompetition clauses cover contractual relations in

---

1. Biever, Drees & Nordell v. Coutts, 305 N.W.2d 33 (N.D. 1981).

2. Beneficial Corp. v. FTC, 542 F.2d 611 (3d Cir. 1976).

more than one state, it may be necessary to comply with the most restrictive jurisdiction. For example, in *Lynch v. Bailey*[3] the accounting firm had offices in New York, Detroit, Cleveland, Pittsburg, St. Louis, Los Angeles, and Seattle. The agreement provided that a withdrawing partner would not practice accountancy within four years of withdrawal within 100 miles of any city in which the partnership was located at time of withdrawal. Since the agreement was unenforceable in Michigan and California because of state statutes there, the court ruled the agreement lacked mutuality and consideration:

> In determining the validity or invalidity of a restrictive clause such as the one here in question, each case must be decided on its own particular facts. On the state of facts here disclosed, we hold that the restrictive clause is, as against this plaintiff, unreasonably broad in its scope, resulting in undue hardship to plaintiff wholly disproportionate to any proper need for defendant's protection, and is against public policy, and invalid and void for lack of mutuality and consideration.

The majority of states enforce noncompetition agreements in accounting practice provided there are reasonable time and territorial restrictions.[4] Reason-

---

3. Lynch v. Bailey, 90 N.Y.S.2d 359 (N.Y. App. Div. 1949).

4. Colorado: Fuller v. Brough, 411 P.2d 18 (Colo. 1966) (agreement that a withdrawing partner could not practice accounting for five years within 45 miles of Greely, Colorado, held valid).

    Delaware: Faw, Casson & Co. v. Cranston, 375 A.2d 463 (Del. Ch. 1977) (agreement not to compete in public accountancy on the Delmarva Peninsula within three years of promotion to manager upheld).

    Florida: Miller v. Williams, 300 So.2d 752 (Fla. App. 1974), (agreement by CPA firm and employee to pay fees to each other for servicing the other's clients after termination was a valid business arrangement and not a contract in restraint of trade). Florida Statutes section 542.12 permit agreements by partners, sellers of goodwill, and employees not to compete within a reasonably limited time and area.

    Illinois: Wolf & Co. v. Waldron, 366 N.E.2d 603 (Ill. App. 1977) (agreement not to service clients of a national accounting firm for two years from termination held valid).

    Minnesota: Haynes v. Monson, 224 N.W.2d 482 (Minn. 1974) (agreement not to engage in bookkeeping, accounting, or tax practice for five years within 50 miles of Austin, Minnesota, held valid).

    New York: Schacter v. Lester Witte & Co., 383 N.Y.S.2d 316 (N.Y. App. Div. 1976) (agreement of withdrawing partners not to service firm clients from two to five years held valid); Lynch v. Bailey, 90 N.Y.S.2d 359 (N.Y. App. Div. 1949) (agreement that withdrawing partners would not practice accountancy for 4 years within 100 miles of 10 cities held void).

    North Carolina: Schultz v. Ingram, 248 S.E.2d 345 (N.C. 1978) (covenant not to perform accounts payable invoice audits over a multistate area for two years from termination held valid); Scott v. Gillis, 148 S.E. 315 (N.C. 1929) (agreement not to service firm clients for three years from termination upheld).

    Oregon: Isler v. Shuck, 589 P.2d 1180 (Or. App. 1979) (agreement to pay 50 percent of gross fees earned from firm clients within three years of termination and to pay 10 percent of gross fees

---

able territorial restrictions may apparently be designated by wording the limitation in terms of servicing clients previously serviced by the terminated individual or (even broader) in terms of servicing clients serviced by the former firm at termination. Some states require strict limitations as to time and territory so that an agreement written in terms of firm clients may be void.[5] A few states limit noncompetition clauses to partners or sellers of businesses.[6] Two

---

earned from own clients (as per list) within two years of termination held valid).

Texas: Peat, Marwick, Mitchell & Co. v. Sharp, 585 S.W.2d 905 (Tex. App. 1979) (agreement that withdrawing partner must not practice in the United States for two years held void); McElreath v. Riquelmy, 444 S.W.2d 853 (Tex. App. 1969) (agreement that a withdrawing partner who serviced firm clients within three years would forfeit his capital account held valid).

Virginia: Foti v. Cook, 263 S.E.2d 430 (Va. 1980) (agreement of withdrawing partners to pay one third of fees collected for three years from any firm client serviced within 24 months of withdrawal held enforceable).

Washington: Racine v. Bender, 252 P. 115 (Wash. 1927) (future employment held consideration for promise signed by employees on time reports not to service firm clients for three years from termination).

5. Georgia: Fuller v. Kolb, 234 S.E.2d 517 (Ga. 1977) (agreement not to provide public accounting services for two years for clients serviced by the firm within two years of termination held void). Georgia Constitution, Article IV, and Georgia statutes section 2–2701 invalidate all contracts which tend to lessen competition or which are in restraint of trade. See Nat Stern, "Enforceability of Restrictive Covenants in Employment Contracts," *Georgia State Bar Journal,* February 1981, pp. 110–18.

    New Hampshire: Smith, Batchelder & Rugg v. Foster, 406 A.2d 1310 (N.H. 1979) (agreement to pay 50 percent of fees received from firm clients for three years held void; orally hiring employees without explaining restrictive covenant presented for signature after substantial change of position held evidence of bad faith).

    South Dakota: Statutes at section 53–9–11 limit noncompetition agreements by employees to 10 years and to a radius of 25 miles "from the principal place of business of the employer, as specified in such agreement." Statutes at section 53–9–10 limit noncompetition agreements by partners to the city or town where the partnership business has been transacted. Statutes at section 53–9–9 limit noncompetition agreements by sellers of goodwill to a specified county or city.

6. California: Noncompetition agreements are void except that under statutes section 16,601 the seller of the goodwill of a business may agree not to compete in a specified county or city. See Swenson v. File, 475 P.2d 852 (Cal. 1970) (agreement not to compete by seller of accounting practice was limited to city or town prior to 1961 and county or city if executed after 1961).

    Louisiana: Under statutes section 921 any noncompetition agreement by an employee is void.

    Michigan: Statutes section 445.766 limit noncompetition agreement to seller of goodwill and to a 90-day restriction where the employer furnishes a route list to the employee for a certain territory where employee is to work.

    North Dakota: Statutes section 9–0806 void noncompetition agreements except for agreements by (1) sellers of goodwill limited to a specified county or city, and (2) partners upon dissolution limited to a specified city where partnership business was transacted.

    Oklahoma: Noncompetition agreements are limited under statutes sections 217, 218, and 219 to sellers of goodwill or partners.

states uphold agreements unrestricted as to time.[7] Since the laws and court decisions are in a state of flux, it is not possible to generalize except to say that the most limited and reasonable restrictions are the most likely to be enforced. Because such agreements are not favored, they will be strictly construed against their applicability.[8]

PRACTICAL POINTER

While some courts hold that continued employment after signing an employment contract constitutes consideration for a covenant not to compete, the recommended practice is to have the noncompetition agreement signed simultaneously with the offer and acceptance of employment. In *Smith, Batchelder & Rugg v. Foster,* 406 A.2d 1310 (N.H. 1979), the court refused to reform and enforce an overly broad restrictive covenant because of a finding of bad faith on the part of the CPA firm. This was based on evidence that the employees were confronted with the written covenant only after substantial change of position in reliance upon the prior oral employment agreement and that during the oral negotiations there was either no discussion of the employment agreement containing the restrictive covenant or only a general reference to it.

THE PROFESSIONAL CORPORATION

AICPA ethics rules now permit practice of public accounting in the form of a professional corporation. Fictitious names are not permitted, and ownership of shares is limited to CPAs or public accountants. As to liability, the AICPA ethics rules provide:

> The stockholders of professional corporations or associations shall be jointly and severally liable for the acts of a corporation or association, or its employees— except where professional liability insurance is carried, or capitalization is maintained, in amounts deemed sufficient to offer adequate protection to the public.[9]

The various states have now enacted laws which permit formation of professional corporations. Under most of these laws the corporation has the effect of providing limited liability.[10] However, under all laws the professional person remains personally liable for work personally performed. Thus there is no effect on liability for incorporation of a sole practitioner.

Advantages of the professional corporation are mainly in the area of pension benefits. There are several disadvantages of professional corporations. Since partners become shareholders and employees, there is increased cost for FICA tax, unemployment tax, and workers' compensation insurance.

PRACTICAL POINTERS

1. Care must be taken to avoid income tax problems when forming a professional corporation. Revenue Ruling 80-198, 1980-2 C.B. 113, indicates that transfer of all assets and liabilities to a professional corporation in exchange for the corporate stock qualifies for nonrecognition of gain under IRC § 351, which covers transfers of assets to a controlled corporation. However, to obtain this status, it is important not to accumulate accounts receivable or to prepay accounts payable in a manner inconsistent with normal business practice in anticipation of incorporation. Where the proprietorship has changed methods of accounting and pursuant to IRC § 481 is spreading the effect over several tax years, the incorporation may require the entire adjustment to be immediately reported. See *Shore v. Commissioner,* 631 F.2d 624 (9th Cir. 1980).

2. Care must be taken to avoid tax consequences when getting out of a professional corporation. See "Two Recent Letter Rulings Define IRS' Position on Tax-Free Break Up of PCs: What Can Be Done," *The Journal of Taxation,* February 1979, pp. 92–97.

The many formalities required for proper corporate existence may cause difficulty. In *Krosnar v. Schmidt Krosnar McNaughton Garrett Co.,*[11] the court held that two CPAs became shareholders in the profes-

---

7. Alabama: Statutes section 8-1-1 permit employees, partners, and sellers of goodwill to agree not to compete within a specified county or city without regard to time limitations. Gant v. Warr, 240 So. 2d 353 (Ala. 1970) (agreement not to compete in CPA practice in three counties for five years held void); Burkett v. Adams, 361 So. 2d 1 (Ala. 1978) (agreement by noncertified PA not to compete for former clients void).

Indiana: Ebbeskotte v. Tyler, 142 N.E.2d 905 (Ind. 1957) (agreement not to service firm clients upheld as to reasonable territory, despite absence of time and territorial restrictions).

8. Derrick, Stubbs & Stith v. Rogers, 182 S.E.2d 724 (S.C. 1971) (restrictive covenant held not to apply to an involuntary withdrawal from the partnership).

9. *CCH AICPA Professional Standards* § ET Appendix C.

10. Incorporation of a professional corporation does not result in limited liability in Arizona, Colorado, Oregon, and Wisconsin. In State Bd. of Accountancy v. Eber, 149 So. 2d 81 (Fla. App. 1963) the court held that the state board rule prohibiting incorporation of an accounting practice could not be construed as prohibiting incorporation under Florida's professional corporation act. For a summary of the various state laws, see *CCH Standard Federal Tax Reports* ¶ 5943.02.

11. Krosnar v. Schmidt Krosnar McNaughton Garrett Co., 423 A.2d 370 (Pa. Super. 1980).

sional corporation despite the fact that no stock book was maintained and apparently no stock certificates were ever issued. The court ruled that the certificate is only evidence of shareholder status. In solving the allocation problem presented upon dissolution, the court pierced the corporate veil and treated the shareholders as equal individuals. The court also ruled that when the CPAs scrambled for business upon breakup of the professional corporation due to personal differences, they owed each other a fiduciary duty of trust and confidence and should have refrained from using their positions to the others' detriment and to their own advantage.

SUMMARY

Solicitation of firm clients while still associated with the firm may constitute an unfair trade practice. The employer may be entitled to an injunction to prevent the former associate from performing services for firm clients for a sufficient length of time to permit it to compete on even terms.

The Federal Trade Commission Act empowers the FTC to order a cessation of advertising which constitutes an unfair or deceptive practice.

Noncompetition agreements in employment and partnership agreements are enforced only if the restraints are reasonably limited in time and territory and are otherwise reasonable considering the interest of the employer and the effect on the employee. The majority of states enforce noncompetition agreements in accounting practice provided there are reasonable time and territorial restrictions. A few states, such as Louisiana, California, and Michigan, refuse to enforce such agreements against employees, regardless of limitations. Because such agreements are not favored, they are strictly construed against their applicability.

Public accounting practice may be conducted in the form of a professional corporation, which in most states results in limited liability. However, the professional person remains personally liable for work personally performed. The chief advantage of the professional corporation is pension benefits. Disadvantages include increased FICA and unemployment taxes and increased cost for workers' compensation insurance.

SUGGESTIONS FOR FURTHER READING

Annot. "Commercial Tax Preparer's Advertising as Unfair or Deceptive Act or Practice under § 5 of Federal Trade Commission Act." 37 *American Law Reports* Fed 81, 1978.

Annot. "Sufficiency of Consideration for Employee's Covenant Not to Compete, Entered Into after Inception of Employment." 51 *American Law Reports* 3d 825, 1973.

Cook, Philip C. "Incorporating the Professional Practice through a Partnership of Professional Corporations." *Georgia State Bar Journal*, February 1981, pp. 102–09.

King, Shepard, and Sharyl L. Poulson. "Is a Partnership of Professional Associations for You?" *Florida Bar Journal*, April 1981, pp. 280–89.

Pomeroy, Harlan. "Restrictive Covenants: What the CPA Should Know." *Journal of Accountancy*, February 1981, pp. 61–68.

Stern, Nat. "Enforceability of Restrictive Covenants in Employment Contracts." *Georgia State Bar Journal*, February 1981, pp. 110–18.

QUESTIONS AND PROBLEMS

1. Do you see anything morally wrong about contacting a prospective client that is now served by a CPA firm with which you were previously associated? Discuss.

2. As a matter of public policy, should the law prohibit noncompetition agreements between:
   a. A CPA firm and its employees?
   b. A CPA firm and its partners?
   c. A purchaser and seller of an accounting practice?

3. What are advantages and disadvantages of the professional corporation?

4. (From the November 1974 Uniform CPA Examination)
   Pickens and Perkins, CPAs, decide to incorporate their practice of accountancy. According to the AICPA Code of Professional Ethics, shares in the corporation can be issued
   a. Only to persons qualified to practice as CPAs.
   b. Only to employees and officers of the firm.
   c. Only to persons qualified to practice as CPAs and members of their immediate families.
   d. To the general public.

5. (From the November 1973 Uniform CPA Examination)
   Smith and Jones, CPAs, wish to incorporate their public accounting practice.
   a. An appropriate name for the new corporation would be the Financial Specialist Corporation.
   b. Smith and Jones need not be individually liable for the acts of the corporation if the corporation carries adequate professional liability insurance.
   c. Smith's 10-year-old son may own stock in the corporation.
   d. The corporation may provide services that are incompatible with the practice of public accounting as long as a non-CPA employee performs the services.

6. (From the May 1974 Uniform CPA Examination)
   Under the AICPA Code of Professional Ethics, which of the following characteristics is true for a professional corporation or association of CPAs?
   a. The name may be impersonal as long as it does not indicate a speciality.
   b. The shareholders must, in all cases, be jointly and severally liable for the acts of the corporation.
   c. The corporation may provide services that are not compatible with the practice of public accounting.
   d. A shareholder who ceases to be eligible to be a shareholder must dispose of all of his shares within a reasonable period.

7. (From the May 1980 Uniform CPA Examination)
   Whipple, Ryan, and Lopez decided to pool their assets and talents in a partnership. The partnership was to

provide management consulting services. The partnership agreement provided the following:

a. All policy questions regarding the scope, nature, billings, size, and future expansion of the business are to be decided by a majority vote of the partners. Each partner shall be bound by the decision reached.

b. Since each party to this agreement has discontinued a profitable individual business at great financial sacrifice, it is mutually agreed that this partnership shall be irrevocable for a period of five (5) years from the date of execution.

For the first year things went smoothly for the partnership. The relationship of the partners was amicable as they integrated the three separate businesses into one.

However, in the middle of the second year, policy disputes began to arise. In virtually every instance, Ryan and Lopez opposed Whipple on matters of expansion and billing rates. At the end of the second year, Whipple announced "he had had enough." He indicated that the ultraconservative thinking of his partners was deplorable and he could not remain in the partnership under the circumstances. He immediately resigned as a partner, reestablished his own business, and actively competed with the partnership. Many of his former clients followed him.

Required:
Answer the following, setting forth reasons for any conclusions stated: What recourse, if any, do Ryan and Lopez, or the partnership, have against Whipple?

12

Problems of Tax Practice

This chapter covers:

- ORGANIZATION OF THE IRS.
- TAX-RETURN PREPARATION.
- PRACTICE BEFORE THE IRS.
- PRACTICE BEFORE THE TAX COURT.
- UNAUTHORIZED PRACTICE OF LAW.
- IRS ACCESS TO BOOKS, RECORDS, AND ACCOUNTANTS' WORKING PAPERS.
- THE ROLE OF THE ACCOUNTANT IN TAX-FRAUD INVESTIGATIONS.
- CIVIL LIABILITIES IN TAX PRACTICE.
- CRIMINAL LIABILITY.

Public accountants who engage in tax practice should be aware of the particular ethical and legal responsibilities that relate to such practice. This chapter begins with a general summary of tax practice and related rules of conduct. The discussion then turns to Internal Revenue Service (IRS) access to books, records, and accountants' working papers, with a glance at the special situation where the accountant assists the attorney in defending a tax-fraud case. The chapter closes with a consideration of civil and criminal liabilities that relate to tax practice.

ORGANIZATION OF THE IRS

The Internal Revenue Code (IRC) provides that the Secretary of the Treasury shall administer and enforce the internal revenue laws. The Code further provides for appointment of the Commissioner of Internal Revenue and the IRS Chief Counsel by the President with the advice and consent of the Senate.

The IRS National Office develops and coordinates national policies and programs. These are administered in the field by 58 District Directors who report to seven Regional Commissioners. Ten Service Centers are under supervision of the Regional Commissioners. Exhibit 12–1 identifies the various regions and districts.

The Regional Counsel in each regional office serves as legal adviser to the Regional Commissioner, while being under the general supervision of the Chief Counsel. The Regional Counsel for the appropriate region represents the IRS in Tax Court; however, all other litigation is handled by the tax division of the Department of Justice or by local U.S. Attorneys.

TAX-RETURN PREPARATION

Section 7701 of the IRC defines *income tax return preparer* as "any person who prepares for compensation, or who employs one or more persons to prepare for compensation, any return of tax . . . or any claim for refund. . . ." Thus the term *income tax return preparer* and related regulations apply to an unlicensed person who prepares a single income tax return for a fee of $2 as well as to attorneys and CPAs.

PRACTICAL POINTER

Request your District Director to place your name on the Tax Practitioners Mailing List so as to receive special releases and an order form for an advance-tax-forms pamphlet (Package X) before the first of each year. Use Form 3975, Tax Practitioner Mailing List Application.

IRC § 6109 requires every income tax return preparer to sign each return prepared and indicate the identifying number of the employer or the social security number of the self-employed preparer, followed by the suffix *SE*. IRC § 6107 requires each preparer to furnish a completed copy of any return or refund claim to the taxpayer. This section also requires each preparer to retain for three years either a completed copy of each return or a list of names and taxpayer identification numbers. IRC section 6060 requires employers of income tax return preparers and self-employed preparers to maintain a record for three years of the name, taxpayer identification number, and place of work for each income tax preparer.

EXHIBIT 12-1
Map of IRS Regions, Districts, and Service Centers

Key:

⊛ Commissioner of Internal Revenue (Washington, D.C.)

○ District Director

★ National Computer Center (Martinsburg, W. Va.)

— Regional Boundary

■ Regional Commissioner

● Service Center

◆ IRS Data Center (Detroit, Mich.)

---- District Boundary

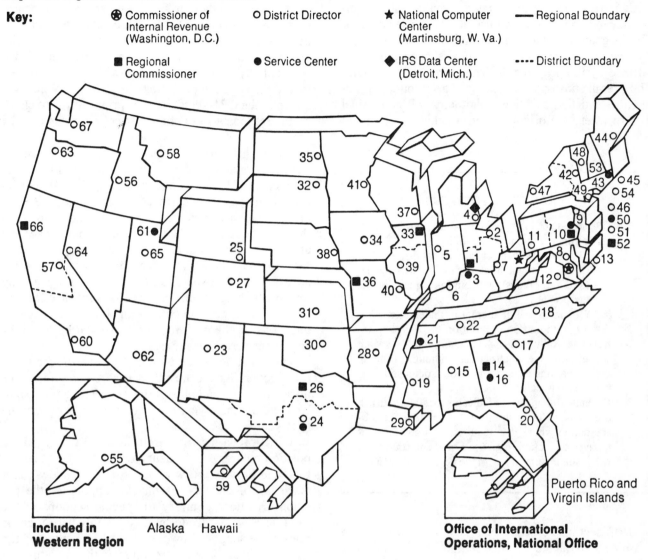

Included in Western Region   Alaska   Hawaii

Office of International Operations, National Office

Puerto Rico and Virgin Islands

Region and District Legend:

Central Region
1 Cincinnati, Ohio
2 Cleveland, Ohio
3 Covington, Ky. (Cincinnati SC)
4 Detroit, Mich.
5 Indianapolis, Ind.
6 Louisville, Ky.
7 Parkersburg, W. Va.

Mid-Atlantic Region
8 Baltimore, Md.
9 Newark, N.J.
10 Philadelphia, Pa.
11 Pittsburgh, Pa.
12 Richmond, Va.
13 Wilmington, Del.

Southeast Region
14 Atlanta, Ga.
15 Birmingham, Ala.
16 Chamblee, Ga.
17 Columbia, S.C.
18 Greensboro, N.C.
19 Jackson, Miss.
20 Jacksonville, Fla.
21 Memphis, Tenn.
22 Nashville, Tenn.

Southwest Region
23 Albuquerque, N. Mex.
24 Austin, Tex.
25 Cheyenne, Wyo.
26 Dallas, Tex.
27 Denver, Colo.
28 Little Rock, Ark.

29 New Orleans, La.
30 Oklahoma City, Okla.
31 Wichita, Kans.

Midwest Region
32 Aberdeen, S. Dak.
33 Chicago, Ill.
34 Des Moines, Iowa
35 Fargo, N. Dak.
36 Kansas City, Mo.
37 Milwaukee, Wis.
38 Omaha, Neb.
39 Springfield, Ill.
40 St. Louis, Mo.
41 St. Paul, Minn.

North Atlantic Region
42 Albany, N.Y.
43 Andover, Mass.
44 Augusta, Maine
45 Boston, Mass.
46 Brooklyn, N.Y.
47 Buffalo, N.Y.
48 Burlington, Vt.
49 Hartford, Conn.
50 Holtsville, N.Y. (Brookhaven SC)
51 Manhattan, N.Y.
52 New York, N.Y.
53 Portsmouth, N.H.
54 Providence, R.I.

Western Region
55 Anchorage, Alaska
56 Boise, Idaho
57 Fresno, Calif.
58 Helena, Mont.
59 Honolulu, Hawaii
60 Los Angeles, Calif.
61 Ogden, Utah
62 Phoenix, Ariz.
63 Portland, Ore.
64 Reno, Nev.
65 Salt Lake City, Utah
66 San Francisco, Calif
67 Seattle, Wash.

Source: *Annual Report 1979: Commissioner of Internal Revenue*, Superintendent of Documents (Washington, D.C.: U.S. Government Printing Office), 83.

Regulations at 26 C.F.R § 1.6695–1 require tax preparers to manually sign returns and claims for refund. This is restricted to the *manual* signature of an individual and does not permit use of a facsimile stamp or firm signature. Where more than one person is involved as tax preparer, the manual signature must be affixed by the preparer having primary responsibility for overall substantive accuracy. The manual requirement is satisfied by filing a photocopy of the original return where the original return contains the manual signature.

PRACTICAL POINTERS

1. IRC section 6694 imposes penalties on tax preparers for understatement of liability:
   a. $100 for negligent or intentional disregard of rules and regulations (including IRS regulations and rulings), with burden of proof on the tax preparer.
   b. $500 for a willful attempt to understate liability, with burden of proof on the IRS.
2. Revenue Ruling 78–344 indicates that following specific taxpayer instructions without consulting the regulations does not provide a defense to the negligence penalty.
3. Revenue Ruling 80–266 indicates that failure to ask the taxpayer for assurances as to existence of substantiation where it is required as a condition of taking a deduction (e.g., travel and entertainment) will result in assessment of the negligence penalty.

IRC section 6695(f) prohibits tax preparers from cashing federal income tax refund checks for their clients; however, regulations exempt banks that act as tax preparers. IRC section 7216 prohibits tax preparers from making unauthorized use of information supplied to them.

California and Oregon regulate tax preparers while exempting CPAs, attorneys, and enrolled agents. (Enrolled agents are discussed at note 13).

AICPA Ethical Standards

Court decisions indicate that AICPA rules constitute minimum standards for all accountants.[1] The AICPA issues *Statements on Responsibilities in Tax Practice* which are found in Volume 1 of *CCH AICPA*

Professional Standards. These standards provide that CPAs must sign any tax returns that they prepare, regardless of whether or not they receive compensation,[2] and in so doing should not modify the preparer's declaration.[3] CPAs who merely review returns may sign as preparers only if they have acquired knowledge substantially equivalent to that which would be acquired in actually preparing the return.[4] Whenever feasible, the CPA should review prior returns to check on the reasonableness of the current return and on the applicability of income averaging.[5]

Although CPAs preparing tax returns are not required to review evidentiary material, clients should be encouraged to provide supporting data. Where information appears incorrect or incomplete, the CPA must make further inquiries to resolve the doubt.[6] Although estimates may be used where generally acceptable and where obtaining exact data is impracticable, they should not be presented so as to imply greater accuracy than exists.[7] The CPA should not sign any return until s/he is satisfied that a reasonable effort has been made to provide correct answers to all relevant questions on the return. Reasons should be given for any unanswered questions.[8]

The resolution of an item depends on the facts and rules governing the taxable year. A compromise or disposition in an administrative proceeding for a similar item in a prior year does not ordinarily govern the later year.[9]

When preparing a tax return, a CPA may take a position contrary to Treasury Department or Internal Revenue Service *interpretations* of the Code without disclosure if there is reasonable support for the position. Positions contrary to specific sections of the Internal Revenue Code may be taken where there is reasonable support; however, in this rare situation the CPA should disclose the treatment in the tax return. In no event may a CPA take a position that lacks reasonable support, even when this position is disclosed in a return.[10]

PRACTICE BEFORE THE IRS

Practice, as defined by IRS regulations, excludes (1) preparing tax returns, (2) serving as a witness for

---

1. See note 37 in Chapter 1. The effect of *Statements on Responsibilities in Tax Practice* is not clear, since they have not been made binding under AICPA ethics rule 204 dealing with technical standards.

2. *CCH AICPA Professional Standards*, TX § 111.02.
3. *CCH AICPA Professional Standards*, TX § 191.13.
4. *CCH AICPA Professional Standards*, TX § 121.04.
5. *CCH AICPA Professional Standards*, TX § 191.10.
6. *CCH AICPA Professional Standards*, TX § 191.07.
7. *CCH AICPA Professional Standards*, TX § 151.02.
8. *CCH AICPA Professional Standards*, TX § 131.02.
9. *CCH AICPA Professional Standards*, TX § 141.05.
10. *CCH AICPA Professional Standards*, TX § 201.02.

the taxpayer, and (3) furnishing information at the request of the IRS. Rather, it involves representing the taxpayer in connection with either office examinations (at an IRS office or through correspondence with an IRS office) or field examinations (at the taxpayer's home or office or at the office of the taxpayer's accountant or lawyer).[11]

Office audits, conducted by tax examiners, are used where the examination is narrowed in scope to a few items which the taxpayer must substantiate. Field audits, conducted by revenue agents, result in more than 90 percent of additional taxes collected but account for less than 25 percent of tax returns audited.

Official Rules of Practice

Practice before the IRS is governed by regulations issued pursuant to statutory authority (31 U.S.C § 1026) authorizing the Secretary of the Treasury to prescribe rules and regulations governing agents, attorneys, or other persons representing taxpayers. These are referred to as "Circular 230" and may be obtained free from the office of any District Director of Internal Revenue.[12] CPAs and attorneys may practice before the IRS without examination. Others are admitted as *enrolled agents* upon passing an examination offered each September or October at IRS district offices.[13] Former IRS employees are enrolled without taking the exam if they have had five years' experience in applying and interpreting the Internal Revenue Code and regulations.

Many persons who prepare tax returns have no license whatever; they are not licensed (as lawyers, CPAs, or PAs) nor enrolled to practice before the Treasury Department. Regardless of their qualifications, any persons who prepare returns may represent the taxpayer at the lowest level of the IRS (revenue agent) with respect to returns that they prepare.[14] If no settlement is reached at this level, taxpayers must thereafter either represent themselves or retain someone admitted to practice before the Treasury Department.

Regulations require that the taxpayer's representative (whether CPA, attorney, or enrolled agent) must file "evidence of recognition" to practice before the service in each case.[15] Furthermore, a power of attorney, executed by the taxpayer, must be filed for the representative to perform any of the following acts:

1. Receive (but must not cash) a refund check.
2. Execute a waiver that effects a settlement of a case.
3. Consent to extend the statute of limitations.
4. Execute a closing agreement under IRC section 7121.
5. Delegate authority to another representative.[16]

The effect of the power of attorney is to authorize the IRS to deal with the representatives instead of the taxpayer. Taxpayer representatives should proceed with caution since any of their admissions are binding on the taxpayer in both criminal and civil cases.[17] No particular form of power of attorney is required; however, the IRS has issued Form 2848 for this purpose.

Negotiating with Revenue Agents

Revenue agents have no authority to negotiate on the basis of controversial legal issues. Only factual matters, such as the percentage of business use for an automobile, may be resolved at the agent level. If agreement on a deficiency is reached, the taxpayer signs Form 870: Waiver of Restrictions on Assessment and Collection of Deficiency in Tax, which usually closes the case. If agreement is not reached, the taxpayer receives a *30-day letter,* which is a letter of transmittal and a copy of the agent's report. The letter explains the taxpayer's right, upon request, to a conference in the appeals office which exercises full settlement authority. In certain circumstances this request must be accompanied by a written protest setting forth the reasons for refusing to accept the findings of

11. 31 C.F.R. § 10.2(a).

12. Circular 230 constitutes part of the Code of Federal Regulations at 31 C.F.R. Subtitle A, Part 10.

Circular 230 includes disciplinary procedures used to disbar persons practicing before the IRS pursuant to 31 U.S.C. § 1026. *See* Annot., "Disciplinary Action under 31 U.S.C.S. § 1026 Authorizing Secretary of the Treasury to Suspend and Disbar Any Person Representing Claimants from Further Practice before the Treasury Department," 50 A.L.R. Fed. 817 (1980).

13. Information can be obtained at IRS district offices by requesting IRS publications 486 and 693, respectively titled *Enrollment and Special Enrollment Examination* and *Sample Special Enrollment Examination*. Although the IRS does not publish answers, questions and suggested answers for past exams are published by both Commerce Clearing House and Prentice-Hall.

14. Circular 230 permits any tax preparer to represent the taxpayer before revenue agents and examining officers. However, this authority does not extend to practice before the appellate division.

15. 26 C.F.R. § 601.503(a). This is part of the conference and practice requirements at Title 26, Part 601, Subpart E, of the Code of Federal Regulations.

16. 26 C.F.R. § 601.502(c)(1).

17. In United States v. O'Connor, 433 F.2d 752 (1st Cir. 1970), conviction of willful failure to file was based on admissions made by taxpayer's lawyer, acting under a power of attorney, that taxpayer lied to protect taxpayer's accountant. Similarly, in United States v. Dolleris, 407 F.2d 918 (6th Cir. 1969), *cert. denied,* 395 U.S. 943, conviction of tax evasion was based on admissions by taxpayer's lawyer, acting under a power of attorney, in conferences held with special agents without taxpayer present. In United States v. Parks, 489 F.2d 89 (5th Cir. 1974), the court ruled: "Admissions of a taxpayer's agent within the scope of his employment, here an accountant, are admissible against the taxpayer in a tax evasion prosecution."

the agent. No written protests are required in office-examination cases; the written protest is required in field examinations involving a total amount of disputed tax, penalty, and interest exceeding $2,500 for any taxable period.

Negotiating at Appellate Conferences

Although the taxpayer is required to file a written protest outlining the dispute only for field examinations involving in excess of $2,500, it is good practice to prepare the protest in all cases. It should include a statement of the facts signed under oath by the taxpayer. Where possible, the taxpayer should attach evidentiary material, such as documentation or affidavits of witnesses. IRS Publication 5 contains instructions for preparing the protest.

The Appeals Officer who represents the IRS is completely independent of the district director responsible for the agent's determination and has full authority to consider the hazards of litigation. The term *hazards of litigation* refers to factors that may affect the outcome of the case if it is litigated. This includes ambiguous facts, uncertain application of the law to known facts, credibility of witnesses, and ability to meet the required burden of proof. Taxpayers usually do not accompany their representatives at the conferences because their lack of objectivity can impede progress. The great majority of cases are settled at the appellate conference.

It is sometimes helpful strategy for the taxpayer to request technical assistance from the national office, especially where there have been settlements in other jurisdictions that are favorable to the taxpayer. This right is lost to the taxpayer once the appellate conference stage is concluded. The appellate organization and technical advice procedure are outlined in Exhibit 12-2.

If a case is settled at the appellate conference level, after concessions by both parties, the taxpayer signs Form 870-AD, which is considered binding on both parties. Cases involving concessions on both sides can be reopened by the IRS only where there is fraud or mathematical errors. Where there are mutual concessions the taxpayer can reopen the case only in unusual circumstances, such as retroactive legislation. If the taxpayer settles at the appellate conference with no concession by the government, Form 870 is signed. In this case the taxpayer relinquishes the right to sue in Tax Court but may still sue for refund in district court.

Taxpayer Access to IRS Manuals

The Freedom of Information Act requires every federal agency to make its interpretations of law available to the public. In *Hawkes v. IRS*[18] the Sixth Circuit held that the IRS is required to make public its Internal Revenue Manual, which constitutes its procedure and policy guidelines for all IRS personnel. This material is now published and updated by Commerce Clearing House in a seven-volume, loose-leaf set titled *Internal Revenue Manual*. Four volumes contain administrative guidelines, while three volumes cover the audit procedures and guidelines. However the courts hold that these manuals do not vest the taxpayer with the right to be treated in accordance with the specified guidelines.[19]

Failure to Negotiate or Settle

If the taxpayer fails to negotiate in response to a 30-day letter or is unable to reach a settlement in the course of negotiations, the IRS will send the taxpayer a 90-day letter. This constitutes a formal Notice of Deficiency and carries with it a presumption of correctness, which must be rebutted by the taxpayer.[20] The taxpayer's available choices for resolution of the dispute at this point are shown in Exhibit 12-3. According to a joint statement prepared by the AICPA and American Bar Association, an attorney should be consulted at this point.[21] The reason is that the tax-

---

18. Hawkes v. IRS, 467 F.2d 787 (5th Cir. 1972).

19. In United States v. Mapp, 561 F.2d 685 (7th Cir. 1977) the court said: "Mapp also contends that the agents handling his case violated two rules contained in the Internal Revenue Service 'Audit Technique Handbook for Internal Revenue Agents.' In the first place, we agree with the Tenth Circuit that these rules were adopted for the internal administration of the service and not for the protection of the taxpayer, and they therefore conferred no rights on the taxpayer." United States v. Lockyer, 448 F.2d 417, 420–21 (10th Cir. 1971). *Accord:* United States v. Caceres, 440 U.S. 741 (1979) (conviction for bribing an IRS agent upheld despite introduction of tape recordings obtained in violation of IRS regulations). *Compare* United States v. Leahey, 434 F.2d 7 (1st Cir. 1970), where the court suppressed evidence obtained in violation of the publicly announced IRS policy requiring special agents to identify the criminal nature of their investigations.

20. Welch v. Helvering, 290 U.S. 111, 115 (1933); Helvering v. Taylor, 293 U.S. 507, 515 (1935); Hinckley v. CIR, 410 F.2d 937, 939 (8th Cir. 1969). In Demkowicz v. Commissioner, 551 F.2d 929 (3d Cir. 1977), the court held that the taxpayers uncontradicted testimony was sufficient to show the assessment erroneous and to shift the burden of going forward with the evidence from taxpayer to the Commissioner.

21. The statement provides:

"Under the Tax Court rules nonlawyers may be admitted to practice.

"However, since upon issuance of a formal notice of deficiency by the Commissioner of Internal Revenue a choice of legal remedies is afforded the taxpayer under existing law (either before the Tax Court of the United States, a United States District Court, or the Court of Claims), it is in the best interests of the taxpayer that the advice of a lawyer be sought if further proceedings are contemplated. It is not intended hereby to foreclose the right of nonlawyers to practice before the Tax Court of the United States pursuant to its rules.

EXHIBIT 12-2
IRS Appeals and Technical Organization (handling of technical advice shown in shaded areas)

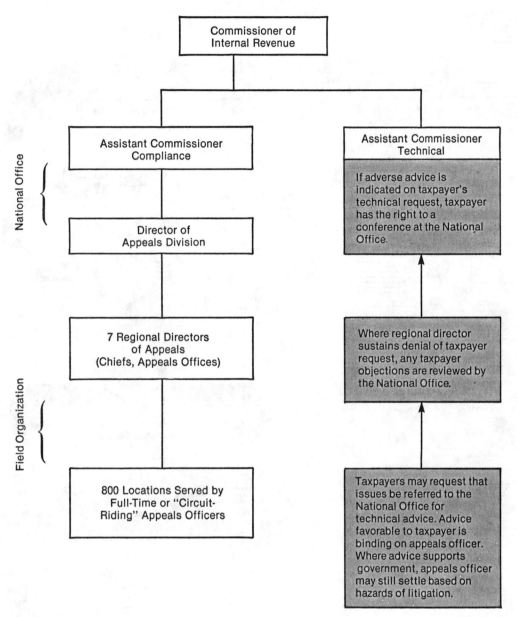

payer has a choice of (1) paying the tax and filing suit for a refund in U.S. District Court or in the Court of Claims and (2) not paying the tax and filing suit in Tax Court. Presumably an attorney must evaluate the choice of forum, since only lawyers may practice in the federal district courts and in the Court of Claims.

"Here also, as in proceedings before the Treasury Department, the taxpayer, in many cases, is best served by the combined skills of both lawyers and certified public accountants, and the taxpayers, in such cases, should be advised accordingly."

The full text of the various joint statements by the AICPA and ABA are published at pages 101–08 of the June 1977 *Journal of Accountancy*.

Note on Exhibit 12–3 that prior to filing suit in either District Court or the Court of Claims, a claim for refund must be filed within two years from payment, and the IRS must either deny the claim or take no action for six months.

PRACTICE BEFORE THE TAX COURT

The Tax Court was known as the Board of Tax Appeals when originally created by the Revenue Act of 1924 as an agency of the Executive Branch. The purpose was to furnish taxpayers a means of litigating tax matters without prior payment of the tax. The name was changed to Tax Court of the United States

EXHIBIT 12-3
Choices for Resolving a Tax Dispute

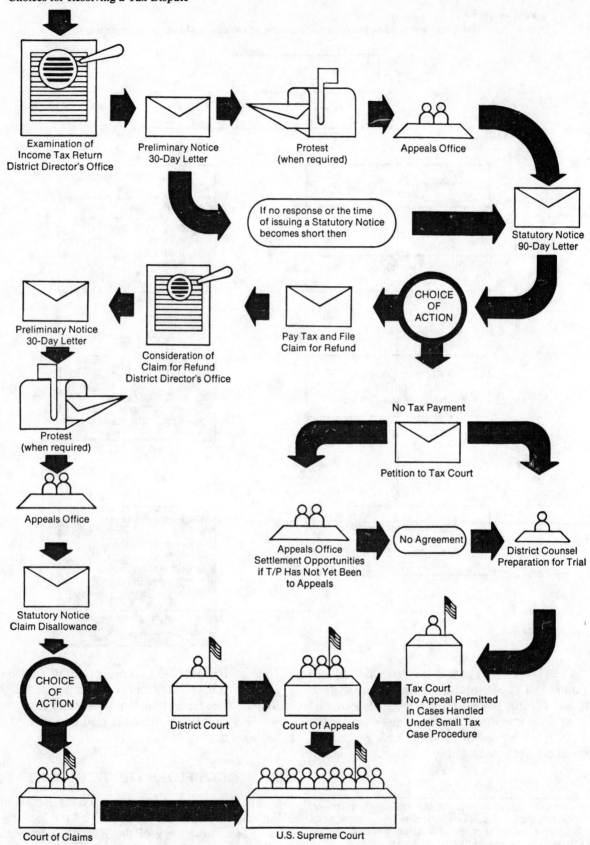

At any stage of procedure:

Agreement and payment may be arranged.

Requests for issuance of a notice of deficiency to allow petition to the Tax Court may be made.

The tax may be paid and a refund claim filed.

Source: *IRS Publication 556: Audit of Returns, Appeal Rights, and Claims for Refund* (Washington, D.C.: U.S. Government Printing Office, 1980) by the Revenue Act of 1942. It was removed from the Executive Branch and redesignated United States Tax Court by the Tax Reform Act of 1969. The statutes creating and governing the Tax Court are at IRC section 7441 and following.

The Tax Court is composed of judges appointed by the President with advice and consent of the Senate for 15-year terms. IRC § 7446 provides that times and places of sessions shall be selected so as to minimize as practicable the inconvenience and expense to the taxpayer. Taxpayers may select the place of trial provided there are courtroom facilities and a sufficient number of cases to be heard.

Rules of Practice

Admission to practice before the IRS does not constitute the right to practice before the Tax Court, nor does admission to practice before the Tax Court constitute the right to practice before the IRS. Admission to practice before the Tax Court is governed by Tax Court Rule 200. Attorneys are admitted to practice upon filing an application and a certificate showing admission to practice law. It is not necessary to be an attorney or a CPA to qualify for practice. Anyone willing to study and acquire the background is admitted to practice upon passing an examination in Washington, D.C., on the last Wednesday of October. Application forms and other information are furnished upon request to Admissions Clerk, United States Tax Court, Box 70, Washington, D.C. 20044.[22]

PRACTICAL POINTERS

1. The Civil Rights Attorney's Fee Award Act of 1976 (42 USC § 1988) provides that "in any civil action or proceeding, by or on behalf of the United States of America, to enforce, or charging a violation of, a provision of the United States Internal Revenue Code, or Title VI of the Civil Rights Act of 1964, the court, in its discretion, may allow the prevailing party, other than the United States, a reasonable attorney's fee as part of the costs."
2. Court decisions indicate that taxpayers may be granted attorney's fees only where all of three conditions are met:
   a. The taxpayer must be a defendant in a court action by the United States (a counterclaim by the government meets this test).
   b. The taxpayer must prevail in the action.
   c. The government action must be unreasonable and unfounded (it is not necessary to show the government acted in *subjective* bad faith).
3. In *Patzkowski v. United States*, 576 F.2d 134 (8th Cir. 1978), the lower court held that the government's *subjective* bad faith was a prerequisite to recovery. The Eighth Circuit reversed, holding it is only "one of several criteria which a district court should consider in exercising its discretion under the Act." For cases awarding attorney's fees, see *In re Ike Slodov*, 79-1 USTC ¶ 9215 (N.D. Ohio 1979), and *United States v. Garrison Constr. Co.*, 77-2 USTC ¶ 9705 (N.D. Ala. 1977).

IRC section 7453 provides that, except for *small tax cases,* proceedings are governed by rules of evidence applicable to nonjury trials in the United States District Court of the District of Columbia and such other rules as may be prescribed by the Tax Court. Jury trials are not available in Tax Court.

Tax Court decisions are designated either *regular* or *memorandum*. Only regular decisions, involving issues not previously decided, are published by the government as *Tax Court of the United States Reports*. Both categories of decisions are published by Commerce Clearing House and Prentice-Hall. When the IRS loses in a regular decision, it indicates in the Internal Revenue Bulletin (compiled each six months into *Cumulative Bulletins*) whether it will follow the decision in similar cases in other federal courts by announcing its acquiescence or nonacquiescence. Such announcements are not made for memorandum decisions nor for decisions of other federal courts.

Decisions of the Tax Court (and all federal district courts) may be appealed to the U.S. Circuit Court of Appeals for the appropriate jurisdiction and then to the U.S. Supreme Court. There are 12 circuits as listed in Appendix C at the end of this book. The Tax Court abides by decisions of the U.S. Supreme Court and of the particular Circuit Court of Appeals to which a decision is appealable. If the particular Circuit Court of Appeals having jurisdiction of the appeal has not passed on the issue, the Tax Court makes its decision independently.

Small Tax Cases

IRC section 7463 establishes a simplified procedure whereby taxpayers may represent themselves in litigating small tax cases that do not involve more than $5,000 of disputed tax. Decisions under this procedure are final and may not be appealed.

22. IRC section 7452 provides: "No qualified person shall be denied admission to practice before the Tax Court because of his failure to be a member of any profession or calling." The November 1974 *Journal of Accountancy* at pages 106–7 contains a discussion by a CPA who passed the exam. He reports that the exam took four hours and that each participant was furnished a copy of the Internal Revenue Code and Rules of the Tax Court.

UNAUTHORIZED PRACTICE OF LAW

Lawyers and accountants have had considerable conflict concerning the overlap of the two professions in the tax area. The AICPA and the American Bar Association (ABA) have worked together and issued a joint statement calling for cooperation and appropriate division of responsibility, but the conflicts are not yet completely resolved. It is agreed, however, that (1) both attorneys and accountants can prepare tax returns and claims for refund, but accountants may not prepare legal documents; (2) an attorney should be consulted when a formal notice of tax deficiency is issued, since this gives the taxpayer the option of going through an administrative process before the Internal Revenue Service (where accountants may represent the taxpayer) or through federal district courts (where only an attorney can represent the taxpayer); (3) an attorney should be consulted when it appears the taxpayer may be subject to arrest; and (4) the terms *tax consultant* and *tax expert* are objectionable for both the accounting profession and legal profession.

In October of 1976 the AICPA and ABA issued a new joint statement incorporating and expanding former positions. It contains what appears to be a change of position on the matter of joint practice:

> While it is proper for an individual to engage in practice simultaneously as a lawyer and as a CPA, that person must comply with all of the provisions of each profession's ethical precepts. Further, a CPA in public practice who is also an attorney providing legal services to a client may, under the Code of Professional Conduct of the AICPA, be prohibited from expressing an opinion on the financial statements of that client if he or she is not considered to be "independent."[23]

Although some state courts have held that tax practice by accountants constituted the unauthorized practice of law,[24] these decisions are apparently overruled by the U.S. Supreme Court decision in *Sperry v. Florida*.[25] In this case the Court upheld Sperry's right to carry on his Florida practice before the Patent Office although he was not a member of The Florida Bar. Application of the *Sperry* reasoning to practice before the IRS indicates that state courts have no authority over the matter.

Section 10.32 of Treasury Department Circular 230 provides:

> Nothing in the regulations in this part shall be construed as authorizing persons not members of the bar to practice law.

While the meaning of this provision is not entirely clear, the apparent effect is to enable certain nonlawyers to practice before the Treasury Department but to limit their authorization to this particular activity.

IRS ACCESS TO BOOKS, RECORDS, AND ACCOUNTANTS' WORKING PAPERS

In order to carry out its legitimate function of enforcing the tax laws, the IRS must examine books, records, and accountants' working papers. Depending upon the particular circumstances, the IRS can obtain access through either the IRS summons or a search warrant. Upon reference of a criminal case to the Justice Department, a federal grand jury can gain access to information by use of the grand jury subpoena.

Practitioners can find themselves caught between IRS enforcement and clients who desire to resist producing data sought by the IRS. Thus it is important for accountants to understand their ethical and legal responsibilites when either they or their clients are required to produce books, records, and working papers.

Scope and Enforcement of the IRS Summons

IRC section 7602 gives the IRS power to summon either the taxpayer or a third party and require either production of records or testimony.[26] Both IRS reve-

23. This quotation and the combined joint statement of the AICPA and ABA is reproduced at pages 104–108 of the June 1977 *Journal of Accountancy*.

24. Lowell Bar Ass'n v. Loeb, 315 Mass. 176, 52 N.E.2d 27 (1943) (tax service enjoined from offering to furnish counsel if return questioned); Matter of New York County Lawyers' Ass'n (the *Bercu* case), 273 App. Div. 524, 78 N.Y.S.2d 209, *aff'd without opinion*, 299 N.Y. 728, 87 N.E.2d 451 (1948) (CPA enjoined from giving tax advice not incidental to regular accounting work and barred from collection of fee); Agran v. Shapiro, 127 Cal. App. 2d 807, 273 P.2d 619 (1954) (CPA denied fee for negotiating reduction of assessment with IRS although it was incidental to tax return preparation practice). *Contra:* Grace v. Allen, 407 S.W.2d 321 (Texas 1966) (CPA and PA held not engaged in unauthorized practice since representation of clients before the IRS was incidental to preparation of tax returns); Noble v. Hunt, 99 S.E.2d 345 (Ga. App. 1957) (CPA entitled to recover fee for practice before the IRS and U.S. Tax Court).

25. Sperry v. Florida, 373 U.S. 379 (1963). Except where federal law specifically provides otherwise, federal courts generally refuse to permit persons not admitted to practice law to represent others in court despite execution of powers of attorney or characterization as "next friend." *See* Weber v. Garza, 570 F.2d 511 (5th Cir. 1978).

26. IRC section 7602 provides:

"For the purpose of ascertaining the correctness of any return, making a return where none has been made, determining the liability of any person for any internal revenue tax . . . the Secretary or his delegate is authorized—

1. To examine any books, papers, records, or other data which may be relevant or material to such inquiry.
2. To summon the person liable for tax . . . or any person having possession, custody or care of books of account . . . or any other person the Secretary or his delegate may deem proper.
3. To take such testimony . . . as may be relevant. . . ."

nue agents (charged with civil enforcement) and IRS special agents (charged with criminal enforcement) carry summonses in their briefcases and routinely sign and serve them. The only requirements are that the purpose must be for determination of tax liability and the data sought must be relevant to this purpose.[27]

The fact that the summons is issued by a special agent in connection with a criminal investigation does not make it improper provided (1) there is also a possibility of a civil tax assessment and (2) the summons is issued prior to recommendation for prosecution to the Department of Justice.[28] If all possibility for the taxpayer's civil liability has ended, the use of the summons becomes solely for criminal purposes and is unenforceable, since it is beyond the scope of the statutory purpose of determining tax liability.[29]

The requirements of relevancy are broadly construed so as to effectuate the purpose of enforcement. Bank records,[30] computer tapes,[31] and handwriting samples[32] are all subject to summons. Although the defense that the IRS is on a fishing expedition is usually rejected, summonses for tax accrual files prepared by the taxpayer,[33] audit programs,[34] and budgets[35] have been held unenforceable as beyond the scope of relevancy.

Where the summons is issued to a third party, such as the taxpayer's bank, accountant, or attorney, IRC § 7609 requires the IRS to notify the taxpayer within 3 days after service of the summons and 14 days prior to the examination. The taxpayer can stay compliance by mailing a notice to the record keeper (with a copy to the IRS) within 14 days of receipt of notice. Since the IRS hearing officers have *no power to enforce* the summons, there is no liability for appearing before the hearing officer and refusing to comply as to specific matters on the grounds of relevance or the Fifth Amendment right against self-incrimination.[36] The proper procedure is to appear in obedience to the summons, answer all unobjectionable questions, and make specific objections to objectionable questions or requests for production. Only after taxpayers are made criminal defendants can they refuse to answer all questions.[37] The IRS hearing officer will apply to a U.S.

27. In United States v. Powell, 379 U.S. 48 (1964) the Court held that once the IRS has made a minimal showing of relevancy, the burden shifts to the taxpayer to show why the summons might represent "an abuse of the court's process" which should not be enforced. Rejecting the notion that the Commissioner must show probable cause to suspect fraud as a condition to enforcement, the Court established a "four-fold test" for a valid summons: (1) the investigation must be conducted pursuant to a legitimate purpose; (2) the inquiry must be relevant to its purpose; (3) information sought must not be within the Commissioner's possession; and (4) the prescribed administrative steps must have been followed.

28. In Donaldson v. United States, 400 U.S. 517 (1971), a special agent issued a summons to taxpayer's accountant and taxpayer objected on grounds the summons was "for the express and sole purpose of obtaining evidence concerning any violation of the criminal statutes." The court held that a joint civil and criminal purpose would support the summons until recommendation for criminal prosecution. In United States v. LaSalle National Bank, 437 U.S. 298 (1978), the U.S. Supreme Court held that the summons is valid if issued prior to recommending prosecution to the Department of Justice unless, after the decision to prosecute, there is a delay merely to gather additional evidence for the prosecution.

29. The taxpayer has two potential methods for asserting the improper purpose defense. In United States v. Wright Motor Co. 536 F.2d 1090 (5th Cir. 1976), the court dismissed the petition for enforcement because the special agent refused to answer questions at a preenforcement deposition. In United States v. Salter, 432 F.2d 697 (1st Cir. 1970), the court questioned the IRS agent as to the purpose of the investigation. The granting of discovery as to purpose has been held to be discretionary with the trial court. *See* United States v. Morgan Guaranty Trust Co., 572 F.2d 36 (2d Cir.), *cert. denied*, 439 U.S. 822 (1978).

For cases supporting the taxpayer's right of discovery, *see* United States v. Genser, 595 F.2d 145 (3d Cir. 1979); United States v. Chase Manhattan Bank, 598 F.2d 321 (2d Cir. 1979), and United States v. Kis, _____ F.2d _____ (7th Cir. 1980).

30. In California Bankers Ass'n. v. Schultz, 416 U.S. 21 (1974), the U.S. Supreme Court upheld the Bank Secrecy Act of 1970. This act requires banks to maintain microfilm copies of customer transactions for use in criminal, tax, or regulatory investigations. It also requires reports of transfer of more than $5,000 into or outside of the United States, and regulations require reports to the IRS of domestic deposits or withdrawals in excess of $10,000.

31. United States v. Davey, 543 F.2d 996 (2d Cir. 1976).

32. United States v. Euge, 444 U.S. 707 (1980) (taxpayers can be required to create handwriting exemplars not in existence at the time of the summons).

33. United States v. Coopers & Lybrand, 550 F.2d 615 (10th Cir. 1977) (IRS had all transaction papers).

34. Ibid. (Auditor did not prepare tax return).

35. United States v. Matras, 487 F.2d 1271 (8th Cir. 1973).

36. In Reisman v. Caplin, 375 U.S. 440 (1963), the attorney for the taxpayers sought injunctive relief against the Commissioner of Internal Revenue. The accounting firm of Peat, Marwick, Mitchell & Co. was retained by the attorney to analyze taxpayers' records in connection with pending Tax Court cases and a criminal investigation of the tax matters. Peat kept taxpayers' records and its related working papers in separate files labeled as property of the attorneys. When a special agent served summonses on Peat, taxpayers' attorney filed suit to enjoin the hearing. In dismissing the suit, the Court noted that the hearing officer is given no power to enforce compliance or to impose sanctions. Although taxpayers can bring suit to enjoin compliance, they cannot enjoin the hearing as Reisman had attempted to do.

37. United States v. Jones, 538 F.2d 225 (8th Cir. 1976); United States v. Hankins, 565 F.2d 1344 (5th Cir. 1978). Although the self-incrimination objection can be asserted in any proceeding, whether civil or criminal, the objection will be sustained only where witnesses reasonably believe the particular information can be used in a criminal prosecution. Thus the Fifth Amendment objection will be denied where the taxpayer is granted immunity from criminal prosecution or where there is only civil liability (including civil fraud) but no possibility for subsequent prosecution.

The rationale in support of the self-incrimination defense was stated by the U.S. Supreme Court in Murphy v. Waterfront Comm'n, 278 U.S. 52, 55 (1964):

"The privilege against self-incrimination . . . reflects many of our fundamental values and most noble aspirations: our unwillingness to subject those suspected of crime to the cruel trilemma of self-accusation, perjury or contempt; our preference for an accusatorial rather than an inquisitorial system of criminal justice;

Commissioner or a U.S. district court for enforcement under IRC sections 7402 and 7604. When an enforcement order is entered directing an accounting firm to comply and no stay pending appeal is granted, the accounting firm must either comply or risk being held in contempt of court.[38]

IRC section 7610 requires payment for fees, mileage, and cost of searching for, reproducing, or transporting books and records. However, no searching, reproducing, or transporting costs are available for the taxpayer or persons acting as officer, employee, agent, accountant, or attorney of the taxpayer at the time of service of the summons.

Summons for Books and Records in CPA's Possession

Unless there are indications of a criminal investigation, CPAs usually cooperate fully with the IRS and turn over books, records, and working papers after obtaining approval from the client. Where a special agent enters the picture, this indicates a criminal-fraud investigation. CPAs cannot practice law, and at this point cooperation is withdrawn and the client is advised to retain counsel. It is best for the client to discuss criminal aspects *only* with a lawyer since the accountant-client privilege is not recognized in federal tax matters.

The CPA can make an initial determination if there are criminal aspects by asking the question: Is there a special agent involved? In *United States v. Tweel*[39] the revenue agent answered no to this question when, in fact, the examination was initiated by the Organized Crime and Racketeering Section of the Department of Justice. In reversing the conviction that resulted from such misrepresentation the court said:

> It is a well-established rule that a consent search is unreasonable under the Fourth Amendment if the consent was induced by the deceit, trickery or misrepresentation of the Internal Revenue agent.

* * * * *

our fear that self-incriminating statements will be elicited by inhumane treatment and abuses; our sense of fair play which dictates 'a fair state-individual balance by requiring the government to leave the individual alone until good cause is shown for disturbing him and by requiring the government in its contest with the individual to shoulder the entire load' . . .; our respect for the inviolability of the human personality and of the right of each individual 'to a private enclave where he may lead a private life' . . .; our distrust of self-deprecatory statements; and our realization that the privilege, while sometimes 'a shelter to the guilty,' is often 'a protection to the innocent.' "

38. United States v. Arthur Andersen & Co., 623 F.2d 720 (1st Cir. 1980), *cert. denied*, 99 U.S. 989 (1980). In a related case at 623 F.2d 725 the court held that the taxpayer's bankruptcy petition does not affect the IRS summons power.

39. United States v. Tweel, 550 F.2d 297 (5th Cir. 1977).

From the facts we find that the agent's failure to apprise the appellant of the obvious criminal nature of this investigation was a sneaky deliberate deception by the agent under the above standard and a flagrant disregard for appellant's rights. The silent misrepresentation was both intentionally misleading and material.

* * * * *

We cannot condone this shocking conduct by the IRS. Our revenue system is based upon the good faith of the taxpayers and the taxpayers should be able to expect the same from the government in its enforcement and collection activities.

The taxpayer cannot object on Fifth Amendment (self-incrimination) grounds when a summons is directed to the taxpayer's accountant. As Mr. Justice Holmes stated in *Johnson v. United States,*[40] "A party is privileged from producing the evidence, but not from its production." The leading case involving a summons to the taxpayer's accountant is *Couch v. United States.*[41] Couch, the sole proprietor of a restaurant, for several years had turned over bank statements, payroll records, and reports of sales and expenditures to her accountant, who acted as an independent contractor. With permission of the taxpayer, a revenue agent began an examination of her books and records in the accountant's office. Upon finding indications of substantial understatement of gross income, a special agent was called to participate in the investigation. At this point, taxpayer withdrew consent, and the special agent issued a summons to the accountant. In the enforcement proceeding which followed, the taxpayer objected to production on both her Fifth Amendment rights and the state accountant-client privilege statute. The U.S. Supreme Court held: (1) the Fifth Amendment is not available to the taxpayer where the summons is directed to taxpayer's accountant, and (2) state accountant-client privilege statutes are inapplicable in federal tax matters.

PRACTICAL POINTERS

1. Obtain a power of attorney from the taxpayer before turning over books and records.
2. Turn over only specific records requested, and keep a log of all records reviewed by the IRS. Ask the agent to execute IRS Form 4564 (Information Document Request) for your records.
3. Use a numbering machine to identify each record and get a receipt on IRS Form 2725 (Document

---

40. Johnson v. United States, 228 U.S. 457 (1913).

41. Couch v. United States, 409 U.S. 322 (1973).

Receipt). The IRS can require production of originals and does not have to accept copies. See, for example, *United States v. Davey*, 543 F.2d 996 (2d Cir. 1976), requiring The Continental Corporation to produce an original computer tape with cost of any duplicate desired by the taxpayer to be made at taxpayer's expense.

4. Where copies are furnished to the IRS, make three sets for reference purposes: (*a*) the IRS, (*b*) the client, and (*c*) the CPA. If the client is represented by counsel, make a fourth set.

5. Where the summons relates to a former client, the IRS may be required to pay for the *value* of the CPA's service in furnishing the information. See *United States v. Davey*, 426 F.2d 842 (2d Cir. 1970), which required the IRS to pay for the *fair value* of information sought from Credit Data Corporation.

Summons for Exposed Books and Records in Taxpayer's Possession

In *Couch* the accountant had possession. The question arises as to whether *taxpayer in possession* can assert the Fifth Amendment defense as to records that have been retrieved from the accountant. In view of the trend of Supreme Court decisions narrowly limiting claims of privilege, the final answer is likely to be no. Meanwhile the lower courts are split. In *United States v. Case*[42] the court stated the view that seems to reflect the thinking of the Supreme Court:

> Respondent seeks to make the documents sought here his "private papers," simply because he obtained them, and possibly retrieved some, from the accountant. This is clearly specious insofar as it relates to anything prepared by the accountant; and it is clear, also, that anything which respondent originally prepared and sent to the accountant ceased to be his "private papers" when it was sent. Recoupment of such documents, even any initially prepared by respondent himself, does not change their character, as something earlier disclosed, and make them again "private."
>
> *   *   *   *   *
>
> Arguments over "ownership" and "right to possession" of the documents, and calling the accounting firm "employees" of respondent, are completely sterile.
>
> *   *   *   *   *

The Fifth Amendment does not provide a privilege against noncompliance with the summons.

Summons for Accountants' Working Papers in Attorneys' Possession

If papers in possession of the taxpayer are protected by the taxpayer's Fifth Amendment claim, they are protected by the attorney-client privilege when transferred to an attorney for the purpose of obtaining legal advice. However, papers that can be obtained from the hands of the taxpayer by the IRS summons do not become protected by transfer to an attorney regardless of the purpose of the transfer.

The leading authority on papers transferred to an attorney is the U.S. Supreme Court opinion on two companion cases decided in 1976.[43] In *Fisher,* the summons related to analyses of the taxpayers' income and expenses, which had been copied by the accountant from the cancelled checks and deposit receipts for the husband's textile waste business and the wife's women's wear shop. In *Kasmir,* the summons required production of accountant's working papers pertaining to books and records of a large medical practice.

In each case the taxpayers transferred the documents to their attorneys after an interview by a revenue agent concerning possible civil or criminal liability under federal income tax laws. Upon learning of the whereabouts of the documents, the IRS served summonses on the attorneys. When the attorneys (Fisher and Kasmir) refused to produce the documents, the IRS sought enforcement. In rejecting the assertion of taxpayers' Fifth Amendment rights, the Court said: "Whether the Fifth Amendment would shield the taxpayer from producing his own tax records in his possession is a question not involved here; for the papers demanded here are not his 'private papers.' "

Concerning the attorney-client privilege the *Fisher* court said:

> Confidential disclosures by a client to an attorney made in order to obtain legal assistance are privileged. . . . The purpose of the privilege is to encourage clients to make full disclosure to their attorneys. As a practical matter, if the client knows that damaging information could more readily be obtained from the attorney following disclosure than from himself in the absence of disclosure, the client would be reluctant to confide in his lawyer and it would be difficult to obtain fully informed legal advice. However, since the privilege has the effect of withholding relevant information from the fact-finder, it applies only where necessary to achieve its purpose. Accordingly it protects only those disclosures—necessary to obtain informed legal advice—which might not have been made absent the privilege. . . . This Court and the lower courts have thus uniformly held that *preexisting*

---

42. United States v. Case, 77-1 USTC ¶ 9130 (So. D. Ill. 1976).

43. Fisher v. United States, 425 U.S. 391 (1976).

documents which could have been obtained by court process from the client when he was in possession may also be obtained from the attorney by similar process following transfer by the client in order to obtain more informed legal advice.

The Search Warrant

The Fourth Amendment of the U.S. Constitution protects against *unreasonable* searches and seizures. This generally requires that (1) a search warrant must be obtained from a neutral and detached magistrate, (2) evidence must establish probable cause that a crime has been committed, (3) the warrant itself must describe with particularity the place to be searched and the items to be seized, and (4) there must be a reasonable nexus between the item to be seized and the criminal behavior alleged.

In *Andreson v. State of Maryland*[44] investigators searched the law office of a sole practitioner attorney and used the evidence for a criminal conviction. The U.S. Supreme Court upheld the search and rejected the attorney's Fourth Amendment objection that the warrant permitted exploratory rummaging in his belongings because at the end of the list of particular documents the warrant added "together with other fruits, instrumentalities and evidence of crime at this time unknown." The Court also rejected his Fifth Amendment defense of compulsory self-incrimination because he was not required to do anything. Andreson was present and free to move about, and his own attorney was with him part of the time.

The IRS can thus obtain a search warrant to seize the taxpayer's books and records, provided the records are adequately described and there is reason to believe they constitute evidence that will aid in a conviction.

The Fourth Amendment protects corporations and businesses as well as individuals. Thus the U.S. Supreme Court held it unlawful where IRS agents made a warrantless entry into an office and seized books and records.[45] Although the IRS can collect taxes by seizure in public places or open areas without a warrant pursuant to IRC section 6331, the warrantless search of private property (including business premises) is improper.

The Grand Jury Subpoena

The Fifth Amendment provides that federal prosecution for serious crimes can only be instituted by "a presentment or indictment of a Grand Jury." The grand jury's responsibilities include its historic functions of determining whether there is probable cause to believe a crime has been committed and the protection of citizens against unfounded criminal prosecutions.[46] It deliberates in secret and is accorded wide latitude to inquire into criminal violations. Since the grand jury does not finally adjudicate guilt or innocence, it has traditionally been allowed to pursue its functions unimpeded by procedural and evidentiary rules governing the conduct of criminal trials. A grand jury investigation may be triggered by tips, rumors, evidence proffered by the prosecutor, or the personal knowledge of the grand jurors. The validity of an indictment is not subject to challenge on the basis that the grand jury acted on the basis of inadequate or incompetent evidence or even on the basis of evidence obtained in violation of defendant's Fifth Amendment privilege against self-incrimination.

In *Bellis v. United States*[47] a grand jury subpoena was served on Bellis, a lawyer, requiring him to produce records of his former partnership with two other lawyers. In ruling that Bellis must produce the records despite his claim of Fifth Amendment protection, the U.S. Supreme Court reasoned that the Fifth Amendment privilege should be "limited to its historic function of protecting only the natural individual from compulsory incrimination through his own testimony or *personal* records." Thus the Fifth Amendment defense is unavailable for records of partnerships, corporations, and unincorporated associations such as labor unions.

Since the subpoena can be issued without notice to the taxpayer under investigation (as is required for a summons) and without a showing of probable cause (as is required for a search warrant), it is a more powerful discovery means than the summons. The accountant served with a grand jury subpoena may not appear and then simply refuse in good faith to comply. When a managing partner in Arthur Young & Co. refused to produce tax accrual files for a client in response to a grand jury subpoena and claimed the accountant-client privilege, a federal district court in Oklahoma held the partner in contempt of court. After spending one night in jail, the partner produced the file.[48]

Although Rule 6(e) of the Federal Rules of Criminal Procedure permits disclosure of grand jury evidence to

---

44. Andreson v. State of Maryland, 427 U.S. 463 (1976).

45. G.M. Leasing Corp. v. United States, 429 U.S. 338 (1977).

46. For the historical function of the grand jury, *see* Costello v. United States, 350 U.S. 359, 361–62 (1956); Blair v. United States, 250 U.S. 273, 279–83, (1919); Hale v. Henkel, 201 U.S. 43, 59 (1906); 4 W. Blackstone, *Commentaries;* G. Edwards, *The Grand Jury* 1–44 (1906); 1 F. Pollock & F. Maitland, *History of English Law* 151 (2d ed. 1909); 1 W. Holdsworth, *History of English Law* 321–23 (7th rev. ed. 1956).

47. Bellis v. United States, 417 U.S. 85 (1974).

48. Sec. Reg. & Law Rep. No. 325, October 29, 1975.

such government personnel as are necessary to assist the government attorney, the rule limits the use of the information to enforcement of federal criminal law. The Seventh Circuit overruled a lower court ruling that permitted IRS access to grand jury materials holding that civil tax enforcement did not justify a "special judicial exception to grand jury secrecy."[49]

The Bank Secrecy Act requires banks to maintain records of the transactions of customers so the records will be available in criminal tax and regulatory investigations and proceedings. The U.S. Supreme Court held in *United States v. Miller*[50] that the act is valid and that a bank depositor has no protectable Fourth Amendment rights when records of his or her account are obtained from the bank, even where the grand jury subpoena duces tecum has technical deficiencies.

The Shrinking Zone of Privacy

Exhibit 12–4 summarizes the shrinking zone of privacy for books, records, and accountants' working papers. *Couch* established the rule that the IRS summons will be enforced as to books and records in the possession of accountants. *Fisher* gave access to accountant working papers in the possession of an attorney despite the taxpayers' claims of privilege. The *Bellis* case involved a grand jury subpoena; however, the reasoning applies to the summons as well. The *Andreson* case shows that even books and records of a sole practitioner are accessible with a search warrant.

THE ROLE OF THE ACCOUNTANT IN TAX FRAUD INVESTIGATIONS

The defense of tax fraud allegations is the province of the attorney and the role of the accountant is limited to assisting counsel. Unless an accountant obtains information while specifically assisting counsel, the accountant will be required to reveal all information to the IRS, including damaging admissions by the client. In *United States v. Kovel*[51] Judge Friendly discussed this distinction:

---

49. *In re* Special February 1975 Grand Jury, 652 F.2d 1302 (7th Cir. 1981).

50. United States v. Miller, 425 U.S. 435 (1976).

51. United States v. Kovel, 296 F.2d 418 (2d Cir. 1961).

In Upjohn Co. v. United States, 101 S.Ct. 677 (1981), the U.S. Supreme Court held that communications to the corporate counsel by corporate employees at all levels are protected by the attorney-client privilege. The attorney-work-product doctrine is broader than the attorney-client privilege and protects an attorney's notes so that the government cannot gain access upon showing "substantial need" or "undue hardship."

Also see *In re* Grand Jury Proceedings, 601 F.2d 162 (5th Cir. 1979), where the conviction of an accountant for refusal to comply with a grand jury subpoena was overturned because the accountant was employed by a lawyer and the working papers were protected from disclosure under the attorney-work-product doctrine.

EXHIBIT 12–4
The Shrinking Zone of Privacy: IRS Access to Books, Records, and Accountants' Working Papers

Type of Material and Holder	IRS Summons (Notice but No Probable Cause)	Grand Jury Subpoena (No Probable Cause or Notice)	Search Warrant (Probable Cause but No Notice)
Records maintained by banks	Can obtain if relevant	Can obtain: Criminal case only (*Miller*)	*Can obtain*
Accountant work papers held by anyone	Can obtain if relevant (*Fisher*)	Can obtain: Criminal case only	Can obtain
Books and records of partnerships and corporations	Can obtain if relevant	Can obtain: Criminal case only (*Bellis*)	Can obtain
Books and records in possession of accountants	Can obtain if relevant (*Couch*)	Can obtain: Criminal case only	Can obtain
Books and records in possession of the individual taxpayer	Cannot obtain in face of Fifth Amendment or attorney-client privilege	Cannot obtain in face of Fifth Amendment or attorney-client privilege	Can obtain (*Andreson*)

What is vital to the [attorney-client] privilege is that the communication be made *in confidence* for the purpose of obtaining *legal* advice *from the lawyer*. If what is sought is not legal advice but only accounting service . . . or if the advice sought is the accountant's rather than the lawyer's, no privilege exists. We recognize this draws what may seem to some a rather arbitrary line between a case where the client communicates first to his own accountant (no privilege as to such communications, even though he later consults his lawyer on the same matter . . .) and others, where the client in the first instance consults a lawyer who retains an accountant as a listening post. . . . That is the inevitable consequence of having to reconcile the absence of a privilege for accountants and the effective operation of the privilege of client and lawyer under conditions where the lawyer needs outside help.

Where the accountant claims protection under the attorney-client privilege, the burden of going forward with the evidence is on the accountant to prove the existence of the privilege. Thus the witness must testify as to circumstances which establish the privilege. The proper practice is for the judge to conduct a preliminary inquiry into the existence of the privilege with the jury excused.

If a tax return is filed, the attorney-client privilege is

waived as to all working papers that support the filed return. Information supplied for preparation of a return is nonprivileged, regardless of whether the preparer is an attorney or a CPA.[52]

Preparing the Defense

Data gathering by the accountant for the defense must parallel methods used by the government. The *specific item method* of proving a tax deficiency involves showing that specific items of revenue were not reported or that nonallowable expenses were deducted. Where the taxpayer keeps inadequate books and records, IRC section 446 empowers the Commissioner to select whatever method that in the Commissioner's opinion clearly reflects income. The Commissioner uses several court-approved methods to reconstruct income for both civil and criminal purposes.

The *net worth method* involves adding the taxpayer's nondeductible expenses to the increase in net worth to determine income.[53] The *cash expenditures method* assumes that the excess of expenditures over reported income is taxable except as otherwise explained. The *bank deposits method* involves showing that deposits from taxable sources exceeded reported revenue. *Analytical methods*, such as estimating revenue of a restaurant based on the proven cost of goods sold[54] or translating use of bed sheets for a motel into gross revenue,[55] are used mostly in corroborating other methods or in civil cases. Because of possible variations, these methods are seldom used as a prime method of proof in a criminal case.

The Accountant as a Witness

Some authorities suggest that the witness who testifies as an expert for the defense should have no personal knowledge of the case and base all testimony on hypothetical facts.[56] The reason is that the accountant who assists counsel in preparing the defense often learns facts that are unfavorable to the taxpayer. This knowledge is unavailable to the government under the attorney-client privilege provided the requisite conditions are met and the accountant does not take the witness stand. Once the accountant testifies as a witness for the taxpayer, the government may fully cross-examine and bring out the unfavorable facts.

Where the accountant engaged to assist counsel previously served as accountant for the taxpayer, it is important to make a clear cutoff point for all working papers and information. This may be difficult for the accountant to accomplish. Information obtained by the accountant *prior to being engaged by counsel* is not privileged. It must be revealed when the accountant is summoned for a formal interrogation by the special agent. Since such proceedings are under oath and recorded by IRS stenographers, it is advisable for the summoned accountant to retain personal counsel and to record the proceedings with a tape recorder or to consider engaging a court reporter.

Miranda Warnings

Most tax fraud cases develop as a result of discoveries in a routine audit by an IRS revenue agent. The revenue agent is instructed to suspend activity and refer the matter to the IRS Criminal Enforcement Division for investigation by a special agent.

IRS administrative procedures require special agents to identify themselves to taxpayers and to give the IRS version of the *Miranda* warning as follows:

> As a special agent, one of my functions is to investigate the possibility of criminal violations of the Internal Revenue Laws, and related offenses.
> Under the Fifth Amendment of the Constitution of the United States, I cannot compel you to answer any questions or to submit any information if such answers or information might tend to incriminate you in any way. I also advise you that anything which you say and any information which you submit may be used against you in any criminal proceeding which may be undertaken. I advise you further that you may, if you wish, seek the assistance of an attorney before responding.

In *Beckwith v. United States*,[57] the taxpayer claimed the above version of the *Miranda* warning was insufficient since it does not advise of the right to remain silent nor of the right to free counsel for those who cannot afford to pay. Two special agents called on the taxpayer at 8:00 A.M. at a private residence, presented credentials and stated they were attached to the Intelligence Division, and advised that one of their functions was to investigate the possibility of criminal

52. United States v. Cote, 456 F.2d 142 (8th Cir. 1972). *See* Annot., "What Constitutes Privileged Communications with Preparer of Federal Tax Returns so as to Render Communications Inadmissible in Federal Tax Prosecution," 36 A.L.R. Fed. 686 (1978).

53. In Holland v. United States, 348 U.S. 121 (1954) the U.S. Supreme Court held that the government can use the net-worth method without first showing that taxpayers' books and records are inadequate. Once the government presents its indirect proof, the burden of going forward with the evidence shifts to defendant. It is not necessary for the government to negate nontaxable sources. However, if the taxpayer provides "leads" as to possible nontaxable sources, the government must show that it has checked these out.

54. Agnellino v. United States, 302 F.2d 797 (3d Cir. 1962).

55. Ibid.

56. Robert S. Fink, "The Role of the Accountant in a Tax Fraud Case," *Journal of Accountancy*, April 1976, pp. 42–48.

57. Beckwith v. United States, 425 U.S. 341 (1976).

tax fraud. After giving the IRS version of the *Miranda* warning, the agents interviewed taxpayer until about 11 o'clock in a friendly and relaxed manner without pressing for answers. Upon request, the taxpayer met the agents at his place of employment and supplied his books to the agents. The taxpayer claimed that his subsequent criminal conviction resulted from his own statements and disclosures and that such statements should have been suppressed because of the IRS failure to give the full *Miranda* warning. In affirming the conviction, the U.S. Supreme Court held that in the usual noncustodial (prearrest) interrogation, the IRS is not required to give *any* warning whatever:

> An interview with government agents in a situation such as the one shown by this record simply does not present the elements which the *Miranda* court found so inherently coercive as to require its holding. Although the "focus" of an investigation may indeed have been on Beckwith at the time of the interview in the sense that it was his tax liability which was under scrutiny, he hardly found himself in the custodial situation described by the *Miranda* Court as the basis for its holding. *Miranda* specifically defined "focus," for its purposes, as "questioning initiated by law enforcement officers *after* a person has been taken into custody or otherwise deprived of his action in a significant way."

* * * * *

> Proof that some kind of warnings were given or that none were given would be relevant evidence only on the issue of whether the questioning was in fact coercive.

When a special agent appears, counsel will usually isolate the taxpayer from interrogation while cooperating to the extent of producing records obtainable from other sources, such as a bank's microfilms. Counsel will take care to see that all evidence is correct since production of falsified evidence is a separate crime.

Where a taxpayer is called as a witness either in judicial proceedings or by the IRS summons, the taxpayer generally must take the stand and either answer the questions or plead the Fifth Amendment on a question-by-question basis. However, once the investigation becomes limited to the taxpayer's *criminal* liability, the taxpayer is no longer required to take the stand. For example, in *United States v. Hankins*,[58] a summons issued to Robert Smith, CPA, called for both testimony and production of working papers relative to a client. Although he was required to produce the working papers related to his client, the Fifth Circuit ruled that after the CPA was given the IRS version of the *Miranda* warning he could no longer be required to testify:

> Of key significance to this issue is the fact that Smith [The CPA] could have no civil liability as a consequence of this investigation, only criminal liability. The *Miranda* warnings given to Smith by the agent prior to any questioning was a clear signal of his potential criminal liability.

> Nevertheless, the government argues that Smith can be compelled to appear, take the witness stand, and either answer the questions the government asks, or plead his Fifth Amendment protection on a question-by-question basis. In the particular circumstances of Smith's situation, we disagree. Were Smith the target of an investigation for robbing a bank, he would unquestionably have the right to stand on silence. There is no significant difference between Smith as a suspected participant in a tax fraud and Smith as a suspected bank robber.

> We hold that Smith cannot be compelled to take the stand by a § 7602 Internal Revenue Service summons. The order that he must do so is reversed.

Conference Opportunities

There are several conference opportunities prior to the government's final decision to prosecute. At the District Director level a conference will be held if requested in writing by the taxpayer or taxpayer's counsel. This will usually be with a group manager or other person associated with the District Chief of Enforcement. This conference almost never deters prosecution, and the taxpayer can learn little more than the alleged statutory offense and the amount of income involved.

If the District Chief of Enforcement recommends prosecution, the case is referred to the Regional Counsel, who will usually grant the taxpayer a meaningful conference. If the Regional Counsel recommends prosecution, the case will go to the tax division of the Department of Justice in Washington. Although a conference will be granted if requested, this conference is usually held in Washington. Once the tax division attorneys refer the case to the U.S. Attorney in the district where the case is to be tried, there is little possibility for avoiding prosecution. However, U.S. Attorneys will usually grant a conference to consider new evidence or concrete data showing a mistake by the government. The U.S. Attorney will present the case to the Grand Jury. Trial responsibility also rests with the U.S. Attorney, who may try the case with or without assistance from tax-division attorneys. Upon request of U.S. Attorneys, tax-division attorneys sometimes represent the government.

CIVIL LIABILITIES IN TAX PRACTICE

Tax practitioners owe duties to clients and investors as well as to the IRS.

---

58.   United States v. Hankins, 565 F.2d 1344 (5th Cir. 1978).

PRACTICAL POINTERS

1. Always base tax advice on carefully stated facts.
2. Caution clients that tax advice is only *your* professional opinion and explain that it is not possible to predict with certainty how the IRS and courts may treat the matter.
3. Whenever tax advice is given orally (such as in a phone conversation), document the assumed facts, advice given, and the date in the client's file. Even better: Send a confirming letter, which eliminates misunderstandings and facilitates billing for the service rendered.
4. Consider the following checklist to avoid liability from tax practice:
   a. Do I have tax working papers to support figures on all returns?
   b. Do I document the client's election in doubtful areas after advising of potential risk and savings inherent in the alternatives?
   c. Do I limit tax advice to written memos stating the assumptions or to oral advice confirmed by such a memo?
   d. Do I require clients to produce and retain documentary evidence to support their returns?
   e. Do I scrutinize client documentation to assure that it is legitimate and review returns for the past several years to check for reasonableness and income-averaging possibilities?
   f. Do I have written agreements covering tax engagements to document the limits of my undertaking?
   g. Do I add a disclaimer to nonaudit-client file copies and mark the pages unaudited?

Liability to Clients

Liability for Penalties and Interest. When public accountants undertake to prepare and file tax returns, they are liable for penalties assessed by the taxing authorities if they negligently fail to file the returns correctly and on time. While the courts apparently have not analyzed the issue, the tax preparer should not be liable for interest where the client had the use of the money.

In *L.B. Laboratories, Inc. v. Mitchell*,[59] decided in 1952, the defendant, a certified public accountant, confirmed by letter an agreement to prepare and file tax returns for the plaintiff. The defendant failed to prepare and file the returns until after the due date, and as a result the plaintiff taxpayer had to pay penalties. The defendant contended that the plaintiff's action was

barred by a two-year statute of limitations for tort. In affirming a judgment for $17,428.43, the court held that the four-year statute of limitation for actions based on written contract applied and that this statute was tolled during the period in which the CPA concealed from the plaintiff that a penalty for late filing had been assessed.[60]

In *Slaughter v. Eugene C. Roddie, d/b/a Roddie Tax Service*,[61] a loss carry-back was filed pursuant to the defendant's suggestion, which resulted in a refund from the federal government of $1,502.27 plus interest of $32.28. Several months later, the plaintiff was notified that his records were to be audited and instructed to report to the IRS office.

At the conclusion of the audit, the plaintiff was informed that he owed the federal government $2,600.00 in taxes, penalties, and interest. After contacting the defendant and receiving no help, the plaintiff employed an attorney, whose fee was $500.00, and shortly thereafter a CPA, whose fee was $750.00. The claim was then compromised for $1,534.64 (the amount of the refund) plus $76.74 penalty, $166.36 interest on the refund, $135.05 as a penalty for failure to file Form 941, and interest on this failure of $53.19. The plaintiff sought recovery on all of this claim against the defendant except the amount that had been refunded to him previously.

The plaintiff had received the following, along with his income tax return prepared by the defendant:

Unconditionally Guaranteed

In the event of an audit we cheerfully appear with you for audit of your return, subject of course to verification of each item on your return by *receipts* or reasonable explanation. We do not accept responsibilities for estimates we are required to make in regard to interest or other items when amounts are unknown at time of preparation. In the event of interest or penalty assessed against this return after accounting by receipts

---

59. L. B. Laboratories, Inc. v. Mitchell, 39 Cal. 2d 56, 244 P.2d 385 (1952).

60. A later California case held that the two-year statute of limitations on a *negligence* claim against a CPA did not start to run until the negligent act was discovered or with reasonable diligence could have been discovered. *See* Moonie v. Lynch, 64 Cal. Rptr. 55 (Court of Appeal, 1st District 1967). *Accord:* Atkins v. Crosland, 417 S.W.2d 150 (Texas 1967) (statute commenced when tax deficiency assessed); Glick v. Sabin, 368 N.E.2d 625 (Appellate Court of Illinois 1977) (cause of action against CPAs accrued when plaintiff knew or should have known of existence of right of action); Isaacson, Stolper & Co. v. Artisan's Savings Bank, 330 A.2d 130 (Del. Supr. 1974) (cause of action against accountant accrued when bank was put on notice of deficiency by IRS); Chisholm v. Scott, 526 P.2d 1300 (N.Mex. Ct. App. 1974) (statute of limitations for malpractice action against CPAs who prepared partnership and individual returns did not start to run until assessment was made by IRS).

For a summary of the authorities on the running of the statute of limitations on a malpractice claim, see Chapter 7 at notes 22-27.

61. Slaughter v. Eugene C. Roddie, d/b/a Roddie Tax Service, 249 So.2d 584 (La. Ct. App. 1971).

we pay all penalties or interest assessed. This guaranty is for the life of the return and no further charges will be made for the above service.

The appellate court held that, based on the guarantee and the defendant's admission of erroneous preparation of the loss carry-back, the defendant was liable for the $76.74 penalty and $166.36 interest on the erroneous refund, plus the $60.00 fee for preparing the erroneous loss carry-back plus $750.00 for the services of a CPA. The claim for $500.00 attorney's fee was disallowed on the ground that attorneys' fees may not be recovered unless based on a specific provision in a contract. The claim in connection with plaintiff's Form 941 was also disallowed, since this was due regardless of defendant's error.

The defendant in this case might have minimized his damages by admitting his error and assisting the plaintiff and thereby saving the fee of $750 for the services of the CPA. In sustaining the CPA's fee in these circumstances, the court said:

> The trial court awarded Eddie M. LeBlanc, Jr., plaintiff's CPA, the sum of $750.00 for services rendered plaintiff. LeBlanc's testimony was to the effect that the loss carry back was so completely erroneous that it constituted a red flag to the IRS examiners. In addition, defendant made no real effort to help plaintiff after he was informed that an audit was forthcoming, and that a deficit of $2,600.00 was found. Had he attended the conferences or made some attempt to help plaintiff alleviate himself from the demands of the IRS, it may well be that plaintiff would not have needed to employ the parties he did. LeBlanc testified that he worked approximately forty hours at $20.00 an hour. Considering the work done by the CPA, we are of the opinion that the fees are reasonable.

Liability for Punitive Damages and Mental Anguish. Negligent tax preparers are generally not liable for mental anguish, but the courts are split as to liability for punitive damages. In a Nevada case[62] the tax preparer erroneously caused plaintiffs to receive refunds, and the following IRS audit resulted in assessment of additional taxes and enforced collection procedures causing severe hardship. In sustaining the jury's award of $100,000 punitive damages, the Supreme Court of Nevada found evidence of fraud to support an award of punitive damages:

> In their public advertising, appellants "guaranteed accurate tax preparation," stating that they would prepare "complete returns—$5 up." Thereby, appellants suggested their employees' expertise in preparing all types of tax returns. Despite this, they made no effort to hire employees with even rudimentary skill in accounting or in the preparation of tax returns. Appel-

lants sometimes administered to new employees a 72-hour course in tax return preparation, but apparently even this minimal training was not a prerequisite to serving the public. The temporary employee who prepared respondents' tax returns had been employed in construction work for several years prior to his employment with appellants, and had received no formal training in the preparation of tax returns, either prior to or during his employment with appellants.

> Appellants' manual instructed their office managers to counter inquiries concerning the qualifications of employees by saying that "[the company] has been preparing taxes for 20 years." The manual further instructed office managers not to refer to an employee as a "specialist or tax expert," but never to correct news reporters or commentators if they referred to employees in this manner.

> In our view, such evidence supports a determination of fraud.

A Maryland case[63] involved husband and wife operators of a service station who for two successive years turned over a box of records to a franchise location of H & R Block, Inc. The Block franchise holder calculated losses, but the IRS, using the same records, calculated income. Upon advice of two other accountants, the taxpayers paid the delinquent taxes, interest, and penalties. In the words of the court:

> Both accountants employed by the Testermans appeared as expert witnesses at the trial. They testified, in essence, that the Block personnel who prepared the returns were woefully inadequate—in terms of education and experience—for the tasks which they had undertaken. The errors Block had made bordered on the absurd. It had understated income for both years by deducting sums "off the top" (from gross income) which the Testermans had drawn periodically from the business for personal use. Also, Block omitted from gross income the amounts paid for expenses from cash receipts at the service station, which, of course, had not been reflected in bank deposits. The records which the Testermans had delivered to Block, however, had accurately reflected all of these transactions.

The Maryland court found that this conduct amounted to negligence but rejected claims for punitive damages because there was no actual malice and rejected claims for mental anguish because there was no physical injury.

Liability for Loss on Prospective Transactions. Public accountants are liable for losses resulting from action taken in reliance on their erroneous tax advice. In *Rassieur v. Charles*,[64] defendant accountants, in connection with preparing the plaintiff's tax returns, advised that she had realized a taxable profit resulting

62. Midwest Supply, Inc., d/b/a H & R Block Company, and H & R Block Co. v. Waters, 510 P.2d 876 (Sup. Ct. Nev. 1973).

63. H & R Block, Inc. v. Testerman, 338 A.2d 48 (Ct. App. Md. 1975).
64. Rassieur v. Charles, 354 Mo. 117, 188 S.W.2d 817 (1945).

168

from the sale of shares of her North American Company stock and that she could sell other securities at a loss before the close of the tax year to offset the loss against profit on North American, thereby decreasing tax liability for the year. The defendants had incorrectly recorded the cost of the plaintiff's North American Company stock, and she actually had sustained a loss, as opposed to a taxable gain. The defendants contended that the plaintiff was not damaged by the sale of her other stock. The court adopted a rule of damages that permitted the plaintiff to be restored to her former position, that is, the difference in sale price and the cost to repurchase the stock after having knowledge of the facts. Since under the federal income tax law, the plaintiff was free to deduct the loss and then repurchase the stock after 30 days from the date of sale, the court held that plaintiff was entitled to recover "the difference between the sales price of her stocks and the cost of replacing them within a reasonable time after the expiration of the 30-day period."

Compare this ruling with *Brackett v. H. R. Block & Company*,[65] where the defendant allegedly made an error, as opposed to giving advice to sell other assets. There the court struck allegations that the plaintiff was forced to sell other property in order to pay the erroneous tax.

Liability for Income Tax on Prospective Transactions. When public accountants give erroneous tax advice, they apparently have a continuing duty to advise of the error, and if they fail to do so, they may incur additional liability because the taxpayer continues to follow the erroneous advice. In *Bancroft v. Indemnity Insurance Co. of North America*[66] the taxpayer was principal stockholder in two corporations, and the CPA erroneously advised that the taxpayer could sell stock in one corporation to the other without incurrence of income tax.

The taxpayer did not act on this advice until four months later, but the court found that since the CPA had been the taxpayer's tax consultant for approximately 17 years, the taxpayer was entitled to believe that if a change had occurred within four months, the CPA would have informed him of such. The taxpayer then engaged in a similar transaction approximately two years and five months after the advice. The court found that but for the erroneous advice the second transfer would not have been effected. Since time passed after the first transaction without objection from the IRS or notice from the CPA, the taxpayer

"was justified in having confidence in the plan and in following the same procedure for sale of the additional stock." The CPA's professional liability insurer was thus liable for the income taxes incurred on both transactions.

Unless the *Bancroft* case is extended to require the public accountant to inform clients of changes which affect past tax advice, the AICPA division of federal taxation seems to have dealt adequately with the problem in its Statements on Responsibilites in Tax Practice. *CCH AICPA Professional Standards* TX § 161.04 requires the CPA to notify a client promptly upon learning of any error.

CCH AICPA Professional Standards TX § 181.05 provides that the CPA assisting with implementing advice must review and revise the advice as warranted by new developments. This same section indicates no such duty is required in the ordinary situation:

> Experience in the accounting and other professions indicates that clients understand that advice reflects professional judgment based on an existing situation. Experience has also shown that clients customarily realize that subsequent developments could affect previous professional advice. Some CPAs use precautionary language to the effect that their advice is based on facts as stated and authorities which are subject to change. Although routine use of such precautionary language seems unnecessary based on accepted business norms and professional relationships, the CPA may follow this procedure in situations he deems appropriate.

Liability for Attorney's Fees. Under the American rule, all parties generally pay their own attorney's fees; however, there is an exception for attorney's fees incurred in resolving a dispute with a third person. In the Illinois case of *Sorenson v. Fio Rito* an attorney was held liable for legal fees incurred by a former client in attempting to obtain refund of penalties and interest resulting from his failure to timely file estate tax returns. For this and related cases see Chapter 5 at note 66.

Liability to Third-Party Investors

Where accountants write tax-opinion letters for use in selling limited-partnership tax shelters, liability has been imposed to third-party investors for recklessness under section 10(b) of the Exchange Act. See the discussion of *Sharp v. Coopers & Lybrand* in Chapter 8 at note 71. Liability to third parties can also be based on aiding and abetting the sale of securities that should have been registered under state blue-sky laws or under federal securities laws. In *Hild v. Woodcrest*

65. Brackett v. H. R. Block & Co., 166 S.E.2d 369 (1969).
66. Bancroft v. Indemnity Insurance Co. of North America, 203 F. Supp. 49 (W.D. La. 1962), *aff'd mem.*, 309 F.2d 959 (5th Cir 1963).

Ass'n[67] the court held the accounting firm of Coopers and Lybrand liable to a limited partner who elected to rescind the sale because the securities were not registered under the Ohio blue-sky law. The court rejected the accounting firm's defense that it did not sell or aid and abet the sale of the limited partnerships because of its active participation in telephoning potential investors and supplying names of others.

Both attorneys and accountants can be held liable under section 12(2) of the Securities Act for misrepresentation in connection with the sale of securities. For a summary of the authorities, see Chapter 8 at notes 50 and 51. Accepting a commission on the sale of investments is a breach of AICPA ethics rule 503 regardless of knowledge of the client. Ethics violation as a basis for malpractice liability is discussed in Chapter 1 at note 37.

Failure to disclose a commission is a breach of a fiduciary duty that gives the client the right to rescind and recover the full investment from the advisor. Cases holding that accountants giving advice are fiduciaries are discussed in Chapter 5 at notes 52–57. The fiduciary duty depends upon the particular circumstances. Thus a CPA/seller of partnership tax shelters was held not liable in *Midland National Bank of Minneapolis v. Perranoski*[68] because he was not a fiduciary with respect to investors who consulted their legal counsel and he had a right to believe that experienced investors would read the partnership agreement before they signed it. For discussion of this case, see Chapter 7 at note 5.

Liability to the IRS

IRC section 6674 provides for imposition of a $100 penalty on tax preparers for each "negligent or intentional" disregard of rules and regulations that results in understatement of liability. This same section provides for a $500 penalty for each "willful" understatement of tax by a tax preparer. Where the $100 penalty has been assessed, only an additional $400 may be imposed for the same understatement. The burden of proof is on the tax preparer for the negligence penalty; however, IRC section 7427 places the burden of proof on the government for the willful penalty. There is no statute of limitations on the willful penalty.

Under IRC section 7407 tax preparers who are guilty of repeated violations may be enjoined from acting as tax preparer.

Right to Rely on Taxpayer's Data

Tax preparers, as a practical necessity, usually rely upon data furnished by the taxpayer. In *Lindner v. Barlow, Davis & Wood*,[69] plaintiff sued defendant CPAs for loss of money erroneously paid as state and federal taxes. The CPAs prepared plaintiffs 1952 and 1953 tax returns based on W-2 forms showing taxes withheld. In doing so they relied upon the W-2 forms as to the taxable status of payments made by Hearst Publishing Company, Inc., to taxpayer as the widow of the former publisher of the San Francisco Examiner. Plaintiff claimed that defendants breached a duty to advise that a doubtful question had arisen as to whether the payments were taxable income and that defendant's malpractice resulted in loss of a refund for years barred by the statute of limitations. In rejecting plaintiff's claim, the court found that the standard of practice in San Francisco did not require defendants to advise plaintiff concerning any doubtful question and that the standard practice permitted the CPAs to rely upon W-2 forms issued by corporate payors as to the taxable status of moneys so reported. The CPAs' case was strengthened by the fact that the return was accompanied by a written statement to plaintiff that it was based on records and information not independently verified.

Engagement Letters for Tax Practice

Where the only service to be performed is preparation of a tax return, the CPA may wish to dispense with a formal engagement letter and substitute a memo something like the one shown in Exhibit 12-5. Other topics for engagement letters for tax practice are suggested by Exhibit 12-6. Since engagement memos are legal contracts, see your personal attorney before using these or other forms.

Some CPAs send a questionnaire or organizer to individual tax-return clients. The questionnaire contains the engagement letter provisions, so that when the client signs, the CPA has a signed engagement letter. This may also contain a representation by clients that they have documentation to support any claimed travel and entertainment expenses.

For a court decision upholding the CPA's right to recover for tax work where there is no engagement letter, see Chapter 5 at note 1. For court decisions upholding the CPA's right to recover a contingent fee in tax practice, see Chapter 5 at notes 12 and 13.

---

67. Hild v. Woodcrest Ass'n, 391 N.E.2d 1047 (Ohio Common Pleas 1977).

68. Midland Nat'l Bank of Minneapolis v. Perranoski, 299 N.W.2d 404 (Minn. 1980).

---

69. Lindner v. Barlow, Davis & Wood, 27 Cal. Rptr. 101 (Dist. Ct. of Appeal 1963).

170

EXHIBIT 12-5
Sample Engagement Memorandum for Tax-Return Preparation

Client _____

Business address _____

Business telephone _____

Home address _____

Home telephone _____

Returns to be prepared:

Return	Due date	Period covered
_____	_____	_____
_____	_____	_____

Scope of engagement — Since only the above returns are to be prepared by us, any and all other returns required by you or your businesses will be prepared by you or others and we have no responsibility for them.

Engagement does not cover review by tax authorities — All returns are subject to review by taxing authorities. The fee for this engagement does not cover any assistance you might need in connection with inquiries, examinations, or assessments by such authorities.

Tax advice excluded — This engagement does not include advice as to the conduct of affairs in the future. All taxpayers are advised, however, to maintain records of any-

thing *affecting* tax returns for the past four years.

Engagement subject to adequate records — This engagement is subject to your furnishing adequate documentation for the current year and copies of returns for the prior four years if they were not prepared by us.

Reliance on information furnished with no independent verification — Returns are to be prepared on the basis of information supplied by the client and by others designated by the client with no independent verification.

Outside computer service — We may at our option process your returns by using an outside computer service.

Fee for *this* engagement — Our fee will be based upon our standard rate of $ _____ per hour plus any out-of-pocket cost for any required long-distance telephone calls or transportation and travel. Our *estimate* of the fee is $ _____ to $ _____, but unforeseen complexities or time requirements could make the fee exceed this estimate.

Payment — Payment will be $ _____ in advance and the balance upon delivery of your return.

APPROVED:

Client: _____

Date: _____

CRIMINAL LIABILITY

Tax crimes are punishable both as specific tax crimes under Title 26 (the Internal Revenue Code) and as general federal offenses under Title 18. The IRC contains criminal provisions for willful

1. Attempt to evade or defeat tax (IRC section 7201).
2. Failure to collect, account for, and pay over tax (IRC section 7202).
3. Failure to keep records, file return of tax or estimated tax, or pay tax (IRC section 7203).
4. Failure to furnish accurate statement to employees (IRC section 7204).
5. Failure to supply correct information to employer (IRC section 7205).
6. Aid or assistance in preparation or presentation of false documents in connection with tax matters (IRC section 7206).
7. Delivery or disclosure to the IRS of any list, return, account, statement or other document known to be false (IRC section 7207).

Item 1 (above) is the basic tax-evasion statute and is broad enough to cover accountants, bookkeepers, and tax preparers who aid and abet the filing of a false return.

Under section 7201 the government must prove a deficiency in payment of tax. However, this requirement can be avoided by prosecuting under section 7206, where conviction has been sustained because of falsely labeling a source of income.[70] Although some provisions are felonies and others are misdemeanors, all contain the willfulness requirement. In *United States v. Pomponio*,[71] the U.S. Supreme Court held that willfulness has the same meaning whether for a felony or misdemeanor. In ruling on the prosecution

---

70. United States v. DiVarco, 343 F. Supp. 101 (N.D. Ill. 1972), *aff'd* 484 F.2d 670 (7th Cir. 1973), *cert. denied* 415 U.S. 916 (1974). *Also see* United States v. Jacobson, 547 F.2d 21 (2d Cir. 1976), *cert. denied*, 430 U.S. 946 (1977), where bypassing the interest income box and labeling the illegal interest as "miscellaneous income" resulted in a felony conviction under 26 U.S.C. § 7206.

71. United States v. Pomponio, 429 U.S. 10 (1976).

EXHIBIT 12-6
Topics for Engagement Letters for Tax Practice

Tax Return Preparation:
Tax return preparation often involves application of conflicting authorities and interpretations that present varying possibilities of IRS challenge. Tax preparers are authorized to use their judgment in making such selection; however, it is understood that taxpayer(s) is (are) responsible for any adverse determination by the IRS or the courts.

Tax Advice:
Although this tax advice represents our best professional opinion, we cannot guarantee this result, even with a private ruling from the IRS national office or a determination letter from an IRS district director. Opinions of various courts are often conflicting, and judicial thought, including that of the U.S. Supreme Court, is subject to change. Often a slight change in the facts may alter the result.

Practice before the IRS:
This firm cannot guarantee any results and does not do so, but only guarantees its very best efforts.

Attorney's Fees:
If it should become necessary for _____ , CPAs, to retain an attorney to collect the professional fees specified herein, the client(s) agree(s) to pay attorney's fees and other costs of collection.

Past-due Fees:
Client(s) agree(s) to sign a _____ day promissory note bearing interest at _____ per cent per month (including provision for costs of collection and attorney fees) for all fees that become past due.

Compensation as a Witness:
Client(s) agree(s) to pay the rate of $_____ per hour for each hour expended as a witness called by any party in connection with work performed for the client.

for willfully filing a false return, the Court said that *willfulness* is satisfied by the voluntary and intentional violation of a known legal duty without regard to the presence of evil motive.

The government usually charges multiple offenses combining criminal tax offenses from the IRC with the general criminal provisions in the U.S. Criminal Code. Particularly broad coverage is provided under 18 U.S.C. section 1001, since it relates to false oral and written statements whether sworn or unsworn. Of cases referred from the Enforcement Division to IRS Counsel, about 30 percent are closed without prosecution due to decisions of Counsel, the Department of Justice, and U.S. Attorneys—each of these three units declines to prosecute approximately equal parts of the 30 percent. Of taxpayers prosecuted, around 75 percent plead guilty. The majority of those remaining are convicted after trial.

Criminal convictions of tax preparers fall into distinct categories:

1. Tax-preparer embezzlement from client and government.
2. Tax-preparer assistance for the client's tax fraud.

Embezzlement by Tax Preparers

United States v. Donovan[72] illustrates the conviction of a tax preparer under IRC § 7201. The tax preparer allegedly obtained money from clients representing that he would transmit the tax return and the tax to the IRS and then failed to file the return or to pay over the tax. The preparer claimed that he could not be convicted of a § 7201 violation without proof of "some positive affirmative act in an attempt to defeat or evade the tax in addition to allegations of mere acts of omission." However, the court reasoned that the affirmative acts of preparing returns, collecting money, promising to file returns and to pay taxes constituted the willful *attempt* to evade constituting the felony prescribed in section 7201 instead of the mere misdemeanor for willful failure to file prescribed in section 7203.

In the earlier embezzlement case of *Leathers v. United States*,[73] the client was proprietor of a fish and crab processing plant near North Bend, Oregon, operated under the name of "Peterson's Sea Foods." It was alleged that the tax preparer had confidence of the client who was an unlettered man unfamiliar with his own books, that the tax preparer collected $10,000 and a note for approximately $10,000 more, that the tax preparer then prepared and signed a return showing only $3,401.25 due and pocketed the difference. In rejecting the preparer's contention that there was insufficient proof to sustain the jury verdict and conviction under a former version of the current tax evasion statute, the court said:

> Also significant is the fact that after the Government began investigating the 1946 tax return, Leathers went to Peterson and talked to him at length about the income tax and tried to persuade Peterson to destroy his records. This is strong evidence of guilt. "It is today universally conceded that the fact of an accused's flight, escape from custody, resistance to arrest, concealment, assumption of a false name, and related conduct, are admissible as evidence of consciousness of guilt, and thus of guilt itself." Wigmore on Evidence, 3d Ed., § 276.

Aiding and Assisting under Section 7206

Where the tax preparer's client, instead of the preparer, obtains the monetary benefit of the false return, one of the government's favorite provisions for prosecution is section 7206 for aiding, assisting, or counseling the preparation of false documents. A number of

---

72. United States v. Donovan, 250 F. Supp 463 (1966).
73. Leathers v. United States, 250 F.2d 159 (9th Cir. 1957). The tax preparer was quoted as saying to the taxpayer: "It will go a lot better if you got any of those record, throw them in the crapper."

tax return preparers have been convicted under this provision.[74]

Conspiracy to Defraud

Conspiracy to defraud the United States is a felony under 18 U.S.C. § 371. In *United States v. Baskes*,[75] a Chicago tax attorney specializing in federal income taxation and real estate planning was convicted of conspiring with others to defraud the United States by impeding and obstructing the assessment and collection of income and gift taxes by the IRS. The court rejected the defense that illegally seized evidence led to the prosecution because the documents involved had been seized at the same time and from the same briefcase as in the *Payner*[76] case. The U.S. Supreme Court held in *Payner* that a taxpayer has no standing to complain of an illegal seizure of a third party.

Aiding and Abetting

Aiding and abetting any federal crime is made a separate offense under 18 U.S.C. § 2. Thus in *Standefer v. United States*[77] the U.S. Supreme Court sustained the conviction of the head of Gulf Oil Company's tax department for aiding and abetting a revenue official in accepting unauthorized compensation, despite prior acquittal of the IRS agent on some of the counts.

SUMMARY

This chapter presents an overview of some of the legal and ethical problems relating to tax practice. *AICPA Statements on Responsibilities in Tax Practice* provide general ethical standards for conducting a tax practice. Practice before the IRS is governed by Circular 230, while the U.S. Tax Court has its own set of rules.

The accountant in tax practice is sometimes caught between the competing interests of the public (as rep-resented by the IRS) and the particular client. In this role the accountant must protect the client's interest but only within the legal and ethical boundaries prescribed for professionals. The situation has become more difficult because of the shrinking zone of privacy of individuals as compared with the legitimate interest of the IRS in making sure that all citizens pay their fair share of taxes.

In tax-fraud matters, it is important to remember that only an attorney may practice law. Anything the client tells the accountant must be revealed if the accountant is questioned by the IRS. However, if the accountant is engaged by counsel to assist in a criminal defense, the accountant's work is then protected by the attorney-client privilege. If an accountant assisting counsel takes the witness stand, all relevant questions must be answered on cross-examination.

Accountants are liable to clients for penalties incurred as a result of their negligence. If the work is performed in a grossly incompetent manner, some courts may impose punitive damages. Accountants generally have a right to rely on data supplied by taxpayers without making independent verifications.

Tax preparers who aid and abet tax evasion are subject to IRS civil fines, injunction to prohibit further work as tax preparer, and criminal prosecution.

SUGGESTIONS FOR FURTHER READING

Annot. "Disciplinary Action against Attorney or Accountant for Misconduct Related to Preparation of Tax Returns for Others," 81 *American Law Reports* 3d 1140, 1977.

Annot. "Disciplinary Action under 31 U.S.C.S. § 1026 Authorizing Secretary of the Treasury to Suspend and Disbar Any Person Representing Claimants from Further Practice before the Treasury Department," 50 *American Law Reports* Fed. 817 (1980).

Annot. "Right of Member, Officer, Agent, or Director of Private Corporation or Unincorporated Association to Assert Personal Privilege against Self-Incrimination with Respect to Production of Corporate Books or Records," 52 *American Law Reports* 3d 636, 1973.

Annual Report 1980: Commissioner of Internal Revenue, Superintendent of Documents, U.S. Government Printing Office, Washington, D.C.

"The Attorney-Client Privilege: Fixed Rules, Balancing, and Constitutional Entitlement," 91 *Harvard Law Review* 464–87.

Balter, Harry Graham. *Tax Fraud and Evasion*. 4th ed. Boston: Warren, Gorham & Lamont, Inc., 1976.

Fink, Robert S. "The Role of the Accountant in a Tax Fraud Case," *Journal of Accountancy*, April 1976, pp. 42–48.

Schmid, Paul F., and John L. Tully, Jr. *Practice before the IRS*, Tax Management No. 147, 4th ed., 1977.

Weiss, Richard "How to Evaluate the Cost and Content Factors When Selecting a Tax Library," *Taxation for Accountants*, February 1978, pp. 86–92.

QUESTIONS AND PROBLEMS

1. Describe the circumstances under which a tax preparer may take positions contrary to the IRS when preparing tax returns.

---

74. United States v. Bernes, 602 F.2d 716 (5th Cir. 1979), Atlanta CPA convicted on testimony of taxpayers and their records which were introduced into evidence; United States v. Warden, 545 F.2d 32 (7th Cir. 1979), Chicago CPA's fee was contingent on amount of refund and evidence indicated inflated or fabricated deductions; United States v. Egenberg, 441 F.2d 441 (2d Cir. 1971), CPA convicted of bribery of IRS agents as well as making false statements (18 U.S.C. § 1001) and aiding and assisting the filing of false returns; United States v. Dobbs, 506 F.2d 445 (5th Cir. 1975), father and son tax preparers added to deductions submitted by taxpayers; United States v. Miller, 529 F.2d 1125 (9th Cir. 1976), clients testified that the returns were false and contained deductions which they had not furnished. *See* Annot., "Tax Preparer's Willful Assistance in Preparation of False or Fraudulent Tax Returns under § 7206(2) of Internal Revenue Code," 43 A.L.R. Fed. 128 (1979).

75. United States v. Baskes, 80-2 U.S.T.C. 9679 (7th Cir. 1980).

76. United States v. Payner, 444 U.S. 822 (1980).

77. Standefer v. United States, 447 U.S. 10 (1980).

2. Describe the opportunities for negotiating the reduction of a tax assessment at each of the following levels:
   a. Revenue agent.
   b. Appellate conference.
3. Under what circumstances may accountants practice before the United States Tax Court?
4. What is a "small tax case" in the United States Tax Court? How does the result reached differ from the result in other cases?
5. Describe the appropriate conduct of an accountant who is served with an IRS summons.
6. Under what circumstances are accountant working papers protected from the IRS summons by the attorney-client privilege?
7. Do tax preparers have liability exposure beyond the client for whom the return is prepared? Explain.
8. Under current laws and ethics rules
   a. Lawyers cannot prepare tax returns.
   b. CPAs cannot prepare legal documents.
   c. Lawyers may issue audit reports.
   d. Both lawyers and accountants may use the descriptions "tax consultant" or "tax expert."
9. In the case of *Fisher v. United States,* Fisher was
   a. An accountant.
   b. An attorney.
   c. Proprietor of a restaurant.
   d. A taxpayer engaged in medical practice.
10. In the case of *Couch v. United States,* Couch was
    a. An accountant.
    b. An attorney.
    c. Proprietor of a restaurant.
    d. A taxpayer engaged in medical practice.
11. In the *Fisher* case the summons related to
    a. Accountant's working papers consisting of write-up work prepared from the taxpayer's canceled checks and deposit receipts.
    b. Books, records, bank statements, canceled checks, deposit ticket copies, working papers, and other documents pertaining to tax liability of taxpayer.
    c. Bank microfilm records pertaining to taxpayer's account.
    d. An original computer tape, which constituted part of taxpayer's books and records.
12. In the *Couch* case the summons related to
    a. Accountant's working papers consisting of write-up work prepared from the taxpayer's canceled checks and deposit receipts.
    b. Books, records, bank statements, canceled checks, deposit ticket copies, working papers, and other documents pertaining to tax liability of taxpayer.
    c. Bank microfilm records pertaining to taxpayer's account.
    d. An original computer tape, which constituted part of taxpayer's books and records.
13. *Bellis v. United States* involved
    a. An IRS summons issued by a revenue agent.
    b. An IRS summons issued by a special agent.
    c. A subpoena to appear before Congress.
    d. A grand jury subpoena.
14. The records involved in *Bellis* were
    a. Phonograph records in possession of the taxpayer.
    b. Books and records of a law partnership.
    c. Accountants' working papers.
    d. Medical records for a large clinic.
15. The Fifth Amendment defense to production of documents is
    a. Available only where a taxpayer is physically placed on the rack.
    b. Generally unavailable to partnerships and corporations.
    c. Generally available to partnerships and corporations.
    d. Available to labor unions, whether national or local.
    e. Available only for the inner sanctum of large business enterprises.
16. In the case of *Beckwith v. United States* the Court held that
    a. IRS special agents involved in a criminal investigation need not inform taxpayers of their constitutional rights prior to a noncustodial interrogation.
    b. IRS special agents involved in a criminal investigation must inform taxpayers of their constitutional rights prior to a noncustodial interrogation.
    c. The IRS must warn taxpayers whenever the IRS is out to get them.
    d. IRS agents must administer a *Miranda* warning before the taxpayer is placed in handcuffs.
17. (From the May 1980 Uniform CPA Examination)
    In accordance with the *AICPA Statements on Responsibilities in Tax Practice* where a question on a federal income tax return has not been answered, the CPA should sign the preparer's declaration only if
    a. The CPA can provide reasonable support for this omission upon examination by IRS.
    b. The information requested is *not* available.
    c. The question is *not* applicable to the taxpayer.
    d. An explanation of the reason for the omission is provided.
18. (From the May 1980 Uniform CPA Examination)
    For the first time in the history of federal income tax law, Congress enacted legislation in 1976 that imposed civil liabilities and penalties upon individuals who are guilty of certain misconduct in connection with their preparing income tax returns for a fee. Prior provisions of the Internal Revenue Code which dealt with criminal fraud remained unchanged.

    Required:
    Answer the following, setting forth reasons for any conclusions stated. What potential civil liabilities and penalties to the United States government should the practitioner be aware of in connection with the improper preparation of a federal income tax return, and what types of conduct would give rise to these liabilities and penalties?

13

Auditing, Accounting, and Management Advisory Services

This chapter covers:

- AUDITING.
- WRITE-UP WORK AND UNAUDITED FINANCIALS.
- MANAGEMENT ADVISORY SERVICES.
- FORECASTS AND PROJECTIONS.
- INTERIM REPORTING.
- MARKET-VALUE REPORTING.
- MATERIALITY.

AUDITING

The auditing function presents the greatest dollar exposure to malpractice liability. This risk has two distinct aspects:

1. Defalcation losses that continue after an audit should have revealed the fraud.
2. Investor and creditor losses that result from reliance upon the audited financial statements.

Defalcation Losses

While liability has been imposed for failure to discover embezzlement when the engagement was limited to bookkeeping[1] or preparing unaudited financials,[2] standard auditing procedures include steps designed to detect kiting of checks and lapping. Kiting of checks involves drawing, but not recording, a check on one bank account and depositing it in another so that the funds appear in both before clearing the first. Lapping involves a continuing process of delayed deposits whereby cash deposits by later customers are recorded to make good cash deposits by earlier customers.

Ordinary audit procedures involve testing for kiting by (1) obtaining a direct confirmation from the bank with cancelled checks (sometimes called a "cutoff" bank statement if obtained at the balance sheet date), (2) preparing a schedule of interbank transfers, and (3) accounting for unissued checks. Ordinary audit procedures for lapping involve confirmation of accounts receivable and comparing the composition of cash and checks on bank deposit slips with the records of cash receipts.

The suit for defalcation losses is ordinarily brought by the client, or the client's bonding company upon payment of the client's loss, to recover for losses that take place after the fraud should have been discovered. For both the client and the bonding company the test of liability is negligence.

Consider *National Surety Corp. v. Lybrand*[3] where the cashier in a brokerage firm confessed to defalcations amounting to $329,300 over a period of several years. Action was brought against the auditors for their failure to discover the embezzlement, which was accomplished through "lapping" and "kiting." Defendants were charged with (1) failure to perform their contract to audit, (2) breach of warranty in the audit reports, (3) negligent audit work, and (4) fraudulent misrepresentation of material facts in the reports of financial condition. It was claimed that if the embezzlement had been discovered, subsequent losses could have been prevented and previous losses might have been recovered.

The system used for lapping, or late deposits, was "to place a customer's check in the petty cash box, instead of immediately depositing it, then extract from the petty cash the amount of the check in cash, and deposit the check in the bank one or more days later." As a result of this practice, the records of the firm and the bank deposit slips would not correspond. When a customer would give a check, the cashier would take an equal amount of cash as his own and later prepare for the item a deposit slip which might list several checks or a combination of checks and cash to make

---

1. Bonhiver v. Graff, 248 N.W.2d 291 (Minn. 1976).
2. 1136 Tenants' Corp. v. Max Rothenberg & Co., *see* Chapter 5 at note 47.
3. National Surety Corp. v. Lybrand, 9 N.Y.S.2d 554 (App. Div. 1939).

up the same total. But the auditors failed to discover this inconsistency between composition of receipts and deposits.

The cashier knew when audits were to be made and kiting was accomplished at the time of the audit so as to cover the shortage. The firm maintained about 27 bank accounts, and by writing, but not recording, a check on Bank A and depositing the check in Bank B on the audit date it could be made to appear that the same funds were in both banks, since the check was not subtracted from the balance of Bank A until after the audit was completed.

The court noted that cash in bank can be verified absolutely and that the authorities on auditing discussed procedures for detection of kiting and lapping. The court said:

> In Dicksee's *Manual on Auditing* (American Edition, 1909, edited by Robert H. Montgomery, one of the defendants herein), it is said (p. 40): " . . . A list of checques outstanding should be retained, and it should be ascertained afterwards, either by a second writing up of the pass book or by inquiry of the bank, whether the amounts agree. If the time of the proposed audit is known, fraud may easily be committed and the cash inflated by drawing a checque at the last moment which will be 'outstanding.' "

> In Montgomery's own treatise on "Auditing— Theory and Practice" (1912), he says (p. 94): "When the cash balance consists of several bank accounts or funds, care must be taken to see that the entire balance is verified simultaneously. Instances are known where auditors have been deceived through one balance, after being inspected, having been transferred and used on a later day in connection with another balance."

> Safeguards against fraud are discussed in *Bell and Powelson on Auditing* (1924), at page 71:

>> The reason for thus testing individual deposits, and especially the composition thereof, is to detect any evidence of temporary misappropriations of cash which have been restored, or of the somewhat similar form of fraud known as "kiting," which involves a series of unauthorized "borrowings," one being used to repay the other. . . .

>> When there is more than one bank account, a test should always be made of deposits during the last days of the audit period. The particular purpose of this is to detect a deposit in one bank of an unrecorded check on another bank to conceal a shortage in the first bank, which check cannot reach the second bank in time to be charged by it in the audit period and will not appear as outstanding.

> And, at page 73, it is said: "For the same reason that all checks supposed to have been issued should be accounted for, it is necessary, so far as practicable, to determine that none have been issued which were not supposed to have been. Knowing that all current numbers of checks would be accounted for by the auditor,

the person desiring to issue a fraudulent check would be likely to use one that was not current. For that reason, the auditor should see that no checks have been abstracted from the back of the check book, if they are in book form."

* * * * *

The evidence in this case discloses similar conditions at the time of all the audits in question. It was for the jury to say whether the practice of "lapping" and "kiting" of checks should have put the defendants upon inquiry which would have led to discovery of the defalcations, and whether, if defendants had exercised ordinary care and used proper methods of accounting as established by the expert testimony, they would have observed checks drawn out of numerical order. If they had checked "outstandings," they would have noted that the check or checks used by Wallach at the audit dates were returned with the cancelled vouchers accompanying the next bank statement. Again, if there had been any substantial compliance with the requirements for verifying cash in banks, the cash shortages would have been detected, as the jury might have found. Their representations that there had been a verification of cash was a pretense of knowledge when they did not know the condition of the bank accounts and had no reasonable basis to assume that they did.

Reliance on Audited Financial Statements

Accounts Receivable. A number of cases have involved reliance on audited financials that include overstated accounts receivable. These have resulted in liability where the auditor (1) failed to recognize that accounts were overstated because they were uncollectible,[4] (2) used a "subject to realization" qualification instead of correctly valuing the receivables,[5] and (3) used a "subject to realization" qualification for a receivable on a real estate sales contract that was never closed.[6] One audit procedure is to rely on collections during field work. However, this must be used with care since funds recorded as collections have turned out to be bank loans or transfers of funds.

Inventories. There are three critical points in the inventory audit:

1. If there is weak internal control or if no reliable perpetual inventory account is maintained, the inventory audit in general and the testing of inventory counts in particular must be greatly extended.
2. The auditor must either control or observe the client's control of all inventory count tags and reflect evidence in the working papers of this control.

---

4. State Street Trust Co. v. Ernst, 15 N.E.2d 416 (App. Div. 1938).

5. *In re* London and General Bank, [1895] 2 Ch. 673.

6. Herzfeld v. Laventhol, Krekstein, Horwath & Horwath, 540 F.2d 27 (2d Cir. 1976).

176

3. If the inventory appears out of line with industry norms or there are errors in items test counted, the auditor should not accept management explanations, but rather should greatly extend the testing assuming (1) the correct inventory is within industry norms and (2) the error rate in the sample prevails throughout.

As to difficulties encountered by auditors in these respects, see excerpts from *SEC Accounting Series Releases* reproduced in Exhibits 13-1 and 13-2.

EXHIBIT 13-1
Excerpt from *SEC Accounting Series Release No. 157*, **"Arthur Andersen & Co."** (1974)

By recreation of inventory records, it was calculated that the $9.2 million book inventories of Crown at October 31, 1971 were overstated by approximately $4.4 million, and that income for fiscal years 1970 and 1971 was overstated. Of this total shortage, approximately $2.5 million occurred at Crown's Roxboro plant. The Roxboro physical inventory had been observed by Arthur Andersen.

In connection with this observation, the Arthur Andersen auditors did not adequately control inventory count tags, even though the firm's own procedures require such control. Accordingly, Crown personnel were able to alter certain tags and to create other tags which were included with actual count tags prior to the tabulation of the inventory. In addition, the fraudulent tags were printed out in numerical sequence on the inventory tabulation listing and indicated quantities of aluminum coil in units of 50,000 pounds per coil, which are quantities in excess of that which could have been reasonably expected to be physically contained in the Roxboro plant or any other plant. The plant did not manufacture or purchase aluminum coils in excess of 5,000 pounds. The auditors and any reviewers of the inventory work papers did not notice this block of 100 tags which constituted a substantial portion of the total inventory on the computer listing with quantities 10 times as large as the largest actual inventory item. Normal inventory auditing procedures would require that special attention be paid to the largest items in the inventory.

EXHIBIT 13-2
Excerpt from *SEC Accounting Series Release No. 196*, **"In re Seidman & Seidman"** (1976)

It appears that about 50 percent of the $32.1 million reported CMH portion of year-end inventory was in fact non-existent. This overstatement of inventory substantially inflated Cenco's consolidated pre-tax income.

During the 1973 audit of CMH, Seidman & Seidman reached two significant audit conclusions which pertained to the CMH inventory accounting system. The first was that the CMH internal controls over inventory continued to be inadequate. The second was that, as in prior years, CMH did not have reliable general ledger inventory balances or perpetual inventory systems. The auditors therefore believed that CMH was forced to rely almost entirely on the results of the physical inventory. In our opinion, the conditions as they believed them to exist required extensive audit testing of inventory. It is our judgment that Seidman and Seidman did not give adequate audit effect to the clear requirements of these conclusions. Under the circumstances, the Commission also believes that the audit program for CMH inventory should have expressly noted these internal control deficiencies and included appropriately detailed instructions concerning the nature and scope of audit tests.

Accounts Payable

Confirmation of accounts payable is not a standard auditing procedure. When it is deemed prudent to apply this procedure, the auditor may want to first consult the client's counsel as to whether there may be valid reasons for nonpayment. The reason for this precaution is that audit confirmation of obligations may waive the statute of limitations or other client defenses.

Consider *Buxton v. Diversified Resources Corp.*[7] where plaintiff sued on a $20,000 loan and the defendant corporation asserted the Utah statute of limitations as a defense to the claim. From 1971 through 1973 audit confirmation letters had been signed by the controller for the $20,000 obligation. In 1974 and 1975 the president signed letters in the following form requesting confirmation to the auditors of an obligation of $20,000 plus interest:

> Our auditors are making an examination of our financial statements, which indicate the following amount payable to you on notes: . . . Please confirm the accuracy of the above information.

The court held (1) the president had authority to sign the audit confirmations, (2) the confirmations constituted a written acknowledgement of the debt which extended the statute of limitations, and (3) the debtor was estopped from asserting the statute of limitations defense because the obligor had been lulled into inaction.

The court based its decision on *Victory Investment Corp. v. Muskogee Electric Traction Co.*,[8] where the court, applying Oklahoma law, held that submitting a balance sheet to the trustee for bondholders with the obligation shown as a current liability extended the statute of limitations on the bonds.

Subsequently Discovered Facts and Subsequent Events

A combination of court cases and new AICPA auditing rules are moving the auditor rapidly to the duty to see that the SEC and the public are made aware of any information coming to the auditor's attention that may affect *either audited or unaudited* financial statements filed with the SEC or disseminated to the public. The auditor's failure to adhere to this duty may well result in liability to third parties.

A 1967 decision in *Fischer v. Kletz*[9] involved allegations by stockholders and debenture holders that the

7. Buxton v. Diversified Resources Corp., 643 F.2d 1313 (10th Cir. 1980).
8. Victory Inv. Corp. v. Muskogee Elec. Traction Co., 150 F.2d 889 (10th Cir.), *cert. denied*, 326 U.S. 774 (1945).
9. Fischer v. Kletz, 266 F. Supp. 180 (S.D.N.Y. 1967).

auditors (Peat, Marwick, Mitchell & Co.) certified to false 1963 financial statements of Yale Express System, Inc., and failed to properly disclose subsequently acquired information. While the auditors were in the course of conducting special studies of Yale's past and current income and expenses in 1964, the auditors allegedly discovered that figures in the 1963 annual report were substantially false and misleading, but did not disclose this finding to the exchanges, the SEC, or the public at large until May 5, 1965, when the results of the special studies were released.

Since the suit involved claims under the federal securities laws, it was filed in federal court. The complaint also included a count for common-law deceit on the basis of failure to disclose information acquired after the audit; the count was based on the pendent jurisdiction of the court. The court noted that since it was sitting in New York, it should apply New York law in deciding the common-law claim, but no New York cases were found on the point.

Although the general rule is that there is no liability in deceit for nondisclosure, Prosser cites an exception:

> Again, one who has made a statement, and subsequently acquires new information which makes it untrue or misleading, must disclose such information to any one whom he knows to be still acting on the basis of the original statement—as, for example, where there is a serious decline in the profits of a business pending its sale.[10]

In applying the rule to this case, the question is whether an auditor has such a duty to a third party; that is, whether the breach of such a duty by an auditor is only negligence (no liability to unforeseen third parties) or intentional misrepresentation such as to subject the auditor to third-party liability. The court held that a duty to disclose, by its nature, creates an objective standard that does not require proof of subjective intent. The court also reasoned that "intent can be sensibly imputed to a defendant who, knowing that plaintiff will rely upon his original representations, sits by silently when they turn out to be false."

The auditor contended that the duty imposed on a party to a business transaction to disclose that a prior representation was false and misleading was not relevant to auditors. It was argued that a "party to a business transaction" could not include auditors because auditors have no opportunity for personal gain by virtue of nondisclosure. But the court rejected this contention:

> Generally speaking, I can see no reason why this duty to disclose should not be imposed upon an accounting firm which makes a representation it knows

will be relied upon by investors. To be sure, certification of a financial statement does not create a formal business relationship between the accountant who certifies and the individual who relies upon the certificate for investment purposes. The act of certification, however, is similar in its effect to a representation made in a business transaction: both supply information which is naturally and justifiably relied upon by individuals for decisional purposes. Viewed in this context of the impact of nondisclosure on the injured party, it is difficult to conceive that a distinction between accountants and parties to a business transaction is warranted. The elements of "good faith and common honesty" which govern the businessman presumably should also apply to the statutory "independent public accountant."

The court noted that the liability question involves a balancing of interests. The effect of imposing liability on accountants must be balanced with the interest of investors in being afforded some degree of protection by and from accountants, whose representations are relied upon for decisional purposes. The court, refusing to decide such a policy issue until full development of the facts, denied the motion to dismiss the third-party common-law claim for deceit.

The AICPA apparently did not take a position on the disclosure of subsequently acquired information until October 1969. AICPA rules were then modified to provide that an auditor is under no obligation:

> to make any further or continuing inquiry or perform any other auditing procedures with respect to the audited financial statements covered by that report, *unless new information which may affect his report comes to his attention.*[11] (Emphasis added.)

When the auditor becomes aware of information that was not known at the date of the report, but that, if known, could have affected the report, the auditor must conduct an investigation. If the information would have affected the report and persons are currently relying on the financial statements, then the auditor must prepare a revised report and see that the client discloses such report to persons relying on the prior report and to the SEC, stock exchanges, and any other regulatory agencies. If the client will not cooperate, then the auditor must notify the client not to associate the audit report with the financial statements and must report the situation to regulatory agencies, including the SEC and stock exchanges, and to each person specifically known to be relying on the financial statements and audit report.

AICPA rules also deal with the disclosure of events occurring between the balance sheet date and issuance of the auditor's report. They provide:

---

10. W. Prosser, *Law of Torts* 696, 4th ed. (1971).

11. *CCH AICPA Professional Standards,* AU §561.03.

1. Events that provide additional evidence with respect to conditions that existed at the date of the balance sheet should be used in revising estimates used in preparing financial statements. For example, events affecting realization of receivables and inventories and determination of estimated liabilities ordinarily require adjustment of the financial statements.

2. Events that provide evidence with respect to conditions that did not exist at the date of the balance sheet should *not* result in adjustment of the financial statements; however, *disclosure* must be made if "required to keep the financial statements from being misleading." If the event is significant, disclosure can best be made by supplementing the historical financial statements with pro forma data, giving effect to the event as if it had occurred at the date of the balance sheet.[12]

AICPA rules specify that the date of completion of field work should be used as the date of the independent auditor's report. If there is a subsequent event that occurs before issuance of the report, the auditor has two methods available for dating the report:

> He may use "dual dating," for example, "February 16, 19____, except for Note ____ as to which the date is March 1, 19____," or he may date his report as of the later date. In the former instance, his responsibility for events occurring subsequent to the completion of his field work is limited to the specific event referred to in the note (or otherwise disclosed). In the latter instance, the independent auditor's responsibility for subsequent events extends to the date of his report. . . .[13]

When auditors are associated with registration of new securities under federal law, they are responsible for investigating subsequent events up to the effective date of the registration statement. This responsibility may extend even to the duty to see that the SEC and public are made aware of subsequent events that make *unaudited* statements misleading.

Public accountants should consider whether they have a responsibility to disclose known facts that make financial statements misleading whenever they are *publicly* associated with either audited *or unaudited* financial statements.

Special Disclosure Problems

Correcting Accounting Errors. Whenever an auditor returns for a subsequent audit and discovers that an accounting error makes the prior audit report misleading, the audit report must be withdrawn as discussed above. Also, the journal entry to correct the error must be a prior period adjustment with full disclosure in a footnote, and the erroneous financials must be restated when presented for comparative purposes with the current year figures. The case of *United States v. Natelli* involved a criminal conviction of a CPA who failed to disclose the correction or withdraw the auditor's opinion. This case is discussed in Chapter 9 and the court's opinion is reproduced in Chapter 15.

Footnote Disclosures. Special care must be taken to disclose and properly account for transactions that may involve illegal or improper transactions. One problem that commonly arises is the receivable or loan to the officer/director of a closely held corporation. In some states a loan to a director is illegal. Such transactions must be approved by a majority of the disinterested board, and minutes ratifying all acts would not be adequate for this purpose. In addition to the necessity for disclosing who got the money and the legalities, there may be a valuation problem. For example, if there is a noninterest-bearing demand note which has been on the books three years, should it be valued at present value? If so, what period should be used? The rule for such matters is full disclosure of all relevant facts. *United States v. Simon* involved criminal conviction of CPAs who the government argued should have disclosed in their footnote that the president, who was looting the company, got the money represented by the receivable. This case is discussed in Chapter 9 and the court's opinion is reproduced in Chapter 15.

Going-Concern Problems. Since all accounting rules are based on the going-concern assumption, a serious threat to this assumption should be disclosed in reports on audited or unaudited financials. One way to test the seriousness of the problem is to require the client to prepare a financial forecast, which will carry you through next year's audit field work to show that the company can remain viable. Then evaluate the assumptions and likelihood that the firm may be unable to sustain operations through that period. If there is serious doubt, the auditor should consider disclaiming or qualifying the opinion with an explanation of the nature of the particular going-concern problem.

Other. Division of audit responsibility with other auditors is discussed in Chapter 7 at note 15. The legal effect of disclaimers and qualified opinions is discussed in Chapter 5 at note 11.

WRITE-UP WORK AND UNAUDITED FINANCIALS

"Write-up work" involves performing bookkeeping functions and actually writing up or creating basic client records. An engagement to prepare unaudited financial statements may or may not include write-up work. The legal effects of labeling financial statements as unaudited is discussed in Chapter 5 at note 33.

---

12. *CCH AICPA Professional Standards,* AU §560.
13. *CCH AICPA Professional Standards,* AU §530.

AICPA standards for unaudited work are established by its Accounting and Review Services Committee. In its *Statement on Standards for Accounting and Review Services No. 1 (SSARS No. 1)* it divided engagements for preparation of unaudited financials of nonpublic entities into two categories: (1) compilation and (2) review. A compilation involves preparing financial statements from information supplied by management without achieving any assurance as to compliance with GAAP, and the report is similar to a disclaimer. A review involves inquiry and analytical procedures to provide limited assurance of compliance with GAAP, and the report is worded in terms of negative assurance.

Limiting "Negligence" Liability for Compilations

While both compilations and reviews are considered general-purpose financial statements for submission to third parties, there is more likelihood of misleading third parties who rely on compilations that are sometimes prepared on the basis of omission of footnotes and supplemental disclosures. Review reports are ordinarily full-disclosure reports containing all footnotes and supplemental disclosures. Therefore, as a matter of firm policy, some public accountants may want to consider limiting compilations to internal use only. Of course the client can breach the agreement and present the financials to third parties without the knowledge of the CPA. However, CPAs would have the well-established defense that they did not foresee the use or reliance of the third party, so that the third party would be required to prove knowing misrepresentation or gross negligence in order to recover from the CPA.

Exhibit 13–3 is presented as a starting point for consideration. Do not use any contract form until you first consult your personal attorney on your particular situation.

EXHIBIT 13–3
Sample Engagement Letter for Restricting Compiled Financials to Internal Use

---

Dear Sirs:

This will confirm the terms of our engagement to *compile* from data that you supply and without verification or review on our part the following financial statements: _____ _____. We will also prepare the following tax returns:

Date due   *Governmental unit*   *Period covered*

We will be compensated for travel and transportation expenses, long-distance telephone calls, and other out-of-pocket expenses plus hourly rates for time expended as follows:

Position   *Hourly rate for each*

Partner
Manager
Senior
Junior

Our estimate of the total fee is $ _____ . The fee is to be paid $ _____ in advance upon your confirmation of this agreement, with balance to be paid immediately when either progress or final bills are rendered.

It is the policy of this firm to *compile* financial statements *only* for internal use. We have adopted this policy in recognition of the fact that the public places greater reliance upon statements with which a CPA is associated and that such reliance may be misleading where no review has been conducted. Each page of the statements we prepare will be labeled "Unaudited compilation for internal use only: Disclosures may not be complete, and accuracy has not been verified."

It is our understanding that you agree to use compiled financial statements prepared by us for internal use only and that you assume full responsibility and liability if, by your actions, these compiled statements should come into view of third parties, including, but not limited to, lenders, creditors, and prospective purchasers. We also understand that you will hold us harmless from any and all liability that we may incur as a result of said third parties placing reliance upon said unaudited financial statements.

This engagement specifically excludes all checking including, but not limited to, review, evaluation, and recommendations concerning internal controls and verification of account balances, invoices, checks, and other records and data. We do not undertake to discover any fraud or irregularities caused by directors, officers, employees, agents, partners, proprietors, or others, and we are specifically relieved of all responsibility therefore. We may, at our option, make suggestions concerning internal control or systems to facilitate this and possible future engagements to *compile* financial statements and tax returns. Such suggestions do not imply the undertaking of the review of internal controls, verifications, or search for fraud specifically disclaimed herein.

Please confirm your agreement with the terms of this engagement by signing and returning the enclosed copy of this letter.

Sincerely,
X Y Z
Certified Public
Accountants

The terms of your engagement as outlined above are accepted.

ABC Corporation

By _____
   President

Date _____

Affix Seal:

180

Known Inadequacies of Client Personnel

Paragraph 11 of *SSARS No. 1* states:

> To compile financial statements, *the accountant should possess a general understanding of* the nature of the entity's business transactions, the form of its accounting records, *the stated qualifications of its accounting personnel*, the accounting basis on which the financial statements are to be presented, and the form and content of the financial statements. The accountant ordinarily obtains knowledge of these matters through experience with the entity or inquiry of the entity's personnel. *On the basis of that understanding, the accountant should consider whether it will be necessary to perform other accounting services, such as assistance in adjusting the books of account or consultation on accounting matters when he compiles financial statements.* (Emphasis added.)

Where the CPA knows that client personnel do not know FIFO from LIFO, the CPA should do enough price testing of inventory to see that the method adopted is being properly applied. Similarly when the CPA knows the client personnel are unsophisticated and are not using an aging schedule to determine the bad debt provision, the CPA should assist and either prepare the aging schedule or supervise client personnel in preparing it.

Using Suspense Accounts on Published Statements

Even when performing a compilation, paragraph 12 of *SSARS No. 1* warns that the CPA may "become aware that information supplied by the entity is incorrect, incomplete, or otherwise unsatisfactory for the purpose of compiling financial statements." At this point the CPA must obtain additional or revised information or withdraw from the engagement.

Consider whether issuing compiled financial statements containing a suspense account would violate this admonition by indicating that the information is incomplete or unsatisfactory. If the amount in suspense is small, it might be the result of offsetting debits and credits. If unraveling the suspense account leads to the discovery of fraud, it can hardly be argued that it was immaterial.

PRACTICAL POINTER

Liability is not necessarily reduced where the public accountant wears a management hat in connection with performing accounting services. In *Security-First National Bank of Los Angeles v. Lutz*, 297 F.2d 159 (9th Cir. 1961), *further proceedings as to damages*, 322 F.2d 348 (9th Cir. 1963), the court held an accountant liable to a third party based on the rule that an accountant who serves as a director and makes entries on the books is a fiduciary under California law. An accountant who served as a director while performing bookkeeping services was held liable to investors under federal law in *Blakely v. Lisac*, 357 F. Supp. 255 (D. Ore. 1972).

For other cases where wearing the management hat has resulted in liability for breach of a fiduciary duty, see Chapter 5 at notes 53 through 55.

MANAGEMENT ADVISORY SERVICES

There has been very little reported litigation involving management consulting. One reason is that problems in this area are usually resolved by going back into the field and correcting deficiencies. The case of *Clements Auto Co. v. Service Bureau Corp.*[14] reveals some of the potential liability. Service Bureau Corp. (a wholly owned IBM subsidiary) provided in its contract that New York law would control. However, the court held that the provision disclaiming all warranties was contrary to Minnesota public policy and as such did not relieve defendant from liability for misrepresentation. The engagement involved installation of an inventory-control system, and the court upheld damages for cost of executive salaries for supervision, increased cost of clerical and office supplies, cost of leasing related equipment, as well as the amount paid for the system.

In contrast with *Clements Auto*, the court in *Farris Engineering Corp. v. Service Bureau Corp.*[15] applied New Jersey law, looked to New York law as the place of contracting, and upheld the contractual clause limiting damages to the fee paid. Similarly, in *IBM v. Catamore Enterprises, Inc.*[16] the court upheld the validity of clauses in IBM's contract limiting damages to the amount paid for services and requiring claims to be made in one year:

> We must now consider the validity of the provision limiting the period of IBM's liability to one year following the accrual of the cause of action. Catamore,

---

14. Clements Auto Co. v. Service Bureau Corp., 444 F.2d 169 (8th Cir. 1971). In Sanitary Linen Service Co. v. Alexander Proudfoot Co., 435 F.2d 292 (5th Cir. 1970), the court rejected the claim for promised savings of $1,000,000 because there was no express promise to effect a savings and held there is no implied warranty in a contract for services. However, the court found that Proudfoot had been unsuccessful in providing the promised short-interval scheduling system for plaintiff's laundry service, and based on this failure of consideration gave plaintiff judgment for all fees paid to Proudfoot.

15. Farris Engineering Corp. v. Service Bureau Corp., 406 F.2d 519 (3d Cir. 1969). By completing the contract in New York, Service Bureau made New York the place of contracting.

16. IBM v. Catamore Enterprises, Inc., 548 F.2d 1065 (1st Cir. 1976).

not surprisingly, complains that it is unfair for IBM to attempt so to curtail its risks and liabilities. The short answer to their complaint is such clauses, providing the time limitation is reasonable, are valid under New York laws. . . . We observe that a small consumer may often be required to deal with a large supplier on the latter's terms—perhaps the forces of competition are the only check to one-sided dealings. In any case, it seems to us that when a supplier and its customer, neither of whom is helpless in the market place, agree on terms limiting the period of liability for future services to one year, those terms must be respected.

PRACTICAL POINTERS

1. Familiarize yourself with the *AICPA Statements on Management Advisory Services*. These standards provide (MS § 101.04):

   The definitions set forth in the March 1, 1973, Code of Professional Ethics are applicable throughout these standards. The term "practitioner" as used herein pertains to all those, whether CPAs or not, who perform management advisory services in CPA firms.

2. Consider this from 57 Am. Jur. 2d, *Negligence* § 21:

   Contracts which do not purport to exempt a party thereto from liability for his own negligence, but which amount to a contract to indemnify another party if he incurs liability, or which limit a party's liability for negligent acts, may provide some degree of protection from claims predicated on negligence without contravening public policy limitations.

3. The IBM exculpatory clause, as quoted by the court with approval in *Catamore* was as follows:

   Limitation of liability

   The Customer agrees that IBM's liability hereunder for damages, regardless of the form of action, shall not exceed the total amount paid for services under the applicable Service Estimate or in the authorization for the particular service if no Service Estimate is made. This shall be the Customer's exclusive remedy.

   The Customer further agrees that IBM will not be liable for any lost profits, nor for any claim or demand against the Customer by any other party.

   No action, regardless of form, arising out of the services under this Agreement, may be brought by either party more than one year after the cause of action has accrued, except that an action for nonpayment may be brought within one year of the date of last payment.

   IBM does not make any express or implied warranties, including, but not limited to, the im-

plied warranties of merchantability and fitness for a particular purpose.

In no event will IBM be liable for consequential damages even if IBM has been advised of the possibility of such damages.

FORECASTS AND PROJECTIONS

The issues concerning disclosure of forecasts and projections are the same as for financial reporting generally:

1. What quantitative and qualitative standards should govern disclosure?
2. How can all members of the investing public gain equal access to information?

SEC Rules

In 1973 the SEC announced a change in its long-standing policy prohibiting forecasts and projections in SEC filings in recognition of the fact that many publicly traded firms release projections of various kinds, such as sales or earnings, to the financial press. SEC rules now permit filings to contain forecasts "which are made in good faith and have a reasonable basis, provided they are in an appropriate format and accompanied by information adequate for investors to make their own judgments."[17]

Although no firms are required to make or publish projections or forecasts, once public statements—including forecasts or projections—are made by management, the firm subjects itself to responsibility. For this reason, few firms are expected to make regular forecasts in their annual reports.

AICPA Rules

AICPA ethics rules provide:

Rule 201E—Forecasts. A member shall not permit his name to be used in conjunction with any forecast of future transactions in a manner which may lead to the belief that the member vouches for the achievability of the forecast.

Interpretation 201-2 offers some guidance to the CPA associated with a forecast:

201-2—Forecasts. Rule 201 does not prohibit a member from preparing, or assisting a client in the preparation of, forecasts of the results of future transactions. When a member's name is associated with such forecasts, there shall be a presumption that such data may

---

17. *SEC Release No. 33-5699* (April 23, 1976), CCH Fed. Sec. L. Rep. ¶ 80,461 (1976).

be used by parties other than the client. Therefore, full disclosure must be made of the sources of the information used and the major assumptions made in the preparation of the statements and analyses, the character of the work performed by the member, and the degree of the responsibility he is taking.

The AICPA has issued "financial forecast"[18] guidelines for the preparation,[19] presentation,[20] or review[21] of financial forecasts. It has also recognized that auditors may have a duty to speak when published forecasts, projections, or "financial forecasts," containing their audited financials, are conflicting and inconsistent with known facts so as to be materially misleading.[22]

Liability for Inaccurate Factual Basis

Liability is not imposed for honest errors in forecasting.[23] Where material facts are fully disclosed in the exercise of fair and honest business practices, there is no liability.[24] However, forecasts that are remote, contingent, or conjectural may violate federal securities laws and result in liability to investors. In cases *not involving accountants*, courts have granted injunctions against using misleading projections in the sale of securities,[25] have enjoined the voting of proxies

18. A "financial forecast" for an enterprise is an estimate of the most probable financial position, results of operations, and changes in financial position for one or more future periods.

19. *Management Advisory Services Guideline No. 3:* "Guidelines for Systems for the Preparation of Financial Forecasts" (New York: American Institute of Certified Public Accountants, 1975).

20. *Statement of Position of the Accounting Standards Division: Presentation and Disclosure of Financial Forecasts* (New York: American Institute of Certified Public Accountants, 1975).

21. *Guide for a Review of a Financial Forecast* (New York: American Institute of Certified Public Accountants, 1980). This publication describes procedures an accountant should apply in reviewing a financial forecast and provides guidance on the form and content for the accountant's report. While the accountant states whether (1) the forecast is presented in accordance with AICPA guidelines and (2) the underlying assumptions are reasonable, the accountant is instructed to disclaim responsibility for (1) updating and (2) the attainment of the forecast.

22. *CCH AICPA Professional Standards*, AU § 550.

23. In *Dolgow v. Anderson* stockholders of Monsanto Chemical Company sued Monsanto and its principal officers and directors, claiming that defendants manipulated stock prices to their advantage by making bullish predictions about the firm's future while selling their Monsanto stock and thereby violated section 10(b) of the Securities Exchange Act. The lower court held that a suit cannot proceed as a class action unless the plaintiffs can show a high probability of winning on the merits, and both denied plaintiffs' right to proceed as a class action and granted defendants' motion for summary judgment. 43 F.R.D. 472 (E.D.N.Y. 1968). The United States Court of Appeals for the Second Circuit reversed both the granting of summary judgment and the disallowance of the class action. 438 F.2d 825 (2d Cir. 1970). Upon remand, the district court reviewed the evidence developed in pretrial discovery and again granted summary judgment. This time the Second Circuit sustained the lower court. 464 F.2d 437 (2d Cir. 1972).

The value of this case as a precedent is doubtful. Attorney Harold S. Bloomenthal notes in his *Securities and Federal Corporate Law*, volume 3A, page 11-86, that some courts have been overtly hostile to class actions. At page 11-87 he gives this analysis of the Second Circuit's decision to affirm the lower court in *Dolgow*: "What it appears to have done is avoid a determination of the issue out of deference to a district court judge (Jack B. Weinstein) for whom it has considerable respect. What Judge Weinstein appears to have done is to go to extraordinary lengths to restrict the use of class actions as a basis for a strike suit, in the process denying plaintiffs both the right to maintain a class action and the right to a jury trial. One cannot but speculate about the further agonizing that would have resulted if the circuit court had concluded that the entry of the second summary judgment was inappropriate as it might well have done." It appears that no other courts have followed *Dolgow*, but several have rejected it. Miller v. Mackey Int'l, 452 F.2d 424 (5th Cir. 1971); Fogel v. Wolfgang, 47 F.R.D. 213 (S.D.N.Y. 1969); Mersay v. First Republic Corp. of Am., 43 F.R.D. 465 (S.D.N.Y. 1968).

24. In Kohler v. Kohler Co., 319 F.2d 634 (1963), the plaintiff owned over 21,000 of the 200,000 shares of Kohler Co. (a closely held corporation) and had been an employee, director, and secretary of the firm. When he indicated a desire to sell, the firm sent a partner from Ernst & Ernst (auditor for Kohler Co.), who projected values of Kohler Co. stock using comparative ratios of publicly traded competitors—Crane and American Standard. The plaintiff ascertained the percentage ratio of market value to book value for both Crane and Standard and averaged the two. He then applied the average to Kohler Co. book value of $155.60 per share, which resulted in a figure of $117.48. He commented that the calculation would justify a price of $120 per share, and the parties contracted at that price. The plaintiff then sued both Kohler Co. and the auditor, contending among other things, that the figures used were not comparable because Kohler Co. funded and amortized its past service cost while American-Standard and Crane Company did not. The United States Court of Appeals for the Seventh Circuit affirmed dismissal. Since the firm both selected proper accounting methods and made a full disclosure of them, it had no duty to explain or justify its accounting procedures to the plaintiff, who was no novice in stock transactions or the company's activities and who had himself initiated the transaction.

25. In SEC v. F. S. Johns & Co., 207 F. Supp. 566 (D.N.J. 1962), the defendant published a report indicating that several projects "in negotiation nearing completion" would make it possible to project earnings of between forty-five cents and fifty cents a share within six months and that highly profitable results were projected for the calendar year. When the defendant's only justification was that the statements were not misleading because they related to matters in the future, the court held that defendant could not rely on the literal truth of a statement that—in the light of undisclosed facts—was nothing more than a half-truth. The court said: "Nor may refuge be sought in the argument that representations made to induce sale of stock dealt merely with forecasts of future events relating to projected earnings and the value of the securities except to the extent that there is a rational basis from existing facts upon which such forecast can be made, and a fair disclosure of material facts."

In SEC v. R. A. Holman & Co., 366 F.2d 456 (2d Cir. 1966), the court held there was no adequate factual basis for a securities salesman's representation that the stock of a boat manufacturer would rise to specified higher prices as a result of enthusiasm generated by a forthcoming boat show or more participation by Grumman Aircraft in the firm's management.

For other examples of SEC enforcement action in connection with improper use of forecasts, *see* SEC v. Glen Alden Corp., CCH Fed. Sec. L. Rep. ¶92,280 (1968) (injunction); In the Matter of Investors Management Co., Inc., CCH Fed. Sec. L. Rep. ¶78,163 (1971) (censure by the Commission); In the Matter of Merrill Lynch, Pierce, Fenner & Smith, CCH Sec. L. Rep. ¶77,629 (suspension of certain activities and censure of certain individuals).

where predictions were speculative in nature,[26] and have imposed liability for damages on those making baseless estimates.[27]

In *Sprayregen v. Livingston Oil Co.*[28] the court refused to dismiss a complaint against the corporation, three directors, and the accounting firm of Peat, Marwick, Mitchell & Co., where it alleged that two directors, with approval of a third, predicted earnings in a speech in New York City before the New York Society of Security Analysts although they knew the fig-

ures, which had been prepared by the accountants, were erroneous. Similarly, in *Marx v. Computer Sciences Corp.*[29] the Ninth Circuit held it was error to dismiss a section 10(b) action based on an erroneous forecast in a speech by an officer and director of Computer Sciences Corp. at a meeting of the New York Society of Security Analysts. The court held that it was for the jury to decide whether liability should be imposed for (1) ignoring facts seriously undermining the accuracy of the forecast or (2) failure to reveal, along with the forecast, that the company was having serious operational problems with a major new product.

Liability for Failure to Disclose Underlying Assumptions

Whenever projections or forecasts are made public, the communication should clearly indicate the true state of affairs, including any critical underlying assumptions. In *Beecher v. Able,* the plaintiffs purchased $75 million of convertible debentures issued by the defendant, Douglas Aircraft Company, in 1966. The court held that the prospectus was materially misleading[30] and awarded the plaintiffs damages for their losses.[31]

The Douglas registration statement became effective July 12, 1966, and contained the statement that ". . . it is very likely that net income, if any, for fiscal 1966 will be nominal." The actual result was a disastrous net loss of $52 million.

In examining the required standard of conduct, the court noted that the "due-diligence" defense available to accountants and other experts is not available to an issuer and that an issuer is liable if the registration statement is materially false. In terms of an earnings forecast the court said:

> Plaintiffs concede that an earnings forecast is not actionable merely because the facts do not turn out as predicted. . . . However, investors are likely to attach great importance to income projections because they speak directly to a corporation's likely earnings for the future and because they are ordinarily made by persons who are well informed about the corporation's prospects. Therefore, in view of the policy of the federal securities laws of promoting full and fair disclosure, a high standard of care must be imposed on

---

26. In Union Pacific R. Co. v. Chicago and Northwestern Ry. Co., 226 F. Supp. 400 (N.D. Ill. 1964), the defendant predicted merger savings of $25 million and made an additional prediction of earnings for an assumed three-way merger. The court found both the estimates and event speculative and without basis so as to imply underlying facts that were not true: "Predictions, estimates, and opinions . . . allow facts to be suggested or implied without direct statement. Even if they do not tend to induce belief in any particular fact, they nonetheless import the existence of unspecified facts which support the conclusion. The shareholder may be led readily to assume, contrary to fact, that the predictor has special knowledge or unique information to bear out fully his prediction, and be induced to rely upon a supposed expert judgment of the mysteries of finance."

27. In Green v. Jonhop, Inc., 358 F. Supp. 413 (D. Ore. 1973), the plaintiff stock purchaser obtained a judgment against the underwriter, who made a market for the stock; the principal shareholder, who was director and executive vice president; and the issuing corporation. The court found that the underwriter circulated a misleading projection that 1969 sales would be $1 million and recommended purchase of the stock without mentioning previous substantial losses: "American Western had no basis for making such an estimate and made no investigation of its accuracy. . . . It is a violation of the anti-fraud provisions of the 1934 Act to recommend a security without an adequate and reasonable basis."

In holding the corporate issuer and the director liable, the court held that when they learned of the misleading statements that the underwriter was circulating, they had an obligation first to notify the underwriter to cease the conduct and then to report the conduct to the SEC and/or issue a public statement correcting or disaffirming the inaccurate information: "Jones' and Jonhop's silence and inaction encouraged reliance by the public on the misrepresentations and omissions in the comment, since it was well known that American Western was the underwriter and principal dealer in Jonhop stock. Such acquiescence through silence is a form of aiding and abetting cognizable under § 10(b) and Rule 10b-5. Brennan v. Midwestern United Life Ins. Co. 417 F.2d 147 (7th Cir. 1969), *cert. denied*, 397 U.S. 989. . . ."

In Blakely v. Lisac, 357 F. Supp. 255 (D. Ore. 1972), a president and director was held liable to the class of shareholder plaintiffs for their losses resulting from a baseless forecast of sales of $4 million and a profit (with no mention of prior losses). These forecasts were given to a reporter, who published them in a newspaper article in the *Oregonian*. (Although this case did involve an accountant, the accountant was apparently not involved in any of the forecasting aspects. The accountant's liability aspects are discussed in Chapter 8.)

In Derdiarian v. Futterman Corp., 38 F.R.D. 178 (S.D.N.Y. 1965), the court approved a settlement where the plaintiffs claimed their losses resulted from a baseless cash flow projection in a prospectus. In earlier proceedings in the same case, 223 F. Supp. 265 (1953), this court held that an action for damages under the federal securities laws survives the death of the alleged wrongdoer.

28. Sprayregen v. Livingston Oil Co., 295 F. Supp. 1376 (S.D.N.Y. 1968).

29. Marx v. Computer Sciences Corp., 507 F.2d 485 (9th Cir. 1974).

30. Beecher v. Able, 374 F. Supp. 341 (S.D.N.Y. 1974). See "Douglas Aircraft's Stormy Flightpath," *Fortune,* December 1966, pp. 166–67; "Why Douglas is in a Downdraft," *Business Week,* October 23, 1966, p. 176.

31. Beecher v. Able, CCH Fed. Sec. L. Rep. 95,016 (S.D.N.Y. 1975).

184

those who, although not required to do so, neverthe-less make projections.

Consequently, this court holds that an earnings forecast must be based on facts from which a reasonably prudent investor would conclude that it was highly probable that the forecast would be realized. Moreover, any assumptions underlying the projection must be disclosed if their validity is sufficiently in doubt that a reasonably prudent investor, if he knew of the underlying assumptions, might be deterred from crediting the forecast. Disclosure of such underlying assumptions is ". . . necessary to make . . . [the forecast] . . . not misleading. . . ." 15 U.S.C. § 77k(a).[32]

The court found it likely that an appreciable number of ordinary prudent investors would have read the "income, if any" passage as a break-even forecast or could have concluded that the company's failure to mention the likelihood of substantial losses, together with its reference to the improbability of substantial profits, was meant to exclude the likelihood of substantial losses.

The court then concluded that Douglas did not meet the required standard of conduct. Although the Douglas internal forecast at the time was relatively close to break-even, the court noted that this was based on an assumption of significant improvements in assembly performance, which was in turn based on assumptions that some of the problems (obtaining skilled labor and prompt delivery of parts) besetting the Aircraft Division would be partially resolved. All previous forecasts for the year had failed.

The court concluded that the prospects of making improvements sufficient to avoid substantial losses were far too uncertain to warrant a forecast that included the suggestion that Douglas would have no substantial losses in fiscal 1966. In this situation, the court found that Douglas was required to disclose its assumptions to avoid a misleading forecast:

Douglas was required to disclose that the forecast was based on an assumption that conditions in the Aircraft Division would have to improve before the company could expect to avoid substantial losses and that earlier forecasts in 1966 had to be modified. Disclosure of these facts was required in order to make the statement about the defendant's earnings prospects not misleading.

The assumption that conditions would improve sufficiently for the company to avoid substantial losses was material since the assumption was sufficiently doubtful that reasonable investors, had they been informed of the assumption, might have been deterred from crediting the forecast.

The court similarly finds that disclosure of the fact that previous forecasts had failed was required since disclosure might have placed investors on notice either that Douglas' forecasting techniques were faulty or that the adverse conditions affecting the Aircraft Division made income forecasting unusually difficult. In either case, reasonable investors might have thereby been deterred from crediting the forecast.[33]

Based on this case, the prudent course of conduct is to disclose critical assumptions that are necessary to permit the attainment of a forecast.

Duty to Correct Erroneous Forecast

Section 10(b) of the Exchange Act imposes a duty to revise forecasts which have become misleading despite the fact that the forecast was accurate when made. In *Ross v. A. H. Robbins Co.*[34] the court held there was a duty to correct the projection of a favorable future for the firm's product:

The mere passage of time would not alone deter the trader in the market from relying on these statements. Such reliance does not appear to this Court to be unreasonable. The defendants therefore had a duty to correct these prior statements when they became aware of subsequent events which rendered those statements misleading.

In contrast with the duty of a corporation to correct its own erroneous forecast, there is no duty to correct erroneous earnings projections of financial analysts when they appear in the press unless the firm has become so involved in projections by outsiders that it has assumed such a duty.[35]

Liability for Insider Use of Nonpublic Forecasts

Anyone affiliated with the issuer, whether officer, director, stockholder, underwriter, auditor, or attorney, who gains access to nonpublic forecasts and uses them for personal benefit or transmits the information to others who so use it is in violation of federal securities laws and liable to those who trade without the information.[36]

---

32. Beecher v. Able, 374 F. Supp. 348.

33. Ibid. at p. 354.

34. Ross v. A. H. Robbins Co., CCH Fed. Sec. L. Rep. ¶ 96,737 (S.D.N.Y. 1979).

35. Elkind v. Liggett & Myers, Inc., 635 F.2d 156 (2d Cir. 1980).

36. Shapiro v. Merrill Lynch, Pierce, Fenner & Smith, Inc., 495 F.2d 228 (2d Cir. 1974). In order to impose liability under section 10(b) of the Exchange Act, plaintiff must meet the scienter requirement by showing the tipper knowingly tipped material information for use of the tippee.

ICC Lack of Power to Inspect Budgets and Forecasts

In *Burlington Northern, Inc. v. ICC*,[37] a three-judge panel held that the Interstate Commerce Commission could not require the Burlington Northern (a common carrier by railroad) to produce its budget and income forecasts for submission to a Senate committee. The inquiry concerned legislation to provide financial assistance to railroads and the attempt to determine the extent of their need for financial assistance. In the face of public information that Burlington continued its quarterly dividend of $8,615,000 notwithstanding a substantial loss in that quarter, four of the nine judges voted for a rehearing before the full court. The rehearing was denied because it was not favored by five of the judges. The four-judge panel based its position on the need for implementing the remedial purpose of regulation. They noted that latitude for investigation by a regulatory commission adds flexibility to the implementation of legislative policy "to make investigations of abuses and problems that may call in part for use of existing administrative authority and in part for new legislation."

INTERIM REPORTING

Accounting and Auditing Rules

The SEC requires reporting companies (those having 500 or more stockholders and assets in excess of $1 million) to file balance sheets at the end of the current and corresponding prior-year quarter, income statements for the current and corresponding prior-year quarter, and other specified data. Although some stock exchanges require quarterly reports to shareholders, the SEC does not.

The SEC lacks specific authority to require audits of quarterly data; however, the SEC does require firms having actively traded securities to append a footnote to the annual financials which discloses comparative quarterly net sales, gross profit, income before extraordinary items, and net income. *SEC Accounting Series Release No. 177* requires the auditor to perform a limited review of the footnote, which is otherwise considered unaudited. This limited review procedure applies to firms listed on the New York and American Stock Exchanges and those carried on the National Association of Securities Dealers Automatic Quotation System (NASDAQ).

The standards for limited review of quarterly data were developed by the AICPA and are contained in *CCH AICPA Professional Standards*, AU § 720. These include:

1. An understanding of the accounting system and its internal controls.
2. Analytical review of interim financials to determine that relationships are within expected norms.
3. Reading minutes of meeting of stockholders, directors, and committees.
4. Inquiry of accounting officers.

AICPA standards provide that a report based on the limited review "should be addressed to the entity's board of directors and should be dated as of the completion of the review.[38] This report covers deviations from GAAP and weaknesses in internal control. According to the standards, the report is designed for the board, may be furnished to management, but may not be released to the public.

Where the auditor takes no exception to the quarterly data, there is no need to mention the limited review in the auditor's report on the annual financials, provided the quarterly data is labeled as unaudited. However, where there are exceptions, internal control weaknesses, or limitations on scope of the review, AU § 519.14 requires the auditor to include a full disclosure of the matter in the annual audit report.

Court Decisions

In *Republic Technology Fund, Inc. v. Lionel Corp.*[39] the plaintiffs, pursuant to a merger, exchanged their common stock of Hathaway Instruments, Inc., for convertible preferred stock of Lionel. Lionel's unaudited financials for the six months ending June 20, 1961, were used both in the Form S-1 registration statement (filed with the SEC to register the Lionel shares to be issued in the merger) and in the proxy materials submitted to both Hathaway and Lionel stockholders to obtain approval of the merger.

The unaudited six-months' figures showed a loss for Lionel of $84,000. However, after the year-end adjustments, the six-month loss of Lionel proved to be $1,898,609. Plaintiffs alleged that failure to provide for necessary year-end adjustments made the six-months' figures misleading and claimed damages under section 17 of the Securities Act of 1933 and section 10(b) of the Securities Exchange Act of 1934.

The year-end adjustments not reflected in the June 30 interim statement included:

1. Inventory write-downs of $1,476,776.

37. Burlington Northern, Inc. v. ICC, 323 F. Supp. 273, *aff'd*, 462 F.2d 280 (D.C. Cir. 1972), *cert. denied*, 409 U.S. 891 (1972).

38. *CCH AICPA Professionals Standards*, AU § 720.20.

39. Republic Technology Fund, Inc. v. Lionel Corp., 483 F.2d 540 (1973).

2. Sales returns and allowances of $166,000.
3. Write-off of research and development of $389,983.
4. Write-off of deferred selling, advertising, and service expenses of $249,000.

Furthermore, Lionel's Anton-Imco division carried an asset item of $998,000 for goodwill, despite a $189,000 loss for the first six months of 1961. Although the interim statements included no adjustment for these items, Mr. Easton (the senior managing accountant for S. D. Leidesdorf & Co., independent certified public accountants), who worked on the Lionel audits in 1960 and 1961, testified "to the effect that the interim statement was accurate (in addition to being in accordance with the same generally accepted accounting principles used in Lionel's year-end statements and its prior financial statements)." He testified, concerning the goodwill item, that the operating loss was outweighed by the fact that the firm was only in its first year of operation as a Lionel subsidiary and, in his words, was "engaged in the development of a new machine—I believe it was a money sensor, a money changing device—and based on all the information that was available at that time the prospects for success seemed very reasonable."

The United States Court of Appeals for the Second Circuit, in holding that the lack of disclosure concerning the goodwill constituted a misrepresentation, said:

> We cannot accept Mr. Easton's evaluation as a matter of law. The notes to the consolidated interim statements of income contain the following statement: "This company recently designed and developed a currency recognizing device, several prototype models of which have been built up to this time. The device has not yet been marketed and there is no assurance at this time as to whether it will be a profitable item." Nowhere do the notes in any way indicate that Anton-Imco had shown a $189,000 loss as of June 30 or that the retention of $998,000 as its good will was based upon the prospects of success of this currency recognizing device which had not yet been marketed, Cf. Petersen Engine Co., Inc., 2 S.E.C. 893, 906 (1937); Lewis American Airways, Inc., 1 S.E.C. 330, 342 (1936) (misleading to designate "patent applications" as "patent rights" or "patents" under intangible assets heading in a balance sheet). Indeed, since the interim statements do not include a balance sheet but only consolidated statements of income they contained no reference at all to the good will item. This makes them, in our view, all the more misleading. The person viewing the statements would have no reason to suspect that the consolidated earnings were at least subject to question since despite a loss on the part of a major division for the first half-year, its good will was still being carried at a full initial valuation equivalent to about 8 percent of the Lionel total book value. Cf. R. Mautz, Financial Reporting by Diversified Companies

157–58 (1968) quoted in T. Fiflis & H. Kripke, Accounting for Business Lawyers 556–57 (1971) (investor needs to know "relative importance" of several industries comprising a diversified corporation accurately to forecast future prospects). This is particularly so when the notes emphasize optimistic items, e.g., calling attention to the fact that the interim statement did not include certain "special items" (including such things as elimination of a $22,444 reserve for certain employee benefits) that would have improved the earnings by $.10 per share in toto for the first six months of 1961. In other words, the voters on the merger were being shown the frosting on the cake with no allusion in the statements to the fact that a substantial part of the cake itself was dried out, if not mildewed. Cf. Globe Aircraft Corp., 26 S.E.C. 43, 46–47 (1947).

> At the very least, good disclosure accounting would have required the notation of some uncertainty regarding the overall interim Lionel profit picture based on this item alone, uncertainty which should have been footnoted, to avoid misleading the stockholder. See SEC Accounting Series Release No. 62, 4 CCH Fed. Sec. L. Rep. ¶ 72,081 at 62,149 (1947) (footnoted explanation must be included in a summary earning statement if the information it would contain is of such "special significance [that] . . . its omission would be likely to give rise to misleading inferences"). Cf. Metropolitan Personal Loan Corp., 7 S.E.C. 234, 239 (1940) (even assuming deferred asset account could be written off in a single year, footnoted explanation required to make income statement not misleading). While stockholders who are voting on a merger are not to be treated like "children in kindergarten," cf. Gerstle v. Gamble-Skogmo, Inc., supra, 478 F.2d at 1297, they are entitled to disclosure of the bitter with the sweet. They are at least entitled to assume that the interim financial statements furnished them by their own company or the other party to the merger will give them better than "ballpark" figures and be based on principles of conservatism which the American Institute of Certified Public Accountants speaks of as "a general tendency toward early recognition of unfavorable events and minimization of the amount of net assets and net income." I APB Accounting Principles § 1022.27 at 140 (CCH ed. 1971). The stockholders are entitled to assume that uncertainty concerning profit or loss should be at least footnoted in the first financial statement issued after the uncertainty arises.[40]

The court also held that the interim statement was misleading in failing to include some adjustment for write-off of research and development and said:

> Research and development (R&D) costs totaling $226,983 in the toy and train division and $163,000 in Lionel Labs were written off at year's end. It is no answer, we feel, to say as both Mr. Easton testified and the court "found" (again, basically repeating Easton's testimony) that "Lionel reviewed its research

---

40. Ibid., pp. 546–47.

and development projects as at June 30" and when Easton's firm, Liedesdorf, made the year-end audit it found nothing to indicate that an adjustment for R&D expense write-off should have been made at June 30. Such findings tell us nothing about the basis for Lionel's and Liedesdorf's conclusions. It is a partial answer to say, as appellee's brief points out, that in fact $40,205.99 of R&D expense was written off at June 30, but an examination of the exhibit to which this refers shows that this was in the *electronics* division, for "abandoned projects." There remains unexplained why no adjustment was made at June 30 in the *toy and train* division, and here too we think the burden of going forward was upon Lionel. Here too we are talking about a substantial write-off item which at year's end represented about 2 per cent of the book value of the company, as well as several cents a share profit (or loss).[41]

The court also found that an adjustment for the raw material price variance should have been applied to the interim statements and remanded the case to the lower court for findings in accordance with the opinion.

In *Kaiser-Frazer Corp. v. Otis & Co.*,[42] an inventory adjustment was allocated wholly to increasing last-quarter earnings in an unaudited tabulation, whereas the allocation should have been prorated to prior periods. It was held that accompanying disclosure with a footnote was inadequate to correct the misleading impression. Because of the misleading registration statement, the court found Kaiser-Frazer's contract to sell stock to defendant was against public policy and unenforceable.

MARKET-VALUE REPORTING

The duty to disclose market values must necessarily depend upon the circumstances. The duty increases in direct proportion to the increases in (1) the reliability of known information, (2) the magnitude of the difference between market value and book value, and (3) the probability of liquidation of assets and realization of the gain or loss either through sale of individual assets or through liquidation of the entire firm. Some courts now hold that the third criterion is critical in finding a duty to report market values. Other courts may well relax the third criterion when the first two criteria are sufficiently met.

In *Speed v. Transamerica Corp.*[43] it was held that the majority shareholder (Transamerica) violated rights of minority shareholders by offering to buy minority shares in Axton-Fisher Tobacco Company without disclosing that (1) there was an unrecorded

appreciation in value of the tobacco inventory and (2) the parent intended to realize it by liquidating the subsidiary. Similarly, in *Gerstle v. Gamble-Skogmo, Inc.*,[44] it was held that minority shareholders were misled in approving the merger of General (General Outdoor Advertising Co., Inc.) into Skogmo (Gamble-Skogmo) when proxy statements failed to disclose: (1) appreciation in value of advertising plants over book value and (2) intent to sell the appreciated properties after the merger. Although General had appraisals of the remaining plants and firm offers indicating that market values greatly exceeded book values, the court's finding of materiality was based on the failure to disclose the intent to sell. This intent made the existence of the value difference material to the vote on the merger.

In *SEC v. Bangor Punta Corp.*[45] the court held that a registration statement and a prospectus pertaining to an offer to exchange Bangor Punta stock for Piper Aircraft Company stock were misleading because of the failure to disclose that the carrying value of the Bangor and Aroostook Railroad (BAR) acquired in a combination was almost four times the offer of a willing buyer. The book value was $18.4 million, and the highest offer for a sale was $5 million. It is not clear what effect negotiations for the sale had on the court's ruling. If the sale had not been made, Bangor Punta would have had to invest $5 million in capital outlays for the railroad to break even over the next five years.

The court required Bangor Punta to offer rescission to shareholders who had accepted the offer to exchange their Piper stock for Bangor Punta stock.

In *Speed, Skogmo,* and *Bangor Punta* the market values were known with a high degree of certainty. In both *Speed* and *Skogmo* there was a failure to disclose that assets were undervalued, while in *Bangor Punta* there was a failure to disclose that assets were *overvalued*. The *Speed* and *Skogmo* courts considered the intent to liquidate undervalued assets as critical to finding a duty to disclose market values, while the *Bangor Punta* court might have found a duty to disclose market value of assets even in absence of any intent to liquidate the misstated assets.

MATERIALITY

Materiality in Conducting an Audit versus Materiality in Financial Reporting

No little confusion has surrounded the use of the words *material* and *materiality* in the accounting pro-

---

41. Ibid., p. 549.

42. Kaiser-Frazer Corp. v. Otis & Co., 195 F.2d 838 (2d Cir.), 344 U.S. 856 (1952).

43. Speed v. Transamerica Corp., 99 F. Supp. 808 (D. Del. 1951), *aff'd*, 235 F.2d 369 (3d Cir. 1956).

44. Gerstle v. Gamble-Skogmo, Inc., 298 F. Supp. 66 (E.D.N.Y. 1969), 332 F. Supp. 644 (E.D.N.Y. 1971), *aff'd*. 478 F.2d 1281 (1973).

45. SEC v. Bangor Punta Corp., 331 F. Supp. 1154 (S.D.N.Y. 1971), *aff'd*, 480 F.2d 341 (2d Cir. 1973).

fession. The reason for this confusion is that authors use the words in various contexts with various meanings without making careful distinctions for the differing uses. Materiality in the context of applying audit procedures is quite different from materiality in the context of financial reporting. For example, an item that might be material in the context of an auditor's examination of cash or verification of inventory may have no relevance whatever for financial reporting. A *general* definition of materiality is broad enough to cover both uses of the word:

> *Materiality*—The quality or state of being something requiring serious consideration by reason of being either certainly or probably vital to the proper settlement of an issue.[46]

This definition embraces the *auditor's examination* of cash or inventory in order to identify those things "requiring serious consideration" *by the auditor*. It also embraces the matter of *financial reporting,* and in this context it relates to those things about cash and inventory that require serious consideration *by the investor*. In both cases the matters that are material are those that may be vital. But in the first case the importance is viewed from the auditor's position (in conducting an examination in accordance with professional standards), and in the second case importance is viewed from the investor's position. Of course, the *means* of determining materiality in both cases will be by the exercise of professional judgment of the auditor.[47]

The overlooked fact that causes most of the confusion is that in applying professional judgment to determine the materiality of an item for financial reporting purposes, the auditor must of necessity look to the probable importance of the item to the "average investor" or "reasonable-person investor." As early as 1895, the terms *material* and *materiality* as they relate to financial reporting were identified with the investor's point of view. Lord Davey's 1895 report defined materiality as follows:

> Every contract or fact is material which would influence the judgment of a prudent investor in determining whether he would subscribe for the shares of debentures offered by the prospectus.[48]

SEC rules related to financial reporting adopt a similar point of view:

> The term "material" when used to qualify a requirement for the furnishing of information as to any subject limits the information required to those matters as to which an average prudent investor ought reasonably to be informed before purchasing the security registered.[49]

Once the materiality of an item in the conduct of an audit is distinguished from materiality in financial reporting, the distinction for liability can also be perceived. Thus the duties of a CPA to uncover an impropriety in the course of the audit and to report the matter once it is discovered are entirely different. For example, the CPA's duty to discover management fraud depends on the materiality of the fraud, its effect on financial position, the pervasiveness of it, and the likelihood of discovery through standard professional procedures. However, once management fraud is discovered, the duty to disclose depends on whether the prototype investor would find the matter of importance. These are two entirely different tests of materiality, which must not be confused.

Illegal political contributions provide a good illustration of the distinction. An auditor probably has no duty to discover a $100,000 illegal campaign contribution (or bribe) made by a major business firm. It would probably not be material either to financial position, to income, or to major elements of financial position. However, once the auditor stumbles onto the practice, the duty to *disclose* (as opposed to the duty to find) is determined by the probable importance (to the reasonable prototype investor) of the fact that top management is engaged in felonies consisting of illegal campaign contributions (or bribes).[50]

Materiality and the Audit

Materiality in the context of applying procedures in the course of an audit relates to the relative importance of the matter in terms of professional auditing standards. It embraces questions such as: (1) Did the auditor fail to exercise due care required by professional standards in failing to discover a deficiency in internal control? (2) Was the omission material to the exercise of due professional care?

---

46. By permission. From *Webster's Third New International Dictionary* © 1981 by G. & C. Merriam Co., Publishers of the Merriam-Webster Dictionaries.

47. The definition of materiality in Eric L. Kohler, *A Dictionary for Accountants,* 4th ed. (Englewood Cliffs: Prentice-Hall), p. 278 includes this: *"Value judgments* are the usual and often the only means of determining relative importance; they are based on such factors as the relative size and general characteristic of the item and the assumed responsibilities of management to stockholders, employees, and the public."

48. This is quoted in "Toward Standards for Materiality," *Journal of Accountancy,* June 1973, p. 62 from Lord Davey Report, Cmd. 7779 (1895) par. 14(5).

49. 17 C.F.R. § 230.405(1).

50. Compare the view of David B. Isbell, an attorney, in "An Overview of Accountants' Duties and Liabilities under the Federal Securities Laws and a Closer Look at Whistle-Blowing," 35 *Ohio St. L.J.* 261–79 (1974). He states: "Thus if the question is asked whether an auditor has an obligation to report his corporate client's illegal contributions in the last presidential campaign to the Special Prosecutor's office, the answer, if the penalties to which the client is subject would not be financially material, is no."

EXHIBIT 13-4
The Effect of Materiality on Audit Reports

Circumstances for Departure from Standard Audit Report	*Required Type of Report*	
Limitation on scope	**Qualified** "except for" Opinion paragraph refers to possible effects on financial statements.	**Disclaimer** Separate paragraph discloses limitation—no reference to procedures performed.
Opinion based partly on report of another auditor	**Unqualified** Scope paragraph discloses reliance and opinion paragraph refers to report of other auditors.	
Departure from GAAP	**Qualified*** "except for"	**Adverse*** Separate paragraph discloses substantive reasons and principal effects.
Departure from an official pronouncement	**Qualified†** "except for"	**Adverse†** Separate paragraph discloses substantive reasons and principal effects.
Lack of consistency	**Qualified*** "except for"	**Disclaimer as to consistency*** Middle paragraph explains inadeqaute records or principles for prior year. Opinion paragraph omits consistency reference.
Uncertainty	**Qualified** "subject to"	**Disclaimer** Separate paragraph discloses substantive reasons.
Emphasis of a matter	**Unqualified** Separate paragraph discusses matter, such as insider transactions.	
	Lesser Greater Materiality (risk)	

* Where there is an accounting change to an incorrect principle, it is not necessary to disclaim consistency, since the opinion will be a departure from GAAP.

† Where the departure is *necessary* to make the financials not misleading, an unqualified opinion is issued with an explanation of the circumstances.

Source: Denzil Y. Causey, Jr., "Newly Emerging Standards of Auditor Responsibility," *Accounting Review*, January 1976, p. 25.

Materiality and Financial Reporting

Materiality has an important, but complex and confusing, role in financial reporting. Exhibit 13-4 shows the effect of materiality on an auditor's report.[51] Exhibit 13-5 depicts a legal scale of materiality. The legal standard for materiality in each case is formulated in terms of the impact of the misstatement *on the user* of the financials.

Stop number 5 on the legal scale (Exhibit 13-5) is sufficient for imposing criminal liability as well as civil. One court said, in upholding the criminal conviction of a CPA:

The scheme need not be fraudulent upon its face or misrepresent any material fact. All that is necessary is that it be a scheme reasonably calculated to deceive persons of ordinary prudence and comprehension.[52]

Stop number 4 on the scale also represents a degree of materiality sufficient to impose criminal liability. It is the kind of situation apt to be most upsetting to auditors in a civil case. If the auditor tries to show compliance with GAAP, the courts may hold (and have held) that compliance with GAAP in such circumstances is not a conclusive defense.[53]

Stop number 3 on the scale represents materiality required by the earlier cases as a condition to imposing

51. *CCH AICPA Professional Standards*, AU § 509.

52. United States v. Bruce, 488 F.2d 1224 (5th Cir. 1973), *cert. denied*, Oct. 15, 1974.

53. United States v. Simon, 425 F.2d 796 (2d Cir. 1969), *cert. denied*, 397 U.S. 1006 (1970).

EXHIBIT 13-5
The Legal Scale of Materiality

Standards of Materiality		*Effect Produced by Information Meeting the Standard*
Reasonably calculated to deceive	←—⑤—→	Probable loss of investment
No warning of impending disaster	←—④—→	Possible loss of investment
Determining factor for a prudent or conservative investor	←—③—→	Deterrent to a prudent investor interested in the type of security involved.
Substantial factor influencing conduct of reasonable investors including speculators	←—②—→	Possible effect on the value of the corporation's stock or securities
Matters of only trifling importance	←—①—→	Remote or no effect

Source: Denzil Y. Causey, Jr., "Newly Emerging Standards of Auditor Responsibility," *Accounting Review*, January 1976, p. 26.

civil liability on auditors.[54] In *TSC Industries, Inc. v. Northway, Inc.*[55] the U.S. Supreme Court held that stop 2 on the scale is the appropriate criterion. The item is not required to be a "determining factor" as in stop 3; it is now sufficient if there is a substantial likelihood or probability that the matter would affect investment decisions.

The Supreme Court's materiality decision related to disclosures in a proxy statement soliciting stockholder approval of a proposed merger. However, the Court's criterion applies in all cases under federal securities laws.[56] The *TSC* Court stated the criterion thus:

> An omitted fact is material if there is a substantial likelihood that a reasonable shareholder would consider it important in deciding how to vote. . . . It does not require proof of a substantial likelihood that disclosure of the omitted fact would have caused the reasonable investor to change his vote. What the standard does contemplate is a showing of a substantial

likelihood that, under all the circumstances, the omitted fact would have assumed actual significance in the deliberations of the reasonable shareholder. Put another way, there must be a substantial likelihood that the disclosure of the omitted fact would have been viewed by the reasonable investor as having significantly altered the "total mix" of information made available.

SUMMARY

Auditing involves the biggest dollar exposure to malpractice liability. The auditor is liable for defalcation losses that take place after the fraud would have been revealed by application of ordinary audit procedures. Auditors continue to have difficulty with overstated inventories and receivables.

Write-up work involves bookkeeping, but preparation of unaudited financials may or may not involve bookkeeping procedures. Where the public accountant knows that the data are incomplete, inaccurate, or unsatisfactory, it is necessary to obtain revised information or withdraw. Where client personnel are not qualified accountants, public accountants should insist on aging schedules for accounts receivable and do some inventory price testing. Suspense accounts should never appear on published financial statements because (1) the amount may be the result of offsetting debits and credits or (2) it could result in liability if its investigation reveals fraud.

While it is against public policy to permit professional persons to contract away all responsibility for their work, contracts for management advisory services can contain reasonable limitations of liability or may provide that the client assumes certain risks.

---

54. Escott v. BarChris Construction Corp., 283 F. Supp. 643 (S.D.N.Y. 1968). The *BarChris* court defined materiality as matters that would affect the investment decision—not minor inaccuracies or errors as to irrelevant matters. Since the *BarChris* convertible debentures were rated "B" and were characterized as speculative, the judge reasoned that investors were attracted by the conversion feature (that is, the growth potential for the stock) and that an erroneous statement of 1960 earnings at $.75 a share instead of $.65 was not material. However, in analyzing the December 31, 1960, balance sheet, he observed that "there must be some point at which errors in disclosing a company's balance sheet position become material, even to a growth-oriented investor" and held that a balance sheet error that resulted in a ratio of current assets to current liabilities of 1.9 as opposed to 1.6 was material.

55. TSC Industries, Inc. v. Northway, Inc., 426 U.S. 438 (1976).

56. Alton Box Board Co. v. Goldman, Sachs & Co., 560 F.2d 916 (8th Cir. 1977).

SUGGESTIONS FOR FURTHER READING

AICPA Computer Services Executive Committee. *The Auditor's Study and Evaluation of Internal Control in EDP Systems.* New York: American Institute of Certified Public Accountants, 1977.

Copeland, Ronald M., and Ted D. Englebrecht. "Statistical Sampling—An Uncertain Defense against Legal Liability." *The CPA Journal,* November 1975, pp. 23-27.

Elliott, Robert K. "Groundrules for Financial Forecasts." *Management Focus,* May/June 1981, pp. 15-19.

QUESTIONS AND PROBLEMS

1. What are three critical points to consider in an inventory audit?
2. What effect does confirmation of payables have on the client's statute of limitations?

Verification of Cash

3. (From the May 1971 Uniform CPA Examination)

    The cashier of Baker Company covered a shortage in his cash working fund with cash obtained on December 31 from a local bank by cashing an unrecorded check drawn on the Company's New York bank. The auditor would discover this manipulation by
    a. Preparing independent bank reconciliations as of December 31.
    b. Counting the cash working fund at the close of business on December 31.
    c. Investigating items returned with the bank cutoff statements.
    d. Confirming the December 31 bank balances.
4. (From the November 1971 Uniform CPA Examination)

    Kiting most likely would be detected by
    a. Tracing the amounts of daily deposits from the cash receipts journal to bank statements.
    b. Confirming accounts receivable by direct communication with debtors.
    c. Preparing a four-column proof of cash.
    d. Preparing a schedule of interbank transfers.
5. (From the May 1973 Uniform CPA Examination)

    Lapping would most likely be detected by
    a. Examination of canceled checks clearing in the bank cutoff period.
    b. Confirming year-end bank balances.
    c. Preparing a schedule of interbank transfers.
    d. Investigating responses to account-receivable confirmations.

Subsequently Discovered Information and Subsequent Events

6. Does an auditor have any responsibility for disclosure of information discovered after an audit report is issued? If so, what is the extent of the duty and how is it discharged?

7. (From the May 1971 Uniform CPA Examination)

    An example of an event occurring in the period of the auditor's field work subsequent to the end of the year being audited which normally would not require disclosure in the financial statements or auditor's report would be
    a. Decreased sales volume resulting from a general business recession.
    b. Serious damage to the company's plant from a widespread flood.
    c. Issuance of a widely advertised capital stock issue with restrictive covenants.
    d. Settlement of a large liability for considerably less than the amount recorded.
8. (From the May 1971 Uniform CPA Examination)

    Subsequent to rendering an unqualified report on the financial statements of Rosenberg Company for the year ended December 31, 1970, a CPA learns that property taxes for the year 1970 have been significantly underaccrued. This resulted from the Company's disregard of a taxing authority ruling that was made prior to completion of the CPA's examination but was not brought to his attention. Upon learning of the ruling the CPA's immediate responsibility is
    a. Advisory only, since he did not learn of the ruling until after completion of his examination.
    b. To make certain that the 1970 income statement is restated when the December 31, 1971, financial statements are prepared.
    c. To immediately issue a disclaimer of opinion relative to the 1970 financial statements.
    d. To ascertain that immediate steps are taken to inform all parties to whom this information would be important.
9. (From the November 1971 Uniform CPA Examination)

    On November 4, 1971, two months after completing field work and rendering an unqualified opinion as to the financial statements of Lambert Collieries for the year ended June 30, 1971, a CPA learns of four situations concerning this client which were not previously known to him. The CPA is required to determine that appropriate disclosure is made to persons relying upon the audited financial statements for the year ended June 30, 1971, in the situation of the
    a. Flooding of one of Lambert's two mines on October 15, 1971. This mine was acquired in 1967.
    b. Discovery on October 25, 1971, of a defect in the title to the other mine, also acquired in 1967.
    c. Settlement on November 3, 1971, of a damage suit against Lambert at an amount significantly lower than that reported in the audited balance sheet.
    d. Decline in coal prices by $2 per ton on October 1, 1971. Net income for the coming year is expected to decrease 50 percent as a result.
10. (From the May 1975 Uniform CPA Examination)

    Which of the following material events occurring subsequent to the balance sheet date would require an adjustment to the financial statements before they could be issued?
    a. Sale of long-term debt or capital stock.

b. Loss of a plant as a result of a flood.

c. Major purchase of a business, which is expected to double the sales volume.

d. Settlement of litigation, in excess of the recorded liability.

11. (From the May 1975 Uniform CPA Examination)

Harvey, CPA, is preparing an audit program for the purpose of ascertaining the occurrence of subsequent events that may require adjustment or disclosure essential to a fair presentation of the financial statements in conformity with generally accepted accounting principles. Which one of the following procedures would be least appropriate for this purpose?

a. Confirm as of the completion of field work accounts receivable which have increased significantly from the year-end date.

b. Read the minutes of the board of directors.

c. Inquire of management concerning events which may have occurred.

d. Obtain a lawyer's letter as of the completion of field work.

12. (From the May 1973 Uniform CPA Examination)

On April 14, 1973, a CPA issued an unqualified opinion on the financial statements of the Emerson Company for the year ended February 28, 1973. A structural defect in Emerson's recently completed plant first appeared in late 1972, but the CPA did not learn of it until April 25, 1973. On May 1, 1973, the CPA learned that the defect would cause material losses to the Company. The CPA's primary responsibility is

a. To determine that immediate steps are taken to inform all parties who are relying on information contained in the statements.

b. To make certain that the Company plans to provide for the losses in its financial statements for the year ended February 28, 1974.

c. To withdraw his unqualified opinion on the financial statements for the year ended February 28, 1973, and issue a disclaimer of opinion or an appropriately qualified opinion.

d. Advisory only, since the structural defect was not disclosed until after the completion of field work.

13. (From the May 1974 Uniform CPA Examination)

When a CPA has concluded that action should be taken to prevent future reliance on his report, he should

a. Advise his client to make appropriate disclosure of the newly discovered facts and their impact on the financial statements to persons who are known to be currently relying or who are likely to rely on the financial statements and the related auditor's report.

b. Recall the financial statements and issue revised statements and include an appropriate opinion.

c. Advise the client and others *not* to rely on the financial statements and make appropriate disclosure of the correction in the statements of a subsequent period.

d. Recall the financial statements and issue a disclaimer of opinion which should generally be followed by revised statements and a qualified opinion.

14. (From the November 1974 Uniform CPA Examination)

On January 15, 1974, before the Longview Co. released its financial statements for the year ended December 31, 1973, Agie Corp., a customer, declared bankruptcy. Agie has had a history of financial difficulty. Longview estimates that it will suffer a material loss on an account receivable from Agie. How should this be disclosed or recognized?

a. The loss should be disclosed in footnotes to the financial statements, but the financial statements themselves need not be adjusted.

b. The loss should be disclosed in an explanatory paragraph in the auditor's report.

c. No disclosure or recognition is required.

d. The financial statements should be adjusted to recognize the loss.

15. (From the May 1978 Uniform Examination)

On February 13, 1978, Fox, CPA, met with the audit committee of the Gem Corporation to review the draft of Fox's report on the company's financial statements as of and for the year ended December 31, 1977. On February 16, 1978, Fox completed all remaining field work at the Gem Corporation's headquarters. On February 17, 1978, Fox typed and signed the final version of the auditor's report. On February 18, 1978, the final report was mailed to Gem's audit committee. What date should have been used on Fox's report?

a. February 13, 1978.

b. February 16, 1978.

c. February 17, 1978.

d. February 18, 1978.

Forecasts

16. To what extent may CPAs become associated with forecasts, and what conditions must such associated CPAs observe?

17. Will liability be imposed on those who issue inaccurate forecasts? Explain.

18. (From the May 1975 Uniform CPA Examination)

A CPA's report accompanying a cash forecast or other type of projection should

a. Not be issued in any form because it would be in violation of the AICPA Code of Professional Ethics.

b. Disclaim any opinion as to the forecast's achievability.

c. Be prepared only if the client is a not-for-profit organization.

d. Be a qualified short-form audit report if the business concern is operated for a profit.

Interim Reporting

19. (From the May 1978 Uniform CPA Examination)

When making a limited review of interim financial information, the auditor's work consists primarily of

a. Studying and evaluating limited amounts of documentation supporting the interim financial information.

b. Scanning and reviewing client-prepared, internal financial statements.

c. Making inquiries and performing analytical procedures concerning significant accounting matters.

d. Confirming and verifying significant account balances at the interim date.

20. (From the May 1978 Uniform CPA Examination)

If, as a result of a limited review of interim financial information, a CPA concludes that such information does *not* conform with generally accepted accounting principles, the CPA should

a. Insist that the management conform the information with generally accepted accounting principles and, if this is not done, resign from the engagement.

b. Adjust the financial information so that it conforms with generally accepted accounting principles.

c. Prepare a qualified report that makes reference to the lack of conformity with generally accepted accounting principles.

d. Advise the board of directors of the respects in which the information does *not* conform with generally accepted accounting principles.

21. Do net operating losses threaten the value of goodwill shown on a quarterly balance sheet? Discuss.

Market-Value Reporting

22. Explain how each of three different factors can affect the duty to disclose market values.

23. How is the applicability or inapplicability of the "going-concern" assumption related to the duty to report market values?

Materiality

24. Explain the distinction between materiality in connection with an audit examination and materiality in connection with financial reporting.

25. What is the legal test of materiality for imposing liability on those responsible for misrepresentation?

26. (From the November 1971 Uniform CPA Examination)

The concept of materiality is important to the CPA in his examination of financial statements and expression of opinion upon these statements.

Required:

Discuss the following:

a. How are materiality (and immateriality) related to the proper presentation of financial statements?

b. In what ways will considerations of materiality affect the CPA in

(1) Developing his audit program?

(2) Performance of his auditing procedures?

c. What factors and measures should the CPA consider in assessing the materiality of an exception to financial statement presentation?

d. How will the materiality of a CPA's exceptions to financial statements influence the type of opinion he expresses? (The relationship of materiality to each type of auditor's opinion should be considered in your answer.)

27. (From the May 1975 Uniform CPA Examination)

Which one of the following statements is correct concerning the concept of materiality?

a. Materiality is determined by reference to guidelines established by the AICPA.

b. Materiality depends only on the dollar amount of an item relative to other items in the financial statements.

c. Materiality depends on the nature of an item rather than the dollar amount.

d. Materiality is a matter of professional judgment.

28. (From the November 1974 Uniform CPA Examination)

On January 2, 1974, the Retail Auto Parts Co. received a notice from its primary suppliers that effective immediately all wholesale prices would be increased 10 percent. On the basis of the notice, Retail Auto Parts Co. revalued its December 31, 1973, inventory to reflect the higher costs. The inventory constituted a material proportion of total assets; however, the effect of the revaluation was material to current assets but *not* to total assets or net income. In reporting on the company's financial statements for the year ended December 31, 1973, in which inventory is valued at the adjusted amounts, the auditor should

a. Issue an unqualified opinion, provided the nature of the adjustment and the amounts involved are disclosed in footnotes.

b. Issue a qualified opinion.

c. Disclaim an opinion.

d. Issue an adverse opinion.

29. (From the May 1974 Uniform CPA Examination)

A CPA has not been able to confirm a large account receivable, but he has satisfied himself as to the proper statement of the receivable by means of alternative auditing procedures. The auditor's report on the financial statements should include

a. A description of the limitation on the scope of his examination and the alternative auditing procedures used, but an opinion qualification is not required.

b. An opinion qualification, but reference to the use of alternative auditing procedures is not required.

c. Both a scope qualification and an opinion qualification.

d. Neither a comment on the use of alternative auditing procedures nor an opinion qualification.

30. (From the May 1974 Uniform CPA Examination)

During the year ended December 31, 1973, Holly Corporation had its fixed assets appraised and found that they had substantially appreciated in value since the date of their purchase. The appraised values have been reported in the balance sheet as of December 31, 1973; the total appraisal increment has been included as an extraordinary item in the income statement for the year then ended; and the appraisal adjustment has been fully disclosed in the footnotes. If a CPA believes that the values reported in the financial statements are reasonable, what type of opinion should he issue?

a. An unqualified opinion.

b. A "subject to" qualified opinion.

c. An adverse opinion.

d. A disclaimer of opinion.

31. (From the May 1973 Uniform CPA Examination)

The opinion paragraph of a CPA's report begins: "In our opinion, based upon our examination and the report of other auditors, the accompanying consolidated balance sheet and consolidated statements of income and retained earnings and of changes in financial position present fairly. . . ." This is

a. A partial disclaimer of opinion.

b. An unqualified opinion.

c. An "except for" opinion.

d. A qualified opinion.

32. (From the May 1972 Uniform CPA Examination)

The use of an adverse opinion generally indicates

a. Uncertainty with respect to an item that is so material that the auditor cannot form an opinion on the fairness of presentation of the financial statements as a whole.

b. Uncertainty with respect to an item that is material, but not so material that the auditor cannot form an opinion on the fairness of the financial statements as a whole.

c. A violation of generally accepted accounting principles that has a material effect upon the fairness of presentation of the financial statements, but is not so material that a qualified opinion is unjustified.

d. A violation of generally accepted accounting principles that is so material that a qualified opinion is not justified.

33. (From the May 1972 Uniform CPA Examination)

The use of a disclaimer of opinion might indicate that the auditor

a. Is so uncertain with respect to an item that he cannot form an opinion on the fairness of presentation of the financial statements as a whole.

b. Is uncertain with respect to an item that is material but not so material that he cannot form an opinion on the fairness of presentation of the financial statements as a whole.

c. Has observed a violation of generally accepted accounting principles that has a material effect upon the fairness of presentation of financial statements, but is not so material that a qualified report is unjustified.

d. Has observed a violation of generally accepted accounting principles that is so material that a qualified opinion is not justified.

34–38. (From the November 1973 Uniform CPA Examination)

Items in 34 through 38 are based on the following information:

The auditor's report must contain an expression of opinion or a statement to the effect that an opinion cannot be expressed. Four types of opinions or state-

ments which meet these requirements are generally known as

a. An unqualified opinion.

b. A qualified opinion.

c. A disclaimer of opinion.

d. An adverse opinion.

For each of the situations presented in items 34 through 38, indicate the type of opinion or statement which should be rendered by reference to the appropriate letter from the above list.

34. Subsequent to the close of Holly Corporation's fiscal year a major debtor was declared a bankrupt due to a rapid series of events. The receivable is significantly material in relation to the financial statements and recovery is doubtful. The debtor had confirmed the full amount due to Holly Corporation at the balance-sheet date. Since the account was good at the balance-sheet date, Holly Corporation refuses to disclose any information in relation to this subsequent event. The CPA believes that all accounts were stated fairly at the balance-sheet date.

35. Kapok Corporation is a subtantial user of electronic data processing equipment and has used an outside service bureau to process data in years past. During the current year Kapok adopted the policy of leasing all hardware and expects to continue this arrangement in the future. This change in policy is adequately disclosed in footnotes to Kapok's financial statements, but uncertainty prohibits either Kapok or the CPA from assessing the impact of this change upon future operations.

36. The financial statements of Reid Corporation for the year ended December 31, 1972, were accompanied by an unqualified opinion. Reid wishes unaudited financial statements prepared for the three months ended March 31, 1973.

37. The president of Lowe, Inc., would not allow the auditor to confirm the receivable balance from one of its major customers. The amount of the receivable is material in relation to the financial statements of Lowe, Inc. The auditor was unable to satisfy himself as to the receivable balance by alternative procedures.

38. Sempier Corporation issued financial statements that purported to present financial position and results of operations but omitted the related statement of changes in financial position (the omission is not sanctioned by *APB Opinion No. 19*).

39. (From the May 1978 Uniform CPA Examination)

If the auditor believes that required disclosures of a significant nature are omitted from the financial statements under examination, the auditor should decide between issuing

a. A qualified opinion or an adverse opinion.

b. A disclaimer of opinion or a qualified opinion.

c. An adverse opinion or a disclaimer of opinion.

d. An unqualified opinion or a qualified opinion.

PART TWO
CASES

14

Cases on
Common-Law
Liability

This chapter includes:

- WHITE v. GUARENTE.
- UNITED STATES NATIONAL BANK OF OREGON v. FOUGHT.
- BONHIVER v. GRAFF.

WHITE v. GUARENTE*

Court of Appeals of New York, 1977
372 N.E.2d 315

This landmark case is a sequel to Ultramares *and decided by the same court almost 50 years later. It holds that the auditor/tax preparer may be liable for negligence to the defined class of limited partners.*

COOKE, Judge.

The issue posed is whether accountants retained by a limited partnership to perform auditing and tax-return services may be held responsible to an identifiable group of limited partners for negligence in the execution of those professional services. We hold that, at least on the facts here, an accountant's liability may be so imposed.

Plaintiff is a limited partner in Guarente-Harrington Associates (Associates), a limited partnership formed in early 1968 for the stated purpose of serving "as a

---

*The court's footnotes are omitted.

hedge fund through which the funds of its Partners may be utilized in investing and trading in marketable securities and rights and options relating thereto." The general partners are defendants William E. Guarente and George F. Harrington. In September, 1968, Associates retained defendant Arthur Andersen & Co. (Andersen), a partnership engaged in the general practice of public accountancy, to perform an audit and prepare the tax return of Associates. Such an audit was required by the partnership agreement.

Among the partnership agreement stipulations were provisions: that the initial capital contribution of each limited partner shall not be less than $250,000; that *no partner* may withdraw any part of his interest in the partnership, except at the end of any fiscal year *upon giving written notice of such intention not less than 30 days prior to the end of such year*; that the books and records of the partnership shall be audited as of the end of each fiscal year by a certified public accountant designated by the general partners; and that proper and complete books of account shall be kept and shall be open to inspection by any of the partners or his or her accredited representative.

The complaint purports to embrace five causes of action, four against the two general partners individually, and the fifth against Andersen, the accounting firm. It is this last cause, the gravamen of which is for professional malpractice, with which we are here concerned. It is alleged that there are approximately 40 limited partners. Plaintiff moved for leave to serve an amended and supplemental complaint and defendant Andersen moved for dismissal of the cause of action asserted against it pursuant to CPLR 3211 (subd. [a], par. 7) on the ground that the pleading fails to state a cause of action, or, alternatively, for a severance of said cause from those asserted against the general partners. The motions were consolidated for disposition and Special Term dismissed the complaint as to Andersen for failure to state a cause of action and directed that judgment be entered dismissing the complaint against Andersen on the merits, as well as ordering a severance of the cause against Andersen, denying the motion to dismiss the causes against the general partners and granting leave to plaintiff to serve an amended and supplemental complaint only on defendant general partners, individually. Plaintiff appealed from so much of Special Term's order as dismissed the complaint against Andersen for failure to state a cause of action and the Appellate Division affirmed.

The cause of action directed against Andersen alleges, *inter alia*, that between September 1, 1969, and March 31, 1970, Andersen knew or should have known that Guarente and Harrington were engaging in withdrawal of funds from their capital accounts in violation of the partnership agreement, that on March 31, 1970, Andersen issued its auditor's report with financial

196

statements of Associates for the fiscal year ending October 31, 1969, and that Andersen violated its professional duties and was guilty of professional misconduct: in that it failed to notify all partners that Guarente and Harrington made withdrawals of funds without proper notice, that the general partners had neglected to prepare and distribute the annual schedule required by the partnership agreement, and that withdrawals were made between November 1, 1969, and March 20, 1970, but were calculated and reported as being retroactive as of October 31, 1969; and in that the audit reports and financial statements were inaccurate and misleading in failing to state that disbursements for various management expenses other than salaries were made in violation of the partnership agreement and in carrying forward without critical comment misrepresentations as to the value of restricted securities held by Associates. From the evidentiary material submitted to Special Term by plaintiff (see *Guggenheimer v. Ginsburg,* 43 N.Y.2d 268, 401 N.Y.S.2d, 182, 372 N.E.2d 17 [decided herewith]), the thrust of plaintiff's claim of malpractice against Andersen centers on the accounting firm's alleged failure to comment on the withdrawal by the general partners of $2,000,000 of their $2,600,000 capital investment based on back-dated oral notices, avoiding six months of losses prior to actual withdrawal, and the lumping together of the $2,000,000 withdrawals with $49,144 in withdrawals by limited partners so that a reader of the financial statement would not be likely to realize that the two general partners had withdrawn a major portion of all their investments. Emphasis is also placed on the acceptance of the valuations of the general partners of restricted securities without adequate checking.

Citing *Ultramares Corp. v. Touche,* 255 N.Y. 170, 174 N.E. 441, and contending that plaintiff does not stand in privity with it, defendant Andersen maintains that plaintiff lacks capacity to sue and may not recover for these alleged acts of negligence (see Siegal, "Practice Commentaries," McKinney's Cons. Laws of N.Y., Book 7B, CPLR 3211.13, pp. 19–20). *Ultramares*, however, presented a noticeably different picture than that here, since there involved was an "indeterminate class of persons who, presently or in the future, might deal with the [debtor-promisee] in reliance on the audit" (p. 183, 174 N.E. p. 446). There it was stated at pages 180, 181, 174 N.E. at page 445: "In the field of the law of contract there has been a gradual widening of the doctrine of *Lawrence v. Fox,* 20 N.Y. 268, until today the beneficiary of a promise, clearly designated as such is seldom left without a remedy (*Seaver v. Ransom,* 224 N.Y. 233, 238 [120 N.E. 639]). Even in that field, however, the remedy is narrower *where the beneficiaries of the promise are indeterminate or general.* Something more must then

appear than an intention that the promise shall redound *to the benefit of the public or to that of a class of indefinite extension.* The promise must be such as to 'bespeak the assumption of a duty to make reparation directly to the individual members of the public if the benefit is lost' (*Moch Co. v. Rensselaer Water Co.,* 247 N.Y. 160, 164 [159 N.E. 896]; American Law Institute, Restatement of the Law of Contracts, § 145)." (Emphasis added.) Indeed, the import of *Ultramares* is its holding that an accountant need not respond in negligence to those in the extensive and indeterminable investing public-at-large.

Here, the services of the accountant were not extended to a faceless or unresolved class of persons, but rather to a known group possessed of vested rights, marked by a definable limit and made up of certain components (see *Ultramares Corp. v. Touche,* 255 N.Y. 170, 182–185, 174 N.E. 441, 445–447, *supra*). The instant situation did not involve prospective limited partners, unknown at the time and who might be induced to join, but rather actual limited partners, fixed and determined. Here, accountant Andersen was retained to perform an audit and prepare the tax returns of Associates, known to be a limited partnership, and the accountant must have been aware that a limited partner would necessarily rely on or make use of the audit and tax returns of the partnership, or at least constituents of them, in order to properly prepare his or her own tax returns. This was within the contemplation of the parties to the accounting retainer. In such circumstances, assumption of the task of auditing and preparing the returns was the assumption of a duty to audit and prepare carefully for the benefit of those in the fixed, definable and contemplated group whose conduct was to be governed, since, given the contract and the relation, the duty is imposed by law and it is not necessary to state the duty in terms of contract or privity (cf. *Glanzer v. Shepard,* 233, N.Y. 236, 239, 135 N.E. 275, 276; see also, *Scholen v. Guaranty Trust Co. of N.Y.,* 288, N.Y. 249, 253, 43 N.E.2d 28, 30; 1 Harper and James, Torts, § 7.6 p. 546).

In *Glanzer v. Shepard,* a judgment in favor of plaintiffs was upheld where defendants, public weighers engaged by the seller of beans, reported negligently the weight of a quantity of the commodity thus causing plaintiffs, the buyers, to overpay the sellers. Thus, there was involved a negligent misrepresentation which induced a third party to act to his disadvantage.

Judge Cardozo, who wrote both *Glanzer* and *Ultramares*, distinguished *Glanzer* in this fashion: "Here was something more than the rendition of a service in the expectation that the one who ordered the certificate would use it thereafter in the operations of his business as occasion might require. Here was a case where the transmission of the certificate to another was not merely one possibility among many, but the 'end and aim of the transaction,' . . . The intimacy of the resulting nexus is attested by the fact that after stating the case in terms of legal duty, we went on to point out that viewing it as a phase or extension of *Lawrence v. Fox* . . . , or *Seaver v. Ransom*, 224, N.Y. 233, 120 N.E. 639 . . . , we could reach the same result by stating it in terms of contract.'' (*Ultramares, supra,* at p. 182, 174 N.E. at p. 445.) Here, too, the furnishing of the audit and tax return information, necessarily by virtue of the relation, was one of the ends and aims of the transaction.

In *Hochfelder v. Ernst & Ernst*, 503 F.2d 1100, 1107, revd. on other grounds 425 U.S. 185, 96 S.Ct. 1375, 47 L. Ed. 2d 668, the court, in discussing recent inroads on the reach of *Ultramares,* stated: "The courts in diminishing the impact of *Ultramares* have not only embraced the rule of *Glanzer*—liability to a foreseen plaintiff—but have extended an accountant's liability for negligence to those who, although not themselves foreseen, are members of a limited class whose reliance on the financial statements is specifically foreseen.'' Here, plaintiff was a member of a limited class whose reliance on the audit and returns was, or at least should have been, specifically foreseen.

As to duty imposed, generally a negligent statement may be the basis for recovery of damages, where there is carelessness in imparting words upon which others were expected to rely and upon which they did act or failed to act to their damage (*Nichols v. Clark, MacMullen & Riley*, 261 N.Y. 118, 125, 184 N.E. 729, 731), but such information is not actionable unless expressed directly, with knowledge or notice that it will be acted upon, to one to whom the author is bound by some relation of duty, arising out of contract or otherwise, to act with care if he acts at all (*Courteen Seed Co. v. Hong Kong & Shanghai Banking Corp.*, 245 N.Y. 377, 381, 157 N.E. 272, 273). Indeed, the rule thus enunciated was specifically approved in *Ultramares* (*supra*, at p. 185, 174 N.E. at p. 446; see, also, *International Prods. Co. v. Erie R. R. Co.*, 244 N.Y. 331, 337–38, 155 N.E. 662, 663–64; *Everson v. First Trust & Deposit Co.*, 46 A.D.2d 722, 360 N.Y.S.2d 338; *Dorsey Prods. Corp. v. United States Rubber Co.*, 21 A.D.2d 866, 251 N.Y.S.2d 311, *aff'd.* 16 N.Y.2d 925, 264 N.Y.S.2d 917, 212 N.E.2d 435).

Defendant Andersen's contention, that plaintiff falls beyond the bounds of protected parties, rests primarily on the theory that its contract with the limited partnership circumscribed the extent of its obligation and the outer limits of its care. This reasoning fails to recognize that "[t]he duty of reasonable care in the performance of a contract is not always owed solely to the person with whom the contract is made . . . It may inure to the benefit of others" (*cf. Rosenbaum v. Branster Realty Corp.*, 276 App. Div. 167, 168, 93

N.Y.S.2d 209, 212; see, also, *Wroblewski v. Otis Elevator Co.*, 9 A.D.2d 294, 296, 193 N.Y.S.2d 855, 857). While *Ultramares* made it clear that accountants were not to be liable in negligence on the generalized basis that a contract for professional services creates liability in favor of the general populace, this plaintiff seeks redress, not as a mere member of the public, but as one of a settled and particularized class among the members of which the report would be circulated for the specific purpose of fulfilling the limited partnership agreed-upon arrangement.

Accordingly, the order of the Appellate Division should be reversed and the motion to dismiss the complaint as against defendant Arthur Andersen & Co. denied, with costs to abide the event.

UNITED STATES NATIONAL BANK OF OREGON v. FOUGHT*

Court of Appeals of Oregon, 1980
612 P.2d 754

This case demonstrates how the failure to report a breach of contract by the client becomes fraud by the CPA, resulting in civil liability to a third party.

GILLETTE, Presiding Judge.

This was an action by the plaintiff bank against two certified public accountants. The trial judge entered judgment for defendants, and plaintiff appeals. The determinative issue is whether the plaintiff bank pled and proved that the defendants defrauded the bank. While the trial court found that the defendants' conduct was "on the very edge of fraud," the court held for the defendants because it determined that the plaintiff had neither pled nor proven the requisite intent to defraud. We find that the court erred as a matter of law by employing an incorrect definition of fradulent intent, and reverse.

The bank was a creditor of Millers International, Inc. (Millers), a jewelry manufacturer and retailer. The defendants are accountants who had performed accounting and auditing services for Millers for several years.

By August, 1976, the bank had loaned large sums to Millers, Millers was in financial difficulty, and the loans were in default. As a result, the bank and the president of Millers, Mr. C. Kenneth Miller, signed an agreement under which Millers was to place all of its receipts in a bank-controlled, cash collateral account. All checks written on the account had to be approved by the bank.

Lists of checks, to be approved by the bank, were

---

* Except for one excerpt, the court's footnotes are omitted.

prepared by defendants' employees and taken to the bank by Mr. Miller or defendant Jones. The bank had been told to rely on defendants for financial information.

In November, 1976, Mr. Miller began to divert funds from Millers and from the cash collateral account. He used at least some of these funds to pay bills for which he knew the bank would not approve payment. The defendants knew what Miller was doing. However, as the trial court found,

> Despite this knowledge, defendants continued to prepare financial information and defendant Jones would personally present lists of checks for payment, without disclosing the unauthorized diversions. During this entire period of time, the defendants were aware of the terms of the letter agreement and the provision for deposits of Millers, Inc. receipts to the cash collateral account.

The bank was unaware of the diversions until, in December, 1976, it discovered a discrepancy between cash receipts and deposits to the cash collateral account. A meeting was held in January, 1977, to investigate the discrepancy. Defendants attended this meeting, but they did not inform the bank that Miller was violating the agreement. Defendant Fought said that he "would look into" the matter of the discrepancy.

When the bank's accountants later examined the records of Millers, Inc., and reconciled the cash receipts to the deposits to the cash collateral account, they discovered a shortage of $105,706.67. This action followed.

In their cross-appeal, and for the first time in this case, the defendants argue that the trial court's disposition of the case may be justified because the bank's pleading was insufficient to state a cause of action for fraud.

The bank's amended complaint describes the parties, the defendants' services as accountants and bookkeepers for Millers, and the cash collateral account agreement between Millers and the bank. The complaint alleges that the defendants knew of the agreement. The complaint outlines Mr. Miller's diversions from the case collateral account. The complaint then recites that,

* * * * *

VIII

The actions of C. Kenneth Miller alleged above were done with the full knowledge of defendants. Notwithstanding this knowledge, defendant James Jones continued to present to plaintiff certified lists of checks and neither defendant disclosed to the Bank the actions of C. Kenneth Miller.

IX

During November and December of 1976 and January of 1977, plaintiff relied on the financial statements prepared by defendants and the lists of checks presented by James Jones as indicating that the only funds available to pay obligations of Millers International, Inc. were those in the cash collateral account and that all funds receivable by Millers International, Inc. were being deposited in the cash collateral account. Such representations were false when made and known by defendants to be false. Defendants further knew, or should have known, that plaintiff was relying on such representation.

X

As a result of defendants' acts, plaintiff has been damaged in the amount of $105,706.67.

The elements of actionable fraud consist of: (1) a representation; (2) its falsity; (3) its materiality; (4) the speaker's knowledge of its falsity or ignorance of its truth; (5) his intent that it should be acted on by the person and in the manner reasonably contemplated; (6) the hearer's ignorance of its falsity; (7) his reliance on its truth; (8) his right to rely thereon; (9) and his consequent and proximate injury. *Conzelmann v. N. W. P. & D. Prod. Co.,* 190 Or. 332, 350, 225 P.2d 757 (1950) (citations omitted); *see also Gardner v. Meiling,* 280 Or. 665, 671, 572 P.2d 1012 (1977); *Williams v. Collins,* 42 Or. App. 481, 485–486, 600 P.2d 1235 (1979).

Defendants argue that the bank's complaint fails to state a cause of action for fraud because it does not allege that "the list of checks and receipts presented by defendants were *material,* were prepared with the *intent to defraud* the bank, that plaintiff had a *right to rely* on the representations, or that plaintiff was *ignorant of the falsity* of the statements." (Emphasis added). We agree with defendants that these elements of fraud are not explicitly stated in plaintiff's complaint. However, until this appeal, defendants did not challenge the sufficiency of the complaint. A complaint is liberally construed when it is attacked for the first time on appeal. *Williams v. Collins, supra,* 42 Or. App. at 487, 600 P.2d 1235; *see also Fulton Ins. v. White Motor Corp.,* 261 Or. 206, 219, 493 P.2d 138 (1972). Moreover, as the Supreme Court has emphasized, while *Conzelmann* and other cases

> . . . list nine requirements to sustain fraud, . . . they unduly fractionalize the essential elements. As an illustration, it is unnecessary to allege or find the hearer's ignorance of the falsity of a statement if it is alleged and found that the hearer relied upon it, because ignorance of the falsity of the statement *is necessary* to reliance. Also, while an allegation or finding of reliance is an allegation or finding of fact, whether or not a person *has a right* to rely is a conclusion which the law draws from facts and is not an allegation or finding of fact . . . *Briscoe v. Pittman,* 268 Or. 604, 610, 522 P.2d 886, 889 (1974). (Emphasis in original.) *See also Williams v. Collins, supra.*

Here, as in *Briscoe,* while the complaint does not recite that the plaintiff was ignorant of the falsity of the defendants' representation, this omission is immaterial because the complaint alleges that the plaintiff relied on the misrepresentation and ". . . ignorance of the falsity of the statement *is necessary* to reliance." Ibid. Applying the same logic, the failure to allege that the misrepresentation was material is also not a fatal defect in the complaint. The complaint alleges the terms of the cash collateral agreement, the defendants' misrepresentation and the plaintiff's detrimental reliance resulting in damage to the plaintiff. The materiality of the misrepresentation is apparent in these allegations.

With respect to the element of "right to rely," *Briscoe* holds that the allegation that ". . . a person *has a right* to rely is a conclusion which the law draws from facts and is not an allegation or finding of fact." 268 Or. at 610, 522 P.2d at 889. (Emphasis in original).

"Intent to defraud" is the intent that the misrepresentation ". . . should be acted on by the person and in the manner reasonably contemplated." *Conzelmann, supra,* 190 Or. at 350, 225 P.2d at 764. The bank's complaint alleges that it relied on financial information, provided by defendants, as indicating that all receipts were being deposited in the cash collateral account, which was the only source of funds available to pay Millers' obligations. The complaint recites that the defendants' representations were false and known by defendants to be false. Finally, the complaint alleges that defendants *knew* or should have known that the bank was relying on the representations. The import of these allegations is that the defendants misrepresented financial information with the knowledge and intent that the misleading information would be acted upon by the bank and in the manner reasonably contemplated.

We find that the bank's complaint is sufficient to state a cause of action for fraud, at least where defendants have not challenged the complaint until this appeal. The complaint "served its principal function" and placed defendants on notice of plaintiff's claim for fraud. *Weiss v. Northwest Accept. Corp.,* 274 Or. 343, 351, 546 P.2d 1065 (1976).

As we have noted, despite the trial court's observation that the defendants' conduct was "on the very edge of fraud," the court held for the defendants because the court determined that the plaintiff had failed to prove that the defendants intended to defraud the bank.

The trial court's findings, which we have already summarized and which are supported by the evidence, incorporate all the elements of fraud except for the requisite intent. The trial court concluded that,

What defendants Fought and Jones did do was to present a list of checks to the plaintiff, knowing them

to be false, and by nonverbal conduct representing them as true, knowing the bank was relying on the false lists to its damage. . . .

The trial court found that the bank was damaged in the amount of $105,706.67.

Despite these conclusions, the trial court felt that the final question was,

Were the actions of the CPAs done with intent to defraud the bank or were they done due to a good faith, but false interpretation of their ethical duty to their client?

Solely because the trial court felt that the defendants were motivated by "good faith," the trial court held that the plaintiff had failed to prove the intent to defraud. The plaintiff argues that the trial court erred by employing an incorrect legal definition of the intent to defraud. We agree.

The intent to defraud does not consist of bad motives. Rather,

. . . [t]he requisite intent to mislead consists of a defendant misrepresenting a material fact for the purpose of misleading the other party or *with knowledge he is misleading the other party* or in reckless disregard of the fact he is misleading the other party. . . . *Elizaga v. Kaiser Found. Hospitals,* 259 Or. 542, 547–548, 487 P.2d 870, 873 (1971) (emphasis added); *see also Gardner v. Meiling, supra; Weiss v. Northwest Accept. Corp., supra; Conzelmann v. N. W. P. & S. Prod. Co., supra.*

In discussing the intent underlying an intentional misrepresentation, Prosser observes that

. . . [t]he fact that the defendant was disinterested, that he had the best of motives, and that he thought he was doing the plaintiff a kindness, will not absolve him from liability, so long as he did in fact intend to mislead. W. Prosser, *Law of Torts,* § 107, p. 700 (4th ed. 1971) (footnotes omitted).

The trial court found that the defendants acted with the knowledge that they were misleading the bank. The defendants intended to defraud the bank.[1] Under such circumstances, the defendants were guilty of fraud.

Reversed and remanded for entry of a judgment in favor of plaintiff.

---

1. The parties disagree as to whether the defendants had a duty to disclose their client's fraudulent actions to the bank. However, as plaintiff noted below, this "is not a mere silence case. . . ." The trial court found that, in presenting the false lists of checks to the bank, the defendants had affirmatively misrepresented the list as being true. "Restatement (Second) of Torts, §§ 550, 551 (1977) states that nondisclosure is actionable when there is a duty to speak, but notes no such duty requirement where there has been an active concealment . . . "

BONHIVER v. GRAFF*

Supreme Court of Minnesota, 1976
248 N.W.2d 291

Although the CPAs never produced completed financial statements, they were held liable (for their erroneous working papers) to the client corporation (as represented by the receiver) and to a third-party general agent.

SHERAN, Chief Justice.

* * * * *

The facts relevant to this appeal are as follows: Defendant Schwartz, Frumm & Company (hereafter, Schwartz, Frumm) is a firm of certified public accountants with its office in Chicago, Illinois. Defendant Philip Graff, a duly certified public accountant, worked for Schwartz, Frumm from November 1960 to December 1964.

Prior to 1963, members and employees of Schwartz, Frumm had done some accounting work for Phillip Kitzer, Sr., with respect to a garage owned by him and with respect to Adequate Mutual Insurance Company (Adequate Mutual). The firm corrected for refiling the annual "convention statement" submitted by Adequate Mutual for the year 1961 or 1962. As originally filed, the statement was unacceptable to the Illinois Department of Insurance. In May 1963, at the request of Kitzer, Sr., and Phillip Kitzer, Jr., Leonard Frumm and an employee, James Holly, journeyed from Chicago to Minneapolis to inspect the books of American Allied Mutual Insurance Company (American Allied Mutual). The Kitzers were interested in purchasing American Allied Mututal for $100,000. Frumm and Holly spent about 10 hours inspecting American Allied Mutual's books, and reported to Kitzer, Sr., that American Allied Mutual was impaired. Frumm and Holly recommended to the Kitzers that they not purchase the company for the price requested, but they purchased it anyway for $20,000.

Upon purchasing American Allied Mutual, the Kitzers transferred its assets and liabilities to a newly formed stock company—American Allied Insurance Company (American Allied). Schwartz, Frumm employees assisted the Kitzers in connection with this acquisition. All of the stock of American Allied was owned by the Kitzers.

* * * * *

In November 1963, Holly left Schwartz, Frumm to become a vice president of American Allied. In August 1964, Holly contacted Frumm and requested help in getting American Allied's books up to date as of June 30, 1964. Frumm sent Graff to St. Paul to do the work. Graff made various entries in the books and records of American Allied and prepared workpapers in the course of his work. On October 5, 1964, the commissioner of insurance of the state of Minnesota sent a team of examiners to examine the books of American Allied. Those examiners worked in the same room with Graff, examined his workpapers, and relied upon the entries he had made in the books, a standard practice. Graff at times personally furnished information to the examiners, and testified that he considered his work to be the "starting point" for the examiners. By his examiners' reliance upon Graff's entries, the commissioner was led to believe that American Allied was solvent, when in fact the company was insolvent. Had the examination disclosed that the company was insolvent, its continued operation would have been challenged by the commissioner. . . .

Because a number of Graff's entries were erroneous, the examination did not disclose American Allied's insolvency. During the existence of American Allied, the Kitzers embezzled over $2,000,000 from the company. Graff's errors involved his failure to investigate and discover the true nature of a number of transactions by which this fraud was taking place. Those errors, upon which the defendants' liability was established, were described in detail in the trial court's findings. Basically, they involved transactions between two companies wherein a payment would be recorded in one manner on American Allied's books and in a different manner on the books of the other party to the transaction. The books of the other parties—often related companies, such as Bell Mutual, Bell Casualty, or United States Mutual—were readily available to Graff. The court found that his failure to examine those books was negligence.

In the spring of 1965, rumors began circulating that American Allied was insolvent. The commissioner of insurance, at a meeting with several concerned parties, including Frank J. Delmont, intervenor, gave assurances that American Allied was solvent. In reliance upon those assurances, Delmont, an insurance agent who had become a general agent of American Allied, continued to write insurance with American Allied. American Allied was allowed to continue to do business until June 10, 1965. During the period September 1964 to August 1965, the Kitzers withdrew $849,078.60 in cash.

Bonhiver instituted this action in October 1970. Delmont instituted a class action in Federal court on December 31, 1970. He intervened in this action on behalf of the class on March 5, 1974. After a court trial, Bonhiver was awarded damages of $88,350.94, Delmont was awarded damages of $29,000, and the class action was dismissed. The trial court denied plaintiff's

---

* The court's footnotes are omitted.

post-trial motion for amended findings or a new trial on the issue of damages, and also denied defendants' and intervenors' motions for amended findings. Defendants appealed and the other parties filed notices of review. We affirm.

* * * * *

Defendant Graff left the employ of Schwartz, Frumm November 5, 1964. The last act of negligence chargeable to Schwartz, Frumm occurred either by that date or at some other time in November 1964. The Kitzers were withdrawing money continuously during this period. Thus, as of some time in November 1964, the company's cause of action against Schwartz, Frumm had accrued: All of the negligent acts chargeable to Schwartz, Frumm had been committed and damage to American Allied had occurred.

A civil action is commenced against each defendant when the summons is served upon him or is delivered to the proper officer for service. Rule 3.01, Rules of Civil Procedure. Minn. St. 540.152 provides that service upon the secretary of state shall have the same effect as service upon a nonresident association doing business within the state and causing injury within the state. Schwartz, Frumm is such a nonresident association. The requirements of Minn. St. 540.152 were complied with on October 16, 1970. The action was thus commenced by Bonhiver against Schwartz, Frumm within the six-year period of the statute of limitations. Service was made on Graff on October 27, 1970, also within six years of the alleged acts of negligence.

Delmont intervened in this action on March 5, 1974. But he had originally filed suit in federal court on December 31, 1970. His damages included loss of good will, loss of earnings, and loss of premiums paid. These damages were not sustained until after the American Allied collapse in the summer of 1965, consequently his cause of action did not arise until then. His institution of the action in December 1970 was thus timely.

Defendants claim that Bonhiver, as receiver for American Allied, cannot maintain this action, as defendants are charged simply with failing to discover the fraud committed by the company's own officers. Whether or not the company would be precluded from bringing this suit (the company was the victim of the fraud, and not the perpetrator), "[t]he receiver represents the rights of creditors and is not bound by the fraudulent acts of a former officer of the corporation." *Magnusson v. American Allied Ins. Co.,* 290 Minn. 465, 473, 189 N.W.2d 28, 33 (1971). See, also, *German-Am. Finance Corp. v. Merchants & Mfrs. State Bank,* 177 Minn. 529, 225 N.W. 891, 64 A.L.R. 582 (1929). Bonhiver is thus not barred from bringing this action.

Plaintiffs' cause of action is not barred by intervening negligence. In this regard, the trial judge wrote:

> Subordinates of the state Commissioner of Insurance were suspicious of the reports and statements and implored the Commissioner to take drastic action long before he did. Nevertheless, the Commissioner steadfastly held to the opinion that the American Allied Insurance Company was not insolvent as late as March of 1965. The fact that the Commissioner did not heed the advice of his subordinates does not negate or lessen the negligence of the defendants in departing from their standards of care. It is unfortunate that the Commissioner did not accept the advice of his subordinates. Regrettably, he called a conference in March of 1965, consisting of insurance agents and many others, who did business with American Allied Insurance Company, to assure them that the Company was solvent, and that the rumors circulating to the contrary were false. That foolhardiness or stupidity does not mitigate in favor of the defendants.

In Minnesota intervening negligence, to be a superseding efficient cause, must be "in no way caused by defendant's negligence." *Medved v. Doolittle,* 220 Minn. 352, 357, 19 N.W.2d 788, 791 (1945). Here, the commissioner's steadfast belief that American Allied was solvent was caused by defendants' negligence. It was their entries which led to the appearance of solvency and upon which the commissioner relied. Thus, the commissioner's negligence was, at most, concurrent but not intervening.

Two expert witnesses were called by plaintiff, Howard M. Guthmann, a certified public accountant and president-elect of the Minnesota Society of Certified Public Accountants, and Richard D. Thorsen, a certified public accountant, past president of the Minnesota Society of Certified Public Accountants, and past chairman of the State Board of Accountancy. Both witnesses, upon hypothetical questions, stated that the defendants did not use the ordinary and reasonable standard of care exercised by the ordinary, careful certified public accountant. The only expert witnesses to testify to the contrary were defendants themselves. There is, therefore, sufficient evidence to sustain the trial court's finding that defendants' actions were negligent.

Defendants dispute liability because they did not produce a complete, certified set of financial statements, but only a set of unaudited workpapers which were themselves incomplete.

Schwartz, Frumm was never asked to produce complete financial statements. It was engaged to bring American Allied's books up to date, a job which was never, in fact, completed.

All accountant malpractice cases called to our attention have involved accountants who prepare or certify completed financial statements. See, eg., *Rusch*

Factors, Inc. v. Levin, 284 F. Supp. 85 (D.R.I.1968); *Ryan v. Kanne,* 170 N.W.2d 395 (Iowa 1969); *Shatterproof Glass Corp. v. James,* 466 S.W.2d 873 (Tex. Civ. App. 1971); *Hochfelder v. Ernst & Ernst,* 503 F.2d 1100 (7 Cir. 1974), reversed, 425 U.S. 185, 96 S. Ct. 1375, 47 L. ED. 2d 668 (1976). No case cited by the parties passes on the liability of a certified public accountant when his work product is not a completed financial statement but is rather a set of unfinished workpapers and adjusting entries. Only one case passes on the liability of a certified public accountant with respect to an "unaudited" financial statement.

In *United States v. Natelli,* 527 F.2d 311 (2 Cir. 1975), the defendant accountants were convicted of making materially false statements in proxy statements filed with the Securities and Exchange Commission. Such a proxy statement required an unaudited ninemonth statement of earnings to be attached. This statement turned out to be false, and the court discussed the defendant's liability with respect to it, stating:

* * * * *

We do not think this means, in terms of professional standards, that the accountant may shut his eyes in reckless disregard of his knowledge that highly suspicious figures, known to him to be suspicious, were being included in the unaudited earnings figures with which he was "associated" in the proxy statement. 527 F.2d 320.

We note that in *Natelli* the court was concerned with the level or degree of a breach of duty which is sufficient to subject an accountant to criminal penalties. To establish liability for negligence in the case at bar, plaintiff and the intervenors need only show a breach of the ordinary standard of care.

Natelli passed upon liability for an unaudited, but completed, financial statement. While no reported case has passed on the liability of an accountant for malpractice in producing workpapers and adjusting entries, it is our opinion that such liability must be imposed upon the defendants on the facts of this case.

This case is a most unusual one; Schwartz, Frumm had investigated American Allied Mutual in 1963 and found that it was impaired. This alerted them to the fact that they were dealing with a "sick cat." Then, in October 1964 Graff personally showed his workpapers and adjusting entries to the state examiners, and he knew that they were relying upon them in conducting their statutorily required examination of American Allied. This was a representation that the assets indicated by those entries were owned by American Allied and could be counted by the commissioner in his examination. The defendants' actual knowledge that the commissioner was relying upon these representations renders them liable for their negligence in making them.

Restatement, Torts 2d, Tent. Draft No. 12, § 552 provides as follows:

§ 552 Information Negligently Supplied for the Guidance of Others.
1. One who, in the course of his business, profession or employment, or in a transaction in which he has a pecuniary interest, supplies false information for the guidance of others in their business transactions, is subject to liability for pecuniary loss caused to them by their justifiable reliance upon the information, if he fails to exercise reasonable care or competence in obtaining or communicating the information.
2. Except as stated in subsection 3, the liability stated in subsection 1 is limited to loss suffered:
   a. By the person or one of the persons for whose benefit and guidance he intends to supply the information, or knows that the recipient intends to supply it.
   b. Through reliance upon it in a transaction which he intends the information to influence, or knows that the recipient so intends, or in a substantially similar transaction.
3. The liability of one who is under a public duty to give the information extends to loss suffered by any of the class of persons for whose benefit the duty is created, in any of the transactions in which it is intended to protect them.

The actions of the defendants fall within the above section. With respect to subsection 1, it is clear that defendants, in the course of their business, supplied false information to American Allied and the commissioner of insurance, that those parties justifiably relied upon the information, and that defendants failed to exercise reasonable care or competence in communicating it. With respect to subsection 2*a,* the defendants supplied the information to both American Allied and the commissioner; with respect to subsection 2*b,* these parties relied upon it in determining whether the operation of American Allied could continue. Because of the continued operation, American Allied suffered an additional loss of $849,078.60 to the Kitzers.

The fact that no previous accounting malpractice case deals with liability for erroneous workpapers or adjusting entries does not unduly concern us, for in the normal case no representations are made by use of such work product; rather, the accountants prepare complete financial statements from their workpapers and distribute the completed statements. The workpapers remain the property of the accounting firm and not of the client. In this case, however, the defendants personally displayed their workpapers to the state examiners and knew that the examiners were relying upon them.

Defendants not only had actual knowledge of the fact that representations were being made by use of the workpapers and adjusting entries, but they made those representations themselves—by personally handing over the workpapers and adjusting entries.

On the facts of this case, therefore, we hold that defendants can be held liable for negligent misrepresentation even though they had not produced an audited or completed financial statement.

* * * * *

No case passing on accountants' malpractice liability has considered their liability to agents of an insurance company client. Two distinct questions are presented: (1) Under what circumstances can accountants be held liable to third parties for negligent misrepresentation? (2) Do those circumstances exist here so as to render the defendants liable to Delmont, an American Allied agent? Delmont's claim is that he relied upon the representations of the commissioner of insurance, who in turn relied upon the representations of defendants. Thus, it is claimed that through the chain of reliance defendants are liable to Delmont.

* * * * *

As is indicated above, the extent of an accountant's liability for malpractice is not settled. If that liability is to be drawn somewhere short of foreseeability, it must be drawn on pragmatic grounds alone. Once it is admitted that a certain number of people have been injured as a result of an accountant's malpractice, there is no logical justification for denying any of them relief based upon the "limited" or "unlimited" nature of their "class," or whether the reliance of the particular injured parties was or was not "specifically foreseeable." Distinctions based upon those factors are grounded in Mr. Justice Cardozo's fear that otherwise accountants would be exposed "to a liability in an indeterminate amount for an indeterminate time to an indeterminate class." *Ultramares Corp. v. Touche*, 255 N.Y. 170, 179, 174 N.E. 441, 444.

* * * * *

Wherever the line will eventually be drawn between those who can recover from the negligent accountant and those who cannot, we feel that on the facts of this case Delmont falls on the side of those who can recover. Delmont was one of two general agents of American Allied. When rumors of American Allied collapse began to spread, Delmont suspended American Allied sales, and Frank Delmont personally went to the commissioner in order to determine the status of the company. When the commissioner reassured Delmont that American Allied was financially sound, he resumed sales. This personal reliance, indirect though it may be through the commissioner, was reasonable on the part of Delmont and sufficient to accord him protection against defendants' negligence.

* * * * *

15

Cases under Federal Securities Laws

This chapter includes:

- HERZFELD v. LAVENTHOL, KREKSTEIN, HORWATH & HORWATH.
- UNITED STATES v. SIMON.
- UNITED STATES v. NATELLI.

HERZFELD v. LAVENTHOL,
KREKSTEIN, HORWATH & HORWATH*

United States Court of Appeals
for the Second Circuit, 1976
540 F.2d 27

While the Hochfelder *case greatly limited accountants' liability under federal securities laws, this case demonstrates that such laws remain a potent source of civil liability including situations where no SEC filings are involved.*

MOORE, Circuit Judge.

Laventhol, Krekstein, Horwath & Horwath, a firm of certified public accountants ("Laventhol"), appeals from an amended judgment for the amount of $153,000, entered against it and in favor of plaintiff, Gerald L. Herzfeld ("Herzfeld") after a trial to the Court. Allen & Company and Allen & Company, Incorporated (referred to collectively as "Allen") appeal from that portion of the judgment which awarded

---

*Except for one excerpt, the court's footnotes are omitted.

Laventhol contribution against them and which dismissed their counterclaims against Laventhol. The opinion of the lower court is reported at 378 F. Supp. 112 (S.D.N.Y. 1974) (MacMahon, *J.*). We affirm the Herzfeld award and the dismissal of the Allen counterclaims. We reverse the Laventhol contribution award against Allen, and dismiss Laventhol's third-party contribution complaint.

Originally, Herzfeld had sued Laventhol and eleven other defendants primarily to recover $510,000 which he claimed that he had paid for certain securities of Firestone Group, Ltd. ("FGL"), namely, two FGL units, each unit consisting of a $250,000 FGL note and 5000 shares of FGL stock at $1 a share, a total of $255,000 per unit. The substance of Herzfeld's charges was that the representations made to him by the defendants in connection with the purchase were materially misleading and that there were omissions of material facts, all of which were inducing factors, and on which he relied, in making his purchase and in not exercising his right of rescission. Herzfeld predicated his suit upon alleged violations of the securities laws of the United States, Section 352-c of the New York General Business Law and common law fraud.

That suit was settled by all defendants except Laventhol for $357,000. Thereafter, by an amended complaint, Herzfeld sought to recoup the balance ($153,000) of the $510,000 from Laventhol. Laventhol thereupon, as a third-party plaintiff, sued nine settling defendants to recover, by way of contribution, a portion of such amount, costs and attorneys' fees for which it might be liable in the new Herzfeld suit. In their answer, Allen asserted counterclaims against Laventhol.

The specific facts are particularly important in determining the rights of the parties, Herzfeld, Laventhol and Allen, and are best developed in chronological order.

FGL was a California company engaged principally in the business of purchasing real estate and thereafter syndicating or reselling it. In November 1969, FGL planned to raise $7,500,000 by the private placement through Allen and Company, Incorporated, of the aforementioned units. Lee Meyer, a defendant, was an Allen vice president and also a FGL director.

Through friends, Herzfeld became interested in the venture. A purchase agreement, entitled "Note and Stock Purchase Agreement," dated November 10, 1969, was delivered to Herzfeld by FGL with an accompanying letter which advised him that the closing date for the sale of the notes would be December 16, 1969, "to permit the preparation of audited financial statements, as at and for the eleven months ended November 30, 1969, copies of which will be delivered to you." The letter added that these "audited statements will serve as the basis for confirming the unaudited Projected Financial Statements annexed to the Note and Stock Purchase Agreement as Exhibit B.''

Exhibit B was a balance sheet and income statement. It portrayed FGL as a strikingly profitable corporation with over $20 million in assets, a net worth of close to a million dollars, sales of over $17 million, deferred income of $2.7 million and an after-tax income of $315,000. FGL warranted that it fairly presented its financial condition as at November 30, 1969.

Herzfeld read the entire income statement and the balance sheet and noted that it represented FGL as being very profitable, with earnings of approximately $2 a share for the period ending November 30, 1969. He then signed the agreement to purchase two units thereunder.

To prepare the promised audit (to be as of November 30, 1969), FGL retained Laventhol as the accountants for the task. The Herzfeld-Laventhol lawsuit and this appeal therefrom involve only the deeds and alleged misdeeds of Laventhol in making its audit which was submitted to FGL and thereafter to the security purchasers, including Herzfeld. However, the third-party claim and cross-claims, hereinafter referred to, necessitate a review of the activities of Allen in the transaction.

The spotlight of Herzfeld's claim of a materially misleading audit, knowingly made with admitted awareness of the facts, focuses upon Laventhol's accounting treatment of two real estate transactions in, which FGL allegedly engaged in late November 1969, referred to herein as the FGL–Monterey purchase and the FGL–Continental sale. Purporting to reflect these transactions are two agreements. Each agreement is on an identical printed form entitled "AGREEMENT FOR SALE OF REAL ESTATE" and certain typewritten provisions have been inserted therein. The first is dated November 22, 1969 and is between Monterey Nursing Inns, Inc. ("Monterey") as seller and FGL as buyer. The transaction was subject to two conditions: (1) the buyer's approval of a preliminary title report and CC&R's[1] of Record on each property (there is no evidence that any such documents were ever prepared, delivered or approved); and (2) execution of a NNN lease per terms of "Exhibit D attached hereto" (no such exhibit appears to have been attached). Twenty-three (23) nursing homes were the subject of the sale "as per Exhibit 'A' attached hereto" (no such exhibit appears to have been attached). The purchase price is stated as $13,362,500, $5,000 of which was payable before November 30, 1969 (i.e., upon the signing of the contract).

On an identical printed form with almost identical typewritten inserts is an agreement by FGL as seller to sell to Continental Recreation Company, Ltd. ("Continental") as buyer. Again, there is no Exhibit A listing the properties. The purchase price is stated as $15,393,000 with $25,000 as a down payment, other payments to be made in 1970 and thereafter.

This purchase and sale of nursing homes, if ever consummated, would have been the largest single transaction in the history of FGL. Placing these two purported agreements side by side, if the obligations therein were ever fulfilled in the future, FGL would have bought Monterey for $113,362,500 and sold it for $15,393,000, thus producing a profit, when, as and if the transactions were consummated, of $2,030,500, no part of which was even contemplated as having been received prior to November 30, 1969, and only payments of $5000 by FGL to Monterey and $25,000 from Continental to FGL may have been made.

A comparison of the financial condition of FGL with and without these transactions demonstrates the importance of them to FGL:

	Monterey Included	Monterey Excluded
Sales	$22,132,607	$6,739,607
Total current assets	6,290,987	1,300,737
Net income	66,000	[169,000]
Deferred profit	1,795,000	—0—
Earnings/share	$0.10	[0.25]

Thus, the accounting treatment of these transactions determined the health of FGL's financial picture. Laventhol knew this was so. By this treatment, namely, immediate recognition of a so-called profit, Laventhol notes, dated November 30, 1969, reveal the conversion of estimated $772,108 losses into a $1,257,892 gain by the addition of the $2,030,500 "profit." These work papers contain the following entries:

Estimated loss 4 months ended 4/30/69	200,000
Estimated loss 7 months ended 11/30/69	572,108
Loss before sale to Continental Recreation	772,108
Profit on sale to Continental Recreation	2,030,000 [sic]
Profit before income taxes	1,257,892 [sic]

Little wonder that when at the outset a Laventhol partner was discussing the situation from an accounting standpoint, he referred to it as a "fictitious or proposed or artificial transaction." Appendix ("App.") p. 887. But Laventhol undertook the task, albeit it had to engage in considerable soul-searching during it. Laventhol also learned that Monterey transactions were nowhere recorded in the FGL books and that there were no corporate minutes or resolutions approving or even adverting to the transactions. The

---

1. Covenants, Conditions and Restrictions.

absence was remedied by Laventhol, who prepared adjusting entries and ordered the FGL controller to enter them in the FGL books. Illustrative is the letter from Laventhol's audit manager to FGL's controller enclosing "the journal entries which we *generated* for the financial statements at November 30" (emphasis added). These very entries were prepared by Laventhol as if the transaction had been consummated: yet the agreements on their face showed that no profits could result therefrom until long after November 30.

Under date of November 30, 1969, appears as a general journal entry (Journal No. 9) an item "Profit on sale $2,030,500" and also a credit of $3,995,000 "to record purchase and sale of various hospitals from Monterey. . . ." A further Laventhol paper, dated December 6, 1969, reverses a tax liability entry on the Continental sale which reads that Laventhol "will not record as sale since not enough deposit was given to Firestone."

The November 22 and 26 contracts came to Laventhol's attention on or about December 1st through its partners, Chazen and Lipkin, and Schwabb, the audit manager. Schwabb sought Lipkin's advice about the proper way to report the transactions in the audit. Lipkin sought to gather the pertinent information by meeting with Scott, a FGL vice-president, and Firestone. Scott told him that FGL was busy acquiring the necessary documentation. Firestone said that the agreements were legitimate and described Continental's principal, Max Ruderian, as an experienced real estate operator and a wealthy individual. Laventhol learned that Continental had a net worth of $100,000 and that its assets consisted of "miniature golf courses plus other assets." Ruderian's business practice was to "buy and resell prior to final payment on his sales contracts."

Lipkin also examined the sales contracts. He was an attorney but had only practiced one year. He concluded that the contracts were legally enforceable. He consulted another Laventhol partner who assured him that there need be no concern about Ruderian. Ruderian's references concurred in the appraisal.

Lipkin also consulted over the telephone with a Los Angeles attorney. The attorney did not see the contracts, nor were the contracts in their entirety read to him, despite the fact that his offices were only one-half hour away by cab. Nevertheless, the attorney gave a telephone opinion that they were valid and enforceable.

The first tangible results of Laventhol's accounting efforts appear in its audit enclosed in its letter to FGL, dated December 6, 1969. In the consolidated balance sheet as of November 30, 1969, the amount of $1,795,500 was recorded "as unrealized gross profit." The same characterization was given to this assumed profit in the income statement with a reference to an explanatory Note 4. This Note only explained the $1,795,500 by stating that "because of the circumstances and nature of the transactions, $1,795,500 of the gross profit thereon will be considered realized when the January 30, 1970, payment is received." The $1,795,500 was apparently arrived at by first adding the $25,000 paid upon execution of the Continental agreement, the $25,000 not yet due (until January 2, 1970) and $185,000—a liquidated damage figure for nonperformance. These amounts totalled $235,000. They were apparently considered as received and were deducted from the then fictitious profit of $2,030,500, resulting in the figure of $1,795,500. This first December 6, 1969, report is marked "Withdrawn & Superseded."

The reason for the withdrawal is found in the testimony that FGL wanted the audit to reflect the entire amount of $2,030,500 as pre-November 30, 1969, income resulting from a sale by FGL to Continental. On December 4, 1969, Chazen and Lipkin met with FGL officers. Firestone objected to the tentative accounting treatment of the Monterey transactions, and FGL threatened to withdraw its account and sue Laventhol if the private financing did not go through.

A second report (also dated December 6, 1969) was then submitted by Laventhol. In the income statement "unrealized gross profits (Note 4)" was changed to "Deferred gross profit (Note 4)" and Note 4, itself to read:

> Of the total gross profit of $2,030,500, $235,000 is included in the Consolidated Income Statement and the balance $1,795,500 will be considered realized when the January 30, 1970, payment is received. The latter amount is included in deferred income in the consolidated balance sheet.

It was this second report which was distributed to the investors, including Herzfeld.

Unlike the initial report, the opinion letter accompanying this second and final report was qualified. It stated:

> In our opinion, subject to collectibility of the balance receivable on the contract of sale (see Note 4 of Notes to Financial Statements) the accompanying consolidated balance sheet and related consolidated statements of income and retained earnings present fairly the financial position of [FGL]. . . .

Recognizing the difference between the financial statements (Exhibit B to the purchase agreement of November 10, 1969) and the Laventhol audit (December 6, 1969) submitted to Herzfeld and others, on December 16, 1969, FGL attempted to explain by a letter of that date the shift of $1,795,500 from a current to a deferred basis. The financial statements and the qualified opinion letter accompanied the FGL letter which purported to "explain" the distinctions between unaudited projections originally contained in the Agreement and Laventhol's report. No claim is made that Laventhol in any way participated in, or was responsible for, this FGL letter.

The FGL letter reads:

> One transaction which is reflected in the November 30 audited financial statements has been treated as producing deferred gross profit rather than current gross profit. While the combination of current and deferred income is actually higher than projected ($1,411,557 as compared with $1,360,000 projected) the shift of $1,795,500 of gross profit on this transaction from a current basis to deferred basis by the auditors has reduced current net income below that originally projected. . . .
>
> Deferred income shown on the audited balance sheet has been increased to $2,834,133 as against $1,421,000 projected. A breakdown of the components of the deferred income account is shown in the audited financial statements. . . .
>
> If for any reason you find that the changes reflected in the audited financial statements are of a nature which would have resulted in a change in your investment decision, we will arrange to promptly refund to you your subscription payment. . . .
>
> Allen & Company will undertake to replace any cancelled subscriptions with others on the same terms and conditions so that in any event the Firestone Group, Ltd. will have available to it the proceeds from the sale of at least 25 units.

Herzfeld read this letter outlining the differences, the "Consolidated Statement of Income and Retained Earnings" and noted the deferred gross profit item of $1,795,500. He did not read the Laventhol opinion letter or Note 4. Apparently, relying on what he had seen, he was satisfied with his investment and did not take advantage of the rescission offer.

Neither the Monterey nor the Continental transactions were consummated, and somewhat over a year later FGL filed a petition under Chapter XI of the Bankruptcy Act. A 10% dividend was eventually paid. This 10% payment was included in the $357,000 Allen settlement, leaving a balance of $153,000 unpaid on Herzfeld's original investment, for which, by this suit, he claims that Laventhol, because of its materially misleading audit, is responsible.

The Trial Court first considered Herzfeld's claim under § 10(b) of the Securities Exchange Act of 1934, and Rule 10b-5 thereunder. 15 U.S.C. § 78j(b); 17 C.F.R. § 240.10b-5. The Court found that "Laventhol knew that its audited report was required for the FGL private placement and that investors would be relying on the financial statements"; that Laventhol had access to information concerning FGL which was not available to investors. As to Laventhol's legal duty, the Court held that it was the policy of the securities laws that investors be provided "with all the facts

needed to make intelligent investment decisions [which] can only be accomplished if financial statements fully and fairly portray the actual financial condition of the company." 378 F. Supp. at 122.

After analyzing the facts, the Court concluded that "the Laventhol report was materially misleading." Id. at p. 124. The Court found that Note 4, claimed by Laventhol to be fully explanatory, was misleading: (1) in not disclosing that Continental, obligated to pay almost $5,000,000 had assets of only some $100,000; (2) in affirmatively stating that FGL had "acquired" the nursing homes (when it had not); (3) in reporting that $1,795,500 was deferred income; and (4) in stating that there was a leaseback (when apparently no such lease existed). The Court's conclusion was that "the inclusion of the Monterey transaction in sales and income was misleading without a full disclosure by Laventhol of all the material facts about the transactions." Id. at p. 125.

Examining the report as a whole, the Court also found ten materially misleading omissions in Laventhol's failure to disclose (1) Continental's net worth; (2) the printed form language which suggested that they were mere options; (3) the absence of Ruderian's personal liability; (4) Ruderian's practice of reselling property before he paid for it; (5) the absence of any records of the Monterey transactions in FGL books; (6) the relative importance of the contracts; (7) the loss FGL would suffer if the sales fell through; (8) the absence of any title search; (9) that FGL had not acquired title; and (10) that the attorney ventured his opinion about the enforceability of the contract without having examined the printed forms.

The Court held that Laventhol had the necessary *scienter* (merely the Latin adverb for "knowingly"), namely, "knowledge of the fact that the figures created a false picture . . .," and in addition, that Laventhol "had actual knowledge of the omitted facts which render[ed] its report misleading." Id. at p. 127. In light of Laventhol's concession that it was actually aware of the facts which the Trial Court correctly determined made Laventhol's affirmations misleading, we need not dwell upon the particular evidentiary items which the Court invoked to supplement its rationale.

The Laventhol report, if not the original inducing factor for the purchase, was read by Herzfeld. The Court therefore concluded that "The report's false picture of FGL's financial condition was, thus, a substantial, even crucial, factor in convincing Herzfeld that his investment decision to purchase the securities was right," Id. at p. 129, and that Herzfeld had shown sufficient reliance thereon. Characterizing the case as one of affirmative misrepresentations, the Court held that the correct test was whether the misrepresentations were a substantial factor in Herzfeld's decision to go through with his purchase of the FGL securities and determined that the Laventhol material was such a factor.

Laventhol contends that the Court erred and would have us attribute Herzfeld's purchase of the securities to his own enthusiasm, his acquaintance's touting, the FGL letter which accompanied the Laventhol report—in short, to everything but the Laventhol material. As to the Laventhol material, Laventhol argues that Herzfeld ignored it and emphasizes that Herzfeld read neither the opinion letter nor footnote 4 to which both the opinion letter and the income statement referred. This, to Laventhol, is fatal because it contends, *inter alia*, that the only statement made by an auditor upon which an investor is entitled to rely is the auditor's opinion letter. We agree with none of these arguments.

The Trial Court invoked the appropriate reliance test. Generally speaking, a plaintiff in a Rule 10b-5 damage action must prove that the misrepresentation was a "substantial factor" in his securities activities. *Titan Group Inc. v. Faggen,* 513 F.2d 234, 238–39 (2d Cir.), *cert. denied,* 423 U.S. 840, 96 S. Ct. 70, 46 L. Ed. 2d 59 (1975). *Globus v. Law Research Serv. Inc.,* 418 F.2d 1276, 1291–92 (2d Cir. 1969), *cert. denied,* 397 U.S. 913, 90 S. Ct. 913, 25 L. Ed. 2d 93 (1970).

The Trial Court correctly applied the "substantial factor" test. Even assuming that persons other than Laventhol first aroused Herzfeld's interest in FGL, or that the FGL cover letter which accompanied the Laventhol material may have influenced Herzfeld somewhat, these considerations do not defeat Herzfeld's claim. Herzfeld was not required to prove that the Laventhol material was the sole and exclusive cause of his action, he must only show that it was "substantial," *i.e.,* a significant contributing cause.

The Laventhol material was clearly a substantial factor. Looking at the transaction as a whole, it becomes clear that the investment decision was predicated upon confirmation of the Agreement's financial presentation by the Laventhol audit. The FGL letter explicitly informed the tentative investors of this fact and the Agreement itself conditioned its financial data on the auditor's confirmation. Herzfeld examined the Agreement and its income statement which suggested that FGL was a "very profitable company." When the Laventhol material was distributed he checked its income statement which provided the crucial corroboration of the Agreement's picture of corporate health. As the Trial Court observed "He paid particular attention to the earnings indicated and was very impressed by the deferred gross profit of $1,795,000. [sic] The latter figure, he understood, meant 'that this is a profit that the company had made and was going to pick up in a subsequent accounting period.' " In reliance upon this

corroborative Laventhol financial statement, Herzfeld completed his investment in FGL securities.

In view of our imposition of liability on the ground that the Laventhol audit was materially and knowingly misleading and that Herzfeld relied thereon, we need not pass upon the questions whether there was a violation of New York State statutory or common law.

The issue here is not one of negligence, but of the "materially misleading" treatment of facts known to Laventhol in its submitted audit.

The function of an accountant is not merely to verify the correctness of the addition and subtraction of the company's bookkeepers. Nor does it take a fiscal wizard to appreciate the elemental and universal accounting principle that revenue should not be recognized until the "earning process is complete or virtually complete," and "an exchange has taken place." Insofar as FGL's interest in the Monterey transactions is concerned, the earning process had hardly commenced, let alone neared completion. As of November 30, 1969, FGL had paid only $5,000 cash out of $13.2 million dollar purchase price and accepted a $25,000 "deposit" under a $15.3 million contract. Conditions for closing were unsatisfied. There remained the consummation of its purchase from Monterey, the furnishing to Continental of current title reports, and the delivery of the CC&R's and a copy of a lease. By the close of November 30, 1969, title had not passed. Nor was this the exceptional instance of a conditional sale or a long-term lease with purchase option, where the retention of title does not vitiate the economic reality of a consummated exchange.

Reference to the SEC's Accounting Series Release No. 95, 28 F.R. 276, 5 CCH Fed. Securities Rep. ¶ 72,117, p. 62,272 ("ASR # 95") points toward the same conclusion. That release lists several factors whose presence, according to the SEC, singly or in combination, raises a question of the propriety of current recognition of profit in real estate transactions. Not less than three of these factors inhere in the Monterey transaction, including (1) evidence of financial weakness of the purchaser (Continental's insignificant net worth relative to the resale property price); (2) substantial uncertainty as to amount of proceeds to be realized because of form of consideration—e.g., nonrecourse notes; (3) small or no down payment. Because the FGL offer was a private placement, ASR # 95 was not directly applicable to Laventhol's audit. But since ASR # 95 merely codifies basic principles of accrual accounting theory, we do not reject its corroboration of our own independent conclusions.

If the hoped-for profit of $2,030,500 were ever to be realized, it could only come after the transactions had been consummated—and consummation was never even contemplated before the audit date, November

30, 1969. FGL's profit till for this transaction as of that date was as bare of profits as Mother Hubbard's cupboard, bare of bones.

An accountant should not represent on an audited statement that income and profit exist unless underlying facts justify that conclusion. Here, the underlying facts known to Laventhol dictated precisely the contrary course, namely, that income should not have been recognized for the accounting period ending November 30, 1969. And were it not for Laventhol's disregard of Statements on Accounting Procedure No. 33, Ch. 2, p. 16 (1963) ("SAP 33") it would have confronted additional evidence pointing in the same direction. SAP 33 states:

> Sufficient competent evidential matter is to be obtained through inspection, observation, inquiries and confirmations to affirm a reasonable basis for an opinion regarding the financial statements under examination.

Laventhol knew that the issuance of FGL securities depended upon a correct ascertainment of that condition. It is undisputed that, without the Monterey-Continental transactions, for the eleven months preceding November 30, FGL has sustained a loss of $772,108. Query: by what accounting legerdemain was this figure converted into a substantial profit? The Monterey purchase added nothing to the FGL till. To the contrary, it reduced it by $5,000 (if the check was honored). The Continental sale produced a down payment of $25,000 (if made) but no profit. In fact, if the hoped-for profit of $2,030,500 were ever to be realized, it could only come after the transactions had been consummated—and consummation was never even contemplated before the audit date, November 30, 1969.

Laventhol points to the Trial Court's finding that the Monterey-Continental transactions were not "phony." This finding, however, only implies that there were signed agreements between the parties. By no stretch of the imagination does it imply that profits of $2,030,500 were realized therefrom before November 30, 1969, or would be at any time until consummation. In fact, both agreements showed on their face that the principal payments were to be made in 1970.

In such circumstances, the recognition of Monterey transactions was a materially misleading statement which, once included at the top of the income statement as a sale, resulted in, or necessitated, compensating adjustments which distorted all the financial figures which followed. A reasonable man in Herzfeld's position might well have acted otherwise than to purchase the FGL securities, had the truth been told and the Monterey transactions not been misleadingly represented as a consummated purchase and sale. *See*

Chasins v. Smith, Barney & Co., 2 Cir., 438 F.2d 1167 (1970); *SEC v. Texas Gulf Sulphur*, 401 F.2d 833, 849 (2d Cir.) (*en banc*) *cert. denied sub nom. Coates v. SEC*, 394 U.S. 976, 89 S.Ct. 1454, 22 L. Ed. 2d 756 (1968).

This misleading impression was aggravated by Laventhol's labeling of the $1,795,500 as "deferred" as opposed to "unrealized" gross profit. Such nomenclature conveyed the erroneous impression that all that profit was so much cash in hand and would be recognized periodically *in futuro* just as if it were prepaid interest or management fees. But as Laventhol well knew, net cash had increased only $20,000, and the transaction was still in doubt.

Having engendered its own quandary, it ill behooves Laventhol to seek the solace of *SAP 33*, which concerns the rendition of a qualified auditing opinion. But even assuming the propriety of allowing Laventhol as extricate itself by the simple expedient of disclaiming or qualifying its opinion of the very financial statements which it concocted, Laventhol did not follow the route proscribed by *SAP 33*. At Chapter 10, page 58, *SAP 33* provides, *inter alia*:

> When a qualification is so material as to negative an expression of opinion as to the fairness of the financial statement as a whole, either a disclaimer of opinion or an adverse opinion is required.

* * * * *

> When a qualified opinion is intended by the independent auditor, the opinion paragraph of the standard short-form report should be modified in a way that makes clear the nature of the qualification. It should refer specifically to the subject of the qualification and should give a *clear explanation of the reasons for the qualification* and of the effect on financial position and results of operations, if reasonably determinable. (Emphasis added.)

But Laventhol did not provide a *clear explanation of the reasons for the qualification*. A simple note would have sufficed saying in substance:

> Agreements for the purchase of Monterey Nursing Inns, Inc., for $13,362,500 and the sale thereof to Continental Recreation, Inc. for $15,393,000, have been executed. When, as and if these transactions are consummated, FGL expects to realize a profit of $2,030,500.

Instead, Laventhol chose to delete from its first so-called explanatory Note 4, the sentence "Because of the circumstances and nature of the transaction, $1,795,500 of the gross profit therein will be considered realized when the January 30, 1970, payment is received" and substituted therefor the sentence "Of the total gross profit of $2,030,500, $235,000 is included in the Consolidated Income Statement and the balance, $1,795,500 will be considered realized when the January 30, 1969, payment is received." The substituted note also changed "unrealized gross profit" to "deferred income." Even in the first Note, there is no explanation of what were the circumstances and nature of the transaction or, in the second Note, how or why $235,000 could qualify as gross profit or income as of November 30, 1969.

From the very outset of the audit, the danger signals were flashing.

1. Even if Laventhol accepted the agreements as not "phony," on the face of the Monterey agreement were two conditions to be performed, i.e., approval by FGL of a title search and a lease back. There was no proof that they were performed or that Laventhol made any effort to verify these facts.
2. Normally on transactions of such magnitude and vital importance, corporate minutes, resolutions and other corporate papers authenticating the transaction would be examined. No proof of such examination was presented.
3. Laventhol demonstrated an awareness that the legality of the agreement with Continental might be important. However, a telephone call to an attorney, who did not even see or read the agreement and who only heard such excerpts as Laventhol's partner chose to read to him, scarcely qualifies as a legal opinion as to enforceability.
4. As for Continental, Laventhol knew that it had contractually committed itself to pay $15.3 million to FGL and that Continental had assets of only some $100,000, consisting mostly of miniature golf courses. Laventhol was aware that Max Ruderian was a well-known, successful, and wealthy real estate operator and had signed the Continental agreement, but there is no document which evidences that Ruderian's wealth was in any way committed to the Continental purchase.
5. The absence of entries of the transactions on FGL's books and the necessity for Laventhol to create journal entries thereof.
6. Laventhol, whose duty it was to reveal the truth rather than be subservient to the dictates of its clients, FGL, should have taken warning from FGL's pressurizing tactics to change "unrealized profits" to "deferred."

In sum, we affirm the result reached by the Trial Court in holding that the Laventhol report contained materially misleading omissions and misrepresentations. The term *result* is used advisedly. Although we agree with the facts as found by the Trial Court, we do not accept its opinion that all of the 10 items specified therein were required to be included in Laventhol's report. The vice of the report was its representation

that the Monterey transactions were consummated and the concomitant statement that current and deferred profit had been realized. This would have been remedied by simply not recognizing the sales as completed transactions for the accounting period ending November 30, 1969. A specific listing of the facts which dictated that treatment would have been unnecessary.

There remains for consideration the effect, if any, of the Supreme Court's recent decision in *Ernst & Ernst v. Hochfelder,* 425 U.S. 785, 96 S. Ct. 1375, 47 L. Ed. 2d 668 (1976). In that case, a firm of accountants petitioned the Court to review a decision of the Seventh Circuit. The Court of Appeals had reversed a decision of a trial court granting summary judgment in favor of the accountants and against securities purchasers in an action based upon an alleged negligent audit by Ernst & Ernst. The gist of the charge was that the accountants "failed to utilize 'appropriate auditing procedures' in its audits of First Securities, thereby failing to discover internal practices of the firm said to prevent an effective audit." *Hochfelder, supra*, 96 S. Ct. at 1379.

The Supreme Court clearly defined the scope of its decision as "whether a private cause of action for damages will lie under § 10(b) and Rule 10b-5 in the absence of any allegation of 'scienter'—intent to deceive, manipulate, or defraud. [footnote omitted]" Id. at 1381. There is no question here that Herzfeld's amended complaint against Laventhol adequately alleged scienter in that Laventhol

> (a) employed a device, scheme or artifice to defraud plaintiff; (b) made untrue statements of material facts or omissions to state material facts necessary in order to make the statements made, in light of the circumstances under which they were made, not misleading; and (c) engaged in transactions, practices and a course of business which operated as a fraud and deceit on plaintiff. App. p. 112a.

The difference, therefore, between the factual situation before the Supreme Court in *Hochfelder*, where "throughout the lengthy history of this case respondents have proceeded on a theory of liability premised on negligence, specifically disclaiming that Ernst & Ernst had engaged in fraud or intentional misconduct. [footnote omitted]" Id. at 1391 and the case before us involving affirmative acts by Laventhol which were materially misleading, is clear. The accountants here are not being cast in damages for negligent nonfeasance or misfeasance, but because of their active participation in the preparation and issuance of false and materially misleading accounting reports upon which Herzfeld relied to his damage.

Nor does Herzfeld's failure to read the opinion letter or "explanatory" footnote vitiate his reliance upon the figures in the financial statement which he did examine. The opinion letter and "explanatory" footnote were as misleading as the figures in the financial statement. None of these discrete portions of the Laventhol audit adequately disclosed the serious question marks surrounding the Monterey transaction.

In his initial complaint, Herzfeld sought compensatory damages and punitive damages for $1 million from Laventhol, Allen and 10 other defendants. In 1971 Herzfeld settled with and released all defendants except Laventhol in exchange for $357,000. The District Court, *per* Palmieri, *J.*, over Laventhol's objection, approved the settlement and dismissed the complaint as to the settling defendants with the proviso that "Laventhol, if it is so advised, can bring third-party actions against any of the settling defendants."

In its third-party complaint against Allen, FGL, Charles Allen, Lee W. Meyers, Irwin H. Kramer, Richard M. Firestone, Martin A. Scott and David Baird, Laventhol sought, by way of indemnification and contribution to recover from these third-party defendants for the amount of any judgment, costs, expenses and attorneys' fees for which Laventhol might be liable in the Herzfeld suit against it. In their answer, in addition to denials, certain third-party defendants, Allen, Charles Allen and Irwin H. Kramer, asserted counterclaims against Laventhol for damages in the amount of $1,890,000. The basis for these claims is that they were the assignees of all rights of purchasers of the units. No proof was adduced from these purchasers as to the circumstances under which they purchased the FGL units or the extent of their knowledge, if any, of the facts.

The Trial Court dismissed the third-party complaint against Kramer for lack of proof. However, as to Allen, the Court found that "Allen plainly failed to fulfill its duty of full and fair disclosure to investors." It premised this conclusion on the fact that Meyer was a director of FGL and a vice-president of Allen. However, it denied Laventhol a right to indemnity from Allen on the theory that "one who intentionally joins in the perpetration of a fraud is denied a right of indemnity for others participating in the wrong, whether the claim is predicated on violation of the securities laws or the common law [footnote omitted]." 378 F. Supp. at 135.

The Court believed that "Laventhol's claim for contribution rests on firmer ground," namely, Allen's knowledge through its officer, Meyer, that there were major discrepancies between the audited and unaudited reports and that Meyer attended a conference at which the contents of the proposed December 16th letter were discussed. After trial the Trial Court computed damages on the main claim, subtracted the settlement from the total and, finding Allen *in pari delicto* with Laventhol, ordered Allen to pay one half of the remainder, i.e., $76,500.

The Allen-Herzfeld settlement for $357,000 and its significance must be given closer attention. We do not find the ground as firm as the Trial Court. The cases cited by the Court and in the Laventhol brief each deal with facts quite different from those here presented. The Court used as its foundation stone the principle that a wrongdoer should [not] be permitted "to escape loss by shifting his entire responsibility for damages to another party" and that "to deny contribution would be to dilute the deterrent effect of the securities laws, since Allen, a participant in Laventhol's fraud, would escape responsibility for its wrongdoing." 378 F. Supp. at 135.

Neither principle is applicable to the facts before us. A review of the facts as found by the Trial Court vis-à-vis the Allen-Laventhol relationship, shows that the Laventhol report which was the source of the false and misleading audit was dated as of, and was issued on, December 6, 1969. There is no suggestion that Allen had anything to do with its preparation. Allen's liability to Herzfeld resulted from its sale of securities with knowledge of the false and misleading nature of the figures in Laventhol's December 6th report. This knowledge came to Allen through its vice president, Meyer. Only after the report in final form was received, did Meyer participate in discussions which had, for their purposes, the making of changes favorable to FGL therein. But this proof only strengthened Herzfeld's case against Allen because it made Allen also liable for selling the securities on the basis of the Laventhol report. However, this liability had been extinguished as to Allen and its codefendants (except Laventhol) by the $357,000 settlement.

Quite apart from any degree of difference in culpability, had the original Herzfeld suit been tried against the Allen group and Laventhol, and, even on the theory of joint Laventhol-Allen liability, they had been held to be joint tortfeasors and compelled to restore to Herzfeld his $510,000 loss (excluding any claim for punitive damages), the respective amounts payable as joint tortfeasors (and on the Court's *pari delicto* theory) whether by judgment, contribution or principles of equity, should have been $255,000 each. Allen, however, to make peace with Herzfeld, had paid him $357,000 (on behalf of itself and others than Laventhol) and thus had removed itself from the category of a tortfeasor defendant. In Herzfeld's subsequent suit to recoup from Laventhol the balance of his $510,000 (namely, $153,000), Allen was not made a defendant and could not properly have been by dint of the settlement. Thus, Allen is not a joint feasor, vis-à-vis Herzfeld, in the present suit.

Allen had already paid Herzfeld far more than half of Herzfeld's loss. It neither escaped responsibility nor the deterrent effect of its settlement, but by the settlement its tortfeasor status had been removed. The pro-

212

cedural principle to which the Trial Court referred, i.e., to simplify the litigation "by bringing in the third party into the prime action . . ." is the very eventuality Allen sought to (and in our opinion did) avoid by its settlement. New York General Obligations Law § 15–108 (23A McKinney's Supp. 1975) supports this doctrine.

As to Allen's attempt to sue as an assignee, putting to one side the question whether any assignments were ever consummated, Allen was not entitled to recover on the claims because it failed to prove a necessary element common to all the assignor's claims. Allen, as assignee, stood only in the shoes of its assignors. However, of all the purported assignors only one was questioned about his reliance upon the Laventhol audit, and it appears that he relied predominantly on the fact that Allen's name was behind the placement. No evidence was adduced sufficient to establish a claim by these purchasers against Laventhol. Accordingly, we affirm the dismissal of Allen's counterclaims with prejudice.

Despite this manifest insufficiency of proof as a matter of law, Allen contends that it is entitled to a new trial on the issues. We disagree. Allen had its day in court; it is entitled to no more. Nor is there any reason to remand the counterclaims to the district court for it to enter specific findings corroborating the insufficiency. While F.R.C.P. rule 41(b) requires findings of fact pursuant to F.R.C.P. rule 52(a) where a claim tried before a court is dismissed for insufficiency, in this case a remand to cure the defect would be pointless. The record is barren as to reliance and consequently points to but one conclusion.

The judgment in favor of Herzfeld against Laventhol in the amount of $153,000 with costs and with interest at the rate of 7½% from January 1, 1971, to September 1, 1972, and at the rate of 6% from September 1, 1972, to the date of payment, is affirmed; the judgment in favor of third-party plaintiff Laventhol against third-party defendant Allen in the amount of $76,500 with costs and one half the interest payable by Laventhol under the judgment rendered against it is reversed; and the dismissal of the counterclaim of Allen against Laventhol is affirmed without costs.

UNITED STATES v. SIMON*

United States Court of Appeals
for the Second Circuit, 1969
425 F.2d 796

This American criminal case established two revolutionary principles: (1) Compliance with generally accepted accounting principles is not a conclusive de- *fense to criminal fraud, and (2) the auditor must disclose known misconduct of the client or client's officers which may reasonably affect audited financial statements.*

FRIENDLY, Circuit Judge:

Defendant Carl Simon was a senior partner, Robert Kaiser a junior partner, and Melvin Fishman a senior associate in the internationally known accounting firm of Lybrand, Ross Bros. & Montgomery. They stand convicted after trial by Judge Mansfield and a jury in the District Court for the Southern District of New York under three counts of an indictment charging them with drawing up and certifying a false or misleading financial statement of Continental Vending Machine Corporation (hereafter, "Continental") for the year ending September 30, 1962. After denying motions for acquittal or a new trial, the judge fined Simon $7,000 and Kaiser and Fishman $5,000 each.

Count One of the indictment was for conspiracy to violate 18 U.S.C. §§ 1001 and 1341 and § 32 of the Securities Exchange Act of 1934, 15 U.S.C. § 78ff. Section 1001 provides:

Whoever, in any matter within the jurisdiction of any department or agency of the United States knowingly and willfully falsifies, conceals or covers up by any trick, scheme, or device a material fact, or makes any false, fictitious or fraudulent statements or representations, or makes or uses any false writing or document knowing the same to contain any false, fictitious or fraudulent statement or entry, shall be fined not more than $10,000 or imprisoned not more than five years, or both.

Section 1341 makes criminal the use of the mails in aid of "any scheme or artifice to defraud." Section 32 of the Securities Exchange Act renders criminal the willful and knowing making of a statement in any required report which is false or misleading with respect to any material fact. Counts Three and Six charged two mailings of the statement in violation of 18 U.S.C. § 1341. Nothing turns on the different phrasings of the test of criminality in the three statutes. The Government concedes it had the burden of offering proof allowing a reasonable jury to be convinced beyond a reasonable doubt not merely that the financial statement was false or misleading in a material respect but that defendants knew it to be and deliberately sought to mislead.

While every criminal conviction is important to the defendant, there is a special poignancy and a corresponding responsibility on reviewing judges when, as here, the defendants have been men of blameless lives and respected members of a learned profession. See *United States v. Kahaner*, 317 F.2d 459,467 (2 Cir.), *cert. denied*, 375 U.S. 836, 84 S. Ct. 74, 11 L. Ed. 2d 65 (1963). This is no less true because the trial judge,

* The court's footnotes are omitted.

wisely in our view, imposed no prison sentences. On the other hand, as we observed in the *Kahaner* opinion, our office is limited to determining whether the evidence was sufficient for submission to the jury and, if so, whether errors prejudicial to the defendants occurred at the trial.

I

The trial hinged on transactions between Continental and an affiliate, Valley Commercial Corporation (hereafter, "Valley"). The dominant figure in both was Harold Roth, who was president of Continental, supervised the day-to-day operations of Valley, and owned about 25 percent of the stock of each company.

Valley, which was run by Roth out of a single office on Continental's premises, was engaged in lending money at interest to Continental and others in the vending machine business. Continental would issue negotiable notes to Valley, which would endorse these in blank and use them as collateral for drawing on two lines of credit, of $1 million each, at Franklin National Bank ("Franklin") and Meadowbrook National Bank ("Meadowbrook"), and would then transfer to Continental the discounted amount of the notes. These transactions, beginning as early as 1956, gave rise to what is called "the Valley payable." By the end of fiscal 1962, the amount of this was $1,029,475, of which $543,345 was due within the year.

In addition to the Valley payable, there was what is known as the "Valley receivable," which resulted from Continental loans to Valley. Most of these stemmed from Roth's custom, dating from mid-1957, of using Continental and Valley as sources of cash to finance his transactions in the stock market. At the end of fiscal 1962, the amount of the Valley receivable was $3.5 million, and by February 15, 1963, the date of certification, it has risen to $3.9 million. The Valley payable could not be offset, or "netted," against the Valley receivable since, as stated, Continental's obligations to Valley were in the form of negotiable notes which Valley had endorsed in blank to the two banks and used as collateral to obtain the cash which it then lent to Continental.

By the certification date, the auditors had learned that Valley was not in a position to repay its debt, and it was accordingly arranged that collateral would be posted. Roth and members of his family transferred their equity in certain securities to Arthur Field, Continental's counsel, as trustee to secure Roth's debt to Valley and Valley's debt to Continental. Some 80 percent of these securities consisted of Continental stock and convertible debentures.

The 1962 financial statements of Continental, which were dismal by any standard, reported the status of the Valley transactions as follows:

ASSETS
Current Assets:

* * * * *

Accounts and notes receivable:

* * * * *

Valley Commercial Corp., affiliate (Note 2)	$2,143,335

* * * * *

Noncurrent accounts and notes receivable:

Valley Commercial Corp., affiliate (Note 2)	1,400,000

* * * * *

LIABILITIES
Current Liabilities:

* * * * *

Long-term debt portion due within one year	$8,203,788

* * * * *

Long-term debt (Note 7)

* * * * *

Valley Commercial Corp., affiliate (Note 2)	486,130

* * * * *

NOTES TO CONSOLIDATED FINANCIAL STATEMENTS

2. The amount receivable from Valley Commercial Corp. (an affiliated company of which Mr. Harold Roth is an officer, director, and stockholder) bears interest at 12 percent a year. Such amount, less the balance of the notes payable to that company, is secured by the assignment to the Company of Valley's equity in certain marketable securities. As of February 15, 1963, the amount of such equity at current market quotations exceeded the net amount receivable.

7. . . . The amounts of long-term debt, including the portion due within one year, on which interest is payable currently or has been discounted in advance, are as follows:

* * * * *

Valley Commercial Corp., affiliate $1,029,475

The case against the defendants can be best encapsulated by comparing what Note 2 stated and what the Government claims it would have stated if defendants had included what they knew:

2. The amount receivable from Valley Commercial Corp. (an affiliated company of which Mr. Harold Roth is an officer, director and stockholder), which bears interest at 12 percent a year, was uncollectible at September 30, 1962, since Valley had loaned approxi-

mately the same amount to Mr. Roth who was unable to pay. Since that date Mr. Roth and others have pledged as security for the repayment of his obligation to Valley and its obligation to Continental (now $3,900,000, against which Continental's liability to Valley cannot be offset) securities which, as of February 15, 1963, had a market value of $2,978,000. Approximately 80 per cent of such securities are stock and convertible debentures of the Company.

Striking as the difference is, the latter version does not reflect the Government's further contention that in fact the market value of the pledged securities on February 15, 1963, was $1,978,000 rather than $2,978,000 due to liens of James Talcott, Inc., and Franklin for indebtedness other than Roth's of which defendants knew or should have known.

II

Although the facts set forth up to this point were uncontroverted, there were some sharp disagreements concerning just what defendants knew and when they learned it. Issues of credibility, however, were for the jury, and we here set forth what the jury could permissibly have found the further facts to be.

Roth engaged the Lybrand firm as Continental's auditors in 1956. George Shegog was the partner in charge; Simon was "second partner" but had no responsibility save for the review of SEC filings. Upon Shegog's death, early in 1960, Simon became the partner in charge. Kaiser was first assigned to the Continental audit as "audit manager" for the 1961 audit. Fishman had been assigned to the Continental audit in 1957 as a young junior accountant; in 1962 he was promoted to be manager of the Continental audit for that year, and Kaiser was retained as "second partner." The day-to-day supervision of the audit was the responsibility of Richard McDevitt. As is usual, the structure was pyramidal in terms of time spent.

The Valley receivable had attracted attention early in Lybrand's engagement. In the late fall of 1958, Yoder, who was then manager of the Continental audit, discussed it with Roth. In a memorandum which was read by Fishman at the time and remained in the Lybrand audit files, Yoder recorded that during fiscal 1958 Continental had made net cash payments to Valley of $1,185,790, which "appeared to be for no other purpose than to provide Valley with cash." He recorded also that since September 30, Continental had made additional payments to Valley of $824,752 which were used "to finance the acquisition of capital stock of U.S. Hoffman Machine Corporation by Mr. Roth, or for loans by Valley to U.S. Hoffman." He also stated that he was informed that the receivable should be applied to notes of Continental and its subsidiaries which represented the Valley payable, and that he had

agreed provided that the notes, which Valley had pledged as collateral for its borrowings from Franklin and Meadowbrook, were surrendered and made available for Lybrand's inspection. In a memorandum to Simon in November 1960, Yoder again discussed the Valley receivable, noting that the payments were frequent, in round amounts, and unaccompanied by written explanations. He observed that during the 1960 fiscal year the receivable had ranged from $695,000 in October 1959 to $398,000 in September 1960 with a high of $1,583,000 in April 1960.

In 1961 and 1962, the cash payments giving rise to the Valley receivable continued to be frequent, in round amounts, and without written explanation. Moreover, the balance in the Valley receivable account characteristically was parabolic, rising after the end of one fiscal year and falling prior to the end of the next. The payments and repayments and the year-end balances for 1958–1962 are shown by the following table:

Year	Advances to Valley	Repayments by Valley	Receivable at Year-End
1958	$3,356,239	$2,583,172	$ —0—
1959	4,586,000	3,510,451	$ 384,402
1960	2,511,000	2,670,500	397,996
1961	2,390,674	1,520,000	848,006
1962	4,708,000	1,986,500	3,543,335

Although the figure for the end of 1961 was more than double that at the end of the two preceding years, and had increased to about $2 million by December 31, 1961, prior to the certification date, the 1961 financial statement made no comment on the "receivable, and none of the defendants asked whether Continental's directors had been informed of the transactions. Simon merely warned Roth that an examination of Valley's books would be required if the receivable at the end of fiscal 1962 was as large as at the end of 1961.

When Fishman visited Continental's office in early September 1962 in preparation for that year's audit, he was told that as of July 31 the Valley receivable had reached $3.6 million. He was told also that Continental was operating a check float in excess of $500,000 daily, that cash was "tighter than ever," and that Continental's Assistant Comptroller had spent most of July and August "juggling cash." Fishman reported this to Simon and Kaiser, noting that "all in all, it promises to be an 'interesting' audit."

The cash audit, conducted in early October 1962, showed how stringent cash had become. The $286,000 in hand on September 30 resulted only from 30-day loans of $1.5 million from Franklin and Meadowbrook four days earlier. The Valley receivable was found to be around $3.5 million, and Fishman told Roth in late

October that this was so large that "there could be a problem with the year-end audit." In answer to a question by Fishman in November why Valley needed so much money, Kalan, Continental's Assistant Comptroller, said that "Roth needed the money to maintain the margin accounts on the U.S. Hoffman stock and bonds and the Continental stock and bonds."

Early in November Fishman met with Kaiser and reviewed the history of the Valley receivable. A memorandum of November 12 from Fishman to Kaiser, with a copy to Simon, "anticipated that September 30, 1962, Continental's balance sheet will show a net receivable from Valley of approximately $1,000,000 representing the excess of cash transfers to Valley over notes issued to Valley" and stated an intention to review the collectibility of the "net receivable" by examining "the latest available financial statements of Valley and other documentation."

In December, Fishman phoned Simon that the Valley receivable as of September 30 was about $3.5 million. Simon instructed Fishman to tell Roth that Lybrand would need the financial statements of Valley in order to evaluate the receivable's collectibility. Roth called Simon and said that Valley's audit was not yet finished and that the statements would be made available when it was. There were similar conversations during January 1963.

Meanwhile, according to Roth, he had contacted Simon in December and said that although Valley had a net worth of $2 million, it was not in a position to repay its $3.5 million debt to Continental as it had lent him approximately the same amount which he was unable to repay. He suggested that he secure the indebtedness with his equity in stocks, bonds and other securities of Continental and Hoffman International if this would be acceptable. Roth called Simon some ten days later and received the latter's assent. On December 31, Roth placed Arthur Field, counsel for Continental, in charge of preparing the assignments.

Late in January 1963, Fishman visited Roth and showed him a draft of Note 2 substantially identical with the final form; he told Roth that Simon wanted to see him. They met in the Lybrand office on February 6. Defendants conceded that at this meeting Roth informed Simon that Valley could not repay Continental and offered to post securities for the Valley receivable, and also to post as collateral a mortgage on his house and furnishings. Simon agreed that if adequate collateral were posted, a satisfactory legal opinion were obtained, and Continental's board approved the transactions, Lybrand could certify Continental's statements without reviewing Valley's, which still were not available. There was also a discussion of verification procedures. Simon determined that Roth, with a Lybrand employee listening on an extension phone, would call the various banks and brokers then holding Roth's

securities to confirm the "amount of securities pledged and the amount due to them."

On February 12, Roth told Simon that Field had the collateral ready for verification. Simon instructed Kaiser to go to Field's office. Finding that Field had made the proposed assignments run to Valley, Kaiser called this "ridiculous" and asked, "If the securities or if the cash equity gets back into Valley Commercial Corporation, what is to stop Harold Roth from taking the money out again as he did before?" On Kaiser's direction Field made the assignments run to himself as trustee for Valley and Continental. Field also discussed the available collateral and exhibited to Kaiser some handwritten notes prepared by Field and Miss Gans, secretary to Roth. These showed that the bulk of the collateral would consist of an equity in Continental stock and debentures. Kaiser made a number of calls having reference to this information and prepared notes of them which he later showed Simon; as developed in section V of this opinion, the Government alleges these demonstrated a complete encumberance of all of Roth's securities held by Franklin, Meadowbrook, and James Talcott, Inc. ("Talcott"). At Kaiser's request Field prepared a letter stating that $3.5 million in collateral was being posted and outlining the mechanics of the collateralization. On the following business day, Simon called to request that Field amend the letter to include an opinion that the collateral adequately secured the Valley receivable; the amended letter was sent on February 15 or 18. Meanwhile Field had informed Simon and Kaiser on February 13 that Continental's board of directors had disapproved of the loans to Valley.

On Friday, February 15, Kaiser assigned James Harris, a supervisor who had no previous connection with the Continental audit, to confirm the collateral. Kaiser explained the agreed procedure and introduced him to Roth and Miss Gans, but did not warn him of the possibility of encumbrances at Franklin, Meadowbrook, and Talcott. The telephone calls began around 10 A.M. and continued until later afternoon when Miss Gans "started having difficulty in reaching some of the people at some of these financial institutions." The calls ended, and Harris totaled the then quoted market price of the confirmed securities, subtracted the indebtedness disclosed over the telephone, and arrived at an equity interest of some $3.1 million, this including an equity of $1.2 million in stock held at Franklin, Meadowbrook, and Talcott. He telephoned Kaiser the results. Meanwhile Roth removed some $100,000 in odd securities from an office safe and offered them if Harris didn't have enough. The offer was declined. The schedule was then delivered to McDevitt, who applied the closing market quotations of February 15; these reduced the value to $2,978,000.

The three defendants met at Continental's plant on

Saturday, February 16, and prepared a printer's draft of the financial statements. Simon telephoned Roth and discussed the proposed statement, including Note 2. In the course of the conversation he requested payment of some $13,000 still owing for the 1961 audit. On Roth's instructions Kalan gave Simon a check, saying "This is going to bounce."

On Monday, February 18, Simon reviewed a printer's proof of the statements. At that time, for reasons which were not developed at trial but are now conceded to be proper, he moved from noncurrent into current assets $1,433,104, representing a receivable from the sale of certain vending routes. At the same time, he dropped from current assets to noncurrent assets some $1,400,000 of the Valley receivable, which Roth caused to be refinanced by Valley's issuance of long-term notes in that amount. Although Simon testified that he made this change solely because of the issuance of the notes, in which he had no part, Roth testified that Simon had earlier told him that some of the $3.5 million Valley receivable would have to go "below the line"—i.e., into noncurrent assets.

The financial statements were mailed as part of Continental's annual report on February 20. By that time the market value of the collateral had declined some $270,000 from its February 15 value. The value of the collateral fell an additional $640,000 on February 21. When the market reopened on February 25 after the long Washington's birthday recess, it fell another $2 million and was worth only $395,000. The same day a Continental check to the Internal Revenue Service bounced. Two days later the Government padlocked the plant and the American Stock Exchange suspended trading in Continental stock. Investigations by the SEC and bankruptcy rapidly ensued.

III

The defendants called eight expert independent accountants, an impressive array of leaders of the profession. They testified generally that, except for the error with respect to netting, the treatment of the Valley receivable in Note 2 was in no way inconsistent with generally accepted accounting principles or generally accepted auditing standards, since it made all the informative disclosures reasonably necessary for fair presentation of the financial position of Continental as of the close of the 1962 fiscal year. Specifically, they testified that neither generally accepted accounting principles nor generally accepted auditing standards required disclosure of the makeup of the collateral or of the increase of the receivable after the closing date of the balance sheet, although three of the eight stated that in light of hindsight they would have preferred that the makeup of the collateral be disclosed. The witnesses likewise testified that disclosure

of the Roth borrowings from Valley was not required, and seven of the eight were of the opinion that such disclosure would be inappropriate. The principal reason given for this last view was that the balance sheet was concerned solely with presenting the financial position of the company under audit; since the Valley receivable was adequately secured in the opinion of the auditors and was broken out and shown separately as a loan to an affiliate with the nature of the affiliation disclosed, this was all that the auditors were required to do. To go further and reveal what Valley had done with the money would be to put into the balance sheet things that did not properly belong there; moreover, it would create a precedent which would imply that it was the duty of an auditor to investigate each loan to an affiliate to determine whether the money had found its way into the pockets of an officer of the company under audit, an investigation that would ordinarily be unduly wasteful of time and money. With due respect to the Government's accounting witnesses, a SEC staff accountant, and, in rebuttal, its chief accountant, who took a contrary view, we are bound to say that they hardly compared with defendants' witnesses in aggregate auditing experience or professional eminence.

Defendants asked for two instructions which, in substance, would have told the jury that a defendant could be found guilty only if, according to generally accepted accounting principles, the financial statements as a whole did not fairly present the financial condition of Continental at September 30, 1962, and then only if his departure from accepted standards was due to willful disregard of those standards with knowledge of the falsity of the statements and an intent to deceive. The judge declined to give these instructions. Dealing with the subject in the course of his charge, he said that the "critical test" was whether the financial statements as a whole "fairly presented the financial position of Continental as of September 30, 1962, and whether it accurately reported the operations for fiscal 1962." If they did not, the basic issue became whether defendants acted in good faith. Proof of compliance with generally accepted standards was "evidence which may be very persuasive but not necessarily conclusive that he acted in good faith, and that the facts as certified were not materially false or misleading." "The weight and credibility to be extended by you to such proof, and its persuasiveness, must depend, among other things, on how authoritative you find the precedents and the teachings relied upon by the parties to be, the extent to which they contemplate, deal with, and apply to the type of circumstances found by you to have existed here, and the weight you give to expert opinion evidence offered by the parties. Those may depend on the credibility extended by you to expert witnesses, the definiteness with which they testified, the reasons given for their opinions, and all the other facts affecting credibility, . . . ''

Defendants contend that the charge and refusal to charge constituted error. We think the judge was right in refusing to make the accountants' testimony so nearly a complete defense. The critical test according to the charge was the same as that which the accountants testified was critical. We do not think the jury was also required to accept the accountants' evaluation whether a given fact was material to overall fair presentation, at least not when the accountants' testimony was not based on specific rules or prohibitions to which they could point, but only on the need for the auditor to make an honest judgment and their conclusion that nothing in the financial statements themselves negated the conclusion that an honest judgment had been made. Such evidence may be highly persuasive, but it is not conclusive, and so the trial judge correctly charged.

Defendants next contend that, particularly in light of the expert testimony, the evidence was insufficient to allow the jury to consider the failure to disclose Roth's borrowings from Valley, the makeup of the collateral, or the postbalance sheet increase in the Valley receivable. They concentrate their fire on what they characterize as the "primary, predominant and pervasive" issue, namely, the failure to disclose that Continental's loans to Valley were not for a proper business purpose but to assist Roth in his personal financial problems. It was "primary, predominant and pervasive" not only because it was most featured by the prosecution but because defendants' knowledge of Roth's diversion of corporate funds colored everything else. We join defendants' counsel in assuming that the mere fact that a company has made advances to an affiliate does not ordinarily impose a duty on an accountant to investigate what the affiliate has done with them or even to disclose that the affiliate has made a loan to a common officer if this has come to his attention. But it simply cannot be true that an accountant is under no duty to disclose what he knows when he has reason to believe that, to a material extent, a corporation is being operated not to carry out its business in the interest of all the stockholders but for the private benefit of its president. For a court to say that all this is immaterial as a matter of law if only such loans are thought to be collectible would be to say that independent accountants have no responsibility to reveal known dishonesty by a high corporate officer. If certification does not at least imply that the corporation has not been looted by insiders so far as the accountants know, or, if it has been, that the diversion has been made good beyond peradventure (or adequately reserved against) and effective steps taken to prevent a recurrence, it would mean nothing, and the reliance placed on it by the public would be a snare and a

delusion. Generally accepted accounting principles instruct an accountant what to do in the usual case where he has no reason to doubt that the affairs of the corporation are being honestly conducted. Once he has reason to believe that this basic assumption is false, an entirely different situation confronts him. Then, as the Lybrand firm stated in its letter accepting the Continental engagement, he must "extend his procedures to determine whether or not such suspicions are justified." If as a result of such an extension or, as here, without it, he finds his suspicions to be confirmed, full disclosure must be the rule, unless he has made sure the wrong has been righted and procedures to avoid a repetition have been established. At least this must be true when the dishonesty he has discovered is not some minor peccadillo but a diversion so large as to imperil if not destroy the very solvency of the enterprise.

On this dominating issue of Roth's diverting corporate funds we do not have a case where the question is whether accountants may be subjected to criminal sanction for closing their eyes to what was plainly to be seen. Fishman was proved to have known what was going on since 1958, Simon must have had a good idea about it from the spring of 1960 when Roth informed him that he had borrowed $1,000,000 from investment bankers to make a repayment to Valley, and the jury could infer that Kaiser also was not unaware. If Roth's testimony was believed, the defendants knew almost all the facts from December 1962. In any event they concede knowledge prior to the certification. Beyond what we have said, Field testified that at a meeting in February 1963 before the statements were certified, he, Simon and Kaiser discussed "how it was possible for a man like Harold Roth . . . for a man like that to go wrong and to take out this money through the circuitous method of having it first go into Valley and then to withdraw it immediately by himself. . . . '' The jury could reasonably have wondered how accountants who were really seeking to tell the truth could have constructed a footnote so well designed to conceal the shocking facts. This was not simply by the lack of affirmative disclosure but by the failure to describe the securities under circumstances crying for a disclosure and the failure to press Roth for a mortgage on his house and furnishings, description of which in the footnote would necessarily have indicated the source of the collateral and thus evoked inquiry where the money advanced to Valley had gone.

Turning to the failure to describe the collateral, defendants concede that they could not properly have certified statements showing the Valley receivable as an asset when they knew it was uncollectible. That was why Roth proposed collateralization and they accepted it. As men experienced in financial matters, they must have known that the one kind of property ideally unsuitable to collateralize a receivable whose collectibility was essential to avoiding an excess of current liabilities over current assets and a two-thirds reduction in capital already reduced would be securities of the very corporation whose solvency was at issue—particularly when the 1962 report revealed a serious operating loss. Failure to disclose that 80 percent of the "marketable securities" by which the Valley receivable was said to be "secured" were securities of Continental was thus altogether unlike a failure to state how much collateral were bonds or stocks of General Motors and how much of U.S. Steel. Indeed one of the defense experts testified that disclosure would be essential if Continental stock constituted more than 50 percent of the collateral. Beyond this, we are not here required to determine whether failure to reveal the nature of the collateral would have been a submittable issue if the Valley receivable had constituted an advance made for legitimate business purpose. Defendants' conduct had to be judged in light of their failure to reveal the looting by Roth. Since disclosure that 80 percent of the securities were Continental stock or debentures would have led to inquiry who could furnish so much, the jury could properly draw the inference that the failure to reveal that the bulk of the pledged securities was of the one sort most inappropriate to "secure" the Valley receivable, rather than being a following of accepted accounting principles, was part of a deliberate effort to conceal what defendants knew of the diversion of corporate funds that Roth had perpetrated.

We are likewise unimpressed with the argument that defendants cannot be charged with criminality for failure to disclose the known increase in the Valley receivable from $3.4 to $3.9 million. Here again the claim that generally accepted accounting practices do not require accountants to investigate and report on developments since the date of the statements being certified has little relevance. Note 2 stated "As of February 15, 1963, the amount of such equity at current market quotations exceeded the net amount receivable." This means the net amount receivable as of February 15. If the receivable remained at the $3.9 million level it had attained at December 31, 1962, and there is nothing to indicate its reduction, the collateral of $2.9 million verified by Harris barely equaled even the "net receivable, since the collateral, supplied long after September 30, 1962, although this also was not disclosed, concededly was security for advances after September 30 as well as before. The jury was thus entitled to infer that the failure to reveal the increase in the Valley receivable was part of an effort to create an appearance of collectibility which defendants knew to be false. Indeed one of the defense experts agreed that the increase in the receivable was a material event that required disclosure in the absence of sufficient collat-

eral. Moreover, this issue, like the others, must be considered in context. The jury could find that failure to reveal the known increase in the Valley receivable, rather than being motivated by adherence to accepted accounting principles, was due to fear that revelation of the increase would arouse inquiry why a company in the desperate condition of Continental would go on advancing money to an affiliate and thus lead to discovery of Roth's looting.

IV

Defendants properly make much of the alleged absence of proof of motivation. They say that even if the Government is not bound to show evil motive, and we think it is not, see *Pointer v. United States,* 151 U.S. 396, 14 S. Ct. 410, 38 L. Ed. 208 (1894), lack of evidence of motive makes the burden of proving criminal intent peculiarly heavy, and the Government did not discharge this.

It is quite true that there was no proof of motive in the form usual in fraud cases. None of the defendants made or could make a penny from Continental's putting out false financial statements. Neither was there evidence of motive in the sense of fear that telling the truth would lose a valuable account. Continental was not the kind of client whose size would give it leverage to bully a great accounting firm, nor was it important to the defendants personally in the sense of their having brought in the business. One would suppose rather that the Continental account had become a considerable headache to the Lybrand firm generally and to the defendants in particular; they could hardly have been unaware of the likelihood that the many hours the firm had devoted to the 1962 audit would not be compensated and that another might never occur. Ordinary commercial motivation is thus wholly absent.

The Government finds motive in defendants' desire to preserve Lybrand's reputation and conceal the alleged dereliction of their predecessors and themselves in former years—the failure to advise Continental's board of directors of Roth's role in creating the Valley receivable, see N.Y. Stock Corporation Law, McKinney's Consol Laws, c. 59, § 59; the failure to expand the scope of the audit for those years to determine the nature and collectibility of the Valley receivable, despite the injunction in a well-known text originally authored by one of the founders of the Lybrand firm, that receivables from affiliates must be scrutinized carefully to determine they "are what they purport to be"; and the certification of the 1961 statements despite Simon's warning to Roth that a further increase in the receivable would necessitate an examination of Valley's books. The apparent failure of the defendants to consult with the Lybrand executive committee, or with the partner in the firm to whom "problems" in audits were supposed to be referred, on what would seem highly important policy questions concerning the 1962 audit adds force to these arguments.

The main response is that if the defendants had wanted to cover up any past delinquencies they would not have insisted on financial statements so dismal in other respects. It is alleged that defendants demanded certain adjustments which good accounting practice permitted but did not require. It is said also that defendants must have known the statements were so unfavorable, even with the limited disclosure in Note 2, that Continental was bound to fold and a full investigation would follow. The argument is impressive but not dispositive. Defendants may have harbored the illusion that the dexterity of Continental's treasurer in "juggling cash" would enable it to survive. Moreover, men who find themselves in a bad situation of their own making do not always act with full rationality.

Even if there were no satisfactory showing of motive, we think the Government produced sufficient evidence of criminal intent. Its burden was not to show that defendants were wicked men with designs on anyone's purse, which they obviously were not, but rather that they had certified a statement knowing it to be false. As Judge Hough said for us long ago, "while there is no allowable inference of knowledge from the mere fact of falsity, there are many cases where from the actor's special situation and continuity of conduct an inference that he did know the untruth of what he said or wrote may legitimately be drawn." *Bentel v. United States,* 13 F.2 327, 329, *cert. denied,* 273 U.S. 713, 47 S. Ct. 109, 71 L. Ed. 854 (1926). See also *Aiken v. United States,* 108, F.2d 182, 183 (4 Cir. 1939). Moreover, so far as criminal intent is concerned, the various deficiencies in the footnote should not be considered in isolation. Evidence that defendants knowingly suppressed one fact permitted, although it surely did not compel, an inference that their suppression of another was likewise knowing and willful.

In addition to all that has been said on this score in the previous section of this opinion, a strong indication of knowing suppression lay in the evidence concerning the erroneous reduction of the Valley receivable by the $1 million of notes payable. Defendants say that this was mere negligence; that, beginning with Fishman's memorandum of November 12, 1962, they were "thinking net." But the jury was not bound to accept this. Even if the jury believed that Fishman had negligently slipped into error in November 1962, despite his peculiar awareness of the impossibility of netting, which it was not required to do, it truly taxed credulity to suppose that, with all the attention that was given to the Valley receivable over the next three months, none of these defendants, experienced in the business of Continental, ever mentioned to the others that the critical figure was not the net receivable but the gross, as

indeed the body of the financial statements showed, so that $3 million of collateral would not secure the receivable. Indeed Simon and Kaiser swore in depositions taken in a civil suit brought by Continental's bankruptcy Trustee and before the grand jury that they had known in February 1963 that the Continental notes were pledged so that netting was impossible, and made the implausible contention, as did Fishman in his grand jury testimony, that Note 2 had not netted. Defendants' attempt to escape from all this by alleging that they learned of the pledges of the Continental notes only in discussions with a Valley employee in May 1963, may have made matters worse for them with the jury rather than better. For the employee denied the conversation, and the story was inconsistent with the failure to net in the financial statements themselves and with other evidence.

The Government furnished added evidence of criminal intent in the shape of conflicting statements by the defendants and contradictions by other witnesses. Simon and Fishman had testified before the Referee in Continental's bankruptcy proceedings that they had discussed, together with Kaiser, whether disclosure need be made of the nature of the collateral, and had rejected this as unnecessary. Yet Simon testified at trial that no consideration had been given to this, and Fishman could not recall any discussion. Simon and Fishman swore to the Referee that they had not known of Roth's borrowings from Valley until March 1963. On the other hand, Fishman admitted before the grand jury that he had known of them as early as 1958; Roth testified to telling Simon about them in December 1962; all the defendants now admit they were fully informed before the certification in February 1963; and counsel for Continental's trustee testified that Simon had admitted knowing the facts "a long time" before that. When we add the delay in getting at the critical matter of the Valley receivable, the failure to follow up Roth's offer or a mortgage on his house and furniture, and the last-minute changes in the balance sheet, we find it impossible to say that a reasonable jury could not be convinced beyond a reasonable doubt that the striking difference between what Note 2 said and what it needed to say in order to reveal the truth resulted not from mere carelessness but from design. That some other jury might have taken a more lenient view, as the trial judge said he would have done, is a misfortune for the defendants but not one within our power to remedy.

V

In this last section of the opinion we will treat defendants' arguments concerning securities of Roth held by Franklin and Talcott, and the judge's handling of questions by the jury on this and another matter.

Kaiser's notes of his interview of February 12, 1963, with Field, which he showed to Simon on the next day, contained the following:

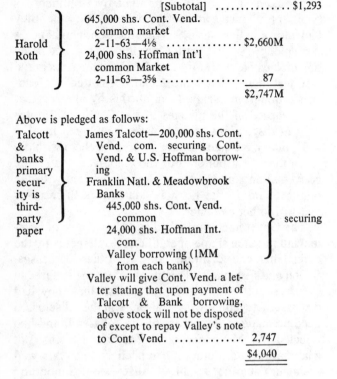

```
                              [Subtotal]  .............. $1,293
                      645,000 shs. Cont. Vend.
                        common market
 Harold               2-11-63—4⅛  .............. $2,660M
 Roth                 24,000 shs. Hoffman Int'l
                        common Market
                      2-11-63—3⅝  ................    87
                                                   $2,747M

Above is pledged as follows:
 Talcott              James Talcott—200,000 shs. Cont.
 &                      Vend. com. securing Cont.
 banks                  Vend. & U.S. Hoffman borrow-
 primary                ing
 secur-               Franklin Natl. & Meadowbrook
 ity is                 Banks
 third-                 445,000 shs. Cont. Vend.
 party                    common                              securing
 paper                  24,000 shs. Hoffman Int.
                          com.
                        Valley borrowing (1MM
                          from each bank)
                      Valley will give Cont. Vend. a let-
                        ter stating that upon payment of
                        Talcott & Bank borrowing,
                        above stock will not be disposed
                        of except to repay Valley's note
                        to Cont. Vend.  ..............  2,747
                                                       $4,040
```

Neither Kaiser nor Field communicated to Harris this indication that the securities held by Franklin, Meadowbrook and Talcott were subject to liens arising from borrowings other than Roth's. When Roth called Meadowbrook, with Harris listening on an extension phone, the bank stated that it held 23,600 shares of Hoffman International stock worth $80,000 which was "Security on Valley obligation," as it later confirmed in writing. Although Harris recorded this on his worksheet, he nevertheless included the $80,000 in the collateral, which defendants admit to have been an error although assertedly an inconsequential one. Franklin said it held 144,484 shares of U.S. Hoffman, 24,411 of Hoffman International, and 585,600 of Continental against a loan of $1,525,000 to Roth, as it subsequently confirmed in writing. Harris's computation, as later revised by McDevitt, included an equity of $900,000 in these securities. There was an erasure, innocent on defendants' view, in the "Comments" column of Harris's work sheets in regard to Franklin. The worksheets with respect to Talcott showed a holding of 67,000 Continental shares as "Collateral on indebtedness of Con. Vend. Mach. to Hoffman Mach." Harris included these shares as $270,000, their full market value. Harris's report did not show to whom he had talked at Talcott, and no written confirmation was received.

The Government was allowed to prove by internal records of Franklin that the securities there constituted collateral for Valley's debt of $944,269 in addition to Roth's personal debt. It was also allowed to prove by internal records of Talcott that Roth had pledged 25,000 Continental shares to secure the payment of Hoffman International notes discounted by U.S. Hoffman and 40,000 shares to guarantee loans by Talcott to Crescent Vending, a total liability exceeding $1 million. The court made clear to the jury that the contention was not that the defendants had seen the Franklin or Talcott records but rather that "they should have known, and shut their eyes to the inquiry." Defendants contend that even this limited use of the records was improper.

We have little difficulty in sustaining the court's ruling with respect to Kaiser and Simon. Kaiser's interview with Field, the notes of which were shown to Simon, indicated the unavailability of the securities held at the two banks and Talcott. The jury could take the failure to pass this information on to Harris and the acceptance of his schedules without further inquiry despite their confirmation of the unavailability of the stock at Meadowbrook and Talcott to be evidence of willingness to be satisfied with anything that would create the appearance of adequate security. Although defendants contend that the force of Kaiser's notes of February 12 was dissipated by another schedule given by Field allegedly on February 14 (which the Government disputes), making no reference to liens arising from indebtedness other than Roth's, this was a matter for the jury. The effect of Franklin's confirmation is dissolved if the only question propounded to it was the amount of Roth's indebtedness; furthermore, the jury was not required to accept the innocent explanation of the erasure. As to Kaiser and Simon the Government was thus entitled to show, under proper instructions, what proper inquiry would have revealed. On the other hand the evidence would have been admissible against Fishman only on the basis that, his membership in a conspiracy having been sufficiently shown, further evidence of the derelictions of the other conspirators was also admissable against him. While he would have been entitled to an instruction making that clear, none was sought.

During the evening after the case was submitted, the jury, which had been conferring for several hours, reported it was deadlocked, but the judge instructed it to deliberate further. Before leaving the courtroom it then asked three questions:

"Is there evidence, undisputed or otherwise, that the $2.9 million collateral had prior liens?"
That is question No. 1.
Question No. 2:
"Where did the proceeds of the home and furnishings mortgage go?"

Now 3:

"Was there testimony to the effect that the $2,900,000 was reduced to $1,700,000?"

After an endeavor to answer these had led to extended colloquy, the judge dismissed the jury for the night, heard counsel again the next morning, and then addressed the jury.

Instead of answering the first question categorically, the judge made a painstaking summary of all the evidence in which he developed the conflicting contentions and the inferences the jury could draw or not as it saw fit. With a single exception discussed in the margin, defendants make no criticism of the summary, and we can find no basis for any. The judge then said he would defer answering the third question because he did not understand the meaning of the words "reduced to." While it might have been better if the judge had simply referred back to what he had already said, we see no error of which the defendants can complain. The judge's detailed answer to the first question provided the best possible assistance with respect to the third, and he could not properly have given the categorical negative answer the defendants desired.

We likewise see no basis for criticizing the judge's answering of the second question by reading to the jury the relevant testimony of Simon and Field. This made clear that, although Roth had assigned the mortgages to Valley and Continental ultimately received them, they were not included in the collateral for the payment of the Valley receivable which constituted the basis for defendants' assertion of adequate collateralization.

We have carefully reviewed the few other arguments made by the defendants but do not consider them of sufficient importance to justify prolonging this already long opinion. This was a trial bitterly but honorably fought, by exceedingly capable and well-prepared counsel, before an able judge experienced in complicated litigation and a highly intelligent jury. Finding that the evidence was sufficient for submission to the jury and that no legal errors were committed, we must let the verdict stand.

Affirmed.

UNITED STATES v. NATELLI

United States Court of Appeals
for the Second Circuit, 1975
527 F.2d 311

Where an auditor covers up past errors that are greatly material, criminal liability will be imposed under federal securities laws.

GURFEIN, Circuit Judge.

Anthony M. Natelli and Joseph Scansaroli appeal from judgments of conviction entered in the United States District Court for the Southern District of New York on December 27, 1974, after a four-week trial before the Hon. Harold R. Tyler and a jury. Judge Tyler imposed a one-year sentence and a $10,000 fine upon Natelli, suspending all but 60 days of imprisonment, and a one-year sentence and a $2,500 fine upon Scansaroli, suspending all but 10 days of the imprisonment.

Both appellants are certified public accountants. Natelli was the partner in charge of the Washington, D.C., office of Peat, Marwick, Mitchell & Co. ("Peat"), a large independent firm of auditors, and the engagement partner with respect to Peat's audit engagement for National Student Marketing Corporation ("Marketing"). Scansaroli was an employee of Peat, assigned as audit supervisor on that engagement.

Appellants were charged and tried only on Count Two of a multicount indictment against other defendants connected with Marketing.

Count Two of the indictment charged that, in violation of Section 32(a) of the Securities Exchange Act of 1934, 15 U.S.C. § 78ff(a),[1] four of Marketing's officers and the appellants, as independent auditors, "willfully and knowingly made and caused to be made false and misleading statements with respect to material facts" in a proxy statement for Marketing dated September 27, 1969, and filed with the Securities Exchange Commission (SEC) in accordance with Section 14 of the 1934 Act, 15 U.S.C. § 78n.

The proxy statement was issued by Marketing in connection with a special meeting of its stockholders to consider *inter alia* a charter amendment increasing its authorized capital stock and the merger of six companies, including Interstate National Corporation ("Interstate") into Marketing.

Count Two of the indictment further charged that appellants, in attempting to reconcile net sales and earnings as originally reported in the annual report for the fiscal year ending August 31, 1968, with the amounts shown in the statement of earnings in the proxy statement, filed less than a year later, created an explanatory footnote that was materially false and mis-

---

1. Section 32 provides in relevant part: "Any person . . . *who willfully and knowingly makes, or causes to be made, any statement in any application, report, or document required to be filed under this chapter or any rule or regulation thereunder* or any undertaking contained in a registration statement as provided in subsection (d) of section 78o of this title, *which statement was false or misleading with respect to any material fact,* shall upon conviction be fined not more than $10,000, or imprisoned not more than two years, . . ." (Emphasis added.)

leading.[2] It was alleged that "as the defendants well knew but failed to disclose. . . (*a*) approximately one million dollars, or more than 20 percent, of the 1968 'net sales originally reported' had proven to be nonexistent by the time the proxy statement was filed and had been written off on [Marketing's] own internal books of account; (*b*) net sales and profits of 'pooled companies reflected retroactively' were substantially understated; and (*c*) net sales and profits of [Marketing] were substantially overstated."

Count Two charged further that the proxy statement also contained an unaudited statement of earnings for the nine months ended May 31, 1969, which was materially false and misleading in that it stated "net sales" as $11,313,569 and "net earnings" as $702,270, when, in fact, as the defendants well knew, "net sales" for the period were less than $10,500,000 and Marketing had no earnings at all.

In order to understand the theory of the government's case, we must retrace our steps to the beginning of the Peat engagement at Marketing. The jury could permissibly have found the following facts.

Marketing was formed in 1966 by Cortes W. Randell. It provided to major corporate accounts a diversified range of advertising, promotional and marketing services designed to reach the youth market. In April 1968 Marketing had its first and only public offering of stock. Peat was not its auditor at the time.

Peat took on the engagement in August 1968 after checking with the previous auditors that there had been no professional disagreement with management. Natelli, the partner in charge of Peat's Washington office, undertook the engagement to audit the financial statements of Marketing for the fiscal year ended August 31, 1968, and Natelli assigned Scansaroli to serve as supervisor on the engagement.

In late September or early October 1968 (after the close of the fiscal year), Randell and Bernard Kurek, Marketing's Comptroller, met with both appellants and discussed the method of accounting that Marketing had been using with respect to fixed-fee programs. In the fixed-fee program, Marketing would develop overall marketing programs for the client to reach the

youth market by utilizing a combination of the mailings, posters and other advertising services offered by Marketing. Randell explained that Marketing and the client agreed upon a fixed fee to be charged for participating in the various programs. Randell stated that the company believed that it was proper to recognize income on these fixed-fee contracts at the time the clients committed themselves to participate in the programs presented to them by the account executives, and that this was the accounting method that had been used in preparing the financial statements for the period ended May 31, 1968, which had been distributed to stockholders.

After considering alternative methods of accounting, Natelli concluded that he would use a percentage-of-completion approach to the recognition of income on these commitments, pursuant to which the company would accrue that percentage of the gross income and related costs on a client's "commitment" that was equal to the proportion of the time spent by the account executive on the project before August 31, 1968, to the total time it was estimated he would have to spend to complete the project.

The difficulty immediately encountered was that the "commitments" had not been booked during the fiscal year, and were not in writing. The Marketing stock which had initially been sold at $6 per share was selling in the market by September 1968 for $80, an increase of $74 in five months. A refusal to book the oral "commitments" would have resulted in Marketing's showing a large loss for the fiscal year—according to Kurek's computations, a loss of $232,000.

Scansaroli, upon Natelli's order, attempted to verify the "commitments," the sales not previously included in the company records, in a rather haphazard manner by telephone to representatives of companies which had purportedly indicated some intent to use Marketing's services. Pursuant to Randell's urging, Scansaroli did not seek any written verifications. He accepted a schedule prepared by Kurek which showed about $1.7 million in purported "commitments." He also received from the account executives forms indicating estimates of the gross amount of the client's commitment, the printing and distribution costs to be incurred on the program, and the account executive's estimate of the percentage of completion of the program.

On the basis of the above, Natelli decided not only to recognize income on a percentage-of-completion basis, but to permit adjustment to be made on the books after the close of the fiscal year in the amount of $1.7 million for such "unbilled accounts receivable." This adjustment turned the loss for the year into a handsome profit of $388,031, showing an apparent doubling of the profit of the prior year.

Appellants were not charged with a criminal viola-

---

2. The footnote read in relevant part: "Net sales and earnings as originally reported to stockholders in the annual report [for the year 1968] and the amounts as shown in the statement of earnings in this proxy statement are reconciled as follows:

Net sales: *1968*
Originally reported .... $ 4,989,446
Pooled companies reflected retroactively 6,552,449
Per statement of earnings $11,541,895

Net earnings:
Originally reported .... $ 388,031
Pooled companies reflected retroactively 385,121
Per statement of earnings .... $ 773,152

tion with respect to this decision. It may be observed, however, that in the footnote to the audited financial statement for 1968 explaining this method of accounting for "Contracts in Progress," no indication is given of the flimsy nature of the evidence that such client "commitments" actually existed.

After the 1968 audit had been given a full certificate by the auditors on November 14, 1968, Natelli in December 1968 told the officers of Marketing that in the future Peat would allow income to be recorded only on written commitments, supported by contemporaneous logs kept by the account executives with respect to each contract. A form letter was drafted to spell out a binding contractual commitment to be signed by each client.

In the meantime, following the issuance of the 1968 audited annual report and before the September 1969 proxy statement, seven companies were acquired largely in exchange for Marketing stock, in reliance on the 1968 annual report.

Things began to happen with respect to the $1.7 million of "sales" that had been recorded as income after fiscal year end. Within five months of publication of the annual report, by May 1969, Marketing had written off over $1 million of the $1.7 million in "sales" which the auditors had permitted to be booked.

Of the total $1 million written off, $748,762 was attributable to "sales" purportedly made by one Ronald Michaels, an account executive who was fired for taking kickbacks and who was said to be dishonest. The other quarter of a million dollars of sales written off had nothing to do with Michaels. When accrued costs were taken into account, the effect of the write-off of the Michaels contracts was to reduce 1968 income by $209,750. It appeared that of the $1 million of sales requiring retroactive write-off, $350,000 had already been written off by the company by subtracting these "sales" from 1969 *current* year figures. An additional $678,000 was to be written off sales for the prior year 1968, and appellants were asked to design the write-off. The write-off suggested by appellants was accepted and entered in the general ledger as a journal voucher entry sometime in late April or early May.

That entry wrote off the $678,000 retroactively as a deduction from 1968 sales. Instead of reducing 1968 earnings commensurately, however, no such reduction was made. Appellants were informed by tax accountants in Peat's employ that a certain deferred tax item should be reversed, resulting in a tax credit that happened to be approximately the same amount as the profit to be written off. Scansaroli "netted" this extraordinary item (the tax credit) with an unrelated ordinary item (the write-off of sales and profits). By this procedure he helped to conceal on the books the actual write-off of profits, further using the device of rounding off the tax item to make it conform exactly as the

write-off.[3] The effect of the netting procedure was to bury the retroactive adjustment which should have shown a material decrease in earnings for the fiscal year ended August 31, 1968.

THE PROXY STATEMENT

A. The Footnote

As part of the proxy statement, appellants set about to draft a footnote purporting to reconcile the Company's prior reported net sales and earnings from the 1968 report with restated amounts resulting from pooled companies reflected retroactively. The earnings summary in the proxy statement included companies acquired after fiscal 1968 and their pooled earnings. The footnote was the only place in the proxy statement which would have permitted an interested investor to see what Marketing's performance had been in its preceding fiscal year 1968, as retroactively adjusted, separate from the earnings and sales of the companies it had acquired in fiscal 1969.[4]

At Natelli's direction, Scansaroli subtracted the written-off Marketing sales from the 1968 sales figures for the seven later acquired pooled companies without showing any retroactive adjustment for Marketing's own fiscal 1968 figures. There was no disclosure in the footnote that over $1 million of previously reported 1968 sales of Marketing had been written off. All narrative disclosure in the footnote was stricken by Natelli. This was a violation of Accounting Principles Board Opinion No. 9, which requires disclosure of prior adjustments which affect the net income of prior periods.[5]

---

3. This procedure was approved by Natelli, for in the first printed draft of the proxy statement he prepared a footnote which lumped contract losses for 1968 and the tax adjustment, stating that "the net effect of the retroactive adjustment was a $21,000 decrease in net earnings for the year 1968."

4. A vigilant and knowledgeable stockholder who had saved his 1968 financial report could have discovered, by matching it with the balance sheet in the proxy statement, that unbilled receivables for the year ended August 31, 1968, were now $1,015,230 as against $1,763,992 in the earlier document, but he would not know why there was a difference. Footnote "c" read: "Figures for 1968 have been restated in certain instances to make their presentation consistent with current accounting practices. There was no material effect as a result of such restatement."

5. Accounting Principles Board Opinion No. 9, issued December, 1966, reads in relevant part: "26. When prior period adjustments are recorded, the resulting effects (both gross and net of applicable income tax) on the net income of prior periods should be disclosed in the annual report for the year in which the adjustments are made. [The Board recommends disclosure, in addition, in interim reports issued during that year subsequent to the date of recording the adjustments.] When financial statements for a single period only are presented, this disclosure should indicate the effects of such restatement on the balance of retained earnings at the beginning of the period and on the net income of the immediately preceding period." *APB Accounting Principles: Original Pronouncements,* Vol. 2, p. 6562 (1969).

B. The False Nine-Months' Earnings Statement

The proxy statement also required an unaudited statement of nine-months' earnings through May 31, 1969. This was prepared by the Company, with the assistance of Peat on the same percentage-of-completion basis as in the 1968 audited statement. A commitment from Pontiac Division of General Motors amounting to $1,200,000 was produced two months after the end of the fiscal period. It was dated April 28, 1969.

The proxy statement was to be printed at the Pandick Press in New York on August 15, 1969. At about 3 A.M. on that day, Natelli informed Randell that the "sale" to the Pontiac Division for more than $1 million could not be treated as a valid commitment because the letter from Pontiac was not a legally binding obligation. Randell responded at once that he had a "commitment from Eastern Airlines" in a somewhat comparable amount attributable to the nine-months' fiscal period (which had ended more than two months earlier). Kelly, a salesman for Marketing, arrived at the printing plant several hours later with a commitment letter from Eastern Airlines, dated August 14, 1969, purporting to confirm an $820,000 commitment ostensibly entered into on May 14, just before the end of the nine-month fiscal period of September 1, 1968 through May 31, 1969. When the proxy statement was printed in final form, the Pontiac "sale" had been deleted, but the Eastern "commitment" had been inserted in its place.

Soon after the incident at Pandick Press, Douglas Oberlander, an accountant at Peat assigned by Natelli to review Marketing's accounts, discovered $177,547 worth of "bad" contracts from 1968 which were known to Scansaroli in May, as doubtful, but which had not been written off. Oberlander suggested to Kurek that these contracts and others amounting to over $320,000 in addition to the $1 million in bad contracts previously disposed of, be written off. Kurek consulted Scansaroli, who, after consulting with Natelli, decided against the suggested write-off.

The proxy statement was filed with the SEC on September 30, 1969. There was no disclosure that Marketing had written off $1 million of its 1968 sales (over 20 percent) and over $2 million of the $3.3 million in unbilled sales booked in 1968 and 1969. A true disclosure, which was not made, would have shown that without these unbilled receivables, Marketing had no profit in the first nine months of 1969.

Each appellant contends that the evidence was insufficient to support his conviction. We shall consider each appellant separately.[6]

I

Natelli—Sufficiency of Evidence

It is hard to probe the intent of a defendant. Circumstantial evidence, particularly with proof of motive, where available, is often sufficient to convince a reasonable man of criminal intent beyond a reasonable doubt. When we deal with a defendant who is a professional accountant, it is even harder, at times, to distinguish between simple errors of judgment and errors made with sufficient criminal intent to support a conviction, especially when there is no financial gain to the accountant other than his legitimate fee.

Natelli argues that there is insufficient evidence to establish that he knowingly assisted in filing a proxy statement which was materially false. After searching consideration, we are constrained to find that there was sufficient evidence for his conviction.

The arguments Natelli makes in this court as evidence of his innocent intent were made to the jury and presented fairly. There is no contention that Judge Tyler improperly excluded any factual evidence offered. While there is substance to some of Natelli's factual contentions for jury consideration, we cannot find, on the totality of the evidence, that he was improperly convicted.

The original action of Natelli in permitting the booking of unbilled sales after the close of the fiscal period in an amount sufficient to convert a loss into a profit was contrary to sound accounting practice, particularly when the cost of sales based on time spent by account executives in the fiscal period was a mere guess. When the uncollectibility, and indeed, the nonexistence of these large receivables was established in 1969, the revelation stood to cause Natelli severe criticism and possible liability. He had a motive, therefore, intentionally to conceal the write-offs that had to be made.

Whether or not the deferred tax item was properly converted to a tax credit, the jury had a right to infer that "netting" the extraordinary item against ordinary

---

6. Natelli contends that a later incident reveals his lack of intent to deceive. In September 1969, John Johnston, a staff accountant with Peat, was assigned to prepare the audit of Marketing's books for the fiscal year ended August 31, 1969. He discovered the uncollectible contracts found by Oberlander in August and reported them to his superior, William Colona, who had replaced Scansaroli as audit supervisor when Scansaroli joined Marketing as an employee in October. Later in October, Peat was asked to prepare a "comfort letter" in connection with Marketing's acquisition of Interstate National Corporation, to assure Interstate that no adverse information concerning the unaudited statements for the period ended May 31, 1969, had been discovered since the acquisition contract had been signed in August. Colona and Johnston drafted a "comfort letter" noting adjustments which completely wiped out Marketing's first three-quarter earnings for 1969 of $700,000 as they had been carried in the proxy statement. Natelli acquiesced. The draft "comfort letter" did not deter Interstate from closing the transaction, and Peat decided, at the suggestion of Natelli, to send the letter to the other companies being acquired, which had failed to require such a "comfort letter" in their contracts. Natelli urged this at trial as proof of his good faith, and the trial judge fairly stated to the jury his contention in that regard.

earnings on the books in a special journal entry was, in the circumstances, motivated by a desire to conceal.

With this background of motive, the jury could assess what Natelli did with regard to (1) the footnote and (2) the Eastern commitment and the Oberlander "bad" contracts.

A. The Footnote

Honesty should have impelled appellant to disclose in the footnote which annotated their own audited statement for fiscal 1968 that substantial write-offs had been taken, after year end, to reflect a loss for the year. A simple desire to right the wrong that had been perpetrated on the stockholders and others by the false audited financial statement should have dictated that course. The failure to make open disclosure could hardly have been inadvertent, or a jury at least could so find, for appellants were themselves involved in determining the write-offs and their accounting treatment. The concealment of the retroactive adjustments to Marketing's 1968 year revenues and earnings could properly have been found to have been intentional for the very purpose of hiding earlier errors.[7] There was evidence that Natelli himself changed the footnote to its final form.

That the proxy Statement did not contain a formal reaudit of fiscal 1968 is not determinative. The accountant has a duty to correct the earlier financial statement which he had audited himself and upon which he had issued his certificate, when he discovers "that the figures in the annual report were substantially false and misleading," and he has a chance to correct them. See *Fischer v. Kletz*, 266 F. Supp. 180, 183 (S.D.N.Y. 1967) (Tyler, J.). See also *Gold v. DCL Inc.*, 1973 CCH Fed. Sec. L. Rep. ¶ 94,036 at p. 94,168 (Frankel, J.). The accountant owes a duty to the public not to assert a privilege of silence until the next audited annual statement comes around in due time. Since companies were being acquired by Marketing for its shares in this period, Natelli had to know that the 1968 audited statement was being used continuously.

The argument that the disclosure was not material is weak, since applying write-offs only against pooled earnings, without further explanation, conceals the effect of the write-offs on the prior reported earnings of the principal company. It is the disclosure of the true

operating results of Marketing for 1968, now come to light, that was material. Materiality is an objective matter, not necessarily limited by the accountant's own uncontrolled subjective estimate of materiality. See *United States v. Simon*, 425 F.2d 796, 806 (2 Cir. 1969), *cert. denied*, 397 U.S. 1006 (1970). In any event, the Court charged that the earnings figures would have to be "known to be false in a material way"—a subjective test.

B. The Eastern Commitment and the Nine-Months' Earnings Statement

The Eastern contract was a matter for deep suspicion because it was substituted so rapidly for the Pontiac contract to which Natelli had objected, and which had, itself, been produced after the end of the fiscal period, though dated earlier. It was still another unbilled commitment produced by Marketing long after the close of the fiscal period. Its spectacular appearance, as Natelli himself noted at the time, made its replacement of the Pontiac contract "weird."[8] The Eastern "commitment" was not only in substitution for the challenged Pontiac "commitment" but strangely close enough in amount to leave the projected earnings figures for the proxy statement relatively intact. Marketing had only time logs of a salesman relating to the making of the proposals but no record of expenditures on the Eastern "commitment," no record of having ever billed Eastern for services on this "sale," and not one scrap of paper from Eastern other than the suddenly produced letter. Nevertheless, it was booked as if more than $500,000 of it had already been earned.

Natelli contends that he had no duty to verify the Eastern "commitment" because the earnings statement within which it was included was "unaudited."

This raises the issue of the duty of the CPA in relation to an unaudited financial statement contained within a proxy statement where the figures are reviewed and to some extent supplied by the auditors. It is common ground that the auditors were "associated" with the statement and were required to object to anything they actually "knew" to be materially false. In the ordinary case involving an unaudited statement, the auditor would not be chargeable simply because he failed to discover the invalidity of booked accounts receivable, inasmuch as he had not undertaken an audit with verification. In this case, however, Natelli "knew" the history of postperiod bookings and the dismal consequences later discovered. Was he under a duty in these circumstances to object or to go beyond

---

7. Natelli contends that the write-offs were of sales of Michaels, an allegedly corrupt salesman, and that since Michaels had been fired, the problem was not likely to recur. But the Government proved that at a meeting on June 9, 1969, at which Natelli was present, the Controller produced charts showing that of the $1.5 million of 1968 sales analyzed, about $900,000 had been written off. Of these, about $700,000 were sales of Michaels, $200,000 of another salesman, Ganis. (In addition, a third salesman had accounted for $213,000 of the 1968 sales, not a dollar of which had yet been billed.)

---

8. Natelli's explanation that only the suggestion of Randell for *complete* replacement of the Pontiac contract, *without changing the figures at all*, was "weird" is not convincing. Certainly the jury could find otherwise.

the usual scope of an accountant's review and insist upon some independent verification? The American Institute of Certified Public Accountants, Statement of Auditing Standards No. 1—Codification of Auditing Standards and Procedures (1972), 1 *CCH AICPA Professional Standards* §516.00, recognizes that "if the certified public accountant concludes in the basis of facts known to him that unaudited financial statements with which he may become associated are not in conformity with generally accepted accounting principles, *which include adequate disclosure,* he should insist . . . upon appropriate revision. . . ." (Emphasis added.)

We do not think this means, in terms of professional standards, that the accountant may shut his eyes in reckless disregard of his knowledge that highly suspicious figures, known to him to be suspicious, were being included in the unaudited earnings figures with which he was "associated" in the proxy statement.

The auditor's duty is not as restricted as appellants urge where, as here, the auditors, rather than the company, controlled the figures, as is evidenced by Natelli's rejection of the Pontiac contract as one he would not accept for the subsequent audited financial statement for 1969, and where the erroneous figures had previously been certified by his firm. *Cf. Fischer v. Kletz, supra,* 266 F. Supp. at 188, 189 (S.D.N.Y. 1967). We reject the argument of insufficiency as to Natelli, who could have pointed out the error of his previous certification and deliberately failed to do so, our function being limited to determining whether the evidence was sufficient for submission to the jury. *United States v. Simon, supra,* 425 F.2d at 799. We hold that it was. We discuss the objections to the charge below.

There are points in favor of Natelli, to be sure, but these were presented to the jury and rejected. These included, with their counterbalance: his rejection of the Pontiac commitment (with substitution of the Eastern contract); his discussion of the footnote with his superior, Leon Otkiss (without full disclosure to Otkiss of all relevant factors); his insistence on dissemination of the comfort letter (see note 6) (but his failure to disclose the huge past write-offs of Marketing resulting in no profit for 1968 or nine months of 1969).

II

Scansaroli—Sufficiency of Evidence

The claim of Scansaroli with respect to insufficiency of the evidence is somewhat more difficult. As Judge Tyler noted after both sides had rested, "It is a close question, I think frankly as to Scansaroli, as I see it. Certainly if I were the factfinder, I would be more troubled with his case for a variety of reasons."

Scansaroli contends that there was insufficient evidence to prove beyond a reasonable doubt that (1) he participated in a criminal act with respect to the footnote or (2) that he made an accounting judgment permitting Marketing to include in sales certain contracts-in-progress with the requisite criminal intent. We hold that there was enough evidence to establish the former, but not the latter. For reasons relating to the form of the charge, we will reverse and remand for a new trial.

A. The Footnote

The essence of Scansaroli's argument on his conviction with respect to the false footnote is that he was really convicted for his conduct during the 1968 audit, for which he was not indicted. This misses the thrust of the Government's claim. The unjustifiable manner of treating the unbilled commitments in the 1968 audit bore upon the illegal acts connected with the 1969 proxy statement in two ways: (*a*) it created a motive to conceal the accounting errors made in the 1968 audit: and (*b*) the 1968 audited statement was part of the 1969 proxy statement and was not disclosed therein to have been wrong in the light of the subsequent known write-offs. In view of the established motive to conceal, the jury could properly find, as we have seen, that both the netting of the tax credit against earnings and the subsequent subtracting of the write-offs from the pooled earnings in the footnote without further explanation were done in order to conceal the true retroactive decrease in the Marketing earnings for fiscal 1968.

There is some merit to Scansaroli's point that he was simply carrying out the judgments of his superior, Natelli. The defense of obedience to higher authority has always been troublesome. There is no sure yardstick to measure criminal responsibility except by measurement of the degree of awareness on the part of a defendant that he is participating in a criminal act, in the absence of physical coercion such as a solider might face. Here the motivation to conceal undermines Scansaroli's argument that he was merely implementing Natelli's instructions, at least with respect to concealment of matters that were within his own ken.

We think the jury could properly have found him guilty on the specification relating to the footnote. Scansaroli himself wrote the journal entry in Marketing's books which improperly netted the tax credit with earnings, the true effect never being pointed out in the financial statement. This, with the background of Scansaroli's implication in preparation of the 1968 statement, could be found to have been motivated by intent to conceal the 1968 overstatement of earnings.

Scansaroli participated in the decision to subtract in the proxy statement footnote $678,000 of written-off Marketing sales from the figures for later-acquired pooled companies instead of from its own figures, without further disclosure. Even if Scansaroli did not write the footnote, he supplied the misleading computations and subtractions though he was conscious of the true facts.

B. The Eastern Commitment

Having concluded that there was sufficient evidence to convict both appellants on the footnote specification, we turn to the nine-months' earnings statement which, in turn, included two items, the Eastern contract and the doubtful commitments discovered by Oberlander. We put aside the decision to ignore Oberlander's questioning of certain commitments on the ground that, if it stood alone, the evidence would have been too equivocal to support proof beyond a reasonable doubt that this was not a mere error of judgment.

With respect to the major item, the Eastern commitment, we think Scansaroli stands in a position different from that of Natelli. Natelli was his superior. He was the man to make the judgment whether or not to object to the last-minute inclusion of a new "commitment" in the nine-month statement. There is insufficient evidence that Scansaroli engaged in any conversations about the Eastern commitment at the Pandick Press or that he was a participant with Natelli in any check on its authenticity. Since in the hierarchy of the accounting firm it was not his responsibility to decide whether to book the Eastern contract, his mere adjustment of the figures to reflect it under orders was not a matter for his discretion. As we have seen, Natelli bore a duty in the circumstances to be suspicious of the Eastern commitment and to pursue the matter further. Scansaroli may also have been suspicious, but rejection of the Eastern contract was not within his sphere of responsibility. Absent such duty, he cannot be held to have acted in reckless disregard of the facts.

III

Appellants contend that the trial court erroneously instructed the jury on the issue of knowledge. We do not agree.

The thrust of appellant's argument, as we understand it, is that the judge charged that each appellant could be convicted "if [his] failure to discover the falsity of [Marketing's] financial statements was the result of some form of gross negligence." We do not read

the charge that way. It followed the charge of Judge Mansfield which was sustained in *United States v. Simon, supra*.[9]

It was a balanced charge which made it clear that negligence or mistake would be insufficient to constitute guilty knowledge. See *United States v. Bright*, ____ F.2d____, Slip Op. 3625 (2 Cir., May 21, 1975). Judge Tyler also carefully instructed the jury that "good faith, an honest belief in the truth of the data set forth in the footnote and entries in the proxy statement would constitute a complete defense here." On the other hand, "Congress equally could not have intended that men holding themselves out as members of these ancient professions [law and accounting] should be able to escape criminal liability on a plea of ignorance when they have shut their eyes to what was plainly to be seen or have represented a knowledge they knew they did not possess." *United States v. Benjamin*, 328 F.2d 854, 863 (2 Cir.) *cert. denied, sub nom. Howard v. United States*, 377 U.S. 953 (1964); and see *United States v. Brawer*, 482 F.2d 117, 128–29 (2 Cir. 1973).

One of the bases for attack on the charge is that in charging "reckless disregard for the truth or falsity" or "closing his eyes," there must also be an instruction like "and with a conscious purpose to avoid learning the truth."

It is true that we have favored this charge in false statement cases, *United States v. Sarrantos*, 455 F.2d 877, 880–82 (2 Cir. 1972), while noting that both phrases "mean essentially the same thing," *id.* at 882; and in cases involving knowledge that goods were stolen, *United States v. Brawer*, supra, 482 F.2d at 128–29 (2 Cir. 1973); *United States v. Jacobs*, 475 F.2d 270, 287 (2 Cir.), *cert. denied*, 414 U.S. 821 (1973). The dual instruction is not necessarily required, however, when the defendant is under a specific duty to discover the true facts, the facts tendered are suspect, and he does

---

9. Judge Tyler charged, in pertinent part, as follows: "While I have stated that negligence or mistake do not constitute guilty knowledge or intent, nevertheless, ladies and gentlemen, you are entitled to consider in determining whether a defendant acted with such intent if he deliberately closed his eyes to the obvious or to the facts that certainly would be observed or ascertained in the course of his accounting work or whether he recklessly stated as facts matters of which he knew he was ignorant.

"If you find such reckless deliberate indifference to or disregard for truth or falsity on the part of a given defendant, the law entitles you to infer therefrom that that defendant wilfully and knowingly filed or caused to be filed false financial information of a material nature with the SEC.

"But such an inference, of course, must depend upon the weight and credibility extended to the evidence of reckless and indifferent, conduct, if any.

"I repeat: Ordinary or simple negligence or mistake alone would be insufficient to support a finding of guilty knowledge or wilfulness or intent."

nothing to correct them. In *United States v. Benjamin, supra,* 328 F.2d at 862, this court said, regarding an accountant, that "the Government can meet its burden by proving that a defendant deliberately closed his eyes to facts he had a duty to see." And *United States v. Simon, supra,* which affirmed the conviction of an accountant, as we have seen, sustained a charge in the very language Judge Tyler tracked.

While the facts in each case are not precisely the same, we think this appeal quite analogous to *Simon, supra,* because Natelli was suspicious enough of the Eastern contract to check it with Kelly, the account executive in house, but not to take the next step of seeking verification from Eastern, despite his obvious doubt that it could be booked as a true commitment. And with respect to the footnote, we think the language of this court in *Simon* to be quite pertinent, "The jury could reasonably have wondered how accountants who were really seeking to tell the truth could have constructed a footnote so well designed to conceal the shocking facts." 425 F.2d at 807.

Appellants argue strenuously, however, that *United States v. Simon, supra,* involved an audited statement while the nine-months' statement here involved was an unaudited statement, and, that hence, the duties of appellants here were different from those enunciated in *Simon.* They urge as a corollary that the District Court failed to instruct the jury on the difference, and that his failure to do so was reversible error.

It is true that the point on appeal might have been eliminated if the judge had charged on the differences in the abstract. But in the circumstances he was not required to do so. As we have seen, *supra,* Point I, the duty of Natelli, given this set of facts, was not so different from the duty of an accountant upon an audit as to require sharply different treatment of that duty in the charge to the jury.

We agree with Judge Tyler when he charged the jury that they could find Natelli "knew" of the falsely material fact if he acted in "reckless disregard" or deliberately closed his eyes to the obvious. The issue on this appeal is not what an auditor is *generally* under a duty to do with respect to an unaudited statement, but what these defendants had a duty to do in these unusual and highly suspicious circumstances. *Cf. United States v. Simon, supra,* 425 F.2d at 806-07. Nor was a proper charge requested.

The duly requested supplemental charge on Natelli's duty with respect to the unaudited earnings statement was properly denied. It read:

> The defendants *only* responsibility as to this statement [unaudited statement of earnings for the nine months ended May 31, 1969] was to be satisfied that, *as far as they knew,* the statement contained no misstatement of material facts. (Emphasis added.)

This requested charge was not correct, for even on an unaudited statement with which Natelli was "associated" and where there were suspicious circumstances his duty went further, as we have seen. As the Court correctly charged, Natelli was culpable if he acted in "reckless disregard" of the facts or if he "deliberately closed his eyes."

We expound no rule, to be sure, that an accountant in reviewing an unaudited company statement is bound, without more, to seek verification and to apply auditing procedures. We lay no extra burden on the normal activities of accountants, nor do we assume the role of an Accounting Principles Board. We deal only with such deviations as fairly come within the common understanding of dishonest conduct which jurors bring into the box as applied to the particular conduct prohibited by the particular statute.

It was not for Judge Tyler in his instructions to deal with the abstract question of an accountant's responsibility for unaudited statements, for that was not the issue. So long as we find that the Judge explicated the proper test applicable to the facts of this case, the duty inherent in the circumstances, and we do, we must also find that he gave the appellants a fair charge.

IV

The Charge on "Unanimity"

The trial judge charged as follows:

> Now, I instruct you that if you find that the proxy statement was false in either one of these two respects that is sufficient to support a conviction.

As we have seen there were two specifications of falsity in Count Two, namely, the footnote and the earnings statement. The defense requested that the court advise the jury that in order to convict, they must be unanimous on which, if either, of the two specifications had been proven materially false beyond a reasonable doubt.[10] This request was refused, and the court did not charge accordingly.

Appellants now contend that the charge given left the jury free to convict if only six of them believed the proxy statement to be materially false in the other respect. Appellants conclude that even if the evidence was sufficient to warrant the submission of each of the allegedly false statements to the jury, the conviction still cannot stand, since it cannot be determined whether the jury did in fact unanimously agree on a single specification of falsity. Appellants cite no au-

---

10. This was not a request for a special verdict. *CF. United States v. Spock,* 416 F.2d 165, 180-83 (1 Cir. 1969); and *see* United States v. Adcock, 447 F.2d 1137 (2 Cir. 1971).

thority directly in point. The government cites no direct authority in this circuit, but cites two cases in the Ninth Circuit, *United States v. Friedman,* 445 F.2d 1076, 1083–84, *cert. denied, sub nom. United States v. Jacobs,* 404 U.S. 958 (1971) and *Vitello v. United States, supra,* 425 F.2d at 422–23, as directly in point. However, these cases are distinguishable.

In *Friedman,* the indictment alleged a conspiracy to violate several substantive statutes. The jury found appellants guilty of the conspiracy and of acts charged in particular substantive counts, thus indicating which violations in the conspiracy count the jury had found unanimously.

Vitello turned largely on the failure of counsel to object at trial. The court noted, however, that it would have had to follow *Yates v. United States,* 354 U.S. 298, 311–12 (1957) if "there was insufficient evidence to be submitted to the jury on any one or more of the specifications of falsity." 425 F.2d at 419.

The charge given by Judge Tyler is a charge generally given in this circuit. It is assumed that a general instruction on the requirement of unanimity suffices to instruct the jury that they must be unanimous on whatever specifications they find to be the predicate of the guilty verdict. We do not say it would be wrong for a trial judge to give the charge requested, but it is not error to refuse it.[11] And we do not change that rule.

The court properly charged that the jury needed only to find a defendant guilty on either of the two specifications in order to convict. Inasmuch as the evidence was sufficient to support Natelli's conviction on either specification, the charge given presents no problem to affirmance as to him.

A difficulty does arise, however, if it is found as a matter of law that there should have been a directed verdict for a defendant on one of the specifications for insufficiency of evidence. The verdict then becomes ambiguous, for the jury could have rejected the specification which the appellate court holds sufficiently proved, and have convicted only on the specification held to be insufficiently proved. In that event, there seems to be no alternative to remand for a new trial. That is the general principle. *Yates v. United States,*

supra: Stromberg v. California, 283 U.S. 359, 367–68 (1931). See *United States v. Jacobs, supra,* 475 F.2d at 283 and cases cited therein.

It is true, of course, that sometimes, as in conspiracy to violate two different substantive statutes, the same evidence may support conviction of conspiracy to violate either or both. See e.g., *Jacobs, supra,* 475 F.2d at 283–84.

When there is more than one specification as a predicate for guilt, each dependent on particular evidence which is unrelated to the other, it would be sound practice to instruct the jury that they must be unanimous on a particular specification to convict. Since that was not done here and since we have found that Scansaroli was not culpable on the earnings statement specification, the essence of which was the inclusion of the Eastern commitment, we must reverse his conviction and remand for trial on the footnote specification alone. We realize that we are reversing a conviction involving only 10 days of jail time. Whether it is important enough for the United States to retry him in the circumstances is a matter for decision by the United States Attorney on which we cannot pass judgment.

V

Appellants contend that Count Two of the indictment should be dismissed for lack of proper venue. Prior to trial, appellants had jointly moved to dismiss Count Two on the ground that proper venue lay only where the proxy statement had been filed with the Securities and Exchange Commission, the District of Columbia. The trial court denied the motion. We must consider the issue with the recognition that venue in criminal cases may raise "deep issues of public policy." See *United States v. Johnson,* 323 U.S. 273, 276 (1944).

Section 27 of the Securities Exchange Act, 15 U.S.C. § 78aa, provides that criminal proceedings for violations of the Act are to be brought in a district where "any act or transaction constituting the violation occurred." Appellants contend that the only critical act here was the filing of the proxy statement containing the false statements in the District of Columbia where it was delivered to the Commission, which is also where appellants' and Marketing's principal offices were. The government contends that there is venue for a charge of violation of Section 32 of the 1934 Act, 15 U.S.C. § 78ff,[12] in the Southern District of New York as well. The government asserts that it has proved that the false footnote and the false nine-

---

11. In reaching this result, we believe that we are following United States v. Remington, 191 F.2d 246, 250 (2 Cir. 1951) (L. Hand, A. Hand & Swan, *JJ.*). There the defendant was convicted of perjury in falsely testifying before the Grand Jury that he had never been a member of the Communist Party. He had requested a charge that "all jurors must be convinced that the accused was a member of the Party 'at a particular time and place,' and if some thought he was at one time only and some another, they could not convict him." Judge Swan agreed that "that request was right and should be given if there is a new trial" but he refused to label it reversible error to refuse the charge "since the substance of it was probably covered, though not so explicitly, by the charge that the jury must be unanimous."

---

12. See note 1, *supra*.

months' earnings statement were prepared in Manhattan, and that this suffices.[13]

In denying the pretrial motion, the District Court held that the gravamen of the violation under Section 32 was the making of the false statement, not the filing, the words of the statute "required to be filed" merely describing a category of documents rather than the essence of the offense. The government, in support, notes the general venue provision for continuing offenses.[14]

Appellants retort that section 27 of the 1934 Act stands apart from the continuing offense statute, arguing that it comes within the exception used when Congress has specifically provided for alternate venue. Appellants find support in *Travis v. United States,* 364 U.S. 631 (1961) which held that the proper venue for an offense under 18 U.S.C. § 1001, the False Statements Act, was not the district in which the false statement was made, but only the district where the affidavit had to be filed, the District of Columbia. The rationale of the decision, as we read it, was that section 1001 proscribes false statements "in any matters within the jurisdiction of any department or agency of the United States" and the the National Labor Relations Board had no such "jurisdiction" under section 9(h) of the National Labor Relations Act as amended,[15] until the non-Communist affidavit required by the statute as a precondition to N.L.R.B. investigation was actually filed in Washington, D.C.[16]

The majority opinion in *Travis* was careful to note that "[t]he decisions are discrete, each looking to the nature of the crime charged." 364 U.S. at 635. And this court has annotated *Travis* by stating that "the decision surely was meant to be confined to the facts based on the unusual statute involved." See *United States v. Slutsky,* 487 F.2d 832, 839 n.8 (2 Cir. 1973), *cert. denied,* 416 U.S. 937 (1974). See also *United States v. Ruehrup,* 333 F.2d 641, 643 (7 Cir.), *cert. denied,* 379 U.S. 903 (1964); *Imperial Meat Co. v. United States,* 316 F.2d 435, 440 (10 Cir.), *cert. denied,* 375 U.S. 820 (1963).

Appellant seeks to come within the *Travis* holding by arguing that just as in *Travis* where the filing of the non-Communist affidavit was simply a prerequisite to future conduct, resort to NLRB processes, so the filing of a proxy statement is merely the prerequisite to future conduct, the solicitation of proxies. The argument is unsound.

In *Travis,* the labor board had no jurisdiction to make an investigation of labor practices "unless there is on file with the Board" a non-Communist affidavit. Here the filing of the proxy statement is part of the continuous process of the solicitation of proxies. Proxy statements are filed only at such time as the persons filing require proxies for some corporate purpose.[17] The filing and solicitations are part of the same process. We hold that there was venue in the Southern District of New York.

We have considered the other arguments raised by appellants and find them without merit. Judgment affirmed as to appellant Natelli; as to appellant Scansaroli judgment reversed and remanded for a new trial.

---

13. Appellants do not seriously contend that there was no preparation in the Southern District as a matter of fact.

14. 18 U.S.C. § 3237(a) reads: (a) Except as otherwise expressly provided by enactment of Congress, any offense against the United States begun in one district and completed in another, or committed in more than one district, may be inquired of and prosecuted in any district in which such offense was begun, continued, or completed.

15. 61 Stat. 136, 146, amended, § 1(d), 65 Stat. 601, 602, repealed, § 201(d) of the Labor-Management Reporting and Disclosure Act of 1959, 73 Stat. 519, 525.

16. If the "jurisdiction of the agency" exists where the false statement is made, however, the continuing offense statute is applicable to venue even in section 1001 cases. United States v. Candella, 487 F.2d 1223 (2d Cir. 1973), *cert. denied,* 415 U.S. 977 (1974).

---

17. We may note, that paradoxically, in most cases arising under the 1934 Act, the defendants would presumably contend that they wished to be tried in their home districts rather than in the District of Columbia. Here the appellants happen to live and work in the District of Columbia and have been tried elsewhere, a rather unusual situation.

Appendix A

CALIFORNIA

Legal Relationships with Tax Clients

Lindner v. Barlow, Davis & Wood, 27 Cal. Rptr. 101 (Cal. App. 1962). The CPAs were held not liable for negligence, since they followed the customary professional practice in relying upon Forms W–2 as to the taxability of payments.

L.B. Laboratories v. Mitchell, 244 P.2d 385 (Cal. 1952). A CPA was held liable for penalties that resulted from his negligence in failing to prepare the client's return on a timely basis.

Working Papers

California Code of Ethics, Section 68:

A licensee of the Board, after demand by or on behalf of a client, for books, records or other data that are the client's records shall not retain such records.

Although, in general the accountant's working papers are the property of the licensee, if such working papers include records which would ordinarily constitute part of the client's books and records and are not otherwise available to the client, then the information on those working papers must be treated the same as if it were part of the client's books and records.

Liability to Third Parties: Unaudited Financials

Security-First National Bank of Los Angeles v. Lutz, 297 F.2d 159 (9th Cir. 1961). The court applied California law and held an accountant liable to a former limited partner in connection with material misrepresentation in obtaining the limited partner's consent to incorporation. The court based liability on California Civil Code § 1573, which defines construc-

tive fraud as a breach of duty without fraudulent intent imposed where a fiduciary relation exists between the parties. The finding that the accountant was a fiduciary was based on the fact that he was a director and that he made bookkeeping entries and prepared financial reports.

Liability to Third Parties: Other

Lucas v. Hamm, 364 P.2d 685 (Cal. 1961). An attorney is liable for negligence to beneficiaries under a will; however, an error involving the rule against perpetuities does not amount to negligence.

Regulation of Accounting Practice

People v. Hill, 136 Cal. Rptr. 30 (Cal. App. 1977). The court enjoined an unlicensed person from using the term *accounting.*

Murrill v. State Board of Accountancy, 218 P.2d 569 (Cal. App. 1950). The court upheld revocation of the license of a public accountant who entered a plea of guilty when charged with willful failure to file a tax return.

Noncompetition Agreements

Swenson v. File, 475 P.2d 852 (Cal. 1970). Agreements not to compete in accounting practice executed prior to 1961 had to be limited to the particular *cities or towns* where the business was transacted; agreements executed after 1961 must be limited to the *counties or cities* where the business is transacted.

The California Business & Professional Code § 16,600 provides: "Except as provided in this chapter, every contract by which anyone is restrained from engaging in a lawful profession, trade or business of any kind is to that extent void." Section 16,601 permits the seller of good will of a business to refrain from carrying on a similar business "within a specified county or counties, city or cities," where the sold business was carried on so long as the buyer or a transferee carries on a similar business.

Defenses: Causation

Vanderbilt Growth Fund, Inc. v. Superior Court, 164 Cal. Rptr. 621 (Cal. App. 1980). Client firms sued Arthur Young & Company (AY) alleging that AY failed to determine that certain restricted securities had not been properly valued. AY's motion for summary judgment was properly granted because AY demonstrated that the securities in question were worthless before and after the audit so that any negligence or breach of contract by AY could not have caused the loss.

Flagg v. Seng, 60 P.2d 1004 (Cal. App. 1936). The court affirmed a judgment for the accountants where the trustee of the bankrupt corporate client claimed damages for unjustified dividends. The accountant did not cause the loss, since the directors were familiar with the books and the manner in which they were kept.

Defenses: Statute of Limitations

Lucas v. Hamm, 364 P.2d 685 (Cal. 1961). Whenever a case sounds in both tort and contract, the plaintiff may elect between them and the statute of limitations is determined by plaintiff's election.

Moonie v. Lynch, 64 Cal. Rptr. 55 (Cal. App. 1967). The statute of limitations on a claim against a CPA for negligently preparing a tax return started running when the negligence was discovered or with reasonable diligence would have been discovered.

Heyer v. Flaig, 449 P.2d 161 (Cal. 1969). The statute of limitations on a malpractice suit against an attorney by an intended beneficiary of a will starts to run only upon the death of the client.

Briskin v. Ernst & Ernst, 589 F.2d 1363 (9th Cir. 1978). The California statute of limitations starts running on a fraud claim when the fraud is discovered, and under California law the plaintiff must allege and prove the date of discovery.

Malpractice Insurance

St. Paul Fire & Marine Insurance Co. v. Weiner, 606 F.2d 864 (9th Cir. 1979) (applying California law). Criminal conviction of the insured accountants did not eliminate the carrier's duty to defend civil actions under the policy's affirmative dishonesty exclusion, since the issues and time periods were not identical.

COLORADO

Legal Relationships with Nontax clients

Franklin Supply Co. v. Tolman, 454 F.2d 1059 (9th Cir. 1971) (applying Colorado and Venezuela law). Where purchaser and seller based price on audited book value with each bearing half of the audit fee, the court held that the buyer could not recover for overpricing of inventory from the accounting firm, since the same damages had been previously recovered from the seller.

Rhode, Titchenal, Bauman & Scripter v. Shattuck, 619 P.2d 507 (Colo. App. 1980). Where client did not protest accounting firm's bills and admitted owing sums charged, it was not necessary to prove the reasonableness of the fees.

Working Papers and Accountant-Client Privilege

Colorado by statute has an accountant-client privilege.

People v. Zimbelman, 572 P.2d 830 (Colo. 1977). A criminal defendant cannot invoke the accountant-client privilege where the CPA audited the corporate victim, since the holder of the privilege is the corporation.

Pattie Lea, Inc. v. District Court, 423 P.2d 27 (Colo. 1967). Communications to a corporation's accountant are not privileged from the corporation's stockholders.

Liability to Third Parties: Audited Financials

Stephens Indus., Inc. v. Haskins & Sells, 438 F.2d 357 (10th Cir. 1971) (applying Colorado law). Where the audit engagement relieved the auditors of responsibility for accounts receivable, the auditors' opinion contained a notation that the auditors did not confirm accounts receivable or review their collectibility, and the notes to the balance sheet indicated that accounts receivable had not been adjusted for uncollectible accounts, the court held that auditors could not be liable to a third-party investor. The court expressed the view that Colorado would not impose liability to third parties for ordinary negligence.

Regulation of Accounting Practice

Hentges v. Bartsch, 533 P.2d 66 (Colo. App. 1975). The CPA's license was appropriately revoked for misappropriation of client funds.

Noncompetition Agreements

Fuller v. Brough, 411 P.2d 18 (Colo. 1966). An agreement providing that a withdrawing partner could not practice accounting for five years within 45 miles of Greely, Colorado, was held valid.

Damages

Professional Rodeo Cowboys Association, Inc. v. Wilch, Smith & Brock, 589 P.2d 510 (Colo. Ct. App. 1978). Where the accounting firm's error caused the wrong cowboy to be declared champion, the accounting firm was held liable for costs of settlement of the dispute including attorney's fees of both cowboys and the association.

FLORIDA

Legal Relationships with Tax Clients

Adams v. Fisher, 390 So. 2d 1248 (Fla. App. 1980). In a nontax matter, the client discharged the first attorney hired on a contingent-fee basis and hired a second attorney on a contingent-fee basis. The first attorney was entitled to recover for services performed on the basis of *quantum meruit*, while the second attorney was entitled to recover his full contingent fee.

Jorge v. Rosen, 208 So. 2d 644 (Fla. App. 1968). The court enforced a contingent fee agreement to pay a CPA 20 percent of any refund and 20 percent of any future credit that resulted from processing a claim for refund of federal income taxes.

Working Papers, Accountant-Client Privilege, and Business Records

Florida by statute has an accountant-client privilege.

Goethel v. First Properties Int'l, Ltd., 363 So. 2d 1117 (Fla. App. 1978), both an attorney and a CPA claimed a lien for fees on a corporate client's books and records; however, the court required the books and records returned, upon substitution of a cash bond by the corporation, because the corporation needed the books and records to defend against the claims.

Liability to Third Parties: Audited Financials

Investment Corp. of Florida v. Buchman, 208 S. 2d 291 (Fla. 2d Dist. Ct. App. 1968). Plaintiffs agreed to purchase stock provided an audit revealed no adverse change. In the buyer's suit against the auditor the court held that under Florida law a nonclient must prove fraud or gross negligence despite the fact that the auditor knows the purpose of the audit is for the third party's benefit. *Accord: Canaveral Capital Corp. v. Bruce*, 214 So. 2d 505 (Fla. 3d Dist. Ct. App. 1968); *Dubbin v. Touche Ross & Co.*, 324 So. 2d 128 (Fla. 3d Dist. 1976); *Mulligan v. Wallace*, 349 So. 2d 745 (Fla. 3d Dist. 1977); *Investors Tax Sheltered Real Estate, Ltd. v. Laventhol, Krekstein, Horwath & Horwath*, 370 So. 2d 815 (Fla. 3d Dist. 1979); *Nortek, Inc. v. Alexander Grant & Co.*, 532 F.2d 1013 (5th Cir. 1976).

Liability to Third Parties: Other

McAbee v. Edwards, 340 So. 2d 1167 (Fla. 4th Dist. 1976). An attorney may be held liable for *negligence* to the beneficiary under a will.

Kovaleski v. Tallahassee Title, 363 So. 2d 1156 (Fla. 1st Dist. 1978). A title abstractor may be held liable for *negligence* to a third party.

Regulation of Accounting Practice

Mercer v. Hemmings, 170 So. 2d 33 (Fla. 1965), *appeal dismissed*, 389 U.S. 46 (1967). A requirement for two-years' residence in Florida prior to taking the CPA exam was held void and unreasonable.

The Florida Bar v. Riccardi, 264 So. 2d 5 (Fla. 1972). Bribery of a revenue agent is sufficient cause for disbarment.

Junco v. State Board of Accountancy, 390 So. 2d 329 (Fla. 1980). Florida statutes required one year of experience in the office of a CPA, the state Public Service Commission, or the state auditor general. The refusal to accept experience with the Internal Revenue Service did not violate plaintiffs' rights to equal protection. The court said: "We cannot agree that the fact of employment in the federal system necessarily qualifies a person under Florida law to practice public accounting in this state."

Cenac v. Florida State Board of Accountancy, 399 So. 2d 1013 (Fla. App. 1981). Cenac, a Florida CPA, formed a corporation to consult on Medicare and Medicaid reimbursement and opted to have his CPA certificate inoperative, thus exempting him from reestablishing competency. When asked if he was a CPA, he would answer that he was "nonpracticing." The Florida board revoked his CPA, and the court reversed because the board did not have adequate support for rejecting the hearing officer's finding that Cenac was not practicing.

Noncompetition Agreements

Florida Statutes 542.12 voids contracts restraining the exercise of a lawful profession, trade, or business except that

1. The seller of a business or an employee may agree to refrain from competing within a reasonably limited time and area.
2. Partners may, in anticipation of a dissolution of a partnership, agree to refrain from competing within a reasonably limited time and area.

Miller v. Williams, 300 So. 2d 752 (Fla. App. 1974). An agreement between a CPA firm and its employee to pay each other for servicing the other's clients after termination was a valid business arrangement and not a contract in restraint of trade.

Defenses

Touche Ross & Co. v. Sun Bank of Riverside, 366 So. 2d 465 (Fla. App. 1979). In a suit against an auditing firm for failure to discover fraud, the auditing firm could not sue the client's banks for contribution because there was no common obligation. The court distinguished the auditor's duty to discover the loss from any duty of the bank.

Subrogation

Dantzler Lumber & Export Co. v. Columbia Casualty Co., 156 So. 116 (1934). Upon payment of an embezzlement loss, the insurance carrier is subrogated to the insured's cause of action against a negligent accounting firm.

Jurisdiction

Touche Ross & Co. v. Canaveral International Corp., 369 So. 2d 441 (Fla. App. 1979). A New York partnership can be sued for partnership activities performed in Florida by serving resident partners.

GEORGIA

Legal Relationships with Nontax Clients

Mitchell and Pickering v. Louis Isaacson, Inc., 229 S.E.2d 535 (Ga. App. 1976). The CPA testified as to reasonable value, and testimony by independent experts was not required.

Intercompany Services Corp. v. Kleeb, 231 S.E.2d 505 (Ga. App. 1976). Where client accepted bills as correct when presented, CPA was not required to prove value.

Legal Relationships with Tax Clients

Noble v. Hunt, 99 S.E.2d 345 (Ga. App. 1957). A CPA who represented the taxpayer without an express contract was entitled to recover the amount generally charged by CPAs for the same or similar services. Since the Treasury Department and U.S. Tax Court permit nonlawyers to practice, the court rejected the defense of unauthorized practice of law.

Working Papers, Accountant-Client Privilege, and Business Records

Georgia by statute has an accountant-client privilege.

Gearhart v. Etheridge, 208 S.E.2d 460 (Ga. 1974). Communications by one joint venturer to the joint venture's accountant are not privileged from other venturers.

Whitlock v. PKW Supply Co., 269 S.E.2d 36 (Ga. App. 1980). Tax return preparer refused to deliver or file tax returns until fee was paid and client recovered $5,000 which was the reasonable cost of completing the abandoned obligation.

Ambort v. Tarica, 258 S.E.2d 755 (Ga. App. 1979). In absence of actual damages, client could recover nominal damages for CPA's wrongful withholding of business records.

Liability to Third Parties: Unaudited Financials

MacNerland v. Barnes, 199 S.E.2d 567 (Ga. App. 1973). An accountant who disclaimed because of lack of independence was held not liable to an investor for negligence; however, the court held that the accountant could be liable for negligent performance of an agreement with plaintiff to verify certain major accounts.

Noncompetition Agreements

Fuller v. Kolb, 234 S.E.2d 517 (Ga. 1977). An agreement not to provide public accounting services for two years for clients serviced by the firm within two years of termination was held void.

Defenses

Jankowski v. Taylor, Bishop & Lee, 273 S.E.2d 16 (Ga. 1980). The statute of limitations on a claim for attorneys' malpractice started running when a suit was dismissed because the attorneys failed to appear, despite the fact that the attorneys could have refiled plaintiff's suit within the next 15 months.

ILLINOIS

Legal Relationships with Nontax Clients

Matter of F. W. Koenecke & Sons, Inc., 605 F.2d 310 (7th Cir. 1979). Under agency law of Illinois, an accounting firm was held liable to client for breach of contract to bring books up to date and for diversion of funds by accounting firm's employee.

Reid v. Silver, 354 F.2d 600 (7th Cir. 1965). Plaintiff, who had designed and sold "Rose Marie Reid" bathing suits, entrusted more than $1.4 million to Michael Silver, a CPA, for investment purposes. The court held Silver was a fiduciary and required him to furnish a full and complete accounting of all his actions in handling plaintiff's moneys, property, and business affairs from the beginning of their relationship.

Cereal Byproducts Co. v. Hall, 132 N.E.2d 27, aff'd 155 N.E.2d 14 (Ill. 1956). The auditor was held liable for failure to discover embezzlement by virtue of accepting the bookkeeper's list of accounts receivable not to be confirmed.

Working Papers and Accountant-Client Privilege

Illinois by statute has an accountant-client privilege.

Palmer v. Fisher, 228 F.2d 603 (7th Cir. 1955). The

deposition of a CPA was taken without notice to the opposing party, and the CPA later decided to claim the Illinois accountant-client privilege. The court suppressed the deposition to enforce the Illinois accountant-client privilege, which was held applicable to cases that are in federal court on diversity of citizenship grounds.

Liability to Third Parties: Audited Financials

Shofstall v. Allied Van Lines, Inc., 455 F. Supp. 351 (N.D. Ill. 1978). Plaintiff alleged that defendant, Price Waterhouse & Co., certified financial statements for three years without disclosing the existence of a dividend restriction known to it. The court, applying Illinois law, held that no fiduciary relationship existed between the plaintiff and the investor and dismissed the negligence claim. In refusing to dismiss the fraud claim, however, the court held that an accountant may be liable to a third party for fraud and deceit and that the question of fact could not be resolved on a motion for summary judgment.

Noncompetition Agreements

Wolf & Co. v. Waldron, 366 N.E.2d 603 (Ill. App. 1977). An employee's agreement not to service clients of a national accounting firm for two years from termination was held valid.

Damages

Sorenson v. Fio Rito, 413 N.E.2d 47 (Ill. App. 1980). Where an attorney retained to represent an estate failed to timely file inheritance and estate tax forms, he was held liable for all resulting penalties and interest plus reasonable attorney's fees incurred in an unsuccessful attempt to mitigate penalty and interest charges. Because the negligence was explicit, the court ruled that expert testimony concerning the standard of care was not required.

Defenses

Bronstein v. Kalchiem & Kalchiem, Ltd., 414 N.E.2d 96 (Ill. App. 1980). A suit against an attorney for negligent tax advice was held premature because the matter had not yet been decided by the Tax Court.

Glick v. Sabin, 368 N.E.2d 625 (Ill. App. 1977). Where it was alleged that a CPA designed an inadequate system and failed to conduct an adequate financial review, the statute of limitations started running when the client knew or should have known about the allegations.

Subrogation

Rock River Savings & Loan Association v. American States Insurance Co., 594 F.2d 633 (7th Cir. 1979). Subrogation claims are barred where stockholders or their transferors participate in the fraud that results in loss.

LOUISIANA

Legal Relationships with Nontax Clients

Ronaldson v. Moss & Watkins, 127 So. 467 (La. App. 1930). A Texas CPA's fee claim was held unenforceable because the balance sheet audit was performed in Louisiana.

Harry L. Beacham and Co., Ltd. v. Belanger, 388 So. 2d 101 (La. App. 1980). Where the CPA's invoice had no breakdown for services to a bankrupt corporation and its officer and there was no evidence that the officer agreed to be responsible for both, there could be no quantum meruit verdict against the officer.

Legal Relationships with Tax Clients

Smith v. St. Paul Fire & Marine Insurance Co., 366 F. Supp. 1283 (M.D. La. 1973), *aff'd per curiam*, 500 F.2d 1131 (5th Cir. 1974). An attorney's erroneous advice that a Louisiana judgment of possession would not trigger the alternate valuation date for federal estate tax purposes did not constitute negligence.

Slaughter v. Eugene C. Roddie, 249 So. 2d 584 (La. App. 1971). A tax return preparer was held liable to the client for refund of fee, fee to employ a CPA, plus penalties and interest resulting from an erroneous loss carry-back and claim for refund.

Bancroft v. Indemnity Insurance Co. of North America, 203 F. Supp. 49 (W.D. La. 1962), *aff'd mem.*, 309 F.2d 959 (5th Cir. 1963). When the CPA overlooked IRC § 304 and advised the taxpayer that he could sell stock in one controlled corporation to the other without incurring federal income tax, the CPA's malpractice insurer was held liable for over $35,000 assessed by the IRS.

Working Papers and Accountant-Client Privilege

Louisiana by statute has an accountant-client privilege.

State v. McKinnon, 317 So. 2d 184 (La. 1975). Louisiana's accountant-client privilege statute was held inapplicable to criminal proceedings.

Thomas v. Adams, 271 So. 2d 684 (La. App. 1972). CPA held not liable to client where evidence indicated that CPA had furnished one copy of adjusting entries to client but refused to furnish another copy until fee was paid.

Regulation of Accounting Practice

State v. DeVerges, 95 So. 805 (La. 1923). The law making it a misdemeanor to unlawfully hold oneself out to the public as a CPA was held constitutional.

State v. State Board of CPAs, 113 So. 757 (La. 1927). A Mississippi CPA applied to the Louisiana board for reciprocity under the provision permitting the board to in its discretion register CPAs from other states provided the issuing state grants similar privileges to Louisiana CPAs. The court held that the board could not "in its discretion" refuse to register any such certificate for any reason or for no reason at all, since under the 14th Amendment the board must treat alike all applicants similarly situated and may not arbitrarily discriminate between them.

A federal court invalidated a Louisiana rule that required every member of a multistate accounting firm that practices in Louisiana to be licensed by the board, *Journal of Accountancy*, July 1980, p. 16.

Noncompetition Agreements

Louisiana Revised Statutes § 23:921 provides as follows:

> No employer shall require or direct any employee to enter into any contract whereby the employee agrees not to engage in any competing business for himself, or as the employee of another, upon the termination of his contract of employment with such employer, and all such contracts, or provisions thereof containing such agreement shall be null and unenforceable in any court.

Damages

Louisiana does not permit recovery of punitive damages.

Defenses

Louisiana by statute permits right of contribution against a joint tortfeasor.

MARYLAND

Governmental Examination

Social Security Administration Baltimore F.C.U. v. United States, 138 F. Supp. 639 (D. Md. 1956). The United States was not liable for failure of federal examiners to discover embezzlement by the bookkeeper of a federal credit union. The Federal Tort Claims Act waives the defense of sovereign immunity but does not

create any new duties. Federal statutes making federal credit unions subject to examination by the Bureau of Federal Credit Unions are similar to laws providing for examination of banks by the Comptroller of the Treasury. The purpose of federal examination is for regulatory purposes and not for verification of accounts or discovery of defalcations. Furthermore, the examiners' report expressed no opinion on the financial statements.

Legal Relationships with Tax Clients

Gladding v. Langrall, Muir & Noppinger, 401 A.2d 662 (Md. App. 1979). The court enforced an agreement to pay a substantial contingent fee for an administrative appeal before the IRS, despite only a few hours expended by the CPA firm.

Feldman v. Granger, 257 A.2d 421 (Md. App. 1969). The taxpayer's claim against the accounting firm for taxes, penalties, and interest resulting from failure to timely file a subchapter S election was barred by the statute of limitations which started running upon the taxpayer's receipt of the IRS notice of deficiency.

Working Papers and Accountant-Client Privilege

Maryland by statute provides an accountant-client privilege.

Regulation of Accounting Practice

Comprehensive Accounting Service Co. v. The Maryland State Board of Public Accountancy, 397 A.2d 1019 (Md. App. 1979). The legislature cannot prohibit unlicensed persons from holding themselves out as "accountants" or describing their services as "accounting."

Defenses

Feldman v. Granger, 257 A.2d 421 (Md. App. 1969). Where it is alleged that an accounting firm failed to file a subchapter S election within the statutory filing period, the statute of limitations starts running when the client receives notice from the IRS.

Maryland by statute permits right of contribution against a joint tortfeasor.

MINNESOTA

Legal Relationships with Nontax Clients

Gammel v. Ernst & Ernst, 72 N.W.2d 364 (Minn. 1955). Where purchaser and seller of a dairy agreed to a price based on earnings as determined by Ernst & Ernst with the audit fee split by the parties, the auditors were not acting as quasi arbitrators and were not immune from liability for negligence

City of East Grand Forks v. Steele, 141 N.W. 181 (Minn. 1913). The court held that alleged auditor's negligence in failing to discover embezzlement was an action for breach of contract, and because losses for embezzlement were not within the contemplation of the parties, plaintiff was limited to a refund of the audit fee.

Bonhiver v. Graff, 248 N.W.2d 291 (Minn. 1976). A CPA firm was held liable to the receiver for an insurance company for the deficiency due to creditors. Liability was based on the fact that the CPAs were engaged in writing up the corporate books and that an investigation of the true nature of the transactions would have revealed fraud by the stockholders.

Legal Relationships with Tax Clients

Vernon J. Rockler v. Glickman, Isenberg, Lurie & Co., 273 N.W.2d 647 (Minn. 1978). A CPA firm was held not liable for loss of capital gains treatment, since the loss was caused by the plaintiff broker/dealer being forced to cover short sales out of the investment account and not from erroneous advice of the CPA.

Liability to Third Parties: Unaudited Financials

Bonhiver v. Graff, 248 N.W.2d 291 (Minn. 1976). The court held a CPA liable for negligence to a foreseeable third party.

Regulation of Accounting Practice

In re Jelle, 244 N.W. 548 (Minn. 1932). The court refused to take any disciplinary action whatever where an attorney used money paid for inheritance taxes for his own purposes.

Noncompetition Agreements

Haynes v. Monson, 224 N.W.2d 482 (Minn. 1974). An agreement not to engage in bookkeeping, accounting, or tax practice for five years within 50 miles of Austin, Minnesota, was held valid.

Defenses

Minnesota, without regard to statute, allows the right of contribution from a joint tortfeasor.

Midland National Bank of Minneapolis v. Perranoski, 299 N.W.2d 404 (Minn. 1980). An accountant who promoted a partnership tax shelter was held not liable to a partner/investor. The CPA was not a fiduciary with respect to investors advised by their own lawyers, and the CPA had a right to expect that experienced investors would read a partnership agreement before signing it.

NEW JERSEY

Liability to Third Parties: Unaudited Financials

Coleco Industries v. Berman, 423 F. Supp. 275 (E.D. Pa. 1976), *appeal of other parties*, 576 F.2d 569 (3d Cir. 1977). Applying New Jersey law the court held an accounting firm liable to a foreseeable third-party purchaser for negligence in preparing unaudited financials: "The errors here were not subtle ones. Avoidance of them required neither a costing check nor an inventory. Under these circumstances we make no distinction between an audited and an unaudited statement."

Damages

Stern v. Abramson, 376 A.2d 221 (N.J. Super. 1977). Allegations that gross negligence by auditors caused losses to plaintiff's tobacco store through manager's embezzlement did not constitute malice nor willful and wanton conduct so as to permit recovery of punitive damages.

Defenses

New Jersey by statute permits right of contribution against a joint tortfeasor.

NEW YORK

Legal Relationships with Nontax Clients

Smith v. London Assurance Corp., 96 N.Y.S.2d 820 (N.Y. App. Div. 1905). Complaint stated a good cause of action where it alleged that embezzlement losses resulted from the breach of a specific agreement to frequently check the case account.

Craig v. Anyon, 208 N.Y.S.2d 259, *aff'd* 152 N.E. 431 (N.Y. App. Div. 1925). Return of the fee was required by the auditor's failure to discover embezzlement, but defalcation losses were too remote where the client represented that the employee could be trusted.

National Surety Corp. v. Lybrand, 9 N.Y.S.2d 554 (N.Y. App. 1939). The question of the auditors' liability for negligence in failing to discover embezzlement was a question for the jury.

Stanley L. Bloch, Inc. v. Klein, 258 N.Y.S.2d 501 (N.Y. Sup. Ct. 1965). Where the CPA prepared a balance sheet with no indication as to responsibility assumed, the court assumed it was audited and awarded plaintiff the fee paid plus the fee paid to prepare a corrected statement.

1136 Tenants' Corp. v. Max Rothenberg & Co., 27 App. Div. 2d 830, 277 N.Y.S.2d 996 (1967), *aff'd*, 238 N.E.2d 322 (N.Y. App. 1968). The CPA was held liable for failure to inquire or communicate concerning suspicious circumstances despite a legend on the financials stating "No independent verifications were undertaken thereon."

Working Papers and Accountant-Client Privilege

Inspiration Consol. Copper Co. v. Lumbermen's Mutual Casualty Co., 60 F.R.D. 205 (S.D.N.Y. 1973). Since New York has no accountant-client privilege, working papers prepared as auditor had to be produced in connection with the client's suit against its insurance carrier.

Liability to Third Parties: Audited Financials

Ultramares Corp. v. Touche, 174 N.E. 441 (N.Y. App. 1931). Public accountants may be held liable to clients for negligence, but a third-party lender must prove fraud in order to recover.

O'Connor v. Ludlam, 92 F.2d 50 (2d Cir.), *cert. denied*, 302 U.S. 758 (1937). Jury verdict in favor of accountants upheld.

State Street Trust Co. v. Ernst, 16 N.E.2d 851 (N.Y. App. 1938). Public accountants held liable to a bank based on a finding of gross negligence.

Duro Sportswear, Inc. v. Cogen, 137 N.Y.S.2d 829 (N.Y. App. Div. 1954). Public accountant held liable to purchaser of corporation's shares based on finding of gross negligence.

C.I.T. Financial Corp. v. Glover, 244 F.2d 44 (2d Cir. 1955). The court affirmed a jury verdict for public accountants based on an instruction that in order to establish liability for ordinary negligence, the audit reports had to be for the "primary benefit" of the plaintiff lender.

Fischer v. Kletz, 266 F. Supp. 180 (S.D.N.Y. 1967). Court refused to dismiss action by stockholders who had relied on audited financial statement based on deceit due to public accountants' allegedly remaining silent after discovery of facts that made the audit report misleading.

White v. Guarente, 372 N.E.2d 315 (N.Y. App. 1977). A public accountant performing an audit and preparing the tax return for a limited partnership may be held liable to limited partners for ordinary negligence.

Regulation of Accounting Practice

People v. National Association of Certified Public Accountants, 204 App. Div. 288 (N.Y. 1923). The court enjoined the defendant from conducting an exam and authorizing persons who passed to use the designations "certified public accountant," "C.P.A." or "C.P.A. (N.A.)."

Shander v. Allen, 284 N.Y.S.2d 142 (App. Div. 1967). Revocation of the CPA certificate was held too harsh where a CPA deliberately understated liabilities on an audited balance sheet in order to give the client a chance to stay in business.

McCaffrey v. Couper, 314 N.Y.S.2d 597 (App. Div. 1970), *aff'd without opinion*, 295 N.E.2d 651 (N.Y. App. 1973). Public accountants have no constitutional right to practice under the assumed name of Fiduciary Associates.

Pincus v. Nyquist, 330 N.Y.S.2d 897 (App. Div. 1972). Revocation of a CPA certificate was not an excessive punishment where the CPA was involved in three incidents of bribing IRS agents.

Noncompetition Agreements

Schacter v. Lester Witte & Co., 383 N.Y.S.2d 316 (N.Y. App. Div. 1976). Agreement of withdrawing partners not to service firm clients from two to five years was held valid.

Lynch v. Bailey, 90 N.Y.S.2d (N.Y. App. Div. 1949). An agreement that a withdrawing partner would not practice accountancy within 100 miles of 10 cities that included 20 commercial centers was held void.

Defenses

Shapiro v. Glekel, 380 F. Supp. 1053 (S.D.N.Y. 1974). In a suit by a bankruptcy trustee against auditors on both negligence and contract theories, the court refused to dismiss on grounds of contributory negligence and ruled that this defense applies only where the employer's negligence contributes to the auditors' failure.

Wilkin v. Dana R. Pickup & Co., 347 N.Y.S.2d 122 (N.Y. Sup. Ct. 1973). The court applied the "continuous treatment rule" applicable to medical malpractice and the "continuous representation rule" applicable to legal malpractice where accountants were allegedly negligent in preparing a tax return. Thus the statute of limitations did not start running until the accountant-client relationship was terminated.

New York without statute allows the right of contribution from a joint tortfeasor. The amount is based on relative fault.

Malpractice Insurance

Berylson v. American Surety Co. of N.Y., 220

N.Y.S.2d 532 (N.Y. Sup. Ct.). An accountants' malpractice policy does not cover the cost of defending criminal charges.

St. Paul Fire & Marine Insurance Co. v. Clarence-Rainess & Co., 355 N.Y.S.2d 169 (N.Y. Sup. Ct. 1973), *aff'd without opinion*, 340 N.Y.S.2d 587 (App. Div. 1973). The duty to defend under an accountants' malpractice policy arises whenever some of the theories fall within the coverage.

NORTH CAROLINA

Legal Relationships with Nontax Clients

Respess v. Rex Spinning Co., 133 S.E. 391 (N.C. 1926). Georgia CPAs were allowed to recover their fee where they "prepared their audit in the rough" in North Carolina and returned to Atlanta and made up their report, since practicing involves more than acquiring information for a report.

Legal Relationships with Tax Clients

Austin v. R. W. Raines Enterprises, Inc., 264 S.E.2d 121 (N.C. App. 1980). Because the issue of reasonable value is for the jury, the court reversed a directed verdict for the CPA based on his testimony.

Regulation of Accounting Practice

Duggins v. North Carolina State Board of Certified Public Accountant Examiners, 240 S.E.2d 406 (N.C. 1978). Tax practice under a lawyer, who was a CPA but who was not engaged in accounting practice, did not meet the experience requirement. The court rejected the contention that requiring experience on the staff of a CPA "in public practice" was an unreasonable and discriminatory classification in violation of equal protection clauses of the state and federal constitutions.

Noncompetition Agreements

Schultz v. Ingram, 248 S.E.2d 345 (N.C. 1978). A covenant not to perform accounts payable invoice audits over a multistate area for two years from termination was upheld.

Scott v. Gillis, 148 S.E. 315 (N.C. 1929). The court enforced the employee's agreement that for three years from termination of employment by a CPA firm he would not service the CPA firm's clients that he had serviced during the employment contract.

Defenses

Angel v. Ward, 258 S.E.2d 788 (N.C. App. 1979).

CPA was held not liable for defamation of IRS agent because statements were protected by:
1. The qualified privilege to make nonmalicious comments about public officials.
2. The absolute privilege afforded for judicial and quasi-judicial proceedings, such as the IRS inquiry as to fitness of its employee.

Heating and Air Conditioning Associates, Inc. v. Myerly, 222 S.E.2d 545, *cert. denied*, 225 S.E.2d 323 (N.C. 1976). Court held for CPAs on claim for embezzlement losses because an engagement to prepare an unaudited financial statement does not require checking for accuracy or investigation of honesty of employees.

North Carolina by statute permits right of contribution against a joint tortfeasor.

OHIO

Legal Relationships with Tax Clients

Hild v. Woodcrest Association, 391 N.E.2d 1047 (Ohio Common Pleas 1977). Coopers & Lybrand was held liable for the return of the investment where it prepared financial projections and assisted in the sale of securities that were not registered pursuant to Ohio law.

Liability to Third Parties: Audited Financials

Beardsley v. Ernst, 191 N.E. 808 (Ohio App. 1934). Auditors were held not liable where their report showed that their consolidated statements were based on statements from abroad as to the foreign subsidiaries.

Regulation of Accounting Practice

Ivancic v. Accountancy Board of Ohio, 221 N.E.2d 719 (Ohio App. 1966). Failure to declare the basis for rejecting an application for a CPA certificate is an abuse of discretion.

Doelker v. Accountancy Board, 232 N.E.2d 407 (Ohio 1967). A CPA certificate cannot be revoked *solely* because the CPA is convicted of willful failure to file a tax return since dishonesty or fraud is not an essential element of the offense.

PENNSYLVANIA

Legal Relationships with Nontax Clients

Bauman and Vogel, C.P.A. v. Del Vecchio, 423 F. Supp. 1041 (E.D. Pa. 1976). Where an accounting firm incorporated in New Jersey sued for systems work performed in Pennsylvania, the court granted summary judgment for the defendant because the CPA firm was not licensed in Pennsylvania and the contract was performed in violation of Pennsylvania law.

O'Neill v. Atlas Auto Finance Corp., 11 A.2d 782 (Pa. Super, 1940). The jury found for the CPA on a claim for unpaid fees and against defendant's counterclaim for negligent failure to discover fraud by the bookkeeper.

Working Papers and Accountant-Client Privilege

Pennsylvania has an accountant-client privilege statute.

Rubin v. Katz, 347 F. Supp. 322 (E.D. Pa. 1972). Pennsylvania's accountant-client privilege statute is inapplicable to information obtained in the course of an audit.

Liability to Third Parties: Audited Financials

Landell v. Lybrand, 107 A. 783 (Pa. 1919). The court held that in absence of contract, auditors cannot be held liable for negligence to a third party.

Liability to Third Parties: Unaudited Financials

Coleco Industries, Inc. v. Berman, 423 F. Supp. 275 (E.D. Pa. 1976), *appealed on other issues*, 567 F.2d 569 (3d Cir. 1977). The trial court applied New Jersey and Pennsylvania law and held an accountant liable to a foreseeable third party for *negligence*. Liability was imposed in favor of sellers of stock who warranted the financials because the accountant was aware of the purpose and use of the report. In its note 59, the court rejected the need for expert testimony because the errors were of a mechanical and computational nature.

Liability to Third Parties: Other

Guy v. Leiderbach, 421 A.2d 333 (Pa. Super. 1980). Malpractice liability for negligence to third parties may be imposed upon the court's application of a balancing test to evaluate (1) the extent to which plaintiff was intended to be affected, (2) the foreseeability of injury, (3) the certainty that plaintiff has suffered harm, and (4) the policy of preventing future harm. The court reversed dismissal of a suit against an attorney both on negligence and contract theories by the beneficiary under a will. The will failed because it conveyed New Jersey realty, and New Jersey law prohibits an attesting witness from taking under the will.

Defenses

Pennsylvania by statute permits right of contribution against a joint tortfeasor.

SOUTH CAROLINA

Legal Relationships with Nontax Clients

Computer Servicenters, Inc. v. Beacon Mfg. Co., 328 F. Supp. 653 (D. S.C. 1970). An oral contract to provide data processing services which was not to be performed within one year was within the statute of frauds and unenforceable. Part performance of an employment contract does not relax the requirements of the statute of frauds.

Noncompetition Agreements

Derrick, Stubbs & Stith v. Rogers, 182 S.E.2d 724 (S.C. 1971). The court held that a noncompetition clause in an accounting partnership agreement should be strictly construed and that the restrictive covenant did not apply to an involuntary withdrawal from the partnership.

Defenses

Kemmerlin v. Wingate, 261 S.E.2d 50 (S.C.1979). The court dismissed a malpractice suit against an accountancy firm because there was no evidence tending to establish the standard of care.

TEXAS

Legal Relationships with Nontax Clients

Squyres v. Christian, 242 S.W.2d 786 (Tex. App. 1951). Where the CPA was engaged to advise and counsel concerning financial affairs, there was a fiduciary relationship, which shifted the burden of proof to the CPA when the client alleged that a transaction was fraudulent.

Liability to Third Parties: Audited Financials

Shatterproof Glass Corp. v. James, 466 S.W.2d 873 (Tex. App.-Fort Worth 1971). The court held that CPAs are liable for *negligence* to foreseeable third parties who the CPAs know will rely upon their work.

Regulation of Accounting Practice

Grace v. Allen, 407 S.W.2d 321 (Tex. Civ. App. 1966). The rights to practice before the Treasury Department are federal rights that cannot be impinged upon by states under the guise of regulation of unauthorized practice of law.

Fulcher v. Texas State Board of Public Accountancy, 571 S.W.2d 366 (Tex. App. 1978). The court enjoined an unlicensed person from using the terms *accountant* or *accounting*.

United States v. Texas State Board of Public Accountancy, 592 F.2d 919 (5th Cir. 1979), *cert. denied*, 100 S. Ct. 262 (1979). A state board rule (as contrasted with a state statute) that prohibits competitive bidding is void as a violation of the Sherman Act.

Noncompetition Agreements

Peat, Marwick, Mitchell & Co. v. Sharp, 585 S.W.2d 905 (Tex. App. 1979). An agreement that a withdrawing partner must not practice in the United States for two years was held void.

McElreath v. Riquelmy, 444 S.W.2d 853 (Tex. App. 1969). An agreement that a withdrawing partner who serviced firm clients within three years would forfeit his capital account was held valid.

Defenses

Atkins v. Crosland, 417 S.W.2d 150 (Tex. 1967). Where the accountant preparing a tax return allegedly failed to obtain consent for a change from the cash to accrual method, the statute of limitations started running when the taxpayer received notice from the IRS.

Texas by statute permits right of contribution against a joint tortfeasor.

VIRGINIA

Liability to Third Parties: Audited Financials

Rhode Island Hospital Trust National Bank v. Swartz, Bresenoff, Yavner & Jacobs, 455 F.2d 847 (4th Cir. 1972). A firm of CPAs prepared financial statements in Virginia for delivery to a bank in Rhode Island where the reliance and injury took place. The federal court sat in Virginia exercising diversity jurisdiction and held that Virginia courts would apply the law of Rhode Island under which accountants are liable for *negligence* to foreseeable third parties.

Regulation of Accounting Practice

Burton v. Accountant's Society of Virginia, 194 S.E.2d 684 (Va. 1973). A state statute making it a misdemeanor for unlicensed persons to use the term *public accountant* was held inapplicable to use of the title *accountant*.

Noncompetition Agreements

Foti v. Cook, 263 S.E.2d 430 (Va. 1980). An agreement of withdrawing partners to pay one third of fees collected for three years from any firm client serviced within twenty-four months of withdrawal was held enforceable.

Defenses

Virginia by statute permits right of contribution against a joint tortfeasor.

Appendix B

REPORTERS FOR STATE COURT DECISIONS

Atlantic (A.2d)
  Connecticut
  Delaware
  Maine
  Maryland
  New Hampshire
  New Jersey
  Pennsylvania
  Rhode Island
  Vermont

North Eastern (N.E.2d)
  Illinois
  Indiana
  Massachusetts
  New York
  Ohio

North Western (N.W.2d)
  Iowa
  Michigan
  Minnesota
  Nebraska
  North Dakota
  South Dakota
  Wisconsin

Pacific (P.2d)
  Alaska
  Arizona
  California
  Colorado
  Hawaii
  Idaho
  Kansas
  Montana
  Nevada
  New Mexico
  Oklahoma
  Oregon
  Utah
  Washington
  Wyoming

South Eastern (S.E.2d)
  Georgia
  North Carolina
  South Carolina
  Virginia
  West Virginia

South Western (S.W.2d)
  Arkansas
  Kentucky
  Missouri
  Tennessee
  Texas

Southern (So. 2d)
  Alabama
  Florida
  Louisiana
  Mississippi

Appendix C

UNITED STATES COURTS OF APPEAL

First Circuit (Boston)
  Maine
  Massachusetts
  New Hampshire
  Puerto Rico
  Rhode Island

Second Circuit (New York)
  Connecticut
  New York
  Vermont

Third Circuit (Philadelphia)
  Delaware
  New Jersey
  Pennsylvania
  Virgin Islands

Fourth Circuit (Richmond)
  Maryland
  North Carolina
  South Carolina
  Virginia
  West Virginia

Fifth Circuit (New Orleans)
  Louisiana
  Mississippi
  Texas

Sixth Circuit (Cincinnati)
  Kentucky
  Michigan
  Ohio
  Tennessee

Seventh Circuit (Chicago)
  Illinois

  Indiana
  Wisconsin

Eighth Circuit (St. Louis)
  Arkansas
  Iowa
  Minnesota
  Missouri
  Nebraska
  North Dakota
  South Dakota

Ninth Circuit (San Francisco)
  Alaska
  Arizona
  California
  Guam
  Hawaii
  Idaho
  Montana
  Nevada
  Oregon
  Washington

Tenth Circuit (Denver)
  Colorado
  Kansas
  New Mexico
  Oklahoma
  Utah
  Wyoming

Eleventh Circuit (Atlanta)
  Alabama
  Florida
  Georgia

District of Columbia Circuit (Washington, D.C.)

Appendix D

USING THIS BOOK FOR CPA EXAMINATION PREPARATION

Preparing for the Business Law Exam

According to the 1975 edition of the booklet *Information for CPA Candidates* (hereafter, *Information*), published by the AICPA, the Business Law section of the Uniform CPA Exam will test the student in the following 14 topics:

1. Accountant's legal responsibility.
2. Antitrust.
3. Bankruptcy.
4. Commercial paper.
5. Contracts.
6. Estates and trusts.
7. Federal securities regulation.
8. Forms of business organizations.
9. Insurance.
10. Property.
11. Regulation of the employer and employee relationship.
12. Sales.
13. Secured transactions.
14. Suretyship.

Information defines the content of topic one, the accountant's legal responsibility, as follows:

> Knowledge of the accountant's common-law civil liability to clients and third parties is tested under this topic. The common-law civil liability is based either upon contract or tort (negligence or fraud). Also included is the accountant's civil and criminal liability imposed by federal statutes, such as the Federal Securities Acts of 1933 and 1934. Finally, the accountant's rights regarding work papers and privileged communication are included.
>
> The candidate is expected to be familiar with current developments and recent cases involving accountants.

These topics are covered in Chapters 4 through 9 of this book.

Information also lists the following content for topic seven:

> Knowledge of the Securities Act of 1933 and the Securities Exchange Act of 1934 is tested under this topic. Included are the scope of the 1933 Act's registration requirements, exempt securities, exempt transactions, and the liability of the various parties involved in making a public offering of securities. Included within the coverage of the 1934 Act are the application of the Act's rules to both listed and unlisted corporations, corporate reporting requirements, antifraud provisions, disclosure of insider information, and short-swing profits.

Most of these matters are covered in Chapter 8 of this book.

Preparing for the Auditing Exam

Information specifies that the Auditing examination will cover generally accepted auditing standards (discussed in Chapter 2 of this book), *Statements on Auditing Standards* (Exhibit 13–4 outlines AU § 509), and *Statements on Responsibilities in Tax Practice* (covered in Chapter 12). *Information* at page 6 specifies that the following matters, which are discussed virtually throughout this book, will be tested: "professional relationships with clients, . . . professional independence, professional conduct, and standards of professional practice." Other matters specified for regular testing include "the social significance of auditing, . . . the attest function, the doctrine of due care and concepts of independence, integrity, and professional responsibility." Chapters 1 through 3 and 13 supply considerable information related to these topics.

Appendix E

Chapter 2

16. *d*
17. *d*
18. *a*
19. *a*
20. *c*
21. *c*
22. *a*
23. *a*. Auditor's independence as it relates to third-party reliance upon financial statements suggests that the auditor's professional judgment must be self-reliant and not subordinate to the views of his clients in fact or in appearance.

  Investors, credit grantors, prospective purchasers of businesses, regulatory agencies of government, and others may rely on an auditor's opinion that financial statements fairly reflect the financial position and results of operations of the enterprise which he has audited. To be independent the auditor must not only consciously refuse to subordinate his judgment to that of others, but he must also avoid relationships which would appear likely to warp his judgment even subconsciously in reporting whether or not the financial statements he has audited are in his opinion fairly presented.

  Independence means avoidance of situations that would tend to impair objectivity or create personal bias which would influence delicate judgments or lead a reasonable observer to believe that such objectivity might have been impaired. In its essence, independence is an expression of the personal integrity of the auditor and is primarily a condition of mind, character, and appearance.

  b. (1) An auditor's independence "in fact" refers to his objectivity, to the quality of not being influenced by regard to personal advantage. The auditor is in fact independent if his judgments are uncolored by personal interests, and interest of his client, or other special parties. Thus, independence in fact exists if the auditor exercises an objective state of mind.

  (2) The auditor is independent in appearance when no potential conflict of interests exists which might tend to jeopardize public confidence in the auditor's independence in fact. For there to be independence in appearance, there should be no reason to suspect that any factors exist which may influence the uninhibited exercise of the auditor's professional judgment.

  c. An auditor may be independent in fact, i.e., have an objective state of mind, but appear to third parties not to be independent. This situation arises where potential conflicts of interest exist which might tend to jeopardize public confidence in the auditor's independence in fact.

  For example, an auditor might not appear to be independent through the eyes of third parties, even though he might be independent in fact, if he or one of his partners (*1*) during the period of his professional engagement or at the time of expressing his opinion, had, or was committed to acquire, any direct financial interest or material indirect financial interest in the enterprise, (*2*) during the period of his professional engagement, at the time of expressing his opinion, or during the period covered by the financial statements, was connected with the enterprise as a promoter, underwriter, voting trustee, director, officer, or key employee or (*3*) renders professional services for a fee which would be contingent upon the findings or results of such services, except in certain tax matters when the contingent fee is determined by a court.

  The auditor may not be independent in appearance if there exists the opportunity for personal advantage as a result of his opinions even though he in fact ignores such considerations in rendering his objective, unbiased professional judgment.

  d. (1) No. A CPA would be considered not independent for an examination of the financial statements of a church for which he is serving as treasurer without compensation. The CPA's independence would be impaired in the eyes of someone who had knowledge of all the facts since the CPA would be reporting on his stewardship of the church's funds as its treasurer, even though without compensation.

  (2) No. A CPA would be considered not independent for an examination of the financial statements of a women's club for which his wife is serving as treasurer-bookkeeper even though he is not to receive a fee. The CPA's independence would be impaired in the eyes of someone who had knowledge of all the facts because the CPA might not be considered objective and unbiased in evaluating his wife's stewardship as treasurer and her record keeping as bookkeeper. The fact that the CPA

would not receive a fee would usually not affect his independence.

   e. An opinion such as should accompany financial statements examined by a CPA who owns a material direct financial interest in a nonpublic client is as follows:

> The accompanying balance sheet of XYZ Company as of December 31, 19XX, and the related statements of income, retained earnings, and changes in financial position for the year then ended have been compiled by me (us).
>
> A compilation is limited to presenting in the form of financial statements information that is the representation of management (owners). I (we) have not audited or reviewed the accompanying financial statements and, accordingly, do not express an opinion or any other form of assurance on them.
>
> I am (we are) not independent with respect to XYZ Company.
>
> Each page of the financial statements should be marked "See Accountant's Compilation Report."

29. *a*
30. *d*
31. *b*
32. *d*
33. *a*
34. *b*
35. *d*
36. *a*
37. *c*
38. *d*

Chapter 3

17. *c*
18. *a*
19. *b*

Chapter 4

1. *c*
2. *a*
3. *a.* The working papers belong to the CPA, and he has the right to retain possession thereof because the CPA is not a mere employee, but instead an independent contractor, and the working papers are vital to the CPA if the performance or accuracy of his work is questioned by his client or third parties.
   b. Although the CPA owns the working papers, his ownership is limited inasmuch as he may not assert unrestricted rights as to their use or disposition. For example, he may not sell them, even to another CPA firm, unless he has obtained the client's consent. This restriction against the transfer of working papers arises from the confidential relationship existing between the CPA and his client and would be equally applicable in connection with the sale by a CPA of his entire firm. In addition, the client's consent must also be obtained to effectively pass

ownership of the working papers to the beneficiaries of a deceased CPA under his will or to his heirs at law pursuant to the intestate succession laws. Finally, despite his ownership of the working papers, the CPA may be compelled by court order, which overrides the confidential relationship between the CPA and his client, to disclose their contents. Subject to the aforesaid qualified right to transfer his limited ownership, the CPA's rights as to working papers are deemed to be primarily custodial in nature.

4. *d*
5. *c*
6. *c*
7. *d*
8. *a.* Privileged communication is a rule of evidence under which certain evidence arising out of special confidential relationships is not admissible in court.
   b. The policy factor behind this rule is the social desirability of fostering free and complete discussion and exchange of information between the parties in these special confidential relationships. This policy factor is deemed to outweigh the fact that otherwise valid evidence is being excluded.
   c. (1) Attorney—client.
     (2) Husband—wife.
     (3) Physician—patient.
     (4) Priest—penitent.
     (5) Accountant—client.
   d. The common law does not afford the accountant-client relationship the requisite status necessary to qualify as privileged communication. Thus, only in those states which have expressly changed the common-law rule by statute will evidence arising out of the accountant-client relationship be excluded.
9. *a.* Probably yes; possibly no. Whether Lake must testify turns on whether the case will be governed by the common-law rule (the majority rule) or statutory rule. The common-law rule provides that communications between accountants and clients are not privileged, and the accountant must testify when such testimony is required by legal process. In contrast, statutes in several states stipulate that confidential communications between the accountant and his client are privileged. Where it exists, the privilege can only be waived by the client because it exists for his benefit.

   The accountant's ownership of working papers is not a valid basis for refusing to testify.
   b. Yes. All actions to change the common-law rule have been by statute. No federal statutes have modified the application of the common-law rule; hence, no right of privileged communication is available to Lake in the federal courts except where the federal court is applying state law.

Chapter 5

8. *b*
9. *a.* True
   b. True

c. False

d. True

e. False

10. *a.* No. This is a contract for personal services which has an implied provision of the contract that the party who is to perform the services shall be physically and mentally competent during performance. Therefore if subsequent physical disability prevents performance, the contract is discharged under the principle of impossibility of performance. Keen was prevented from completing the engagement by his paralyzing disability, which resulted in retirement. Keen had no partners or associates who might have taken over for him and completed the work. Therefore Keen's inability to conclude his performance is an "excusable" breach of contract which is not actionable.

b. No. By the terms of the contract, Keen was engaged to perform a completed job, i.e., audit the company's books and prepare a financial report. The firm's only interest lay in this completed engagement which would enable it to submit the contemplated report to the prospective partners. The fact that Keen's compensation was fixed on a per diem basis does not alter the obvious intention of the parties, which was that Keen would submit a completed report and the firm would pay him for the number of days he worked. The work done by Keen, although a substantial amount of the finished job, was of no value to the firm. Therefore Keen is unable to obtain any recovery, either for the agreed per diem fee or the reasonable value of his services, even though his failure to complete the engagement was not his fault.

c. Arthur & Son cannot recover working papers prepared by Keen supporting his intended report to it; the firm can recover papers originating in its offices and loaned to Keen. Working papers are prepared by a CPA for his own use and as a basis for his reports. These papers belong to the CPA and should be retained by him. However, any records belonging to the client remain its property and must be returned by the CPA. The canceled checks, copartnership agreement, and other firm records originated in the firm's offices and were loaned to Keen merely to assist him in his work. They do not become part of the working papers and must be returned to the firm.

11. *d*

12. *c*

13. *c*

14. *d*

15. *d*

Chapter 6

8. *Part a.*

The issue of privity is clearly raised by the CPA firm's contention that the duty of care is to the limited partnership with which it had contracted and not to third-party limited partners, such as Marcall.

The common-law privity limitation, as it applies to CPAs, is currently in a state of change. However, recent cases indicate a gradual erosion of this limitation on the recovery rights of third parties. Because the basis of Marcall's claim is clearly negligence and not fraud, the traditional fraud exception to the privity rule is not available. The following theories undoubtedly would be asserted by Marcall:

(1) The third-party beneficiary doctrine would be asserted based upon the fact that it was clear that the audit was intended to benefit the limited partners. Therefore, although not directly parties to the contract, they may sue as its intended beneficiaries.

(2) The services of the accountants clearly did not extend beyond a class of persons actually known and limited at the time of the engagement. The privity barrier is essentially based upon a reluctance to impose liability against CPAs to the extensive and indeterminable investing public-at-large. However, where the audit was expected to be relied upon by a fixed, definable, and contemplated group whose conduct was to be governed by the audit, the duty of care extends to this class of people. It is not necessary to state the duty in terms of contract or privity.

(3) Although the facts indicate ordinary negligence, it is possible that gross negligence might be present. The dividing line between ordinary and gross negligence is such that liability to third parties could be found on this basis.

(4) Although the audit was performed pursuant to a contract with the limited partnership, the real parties-in-interest were the partners. The partnership is not a separate and distinct entity for this purpose. The general partners signing the engagement letter were doing so as agents for each of the members of the limited partnership.

Part b.

Ordinarily, users of financial statements, other than those who contracted for the audit and those known in advance to the auditor, may not recover for ordinary negligence by the auditor in the performance of an audit. Usually, recovery of damages by third parties must be based on fraud. Actual knowledge of falsity (scienter) is generally required for an action based upon fraud; however, the scienter requirement for an action based upon fraud may be satisfied by either

(1) Showing a reckless disregard for the truth.

(2) Demonstrating that the auditor was grossly negligent.

It appears that the three deficiencies in the audit by Farr & Madison might be sufficient to satisfy either approach. The deficiencies of failure to check the existence of certain receivables, collectibility of other receivables, and existence of security investments, taken collectively, if not individually, appear to show a reckless disregard for the truth by the auditor. In fact, the audit probably lacks sufficient competent evidential matter as a reasonable basis for an opinion regarding the financial statements under examination.

The audit appears to have been conducted in a woefully inadequate fashion, without regard to the usual auditing standards and procedures necessary to exercise due professional care. Therefore, the auditors were grossly negligent in the performance of their duties.

Chapter 7

1. *b*
2. *d*
3. *b*
7. *c*
8. *b*
9. *c*
10. *b*
11. *a*
12. *b*

Chapter 8

3. *b*
4. *d*
14. *c*
15. *c*
16. *d*
17. *d*
18. *c*
19. The Securities Act of 1933 permits an aggrieved party to sue various parties connected with the registration statement for an untrue statement of a material fact in the registration statement or the omission of a material fact required to be stated therein or necessary to make the statements therein not misleading. Those having potential liability include issuers of the security, those who signed the registration statement, every director, underwriter, and expert.

Any acquirer of the security may sue unless it is proved that at the time of such acquisition he knew of such untruth or omission.

The issuing corporation is an insurer of the truth of the registration statement and is liable without proof of negligence. Contrast its liability with that of the accountants and lawyers who are both experts. As such, they are not liable for parts of the registration statement on which they did not render an expert opinion. Moreover, as experts, they have the benefit of the "due-diligence" defense. That is, liability can be avoided if it can be shown by the expert that he had, after reasonable investigation, reasonable ground to believe and did believe at the time such part of the registration statement became effective that the parts for which he gave expert opinion were true and that there was no omission to state a material fact required to be stated.

The act also provides certain defenses based on the amount of damages and their relationship to the misstatements or omissions.

28. *d*
29. *a*
30. *a*

Chapter 9

6. *a.* The Securities Act of 1933.
   b. The Securities Exchange Act of 1934.

c. The Internal Revenue Code of 1954.
d. The Investment Companies Act of 1940.

7. *a.* Pro forma financial statements are special-purpose financial statements reporting the effect of transactions consummated or which may be consummated subsequent to the date of the statements.

b. The following conditions are necessary for giving an opinion on pro forma financial statements:

(1) The subsequent transactions reported in the statements are the subject of a definite (preferably written) contract or agreement. In the absence of a definite agreement there is no auditing evidence to support the auditor's opinion regarding the statements. Moreover, there must be assurance that transactions would be consummated in accordance with a definite plan so that the results can be logically determined.

Certification of pro forma statements is denied when they include an estimate of earnings contingent upon future operations. Forecasts based upon subsequent events beyond the normal control of business management are subject to varying degrees of reliability. To vouch for the accuracy of such a forecast is unethical.

(2) The accountant must be satisfied that the involved parties are responsible and able to carry out the provisions of the agreement. Even though the statements were based upon a formal agreement, they would be misleading if the parties did not have the ability or the intention to carry out the agreement.

(3) The time elapsing between the date of the statements and the contemplated date of the subsequent transactions should be reasonably short—not more than, say, four months. If a longer time elapses there is increased likelihood of major changes in financial condition because of operating results. Furthermore, other post-balance-sheet-date events might occur to impair the reliability of the statements.

(4) Investigation and inquiry should disclose that no other transactions or developments had occurred that would adversely affect the position of the company. This post-balance-sheet-date review should be carried through the date of the completion of the audit field work. Events of material importance occurring after the date of the financial statements must be reported by adjustment or annotation to prevent the statements from being misleading.

(5) The character or purpose of the transaction to which effect is given should be disclosed in the statement heading or elsewhere in the report. Such disclosure would prevent the statements from being misleading.

(6) It is desirable to use the past tense in any description of a statement and in a related auditor's report. Using the past tense is an

additional device to make clear that the contemplated (or consummated) transactions have been definitely covered by contracts and are not forecasts or estimates based upon impending events.

8. *c*
9. *c*
10. *d*

Chapter 11

4. *a*
5. *b*
6. *d*
7. Whipple's withdrawal from the partnership caused a dissolution. The Uniform Partnership Act provides that the dissolution of a partnership is the change in the relation of the partners caused by any partner's ceasing to be associated in carrying on the business. Furthermore, the dissolution was in contravention of the partnership agreement, which provided an irrevocable term of five years. Whipple resigned after two years.

There are several consequences of such wrongful conduct. First, with respect to Whipple, who caused the dissolution wrongfully, the other partners have the right to damages for breach of the agreement. These may be charged against him in an accounting or by an action at law. In addition, if the partners who have not caused the dissolution desire to continue the business in the same name, they may do so during the agreed term of the partnership. In doing so, they may possess the partnership property, provided they secure a bond approved by the court or pay to the partner who caused the dissolution wrongfully, the value of his interest in the partnership, less damages and indemnify him for all present and future liabilities.

The partnership cannot sue in the partnership name according to the common-law rule, since it is not a legal entity. A growing number of states (some 13) have changed this rule, but the Uniform Partnership Act is silent on the point.

The final action that could be taken by the partners is to seek to recover for damages caused as a result of Whipple's establishing his own business in competition with the partnership and to seek some form of injunctive relief in equity that wholly or partly precludes him from competing for the remainder of the five years.

Chapter 12

17. *d*
18. The 1976 Tax Reform Act substantially changed the liability imposed upon individuals who prepare income tax returns for compensation. In addition to disclosure requirements and ethical standards, the act imposed civil liability and penalties and empowered the government to obtain injunctive relief.

The basis for liability under the 1976 Tax Reform Act is an understatement of the taxpayer's federal income tax liability. A final determination of the taxpayer's tax liability by the Internal Revenue Service or the courts is not a necessary condition for establishing an understatement of that liability. Where the understatement is due to the negligent or intentional disregard of the income tax rules or regulations, the penalty is $100. The penalty does not extend to the employer of a tax-return prepared solely by reason of the relationship. In the event of a trial of the question of the proper assessment of the penalty, the preparer has the burden of proving he was not at fault.

Where it is found that the preparer willfully understated the taxpayer's liability, the penalty is $500 per return. Where the willful understatement of liability also constitutes a negligent or intentional disregard for the rules and regulations, as it usually will, the combined penalty is a maximum of $500.

The 1976 Tax Reform Act also established new procedures for return preparers. Noncompliance with these procedures subjects the preparer to the following penalties.
a. $25 for failure to furnish a copy of the completed return to the taxpayer.
b. $50 for failure to retain either a copy of all returns prepared or a list of all taxpayers and their identification numbers.
c. $25 for failure to reflect the preparer's identification number on the tax return.
d. $25 for failure to sign the return.
e. $500 for each taxpayer's income tax check endorsed or otherwise negotiated by the preparer.

Finally, the Internal Revenue Service has the power to seek injunctive relief by enjoining a preparer from engaging in prohibited practices; or, if his conduct has repeatedly violated the proscribed practices, he may be enjoined from practicing as an income tax return preparer.

The specific practices of an income tax return preparer that can initiate an action to enjoin on the part of the service are the following:
a. Conduct subject to disclosure requirement penalties and understatement-of-taxpayer-liability penalties.
b. Conduct subject to criminal penalties under the Internal Revenue Code.
c. Misrepresentation of (*a*) the return preparer's eligibility to practice before the IRS or (*b*) his experience or education as an income tax return preparer.
d. Guarantee of payment of a tax refund or of allowance of a tax credit.
e. Other fraudulent or deceptive conduct that substantially interferes with proper administration of the internal revenue laws.

Chapter 13

3. *c*
4. *d*
5. *d*
7. *a*
8. *d*
9. *b*
10. *d*

11. *a*

12. *a*

13. *a*

14. *d*

15. *b*

18. *b*

19. *c*

20. *d*

26. *a*. An item is material if it would be a substantial factor influencing the conduct of reasonable investors including speculators. To be material it is not necessary for the item to be a determining factor in a decision.

b. (1) The materiality of an account or activity and related internal controls affects the relative audit risk that must determine the audit program.

   (2) When errors or irregularities are discovered, the materiality and sensitivity must be evaluated in determining whether to extend the usual auditing procedures.

c. The CPA must consider the potential impact on those who may use the financials for decision making. A small misstatement may assume major significance if it converts a loss to a profit or results in avoiding an apparent breach of a loan covenant. A small loan to a company officer may be considered material especially if it is in violation of law or is a breach of fiduciary duty.

d. See Exhibit 13–4.

27. *d*

28. *b*

29. *d*

30. *c*

31. *b*

32. *d*

33. *a*

34. *d*

35. *a*

36. *c:* Compilation or review

37. *c*

38. *b*

39. *a*

Index